The
HISTORY
of BHUTAN

The
HISTORY
of BHUTAN

KARMA PHUNTSHO

RANDOM HOUSE INDIA

Published by Random House India in 2013
Second impression in 2014

Copyright © Karma Phuntsho 2013

The photographs in this book are by Karma Phuntsho or
are reproduced by permission.

Random House Publishers India Pvt Ltd
7th Floor, Infinity Tower C, DLF Cyber City
Gurgaon – 122002, Haryana

Random House Group Limited
20 Vauxhall Bridge Road
London SW1V 2SA
United Kingdom

978 81 8400 311 6

Typeset in Times New Roman by R. Ajith Kumar

Printed and bound in India by Replika Press Private Limited

गुरुर्गरीयान्न पितुः परोऽस्ति मातुः परं दैवतमस्ति नान्यत् ॥

ब्ल་མ་ཕ་ལས་སྟེ་བ་གཞན་མེད་ཅིང་། །ལྷ་ཡི་མཆོག་ནི་མ་ལས་གཞན་པ་མེད།།

There is no guru dearer than one's father and no divinity higher
than one's mother.

~ The Buddha in Kṣemendra's *Bodhisattvādānakalpalatā (chap. 92, v. 4)*

ॐ

To my parents

Contents

Preface

WHEN ZHABDRUNG NGAWANG NAMGYAL, the founder of Bhutan, passed away in 1651, his death was concealed through the hoax of a retreat. Meals were served on time, musical instruments were played regularly, orders issued on wooden boards and someone pretending to be him even received gifts and gave blessings from behind a curtain. The Bhutanese public were given the impression that he was in meditation but his Tibetan enemies were not easily convinced. The 5th Dalai Lama suspected that Zhabdrung suffered an inauspicious death after being struck by a fatal illness, which was caused by the Dalai Lama's own occult powers. In contrast, the Mughal governor of Bengal was told that Bhutan's ruler was an ascetic, some 120 years old, living on a vegetarian diet of bananas and milk. Understandably, the mystery of his 'retreat' gave rise to interesting and also conflicting speculations. It certainly also helped an emerging Bhutan sustain its newfound sovereignty as a unified state.

Such an enigmatic scenario is not merely a phenomenon of the distant past. Perceptions of Bhutan even in recent years were imbued with a similar sense of mystery and contrasting views. While many saw Bhutan as a happy country of exceptional natural beauty and cultural exuberance, some held views of Bhutan in less favourable terms as an autocratic third-world state. These perceptions often veered to extremes, with one group romanticizing Bhutan as a modern Shangrila while the other portrayed Bhutan as a genocidal state. Like the mystery concerning the founder's death in the seventeenth century, the intrigue entailed by these biased perceptions in some ways also helped Bhutan underline its security and sovereignty. Similarly, just as the medieval government promoted the 'retreat' hoax, the modern Bhutanese government endeavoured to convince both its citizens and the outside world of Bhutan's special position as a happy land with a rich blend of culture and nature.

However, until recently, most people outside the Indian subcontinent have not even heard of Bhutan. Due to its small size, insignificant economy and the lack of reliable information about it, Bhutan largely remained an obscure country. Consequently, Bhutanese travelling abroad would have to often endure delays at immigration check points and embassies, as immigration officers struggled to locate the country. This changed in the last couple of decades as the travel culture rapidly increased in other parts of the world, and Bhutan, with its high-value tourism policy, has now become an exotic and much-desired travel destination. As a result, the number of tourists who visited Bhutan shot up from 6,392 in 2001 to 1,05,414 in 2012 and included a large number of Indian visitors who travelled by land.

Yet, detailed and objective information on Bhutan is still sparse. Apart from a handful of books by foreign scholars and local Bhutanese writers, most publications are colourful pictorial books or sentimental travelogues by visitors to the country. Most of these sources present a nostalgic account of Bhutan with a heavy dose of Orientalist romanticism and often betray the authors' own subjective susceptibility more than they report the actual situation in Bhutan. In addition to this, the government has actively engaged in a calculated effort of packaging and branding the country as a whole in order to appeal to the external expectation and sensibility. The recent efforts of the government to promote Gross National Happiness as a new economic and development paradigm in forums such as the UN has further complicated people's imagination of Bhutan both at home and abroad. Increasingly, more and more people now describe Bhutan as a happy country, despite the fact that a large percentage of the Bhutanese live in depressing poverty and many Bhutanese youth would willingly grasp the opportunity to work in an American kitchen or European warehouse if given the chance. Moreover, none of the existing sources on Bhutan also adequately discuss the seriousness of the sociocultural transformations, which is fundamentally changing the worldview, cultural ethos and social fabric of Bhutanese society today.

In contrast to popular writings, most of which 'shangrilize' Bhutan, the academic accounts of Bhutan generally provide readers a fairly sober account. Although they are fewer, these writings give readers information about Bhutan in some depth and detail. Yet, many academics approach Bhutan with a prior knowledge of Tibet and often show a naïve tendency to Tibetanize Bhutan. A very good example for demonstrating this is the application of the *la* suffix, which is added after first names in conversations to address people in the honorific form in Tibet. Although the *la* suffix may be added at the end of a phrase or sentence (see Chapter 3), its addition after names is not usual practice in Bhutan and, in some parts of the country, it is even considered pejorative to address poeple with a *la* suffix attached to their names. Many acclaimed scholars on Bhutan, unaware of such cultural and linguistic nuances, confidently use the *la* suffix after a name in imitation of the Tibetan practice.

Such nonchalant Tibetanization of Bhutan can be also found in numerous other cases—even in writings of scholars on the Himalayas and Bhutan. A well-known example is the following introduction to Bhutan by two doyens of Tibetan Studies, Hugh Richardson and David Snellgrove; it is cited by two pioneering historians on Bhutan, Michael Aris and Yoshiro Imaeda, in their introduction of Bhutan.

> Thus, of the whole enormous area which was once the spirited domain of Tibetan culture and religion, stretching from Ladakh in the west to the borders of Szechuan and Yunnan in the east, from the Himalayas in the south to the Mongolian steppes and the vast wastes of northern Tibet, now only Bhutan seems to survive as the one resolute and self-contained representative of a fast disappearing civilisation.[1]

While it cannot be denied that Bhutan is closely linked to Tibet in its religious culture and is now often called the last bastion of the Tibetan Buddhist civilization, the general cultural affinity between Bhutan and Tibet outside of the religious influence is far more tenuous than most experts on Tibet would have us believe. Thus, against the general tendency of Tibetologists to treat Bhutan as an extension of Tibet, we must distinguish one from the other, at least to the extent Japan is distinct from China or Nepal is from India. It will become clear from the following discussion of history that for nearly half a millennium Bhutan and Tibet had separate political and sociocultural existences, which have led to stark differences even in the religious cultures. Such differences have only become further entrenched and distinct after Bhutan's northward link to Tibet was severed in 1959, following the occupation of Tibet by China.

Inaccurate projections by foreign writers, however, are not the only factors that influenced perceptions of Bhutan. If the accounts of Bhutan by outsiders smack of the Orientalist romanticization, naïve Tibetanization or other traces of pro- or anti-Bhutan sentiments, many local Bhutanese have appropriated

---

1 Richardson and Snellgrove (1968), p. 271. Both Aris and Imaeda cite this at the beginning of their histories of Bhutan.

and internalized these external perceptions and projections. Thus, we find many Bhutanese painting the same rosy picture of Bhutan, which an enchanted Western visitor may paint, and promoting it with a patriotic zest as if it were an official dogma although they are fully aware of the problems and challenges that beset the country. They regurgitate the same sentimental and hyperbolic descriptions of Bhutan produced by a nostalgic visitor. This was also true to some extent with the traditional Bhutanese authors writing in classical Tibetan or Dzongkha. They wrote under a strong Tibetan influence and reproduced the perceptions which the Tibetan religious visitors through the ages had of Bhutan. Their discourses on Bhutan are set in the Tibetan cosmological and religious context and embedded in the Tibetan literary culture despite their best efforts to extricate Bhutan from the Tibetan cultural and political domain. These tendencies of internalizing external perceptions are nonetheless tolerable when compared to awry opinions such as Ashley Eden's claim that Bhutan had no tradition or history or the mistaken view still held among some quarters that Bhutan is a political vassal of India. Such viewpoints are too parochial to be considered even worthy of any rebuttal.

Against these tendencies and misconceptions, a new voice of independent Bhutanese writers who draw on Bhutan's rich cultural heritage and history, is now rising. Many Bhutanese today write in English for a global audience and bring the local Bhutanese stories, wisdom and cultures directly to their readers around the world without an intermediary. Not only do they present the original Bhutanese voice but they also help develop the much needed self-representation in scholarly discourses on Bhutan. Through them, Bhutan is beginning to emerge on the international intellectual arena with its own voice.

Like a shy bride gradually removing her veil, Bhutan is today shedding its historical obscurity and isolation and beginning to attract a lot of attention, especially through its policy of Gross National Happiness. It is my hope that this book will aid this emergence of Bhutan by giving some substance to the growing popularity. The book aims to tell the story of Bhutan's past in an unbiased narration and analysis and is the first ever attempt to cover the entire history of Bhutan in detail in English, combining both traditional perspectives and modern historiographical analyses.

While every effort is made to steer away from the undue influence of external perceptions or internal prejudices, I make no claim of cultural or political neutrality. Ideas and opinions arise from sociocultural contexts, and the narratives and analyses in this book are also results of my own exposure to traditional Bhutanese cultural upbringing and education as well as modern Western academic training. Although I am intimately aware of both the blessings of Bhutan and the challenges it is facing, this book is intended neither as praise for Bhutan's successes nor as a critique of its failures. My main concern here is to present an objective story (or a plausible one when evidences are lacking) by weaving the facts or available data together into a readable narrative as no such complete history of Bhutan exists so far.

This book is a byproduct of the project entitled 'The Historical Study and Documentation of the Padma Gling pa Tradition in Bhutan', funded by the UK's Arts and Humanities Research Council at Cambridge University. Through this project and other digitization projects funded by the Endangered Archives Programme of the British Library, I have carried out an extensive digitization of the textual corpus associated with the Pema Lingpa tradition in order to both preserve Bhutan's textual heritage and to compile a historical account of Pema Lingpa's tradition, which is the only religious tradition of local Bhutanese origin. It was in the course of my collection of notes for the history of Pema Lingpa's tradition that I was tempted to undertake a comprehensive study of Bhutan's history; this book is an outcome of such curiosity and intellectual diversion.

From a Buddhist perspective, the foremost project of human existence is self-development and edification. In order to improve the world, a country or community, one must start by improving oneself, something that can be effectively pursued only by first understanding oneself. We are products of a complex historical process and history tells us who we are and why we are who we are. It reveals the roots of our perceptions, prejudices, outlooks and parochialisms and helps us improve ourselves by learning from past mistakes and emulating past achievements. Our past explains our present and informs and guides our future; it is my modest hope that *The History of Bhutan* will help readers better understand the Bhutanese character and contribute towards a process of social edification by fostering the Bhutanese tradition of self-reflection and mindfulness, especially as it pursues its goal of Gross National Happiness.

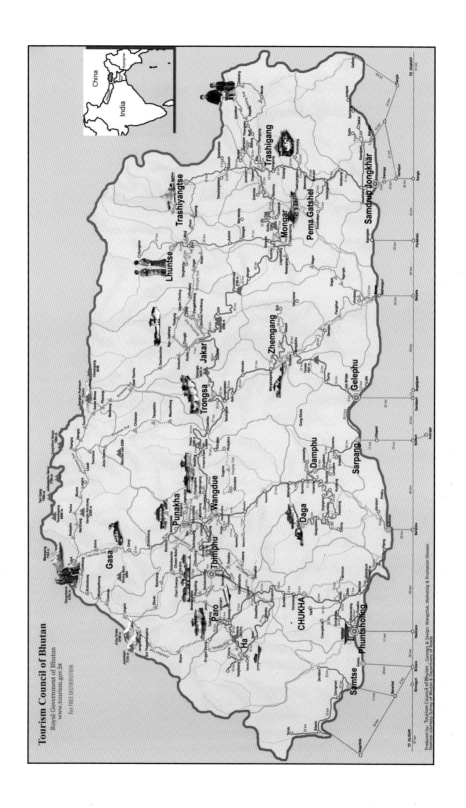

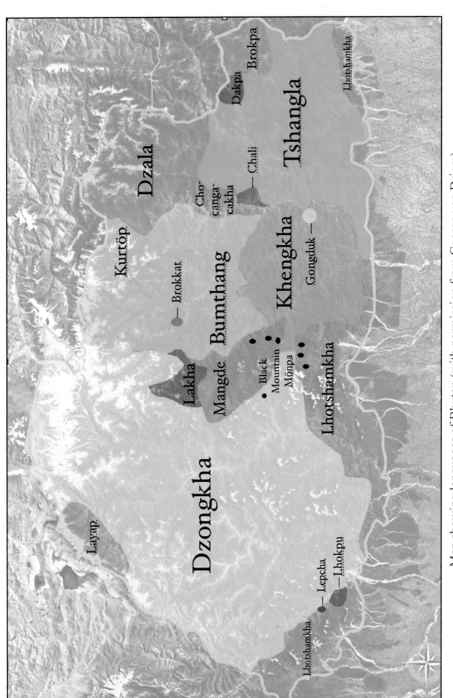

Map showing languages of Bhutan (with permission from George van Driem)

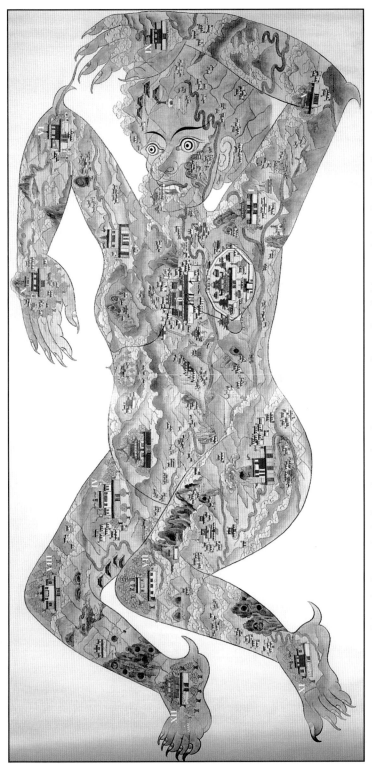

A traditional Tibetan depiction of a supine demoness and temples (with permission from Per Sorenson)

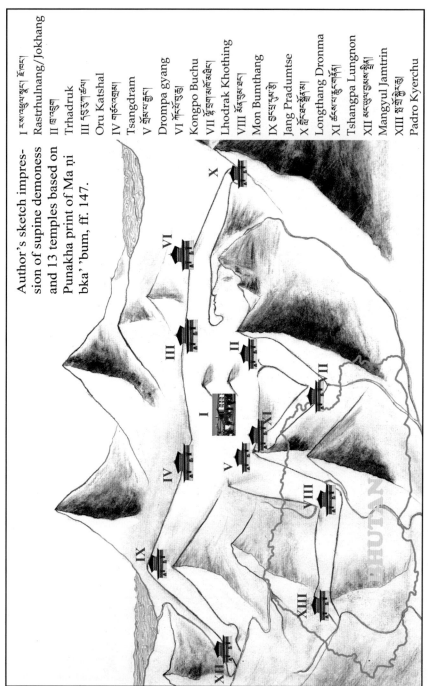

Author's sketch impression of supine demoness and 13 temples based on Punakha print of Ma ṇi bka' 'bum, ff. 147.

I རས་འཕྲུལ་སྣང་། ཇོ་ཁང་། Rastrhulnang/Jokhang
II ཁྲ་འབྲུག Trhadruk
III ཀ་ཙ་ཆུ་ཚལ Oru Katshal
IV གཙང་འགྲམ། Tsangdram
V གྲོམ་པ་རྒྱང་། Drompa gyang
VI ཀོང་པོ་བུ་ཆུ། Kongpo Buchu
VII ལྷོ་བྲག་མཁོ་མཐིང་། Lhodrak Khothing
VIII མོན་བུམ་ཐང་། Mon Bumthang
IX བྱང་ཏྲ་འདུམ་རྩེ། Jang Pradumtse
X ཁོང་མཐིང་སྒྲོན་མ། Longthang Dronma
XI ཚོང་པ་ཀླུང་གནོན། Tshangpa Lungnon
XII མང་ཡུལ་འཇམ་སྲས་སྒྲིན། Mangyul Jamtrin
XIII ཕ་གྲི་སྐྱེར་ཆུ། Padro Kyerchu

Author's depiction of the demoness and temples laid out within the Himalayan landscape

Chokhor valley and Jakar *dzong,* with snowy peaks in the background

Jampa Lhakhang, the temple built on the left knee of the
supine demoness

Paro valley, the medicinal land and a trade route since the seventh century

Kyerchu Lhakhang, the temple built on the left foot of the supine demoness

The temple of Samye in central Tibet

Taktshang or Tiger's Nest, Bhutan's most iconic site, hanging on a cliff

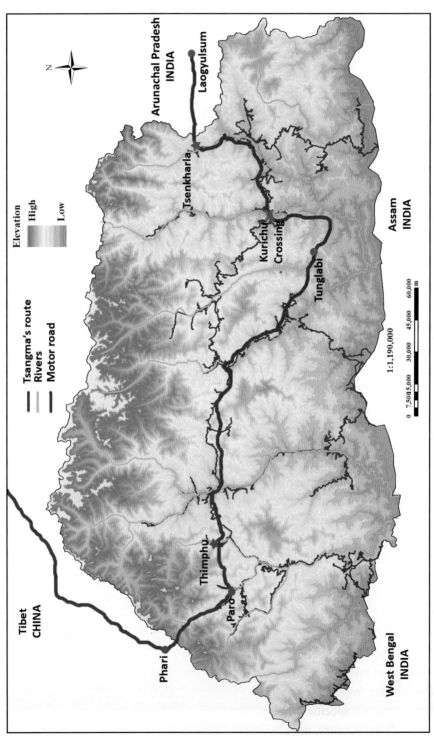

Map showing elevation, ecological zones, motor road network and the route of Prince Tsangma in the ninth century (based on a map by the Royal Government of Bhutan)

The Country and Its Names

THE BUDDHIST PHILOSOPHER DHARMAKĪRTI observed that names are like sticks. A stick does not hit an object on its own. It follows the person who wields it. Names do not apply themselves to their referents; they only follow the wishes of their user. Dharmakīrti's point is that names are purely conventional designations. We cannot give them any objectivity and significance beyond their function as mere nomenclature. They are labels and they change. Druk, now the local name for Bhutan, was once the name of a small establishment in central Tibet, while 'Bhutan', with variations in spelling, was also used for the whole or part of the stretch of highlands north of Bengal. There is no inherent link between a name and its referent. Hence, to understand a place by studying its name may seem misplaced, even ludicrous, like studying the finger pointing at the moon in order to understand the moon. Yet, for the sake of communication, a finger can show the moon. Similarly, studying a place name can reveal the underlying intentions and purposes for giving the name. A toponym can help us understand people's perception of a place, of themselves and their neighbours.

The Bhutanese have etymologies for nearly all their place names. Throughout Bhutan, one can even today find a rich tradition of using toponyms to tell historical and religious narratives. Many stories of people's origin and local cultures are told by stringing together place names. When one listens to such a narration, the whole landscape comes back to life as a stage for legendary and historical events. Through the toponyms, we get glimpses of the elusive past and the names serve as mnemonic tools to remember local legends and histories. Unfortunately, the many names for the country itself do not string together to provide a fabulous national narrative but they do provide us some specific insights into how the Bhutanese and their neighbours perceived the country, which today we call Bhutan.

Mon

Bhutan was called by different names and not all of them were used for the same place and at the same time. Unravelling the origins and significances of these names can be exciting as well as challenging. According to traditional Bhutanese historians, the earliest name for the area roughly covering modern-day Bhutan is Mon, Monyul (Mon country) or Lhomon (Southern Mon). Mon, they explained, is a derivative of *mun*, a Tibetan word for darkness. The inhabitants of the southern borderlands were known to the central Tibetans as *mon pa* (མོན་པ་) or dark people because they were considered to live in a state of socio-spiritual darkness. Unlike central Tibet, where Buddhist civilization had reached its peak by the middle of the eighth century, the people in the borderlands, in the eyes of a central Tibetan, were groping in darkness without the light of the Buddha's wisdom.

The application of the term Mon to areas of Bhutan is attested in many ancient texts written by both Tibetan and Bhutanese authors. However, any suggestion that Mon and Monyul were used as formal or established nomenclature for one area or ethnic group is highly debatable. Scholars are still at a loss as to what the term *mon* exactly meant or is derived from. It may be related to the Chinese word '*mán*', which designates barbarians and was also applied by the Chinese, according to some scholars, to Tibetan groups. Michael Aris, the first Western historian on Bhutan, speculated that the use of the term for central Bhutan may have a direct link to *mán* and *mong* used in eastern Tibet along the Sino-Tibetan frontiers.[1] Interestingly, even as early as the seventh century, Xuanzang, the great Chinese traveller, noted that the people in the frontiers north of Kamarupa kingdom (modern Assam) were akin to the *mán* people of China's southwestern borderlands.[2]

It is further intriguing that the name Mon was used in many parts of the Himalayas stretching from the Karakoram ranges in the west to Arunachal Pradesh in the east. Even today, one can find groups of people called Mon in Pakistan, Bhutan, Tibet and eastern India. It is possible that these groups have a common origin and the term *mon* designated a people who initially inhabited the fertile valleys but were gradually pushed out to remote and rugged areas by dominant groups. Scholars have also speculated that the Mon in Burma and Thailand may be distantly related to the Mon in the Himalayas and that both may have initially started from western China and spread along the sides of the Himalayan watershed. Only further linguistic, archaeological and anthropological study can shed more light on this.

In the case of the name being used for Bhutan, it is more plausible that the term was used loosely to describe the primitive and rural people from the borderlands than as a strict ethnonym. This can be inferred from the use of the term through the centuries. If the Chinese called some Tibetans '*mán*' or barbarians, the Tibetans certainly used Mon to refer to people from their border areas who they considered 'dark' and uncivilized. The use of the term Mon for the ethnic groups in India and Tibet even today carries a connotation of provincialism, and the Bhutanese still use the term to refer to a small group of people in a remote part of central Bhutan. To put it simply, Mon and Monpa are names used with no fixed referent. The Tibetans called the people from the borderland Monpa and these in turn called some other rural minorities Monpa. It even comes down to using Monpa as a pejorative nickname for a simpleton in a village.

Read in this context of malleable application with shifting referents, the use of the name Mon for ancient Bhutan and its etymology are based on a very Tibet-centric worldview. Tibet is assumed to be the centre of Buddhist civilization, and Bhutan and other Himalayan hinterlands are assumed to be on the periphery of this civilized world. Applied in this manner, the term also carries a derogatory connotation; it is not surprising that a big country describes its smaller neighbours condescendingly. What is interesting is that with persistent use and repetition over time, even the population to whom the pejorative name was applied appropriated the name for themselves. Traditional Bhutanese historians, themselves being largely products of Tibetan monastic education, accepted the Tibetan application without questioning. They even went so far as to justify the ancient name by providing an etymology; although the etymology they provided may have been be a very arbitrary and recent effort to explain the ancient term.

Today, we see the same scenario in the use of the name Mon for the groups of people in central Bhutan and eastern India. These groups have generally adopted the name in spite of its derogatory connotation and sometimes even perceive themselves inferior to those who refer to them with this name. However, since the Chinese occupation of Tibet, along with a growing respect for ethnic diversity, the term is now increasingly used as a neutral ethnonym. An intelligent and convincing alternative to the popular etymology of the name may be found in what some Monpa elders in central Bhutan have to say. They claim to be the earliest inhabitants of the country and argue the word Monpa comes from *man pa*, the word for 'old' in some central and eastern Bhutanese languages.

Lhomonkhazhi—the Mon of four approaches

Another name by which Bhutan was known for many centuries is Lhomonkhazhi (ལྷོ་མོན་ཁ་བཞི་)—the southern Mon of four approaches. This name also appears in other variations such as Lhokhazhi (southern land of four approaches) and Monkhazhi (Mon with four approaches/four Mon approaches) and was used to refer to Bhutan or parts of it long before the unification of the country in the seventeenth century. According to the most well-known enumeration, the four approaches are Dungsamkha to the east, Pasakha to the south, Dalingkha to the west and Taktsherkha to the north—places located in the four corners of the country and roughly corresponding to the current state boundary of Bhutan.

However, this enumeration of four approaches in order to explain the ancient name Lhokhazhi presents a problem, as it suggests a territorial unity long before the country was formally united into one state. Could the ancient Bhutanese and their neighbours have perceived the area of modern Bhutan as a geographic unit to be approached via the four approaches even before the country was politically unified? It is very unlikely that they did so given the natural division of the country into many parts by mountain ranges, leading to very pronounced linguistic and cultural differences. It is hard to imagine that valleys in Bhutan shared a striking resemblance, which they did not share with their neighbours in Sikkim and Tawang, before their unification in the seventeenth century. Besides, human mobility in ancient Bhutan was more commonly of a north–south orientation, between Tibet and India and the valleys, rather than laterally among the valleys themselves. Thus, the identification of the four approaches with the four coordinates located at four corners of Bhutan is historically problematic.

To explain this anachronistic appellation, historian John Ardussi argues that the name Lhokhazhi was 'applied originally only to an eleventh-century clan appanage in far western Bhutan, and by stages emerged from the religio-political struggles of the tenth–seventeenth centuries as a Drukpa metaphor for the state of Bhutan as a whole'.[3] He presents a very persuasive explanation for the name, weaving it with the gradual expansion of the unitary political domain for which the name is used. In the order of words, the name was first used to refer to a small area around Paro, then for much of western Bhutan and finally to the whole of modern Bhutan by the middle of the seventeenth century.

Ardussi's theory that the term had an expanding range of reference certainly helps us resolve much of the problem of anachronism. Yet, it is possible that some Bhutanese may have attributed a vague sense of congruity and unity to the areas which constitute modern Bhutan even before the seventeenth century. There is at least one record in which the name Lhokhazhi is used to refer to a country with its loose domain extending as far as Khaling to the east, Chumbi to the west, India to the south and Phari to the north.[4] We shall return to this at the end of the chapter on ancient history. Another interpretation of the name Lhomonkhazhi is found in a local oral tradition.[5] According to this oral enumeration, Lhomonkhazhi is not understood as the southern Mon of four approaches but as the four southern Mon approaches. The name does not imply a unitary land with four approaches but refers to four individual places which lie south of Tibet and also served as significant approaches/doors to Tibet in ancient times. The four approaches are the four main Mon valleys of Paro, Bumthang, Kurtoe and Tawang. Although this is not how the name is commonly understood, it is a viable interpretation and may have been the original purport of the term Monkhazhi. While Lhokhazhi referred to the appanage in western Bhutan with fairly defined boundaries, Monkhazhi may have designated the four valleys.

It seems highly plausible, then, that the early names Lhokhazhi, which initially referred to a clan appanage, and Monkhazhi, which perhaps referred to four Mon valleys south of Tibet, got compounded to form the later designation Lhomonkhazhi. This conveniently combined both the reference to the southern Mon area and the notion of a geographic and territorial unity, and may have suited the purpose of the people, who used the name for the emerging state of Bhutan in the seventeenth century. The final act in this process of naming would have been the identification of the four coordinates at the frontiers with names ending in *kha* or approach. This not only made the name etymologically sound but would have also helped secure and strengthen the territorial integrity of the young nation through even its name.

Whatever its origins and the processes through which it was appropriated, the name got deeply embedded in the Bhutanese historical consciousness. It was commonly used to refer to Bhutan and, even today, the name is frequently used in its modern variation: the Dragon Country of Four Approaches (ཁ་བཞི་འབྲུག་གི་རྒྱལ་ཁབ་). Viewed against the changes in the political boundaries of Bhutan's large neighbours since the seventeenth century, it is a matter of no small achievement that the small country of Lhomonkhazhi has retained more or less the same national boundaries, corresponding to the four approaches. The name Lhomonkhazhi certainly must have played an important part in this by providing a distinct, geographically centred identity.

Menjong—the medicinal country

Another name used for Bhutan, which the Bhutanese invoke frequently in literary speech, is Menjong (སྨན་ལྗོངས་), 'the land of medicinal herbs', a name which must certainly strike a chord for those familiar with Bhutan's botanical diversity. This name was used to refer to the Paro valley even as early as the thirteenth century.[6] Being located on the southern slopes of the Himalayan watershed, Bhutan enjoyed immense botanical richness compared to the relatively arid Tibetan plateau. The country was largely forested and even today about 72.5 per cent of the country is under forest cover, much of it pristine and dense. It is for this reason that the Bhutanese hierarch and historian Gedun Rinchen called Bhutan 'the southern land of forests' in the title of his religious history of the country.

Once again, our point of comparison is Tibet, Bhutan's northern and most important neighbour until 1959, and the significance of the name Menjong can be only properly appreciated with reference to the Tibetan medical tradition. Tibet has an ancient and sophisticated medical system, which is a synthesized amalgam primarily of Indian Ayurvedic, Chinese and Central Asian ideas of health and healing but heavily imbued with the Buddhist theories of the mind–body relationship. It is primarily based on the theory of the three humours of vital energy, bile and phlegm, and the maintenance and restitution of their balance through medical, dietary, lifestyle and behavioural intervention. The *locus classicus* of the tradition is the corpus of four medical texts called *Four Tantra*s which the tradition believes was taught by the historical Buddha in his manifestation as the Medicine Buddha. Thus, this medical system is considered to be Buddhist and referred to, particularly in Bhutan, as 'Buddhist medicine' (*nangpai men*, ནང་པའི་སྨན་) in contrast to biomedicine, often referred to as 'Indian medicine' because it was first introduced from there.

Unlike biomedicine, the traditional medical system uses very little or no chemical medications but places great importance on remedies made from herbs and minerals. It is for this important role of herbs in health and healing and their abundant growth in Bhutan that the country got its laudatory name 'the country of medicinal herbs', although, as noted earlier, it seems the appellation was first applied to Paro and only later to the whole country. It is clear, however, that herbs, like paper (another Bhutanese produce from the local environment), was highly valued across the border in Tibet. Throughout ages, Bhutanese sent freight loads of herbs and paper to Tibet as both gifts and trade items. The 2nd Desi ruler of Bhutan, for instance, made mass distribution of herbs to all doctors of Tibet twice during his reign. Even today, the use of this natural resource continues through the Royal Institute of Traditional Medicine, which promotes indigenous herbal treatment alongside biomedicine throughout the country.

As for most other things, the old Bhutanese provide an interesting explanation for the herbal richness. Long ago, when Princess Wencheng, known to the Bhutanese as Ashe Jaza (Chinese Princess), came to Tibet as a bride for the great seventh-century King Songtsen Gampo, the story goes that she brought with her the science of geomancy and medicine from the court of China. She also carried with her a pouch of medicinal seeds, which he cast into the sky upon her arrival in Tibet with prayers that they may spread across the land. A few seeds landed on Chagpori while the rest were carried by the north wind to the southern mountains of Lhomon. Chagpori later became a renowned centre for medical and astral studies in Tibet and the southern land a rich country for medicinal herbs.[7] As for the story itself, it is perhaps of a Tibetan origin as it betrays the later Tibetan nostalgia with which they trace back all good and great things to the Yarlung dynastic period of Tibet from the mid-seventh to mid-ninth century. Even the botanical richness of the borderland is considered somehow as a work of the great Tibetan dynastic period. Such Tibetan superciliousness no doubt vexed the Bhutanese, leading to neighbourly distaste and even serious conflicts between the two countries. A new contest over a medicinal plant is today taking place along the high mountainous border in the form of competition and confrontation between the Tibetan/Chinese and Bhutanese collectors of the expensive fungi *cordyceps sinensis,* which is said to have helped three Chinese athletes to break world records in running.

Country bestrewn with Tsanden

Bhutan has another botanical epithet: Tsanden Köpaijong (ཙན་དན་བཀོད་པའི་ལྗོངས་)— the country bestrewn with *Tsanden.* This was never used as a name of the country as such but the country is often described with this epithet. Perhaps the earliest use of this epithet for the area of modern Bhutan is in homiletic letters of the Tibetan saint Dorji Lingpa (1346–405) sent to his Bhutanese students and patrons in 1381.[8] Today, the national anthem of Bhutan begins with this epithet. The Himalayan word *tsanden* is a mispronunciation of the Indian word *candan* for sandalwood. The Sanskritic *candan* and Tibetan *tsanden* are pronounced differently but still retain identical spelling when written in Tibetan characters. However, the *tsanden* we are talking about in the Bhutanese context is not sandalwood as all Tibetan dictionaries may have us believe. Sandalwood hardly grows in Bhutan and its role is not significant. Instead in Bhutan, *tsanden* refers to the cypress, particularly the species which now goes by the name Bhutan cypress (*Cupressus corneyana*). It is quite possible that the gigantic cypresses of Bhutan got the name of the aromatic sandalwood as the wood from very mature cypresses produces a similar fragrance. The wood from mature cypress is commonly used in incenses as a major ingredient.

This coniferous tree is now Bhutan's national tree and is commonly seen across the country. The cypress, one can say, holds the highest place in the Bhutanese botanical hierarchy. It is viewed as a special tree, some even ascribing to it a quality of sacredness. Its growth in most unlikely places, to awesome heights rising to over 80 m, an impressive girth of up to 14 m and the large bulbous trunk it accumulates with age all help inspire such numinous feelings about the tree. To this, then, are added religious stories about the tree's origins. One can find cypresses which are considered to have grown from the walking staff used by holy persons, like the large cypress next to the famous Kurjey temple which is believed to have grown from Padmasambhava's staff. It is not uncommon to see a gigantic cypress growing next to an old religious or secular establishment, which confirms the important status given to the cypress in Bhutanese cultural surroundings. For social historians today, these cypress trees are good markers of historically significant places.

Drukyul—the Land of the Thunder Dragon

The names discussed above have generally ceased to be used today as names for Bhutan. Even those that are still current are used only in literary forms of expression, as epithets rather than names. The standard local designation currently used by both the Bhutanese people and their neighbours is Druk (འབྲུག) or Thunder Dragon and, by extension, Drukyul (འབྲུག་ཡུལ), Land of Thunder Dragon, and Druk Gyalkhab (འབྲུག་རྒྱལ་ཁབ), Thunder Dragon country. This is rendered in a much more dramatic fashion in English today as the Land of the Thunder Dragon. Some go even further with an oxymoronic description: the Land of the Peaceful Thunder Dragon.

The dragon appellation is latest among the local names for Bhutan and gained currency only after the unification of the country in the seventeenth century. As such, it does not have the same antiquity as the names discussed above although its initial application to a monastery in Tibet is very ancient. Druk was initially the name given to a place near Nam village, located south of Lhasa along the Kyichu valley in around 1206 CE. Traditional Tibetan and Bhutanese histories offer us a fabulous story of its beginnings. Tsangpa Gyarey (1161−1211), the renowned meditation master and ancestor of Bhutan's founding father, was visiting the Nam area, following the prophetic instructions of his teacher and tutelary deities to set up a spiritual centre, when he is reported to have seen nine dragons there. As he approached, the dragons flew off, triggering a clap of booming thunder in the sky. Subsequently, it rained flowers. Tsangpa Gyarey read these as auspicious omens for the foundation of his centre and thus named the place Druk or Dragon and his tradition, which began to spread out of this and other places, took the derivative name Drukpa or Dragoner, if such a word can be used.

Thus, like the other names for Bhutan which we discussed above, Druk also originates in Tibet. The name Dragon, however,was not given after Bhutan's fauna, in the way that Menjong was given after its flora, although many Bhutanese would still believe that there existed a reptilian creature which could fly and roar in the sky to cause thunder. Nor does the name have any historical connection to the prevalence of the dragon in Chinese culture as an unsuspecting visitor may assume. Apart from a single case of a Bhutanese mission to the court of Manchu Emperor Yongzheng (r.1723−36) in 1734,[9] historical links to China were virtually non-existent and the scanty influence from China on Bhutan was sieved through the Tibetan region. Even today, the borders are practically closed and there is neither a formal diplomatic link nor sociocultural exchanges.

The contemplative Drukpa tradition which Tsangpa Gyarey launched from Druk quickly spread in Tibet and its surrounding areas in the thirteenth century. Soon, the tradition became popular and widespread like 'dust on the soil and stars in the sky' to put it in one of their own idioms. It reached 'as far as a vulture could fly in eighteen days' and the adherents of the Drukpa tradition made the fantastic claim that 'half of the world is followers of the Drukpa tradition, half of them paupers and half of the paupers people with high spiritual achievements'.

With a major Drukpa centre located at Ralung, which is just a few days across Bhutan's northern border, the tradition very quickly found its way to the western valleys of modern Bhutan. The first person to bring this tradition to the main valleys of Bhutan was Drukgom Zhigpo, an eastern Tibetan man who journeyed south on a religious mission, following the instructions of his teachers. In spite of the difficulties he endured, which we will briefly discuss in Chapter 6, Drukgom Zhigpo managed to successfully establish himself in the western valleys, using Buddhism, diplomacy, sorcery and warfare. By the end of his life, he had established the Drukpa tradition in western Bhutan and he could bequeath to his heirs several establishments, estates and the patronage of local chieftains.

Some local historians claim that Bhutan was called Drukyul and her people Drukpa after the conversion of most people to the Drukpa school by Drukgom Zhigpo. However, the actual application of the name appears to have evolved gradually through a complex process. Firstly, we see a great number of religious centres being founded by lamas of the Drukpa order and many of them with names explicitly containing the word Druk, such as Druk Choding, Druk Chökyong Phodrang, Druk Phodrangding and Druk Rabtengang. There was a gradual rise in the number of toponyms containing the word Druk. However, the name was not used to refer to any area or region, let alone the country as a whole, even when Zhabdrung Ngawang Namgyal came to Bhutan in the seventeenth century and began to unify the valleys into one state.

The most common name used for the area that was proto-Bhutan during the sixteenth and seventeenth centuries was still Lhokhazhi, which we discussed earlier, or just Lho—'the south'. A convenient way of referring to the area was often by using a loose term—the southern region (ལྷོ་ཕྱོགས). Zhabdrung's historic departure for Bhutan in 1616, for instance, was commonly described as 'turning the riding pony toward the south' (ཆིབས་ཁ་ལྷོ་ལུ་བསྒྱུར). Some Tibetan authors around this time used the term 'outer south' (ལྷོ་ཕྱི) to refer to Bhutan in contrast to the 'inner south' (ལྷོ་ནང) which referred to the Lhodrak area in southern Tibet. There was a clear decline in the use of the term Mon or Monyul in reference to Bhutan after the unification. However, the primary referent of the name Druk throughout the seventeenth century was still the Namdruk and Druk Ralung establishments in Tibet.

Contrary to what most Bhutanese historians claim, it appears that the names Druk and Drukyul came to be used for the Bhutanese state and the term Drukpa for its people only in the eighteenth century. The earliest record is perhaps the Tibetan biography of Pholhaney by Tshering Wangyal completed in 1733. There the author refers to Bhutan as Lhodruk (ལྷོ་འབྲུག) or Southern Druk and Drukyul (འབྲུག་ཡུལ) or Land of Druk.[10] Although the term Drukyul was still rare, Druk appeared frequently after this. In a letter (in

Persian) written by the 3rd Panchen Lama (1738–80) to the British in 1775, he referred to Bhutan as Dukbo (འབྲུག་པ་) country. We also know from British records of their mission to Bhutan in 1774–75 that the Bhutanese called themselves Drukpa.[11] During the eighteenth and nineteenth centuries, we see a gradual transition from the vague name Lho to Druk and to Drukyul, and the name Druk, which designated the religious school, was used to refer to the country which the religious school has now effectively gained control of.

The use of formal names for the country and its inhabitants was perhaps necessitated by the increasing political interaction with Bhutan's neighbours. By the beginning of the eighteenth century, the Bhutanese state had also reached the point of being a nation with fairly well-defined territorial boundaries, formal administrative structures and an independent political identity, after going through much of the seventeenth century in a process of emergence. Nevertheless, it was only by the beginning of the twentieth century that the name Druk/Drukyul was firmly established and used as a standard name for the country both by its own citizens and its neighbours. This is attested by the phrase 'in our Dragon country' (རང་ཅག་འབྲུག་གི་རྒྱལ་ཁབ་) in the founding document of the monarchy signed by various eminent statesmen and clergy to endorse the hereditary monarchy in 1907. Today, Bhutan is called Druk or Drukyul by its own people and its Tibetan, Sikkimese and Monpa neighbours.

Bhutan—a British legacy

Of the many names we have discussed above, Bhutan's southern neighbours used none of them. We have no knowledge of what name the Assamese, Bengalis and Biharis may have called the new state which was formed to their north over a century before the British took over their own areas. The scanty records we have today show that they called the people from northern highlands Bhoteas or Bhutias, terms which are used even today to refer to people of Tibetan–Mongoloid racial group. The term Bhotea, today, has a pejorative connotation in some places and does not denote a specific nationality. It is quite likely that the areas which now comprise Tibet, Sikkim and Bhutan today were either known to them loosely as the country of Bhoteas or they may have used a name which was similar to what the British later used.

The modern name Bhutan is a British legacy and is partly an outcome of the British ignorance of the countries and the political and demographic setting beyond the Himalayan foothills. Although some people from the Indian plains certainly visited Bhutan as merchants, pilgrims or refugees, the British had very little information on Bhutan when they took over the Bengal and Assam plains and became Bhutan's southern neighbour. The Portuguese Jesuits Estevao Cacella and Joao Cabral, who travelled through Bhutan in 1627 and met its founding father, were the first Europeans to visit Bhutan and in their report dated 4 October 1627, called the country Cambirasi. The origin as well as the etymology of this name has perplexed historians. As farfetched as it may sound, this might have been a poor Portuguese rendering of Lhokhashi and something they picked up after they entered Bhutan. This is highly plausible as the Bhutanese, we have seen above, used the name Lhokhashi at that time and the Jesuits seem to have made a clear distinction between Bhutan and Tibet by using Cambirasi for Bhutan and Potente for Tibet, a distinction they would not have known prior to their arrival in Bhutan.

For our purpose here, the name Potente, which the Jesuits used for Tibet, is an interesting cue. Evoking the romantic idea of a mystical country ruled by a potentate, it resembles the idea of the fabled Christian kingdom of Cathai ruled by Father Prester John, which early European explorers, and perhaps even the two Jesuits, were bent on finding; the name is also clearly a prototype of the name Bhutan.

Potente was one among the medley of names early European explorers and cartographers used to refer to the mountainous area north of the Bengal and Assam plains extending as far as China and Tartary. Other names used include Bottan, Bottaner, Botton, Boutan, Bootan, Butan, Botenti, Pettent, Bhotanta, Porangké, Tobat, Thebet, Thibet and Barontola. These names were used to designate either the whole of the Tibetan world or parts thereof; sometimes two or three of these names appear on the same map referring to different regions and other times they are applied, often synonymously, to the same place.

Until the eighteenth century, no one in India seems to have had a clear knowledge of the political landscape of the north of the Assam plains. The multiplicity of the names and their variations amply suggest a serious confusion and uncertainty among the people who used these names. Ralf Fitch, an adventurous English merchant, is said to have been the first European to have sighted 'Bottaner' to the north of Bengal around 1586 and a book by Giovanni Peruschi published in 1597 contained a map showing a 'Botthanti populi', undoubtedly referring to the Tibetan people. Long after that, the Italian cartographer Cantelli, in his maps produced in 1682 and 1683, placed 'Boutan' in a number of locations between India and the Tartars, and used the names Boutan, Thibet and Barontola in a number of ways. Similarly, Guillaume Delisle, the French father of modern cartography, in his eighteenth-century maps used Boutan as an alternative for Tibet. Jean-Baptiste d'Anville did the same but added the 'Pays de Porangké' roughly where modern Bhutan is located, as did many other mapmakers and writers. Thus, Romola Gandolfo, who has carried out an incisive study of the name Bhutan on European maps, concludes that 'all supposed references to "Bhutan" based on western historical sources produced before 1765 should be understood as having nothing to do with present-day Bhutan: they refer instead to the whole of Tibet, or at least to that large portion of it which was called Greater Tibet and had Lhasa as its capital'.[12]

In spite of what the Jesuits reported in 1627, it is surprising that European explorers and cartographers until 1765 did not really know about the separate geopolitical existence of two separate states. They used the names Boutan and Thibet interchangeably and were not aware of a small Drukpa state north of Bengal but independent of Tibet. It was with such ignorance that George Bogle ventured into uncharted territory in 1774, in what was to be the first British mission to Bhutan and Tibet. The mission came about as a result of the military confrontation between Bhutan and Britain concerning the installation of the King of Cooch Behar, the small north Indian state which subsequently fell under the control of the East India Company.

Bogle and his team made their journey through modern Bhutan, where they stayed for about four months and met the 17th Deb Raja, and finally reached the place of the 3rd Panchen Lama, who they called the Teshoo Lama after his monastic seat of Tashilhunpo. In the course of the mission, Bogle learnt that there were two different countries with distinct political jurisdictions, and referred to the first one initially as the Deb Raja's country and the other as the Teesho Lama's country. Then, he seems to have vacillated between the Deb Raja's country and Boutan, perhaps not being able to make up his mind about which name to choose, and veered towards using Boutan for the Deb Raja's country and Tibet for the Teesho Lama's. Finally, it was in a report dated 30 September 1775, which he wrote after returning from Tibet and while staying in Bhutan, that he decisively nailed the name to the country. 'This country, which I shall distinguish by the name of Boutan', he wrote, referring to the Deb Raja's country, which we now call Bhutan. It was thus an amiable Scotsman named George Bogle who, in a stroke of historical accident, for once and for all distinguished the two countries of

Bhutan and Tibet for the Western world and secured the name Boutan for the Drukpa state.

Bogle's distinction of the two countries changed the imagination of the Himalayan world in Europe. This was further reinforced by the maps of James Rennell, a British surveyor who returned to become a mapmaker in 1777. Rennell's map effectively showed Bhutan as a separate country and also switched the French Boutan to an anglicized Bootan. The orthographic form, Bhutan, which is in currency today, is a later Indianized version although Indians generally pronounce it as Bhotan. Despite the orthographic change, the British still pronounce it Bootan.

Quite oblivious of the gradual development mentioned above, local and Indian scholars have made several efforts to explain the etymology of the name Bhutan. With the nationalistic proclivity to find an ancient justification for modern sociopolitical realities, some proposed that Bhutan derives from the Sanskrit term, Bhoṭānta—the end of Bhoṭa or Tibet. This is to say that Bhutan was at the edge of Tibet but never part of it. Others argue it comes from Bhū-uttan, meaning highland in Sanskrit—*bhū* indicating land and *uttan* elevated. Rejecting these hypotheses, Balaram Chakravarti suggests that the word Bhutan is perhaps simply a derivative of *Bhoṭānām*, that is, of the Bhoṭas, just as Iran is derived from Āryānām.[13] There is no doubt that the main part of the name Bhutan is derived from the word *bod* (བོད་) for Tibet. Even the name Tibet is derived from *Thobod* or high *bod*. Indians rendered *Bod* as *Boṭa* or *Bhoṭa* and one can surmise that the ending *tan* may have come from 'stan', which refers to a ground or land as in the cases of Pakistan and Hindustan. Whatever the historical origins and etymologies may be, the name Bhutan is now used throughout the world and is also what the Bhutanese themselves use when referring to their country in English. The French use the Francocized Bhoutan and the Chinese use the Sinocized Bùdān.

The Land and Its People

THE KINGDOM OF BHUTAN corresponds to the land between 88° 45' to 92° 10' East longitude and 26° 45' to 28° 10' North latitude, with an area of 38,394 sq. km. It is six hours ahead of GMT. Most people, however, use Bhutan's better-known neighbours as reference points.

Bhutan is often introduced in official and travel writings with the locution 'a kingdom sandwiched between the Asian giants of India and China'. This depiction aptly captures Bhutan's location as well as its vulnerable geopolitical situation. It also preserves an ancient Bhutanese predilection to define the country with reference to its immediate neighbours in the north and south.

In the old days, Bhutanese often situated their country due south of Lhasa and Samye in Tibet and north of Bodh Gaya, where the Buddha attained enlightenment and thus the heart of our world according to Buddhist cosmology. These places represent both geocultural centres and spiritual power points and Bhutan's geographical location was presented in relation to them. Further, to mark Bhutan's political boundary and suggest a territorial unity, the Bhutanese for many centuries used the scheme of four approaches which we saw in the discussion of the name Lhomonkhazhi. In this scheme, the extent of Bhutan was clearly marked by the four entry points. However, most traditional authors paid little attention to the state's territorial details as compared to their cosmological interest in positioning Bhutan in the universe as a whole. Thus many of these authors tell the story of Bhutan or a Bhutanese with a staggeringly wide macrocosmic view, as we see in Mahāyāna and Vajrayāna Buddhism.

In this system of thought, the universe we live in is only one of the many trillions of Buddha realms spread across the endless stretch of space and time, which are paradoxically inherently empty, multidimensional, collapsible,

Representation of Buddhist cosmology

expandable, interpenetrable, unobstructed and unlimited. The Buddha realm we live in, or 'our galaxy', is made up of ten billion microcosmic world units, each with the central Mount Meru, sun, moon and four continents. Representations of such a unit in art form are found across Bhutan at temple and *dzong* entrances. At the heart of the southern continent of such a world unit is Bodh Gaya and Bhutan is to be found to its north, often described as the land to be tamed by Padmasambhava. The Bhutanese, as devout Buddhists, believe in the unlimited extent of existence and in the process of reincarnation which takes a person on a cyclic journey through these world systems. Thus, it is not surprising that Bhutanese and other Himalayan Buddhist authors lay out an overly wide cosmological map in order to set the context for the subject of their work, be it a place or a person. Their contextual settings are like maps designed for an alien visitor from a faraway galaxy rather than for a human being on this earth, and it is with such an extraterrestrial view and conceptual mapping that traditional scholars approach the location of Bhutan.

Traditional literatures, however, do not mention the size of the country and even modern records give varying figures. School students were taught just a few years ago that Bhutan is over 47,000 sq. km and many sources still have this figure but the official Bhutanese version today is 38,394 sq. km. The variance is no doubt mainly due to the lack of exhaustive and accurate surveys and a clear demarcation of the border with China. Serious adjustments were made recently to the size and shape of Bhutan and the triangular swathe of mountainous area along the bend leading to the Kulha Khari peak in the north-central part of Bhutan is now no longer part of Bhutan. While the size in some areas changed with more accurate measurements, this area is said to have been always within Chinese control although it was shown as part of Bhutan in Bhutanese and commercial maps. Thus, the recent update in Bhutan's area has brought about visible changes to both the shape and size of the country and has alarmed many Bhutanese and their friends. It is quite possible that there may be further changes to Bhutan's size as its border with China becomes fully demarcated.

Faced with such inconsistent and changing figures for the size of Bhutan, many writers and speakers still take an easy and safe option of relative presentation of Bhutan as a country roughly the size of Switzerland or the Netherlands. It is undoubtedly a small country but in relative terms it is not as tiny as most people assume it to be. One can be surprised that there are nearly a hundred other independent and semi-independent countries, which are smaller than Bhutan and Bhutan's position in global ranking in size is about 134 out of 233, next to Switzerland and the Netherlands.

The lowest part of Bhutan starts at roughly 100 m above sea level and it rises to the high Himalayan watershed, the highest point now being the peak of Gangkar Punsum at 7578 m, which is also claimed to be highest unclimbed point on earth. Kulha Khari, at about 7554 m, was formerly deemed to be the highest point in Bhutan but is now considered neither within Bhutan nor higher than Gangkar Puensum. In the south, the country today begins almost simultaneously with the base of the foothills, although Bhutan controlled large areas of the Assamese and Bengal plains before they were lost to the British. While the northern and southern state borders generally follow the natural boundaries, the eastern and western boundaries with the Indian states of Arunachal Pradesh and Sikkim are political frontiers with no explicit natural demarcation. In addition to the general north–south gradient, the country is laterally divided by deep river valleys and high ranges with plunging sides. For this reason, some people describe Bhutan as a 'vertical country' and facetiously estimate that Bhutan may be as much as half of India if it were fully flattened.

The steep mountainous terrain of Bhutan and the Himalayan region as a whole, according to modern geology, were an outcome of the continental collision of the Eurasian and Indo-Australian tectonic plates some fifty million years ago over the area then occupied by the Tethys Sea, whose bed was pushed up to form the Tibetan plateau and the towering Himalayas. Sedimentary rocks, fossils of the sea animal ammonite and reserves of rock salt are proofs to argue that the plateau and mountains were once under the sea. The Himalayas are thus relatively young compared to the age of the earth and as the Indian plate continues to move into Asia by about 2 cm a year, the Himalayas are still said to be growing by about half a centimetre each year. This rise also makes the region seismically very active.

Bhutan falls entirely on the southern slopes of this tectonic uplift and, therefore, does not share exactly the same past as the Tibetan plateau. If the Tibetan plateau is the roof of the world, as it is often put, Bhutan is the eaves on its steep southern front. Tibet was a seabed thrust upward to form a tableland and it perhaps remained under seawater for a long time, until the seawater was fully drained or dried out. In a striking resemblance to the modern geological theory, ancient Tibetan religious lore has it that Tibet or at least what we call central Tibet was once a big sea. The sea gradually receded, opening up a vast expanse of habitable area, which was filled with a wide range of wild animals including *drong* or wild yak and apes and mythical ogresses. Eventually, it was one meditative monkey, believed to be an incarnation of Avalokiteśvara, who became the progenitor of the Tibetan people, having copulated with an ogress to produce the first 'red-faced' humans in Tibet. According to the lore, this unfortunately happened only after the historical Buddha. A verse allegedly from the Buddhist text, *Manjuśrimūlatantra,* is often cited to show how the Buddha predicted the withdrawal of the sea and growth of a forest of *sal* trees in the future. Tibet was not to be the direct recipient of Buddha's compassion. The Bodhisattva Avalokiteśvara was, therefore, assigned the task of taming the wild country of Tibet in the future and this he did, it is believed, through his numerous incarnations, including the monkey primogenitor, Tibet's great Emperor Songtsen Gampo in the seventh century, and the Dalai Lama in our times. This narrative is accepted as a historical fact by traditional Tibetan historians and forms a part of the standard history of Tibet.

Traditional Bhutanese historians and scholars also generally subscribed to this Tibetan origin myth but they went on to claim that the land which constitutes modern Bhutan existed long before the inland sea receded in Tibet. Bhutan, they argue, existed as an inaccessible hidden land long before Tibet came into existence as country. It is worthwhile citing Gedun Rinchen's poetic portrayal of Bhutan's primeval state:

As for the specific profile, from the outside there were cliff-mountains filled with weapons such as the indestructible rocks, thick forests which were like upstanding tresses of a wrathful [deity], and a landscape which is encircled by interlaced mountains of high elevation, in the corridors of which, like guards at an entrance, terrifying beasts roared. Inside, in the woods of diverse plants which shine like heavenly groves, divine hermit-like deer frolicked. From the soaring mansions of heavenly trees, birds with altruistic thoughts sang the melodies of *dharma*. In between these permeated in a hundred directions the scent of various medicinal herbs and flowers. The bees hummed like they were hard at work in making offerings with no seasonal breaks. In brief, this land, which perfectly fits the description of the sacred land for fulfilment of esoteric tantric practice, was like no other country. The country was naturally endowed with these marvellous qualities right at time of the inception of the world. It was not covered by sea before. Like the Malaya Mountain in Lanka, this is a special hidden land, difficult to be accessed by ordinary and common people.[1]

The Bhutanese monk-historians used a number of Buddhist accounts to argue for Bhutan's existence since very early times. Citing the *Jātaka* tales about the Buddha's former rebirths, they conjectured that the mountains and forests to the north of central India, to which many Bodhisattva figures of the *Jātaka* stories went for solitary retreat or into exile, must coincide with the highlands of Bhutan or Sikkim. From their perspectives, neither Tibet nor Nepal or even Kashmir qualified to be these forested mountains to the north of central India as they were, according to their origin myths, under the sea until many hundreds of years after the time of the Buddha. I shall say more about the journey of one such *Jātaka* character, Prince Drime Kunden, in Chapter 4. Another religious source they use is the legend of the deity Mahākāla, who is one of the main state protectors of Bhutan. When Mahākāla became an all-powerful spirit on earth in a very distant past, long before the Buddha came to this world, his retinue included a hundred Mon people. These, some traditional historians argued, were proto-Bhutanese.

They also recount the event when the Buddha delivered the discourse entitled *Sūryagarbhasūtra*. During this event, rays of light emitted from the Buddha and his disciple and shone on the mountains, rivers and forests to the north. Through this, the land was blessed to be a source of *dharma* in the future. The Buddha then prophesied that his teachings, monastic order and temples will appear in the area thus blessed. To the monk-historians, this mountainous tract in question includes the area of modern Bhutan. Using such arguments, the monk-historians insisted that Bhutan predated Tibet by a significant period of time. They also used the Tibetan lore very effectively to argue that Bhutan is older than Tibet and the earliest inhabitants are not of Tibetan stock born from a red-faced monkey. The monk historians also argued that the Buddha must have himself visited Bhutan as the Buddha is said to have traversed the whole earth in the fourth week after his enlightenment. Thus, the traditional understanding of Bhutan's early history and antiquity is largely informed by Buddhist belief and lore.

Having briefly discussed the location, size and age of the country, let us now turn to a more detailed profile of Bhutan's natural landscape. Extending from the subtropical terai belt to the eternally frozen snow mountains, Bhutan presents an ecological diversity rarely seen elsewhere in a short distance. The mean distance from the subtropical base of foothills in the south to the high peaks in the north is only about 120 km, as the crow flies. Besides, the country is divided by the river valleys plunging as deep as 3000 m. These valleys are often microcosms containing a full range of natural diversity, from the subtropical to alpine flora and fauna. Yet, the most outstanding aspect of Bhutan's ecology is its mostly pristine and untouched condition even in our times when the global ecosystem in general has been rendered very fragile and precarious through human exploitation. It is highly remarkable that Bhutan's ecosystem is still mostly intact and that environmental conservation features as one of the top priorities of the state, including a constitutional guarantee to retain at least 60 per cent under forest cover at all times.

According to the latest official figures, a total of 72.5 per cent of the country's area is under forest cover and 51.44 per cent is declared to be maintained as protected areas, including national parks, wildlife sanctuaries and ecological corridors. There are twelve parks and wildlife sanctuaries spread over the entire country ranging from 4914 sq. km. to 216 sq. km, the newest and the largest one being Wangchuk Centennial Park added only in 2008 to commemorate a hundred years of monarchical rule. These parks and sanctuaries are connected to each other by biological corridors, which make up about 6 per cent of the country. The corridors help avoid fragmentation of the natural habitats and encourage the free flow of genes in order to avert genetic degradation and maintain biodiversity. More details on the parks and corridors, including their floral and faunal diversity, human neighbours and trekking routes can be found in Lhendup Tharchen's *Protected Areas and Biodiversity of Bhutan*. The following excerpt gives us a clear picture of the magnitude of the Bhutan's biodiversity.

> The country's wild biodiversity is outstanding with almost 5500 species of vascular plants including 46 species of rhododendrons, 400 lichen species, 430 orchids, over 200 species of forest mushrooms, over 200 mammals species, 770 species of birds and many species of entomofauna, herpetofauna and aqua fauna still waiting to be discovered.
>
> The country's vast and contiguous tract of sub-tropical and temperate forests, alpine scrubs, meadows and screes, rivers, lakes and wetlands harbour several species of wild flora and fauna of global significance. Of these, 25 species of mammals and 14 species of birds found in Bhutan features in the World Conservation Union's Red List of threatened species. Species which are globally threatened like Tiger, Red Panda, Takin, Golden Langur, Black-necked crane and White-bellied Heron are found in good numbers in Bhutan.[2]

According to Tharchen's record, Bhutan has 5500 plant species out of which 129 are said to be endemic to Bhutan. In addition to the vast number of mammals and birds mentioned above, Bhutan has a large number of reptiles, including fifty-five species of snakes and nineteen species of lizards. Between 800 and 900 species of butterfly are known to exist in Bhutan.

These figures, however, include only species encountered by researchers, and which have been scientifically documented. Given the fact that large stretches of Bhutan's mountains and forests remain largely untouched by even local herders and farmers, it is highly probable that there are plants and animals yet to be discovered. The ecological wealth of Bhutan is still to be fully accounted for and only extensive and thoroughgoing research can reveal the ecological significance of Bhutan's uncharted nature. So far, not even species which the locals claim to exist have been either properly documented or conclusively proven to be a cultural fiction. The yeti or *migö* is a popular example. It is strongly believed to exist by many people in the Himalayas but it has remained elusive to the scientific radar. Another good example in central Bhutan is the case of a shy ape-like bipedal animal, which the Bhutanese call *michung*. The herders in Bumthang claim the *michung*, called *mirkula* in the local vernacular, exists and some even claim to have spotted it but there is no conclusive scientific evidence so far. Thus, Bhutan's ecological richness is not only a bonanza for nature lovers but a potentially rich ecological treasury for scientists to unravel.

The rich composition of Bhutan's flora and fauna is mainly due to the many eco-floristic and climatic zones encompassed by the country. The common model of its three eco-floristic zones of the subtropical lowlands, the temperate midlands and the alpine highlands correspond to the three lateral geopolitical areas of southern, middle and northern Bhutan but it must be noted that they do not match exactly; one can find near-alpine mountaintops even near southern parts of Bhutan and subtropical forests in deep valleys in northern Bhutan.

The Subtropical Lowlands

This zone stretches from the alluvial plains, of which Bhutan has very little, through the terai belt and foothills up to the lesser Himalayan ranges, rising from about 100 m to 1800 m. The vegetation is mainly lowland hardwood and broadleaf deciduous and evergreen forests consisting of a wide range of plants including the rare and endangered aloe wood (*Aquilaria agalocha*).

The hills have a steep south face and subtropical climate with warm winters and hot and humid summers. Due to high precipitation, the region sees a lot of rain in the monsoon season, causing frequent landslides. Here one finds a wide variety of subtropical animals, including elephants, rhinos, Bengal tigers, clouded leopard, golden langur, Indian gaur and black panther and easily over 500 kinds of birds, including the endangered species such as rufous-necked hornbill, great hornbill and white-rumped vulture.

One can assume that the lowland belt was almost completely under forest cover until the twentieth century, with only very sparse human settlements. These small settlements were probably concentrated in the border posts in the southern frontiers, about which one finds some information in the diaries of the British visitors. The heat and humidity of the subtropics, compounded with the fear of malaria, kept the northern Bhutanese farmers from even entering, let alone settling, in the area. The main northern Bhutanese to make it to the lowlands were occasional political envoys, traders visiting Indian trade marts and some cattle herders who would bring their cattle southward to subtropical pastures in the winter. Among the ethnic groups who lived in the lowlands before the twentieth century are two closely related groups known to other Bhutanese as Lhop and Taba Dramtep. These communities, which remained isolated from the rest of Bhutan until very recently, represent a very ancient and primitive culture that is quite different from the mainstream Bhutanese culture. The following description by the ethnographer Francoise Pommaret gives a clear picture of their way of life:

> They live in close-knit communities, marry their cross-cousins and, by and large, are still animists worshipping local deities. They do not cremate their dead, but bury them in wood and stone-slab coffins that form a small mound. A hut erected on the mound protects it from the rain, and a fence is put up around the site. In the past, the personal belongings of the dead person were kept in the hut, but today the family just leave a few coins. The Lhopus are shifting cultivators (growing maize, millet and sorghum); they raise cattle, but they also hunt, fish and gather forest products ... Men and women wore the same kind of wraparound garment called *pakhi* made of nettle fibre, though nowadays they use machine-woven Indian cotton.[3]

The lifestyle and the cultural practices of the Lhop and Taba Dramtep communities are so compellingly old and untouched by Buddhist or other external influence that some have even venture to speculate that they may be the last remnants of the earliest inhabitants of western Bhutan who got pushed out to the peripheries by dominant groups.

The other ethnic group living close to the subtropical lowland in western Bhutan is the Lepcha. The Lepcha no longer fully carry on their distinct cultural practices; they have assimilated into dominant groups and their cultural and linguistic features are akin to the ethnic Lepcha in Sikkim. The subtropical areas close to the central lowlands were inhabited by the people of the Kheng and Mangde regions, who are generally considered to be of the mainstream Bhutanese stock. Similarly, some lowland areas in the east, particularly near Dungsam, saw some eastern Bhutanese settlers.

However, the most significant demographic development in the southern lowlands occurred with the arrival of migrant labourers from Nepal some time around the turn of the twentieth century. Although referred to as Nepalis due to their common origin, these immigrants came from a wide range of ethnic backgrounds. Some belonged to the strict Hindu-Indian castes and subcastes, including Bahun and Chhetri, equated with Brahmins and Kshatriyas, others were Rai and Limbu, who are considered to be the indigenous peoples of eastern Nepal and yet others were Sherpa and Tamang, who considered themselves Tibetan stock and followed Buddhism. The Nepali settlers cleared huge areas of forests to make farmland and became the most dominant people in southern Bhutan. A century on, their common tongue, Nepali, an Indo-European language, is spoken across Bhutan and most of their descendents are citizens of Bhutan. Today, in spite of a bitter ethnic conflict around 1990, the people of Nepali origin make about 25 per cent of Bhutan's population and a more politically correct term Lhotshampa or 'Southerner' is used to refer to them as a whole. The settlement of Lhotshampas in subtropical lowland transformed the demography of the area.

Today, the area covers the districts of Samdrupjongkhar, Pema Gatsel, Shemgang, Sarpang, Tsirang, Chukha and Samtse, and is bordered to the south by the Indian states of Assam and West Bengal and to the east by Arunachal Pradesh and to the west by Sikkim. The region has seen strong economic growth with the introduction of cardamom and orange plantations for export. Cereals such as maize, millet and rice and a wide range of vegetables and fruits are grown in the area. The areca nut, which Bhutanese consume with great penchant, is popularly grown in this area. The nut is eaten wrapped in betel leaves and smeared with lime paste. Although tea is widely grown just across the border in the tea estates of Assam and Bengal, the practice has not really interested the Bhutanese, who nonetheless drink a lot of tea imported from both India and China.

More importantly, the lowlands are now the lifeline for Bhutan, which has become increasingly dependent on imports. They have become the main doorways for businesses with India, Bhutan's principal trading partner and supporter. Due to this, many urban centres have sprung in the areas of former trade centres and frontier posts. These towns include Samtse, Phuntsholing, Sarpang, Gelephu, Ngalam and Samdrupjongkhar, all of them located on the border with India. This has made the population density in the lowlands higher than in the valleys north of it. Economic activity has further increased ethnic diversity by attracting merchants from various parts of north India and Bhutanese from all parts of the country. While demographic changes due to this economic boom were mostly happening in the urban centres, the government's programme to resettle northern Bhutanese in the lowlands to help diffuse potential ethnic tensions and secure political stability in the area has led to a significant rise in the northern settlers in rural parts of the lowlands. Thus, the subtropical lowlands, which were once seen as treacherously hot and too dangerous to travel to, are today a lively region with economic promise and are a popular winter destination for many Bhutanese.

The Temperate Midlands

This zone is the cultural heartland of Bhutan and includes the central valleys, with altitudes ranging from 1000 to 3000 m. The climate is generally moderate with temperatures between 15° and 30° in the summer, frequently dropping below zero in the winter in higher regions. The region receives a lot of rain, with torrential downpours during the peak of monsoon in July and August; there is snowfall in the higher areas in the winter months. In spring, the mountains are bestrewn with blossoms of magnolia and rhododendrons while in autumn the sky is clear, the mountains are full of colours and the valleys turn gold with paddy fields ready for harvest.

The midlands are marked by broad valleys separated by high mountain ranges and split by big rivers, which flow from north to south. These natural barriers divide the various districts of the Bhutan and have historically led to the ethnic and linguistic diversity of the country. The vegetation in the lowest parts of the midlands comprises evergreen broad leaves with thick undergrowth in moist areas and chir pine forests with patchy undergrowth in hot and dry places. With the rise in altitude, the vegetation quickly changes to deciduous forest of trees, including oak, maple and beeches. Further up, the vegetation is a mixture of deciduous and evergreen conifers such as blue pine and Bhutan cypress. In the upper reaches of the midlands, one can find forests of blue pine, spruce, larch, rhododendrons, fir and juniper with a widespread undergrowth of bamboos. A valley like Ura in central Bhutan at 3200 m has forests of primarily pine on the western side, some larch on the eastern side, spruce on the northern side, fir and juniper in the upper regions, all mixed with several kinds of rhododendrons, bamboos, roses and other bushes and shrubs. In these forests, one finds a wide variety of animals, including the red panda, the Himalayan black bear, boars, leopards, wild dog and deer, and a huge range of birds.

The majority of people known to the outside world as Bhutanese live in this zone. In the lower valleys such as Paro, Thimphu, Punakha, Tongsa and Mongar, rice is cultivated widely as are maize, millet, chilli and many varieties of vegetables and fruits. In higher areas such as Haa and Bumthang, the main crops traditionally were bitter and sweet buckwheat, barley and wheat. Vegetables such as turnips, radish, beans and peas and fruits, including apples, apricots, peaches and berries, are also common. Today, most of the farmers grow potato as a cash crop. This tuber is said to have been introduced to Bhutan in 1775 by the Scotsman George Bogle, who led the first official European mission to Bhutan. The farmers in the upper regions of central region now grow potatoes in significant quantities and export them to India, where some of them are valued as high-quality seeds.

Because the valleys in the midlands are separated by natural barriers of mountains and rivers, communication between them was minimal until the main artery of the east–west highway was built in the latter half of the twentieth century. In contrast, most of the valleys had easier access to Tibet and India and many people travelled to Tibet for trade, education or pilgrimage. Fewer people did so to India although the trend is completely reversed now with thousands of Bhutanese visiting India each year for these three reasons, while Tibet has become a very difficult destination for the Bhutanese with the northern border officially sealed. A few Bhutanese, however, visit Tibet on pilgrimage via Nepal or China. Before motor roads came, the physical barriers in the landscape and the consequent lack of mobility had led to a generally isolated growth of cultures and languages across the country. It is only from the middle of the twentieth century that Bhutanese people from different valleys started interacting with each other and converging to form a shared national identity to the degree that we can talk of a single national culture. Thus, the midlands of which we speak as traditional Bhutan was anything but of one tradition or culture.

In the eastern districts of Samdrupjongkhar, Pema Gatsel, Tashigang and Mongar are people whose traditional staple is maize and whose native tongue is Tshangla, which is more known by its other name, Sharchopikha, literally the language of the east. There are at least seven other local languages spoken in these districts and the two neighbouring districts of Tashi Yangtse and Kurtoe. These six districts make up eastern Bhutan in the current administrative and sociopolitical convention. The valleys in the east generally have steep slopes and very narrow riverbeds resembling deep canyons. This has resulted in a shortage of agricultural land, forcing people to etch out a living on steep slopes. Rice is grown in irrigable land but maize, various kinds of millet, potato and chilli are the main crops. Many people lived in bamboo houses on stilts but this is quickly changing with the availability of new building materials and mechanisms. Distilled spirit or *ara* made from the cereals is popular and even women are known to be avid drinkers. They practise cross-cousin marriages, adopt a liberal attitude to sex, and excel in a number of crafts, including woodwork, bamboo crafts and textiles.

Due to their geographic proximity and similarities in the physical features, food culture and textile tradition, it was suggested by scholars that many of the eastern Bhutanese may have been originally closer to the people of eastern India and Burma than to those of central and western Bhutan. This may very well justify the claim that there are three major racial groups in Bhutan today, the first with a close affinity to Burmese, Assamese and other hill tribes to the east, the second with ancient connections to Tibetans in the north and finally, the third who descended from recent immigrants from Nepal. In the first group would fall most people of eastern Bhutanese origin and in the second those from central and western Bhutan. The southern Bhutanese or Lhotshampa make up the third group. However, following linguistic features, it is perhaps more appropriate to talk about four major groups: the western Bhutanese who primarily speak Dzongkha, the central Bhutanese who speak languages of the Bumthangkha group, the eastern Bhutanese who speak Tshangla and the southern Bhutanese who speak Nepali, an Indo-European language. However, any such categorization must be seen as a generalization and not as a hard and fast genetic grouping or cultural transmission. We must remain aware of the linguistic complexity of Bhutan, the common practice of intermarriage between regional elites, the adventurous religious missionaries who started fresh establishments, and of the old Himalayan predilection for group or individual migration in search of greener pastures, all of which point to a diverse and an interwoven ethnographic scenario.

The linguistic complexity is particularly perplexing when it comes to explaining the origins of the midland Bhutanese. To the north of Tshangla speakers both in the upper course of Kholongchu in the Tashi Yangtse district and Kurichu in the Kurtoe district, we find several languages which fall within different subgroups of the Tibetan–Burman language family. Some of them are found to be related to languages spoken in areas which are not directly connected to the places where they are spoken. Chalikha, an East Bodish language spoken in just one village on the fertile eastern slope of Kurichu, is a good example. The village is surrounded by areas where Tshangla and Central Bodish is spoken and cut off from other areas where East Bodish is spoken.

Although it may well be the case that general Tshangla speakers shared ancestral origins with their eastern neighbours, we also have plenty of evidence that people from Tibet and other parts of Bhutan have settled in the eastern regions throughout the centuries, thus diluting any ethnic particularity. A genealogical account by the seventeenth-century monk Ngawang, tracing the roots of the nobilities of eastern Bhutan to the exiled Tibetan Prince Tsangma and the Dorji brothers in the ninth century and Lama Sa-ngag's genealogy of the Nyö family, which also originated in Tibet, sufficiently demonstrate the significance of influence from Tibet and central Bhutan. We shall come across Ngawang's account of Prince Tsangma and the Dorji brothers in the next chapter. What is important to note at this point is that Ngawang, writing his genealogy in 1668, traces the origin of both the nobilities and commoners of eastern Bhutan to Tibet, quite different from the claims made by later monk-historians that Bhutan was inhabited by people long before Tibet. Ngawang also lists some twenty-six different clans of common people who inhabited the eastern regions of Bhutan.

What we learn from genealogical accounts of both Ngawang and Lama Sa-ngag is that the ethnic make-up of the region is far more composite than it may seem. To the written accounts of the genealogists, one may also add the many oral stories about trans-regional religious travels, political deputations, marital exchanges and trade in order to get a clearer picture of an ethnic fusion. However, none of these convergences in the past would even remotely compare to the homogenization and cultural merger now taking place across Bhutan, a process bound to blur ethnic and cultural distinctions.

Further west along the midlands, one finds the region of Bumthang, which is one of the highest areas among what we call here the Temperate Midlands.

Bumthang is composed of the four valleys of Ura, Tang, Chokhor and Chumey, going from east to west. The language spoken here is Bumthangkha and the language spoken in the Kurtoe, Shemgang and Tongsa districts are very closely related to this. Thus, linguistically, Kurtoe would belong more to central Bhutan than to the east. In ancient times, both Kurtoe and Bumthang were contiguously linked to each other and to southern Tibet and their economies and lifestyles would have been more heavily influenced by exchanges with Tibet to the north than with other Bhutanese valleys. Both areas have a rich textile tradition although the materials and patterns used are different. In the distant past, inferring from the woollen *shingkha* tunics found in Bumthang and the cotton and nettle *kushung* tunics, which were worn in Kurtoe, the two valleys may have also shared a dress culture. Today, both these dresses are almost wholly forgotten; only remnants of them are found further east. The few ancient records we have access to today suggest that the area which includes Bumthang and some valleys to the west had a dress which was different from what the Tibetans wore then. This dress is referred to as *lhochey* or dress of the south. It is however difficult to tell if this southern dress was a prototype of the *gho* and *kira* which nearly all Bhutanese wear today or something resembling the archaic tunics.

To withstand the severe cold of the harsh winters, the people of Bumthang traditionally wore thick woollen clothing. In addition, women wrapped their heads with a piece of cloth and both men and women wore furry yak and sheep pelts on their backs both to keep warm and to shield themselves from the heavy load they carried. As recently as the twentieth century, aristocratic ladies in Bumthang also wore aprons over their *kira*, like Tibetan ladies do over their dress. It is common to see women in Ura wear aprons even today and this may indicate a close link between the Ura people and Tibet. Interestingly, there is an ancient saying: The people of Ura are Mon who have descended from Tibet and people of Khothing are Tibetans who have descended from Mon (མོན་བོད་ལས་ཆད་པའི་ཨུ་ར. པ། བོད་མོན་ལས་ཆད་པའི་མཁོ་མཐིང་པ།). The people and culture of Khothing, which is on the other side of Bhutan's border with Tibet, are said to have closely resembled those of Bhutan. Whether this saying is simply figurative speech to underscore the similarity between people of Ura and Tibetans or an indication that people of Ura descended from Tibet is not clear. However, we can see historical cases of Ura's connections to Tibet in the stories of Ura *dung* and Nyö families and remarks by Longchenpa about the presence of the Tibetan royal line in Ura. We will come across these stories in the following chapters. There are also various ethnographic evidences, such as songs and rituals, to indicate close links. Yet, the ethnic closeness to Tibet is not exclusive to Ura. Ura is just a case in point to illustrate the ancestral link between Bumthang and Tibet. It is worth noting here that the ethnic origins of the people of Bumthang, particularly among the elites, are traced back to Tibet either through the legendary Tibetan refugees and their subjects or Tibetan religious masters, who gave rise to many prominent families in Bumthang.

The people of Bumthang cultivated crops such as wheat, barley, bitter and sweet buckwheat and various kinds of vegetables and fruits. If we are to believe Longchenpa (1308–64), the Tibetan philosopher saint who travelled across Bhutan, Bumthang was a heavenly paradise with people living in great prosperity.[4] The large houses had slanting wooden roofs, making them look like celestial mansions from a distance, but ordinary houses were pleasant, with the slanting roofs facing only on one side. There were also many dwellings made of bamboo and cane. 'Medicinal herbs, flowers and fruits grow in abundance. The country is vast, growing nine varieties of crops. There are also many trade items from [various] directions,' he says about the Tang valley. And speaking about Ura, he writes: 'The grass is highly nourishing here and hence livestock thrives more than other places. The trees bear good fruits and the forests are marvellous.'

Longchenpa's account of Bumthang as an abundant place is corroborated more than a century later by Pema Lingpa (1450–1521), who claimed to be his reincarnation and was a native of Bumthang. Pema Lingpa's autobiography gives ample information on the peaceful and prosperous way of life in the Bumthang valleys. For instance, the long list of local cuisine, including *puta, jangmuli, pin* and *khurwa,* in his biography gives a great deal of information on agriculture and the ethno-gastronomic culture of the people of Bumthang in the fifteenth century.[5] Many of these cuisines are still known in Bumthang and considered local delicacies.

The people of Bumthang were also great pastoralists, owning large herds of cattle and yaks. They owned large areas of grazing lands in the neighbouring districts of Kurtoe, Mongar, Mangde, Kheng and some even as far as the lowlands of Sarpang. The cattle were always taken to lower altitudes in the winter and some members of the families also migrated with the cattle to warmer regions. However, the transhumance which the people of Bumthang practised was different from the full migratory patterns practised by some people in western Bhutan. The people of Bumthang often owned rice fields and fruit orchards in warmer areas such as Mangde and Mongar, which they would lease out to locals in the area for share-cropping and would only visit briefly to harvest the crops in autumn. Today, both agricultural and pastoral farming are declining in Bumthang, as in most other parts of Bhutan, as young people favour white-collar jobs and a consumerist lifestyle. The robust tradition of animal husbandry is encumbered by the hard labour associated with it and the stringent environmental regulations restricting the use of forests. The government has tried to substitute traditional animal husbandry with Jersey and Brown Swiss cattle farming with some success.

To the south and west of Bumthang are two districts of Mangde and Kheng, now commonly known as Tongsa and Shemgang after their district headquarters. Both districts extend from high fir forests to the deep valleys with subtropical forests of evergreen plants. On the whole, they lie much lower than Bumthang. However, their topography, like much of eastern Bhutan, is made of very steep slopes and narrow riverbeds. Hence, despite the favourable climate, agricultural productivity is restricted to areas with mild slopes. Nevertheless, the districts produce a great variety of cereals, including rice, maize and millet and a large range of fruits and vegetables. Speaking about the abundance of food in the Mangde region, Longchenpa remarked that it is truly *mang sde*, the region of plenty. He adds: 'In the upper reaches are many groups of forested mountains; in the middle, many grains and abundant medicinal plants and fruits. In the lower regions, rice, millet, peas and other cereals grow in plenty, as does a very good tea plant.' It is not clear if there was cultivation of some indigenous tea or if Longchenpa was referring to some kind of local herbal tea such as the mistletoe (*Serrula elata*), which is quite commonly used by the Bhutanese for hot beverages and often called tea.

The people of Mangde and Kheng, like the people of Mongar and Kurtoe, often maintained a strong religious bond with the lamas of Bumthang. Each autumn, the lamas of Bumthang and their disciples made their journey to perform religious services for the people of the lower regions. They carried their religious relics to bless the populace and in the course of their religious tours collected huge numbers of gifts. These offerings came mainly in the form of grains but also included textiles, fruits, vegetables, dyes, vegetable butter and wood and bamboo products. The people of Kheng are particularly well known for their craftsmanship in bamboo works. Such exchange of agricultural and forest products with spiritual blessings and guidance formed a regular and important component of the economic and social transaction. It also linked communities, establishments and families together in close spiritual and secular alliances. It is a good example of *chöyon* (མཆོད་ཡོན་) or the priest–patron relationship at a very micro level but akin to the same kind of relationship the Yuan and Qing emperors of China had with Tibetan Sakya and Gelukpa lamas. With unprecedented mobility in both physical space and social status and the expanding influence of the State Monk Body, this tradition of a selective priest–patron relationship is fast declining. Moreover, with economic improvement and better communication facilities, there is now widespread access to religious education both within and outside Bhutan, giving rise to a host of new lamas from outside traditional religious families.

Among people in the Mangde and Tongsa regions, the Mon people, numbering about sixty households and 350 members, deserve a special mention. The Monpa live on the eastern and western slopes of Jowo Durshingphu, which is today commonly known by the name Black Mountain for its appearance. They speak a distinct language called Olekha or Monkha, which is not directly related to other languages spoken in the surrounding communities. With a very strong connection to nature, they by and large live a primitive agrarian life, growing wheat, maize and millet and depending on other forest products. Compared to the mainstream Bhutanese in central and western Bhutan, the Monpa communities, like the Lhopus, still remain quite isolated and underdeveloped. It may be recalled here that Mon is an ancient term used by Tibetans to refer to the Bhutanese and other groups along the southern borders. Some scholars have taken this cue of the name to argue the Monpas may be the early inhabitants of the central Bhutanese valleys and they may have got pushed to the peripheral regions. Such an argument, we saw earlier, was used for the Lhops. Although it is difficult to confirm or reject such hypothesis without substantive ethnographic evidence, judging from the location of their settlements, it is also possible that their arrival occurred much later, after the fertile agricultural lands were occupied by other groups. The Monpa settlement of Reti, for instance, is said to have started as late as the time of Ugyen Wangchuk (r.1907–26) to escape the heavy labour tax of transporting cargo from eastern Bhutan to western Bhutan for the government.

To the north of the Monpa are the people who speak the Ngenkha. They extend from the Mangechu valley to the vicinity of the Pelela pass although the north eastfacing slopes of Black Mountain hardly have any human settlements except at the bottom of the valleys. The whole stretch of forest, now opposite the motor road before Chendeji, approaching from Tongsa, was once considered the dangerous domain of the terrifying Nyala demoness.

The village near the Pelela pass heralds the end of what was known as eastern Bhutan in Bhutan's medieval history. The area east of the Pelela pass was metaphorically known as the Eight-spoke Wheel of the East (ཤར་ཕྱོགས་འཁོར་ལོ་རྩིབས་བརྒྱད་) after the unification of the country in the middle of the seventeenth century and made up of eight districts including (1) Mangde, now Tongsa (2) Kheng, now Shemgang (3) Bumthang (4) Zhongar, now Mongar, (5) Kurtoe, now Lhuntse (6) Yangtse (7) Tashigang and (8) Dungsam, now Pema Gatshel.

The Pelela pass distinctly marks the linguistic divide between Dzongkha and non-Dzongkha speakers as well as the historical and sociopolitical boundary between western and non-western Bhutan. Indications that it divided the Bhutanese world into two in the past can be seen in the confusing pair of toponyms, *shar* or East, the name for the valley west of Pelela and *nub* or West, the name for the valley east of Pelela. The names show how the eastern horizon of the western Bhutanese ended with the valley of Shar or East and the western horizon of the central Bhutanese extended just up to the area of Nub or West.

The valleys west of Pelela pass are generally low and warm rice-growing areas with the exception of Haa valley. Thus, the staple food in this part of Bhutan is rice, over a kilo of it being consumed each day by a single adult on the average. Maize, wheat and barley are also cultivated and we have records from both Bhutanese sources and British records about the availability of a wide range of fruits and vegetables. The people in these valleys are also more avid meat-eaters than those to their east but consume less alcohol. Ancient records also talk about their superior physique and bellicosity. They are well known for their literary talent of chanting out extemporaneous poems known as *lozé*. A similar genre of oral literature known as *tsangmo* is found in central and eastern Bhutan.

The people in the western valleys are commonly known as Ngalong, a blanket term used in recent past to refer to all native Dzongkha speakers. Even Dzongkha was known as Ngalongkha, the language of the Ngalong, until it was formally constituted as the official language. Some traditional historians argue, based on the etymology allowed by its modern orthography, that the term Ngalong refers to 'early risers', that is, the early ones to be woken up by the teachings of the Buddha. This would imply that the people of western Bhutan were the earliest to convert to Buddhism. The etymology is, however, a farfetched one and most likely a modern reconstruction. In the early records the term appears mostly as *rngen lung,* the *lung* or valley of *rngan* which either means 'before' or may be a cognate of *brngan* or hunting. It is often coupled with the word *men log*, for which scholars again provide the etymology *mi log* or non-returning. According to them, due to their fertile land and amenable climate, the valleys of Shar and Punakha were occupied by people of Indian origin.[6] There are still oral stories and toponyms being used to indicate some Indian presence here. These immigrants were later expelled using the help of the Tibetan army of King Tri Ralpachen (r. 815–38). In the typical fashion of military expeditions, the Tibetan soldiers, having routed the Indians, found the districts too good for them to resist. They decided to settle in the area and not return to Tibet and thus came to be called *mi log* or non-returners. Whether or not there is any historical truth in the etymology, the term *rngan lung men log* is almost exclusively used for the Shar district in the old records. The term does not cover the Thimphu, Paro and Haa valleys to the west and Dagana and Chukha to the south, which the modern term Ngalong encompasses.

If there is any truth in the story of Indian occupation and Tibetan settlement mentioned above, it suggests that the ethnic origin of the people in the western valleys, particularly of Shar, is likely to be a mixture of both ancient Indians and Tibetans. Besides, the western valleys attracted a lot of religious pilgrims and missionaries from Tibet. We know that the Tibetan religious missionaries dominated the western valleys ever since the thirteenth century and their descendants, particularly the families descending from Phajo Drukgom Zhigpo, make up most of the old nobilities in the region. The valleys were also very well connected to both India and Tibet allowing a great deal of movement for both religious and commercial reasons. This certainly facilitated the arrival of Zhabdrung Ngawang Namgyal in the region in 1616 and has eventually turned the region into the political centre of the new state of Bhutan. This, in turn, enhanced the visibility of this region and attracted even more people, including Europeans.

After the establishment of centralized power in the seventeenth century, central and eastern Bhutanese referred to the western valleys as *zhung*, which means centre or mainstream and by derivation, the government. True to the name, it was here in the valleys of Thimphu and Punakha where the government headquarters of Bhutan remained through centuries except for the first half of the twentieth century when the country was officially run from Bumthang and Tongsa. The Bhutanese valleys, which were socially and commercially oriented to the north until the formation of the unified state, saw a major change in their sociopolitical orientation with the rise of political power in the western valleys of Thimphu and Punakha. They had to deal with each other more than they dealt with their neighbours to the north and south and it certainly must have brought a sudden change in their perception of each other.

Another small component of the demographic mixture of western Bhutan originates in the ancient slave culture. This is also true for some parts of central and eastern Bhutan. Bhutanese marauders in medieval times often raided north Indian villages and kidnapped the people or held Indian travellers captive. These people were then enslaved giving rise to a whole class of serfs, who were known in some parts of the western valleys as *jow* (ཇོ) and *jom* (ཇོམ), a vernacular term for male and female Indian. Through generations, they served the families who owned them as slaves, without any property or fees for their labour. Also, several Tibetan children were kidnapped by Bhutanese traders to be turned into slaves. Before the abolition of slavery by the 3rd King in 1958, this class of people formed the lowest stratum of the traditional Bhutanese society.

Most people of the western valleys lived a migratory life, keeping two homes: a summer home in temperate regions and a winter residence in the warmer subtropical areas. This migratory pattern seems to be common to all the valleys, except perhaps to a lesser degree to Paro. We have some records of such migratory movement happening in medieval times and it can be also inferred from the migration of the State Monk Body between Thimphu and Punakha since their early days. When the families moved from the warm summer estates to higher elevations in spring it was often the slaves of Indian origin who would stay on to look after the fields in the summer. The people of the Shar valley have their summer homes in the highlands of Phobjikha, now well known for the endangered black-neck crane; people in the Thed or Punakha valley went to Thimphu for the summer. These twin valleys were known as Wang, and together with Shar and Paro, they made the tripartite area of western Bhutan.

Of the western midlands, Haa is the only major valley at an elevation too high to cultivate rice. Like in Bumthang, people of Haa grow buckwheat, sweet buckwheat, wheat, barley, turnips and mustards and are ardent pastoralists, with a strong tradition of herding both lowland cattle and highland yak. While they keep their yaks in the higher altitudes throughout the year, they take their lowland cattle to lower subtropical areas in the northern regions of Samtse. Due to their proximity to Tibet via the ancient trade route through Dromo or Chumbi, the narrow triangular stretch of China between

Bhutan and Sikkim today, both the peoples of upper Paro and Haa speak a dialect of Dzongkha which resembles Tibetan. They also share a New Year called Loba, which falls about two months before the common Bhutanese New Year. The New Year for lower Paro precedes even Loba and falls in the tenth Bhutanese month.

The Alpine Highlands

If the term alpine is derived from the Alps, there is one drastic difference between the Alps and Himalayas that we must take note of in using this term for the Himalayas. The alpine zone in Bhutan starts at a much higher altitude of some 4000 m compared to just about 1500 m on the Alps. Trees in Bhutan grow in much higher altitudes than in Europe. The subalpine vegetation of stunted fir, spruce and junipers gradually gives way to dwarf rhododendrons and other shrubs, flowering plants and herbs in alpine meadows. It is in this terrain that many medicinal herbs, including the expensive caterpillar fungus *Cordyceps sinensis*, grow. The alpine meadows make up the wide pastures for grazing highland animals such as yak and sheep. The meadows extend as far as snow lines leading to mountains perennially covered in snow. The main wild animals in the alpine region are pikas, marmots, blue sheep, musk deer, takins and snow leopards. The nebulous and mysterious yeti and the *michung* are said to roam mostly in the alpine and subalpine regions of big mountains.

The people living close to the alpine grasslands are mainly pastoralists as the land and climate turn less conducive for cultivation. However wheat, barley and buckwheat are cultivated by many highland communities as are radishes and turnips, the leaves of which are dried and used as vegetables in the winter. Many highland communities have distinct sociolinguistic and cultural features, which differ from those of the midlands. To the north of western Bhutan are three highland communities of Laya, Lingshi and Lunana. They herd yaks, which feed on grass and dwarf bamboo, and their main source of livelihood is dairy products, which they barter with other items such as rice, salt, clothes and cooking utensils. During the summer, they graze their cattle in the mountain pastures and in autumn before the snow closes their trade routes, they journey to the lowlands to sell their products. Resembling trade in other areas, they exchange their products with other goods although today with a monetized economy, they increasingly sell goods for cash which they then use to buy other things.

The people of these areas speak dialects of Dzongkha, which are not easily intelligible to an ordinary Dzongkha speaker. They have a very distinct culture of dress and living space, which places them much closer to Tibetan pastoral communities than to mainstream Bhutanese. They live in large black tents made out of yak hair and also wear dresses made of the yak hair and sheep wool. The women's dress, to use Pommaret's description, is 'a black skirt with brown vertical stripes, a black jacket, a distinctive conical bamboo hat perched on top of the head and much silver jewellery, including spoons, hanging at the back'.[7] Men wear something similar, minus the jewellery, and have shorter skirts. Sadly, these cultural distinctions are fast disappearing as more and more people take up the mainstream Bhutanese culture.

According to a local myth, the people of these areas are alleged to be descendants of a group once sent off from Tibet as part of a scapegoat ritual. This ritual, which is widely practised in Tibetan communities, purports to pacify and get rid of harmful spirits or deities by banishing them to distant lands fully stocked with necessities and other gifts. Normally, dough effigies of the spirit are made, draped in small pieces of cloths and decked with jewellery. Effigies are also made of wooden moulds of servants, animals and other properties. Symbolic mansions are created weaving threads of different colours. These replicas, to which are added grains, coins, etc. are then mentally transformed by chanting mantras and through the power of visualization to be perceived as real by the spirit, who is then sent off by casting away the effigies at crossroads. Banishing people as part of a scapegoat ritual is not generally known although there is a legendary account of the expulsion of Tibetan Prince Khikha Rathö in this manner; we shall see this in the chapter on the Early Historic period.[8] It is unlikely that the origin of these communities lies in such an arcane ritual. Their close affinity with their northern Tibetan neighbours must be mainly a consequence of geographic proximity. Even today, these villages are more easily accessible to the Tibetan neighbours across the border than to the Bhutanese communities to the south. It was with Tibetans that they mostly bartered their goods until the Chinese occupation in 1959 when the border between Bhutan and Tibet was sealed. With the recent boom of business of the expensive fungus, cordyceps, in these highlands, the inhabitants have seen a sudden rise in their fortunes and in the import of goods from across the border with China.

Going eastward along the northern highlands, one reaches the Lakha people, literally people in the mountains, who live in the upper reaches of the Pelela range. They speak a language which goes by the same name and are well known in the area for bamboo crafts. Though quite different from the fine bamboo work of Kheng, they produce much durable bamboo wares including buckets, bowls, containers, sieves and mats, using high-altitude bamboo. Before cheap imported woollen garments were available, the pastoralists of Lakha were also itinerant merchants selling wool and woollen fabrics.

Further east, another group of people, whom the mainstream Bhutanese categorize as herders, live in the village of Dur. They speak Brokpaikha, the language of herders, and live sedentary lives. Although they have retained the language, they share the village space with speakers of Bumthangkha and have long assimilated into the mainstream culture. The most interesting highland people in the eastern part of Bhutan are herders in the areas of Merak and Sakteng. Like other highlanders, they rear both yak and sheep and barter their products with items from lower regions. They live in hamlets but some of them even migrate to lower areas in the winter. They speak a distinct language, which is closer to the Dzongkha group than to any other language spoken around them and share much in common with the people in the Tawang area of Arunachal Pradesh.

Their distinctive dress, also worn in the Tawang area, has as the main piece a tunic, which is perhaps a vestige of clothing worn much more widely in Bhutan in the past. I provide here Pommaret's description:

> The women wear a short poncho-type dress and a red jacket woven in
> its lower part with geometric or animal designs. The men wear leather
> leggings and woollen trousers; their upper garment consists of sleeveless
> hide vests—worn with the fur on inside—over long-sleeved woollen
> tunics. Both sexes wear a distinctive hat made of yak felt with long twisted
> tufts, said to keep the rain from running onto their faces.[9]

According to their own origin myth, they are supposed to have come from Tibet guided by the female deity Ama Jomo after they rebelled against a despotic ruler.[10] The story begins with the Tibetan ruler commanding his subjects to cut off a hilltop, which was blocking the early sun from shining on his residence. In course of the forced labour to demolish the hill, an intelligent woman sings a song implying that it is easier to chop off the ruler's head than cut off the hill head. The others heed the call and together they assassinate the ruler but the rebellion leads to the exodus of the Brokpa people from their land. They journey southward and settle in what is today Merak and Sakteng. The deity is still today worshipped through

Ache Lhamo, the dance which resembles Tibetan operatic performances.

The two ethnic minorities of Laya-Lingshi and Merak-Sakteng are geographically and figuratively the crown of Bhutan's ethnic landscape. They share the commonalities of a yak- and sheep-based pastoral economy and a culture heavily influenced by or received from neighbouring Tibet. They are both well known for their wealth of dairy products. We even find the same playful proverb about the abundance of butter used in reference to both communities. In western Bhutan, the proverb goes: Laya and Lingshi are a treasury of butter but how embarrassing that there is no butter for decorating the *gtor ma* (ལ་ཡག་གླིང་གཞི་མར་གྱི་མཛོད༎ གཏོར་མ་དཀར་རྒྱན་མེད་པར་ཧྲེ་རེ་རེ༎) In eastern Bhutan, the same, more or less, is said in the rhyme: Merak Sakteng is butter Sakteng but there is no butter for butter decorations (མེ་རག་སག་སྟེང་མི་སག་སྟེང་༎ དཀར་རྒྱན་ཧྲེ་ལེ་སེ་ལ་ལ༎). The Bhutanese excel at butter sculpture or the making of butter decorations, an essential component of *torma* (གཏོར་མ་), the religious-ritual object made out of dough. Bhutanese farmers go without butter for weeks in order to save butter for this purpose. Thus, the lack of butter for this holy purpose jocularly ridicules the claim of the abundance of the butter in these pastoral communities.

Proverbial sayings about the abundance of butter are not the only similarities the Laya-Lingshi and Merak-Sakteng share. Both exotic communities trace their origins to Tibet. If the Laya-Lingshi people were cast away, the Merak-Sakteng lot were a runaway group, according to the stories of their origin. Their similarities may have a lot to tell us about processes of cultural transmissions just as their differences make us reflect on the evolving nature of human perceptions, behaviour and practices. Red, for instance, is the standard colour of the Merak-Sakteng dress while black dominates for the Laya-Lingshi dress culture. What could have affected their choice of colours? Unfortunately, we are still miserably short of a proper ethnographic study of these ethnic groups to understand the underlying reasons. In the meantime, the two groups, along with the Lhopas of the southwest and the Monpas of the south-central, which make up the most archaic and exotic ethnic components of Bhutan, are undergoing rapid change and their distinctiveness is gradually eroding with the deluge of modernization and globalization.

The People

The rough survey of the peoples of Bhutan using their geographic locations and ethno-linguistic distinctions gives one an understanding of their diversity.

There is, however, also a sense of Bhutanese character and personality which is shared by the diverse groups, beside the common identity granted by citizenship. After all, the size of Bhutan's land and population is not so large as to allow any drastic cultural divergence. These shared characteristics and features come in the form of ideas, beliefs and cultural habits, which constitute the Bhutanese personality. The first notable feature is perhaps the deep connection to nature which Bhutanese of all areas and groups share. While this can be said of any pre-modern and non-urban societies, the Bhutanese character is vividly defined by nature in interesting ways. To invoke Bordieu's concept of *habitus*, there is in the Bhutanese case a true internalization of the external environment; in their thought, behaviour, belief, outlook, art and architecture. Similarly, we also see a vibrant externalization of the internal human values and beliefs in the environment. The Bhutanese have a wonderful symbiotic relationship with their environment, which is very different from the extractive and exploitative attitude induced by modern materialism today. Their worldviews, cultural habits and lifestyle are heavily influenced by their interaction with their land and nature and vice versa.

The cultural habits such as that of dress and diet are the most obvious examples of the influence of their immediate environment. The Lhopas wore clothes made from nettle fibres, the people in Bumthang from wool, the people in the east and south from silk and cotton while people in the highlands used clothes made from yak hair. Similarly, from the ceremonial *hontoe* dumplings of Haa made from sweet buckwheat, the rice *mengey* of Shar, the buckwheat *puta* of Bumthang to the corn meals in the east, people's eating habits were shaped by what their land could grow. In addition to the crops they cultivated in the fields and the wood products they got from the forest, nature was the source of a wide range of food, medicine and household items. Bhutan's Department of Forestry has identified about 216 species of medicinal plants, 97 mushroom species, 97 different fruits and nuts, 70 ornamental plant species, 50 bamboo species, 14 cane species, 25 oil and resin species, 20 spices, 38 fibres, 181 fodder, 36 dyes, 12 food crops (yams) and 77 forest vegetables, among the non-wood products the Bhutanese traditionally received from nature. This excludes the obvious provision of clean air, water, medicinal and hot springs and other intangible benefits such as the freshness, serenity, peace and beauty which nature provides and, which have had the most profound impact in shaping the character, worldviews and behaviour and in inspiring the spiritual endeavours and artistic creations of the Bhutanese people.

From a social and scientific point of view, it is plausible that it was the sheer magnitude and the aura of nature around them which gave rise to the animistic belief systems and nature worship that comprise the early Bhutanese worldview. The idea of the mountain deities, for instance, must have initially arisen in the primitive human mind impressed by both the formidable scale and majesty of the lofty mountains and the dramatic meteorological effects and changes which one can experience around them. The impact of such spectacular effects and presence of nature can be felt even more vividly when the human mind feels effervescent from the thin mountain air. To these, one may add the stimulation caused by the sight, sound, smell or taste of elements specific to the mountain atmosphere. For instance, the smell and pollen from two dwarf rhododendrons *Rhododendron anthopogen* and *setosum* called *balu* (བ་ལུ) and *sulu* (སུ་ལུ) locally are known to cause giddiness akin to altitude sickness.[11] Thus, the idea of the mountains being imbued with higher forces must have arisen in people who were awestruck, overwhelmed and entranced by the grandeur as well as such elements of nature. Even the rationalist Sir Francis Younghusband, who led the British invasion of Tibet in 1905, is said to have had some sort of an epiphany on the high mountains of Tibet, which put him after his return to England on a new spiritual career.

Similar experiences and impressions can be said of other natural phenomena. The eerie hair-raising awe of a dense and old forest, the shimmering surface of a lake whose depth is unknown and the gushing torrents of a roaring river can all instil fear as well as amazement. These experiences must have led to the perception of mountains, lakes and rocks as either living entities or as abodes of non-human forces. The ideas may have then led to the host of beliefs in entities such as mountain gods, water spirits and forest guardians and cultural behaviour including rituals of protection, placation, ablution, libation, supplication, etc. or of thanksgiving and commemoration. These rituals, when routinized and observed as customary traditions, gradually become the local festivals and socioreligious events, around which people plan their lives.

Thus nature primarily shaped the Bhutanese world-view and much of their basic sociocultural practices, especially those which were pre-Buddhist, appear to have been local human responses to nature rather than ideas and practices learnt from some established institutions. We know that most of the numerous folk traditions, which involve animistic and shamanistic beliefs and practices and which are today naïvely branded as Bon religious cultures, have nothing to do with the Bon religion of Tibet but are localized rituals directly connected to their immediate surroundings. They are human efforts of negotiation with nature, which consequently help to regulate people's lifestyles and behaviour and through that also the continuity of nature itself. These beliefs and practices were later skilfully incorporated into the Buddhist system, which has further strengthened people's relationship with nature through its concepts of interdependence, non-violence, and respect for life, the sacred landscape and hidden valleys.

In addition to nature's main role in the formation of such beliefs and practices, one must also add the impact nature has on the artistic and literary traditions of Bhutan through both the material resources and the immaterial stimulation and inspiration it provides. Nature is also a major instrument for the advancement of Bhutan's established religious and political systems. For instance, the real spirit of Bhutan's Buddhist heritage mainly thrives in solitude rather than in big settlements and Bhutan's political independence has been partly a result of its natural terrain. The Bhutanese identity is primarily moulded by nature and only secondarily by other things including Buddhism, which is certainly the next most important facet of the Bhutanese person.

Almost all northern Bhutanese are Buddhists and some southern Bhutanese of Nepali origin also follow Buddhism. Most southern Bhutanese are Hindus and there is a growing number of Christians; there is clandestine missionary work in many parts of Bhutan although open evangelical activities are prohibited. For most Bhutanese, Buddhism permeates all facets of their lives (and the same can be said of Hinduism for its Hindu followers). It informs their worldview, lifestyle, social behaviour, economic practices and political thinking. For many of them, it is the single most important purpose of their existence and the highest meaningful pursuit in life. The world of Bhutanese Buddhism, akin to that of Tibet, is a very complex and colourful one, difficult to do any justice to with a discussion here. It includes the enormous body of doctrinal knowledge received from India and Tibet as well as numerous forms of local beliefs and practices that were expediently incorporated into the Buddhist system in the process of a syncretic assimilation. Given this range, Buddhism permeates almost all forms of spiritual expression and practice, unless they are contraposed to Buddhist teachings. Buddhist teachings and practices play a fundamental role in Bhutanese life and, like nature, are dominant factors which shape the Bhutanese personality.

Nature and Buddhism certainly make the most pervasive and powerful dyad which defines the Bhutanese people and culture. A striking example is the case of traditional Bhutanese music. While all the monastic music is Buddhist in content and style, most of the folk songs dwell on either nature or Buddhism. This is in sharp contrast to music today, which is heavily influenced by modern pop and Bollywood music and deals with romance, patriotism or other secular topics. Bhutanese folklore is also largely on the themes involving the wonders of nature and Buddhist figures. The importance of nature and Buddhism in Bhutanese life can also be appreciated through the Bhutanese sense of mind–body dualism. If nature nourishes the body, it is certainly Buddhism which provides the nourishment for the mind.

Nature and Buddhism also determine the occupational classification of the Bhutanese people. Over 60 per cent of the Bhutanese are farmers, in daily contact with nature. While some work on fields and gardens, others look after the animals on the farms or pastures. However, unlike in neighbouring Tibet, where there is generally a clear division between the *zhingpa* (ཞིང་པ་), or agriculturist, and *drokpa* (འབྲོག་པ་), or pastoralist, most families in Bhutan combine the two. It is often the case in traditional Bhutan that one or two members of the family will look after the cattle if the family has a big herd; they will spend much of their time in the pastures away from home while families will live settled lives working on the farms in the village. Although the term *sonam zhingpa* (སོ་ནམ་ཞིང་པ་) is used for the agriculturist, it does not particularly designate the agricultural farmer vis-à-vis the pastoralist. The word *jyop* (འབྲོག་པ་), the equivalent of the Tibetan word *drokpa,* is also used in Bhutan but has lost its original meaning and does not specifically refer to people who are pastoralist by profession. Rather it is a pejorative term used variably to refer to people from the highlands, whether they are pastoralists, agriculturists or something else. It connotes an upland tribal person, one without the sophistication of the mainstream culture.

The agriculturists mostly work on the fields in their immediate environment but many, particularly from higher elevations, own fields in lower districts and thus may move in winter to work in those fields. Bhutanese farmers practise shifting cultivation and carried out slash and burn methods although this is now forbidden by the new environmental regulations. Only about 8 per cent of country is said to be arable land but almost all families own land. Those who are landless are given gifts of land by the King from areas owned by the state. However, the government's ceiling of twenty-five acres per household imposed about thirty years ago has constrained the more progressive farmers and many are leaving farming in favour of trade or other professions. Agricultural farming is no longer seen as a desirable option by most of the educated youth.

This is also true of herding, a profession with an onerous schedule of backbreaking tasks. In contrast to the relatively sedentary life of the agriculturists, the herders have a highly mobile life. Whether of cows or yaks, herds are usually kept in the mountains, grazing on wild grass, shrubs and other fodder plants. Only a few cows for daily milk supply may be kept at home. Pastoralism is traditionally divided into the two categories of herding *lanor* (ལ་ནོར་), or highland cattle, and *thanor* (མཐའ་ནོར་), or lowland cattle. Highland cattle comprise yaks and their female counterpart *jyi* (འབྲི་), and some *dzo/ dzoms* (མཛོ་/མཛོམ་), which are cross-breeds between highland and lowland cattle. Lowland cattle comprise cows, which are mostly offspring of the Indian *mithun*. Highland cattle are normally kept in the alpine and subalpine zones while lowland cattle often migrate between alpine and subtropical zones, covering long distances. They are kept in the lowland in winter and taken to higher elevations in the summer, especially if they are owned by families based in the higher districts. In the average family, a member of the family would live with the cattle to look after them but rich families often employ a herder while those with smaller herds may join hands to herd the animals in turn. The aristocrats in the past had families who would herd their cattle for generations. The grazing lands are generally shared among the farmers of the same village but some families may have exclusive grazing rights in certain areas. The herds are moved from one pasture to another to allow the regeneration of grass and the herders base themselves in sheds built in the middle of a clearing.

Besides cattle, Bhutanese farmers in the higher regions also kept sheep for wool. Sheep farming has drastically dropped across Bhutan in the last few decades with the availability of cheap clothes and wool imported from abroad and the enrolment of children, who would normally herd the sheep, into schools. Similarly, with the motor roads and modern transportation facilities, the role of horses in the local economy has diminished except in areas still inaccessible by motor vehicles. About thirty years ago, in a district like Bumthang, most families owned a few dozen sheep and a few horses. Today, sheep farming is nearly extinct and horses are rare. The few horses one may find are used mainly as riding ponies or pack animals for the tourism industry. The tradition of keeping a pair of *dzo* or bullock for ploughing is also fast disappearing. As strong and sturdy crossbreeds between a *jyi* (female version of yak) and a bull, *dzo*s were used mainly for ploughing fields in the highlands while bullocks were used in most parts of the country. In their place, today, a visitor would find the powerful tractors from India and the power-tillers from Japan. This last one is a dextrous mini-tractor, highly suitable for the Bhutanese terrain which has gained great popularity among ordinary farmers for its dual functionality in tilling fields and carrying things and for also its easy maintenance.

The changes in farming practices have no doubt brought about visible economic benefits and improvement in people's lifestyle and working conditions. Yet, these changes have also entailed a drastic loss of cultural heritage and have disconnected people from the natural environment. Such loss can be seen in the ignorance of the younger generation of even basic terms to refer to traditional farming tools, such as ploughs, yokes, tethers, saddles and trappings and of basic skills of farming. Traditional Bhutanese farmers professed a strong passion for agriculture and animal husbandry and thus possessed a rich local knowledge of the agricultural products and their nutritional and medicinal values, of breeding and animal pedigree and even fascinating stories about the origins of their livestock. This wealth of accumulated cultural knowledge and wisdom, which has been transmitted throughout generations in the past, is now gradually vanishing.

In contrast to the strong tradition of agriculture and animal husbandry, the Bhutanese had no serious interest in floriculture, although the offering of flowers holds a very important place in Buddhist rituals. While food crops and fodder are grown in large areas, flowers are normally given only a small patch in a corner of the family garden. Whatever is grown in the garden is usually offered in the temple or family shrine room, which would have vases particularly designed to hold flowers. Apart from the sacred space of the shrine room, the Bhutanese neither decorated their homes with flowers nor cultivated flowers as a business. Similarly, in spite of the repeated visualization of green lawns and magnificent grounds in Buddhist religious practices, traditional Bhutanese rarely kept a lawn or green space near the house. Perhaps, given the abundance of wild flowers and natural meadows, the effort to grow flowers and maintain lawns was not seen as necessary. However, today, one can find many Bhutanese growing flowers in pots and a few even running nurseries and garden centre businesses.

The occupational composition of the demography is also undergoing rapid change. In the middle of twentieth century, around 90 per cent of the working population would have been farmers, combining both agriculture and animal

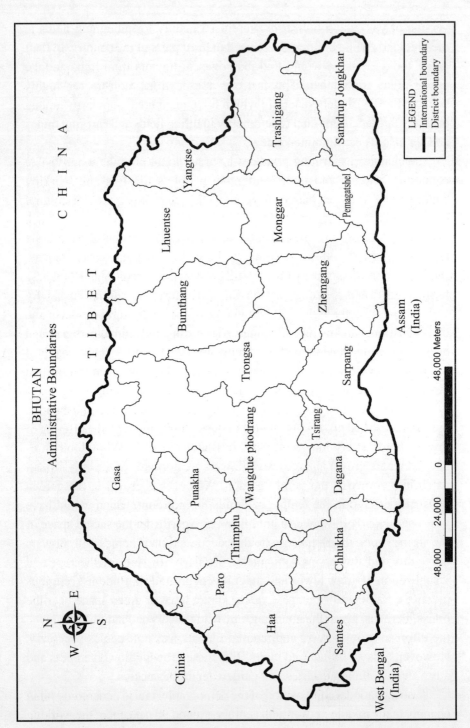

Bhutan administrative map (courtesy: Royal Government of Bhutan)

Gangkar Punsum (7578 m above sea level) is the highest unclimbed
point on earth and highest peak in Bhutan.

Harvesting potatoes with the help of a pair of dzos. Dzos are crossbreed between
the highland jyi cow and the lowland bull and mainly used for ploughing.

A traditional farmhouse in Paro

Women dancers in Haa—1933

husbandry in most cases. A small segment of the farming population also carried out trade but only a small number of individuals were full-time traders, travelling from one valley to another or/and to Tibet and India. A significant segment of the society were clerics, including monks, nuns, lay Buddhist-priests, meditating recluses and village shamans. In 2008, according to the government's register, there are about 10,000 people registered as members of a religious organization. The figure does not include those who are not members of a recognized institution and would thus reflect only about one quarter of the actual religious persons. Assuming that the number of religious persons was twice as high before secular education programmes started as it is now, the number of people who pursued religious careers before the extensive introduction of school education in 1960s is very likely to have been 10–20 per cent of the population.

Thus, traditional Bhutanese society was composed primarily of two occupational groups of people: farmers and clerics. The former was associated with nature and often referred to as *minap jigten minap* (མི་ནགཔ་/འཇིག་རྟེན་མི་ནགཔ་) or world/dark person in allusion to their dark houses, weather-beaten faces and mundane tasks; the latter with Buddhism and normally referred to as *chhop/ lamchhop* (ཆོསཔ/བླམ་ཆོསཔ་) or lama/religious person. Bhutanese aristocrats can also be roughly divided along these lines. Some aristocratic families were secular households and *de facto* farmers with large estates on which they made their slaves work, while others were holders of religious lineages and thus fell in the category of clerics.

These distinctions are, however, no longer applicable. Largely due to the widespread education and development programmes, there is now a rising, new class of bureaucrats and professionals and a growing population of people in the business sector. In 2008, there were nearly 20,000 civil servants, including professionals, employed by the state and a little over 28,000 businesses. Just as membership in monastic institutions is diminishing as only a small number of children today join religious centres compared to over 90 per cent enrolment in schools, the number of farmers is also declining as more and more young people move out of villages to towns in search of easier jobs with salaries. To this, one could also add the fall of the traditional aristocrats with the abolition of slavery and rise of the new middle class. Thus, the social demographic landscape of Bhutan has changed significantly in the last few decades.

The following table with figures from the last three years gives a general idea of the demography in relation to age and sex.

	2010	*2011*	*2012*
Male	363,383	369,476	375554
Female	332,439	338,789	345125
0–14 yrs	213,072	214,828	216972
15–64 yrs	449,531	459,678	469450
65+ yrs	33,219	33,759	34259
Median age (years)	23.4	23.7	24
Population density	18.1	18.4	18.8

Source: National Statistics Bureau: Bhutan at a Glance 2012

Many Tongues

IT IS OFTEN UNCONVINCING to monolingual people from large countries to hear that a small country like Bhutan has more than twenty different languages. Many wonder if one is taking a dialect for a language. We have seen while mapping the land and its people that Bhutan is topographically sharply divided and its people have lived in isolation for centuries. It is not difficult to imagine Bhutan's linguistic diversity after understanding such geosocial segregation. Nevertheless, as a general guideline, let us consider two vernaculars as dialects of the same language if they are mutually intelligible to their speakers without much difficulty and their basic syntactical patterns and vocabulary are the same. Most Bhutanese vernaculars, considered as different languages here, are as different as English and French and considerably more different than Sanskrit and Pali or Hindi and Nepali are. Although they share a lot of vocabulary, especially for technical and modern terms, the languages discussed below are not considered mere dialects but different languages because of their linguistic variations, mutual intelligibility and sociohistorical associations.

To underscore the diversity and precarious situation of almost all Bhutanese languages today, a rough sketch is presented here mainly by summarizing the excellent work on the languages of Bhutan by George van Driem.[1] Like the political map, the linguistic map of Bhutan is not fully established although van Driem's work gives us a clear picture of the number of the languages, their relationships and distribution. He classifies the spoken vernaculars of Bhutan into nineteen languages belonging mostly to the Central and East Bodish genetic groups. The sixteenth edition of *Ethonologue*, the comprehensive catalogue of the world's languages, even lists twenty-five languages for Bhutan. To get a detailed account of all the languages, including their dialects, will require work for many more decades;

some of the minor languages are already on the brink of extinction, spoken fluently only by a handful of people.

All nineteen Bhutanese languages, which van Driem lists, belong to the Tibetan–Burman/Sino-Tibetan language family, except for Nepali, which belongs to Indo-European family. Whether this main family, which is now spoken by the largest number of people in the world after Indo-European, is called Tibeto-Burman or Sino-Tibetan is still debated among linguists and determined not only by linguistic and geographic criteria but perhaps also by political considerations. The real question is about whether Chinese languages fall within the Tibetan–Burman family as a subgroup or Tibet–Burman is to be treated as a subgroup of Sino-Tibetan family. The Tibeto-Burman family, according to van Driem, can be divided into Brahmaputran, Southern Tibeto-Burman, Sino-Bodic and other isolates. Sino-Bodic is further divided into Sinitic (containing Chinese), Bodish-Himalayish, Kirantic and Tamangic. Bhutanese languages fall within the Bodish group, which Shafer divided into West, Central and East Bodish languages. Central Bodish corresponds to Old Tibetan, descendants of which include all modern Tibetan languages. A few of Bhutan's languages fall within this subgroup, but many others fall within the East Bodish group. The rest are as yet unclassified and treated as isolates. Of the nineteen languages, those belonging to the Central Bodish group are spoken in the western and northeastern parts of Bhutan. East Bodish languages are mostly spoken in central Bhutan.

Central Bodish group

Dzongkha

Dzongkha is a modern name for the language spoken in the western valleys. It was known as Ngalongkha or the language of the Ngalong region. This name initially seems to refer to a part of the Shar district but was later used to refer to the entire region of western Bhutan from the Pelela pass to Haa. After the unification of Bhutan, Ngalongkha became the dominant medium for official transactions as the political offices were mainly based in areas where it was spoken. Among the power centres of medieval Bhutan, only Tongsa was out of the Ngalongkha-speaking area. Gradually, Ngalongkha was used as the official language in the administrative offices and monastic centres across the country. As the government offices and monastic institutions were based in the large *dzong*s, Ngalongkha also slowly came to be known as Dzongkha, the language of the *dzong*. However, it appears that the term

Dzongkha probably gained currency only in the latter half of the twentieth century, particularly after Bhutan adopted it as the national language in the 1960s.

Ngalongkha, it must be remembered, was only a spoken vernacular like all local Bhutanese languages. It was a *phalkay* (པལ་སྐད), a commoner's vernacular as opposed to *chökay* (ཆོས་སྐད), the scriptural idiom, which in this case is classical Tibetan, the Latin of the Buddhist Himalayas. All written communications in Bhutan until the introduction of written Dzongkha in the second half of the twentieth century were conducted in classical Tibetan and much of Bhutanese literature even today is composed in this medium. Some authors such as Yontan Thaye are said to have written some things in the local vernacular but apart from oral compositions, nothing significant seems to have been written in Dzongkha until the adoption of Dzongkha as the national language. The main task of putting down Dzongkha in writing by developing a standard orthographic and grammatical structure started only in the 1960s with the school grammar books. This move seems to have been triggered by a cultural consciousness and nationalistic sentiments aimed at establishing a unique linguistic identity for Bhutan and to distinguish Bhutan from Tibet, over which China had by then made serious historical claims. It was thus a way of resisting external claims of linguistic hegemony as well as uniting the country with a lingua franca. Today, Dzongkha is taught in schools; most Bhutanese speak Dzongkha imperfectly and only a few can write in Dzongkha with ease.

The promotion of Dzongkha in the place of classical Tibetan as a written language faced serious challenges in many quarters and continues to do so even today. While the elite, most of whom got educated in Western English-medium schools, were and are still today not capable of writing even government correspondences in Dzongkha, conservative clerics were outraged by the idea of replacing the rich language of religion with a vernacular language. Dzongkha did not have the lexical strength and grammatical sophistication to construct advanced literary works without relying on classical Tibetan and it was feared that promoting Dzongkha instead of classical Tibetan could close the access to the wealth of religious literature available in this medium. Furthermore, Dzongkha was not even spoken by the majority of Bhutanese people. It was perceived to be as hard as learning a foreign language. To make things worse, Dzongkha is disappointingly short of vocabulary to render new technological and scientific terminology. These problems encumber Dzongkha even today and its viability as the national language against the onslaught of English is being tested today more than ever before.

Dzongkha is the only written local language so far and it is written using Tibetan alphabets. Bhutanese use the Uchen (དབུ་ཅན་) script widely for formal documents and books and the Joyig (མགྱོགས་ཡིག་) script for informal writing. This script is considered to be a unique Bhutanese script although there is no evidence that it was commonly used in Bhutan before the twentieth century. The prototype of Joyig, used by some traditional scholars to prove its antiquity, resembles very closely the Tibetan scripts used before the eleventh century and now found in the documents discovered from the Dunhuang caves in Gansu. It also appears from the ancient manuscripts in Bhutan's temples that the Bhutanese wrote a great deal in a variety of Ume (དབུ་མེད་) scripts in the past although most Bhutanese today cannot even read Ume scripts and associate them with Tibetans.

Dzongkha is spoken as their native tongue by people of the Haa, Paro, Chukha, Thimphu, Punakha, Gasa, Wangdiphodrang and Dagana districts and is heavily split into different dialects, some of them nearly unintelligible to other speakers of Dzongkha. The mainstream Dzongkha used in official communication and media is a modern Dzongkha based on these dialects but without the regional accents and variations. All school students are taught Dzongkha for about an hour a day at school while monastic institutions still impart their education in the medium of Dzongkha and classical Tibetan. Thus, monastic scholars are the main users of written Dzongkha but many of them often write in classical Tibetan.

Chocha Ngacha / Tsamangpikha

Like Dzongkha, Chocha Ngacha falls within Central Bodish or the Tibetan group of languages. Interestingly, this language is spoken in an area completely separated from the Dzongkha-speaking areas and squeezed between East Bodish languages. Main users are people in the lower part of the Kurtoe district and the upper part of the Mongar district along the Kurichu valley but there are small communities of Chocha Ngacha speakers in the Tashi Yangtse and Tashigang districts. The name Chocha Ngacha, literally 'you and us', is probably given by speakers of other languages. It is also known as the language of Kurme (ཀུར་སྨད་) or the lower part of Kurilung. It has a striking semblance to classical Tibetan and preserves a great deal of the pronunciation of Tibetan orthography, which is lost in contemporary Tibetan.

Jyokha of Merak and Sakteng

Jyokha literally means the language of the pastoralists. It designates the languages spoken by the *jyop*s, although who *jyop*s are is a highly contested and sensitive issue. This particular Jyokha in the Central Bodish group is spoken in the eastern highlands of Merak and Sakteng by about 5000 people. Jyokha is a Dzongkha rendering and the locals call their language Brokpake. Their Tshangla-speaking neighbours call it Brahmilo, the language of others or Brahmi people.

Jyokha of Dur

The small group of people in Dur in the Bumthang district speak this language, which is closer to Dzongkha and Tibetan than to the Bumthangkha spoken by their neighbours. There are only a few dozen households who speak this language, which is quickly declining in favour of dominant Bumthangkha, Dzongkha and English.

Lakha language

The people of the Sephu area or Lakha, literally 'on the mountain', speak this language—van Driem understood Lakha as the 'language of the mountain passes' but this is contestable as the people are often called Lakhajyop, or pastoralists of Lakha. Thus, kha in Lakha would not refer to the language. The Lakha people are located north of the highway just after crossing the Pelela pass coming from Thimphu. There are said to be over 1200 households who speak this language.

Bökay or Tibetan

Tibetan is spoken by a large number of Tibetan refugees who settled in Bhutan during and after the exodus in 1959. Although most of the younger generation who were born in Bhutan speak the local Bhutanese languages, many of the older Tibetans still speak Tibetan. The Tibetan spoken in Bhutan comprises Khampa dialects from eastern Tibet, Lhodrak dialect from southern Tibet and Ue and Tsang dialects from central Tibet. Tibetan is also spoken by some Bhutanese families living along the Tibetan border and with closer ties to Tibet. Many Bhutanese born before 1959, when relations with Tibet were strong, can communicate in Tibetan.

East Bodish group

Bumthangkha

Bumthangkha is mainly spoken in the four valleys of Bumthang and split into numerous dialects. Even in one administrative block like Ura, with just over 2000 people, there are about five dialects. The dialects are clearly intelligible to each other but there is no standard version of the spoken form like the official Dzongkha. Bumthangkha is spoken as far as Kurtoe, the upper course of Kurichu river to the east and as far as Nubchutoe, the upper course of Mangdechu river to the west. It is also spoken in the Kheng region along the lower courses of Mangdechu and Chamkharchu. In both Kurtoe and Kheng, the language is spoken with substantial variations so that van Driem considered these two as two different languages.

Khengkha

Khengkha is spoken south of Bumthang and as far as the Panbang area in lower Zhemgang. Due to the vast area the language covers and the rough terrain, the difference in the various dialects is intense. The language is closely linked to Bumthangkha and it is plausible that it originated from an older version of Bumthangkha.

Kurtöp

The Kurtöp language is spoken in the northwestern part of Kortoe district around the Lhuntse area. The area is geographically connected to Bumthang, with which it had strong historical relations. The Kurtöp speaking area begins at Tangmachu and extends as far as the last village of Chusa to the north.

Ngenkha

Another cognate of Bumthangkha, this language is spoken in the middle regions of the Mangde valley. It is also known as Mangdebikha, the language of Mangde, which is bordered by Dzongkha to the west, Bumthangkha to the north and east and Khengkha to the south.

Chalibikha

Squeezed between the Tshangla- and Chocha Ngacha-speakers is a village called Chali in the current district of Mongar where this language is spoken. George van Driem speculates that the speakers of Chalipikha may have got separated from the speakers of other East Bodish languages in the surrounding areas with the arrival of the ancestors of modern Chocha Ngacha speakers. To the Bhutanese, it is known as a linguistic hodgepodge, curiously containing English words, or at least something based on them.

Dzalakha

The Dzala speakers are located in the upper course of Kholongchu in the Tashi Yangtse district and extend as far as Khoma in the adjoining district of Kurtoe. It is also known as Yangtsepikha, the language of Yangtse.

Dakpakha

This language is spoken by the people known as Dakpa, who live in the northeastern parts of Bhutan. The language is also spoken in the Tawang region of the Indian state of Arunachal Pradesh and is sometimes called Northern Monpa.

Monkha / Olekha

The Olekha is spoken by the people in the lower slopes of Jowo Durshing or Black Mountain range in central Bhutan. The people are called Monpa by other Bhutanese and some researchers have speculated that they have be remnants of the earliest inhabitants of the country. The language is spoken by a few hundred people and only fluently by a handful of elderly people.

Other Bodic languages

Tshangla

The Tsangla belongs to the Tibeto-Burman family but to the unusual group of ancient languages which linguists have not yet classified into the more well-known subgroups. It is also known as Sharchopikha, the language of the easterners. As the native tongue in the districts of Samdrupjongkhar, Pema Gatsel, Tashigang and Mongar, Tshangla is spoken by a large percentage of people in Bhutan as the eastern districts are more densely populated than other parts of Bhutan. It is also spoken in small pockets of Arunachal Pradesh in India and in southern Tibet, where the language spread with groups which emigrated from Bhutan. Today, with a lot of Tshangla speakers living in towns across Bhutan, the language is also widely spoken in other parts of Bhutan and is one of the languages used by radio stations and the music industry in Bhutan.

Lhopikha

The Lhop language is spoken by the indigenous communities of Lhop and Taba Dramtep in the southwestern district of Samtse and north of Phuntsholing. It is said to be more closely related to Kiranti languages spoken in some parts of modern Nepal than to the Lepcha language spoken by their immediate neighbours. According to the linguist George van Driem, Lhop appears to be a substrate language for Dzongkha in western Bhutan. He writes: 'Linguistic evidence indicates that the Lhop were influenced by some older forms of Dzongkha in the distant past, which suggests that the Lhopus were probably the first aboriginal groups encountered by the early Ngalongs during their southward expansion in ancient time.'[2]

Gongdukpikha

The language of Gongduk is spoken in an isolated area south of Mongar in the Kurichu valley. Now spoken barely by just over a thousand people, van Driem states, 'Gongduk language is one of the two languages in Bhutan which has retained complex conjugations which appear to reflect the ancient Tibeto-Burman verbal agreement system.'

Lepcha

The Lepcha language is spoken in the district of Samtse by a number of villages. The speakers of this language have immigrated to Bhutan from neighbouring Sikkim, where the Lepcha language and culture were once dominant.

Limbu, Rai, Tamang, Sherpa, etc.

A number of Kiranti languages such as Limbu and Rai are also spoken by twentieth-century immigrants from Nepal as are the Tamang and Sherpa languages. Tamang is a branch of the Sino-Bodic subgroup while Sherpa falls within the Central Bodish or Tibetan group of languages. Although there are no entire villages and communities which can be associated with these eastern Nepali languages, a vast number of people who immigrated into Bhutan from Nepal belonged to groups speaking these languages. However, by the time they arrived in Bhutan, Nepali was already a common tongue among them.

Kurux

Bhutan also has also small population of people speaking Kurux or Kurukh, the only Dravidian language spoken in the country. The speakers of Kurux are found along the southwestern border of Bhutan and are closely related to people speaking the same language in West Bengal.

Indo-European languages

Nepali

Nepali belongs to the Indo-European language family which covers most European languages, including English. It was initially spoken by a small Indo-Aryan group called the Khas in western Nepal and was known as Khas Kurā, the language of the Khas. It was not the vernacular of the place we know now as Nepal with its centre in the Kathmandu valley. After the Khas took over the kingdom of Gorkha and gradually over Kathmandu and other parts of Nepal, they adopted this Khas Kurā as the official language of Nepal and named it Gorkhālī. Gorkhālī was then again renamed in the twentieth century and it gained dominance over all the native languages of Kathmandu and other parts of Nepal. Today, it is the official language of the new republic of Nepal. In Bhutan, it is spoken by the people of Nepali origin who have settled in the southern districts of Samtse, Chukha, Sarpang, Tsirang, Dagana and Samdrupjongkhar in the twentieth century. However, the Bhutanese people of Nepali ancestry are referred to by the politically correct term Lhotshampa and their language as Lhotshampikha. Many Bhutanese in the midlands also speak basic Nepali and it is used for radio broadcasting.

Hindi

Some Bhutanese people who live along the border with India speak Hindi, the main language of India. Like Nepali, Hindi belongs to the Indo-European language family and is mostly spoken in north and central parts of India. Due to the influence of Bollywood and interaction with Indian migrant labourers, most Bhutanese speak some Hindi. Until the introduction of English-medium schools, Hindi was also used a medium of instruction in the early schools set up in the country. Beside Tibetan, Hindi was one of the main foreign languages used by the Bhutanese until the later part of the twentieth century.

English

Among the languages commonly spoken in Bhutan, English is certainly the most recent but it is also definitely the fastest-growing language in the country today. The first speakers of English to visit Bhutan were the British envoys in 1774 sent by the East India Company under Lord Hastings. Since then, Bhutan saw a series of English-speaking visitors but the real rise of English in Bhutan as a communal language began only in the second half of the twentieth century with the introduction of English as a medium of instruction in schools. There is no doubt that the Bhutanese predilection for English was partly due to the influence of the southern neighbours, the British Raj in the first half of the twentieth century and independent India in the second half. Exposure to the West and the force of globalization in vogue today are certainly reasons for its intense growth in the recent decades. However, its pervasive presence and rapid growth are certainly due to its inclusion in school education as the main medium of instruction.

English is the only foreign language taught in Bhutanese schools. It is now also the dominant medium of official correspondences and written communication, with most educated people still incapable of reading and writing in Dzongkha with proficiency. Only those who attend monastic colleges or the only regular college for Bhutan's language and culture are able to speak, read and write Dzongkha with good command. Embarrassing and ironic as it may sound, English is now used in Bhutan more than Dzongkha, the national language. Most Bhutanese languages are basic spoken languages lacking in terminologies for sophisticated ideas and spoken by only a small number of people. Even Dzongkha, the national language and the only written Bhutanese language, was until recently the only spoken vernacular and thus still in want of a fully developed grammar and orthography. The Bhutanese languages do not have sufficient vocabulary and literary resources to be able to cope with the rapid expansion of knowledge in the country. Given this scenario, English is now filling the linguistic gap and slowly emerging as an effective lingua franca so much so that even a leading monastic figure has recently suggested that English may be adopted as a national language.

Older Bhutanese, who have not attended secular schools, do not speak or write in English but most of the modern educated elite in Thimphu use English more than local Bhutanese languages at both home and work and some can only communicate fluently in English. Although most literate Bhutanese speak their native tongue with ease, they do the majority of their reading and writing in English rather than in Dzongkha. Because most of the teachers were hired from India when school education was introduced nationwide in the 1960s, older Bhutanese speak English with a mild Indian accent but today more and more people are speaking English with an American accent although the Bhutanese generally speak English with a very mild or no accent.

The linguistic situation in Bhutan is a very complicated and puzzling one. While Bhutan has about sixteen local vernaculars, only one of them is written, and that too, with no established orthographic and grammatical systems. Given this scenario, English is gaining ground rapidly. While the Bhutanese generally grow up speaking multiple languages, most of them, especially in urban areas, speak them as second languages. Many Bhutanese youth do not have a first language with a full proficiency although for cultural and sentimental reasons, they claim a local language as their native tongue. Paradoxically, not all can speak their 'native tongue' fluently. This linguistic conundrum of multiple imperfect tongues with no solid grounding in one as the first language aptly reflects the very fragmented but dynamic personality of many young Bhutanese, who are grappling between the traditional past and postmodern future. They have neither fully relinquished the old world and embraced the new, nor fully inherited the old and rejected the new; they linger in a limbo halfway between tradition and modernity, the East and the West, simplicity and sophistication, between linguistic poverty and proficiency. Out of such a diachronic situation emerges an interesting Bhutanese character, which is aptly captured by the state's search for the Middle Way. Even linguistically, some have found a middle ground in the form of a queer Bhutanese hybrid English, now sometimes called Dzonglish. 'That is the situation mo' is how a young Bhutanese may put 'That is the situation, isn't it?' Similarly, 'it is te' is an emphatic 'it is'. The 'la' suffix is the ubiquitous Bhutanese magic word. 'This is true la' is equivalent to 'I humbly submit that this is true'.

The Bhutanese are on the whole linguistically dextrous and most children still grow up speaking multiple Bhutanese languages. However, the predominance of English, especially in the written medium, poses a serious challenge for the youth to continue learning a different language or stay fluent in their native tongues. Today, most educated Bhutanese are struggling to juggle between linguistic multiplicity and mastery. A few manage to excel in seamlessly blending two ways of life and having a native first language and speaking others with fluency.

The linguistic landscape of Bhutan is changing very fast and dramatically. It is very likely that in a few decades most dialects and many minor languages will be dead. A few major languages may survive the onslaught of English and globalization but will nonetheless have changed significantly. As each word represents an idea, the death of each language will mean the loss of a whole set of ideas and culture. The situation of Bhutan's languages in the long future will be the best yardstick to measure cultural changes, indicating both how much was lost and how much has changed due to the homogenizing affects of modernization.

History and Prehistory

A COUNTRY AND ITS PEOPLE can be only fully understood by unravelling their past. This is definitely true in the case of Bhutan. The Bhutanese have a keen sense of history and a strong connection to the past however nebulous their understanding may be. 'One who is ignorant of his ancestry is like a monkey in the wilderness',[1] goes a well-known saying in Bhutan. History has a very active and instrumental role to play in Bhutan. It is not merely tall tales of the past but an ongoing experience of what has happened. It justifies the present and guides the future. The past events and practices are often used as yardsticks and as points of reference for conducting present-day affairs, ranging from grand state ceremonies to basic personal comportment. Bhutan's policy for cultural preservation is a clear example of the people's robust proclivity to preserve and perpetuate the past.

In the presence of the past

The historical consciousness we find in Bhutan stems from several factors. Firstly, Bhutan has a rich tradition of historical thinking in the forms of both written literature and oral cultures. These include origin myths, national and local narratives, historical accounts, biographies, folk stories, ballads, songs and pilgrimage guides. Quite contrary to the assumption that most Bhutanese as Buddhists imbued with the wisdom of impermanence would not hold onto the past, Bhutanese have an avid sense of history, which partly comes from their deep sense of belonging to the homeland. Another reason is the congruous and continuous nature of Bhutan's history. Bhutan has enjoyed a very harmonious and continuous past with no foreign invasion, occupation, colonization or internal upheaval, which could seriously disrupt the country's rhythm of life or damage its sovereignty. All of Bhutan's neighbours have gone through episodes of tumultuous change leading to serious disjunctions in their histories. Tibet, for instance, had undergone a catastrophic destruction of its ancient heritage in the second half of the last century and Sikkim has very little left of its Buddhist past. In contrast, Bhutan has generally remained stable, enjoying an uninterrupted, close and harmonious connection to its past. The sociopolitical changes brought about by the process we call modernization in the last fifty years are by far the most widespread and profound social transformation in Bhutanese history. Beside, Bhutan's historical continuity is not blemished by any dark chapter which could haunt people's historical memory. All in all, Bhutan's is a very pleasant and honourable past to recall and be part of.

It is thus clear why the Bhutanese are conscious of their history and often draw inspiration from past events both by referring to them and symbolically re-enacting them at state and village functions. Such historical consciousness, coupled with the fervent love of the country, has also given rise to buoyant and even egregious patriotism. Yet, despite a lively awareness of history, Bhutan's history from the point of modern historiography is a poorly charted territory. There is very little written about it and much of what is written, especially in India, is reproduction of earlier works. Most of the works on Bhutanese history also treat specific periods and none has so far attempted to undertake a comprehensive study. In fact, apart from those in classical Tibetan by Bhutanese monk-scholars, there is not a single scholarly book dealing with Bhutan's history as a whole. This deficit in Bhutanese historical studies is clearly seen in the lack of a commonly accepted periodization of Bhutan's past. For our convenience, I introduce the following periodization for mapping the entire history of the Bhutanese.

The years before the introduction of Buddhist culture and the acclaimed founding of the two famous temples of Jampa Lhakhang in Bumthang and Kyerchu Lhakhang in Paro in the middle of the seventh century will be referred to as the Pre-Historic Period (ལོ་རྒྱུས་གོང་རབས་/གནའ་རབས་). I call this period prehistoric, mainly because there is no known historical record, either in writing or oral forms, which is or is alleged to be from this period. The time before the mid-eighth century is not characterized as much by historical features as by the lack of history. Apart from scattered lithic tools, there is hardly any historical evidence tied to a historical place, time and person. Even later accounts of early historical persons and places go only as far back as the middle of the seventh century. Then, I use the term Early Historic Period (ལོ་རྒྱུས་སྔ་མའི་དུས་ཚན་/དུས་རབས་) for the period spanning from the mid-seventh until the mid-seventeenth-century unification of Bhutan as one nation. For this period, we have sporadic historical records in the form of written texts, oral accounts and artefacts, which enable us to speak about these thousand years with some certainty. However, the sources only give a story which is fragmentary, as was Bhutan itself then. The main distinction which separates this period from what preceded it is the introduction of Buddhism.

This period can be divided into the Early Diffusion (སྔ་དར) and the Later Diffusion (ཕྱི་དར), corresponding to the two periods of transmission of Buddhism to Tibet and other Himalayan areas. The Early Diffusion starts with temple building in the seventh century and covers the arrival of the famous guru Padmasambhava in Bhutan. It marks the emergence of Bhutan as a Buddhist country, at least according to later historiography. The period ends with the temporary decline of open Buddhist activity in Tibet and the alleged arrival of Prince Tsangma and the Dorji brothers to Bhutan in the middle of the ninth century. The period of Later Diffusion roughly coincides with the later transmission of Buddhism to Tibet from Nepal and north India. However, the Buddhist transmissions to Bhutan in this period came almost entirely from Tibet through a series of Tibetan lamas travelling southward in search of tranquil solitude, hidden treasures, religious following and patronage. Like Tibet, Bhutan saw a widespread proliferation of Buddhist schools and establishments and the growth of Buddhist influence in the affairs of state as well as the lives of ordinary people.

The period of theocracy which started with the rule of Zhabdrung Ngawang Namgyal and ended at the turn of the twentieth century is the Medieval Period (ཡོ་རྒྱས་བར་མའི་དུས་ཚོན/བར་རབས). The beginning of this period is marked by the unification of the Bhutanese valleys as one nation. This period is comparable to the European Middle Ages in seeing the rise of a centralized religious authority, which wielded strong political power, and the growth of Buddhist-oriented art and architecture, organized scholastic learning, codification of laws and courtly behaviour and an economy based on a feudal system. We know a great deal about this period from both local sources and reports originating from neighbouring countries, including Tibet and British India.

The monarchial rule from 1907 until 1960 or thereabouts will be referred to as the Early Modern Period (དེང་རབས་ཉེ་མ). There was a growing awareness of and interaction with the world outside and some early efforts of modernization began within the country during this period. The period spanning some six decades since the introduction of the legislative assembly, secular education, biomedicine and motor roads is known to most Bhutanese as the Modern Period (དེང་རབས་) and it is during this period that Bhutan saw in earnest the socioeconomic development which characterizes modernity in most parts of the world. It will be shown below that these periods are separated by historical milestones, and each of them is characterized by a different political setting, socioreligious awareness, and to some degree by changes in economy, lifestyle and also styles of art and architecture.

Those who are interested in Bhutan's history in more detail may read Michael Aris's *Bhutan: The Early History of a Himalayan Kingdom* for the Early Historic Period followed by the writings of John Ardussi for both the Early Historic and Medieval Periods until Bhutan's encounter with the British. Another source on Medieval Period is Yoshiro Imaeda's *Histoire médiéval du Bhoutan,* which has been published recently. A few books on Anglo-Bhutanese relations, including A.B. Majumdar's *Britain and the Himalayan Kingdom of Bhutan* and Peter Collister's *Bhutan and the British* partially fill the existing gap for the later part of the Medieval Period covering the eighteenth and nineteenth centuries. One can then return to Aris in his *Raven Crown* for the Early Modern Period. There is ample writing on the Modern Period, including books, articles, government dossiers, reports, academic dissertations, travelogues, memoirs and essays but there isn't yet a compact historical work describing the events in the second half of the twentieth century in a single volume. A significant number of modern Indian writings provide a sketchy overview of the entire history. Sonam Kinga's *Polity, Kingship and Democracy* also provides a comprehensive account of Bhutan's political history. For those with good classical Tibetan, the religious, political and cultural histories by the monk scholars, Tenzin Chögyal, Tshering Dorji, Gedun Rinchen, Phuntsho Wangdi, Pema Tshewang and Lopen Nado are excellent introductions to Bhutan's history. What follows is a gist of the historical works I have mentioned in this paragraph, except those by Imaeda and Kinga which were published after much of this book was written.

The Prehistoric Period

There is indeed very little one can say about this era with any certainty. Ethnology, genetics, linguistics and archaeology, which can help reveal more information about this period are in their infancy, if at all existent, in Bhutan. Some ethnological and linguistic works have been carried out, giving us a general idea about the ethnic distribution and theory that some people in the remote parts of Bhutan may have been earlier inhabitants pushed out by later settlers. Yet there is no sufficient information and material evidence to know what kind of lives people in prehistoric times may have lived. Archaeological works have the greatest potential to reveal further information about this period but so far only two archaeological projects have taken place, both in Bumthang and by Swiss teams. One involved digging after a chance finding of underground structures during a construction and the other is a planned excavation of a *dzong* structure built in much later times. Neither of the projects directly involved sites which could reveal more information on the Prehistoric Period. One can only hope that new archaeological work at sites and on artefacts more likely to be associated with this period and further studies in linguistics and genetics may at some point help us gain a better idea of the remote past. For now, we may have to make do with the very few clues we have of what life might have been before the mid-eighth century.

One of the main clues to prehistoric life is stone implements. A good number of stone adzes can be found in Bhutanese households, some preserved by families for generations as heirlooms and others discovered by farmers by chance from their fields or forests. The Bhutanese generally believed these to be celestial weapons, which are used in the battles between the gods (ལྷ་) and demi-gods (ལྷ་མིན་) in the sky. Thus, they are called sky iron, *namcha* (གནམ་ ལྕགས་) or sky iron axes, *namcha tare* (གནམ་ལྕགས་སྟ་རེ་) and treasured as powerful objects in a receptacle called *yangdrom* (གཡང་སྒྲོམ་) or *yangkhang* (གཡང་ཁང་), the box or house of wealth. This receptacle would contain samples of all items of wealth, including grains, coins and jewellery. It is believed to hold the *yang* or essence of wealth and normally housed in the family storeroom, and used in a ritual to enhance wealth. Curiously, the word *yáng* comes from Chinese for sheep, which symbolizes wealth for pastoralists although in Bhutan this original denotation is lost.

The Bhutanese identification of lithic adzes as celestial axes must have arisen from the confusion between these lithic tools and meteoric stones. Meteorites are believed to be pieces of celestial weapons, which accidentally fall on earth during the battles between the gods and demi-gods. They are thought to land on the earth with lightning and thunder. Needless to say, the belief in the celestial battles between the gods and demi-gods is derived from Indian cosmology, which spread in Bhutan with Buddhist teachings. It is a common practice among Buddhists in Bhutan to meditate on the problems of life and ills of the world and such a meditation includes reflection on the strife-ridden life of demi-gods who are constantly at war with the gods out of jealousy. Thus, the identification of stone adzes with celestial axes represents a case of assimilation of pre-Buddhist ideas and artefacts into the dominant Buddhist discourse.

Michael Aris had one of these adzes examined by Gale Sieveking of the British Musuem, who classed it as an artefact from the Late Stone Age with a suggested date of 2000–1500 BC. Similar stone implements, according to Sieveking, are found commonly in the regions of Myanmar, Yunnan, India (Assam, Bihar and Orissa), Thailand, Vietnam, Malaysia and Indonesia. This helps us safely surmise that some of the Bhutanese valleys were inhabited by people using lithic tools over 4000 years ago and there may have been a Neolithic culture not very different from those which existed in countries listed above. It is quite likely that the agricultural practices in Bhutan, including cultivation of rice, maize and millet, spread from southern China and northeastern India.

In addition to stone tools, historians have also noted the standing megaliths found in many parts of Bhutan. The best-known examples include the megaliths in the Somthrang and Könchogsum temples in Bumthang and the Nabji temple in Zhemgang. Unlike some Tibetan stone pillars marking the foundation of important establishments, Bhutanese megaliths, as far we know, have no inscription and are generally thought of as pagan symbols or objects connected to the dead or death rituals by modern historians. Locally, the megaliths are said to mark geomantic power spots or demarcate political boundaries. The pillar in Somthrang, for instance, is said to mark a sacred point in the middle of four auspicious landmarks on which the temple was built. It is known as the 'self-created stone pillar' (རང་བྱོན་རྡོ་ཡི་ཀ་བ་). A similar significance is attributed to the stone structures in Nyidugkha and Tanabji in Dagana, which are called 'the rock pillars of the sky' (རྡོ་གནམ་གྱི་ཀ་བ་) and 'the cosmic stone steps' (རྡོ་བསྐལ་པའི་བྱིན་ཐེག).[2]

The pillar in Nabji, however, does not hold such geocosmic significance but is said to have been erected in the eighth century by Padmasambhava when the two warring kings were made to take an oath of peaceful reconciliation, a story to which we shall later return. Furthermore, some megaliths, such as the one between Tang and Ura, are said to mark ancient political boundaries. Whether these megaliths existed from the Neolithic period and were later used for the new religious and political purposes is difficult to say and may vary from case to case. If we are to believe the local stories and associate the megaliths with the sites where they are found, most of them were erected in later times but, like the adzes, it is possible that things from earlier times were used to construct later narratives. One can also find megaliths erected in our own times near temples and along the modern motor roads, a fact which duly cautions us that they are not all antique evidences of a Neolithic culture.

However, one can be generally certain that Neolithic tribes inhabited the Bhutanese valleys by 2500 BC. During a recent work on the history of glaciers in northwestern Bhutan, geologists found some charcoal near the glaciers, which is almost certainly a result of human activities, dating as early as 4700 BC. Their studies of the pollen in the sediments of the lakes also revealed a drastic change from natural to human-induced vegetation around 2550 BC. Given these evidences for human activities in harsh climatic areas such as Lunana, it is only highly probable that the temperate and fertile valleys were already occupied by early settlers to some extent. It is also quite likely that the settlers in highlands such as Lunana may have come from the north while the midlands were generally occupied by those who came from the east and the south.

This would then correspond to the general view that archaeologists and linguists currently hold on the origin of people speaking Tibeto-Burman languages. I summarize the very complex and detailed analysis George van Driem provides in his voluminous book on the languages of the Himalayas.[3] The heartland of the Tibetan–Burman people, according to scholars such as van Driem, was in the modern-day Sichuan province of China. From there, the first wave of people moved westward from Sichuan through the Brahmaputra valley and northeastern India as early as the seventh millennium BC. These people are called the Western Tibeto-Burmans and they introduced the Eastern Indian Neolithic technologies in northeastern India and may have met the Austroasiatic people already inhabiting the region. The Bhutanese stone adzes, which we saw earlier, could belong to people of this group and we can assume that some lower regions of Bhutan were occupied by them. The second wave of people out of Sichuan went northward around the same time to settle in the fertile plains of the Yellow river in China. These people, called the Northern Tibeto-Burmans, developed an advanced civilization and by late Neolithic times split into Northwestern (Bodic) and Northeastern (Sinitic) groups. These two are associated with the Proto-Bodic Măjiāyáo culture and the Proto-Sinitic Yăngsháo culture of China. The Măjiāyáo culture based around the modern-day Gansu area then spread in the late fourth and early third millennia BC southward through eastern Tibet to the Himalayan areas, including Bhutan. The cultivated vegetation found in Lunana could be from this period. Another group took the Măjiāyáo culture westward and over the Karakoram ranges to areas around Kashmir. This began the Northern Neolithic culture and it spread eastward again towards the Tibetan plateau, crossing over the watershed whenever topography permitted. The speakers of the Bodish languages are from this group. George van Driem claims that speakers of the East Bodish languages must have crossed the Himalayas into Bhutan long before the beginning of the Christian era but the presence of Central Bodish speakers is of recent date. Despite the lack of clear understanding of the past, we can perhaps safely assume that some people from all three movements settled in Bhutan during different stages in prehistoric times. While there is no doubt that people entered Bhutan from the north at different times in different waves, it is highly plausible that many entered from the east and south as well in ancient times.

In the previous chapter, I have already alluded to the claims made by local historians of Bhutan's connections to India in very early times. Although they are largely conjectural and sometimes even based on mythical accounts, some of the claims are nonetheless plausible and it is worthwhile reiterating all of them here to construct a possible demographic scenario of Bhutan in the Prehistoric Period. Even where the stories may be purely mythical, they help us understand the Bhutanese perception of prehistoric times. The traditional scholars generally approached historical study or any other disciplines from a Buddhist perspective as passed down through its Indo-Tibetan traditions. Thus, their way of looking at Bhutan's past is based on a worldview and mode of enquiry quite different from one adopted in modern historiography.

We have already come across the well-known Tibetan myth of how the Tibetan country was under an inland sea not so long ago. In contrast, Bhutan, all Bhutanese historians argue, existed as a mountainous land long before the sea receded in Tibet and that it was visited by many figures from the Indian plains. A very old but legendary story that most monk-historians recount is that of Prince Drime Kunden (དྲི་མེད་ཀུན་ལྡན) and his exile from the north Indian plains to what is now the Punakha region of Bhutan. The story originates in the Buddhist *Jātakas* and is a very popular Buddhist narrative although it cannot be really construed as a historical account. It concerns one of the previous lifetimes of the Buddha, when he was a Bodhisattva prince with immense generosity. Drime Kunden, who is known by the name Vessantara in some Buddhist traditions, gives away his nation's prized treasures and wealth as alms, earning himself a punitive exile into a dangerous wilderness infested with terrifying beasts. In the course of his exile, he gives away his children as well as his eyes (or wife, according to some versions), thus perfecting his quality of generosity. The Bhutanese link the journey of this charitable prince with the Punakha valley, interweaving the local place names with events in Drime Kunden's journey into exile. The prince leaves his kingdom in north India and travels to the haunted Hashang mountain, which is identified as situated in the hills between the Phochu and Mochu rivers.

This association of the area with Drime Kunden's journey is, however, not a modern construction. It appears in a written record as early as the seventeenth-century biography of Zhabdrung Ngawang Namgyal by Ngawang Pekar.[4] According to the biography, Zhabdrung came across some strange leaves which instantly triggered his memory of flora, fauna and special spots in the area as he remembered his previous life as King Drime Kunden. This story of Drime Kunden's journey into the Punakha valley is reiterated by most local historians to support the primeval arrival of Indians to Bhutan. It may also be noted that the Bhutanese saint Pema Lingpa also tells the story of Drime Kunden in detail in one of his treasure texts. He does not, however, mention any association between Punakha and Drime Kunden's land of exile but concludes that Drime Kunden was one of Padmasambhava's former lives. The traditional historians also allude to other *Jātaka* characters in relation to prehistoric Bhutan but do not give us any detail.[5]

Coming forward to the times of the historical Buddha, these historians suggest that the mountain tribes (རི་རྒྱལ་པ་) and barbaric people (མ་རྒོ་) mentioned in ancient Buddhist scriptures, particularly to the north of the Buddhist heartland, most likely refer to the barbaric Mon tribes who lived in the areas including the Bhutanese mountains. We have already seen their use of the name Mon to refer to Bhutan as a tribal borderland before Buddhism was introduced. What we see in this case is a shift in the reference point. Bhutan is not perceived as a dark, border country in relation to Tibet, which did not even exist at this stage in their trajectory; it is a barbaric borderland in reference to civilized India, where Buddhism was flourishing. They go even as far as to argue that the Buddha himself must have miraculously visited the areas of Bhutan when he traversed the entire world in the fourth week after his enlightenment.

The claims traditional historians make of early human settlement and Indian influence we have seen above and in the previous chapter are generally based on Buddhist stories, which the Bhutanese received in later times. Thus, they are undoubtedly a retrospective projection of later ideas on to the past and tell us more about the Bhutanese perception of the past moulded by Buddhist ideas than about the actual past. However, the stories about the

Indian presence by the eighth century may not be purely constructions based on mythical stories. Despite the lack of concrete evidence, the widespread oral accounts and later historical writings based on them do point to some Indian presence around the eighth century. Speaking about this period, Pema Lingpa states: 'At that time, Kurelung and all the regions of Mon were the home of the Indians. All their houses were made of bamboo, grass and wood.'[6] Similarly, Tenzin Chögyal, the medieval monk-historian, makes this claim:

> Indian settlements with kings, ministers and subjects were established in these southern regions. The country was peaceful, prosperous and powerful. As evidences, even today, there are ruins of the palace of an Indian king next to a cypress in the forests of Tsachuphu and of the settlements of some kings in Jazhag Gönpa. Ratsha Og in Shar is one of the many mispronunciations and should be spelt as Rajā Og (ར་ཇཱ་འོག་ under the rajā).[7]

Both he and later historians use this toponym to argue for the presence of an Indian ruler in the Shar district. How credible are these accounts and if they are at all credible, how far back would such a presence go? We also find in Pema Lingpa's biography another toponym in the Shar district, Jagar Togey Gönpa (རྒྱ་གར་རྟོག་གེ་དགོན་པ་ , Temple of the intellectual Indian), which suggests the presence of Indians in this area.[8] A certain Indian king named Üktön (དབུགས་སྟོན་) is said to have acted as a patron when Tri Songdetsen built Tsilung or Chökhor Lhakhang in Bumthang. Lopen Nado identifies this with the Indian King who was settled in the Shar valley and also helped the Tibetan king Tri Ralpachen build temples in Bhutan.[9] Traditional historians, as we seen earlier, note that the name Menlog (མན་ལོག་) for people of the Shar valley comes from *milog* (མི་ལོག་), or non-returning, which referred to Tibetan soldiers who did not want to return to Tibet after they were sent to expel from this area some of the Indian settlers. However, the account of an ancient Indian presence in the Bhutanese midlands which is by far the most popular, is the story of Sedarkha or Sindharājaā, the King of Bumthang, who invited Padmasambhava to Bhutan in the eighth century and whose account we shall explore in the next chapter. What we can say for now is that there is a general consensus among traditional scholars about the existence of a flow of people and ideas from India into Bhutan.

While most Western scholars have disregarded these accounts as conjectural or mythical, Indian writers on Bhutan happily accepted the theory of the Indian presence but generally had nothing new to say. One scholar took pains to argue, rather strenuously, that Bhutan had rich Buddhist cultural exchanges with its southern neighbours by the fifth century. In his book *A Cultural History of Bhutan*, Chakravarti uses the case of Tönpa (སྟོན་པ་), a preceptor to the king of Prāgjyotiśa (Assam) in the fifth century. According to Kalhaṇa's *Rājataraṅginī*, the chronicle of Kashmiri kings, this guru with a Tibetan name is said to have accompanied the Prāgjyotiśa Princess Amṛtaprabhā, when the latter was married to Prince Meghavāhana of Kashmir. The princess is said to have built a *stūpa* and named it Lhotönpa after the guru in his own language. Chakravarti has not a shadow of doubt that this Tönpa is an esteemed Bhutanese individual and the word Lho in the name referred to Lhoyul or southern country, which we may remember, is a name Tibetans, not Assamese, used to call Bhutan in later times. His main reason for this conclusion is Bhutan's proximity to Prāgjyotiśa (present-day Guwahati). He cites archaeological findings in Assam, particularly Sūryapāhār, to argue for the existence of Buddhist centres in Assam since the beginning of the first millennium and its probable arrival in Bhutan. Thus, he concludes: 'It can be legitimately presumed that Bhutan might have received initiation to Buddhism much earlier than Tibet. Moreover, the constant communication through the duars for trade as well as raids must have brought the Bhutanese people in contact with the Buddhist people of the Assam–Bengal plains much earlier than some writers on Bhutan have presumed.'[10]

Although Chakravarti's arguments seem farfetched and sometimes anachronous, his thesis that the peoples of Bhutan and Assam–Bengal may have a very ancient interaction certainly strikes a special chord with what the traditional Bhutanese historians claim. It is a topic inviting further historical research. For one, we know from the records of the Chinese traveller Xuanzang in the seventh century, who visited Prāgjyotiśa and spent time with the Kamarupa King Bhaskavarman, that there were tribal people who were akin to *mán* people living the southwestern frontiers of China and that Buddhism has spread in the Kamarupa kingdom.[11] If Prāgjyotiśa was a centre of high culture, which seems to be the case according to the records we have, it is perhaps not too farfetched to think that Bhutan, being in close proximity, received some of its peoples and cultures. Another food for thought in this regard is the discovery of treasures in the shape of a shivalinga in Bhutan by later treasure discoverers, in much the same way as similar shivalingas were discovered during modern archaeological excavations in Assam. Thus, a vigorous flow of people between the Assam–Bengal plains and Bhutan in this period certainly cannot be ruled out.

However, one must also be cautious not to fall for suggestions which are sometimes presented as a *fait accompli*. Another Indian attempt to establish an ancient link between India and Bhutan, repeated by a number of Indian writers on Bhutan including Chakravarti and Mehra, is the theory that the people called the 'Tehpoo' were the first to settle in Bhutan. The Bhutanese cultural historian Lopen Nado spurned such a claim as an unreliable report based on 'groundless and careless speech of village fellows'.[12] Aris too dismissed it as 'a quite unfounded claim made in the British colonial writings' and traces the origin of this notion to one 'garbled report on Bhutanese history by Krishna Kanta Bose who spent the year 1815 on deputation to Bhutan'. The account given by Bose states that 'the caste or tribe of Thep' settled in Punakha are the descendants of 'a raja of the Cooch tribe' who had been ousted by the arrival of the 1st Dharmarāja of Bhutan (Zhabdrung Ngawang Namgyal).[13] The account is certainly very muddled[14] as there was certainly no Indian presence in Punakha which Zhabdrung Ngawang Namgyal had to oust when he arrived. Besides, he enjoyed good relations with the rājas of Cooch Behar, who were his contemporaries as we shall see later.

The muddle is probably due to Bose's own misunderstanding. Bose perhaps met locals in Punakha who said they are Thep (contracted from Thedpa) or people of Thed and also that their ancestors came from India. Thed is an old name for the Punakha area and many people in Thed were slaves of Indian origin. Lopen Nado gives us an example in the case of the village of Rinchengang in the lower Thed valley, of which the whole population descended from former Indian slaves.[15] Some of these slaves were probably descendants of Indian travellers and mendicants held in captivity in Bhutan, as reported by an eighteenth-century source,[16] while some may have been bought by Bhutanese merchants from India. Travelling to Bhutan through Cooch Behar in 1783, Samuel Turner, head of the second British mission to Bhutan and Tibet, reports how people in Cooch Behar sold their children as slaves for an insignificant amount and how people borrowed money with their wives as collateral. If the wife produced children, they were divided between the money lender and debtor.[17] Yet, many Indian slaves may have been abducted by the Bhutanese marauders who raided the Indian villages frequently. While it is true that a whole class of people in Thed were descendents of Indian slaves, who were enslaved mostly during the Medieval Period of Bhutanese history, it is however both ahistorical and achronistic to claim, using this as evidence, that the earliest settlers in the Punakha region were of Indian origin. At best, the case of the Indian descendents whom Bose encountered affirms a latter Indian contribution to the demographic composition of the western midlands rather than an ancient case of Indian settlement.

Early Historic Period:
Early Diffusion of Buddhism

WHILE THE CLAIMS of ancient connections to the south remain mythical or conjectural with no substantive material evidence or conclusive written records, Bhutan's link to the north is viewed as being fairly well established. There is a plethora of historical evidence, including oral accounts, written works and material artefacts, confirming Bhutan's very early link with Tibet. Tenzin Dorji, a contemporary scholar, even claims a Tibetan royal connection to eastern Bhutan as early as the death of the 7th King of Tibet, Drigum Tsenpo.[1] Drigum's son, Nyatri, according to Tenzin Dorji, established the castle of Nyakhar in eastern Bhutan after the latter escaped from Tibet following the death of his father, which would be roughly in the first century BC.[2] We have already seen how the genealogist Ngawang also claimed that both the nobilities and common people are descendents of Tibetan stock.

However, the earliest and most well-known Bhutanese assertion of links to Tibet is the popular claim that the two temples of Jampa Lhakhang (བྱམས་པ་ལྷ་ཁང་) in Bumthang and Kyerchu Lhakhang (སྐྱེར་ཆུ་ལྷ་ཁང་) in Paro were built by Songtsen Gampo (c. 605–50), the 32nd King of the Yarlung dynasty which ruled Tibet for much of the first millennium. The story of the foundation of these temples by the Tibetan king is so well known to the Bhutanese that Bhutan's known history effectively begins with this event. It forms an important part of Bhutan's historical and religious consciousness, especially because the two temples are still standing as prominent places of religious worship. To the Bhutanese, the founding of the temple, however, does not presuppose Tibetan rule over Bhutan. Bhutanese historians go to some length to explain that the temples were works of religious piety rather than political domain markers, much like the fabled Buddhist temples built by the Indian Emperor Aśoka in Tibet and like the temples built by the Bhutanese themselves at Kailash in Tibet, in Ladakh and Nepal. The truth may, however, be more complex.

Songtsen Gampo and the two temples

Songtsen Gampo was one of the greatest kings of ancient Tibet. Today, we know a great deal about him, particularly his military successes as an imperial ruler, from old Tibetan sources such as the *Old Tibetan Chronicle* and *Old Tibetan Annals*. These were written in the centuries after his reign but only discovered at the turn of the twentieth century from caves near Dunhuang in the Gansu province of China. These books are among tens of thousands of manuscripts, over 4000 of them in Tibetan, which date from the late eighth to tenth century. They were found by British and French explorers in caves, which are believed to have been sealed in the eleventh century. The manuscripts and wood slips are today in London and Paris. In addition to Dunhuang sources, there are also several pillar inscriptions erected in the centuries after Songtsen Gampo. To this, one must also add the accounts of the Tibetan rulers in ancient Chinese and Arabic sources and a wealth of later Tibetan historical and religious writings from the twelfth century onwards which elaborate on the glory of the ancient imperial period. The chief one among the later written sources is the *Ma ṇi bka' 'bum*, which promotes the idea of Songtsen Gampo as an incarnation of Avalokiteśvara, the Bodhisattva of compassion along with his two queens from Nepal and China who are presented as incarnations of two versions of the female deity Tārā. The book is a rediscovered treasure, a text which is believed to have been written and hidden in earlier times and later discovered by a treasure discoverer (see more on treasures in the following chapter). Although the book as it exists today is a result of cumulative compilation, its core part dates back to at least the twelfth century. It is a long narrative containing, among other things, accounts of Avalokiteśvara's career as a Bodhisattva, the genesis of the Tibetan people, the life story of Songtsen Gampo and a large number of his testaments. Almost every source for Songtsen's life written after this text derive their information from this. It is in this and later Tibetan sources that we find a portrayal of Songtsen Gampo as a great Buddhist king and the pioneer of the Tibetan Buddhist civilization. The Bhutanese temples are attributed to such a religious king but let's capture a profile of the imperial ruler before turning to his career of temple building.

Songtsen Gampo became the Tsenpo (བཙན་པོ་) or King of Tibet just as Tibet was emerging as a strong military power in the region. Under Songtsen's rule, the Tibetan empire rose to become a major, if not the most powerful, player in Central Asia alongside the Chinese and Arabs. Through his military conquests, he extended his dominion across the entire Tibetan plateau and beyond. To the west, he conquered the Zhangzhung kingdom, which covered the large area of western Tibet around Mt Kailash; to the south, he conquered the Kathmandu valley and his troops are said have gone even further into north India; and to the north and east, his troops conquered the Sumpa and Azha countries located around the present-day Qinghai province of China. As was the fashion then, Songtsen Gampo often used marital alliances to build connections with these kingdoms. Marriage was the 'carrot', failure of which followed the 'stick' in the form of a military offensive. To give an example, Songtsen's sister was sent as a bride to the Zhangzhung ruler Ligmigya. The alliance did not last long as the Tibetan princess complained of mistreatment. The marital impasse led to the full invasion of Zhangzhung by Songtsen's army, who indeed made use of the intelligence provided by his sister. Although there is no mention of Songtsen's Nepali bride in the earlier records, the betrothal of the Nepali Princess Bhrikuti to Songtsen, which later books narrate, can also been seen as a political alliance.

Songtsen proposed a similar marriage alliance to the Tang rulers of China but the Tang court initially declined the proposal as they could not imagine the prospect of a Chinese princess being married to a Tibetan ruler. The Chinese, who considered themselves civilized, certainly would have perceived the Tibetans, including their king, as provincial and barbaric. Following the rejection, Songtsen invaded the Azha/Tühüyün country, which was already occupied by Tang forces and his troops marched on to Tang territory in 638 CE. Fearing Songtsen's campaign against China, the Tang court relented and accepted the proposal of a marriage alliance, which certainly eased the relations between the two powers throughout the reign of Songtsen Gampo. In about 640, the Tang emperor received Songtsen's minister Gar Tongtsen, who came to take Princess Wencheng to Tibet. This minister is very affectionately remembered by later Tibetans for the wit and wisdom he employed to win the Chinese bride, whom, according to later sources such as *Ma ni bka' 'bum*, he won through a competition which involved many contenders and a series of brain-teasing challenges. The Chinese records however recalled not only his intelligence but some 5000 ounces of gold he brought with him when he came to fetch the princess. The subsequent saga of Wencheng's journey from the Tang court to Lhasa and her arrival in Tibet is told very poignantly in the later Tibetan written and folk oral literature. Even in Bhutan, folk songs and stories about Wencheng, known locally as Ashe Jaza or 'Chinese Lady', are common to this day. Later Tibetan histories unanimously recount that Wencheng was sought as a bride for Songtsen himself and also allude to her clandestine relationship with the minister Gar Tongtsen on her way to Tibet, but some historians today say that she was intended to marry Songtsen's heir Gungsong Gungtsen, who predeceased his father in 646 CE. Wencheng consequently became the queen of her father-in-law. Whatever the case may be, it is the arrival of Wencheng in Lhasa after a long journey which forms the prelude for the narratives on temple building with which we are concerned.

According to traditional Tibetan accounts, when Wencheng arrived in Lhasa with the famous Buddha statue given to her as a parting gift and as an object of worship by the emperor, the cart on which the Buddha was being transported got stuck in the marshlands of Lhasa. The cart, it was said, was pulled by two strong Chinese men, who would later become the ancestors of the family to which the founder of Bhutan belonged. Unable to move the cart despite all efforts, Wencheng spread out the geomantic and divination chart she carried with her from China and conducted a geomantic survey of the land. It must be remembered that Tibetans viewed China as a major source of astrological, geomantic and divinatory sciences and Wencheng is often attributed with the introduction of these sciences to Tibet although scholars now think it was not her but Princess Jincheng who followed her a few generations later and promoted Chinese culture. Himalayan Buddhism, especially in its popular practice, is heavily ridden with geomantic and divination practices, much of which originated in China. While some such cultural transmission must have taken place at the time of Wencheng, modern historians think that a more robust propagation of Chinese culture and learning, including Buddhist religion, may have taken place not at the time of Princess Wencheng but during the days of the second Chinese princess, Jinsheng, who arrived in Tibet in 710, three generations after Wencheng.

To return to the main story, Wencheng's geomantic analysis revealed that the country of Tibet lay on a supine demoness. The demoness's body stretched across the Himalayan landscape causing it to breed savagery and diabolic forces. The lake of the Othang was the blood of her heart, the two hills around Lhasa symbolized her breasts and her limbs extended to the distant territories. For any prospect of civilization in Tibet and particularly for Buddhism to flourish, the demonic landscape had to be tamed through building a series of temples. The lake of Othang had to be suppressed by a pivotal chapel and the demoness pinned down with temples on her vital points and limbs. According to the later accounts of Songtsen and Wencheng, it was this scheme of subduing the supine demoness which led Songtsen and his Nepali and Chinese queens to build a series of temples. First, the temple of Rasa Thrulnang, now known popularly as the Jokhang and as Tsuglhakhang to local residents of Lhasa, was built on the lake of Othang by Tritsun/Bhrikuti, Songtsen's Nepali queen. According to the narrative, she demanded her right to build the first temple as she was the senior queen. Being granted the right and after many difficulties, she successfully built her temple facing Nepal and on the lake, as Wencheng's prediction suggested, with the support of Songtsen's miraculous power. Wencheng built her temple, known as Ramoche, facing China and installed her Buddha statue in it. The statues were swapped at later times to confuse the Chinese soldiers who came to recover Wencheng's Buddha statue. Today, the Jokhang cathedral, which was built by the Nepali queen but which houses the Buddha brought by Chinese queen is, to put it in the words of Hugh Richardson, 'the Tibetan Holy of Holies'[3] and the most popular destination of Buddhist pilgrimage after Buddhist sites in India.

To subdue the demoness, a further twelve temples were said to have been built: four to pin down the keys points of the shoulders and hips known as 'the four suppressing the districts' (རུ་གནོན་བཞི་), four on the elbows and knees known as 'the four taming the frontiers' (མཐའ་འདུལ་བཞི་) and four on the hands and feet known as 'the four taming outer frontiers' (ཡང་འདུལ་གྱི་བཞི་). In the earliest record of the scheme, Jampa Lhakhang in Bumthang is listed among the temples taming the borders and Kyerchu Lhakhang among the temples taming outer frontiers. Jampa Lhakhang falls on the left knee and Kyerchu Lhakhang on the left foot of the supine demoness. Later histories also talk about 108 temples founded by Songtsen Gampo, 108 being a very common Buddhist numerical metaphor or a substitute for a figure approximating 100. In Bhutan, Anu Lhakhang and Namkhai Lhakhang in Tang, Genye Lhakhang in Chume and Lhakhang Karpo and Lhakhang Nagpo in Haa are said to be from the same period although there is hardly any proof to substantiate the claims.

How credible, then, is the account of Songtsen Gampo's temple building? Did Songtsen Gampo really build the temples attributed to him, including those in Bhutan? The question is particularly critical for determining the earliest cultural and religious event in Bhutan of great historical significance. The Tibetan historical documents we have from the Early Diffusion such as the ones found in Dunhuang are silent on Songtsen's Buddhist policies and the project of temple-building. While they contain accounts of the Chinese princess, they make no mention of the Nepali princess. This has led scholars to question the historicity of the events pertaining to temple-building mentioned above. Michael Aris, who did the first elaborate study of Songtsen's scheme of temple-building, has even categorized the story as a myth rather than as a historical account, one which got embellished with later accruals. Needless to say, Bhutanese and Tibetan historians contest Aris's presentation of this story as a myth. As embellished and legend-laden as it may be due to its long existence and the hallowed admiration with which they viewed the dynastic period, the story of Songtsen's temple building cannot easily be dismissed as a myth. Although the Dunhuang documents pass the Buddhist works of Songtsen Gampo in silence, the pillar inscription of Tri Desongtsen (d.815) make a clear statement about Songtsen's establishment of Rasa (Jokhang) and other temples:

> During the time of the magically sagacious and divine emperor, the ancestor Tri Songtsen [Gampo], as an enactment of the Buddha's doctrine, the temple of Rasa (=Lhasa) and others were built, and the shrines of the Three Precious Jewels were established. During the time of the ancestor Tri Düsong, temples were built including Tritsé in Ling, and the shrines of the Three Precious Jewels were established. During the time of the ancestor Tri Detsukten, temples were built in Kachu in Trakmar and at Chingphu, and the shrines of the Three Precious Jewels were established. Then, during the time of [my] father Tri Songdetsen, temples were built in the center and frontiers, including Samyé at Trakmar, and the shrines of the Three Precious Jewels were established. And [now] in [my] time, I, the divine emperor Tri Desongtsen, have built the temple of Karchung, among other, so that the shrines of the Three Precious Jewels are established.[4]

The inscription, not fully cited here, goes on to show that there was a sustained interest in Buddhism among the ruling kings since Songtsen's reign. The claim is corroborated also by the following edict of Tri Songdetsen, who started at around the age of twenty to promote Buddhism which had suffered some decline during his minority:

> After the Tsenpo [my] father passed into heaven, some of the uncle-ministers had thoughts of rebellion. They destroyed the Buddha's Dharma that had been practices since the time of [my] father and ancestors.[5]

The *Testament of Ba*, parts of which certainly predate the period of Later Diffusion, also contains many references to Songtsen's Buddhist activities and to the two temples associated with Songtsen's queens. It is quite clear that later narratives were based on earlier oral and written records and not pure fabrications. To the Tibetans in later times, Songtsen Gampo is undoubtedly the father of Tibetan Buddhist civilization. Not only did he take the Tibetan nation to unprecedented heights in terms of political and military power, he left three important legacies which came to shape the course of Tibet throughout its history. These legacies would also have a palpable cultural impact on the Himalayan areas such as Bhutan which were technically outside the political sphere of Tibet. First and foremost of Songtsen's achievements in the eyes of later Tibetans is his promotion of Buddhism. He is remembered as a pioneer in bringing Buddhism to Tibet and subsequently also seen as an incarnation of the Buddha, who is the guardian of the Land of Snows.

Secondly, he was responsible for the invention of Tibetan scripts, which came to be used by the entire Buddhist Himalaya. It was during his reign and through his initiative that a minister named Thonmi Sambota is said to have created the Tibetan letters based on north Indian scripts. Modern research has generally confirmed this claim despite strong contention from the adherents of Tibetan Bon tradition that writing existed in Tibet before Songtsen Gampo. Songtsen's third major contribution is in the system of law and structure of governance. He is said to have introduced various Tibetan legal codes and to have enforced 'the sixteen pure laws of man' (མི་ཆོས་གཙང་མ་ བཅུ་དྲུག) and 'the ten virtuous laws of gods' (ལྷ་ཆོས་དགེ་བ་བཅུ). These laws as found in some Bhutanese sources are given below in a table. Many legal documents from the period of Early Diffusion have been found among the Dunhuang manuscripts, some of them possibly preserving Songtsen's original legal codes. Only further study can reveal this.

Another aspect of his legislative initiatives was the creation of administrative divisions for efficient civil and military administration. The country was roughly divided into four *ru* (རུ) or districts and these were further grouped into communities of *tongde* (སྟོང་སྡེ) comprising a thousand households. Such classification of his domain into four districts (རུ་བཞི) and four frontiers (མཐའ་བཞི), which are recorded in Dunhuang manuscripts, lend some credence to the temple scheme we have seen above. It is quite likely that these temples were built during Songtsen's reign with some sort of a scheme, however unclear and off the mark it may have been in terms of physical links due to poor knowledge of the geography. Mapping was not a skill the Tibetans knew much about until very recent times and geomantic considerations prevailed over geographic ones. Further, if we are to take the analogy of seventeenth-century *dzong* constructions under Zhabdrung Ngawang Namgyal's leadership and guess the intent of temple building, it is highly likely that the temples were not merely religious sites built for Buddhist piety but also political statements marking the imperial domain under Songtsen's rule.

The Ten Virtuous Laws of Gods	The Sixteen Pure Laws of Mankind
Saving life (avoid taking life)	Seek refuge and follow the Three Jewels
Chastity (avoid sexual misconduct)	Conform the three doors (body, speech, mind) to *dharma*
Charity (avoid misappropriation)	Serve one's parents and those who have been kind
Honesty (avoid false speech)	Respect the learned and wise
Conciliation (avoid sowing discord)	Honour the elders and those of higher status
Pleasant speech (avoid harsh speech)	Be sincere to all friends and relatives
Useful speech (avoid idle gossip)	Help everyone in the community
Contentment (avoid covetousness)	Emulate the noble and look upward
Loving-kindness (avoid hatred)	Be wise in enjoying food, clothes and wealth
Right view (avoid wrong view)	Never forget a kindness or favour
	Treat everyone with equanimity
	Avoid trickery through scales and measures
	Eschew jealousy
	Do not listen to bad women
	Speak placidly and pleasantly
	Be broad-minded and forbearing

Though the question of whether the two temples were built during the time of Songtsen Gampo as tradition claims remains to be conclusively resolved, there is no disagreement among scholars as to the origins of the Jampa Lhakhang and Kyerchu Lhakhang in the period of Early Diffusion. The architectural and iconographical styles of the temples, which share close resemblance with other temples of Tibet's dynastic period, clearly point to their foundation during the Early Diffusion. Written records such as the *Ma ṇi bka' 'bum* also sufficiently prove their existence by the twelfth century and all available sources place their foundation to the reign of Songtsen Gampo. For the largely illiterate and oral society that Tibetans and Bhutanese communities were until our times, one cannot also discount the rich and uninterrupted oral accounts about the temples. Oral tradition represents the main transmission of knowledge among the people and it indubitably maintains that the temples were first built by Songtsen Gampo.

Padmasambhava and the two kings

The next milestone in Bhutanese history is the arrival of Padmasambhava, the famous tantric teacher from India, which took place some time in the middle of the eighth century, roughly a hundred years after the foundation of the temples. Padmasambhava, or Guru Rinpoche as he is popularly known in Bhutan, is without any doubt the most important and universal of all historical and religious figures in Bhutan. He holds a central place in Bhutan's religion and history. The Bhutanese world is imbued with his presence so much that he can be considered the patron saint of Bhutan. From the grand state festivals to the first prayers toddlers mumble, from the giant monuments to fleeting dreams of hermitic monks, the figure and worship of Padmasambhava permeates Bhutan's spirituality and religious culture. To most Bhutanese, he is both a precious teacher (Guru Rinpoche) and the quintessential divinity. He is often described as the second Buddha and perceived as the embodiment of the enlightened wisdom, compassion and power of all Buddhas. A great number of Bhutanese religious festivals, ceremonies and prayers have him as their focal point of worship or meditation. He is seen as the epitome of enlightened power and beneficence and one particularly kind to the people of the hidden lands such as Bhutan. In fact, traditional Bhutanese historians unanimously claim that Bhutan is the destined field of activity for Padmasambhava just as Tibet is for Avalokiteśvara.

In the theological formulation of Padmasambhava as the focus of prayer and meditation, he is not merely a historical person but an enlightened energy or state of being. The historical figure of Padmasambhava only symbolically represents the divine and enlightened being, which transcends the vicissitudes of life and death and the notions of time and space. In the ultimate reality, he is the primordial Buddha, the enlightened nature immanent in all phenomena and beyond individuality. He is the state one must aspire to reach as indicated by the popular mantra dedicated to him: *oṃ aḥ huṃ vajraguru padma siddhi huṃ* (May I attain the state of the adamantine guru Padma). It is in the context of such theological understanding and apotheosis of Padmasambhava as an enlightened and compassionate divinity that we must understand most of the practices of devotion and rituals pertaining to him. To the Bhutanese, Padmasambhava or Guru Rinpoche is the enlightened being who manifests in multiple forms, effortlessly and simultaneously, to benefit the world according to its needs. First and foremost, he is the precious teacher who can lead one on the noble path of enlightenment, this being the supreme purpose of life from a traditional Bhutanese perspective, but his role is not limited to this. The Bhutanese, like most other Tibetan Buddhists, pray to him for health, wealth, long life, safety, happy rebirth, success in wars, businesses, exams and virtually in all affairs of life.

Even when we try to leave behind the theological realm and come to the domain of historical narratives, Padmasambhava, in the eyes of his followers, is an enlightened being with full control over life and death and, in fact, 'beyond birth and death' (སྐྱེ་འཆི་ལས་འདས་པ་). His life spanned over many centuries and he was already a living legend in India by the time he visited Bhutan and Tibet in order to carry out his mission of taming the wild landscape and spreading the Buddhist teachings. Such presentation of history is no doubt due to a distinctive concept of time and space and the interfusion of theological and historical perspectives found in traditional scholarship, about which we shall see more later.

Using a traditional Buddhist religious, philosophical and historical approach, the accounts of Padmasambhava's life and miracles are narrated in a great detail in nearly two dozen biographical accounts, the most elaborate of which are known as *kathang* (བཀའ་ཐང་). There are about a dozen *kathang* hagiographies, all of which are considered to be treasure texts hidden in the eighth century and revealed in later times. To gain a general idea of the traditional perception of Padmasambhava's life, a synopsis of his mythical biography is presented in the following paragraphs based on the *kathang* literature, including the earliest one attributed to Nyangral Nyima

Özer (1124–92) and the local Bhutanese one revealed by Pema Lingpa (1450–1521). A great of deal of writing is also available on Padmasambhava in Western languages for those interested in secondary work. As a framework for the brief sketch of his long and legendary life, I use his eight characters or manifestations known as *guru tshengye* (གུ་རུ་མཚན་བརྒྱད་), which are associated with eight stages of his life and commonly enacted in a sacred dance during Bhutanese festivals.

Padmasambhava's mission, according to the *kathang* hagiographies, began in Sukhāvatī, the heavenly realm of the Buddha Amitābha. Padmasambhava is an emanation sent forth to this world by the Buddha Amitābha to help the sentient beings after the historical Buddha had passed away. The first mark of his transcendental status is his miraculous birth on a lotus in the middle of a lustrous and immaculate lake, unsullied by the ordinary human womb. He is described as a self-born emanation without father and mother (ཕ་དང་ མ་མེད་རང་བྱུང་སྤྲུལ་པའི་སྐུ་) and his name Padmasambhava/Padmakara (Lotus Born) is obviously derived from this although some sources do record his birth from human parents. The divine character of his person right from birth is summed up in the response he gave to the enquiry about his identity: 'My father is innate awareness and my mother the perfect sphere of reality. I belong to the caste that is non-duality of the reality and awareness and I am from the unborn sphere of truth. I consume conceptions of duality and I live to destroy the afflictive emotions.' If the supernatural birth on a lotus was a compelling sign of his divine and deific origin, *kathang* literature further reinforced this with a prophecy attributed to the historical Buddha, stating that he would return after eight years in the form of Padmasambhava. Thus, Padmasambhava is seen as the immediate incarnation of the Buddha and often given the epithet: the second Buddha.

The miraculous child on the lotus was then brought by the childless King Indrabodhi of Oḍḍiyāna to his palace and appointed as his heir with the name Tshokye Dorji. He was brought up as a beloved prince, in the same fashion as the Buddha was brought up during his early life in the palace, but Tshokye Dorji, like the Buddha, personally longed to follow a spiritual path to benefit all beings. Unable to persuade King Indrabodhi to allow him to renounce the princely life, he resorted to outrageous conduct, and during one of his playful antics, he lost hold of the trident in his hand and killed a minister's son. As a punishment, he was banished from Indrabodhi's country in Oḍḍiyāna. Young Tshokye Dorji then wandered in northern India as an ascetic and undertook different spiritual practices in haunted places such as

Padmasambhava and the eight manifestations

Sitavana, the famous charnel ground. He engaged in esoteric tantric practices including cannibalism and emerged as a spiritual adept with great powers in magic. Adopting a fierce appearance and barbarous lifestyle, he used his power to tame the unruly by 'ritually slaying' the male and copulating with the female in sexual union, these being the two forms of highly advanced and esoteric tantric techniques of subjugation.

Despite his spiritual achievements as a non-conformist mystic, Tshokye Dorji was not able to establish his spiritual authority in mainstream society through the obscure practices on its fringes. To build his religious credibility and show the example of a progressive spiritual path, he received the ordination of a full-fledged Buddhist monk with the new name Śākya Senge. He followed a number of teachers to continue his pursuit of knowledge and mastered astral sciences, medicine, linguistics and languages, alchemy, arts and crafts, earning himself the name Loden Chogsi. His spiritual training under numerous gurus continued for many more years, focusing particularly on the highly esoteric teachings which he would later pass down in Tibet. His name, Padmasambhava, is often associated with this stage of his life. There are particularly two notable sets of transmissions, for which he is remembered in Tibet in later times. The first is the set of teachings known as the Kagye (བཀའ་བརྒྱད་) or Eight Pronouncements, which he received from eight different mystics and is later said to have passed on to his twenty-five Tibetan disciples, including the Tibetan king. The second notable set is that of the Dzogchen (རྫོགས་ཆེན་) technique, which he is said to have received from its pioneers such as Garab Dorji and Śrī Siṃha. This later became very popular as the apex of the religious system of the Nyingma School, which championed the cause of continuing his legacies.

To continue our narrative of his time in India, Padmasambhava earned one further name, Nyima Özer, from his practices in the charnel grounds and the use of magical power to subjugate many malevolent spirits and heretics. When the Buddhist scholars at Bodh Gaya, the epicentre of the Buddhist world, were threatened by non-Buddhist rivals, he appeared miraculously to defeat the non-Buddhist opponents in both intellectual debate and magical contest. For this role as defender of the faith, he was given the name Senge Dradro, 'the lion's roar'. Padmasambhava traversed the Indian subcontinent on his mission to subdue evil forces and to propagate the Buddhist faith. When he visited the kingdom of Zahor to tame its king and people, he did so by entering into a spiritual relationship with the pious Princess Mandarava. The king was outraged by the act and punished him by having him burnt alive but he miraculously transformed the fire into a tranquil lake and reappeared on a blooming lotus in its centre. The king grievously repented his ignorance and rash action and offered his service to Padmasambhava, who was given the name Padma Gyalpo. He performed a similar miracle in his country of Oḍḍiyāna to which he returned to tame King Indrabodhi and his court. The people of Oḍḍiyāna recognized Padma Gyalpo, who was earlier banished from the kingdom for murder. They captured him and burnt him alive only to find the smothering cinders transformed into a tranquil lake after some days and Padma Gyalpo reappear on a blossoming lotus with his consort.

Padmasambhava is said to have even travelled to China and some *kathang*s also claim that he appeared in the form of a Buddhist monk to convert the war-mongering Emperor Aśoka to a peace-loving Buddhist. However, it was while he was in a meditation retreat in the Yangleshod cave in Kathmandu valley with his Newari consort in the middle of the eighth century that his journeys to Bhutan and Tibet purportedly took place. By then, he had already had a long career in India and become a renowned figure with an unmatched prowess in occult practice. The 37th Tibetan King Tri Songdetsen (742–c.797) had just begun to promote Buddhism, which some of his ancestors had introduced in the Tibetan court some generations earlier, and had in fact invited the Bengali abbot Śāntarakṣita to teach in Tibet despite strong opposition against it. When the obstruction from human and non-human denizens of Tibet to Buddhist teachings became too difficult for the peaceful abbot to handle, he was asked to temporarily leave Tibet, and Padmasambhava, the master of occult power, was invited to Tibet to convert the hostile world of Tibet into a conducive field for Buddhism.

Padmasambhava is believed to have subdued almost all the hostile spirits and divinities of Tibet, using his spiritual power, and bound them under oath to serve and protect the Buddhist doctrine. In one of these acts of subjugation of local deities of the Himalayas, he took the wrathful form known as Dorji Drolöd, the last of the eight characters. According to the *kathang* hagiographies, he is said to have assisted the king in building Tibet's first monastery of Samye and in launching the massive translation of Buddhist scriptures into Tibetan although early sources recount that Padmasambhava spent only about eighteen months in central Tibet and they place his departure before the Samye monastery was built in about 779 CE. His active missionary work, technological initiative of irrigation, economic projects of agricultural expansion and above all, his profuse use of occult power eventually made the Tibetan court and the spirits apprehensive and distrustful and he was asked to leave. In a departure as dramatic and incredible as his life and time on earth, he took off from Tibet, according to the traditional sources, riding an extraordinary horse through the sky to the island of Chamara to live there immortally as the subduer of its cannibal inhabitants.

Such spiritual persona based on philosophical theories and expressed through the ritual and semi-historical texts developed many centuries after his life, however, may not fully correspond to the real person of Padmasambhava, who played a very important role in the transmission of Buddhism to Bhutan and the Himalayas in the eighth century. The highly mythological accounts do not leave us with much information that is really tenable in modern historiography. The only well-known biography which was not based on the revealed treasure texts but written by the seventeenth-century scholar Tāranātha based on sparse Indian sources provide some interesting information including Padmasambhava's human birth in a family of the warrior caste in Oḍḍiyāna but even this one provides very little information we can use to understand the personality of Padmasambhava or date him precisely.

Due to intense deification in the standard sources, some scholars even questioned his historicity but it is generally agreed among historians on Tibet, on the basis of a number of pieces of evidence, that Padmasambhava lived and played an important role in the transmission of Buddhism into Tibet during the Early Diffusion. Until recently, scholars have also generally assumed that the apotheosis and cult status of Padmsambhava began in the twelfth and thirteenth centuries with the appearance of his extended biographies and development of rituals of worship focused on him. However, new scholarship on Padmasambhava based on ancient sources strongly suggests that Padmasambhava may have been mythologized and venerated in rituals by the tenth century.[6] It is, therefore, quite likely that the traditional narratives, despite being overladen with later accretions and embellishments, contain in them largely true threads of Padmasambhava's life and activities.

The Bhutanese generally accept Padmasambhava's multiple visits to Bhutan as a historical fact and a great deal of their religious and cultural life are enactments or celebrations of these events. There are, however, no conclusive evidences for his visits to Bhutan even in early Tibetan sources. Here, we will focus on the stories of his arrival in central Bhutan found in later sources and the implications of these stories for Bhutan. Our main written sources are *terchö* (གཏེར་ཆོས་) or treasure texts from the early eleventh century onwards. The texts are traditionally claimed to have been composed in the eighth century and buried by Padmasambhava or one of his disciples to be revealed by a destined *tertön* or treasure-discoverer when the time is ripe. However, for the purpose of historical enquiry, we can only date these texts as far back as the treasure-discoverer. They cannot be taken as contemporary records of events in the eighth century, which the treasure tradition claims them to be.

The narratives in the treasure texts are supplemented by a plethora of oral accounts, a number of which may predate textual records. Yet many may have developed out of the written accounts, spread by educated religious travellers. In comparison to the very limited number of written records on Padmasambhava's visit, the oral narratives are rich and diverse. They are generally localized stories drawing on local legends, toponyms and other aspects of life in the communities. There are a great many place names associated with Padmasambhava's journeys to Bhutan in Bhutanese oral accounts. Ugyen Drak in Zhemgang is a cliff named after Padmasambhava, the master from Ugyen or Oḍḍiyāna (ཨུ་རྒྱན་), because he blessed it. Phrumzur, said to be an aberration of *phurzug* (ཕུར་འཛུགས་) or piercing with the dagger, is a spot in the same area where he pierced his dagger into the rock. Ura, for which the archaic term is Urbay, is said to be the *beyul* (སྦས་ཡུལ་) or hidden land, named after Ugyen Padmasambhava. One of their local deities, some villagers believe, accompanied Padmasambhava from India. A village in western Bhutan is called Yibri (གཡིབ་རི་) or hiding hill, because the natives were hiding when Padmasambhava passed through it. Similarly, in a village in the Shar district, the gushing mountain spring goes underground before reaching the village and comes back to surface some miles below the village. This natural phenomenon is said to have resulted due to the refusal to offer water to Padmasambhava when he passed through the village. Khoma village in Kurtoe is where Padmasambhava found *khoma* (མཁོ་མ་) or the useful lady. The list goes on. Such legends and narratives no doubt help us understand the ubiquity of Padmasambhava in the Bhutanese cultural consciousness but they do not leave us any wiser historically. It is mainly to the written texts and existing monuments that we will have to turn to find any remaining traces of history in the legendary stories of Padmasambhava.

Leaving aside the miraculous journeys Padmasambhava made, we can speak of two visits of Padmasambhava to Bhutan: first from India before he visited Tibet and subsequently from Tibet. Our sources for his arrival from India are treasures texts discovered by Molmokhyil and Ugyen Zangpo, about whom we know virtually nothing. According to Kongtrul's *Biography of Treasure Discoverers*, Molmokhyil lived in the second sexagenary cycle (1087–1146) and Ugyen Zangpo in the fifth (1267–1326). Molmokhyil was a western Tibetan and a descendent of an ancient Tibetan dynasty while Ugyen Zangpo is said to have been from central Bhutan.[7] In his text for preparing a circular chart to be used as a protection against harm by non-human spirits, Molmokhyil gives a background story about a king of Mon named Sedarkha, who was engaged in evil deeds. The eight classes of non-human spirits (སྡེ་ཆེན་ སྡེ་བརྒྱད་), led by Shelging Karpo (ཤེལ་གིང་དཀར་པོ་), punished the king by sending forth diseases, drought and other natural calamities in his country.

According to the story, King Sedarkha falls seriously ill and proclaims that he will share his country and court with anyone who can cure him of the ailments imposed by the eight classes of spirit. A minor ruler of a border district offers to find someone who can cure him in exchange for a measure of gold. When he was given a measure of gold, he reports that in the Yangleshod cave in Nepal, there is someone called Padmasambhava, who is a master of secret mantra and who subjugates entire existence with his power. Upon hearing this, the king swiftly despatches messengers to invite Padmasambhava. When Padmasambhava arrives at Sedarkha's bedside, the latter offers to do anything and give everything if he is cured and the misfortunes caused by the demons and gods are reverted. Padmasambhava asks for no material gains but proposes that the king and his country eschew negative deeds, engage in virtuous actions and follow his spiritual ways. Sedarkha agrees to do so and Padmasambhava meditates for three days at the red cliff of Dorji Tsegpa. Using his power through a circular magical chart, he subjugates Shalging Karpo and his coterie of eight classes of spirits. Later the chart is worn by the king, who is freed from the harms done to him by the spirits, and the country flourishes.

Molmokhyil's account is terse and brief, aimed only at giving a quick background for the story of the protective amulet and the related teachings he discovered. He leaves us with no information about Sedarkha, apart from his being a king of Mon. However, from the name of the cliff, Dorji Tsegpa, we can surmise that the Mon country he is talking about is modern-day Bumthang. This name is used in many other sources to refer to the cliff-cave in Kurjey in Bumthang. Molmokhyil is also considered to be the rebirth of a certain Mon figure of the eighth century from Bumthang called Hamināth. Although the historicity of this character with an Indian name can be questioned, Molmokhyil's identification with him certainly points to a link between Molmokhyil's story and Bumthang where the standard story of Padmasambhava's arrival in Bhutan is set. Thus, if Kongtrul's date for Molmokhyil is to be trusted, we can be certain that stories of Padmasambhava's arrival in Bumthang existed by the beginning of the twelfth century.[8]

If Molmokhyil leaves us asking for more information, our second source by Ugyen Zangpo certainly fulfils the task of providing that. Ugyen Zangpo recounts this story of Padmasambhava's visit in detail and it is his version which has become the dominant narrative of Padmasambhava's arrival in Bhutan. The story is told by Denma Tsemang, one of the students of Padmasambhava, whose rebirth Ugyen Zangpo claims to be. The story starts with Padmasambhava's achievements in India and his residence in the palace of the Indian King Nawoche (སྣ་པོ་ཆེ་), literally big nose in classical Tibetan. Nawoche and his court invite Padmasambhava to their country and the great master blesses the country by 'turning the wheel of dharma', that is, teaching the Buddhist doctrine. It was at that time that the king named Sindharāja became ill and sent messengers to invite him.

Sindharāja, according to this account, was born as Prince Kunjom to a certain King Singala of Kapilavastu in northern India. He was the fourth of seven sons. Due to his wild character and his harassment of the subjects, he was asked to leave the court and pursue a religious life. He initially accepts the proposal but, influenced by his wives and attendants, he later rejects it and destroys thirty villages belonging to the minister who presented the proposal. As a consequence, he and his retinue are banished to the region of Sindha which he rules, assuming the new title Sindharāja. However, after a clash with the neighbouring King Nawoche, he and his retinue are again forced to move from Sindha to eventually settle in Bumthang. In Bumthang, he builds the extraordinary iron castle without doors (ལྕགས་མཁར་སྒོ་མེད་), which Ugyen Zangpo describes with fantastical details. The iron castle has nine floors, five levels of underground passage to enter it, and 108 windows made of precious jewels. Each floor of the palace is decorated with precious metals and stones and when the sun and moon shine on it, the palace radiates to the sky and its surroundings like a rainbow. It is filled with treasures and one entrance is to the river and the other facing west.

It was from such a palace that Sindharāja started to extend his domain as far as Dorjidrak in Tibet and Sindhabari in India. In course of his expansion, his only son Tala Mebar is killed in a conflict with King Nawoche in the Indian plains. In retaliation, Sindharāja burns a thousand settlements in Nawoche's domain. A constant exchange of invasions ensues between Mon and India. Upset by the loss of his son, Sindharāja gives up worshipping his tutelary deities. Instead, he desecrates their domains. The angry spirits hit back by stealing his *lä* (ཟླ) or essence of life. The *lä,* like *wängthang* (དབང་ཐང་) or charismatic presence and *lungta* (རླུང་རྟ) often rendered as wind horse, is a pre-Buddhist concept of quasi-psychological property of life or constituent of a person in addition to the well known psychosomatic components. When a person is deprived of *lä,* the person is seriously destabilized and ruptured. Thus, as a result of losing his *lä*, the king falls gravely ill and his ministers desperately search for a solution when a minor ruler from a border area suggests that Padmasambhava, the Indian tantric master, who is also Nawoche's spiritual guru, may be able to help the king.

Messengers were immediately sent to invite Padmasambhava with seven measures of gold dust, following which the guru arrives in Bumthang. Sindharāja from his sick bed promises to offer anything in return for his health but the guru asks only for a consort with whom he can carry out his spiritual practice to retrieve the *lä*. The king has four daughters who bear the marks of a *ḍākinī* or a spiritually potent woman. Bumden Tshomo, the most virtuous of all, is given as a tantric consort to the guru and the guru starts his retreat in the cave of the red cliff, Dorji Tsegpa. One is to understand that this cliff was the main base of the chief of the spirits, Shalging Karpo, who took the king's *lä*. After seven days of meditation, Padmasambhava left an imprint of his body on the rock face of the cave. Shalging Karpo appears to Padmasambhava and offers an inflated leather pouch in which Sindharāja's *lä* and *srog* or life-force were trapped. 'The air in the pouch is the life-force and the white spider in it is the life essence,' the spirit says. 'Tell the king not to repeat the bad actions. His bad actions have led to the punitive illness.' Padmasambhava and Bumden return to the iron castle and, placing the pouch next to the king's nostrils, reinstate the king's life essence and life force. The luminous white spider disappears into the king.

Some of the oral accounts give us a slightly more dramatic story of Padmasambhava's final subjugation of the king of evil spirits. As the guru enters into deep meditation to use his psychic power to subdue the evil spirits, Shalging Karpo, the chief of the spirits, remains in hiding unwilling to challenge the tantric master. However, on the seventh day, the guru miraculously creates a magnificent spectacle on the ground in front of the cliff. Shalging Karpo is persuaded by his followers to see the unprecedented show. Seduced by the temptation, Shalging Karpo shyly reveals himself in the form of a lion and instantly the guru swoops down on him in the form

Kurjey temples built around the cave where Padmasambhava meditated

The temple of Chagkhar currently standing on the site of the Iron Castle

of a *garuḍa* bird and suppresses him. Such stories of miracles, contests and subjugation of the evil forces form the main thread of Padmasambhava's career in Bhutan and Tibet. It is as a tamer of wild and malevolent forces that he is remembered by posterity in the Buddhist Himalayas.

Following his recovery, King Sindharāja hosts a big celebration. Offering his palace, wealth and realm, he requests Padmasambhava to remain as his lord but the guru declines saying that he has the whole world to serve, that he has no need for a palace for the whole of existence is a palace to him, that he has no need for wealth as the whole world is filled with his wealth and that he has no need for private patrons as all beings are his patrons. Padmasambhava imparts Buddhist teachings to the king and his court and instructs them to live a virtuous life, following the Buddhist religion. 'Do not be miserly, give away wealth in charity. Do not cause violence, let people enjoy a peaceful life,' he admonishes. After hearing Sindharāja's grievances against Nawoche, Padmasambhava persuades Sindharāja and his ministers to come to the border with him to seek conciliation with Nawoche.

Padmasambhava tells them that he will return to Bumthang to give further teachings in the future but he will come from Tibet rather than India. Our author pre-empts Padmasambhava's journey to Bhutan from Tibet which is yet to take place and he does so by presenting it as part of the general narrative of Padmasambhava's visit to Tibet. It is partly put here to indicate Padmasambhava's power to foresee the events yet to unfold. Before he leaves the iron castle, Padmasambhava instructs the people in various Buddhist practices. He appoints caretakers for Jampa Lhakhang and the new site of Kurjey, where he has left the imprint of his body, and leaves butter for butterlamps at these places. By mentioning Jampa Lhakhang here, the author perhaps intends to inform his readers that this temple, which we have discussed above, was already a site of worship when Padmasambhava came to Bumthang.

The story continues with Padmasambhava's return to Nawoche's palace in the Indian plains. Padmasambhava persuades the king to come with him to the border to make peace with Sindharāja. As an earnest devotee of Padmasambhava, the king complies with Padmasambhava's wish. Thus, the two kings and their retinue meet on a spacious ground at the border between Mon and India. Padmasambhava gives them Buddhist teachings and oversees a ceremony of oath taking. A stone pillar is erected and the two parties take vows to live in peace and to not let their troops cross the border demarcated by the pillar. This place, where the peace deal was made, is today identified with Nabji, literally 'the open ground of oath', which lies in the southern end of the Mandgechu valley. A stone pillar known as *nado* (མནའ་རྡོ) or stone of oath, which is believed to have been erected at this meeting, is still found standing on the site. Padmasambhava is said to have hidden various religious treasures in the vicinity and blessed the area as a hidden land.

The native inhabitants of this area are the Monpa tribes, who speak Monkha. We have already discussed the likelihood of their being the earliest people in this region. In their own oral account as recorded by Francoise Pommaret, their ancestors were said to have not been welcoming to Padmasambhava but they were nevertheless appointed as the entrance guardians of this place by him. According to another oral account, one girl named Shelkar Tsodron of this tribe is said to have become a consort of Padmasambhava.[9] To return to our story, after the peace deal was made, Padmasambhava returns to India on a mission to reclaim Bodh Gaya, the spot where the Buddha became enlightened, from the non-Buddhists. From there, he journeys to Nepal and eventually to Tibet in order to tame the wild landscape and help establish the Buddhist tradition in the Tibetan court.

We can see that Ugyen Zangpo's narrative of Padmasambhava's journey from India to Bumthang is clearly connected to Molmokhyil's short account if not a direct extension of it. Ugyen Zangpo may have been aware of Molmokhyil's text or had access to another transmission of the story. Michael Aris suggests that even the name may have gradually evolved from Se'darkha, Sen-mda' kha, Sindha to the fully Indianized Sindhurāja found in later historical literature. The Indianization no doubt is advantageous to those who speculate a strong Indian connection to and influence on ancient Bhutan. It also lends more credence to the account of the royal protagonist being a refugee from India. However, apart from the toponyms such as Chagkhar, Kurjey and Nabji and the numerous oral accounts, there is no other evidence to substantiate the events which take place in the narrative. There is no known textual source which predates Ugyen Zangpo's text corroborating his accounts, apart from the passing association of Kurjey in Bumthang with Padmasambhava found in earlier texts.

There is also currently nothing visibly left in Chagkhar in terms of structural remains which remind one of an important ancient establishment, let alone an enduring iron castle. In fact, the text itself warns the reader in the form of a prophecy that not a single fragment of the iron castle will be left in the future. The castle is predicted to fall simultaneously with the fall of the Tibetan dynastic rule and it is presented as an example for teaching the basic Buddhist message of impermanence and futility of attachment to worldly properties. Reading between the lines, it is probable that whatever fort or castle stood in Chagkhar may have already been erased by the time of Ugyen Zangpo. In 1905, the British political agent John Claude White reports seeing the ruins of a square structure with surrounding ditches, but by the time Michael Aris visited the Chagkhar in the 1970s, there was nothing left of such structures but only fallow fields used for grazing cattle from neighbouring villages. We can learn from this that the speed of change, even in a fairly static society, is so great that our prospect for concrete material evidence is becoming increasingly poor. However, by the same token, this also suggests that many things may have happened as preserved in old stories despite the lack of evidence today. A serious archaeological work in the area may be our last hope of finding any substantive evidence for the famous castle.

A question must also be raised with regard to the name Chagkhar, the iron castle and thence Chagkhar Gyalpo, the king of the iron castle. Aris's speculation that this may have been a Neolithic fort has no base and does not explain the name. Traditional historians generally take the name in its literal sense and would have us believe that there was a castle substantially built out of iron. However, it is quite possible that Chagkhar is just a name given to the castle without any semantic explanation. The word Chagkhar (ঙ্গুঘ্ম'ম্মাম্ম) is rendered in the literary writings as iron castle, where *chag* (written *lcags* ৠঘ্ম') is iron and *khar* (written *mkhar* ম্মাম্ম) is castle. However, it is also possible that the term is a vernacular with no written orthography, an option that no historian has thought of so far. There is a homonymous term in Bumthang vernacular—*chakhar*, found commonly with a *pa* suffix. *Chakharpa*, which is cognate of the classical Tibetan term *rgya gar ba* (ক্ক'ম্মা'ম'), refers to an Indian. Based on such a reading, Chakhar Gyalpo could be an Indian king and Chagkhar Gomae could refer to an Indian building as *mae* denotes a house in the Bumthang dialect. Thus, the castle may have been just an Indian building instead of an iron castle without gates. This would of course concur with the Indian origin of the King Sindharāja. However, we are still left with the problem of the syllable *go* which is prefixed to *mae*. Could *go* refer to first, thus first house? In any case, all interpretations must still remain generally conjectural until any further evidence or more convincing explanation of the toponym is found.

Our problem of giving credence to the narrative is further worsened by the lack of information on its source, Ugyen Zangpo, himself. After a muddled analysis, Michael Aris concludes that Ugyen Zangpo is none other than the famous treasure-discoverer Pema Lingpa, who often addressed himself as Ugyen Pema Lingpa. Aris does not, however, give any good reasons for his conclusion. Gedun Rinchen, Bhutan's first modern historian follows Kongtrul Lodoe Thaye in identifying this Ugyen Zangpo as a student of Dorji Lingpa. In their brief notes on Ugyen Zangpo, both Kongtrul and Gedun Rinchen present a legendary story. Ugyen Zangpo was born in Bumthang and he rediscovered in Kurjey the Dzogchen text entitled *Clear Mirror* (རྫོགས་ཆེན་ཀུན་གསལ་མེ་ལོང་) of which the account of Sindharāja is a part. This text leaves no doubt that the author was very active in Bumthang, particularly around Kurjey.

According to Kongtrul and Gedun Rinchen, Ugyen Zangpo had received the prophecy to build a three-dimensional maṇḍala in Kurjey for the welfare of Bumthang valleys. In order to clarify doubts he had about the maṇḍala, Ugyen Zangpo transports his consciousness to the presence of Padmasambhava, leaving behind his human body temporarily. His return gets delayed by a week and in course of the delay, his attendant discards his corpse in confusion. Unable to re-enter his own body, Ugyen Zangpo desperately looks for a medium. Finally, using the technique of *drongjug* (གྲོང་འཇུག་) or transference of consciousness into another body, he enters the body of a young girl who has just died. He was able to carry on some of his works but did not finish his maṇḍala project. Faced with just this short legendary account, it is difficult to ascertain who Ugyen Zangpo was and when he lived. As we have seen above, Kongtrul places him in the fifth sexagenary cycle (1267–1326) but that is not tenable if he was a student of Dorji Lingpa (1346–1405). Furthermore, Dorji Lingpa himself uses Ugyen Zangpo as his childhood name and Tenzin Chogyal, the famous medieval Bhutanese monk-historian, attributes the account of the maṇḍala project and transference of consciousness to one Drime Lingpa, who he says was one of the antecedent reincarnations of the Gangteng Trulkus.[10]

The mythical and mystical character of our only sources for the accounts of Padmasambhava's first visit, which is accepted as an established fact, amply demonstrates the difficulties we face in understanding ancient Bhutan. The accounts in both oral and written sources are heavily laden with legends as can be expected with a story about a hallowed figure which was passed down through many centuries. There is no doubt that the original story of Padmasambhava's visit, if it ever took place, was incrementally embellished and exaggerated in the subsequent centuries. Thus, the main challenge of a historian is in seeing the kernel from the husk and reaching the original core or basic thread of the accounts and finding vestiges of the real event. The legendary nature of the story, however, was not as much a problem for the learned traditional historians as for modern historical researchers. The monk historians, who are today the main sources for Bhutan's history, saw the world from a very different philosophical perspective. They espoused a philosophical thinking and worldview in which both time and space are illusory and inherently empty of real nature. They espoused the Buddhist view that all phenomena lack an absolute reality. There is no such thing as an absolute fact; there are only multiple conventional truths perceived from different perspectives. The empirical world is a fluid and dynamic experience processed through diverse sociocultural conditioning and perspectives. There is no ultimate point for fixation: truth and falsity are empty and artificial categories. Such philosophical thinking removes any rigid temporal and spatial strictures. Both time and space are viewed as flexible, stretchable, collapsible and interpenetrable.

Furthermore, when fully manifest, the power of the mind surpasses the power of matter. Thus, such things as miracles are simply instances of exercising the mind's power over matter, time and space. An enlightened and liberated mind can transcend the ordinary notions of materiality, temporality and positionality. According to them, this is why Padmasambhava could leave the imprint of his body on a rock and hold texts in a time warp to be revealed by people centuries later. Seeing history from this philosophical point of view allows them to cohesively accommodate the features and events which are dismissed by historical researchers as mythical, ahistorical and anachronistic. Thus, the fantastic stories and chronological problems that are found in the works of traditional historians are not necessarily signs of ignorance or lack of analytical thinking. Ironically, they are a result of a well-established philosophical viewpoint based on very rigorous patterns of analytical thinking, but patterns which are different from those employed in Western historiography. The views derive from a very rich Indo-Tibetan philosophical tradition which employs thorough analytical and rational procedures.

The difficulties faced by a secular historian in verifying the 'truth' from 'mythical' accounts written by a person with such Buddhist philosophical approaches become even greater as we turn to the accounts of the subsequent visit of Padmasambhava to Bhutan from Tibet and the story of the second king who also based himself in Bumthang. According to Ugyen Zangpo, Padmasambhava is said to have returned to Bumthang the year after his first visit. He was accompanied this time by his young Tibetan disciple, Denma Tsemang, whose rebirth Ugyen Zangpo claims to be. It is also to this figure of Denma Tsemang that traditional scholars of Bhutan would trace the origin of the Bhutanese Joyig script, which became popular in the twentieth century. Padmasambhava comes to Bumthang from Tibet via Khenpalung, a region in the northeastern corner of modern Bhutan, from where he is also followed by the Tibetan King Khikha Rathö and his subjects. King Khikha Rathö renounces his kingdom of Khenpalung and its riches in pursuit of spirituality, quite contrary to the other account we will see below. The wealth of Khenpalung is buried as treasures and the whole area concealed as a hidden land to be discovered and opened only in future times. Padmasambhava and the royal entourage seem to approach through the valley of Tang where Padmasambhava bestows teachings to the royal party. Most of Khikha Rathö's group settle around Genye Lhakhang but the Tibetan king, his queens and senior officials continue to Kurjey. When Padmasambhava arrives in the area of Kurjey, he was received by Sindharāja with much pomp and ceremony. Padmasambhava gives teachings to the two kings and their subjects at Kurjey.

The main royal protagonist in Ugyen Zangpo's account is the Indian King Sindharāja and not the Tibetan King Khikha Rathö. Khikha Rathö appears on the side but we must note that he is presented in Ugyen Zangpo's account as an amiable and deeply religious character. Unfortunately, that is not how he was going to be remembered with the emergence of the account of his life in Pema Lingpa's guides to Khenpalung. There are two different versions of Pema Lingpa's accounts among his works: a short one in his *Guide to the Hidden Lands of Sikkim and Khenpalung* and a longer one standing separately called *Guide to the Hidden Land of Khenpalung.*[11] Pema Lingpa's detailed account of the hidden land of Khenpalung presents Khikha Rathö as an inimical and diabolical prince with a dog's mouth and a goat's skull as his name indicates.

Coming from a treasure text, the story understandably begins in the court of Tri Songdetsen, the 37th King of Tibet, who invited Padmasambhava and the Bengali monk Śāntarakṣita to Tibet and established Buddhism as the formal religion of the court. The story begins with the completion of the Samye monastery around 779, and the project to translate the Buddhist scriptures into Tibetan. It is a well-known historical fact that a massive and systematic project of translation of the Buddhist literature from Indic and Chinese sources took place during the late eighth century involving several dozens of Indian scholars and Tibetan translators. The bulk of the Buddhist literature in Tibetan codified later in the canons of Kanjur and Tanjur was translated in the eighth and the first half of the ninth centuries. The following words of Kapstein sum up the translation project of the Tibetan dynastic era:

> The translation of Buddhist canonical scriptures, undertaken by committees including both Tibetan monks and foreign Buddhist scholars, figured prominently among the monastic activities sponsored by the monarchy, and the scope of Tibetan translation activity, continuing under royal patronage into the mid-ninth century, grew to enormous proportions. In both quantitative and qualitative terms the achievement of the Tibetan translators must be ranked among the cultural monuments of the medieval world and the hundreds of texts translated into Tibetan by the imperial translation committees may be counted among the finest achievements of the art of translation in any place or time.[12]

One of the great translators of this period was Vairocana of Pagor. He was trained as a translator and sent to India to bring back Buddhist doctrines. Vairocana is later remembered for bringing a wide range of esoteric tantric doctrines including the teachings belonging to the well-known Dzogchen or Great Perfection tradition. According to our source, Vairocana is accused upon his return by Za Marjen, one of the queens of Tri Songdetsen, and the anti-Buddhist ministers for bringing with him dark magic and harmful spells in the guise of Buddhism. Some accounts have it that the queen made up the accusation as Vairocana, who was a handsome man but one of the first seven monks to be ordained in Tibet, defied her wish for a sexual liaison with him. Embarrassed by Vairocana's defiance of her seduction, Za Marjen falsely accuses Vairocana of raping her. Either way, the king is forced by the court to force Vairocana into exile. Although our source does not pursue Vairocana's story any further, we know that he is later recalled from his exile and becomes the most celebrated translator.

Queen Za Marjen, however, falls out of the king's favour and he avoids her for many years. In course of that time, Za Marjen, overcome by strong sexual urges, copulates with a dog and a goat. This liaison, we are to believe, resulted in the birth of Prince Murum Tsenpo, who had a canine mouth (ཁྱི་ཁ་) and caprine skull (ར་ཐོད་). Upon hearing about Murum Tsenpo and his bestial paternity and appearance, the king asks Za Marjen to bring the prince to him. He subsequently banishes the prince with many followers and subjects as a *lü* scapegoat to the southern borderlands. We may recall the common ritual of sending away scapegoats and ransoms, mainly in the form of effigies of dough, in order to cast away evil harm-doers and misfortunes, which we have touched on in the previous chapter. Murum Tsenpo or Khikha Rathö suffered such a fate and was first settled in Lhodrak Gyid but he was expelled again from there to Khenpalung.

The identification of the hidden land of Khenpalung is an interesting topic for understanding the history and transmission of ideas. Even the name Khenpalung (མཁན་པ་ལུང་), literally 'the valley of Artemisia', evokes a sense of mystery and awe to the Bhutanese. Pema Lingpa and the people who followed him commonly identified Khenpalung with the highlands northeast of Bumthang and northwest of the modern Kurtoe district in Bhutan extending across the current border with China. By the fourteenth century, the region had become a famous destination for spiritual men seeking hidden lands and buried treasures. It was one of the most prominent hidden lands, which are believed to have been concealed by Padmasambhava.

However, the idea of Khenpalung was not limited to Pema Lingpa's world. About half a century before him, Godkyi Demthruchen (1337–1409) 'opened' one hidden land of Khenpalung near the Everest region north of the Arun valley and south of the Latö Lho region of Tibet. Like our Khenpalung, the Nepali Khenpalung is also split by the modern state boundary. We do not yet know how the two Khenpalungs, opened at different times and different places by two different clerics, are related. It is most likely that the idea of a hidden land with this name, associated with Prince Khikha Rathö and waiting to be opened by a destined person, was in vogue across southern Tibet and the cis-Himalayan areas and both Gökyi Demthruchen and Pema Lingpa were exposed to this idea and went on to identify it but in different locations and closer to their own worlds. However, we cannot discount the fact that there may also have been ideas of two different Khenpalungs. Interestingly, Godkyi Demthruchen mentions a Khenpalung of Bud (བུད་ཀྱི་མཁན་པ་ལུང་) and Khenpalung of Lhodrak Gyal (ལྷོ་བྲག་རྒྱལ་གྱི་མཁན་པ་ལུང་).[13] One wonders if there is an orthographic problem here and the work *rgyal* in Khenpalung of Lhodrak Gyal should actually read *rgya* or India. Pema Lingpa's text does explicitly refer to his Khenpalung as 'Khenpalung of India' although there is no mention of a second Khenpalung.[14] One can only conjecture that it may have been called Khenpalung of India because it is located in southern borderlands close to India.

To return our narrative, Khenpalung turns out to be a thriving home for

Khikha Rathö and his entourage. Pema Lingpa gives a detailed description of the many valleys, rivers, ridges, streams, springs, lakes and mountains in the area, which no doubt he must have known very well because he was born not far from it and he spent some time travelling in and across the area. In fact, even his *Guide to the Hidden Land of Khenpalung* was extracted from one of the cliffs there. He narrates the way in which Khikha Rathö and his subjects settled in the various valleys and hills, built houses in a mixture of Indian and Tibetan architectural styles, cultivated various crops, reared livestock and even benefited from the trade between Tibet and India. Khikha Rathö, Pema Lingpa says, also built a close connection with the Indian King Sendha (སེན་མདར་), who we may assume is the same person as Sindharāja whom we have discussed earlier.

After establishing a prosperous community in Khenpalung, Khikha Rathö launched a military invasion of Tibet using the Indian support he had garnered. In Tibet, King Tri Songdetsen had passed away by then and his son King Mutig Tsenpo, Murum Tsenpo's brother, was installed as the ruler of the Tibetan empire. Under the threat of Khikha Rathö's invasion, Mutig Tsenpo sought the intervention of Padmasambhava, who in turn, commanded the god Namthil Karpo to create a heavy storm and lightning. Terrified by the lightning flashes, the troops returned home to Khenpalung. Mutig Tsenpo, however, continued to worry that Khikha Rathö might strike again and destroy the Buddhist shrines built by his father and ancestors unless Khikha Rathö was forced out of Khenpalung and further away from Tibet. To this end, he once again sought Padmasambhava's help.

Padmasambhava travelled to Khenpalung and transformed himself into a fearsome black man. He deceived Khikha Rathö into believing him to be a non-Buddhist rival of Padmasambhava called Hara Nagpo, who wished to destroy the works of Padmasambhava. When he was asked to show his power, he performed a dance on a flat rock, leaving eighteen footprints. Being convinced, Khikha Rathö now requested the black man to help him build a temple as great as the temple built by his father King Tri Songdetsen and Padmasambhava. The black man, however, offered to build something even more wondrous than the temple: a wooden bird holding 500 people to party with all kinds of enjoyments. Immediately carpenters were gathered and the large wooden bird built. For its inauguration, the king and his entourage were all invited to a party in it. When all of Khikha Rathö's court was in it, the black man went on the top of the wooden bird and hit with a hammer the nail, which triggered the unsettling wind.

The wooden bird soared to the sky and Khikha Rathö duly discovered that the black man, none other than Padmasambhava, had tricked him. The wooden bird/plane flew out of Khenpalung to Bumthang and, when the nail which triggered the settling wind was hit, it landed in a place called Karnya. Leaving the king and his entourage there, Padmasambhava returned to Khenpalung to bury all the properties of Khikha Rathö and his court. He sealed the entire hidden land so that no one could find the place until the right time had come. Unable to find their place again, Khikha Rathö and his subjects settled in Kyizum village in Tang. To this day, there is a household who claims descent from Khikha Rathö. Padmasambhava returned to Chakhar palace in Bumthang to visit Sentarāja (Sindharāja).

Pema Lingpa's account does not mention Khikha Rathö coming to Chokhor at the time, but hints in the form of a prophecy that Khikha Rathö will settle in lower Chokhor in future.[15] We have already seen in Ugyen Zangpo's account that he came to Chokhor while most of his people settled around the temple of Genye, which is perhaps to be identified with the little old temple by the roadside in Zu-nge village in Chumey.[16] Local oral accounts in Bumthang also claim that Khikha Rathö and his court eventually settled in the lower part of Chokhor valley. The village of Chamkhar, it is believed, is named after the *khar* (མཁར་) or castle of his *cham* (ལྕམ་) or queens and Jalkhar after the castle of *jelön* (རྗེ་བློན་) or king and ministers. Longchenpa, who travelled through this valley approximately one and a half centuries before our narrative was recovered by Pema Lingpa, reports that at the lower end of the Chokhor valley there are castles and settlements of ancient kings and ministers and that the people there are of noble descent with superior physiques.

At first glance, the narrative, with its accounts of bestial insemination of the queen and the wooden airplane which flies with wind force and magical concealment of the entire region into a time warp, sounds like a very imaginative medieval Bhutanese version of modern science fiction. However, discounting these mythical elements, which must have accumulated during the many centuries the story was passed down, there seem to be traces of historical events which can justify a claim that a Tibetan prince indeed lived in the northeastern part of Bhutan some time around the beginning of the ninth century. Of the many references to Tibetan historical events, the stories of Vairocana's exile and the notoriety of Queen Za Marjen of Tsepong are well known among Tibetan historians. However, the succession of the Tibetan kings after Tri Songdetsen until Tri Ralpachen is far from clear and has puzzled most Western and native Tibetan scholars. Tri Songdetsen is said to have had four sons: Mutri Tsenpo, who died very young, Mune Tsenpo, Murum Tsenpo and Sadnaleg alias Tri Desongtsen. There is a lot of confusion with dates for these figures as well as with the variant use of the names Mutik and Murum for the third and fourth sons in different sources but it appears very likely that Khikha Rathö, the protagonist of our narrative, is the third prince, Murum Tsenpo.

As Mutri Tsenpo died young, Mune Tsenpo inherited the throne when their father, Tri Songdetsen, retired in 797. He appears to have been a devout Buddhist and during his reign, he tried thrice to eliminate the gap between rich and poor through wealth redistribution. Although his project of equalization was unsuccessful, posterity remembers him mainly for this noble act. It might also be this that brought on his early death although most sources say that he was poisoned by his own mother, Za Marjen of Tsepong out of jealousy for his beautiful queen, Gyalmo Tsun of the Phoyong clan. As Mune Tsenpo had no heir, the throne would have passed to the third son, Murum Tsenpo. However, it appears that he was disqualified for killing Wuring, a minister of Nanam clan. The inscriptions of the stone pillar at Zhwa temple in Tibet confirm that Murum Tsenpo did not get along with his father Tri Songdetsen. Perhaps, he was never the preferred choice, due to his ugly appearance, accorded to him by some sources. For his crime, he was banished from Tibet to Lhodrak, which is adjacent to the region of Khenpalung and just north of Bumthang, according to some sources. The sources differ on the reasons and the destinations for his exile but we can be more or less certain that our narrative of Khikha Rathö is based on this story of Murum Tsenpo's exile.

With Murum Tsenpo exiled, the throne went to the fourth son, Sadnaleg alias Tri Desongtsen, who ruled Tibet from 804 to 815 and is also sometimes referred to as Mutik Tsenpo, as in our narrative. Thus, the core thread of our narratives seems to echo the political intrigues at the Tibetan court and it may not be too farfetched to surmise the arrival of an exiled Tibetan prince first in Khenpalung and subsequently in Bumthang, whether or not Padmasambhava played any role in it. Interestingly, the oral stories in the Tang valley narrate a journey of Khikha Rathö from Khenpalung to Tang, using landmarks and toponyms, defying the later dramatization of the journey on a wooden aeroplane. Longchenpa's sighting of castles in Bumthang and the local preservation of the family line descending from Khikha Rathö lends good support to this hypothesis. The latter case is especially striking and convincing given that Khikha Rathö is popularly viewed as an outcaste, an inimical figure rather than as a prince from a hallowed pedigree. Why would a family come to accept and sustain such a family origin if there were no shred of truth in it? Despite the popular portrayal of Khikha Rathö as a bestial, evil figure, it seems that there is at least among some people an implicit acknowledgement of the family's connection to the divine lineage of the Tibetan kings through Khikha Rathö. This is suggested by the important role played by the family in a local festival, a role similar to the ones some leading families play in festivals in other areas. It is quite likely that the fantastical accounts and demonization of Khikha Rathö started only during or slightly before Pema Lingpa's time. We have seen how Ugyen Zangpo, who lived in Bumthang before Pema Lingpa, had only a pious picture to paint of Khikha Rathö.

According to the *Testament of Ba*, the earliest source we have mentioning Padmasambhava's arrival and activities in Tibet, he is supposed to have left Tibet before the construction of the Samye temple. According to this source, it appears that his works of spiritual subjugation of malevolent forces, religious conversion, his socioeconomic project of creating agricultural land and irrigation schemes and his close relation with and influence on King Tri Songdetsen made many in the Tibetan court jealous and apprehensive. Due to the misgivings about his presence in Tibet that many of the Tibetan nobles seem to have had, he was asked to return to India and these people even plotted an ambush on the way to eliminate Padmasambhava but the ambush failed due to the guru's magical power. He is said to have left for the island of Chamara to tame the cannibals, flying on his horse as we saw above.[17]

However, according to most of the later biographical sources, he is supposed to have left Tibet only during the reign of Mutig Tsenpo alias Tri Desongtsen. There are long periods of his absence in the Tibetan court, particularly around the time when Vairocana returned from India and was exiled. According to these sources, Padmasambhava was at this time travelling or in retreat in the cis-Himalayan areas, including Bhutan. One source even notes that he was in Senge Dzong area of Bhutan after he was evicted from Tibet.[18] Now, if we look at these accounts of exile or deportation, Śāntarakṣita was asked to return to the Nepali borders following his first visit and strong opposition to his Buddhist activities from members of the Tibetan court. Similarly, Vairocana, we saw already, was banished to Tsawarong in the eastern border region after his return from India. Namkhai

Nyingpo, another monk and disciple of Padmasambhava, was briefly exiled to Lhodrak. Khikha Rathö, whether historical or mythical, was exiled to the Khenpalung area and we will study two more cases below.

We can clearly see a pattern of the southern and eastern borderlands being used as the main destinations for exile or deportation. If the events in our sources are historical, albeit mythicized and exaggerated, then it is quite plausible that when Padmasambhava did face strong opposition in Tibet after his initial work and was asked to leave, as recorded by the *Testament of Ba*, he did so by coming to Bhutan and connecting up with Sindharāja, his former student and patron in Bumthang. This case becomes even more compelling as we see Padmasambhava being associated with Mon both in the *Testament of Ba* and a biography of Yeshe Tshogyal, his consort and chief Tibetan disciple.[19]

Whatever the case may be, by the middle of the second millennium, his visit or multiple visits to Bhutan were seen as a *fait accompli*. In fact, he is said to have travelled across and blessed every inch of the Bhutanese landscape and of the Himalayas in general. Many valleys and villages across Bhutan have local legends about Padmasambhava's visit and often explain their existence and cultural behaviour in relation to such legendary events as we have already seen. One of the most prominent stories of Padmasambhava's visits is to the Paro valley in western Bhutan. Here, he is sometimes said in oral accounts to have come flying on a tigress. The iconic Taktsang or Tiger's Nest hanging perilously on the cliff has from the early centuries of the second millennium come to be one of the most important holy sites in the Buddhist Himalayas. In Padmasambhava's biographies, it is the site where he assumes the identity of a wrathful figure in order to subdue all the malevolent forces of the Himalayas to make way for the teachings of the Buddha.

In this fearful emanation, Padmasambhava manifests as the guru Dorji Drolöd (རྡོ་རྗེ་གྲོ་ལོད་) or the Adamantine Exuberant Wrath. The form epitomizes his role as the subjugator of the wild Himalayan landscape and all forces in it. Interestingly, the tigress on which he rides is often identified with no other than his Bhutanese consort Tashi Kheudren. This Bhutanese lady is perhaps the only Bhutanese disciple of Padmasambhava about whom we find some information in Tibetan sources.[20] She is said to be from the Mon region, probably Bumthang or Kurtoe, and the daughter of a local king named Hangrey. She first met Yeshe Tshogyal when the latter was meditating in Senge Dzong in northeastern Bhutan. Yeshe Tshogyal took Tashi Kheudren as her student and introduced her to Padmasambhava in Taktshang.[21] As she possessed all the hallmarks of a spiritual partner, Padmasambhava took Tashi Kheudren as his consort in order to undertake the esoteric practice of Vajrakīlaya. As the culmination of this religious meditative practice, Padmasambhava is said to have manifested in the appearance of Dorji Drolöd while Tashi Kheudren, who had already achieved great spiritual heights, transformed herself into a tigress. In these terrifying forms of a wrathful deity and a tigress, the duo is believed to have scared the evil forces of the entire Himalayan region into submission. Also partaking in this ceremony of Vajrakīlaya were other disciples including a young Bhutanese named Saley, Yeshe Tshogyal (Tibet's greatest female Buddhist figure) and her spiritual partners Atsara Saley and Pelgyi Senge. The main cave on the Taktshang cliff site is named after Pelgyi Senge and a *stūpa*, which is said to contain his remains, is still preserved in a shrine at Taktshang.

The Taktshang and Kurjey caves are undoubtedly the two most important and popular places associated with Padmasambhava's journeys to Bhutan. To the Bhutanese and traditional historians, these two monuments also stand as two irrefutable testimonies of Padmasambhava's benevolent works in Bhutan. One can then add to these two places of spiritual eminence and power, countless other power spots, footprints, handprints, springs, trees, temples, relics and narratives which abound across Bhutan to confirm and reinforce the importance of Padmasambhava in the Bhutanese religious and historical consciousness. The Bhutanese historian Pema Tshewang also adds that many Bhutanese, including a certain local man named Hamināthā, who became a disciple of Padmasambhava, followed him to Samye to study.[22] This curious figure with an Indian name was later associated with a few treasure texts, including the earliest record of King Sendarkha in Bumthang. We also find the names Bumden Tshomo and Shelkar Tshodön, which are both enumerated among Padmasambhava's consorts although it is not clear whether they refer to the same or different persons. Tertön Tshering Dorji, in the account of his previous rebirths, also claims that King Tri Songdetsen had a queen from Paro named Mendey Zangmo.[23] Her daughter, Saley Ödron, is believed to have been a student and consort of Padmasambhava.

Based on the sporadic records of Buddhist activities, most of which are also from much later times, it is very difficult to judge to what extent Buddhism had spread in the area of Bhutan by Padmasambhava's time. Ugyen Zangpo's accounts certainly claim that there were religious sermons bestowed by Padmasambhava and practices taken up by his disciples at Kurjey on a communal scale. King Sindharāja, who was the main patron, is said to have also supplied paper to Tibet for the vast literary work which was going on in Samye. Similarly, the biographies of Padmasambhava and Yeshe Tshogyal also mention their religious activities in Taktshang and Senge Dzong. The later accounts of this period also assert the existence of several temples which were already built during Songtsen Gampo's time. While there is some material evidence for the existence of the temples, there is very little we can say with certainty on the spread and influence of Buddhism in either the ruler's court or among the populace.

Relying on literary and material evidence, one thing we can say with certainty about this era is that there was an unparalleled explosion of Buddhist religion and culture in neighbouring Tibet. Padmasambhava played an important role in this cultural diffusion so much so that the later traditions which derived from this early diffusion took him as their primary figure. This diffusion in Tibet had a far-reaching impact not only on Tibet but on many areas around Tibet. It is very likely that the diffusion had at its time some influence on people's life in Bhutan, which lay at the fringes of Tibetan political configuration then. Some Bhutanese might have also participated in the religious works in Samye, which saw the convergence of people from many places. If later memories are correct, many Bhutanese may have also adopted Buddhism, preparing a favourable ground for Buddhist visitors in the following centuries and Bhutan may have been a concourse of Indian and Tibetan ideas and people, as Pema Lingpa seems to suggest in his guides to Khenpalung. Whatever the case may be, Padmasambhava's visits to Bhutan form a major milestone in Bhutanese history. In later times, many Bhutanese religious figures, including Bhutan's foremost saint Pema Lingpa, would also claim to be rebirths of the personages from this early ancient period.

The refugees

Since ancient times, Bhutan has been a well-known destination for Tibetans who were banished from their country, escaping into exile, searching for Buddhist devotees or simply seeking to start a new life. This trend continues in our times. When one looks at ancient Bhutanese history with such understanding, it is easier to appreciate the traditional claims that there was a significant Buddhist culture established in Bhutan during the Tibetan dynastic period through the works of Padmasambhava. This is particularly plausible as events and intrigues in the Tibetan court spilled over to Bhutan in many ways. We have already seen the story of Khikha Rathö and his subjects although much of it sounds mythical. The next case we come across is the arrival of Prince Tsangma. King Tri Desongtsen of Tibet, whom we saw earlier as the younger brother of Murum Tsenpo alias Khikha Rathö, had three sons. Modern historians on Tibet generally agree that Tsangma was the eldest of the three sons although many traditional sources consider him a younger brother of Tri Ralpachen. However, his historicity is not contested and historians also generally agree that he had a strong religious inclination, which made him pass the throne to his brother. Some accounts even talk of him as a monk. The second brother Udum Tsenpo alias Lang Darma is said to have been denied the throne on the grounds of his character. Thus, the Tibetan throne went to Tri Ralpachen, the last of the three great Buddhist kings of Tibet in the dynastic era. Songtsen Gampo, Tri Songdetsen and Tri Ralpachen are remembered by posterity as the royal trio, who respectively introduced, widely propagated and consolidated the Buddhist system in Tibet.

The arrival of Tsangma in Bhutan must be recounted in the context of Tibetan political and religious conflicts. More than 200 years after the introduction of Buddhism, Tibet's royal court was anything but peaceful and non-violent. The Tibetan empire was maintained through successive military campaigns in all directions. As we have already seen, the court was marred with violent disputes, plots and controversies. A series of such plots and subplots were to unfold, culminating in the assassination of two kings and the final disintegration of the great Tibetan empire by the middle of the ninth century.

Despite initial expectations, Tri Ralpachen turned out to be a strong ruler who held fast Tibet's territorial integrity and almost fanatically promoted its new court religion. He is today well known for the bilingual treaty he signed with China around 821 or 822, which established the Sino-Tibetan border and the pillars erected with the inscription of the treaty in Tibetan and Chinese. However, it was his devotion to the Buddhist tradition, for which posterity remembers him affectionately, but which was to become the main cause of his downfall and that of his great empire. Tri Ralpachen showed uncompromising support for Buddhism. Later stories have it that he would attach two stretches of cloth to his tresses and have the monastic and lay Buddhist clergies sit on them as a mark of his deep respect to them. Tri Ralpachen is proudly remembered by later Buddhists for his draconian laws concerning the treatment of Buddhist clergy. Anyone who even looked askance at a monk was to have his eyes gouged out and anyone pointing a finger at a monk with disrespect was to have his fingers chopped off.

Certainly, these are later exaggerations to underscore his high regard for the monks and should not be taken literally. They do, however, point out that he was unrelenting in his support to the Buddhist clergy. Monks were appointed as royal tutors, advisers and ministers and monasteries were granted large appanages. According to later sources, each monk was given seven households for his support and the tradition of monastic estates is supposed to have started during his reign. Much of tax collected from the people was used to support the monastic community, build temples and fund the large translation projects. He commissioned a large project to improve earlier translations and systematize translation methods.

In the end, these costs for monastic and intellectual projects and expenses for endless military campaigns drained out the royal coffers. It was probably such an economic crisis which triggered the tensions and conflicts which were to ensue in the Tibetan court. The later Tibetan historiography put the blame wholly on the simmering tension between the Buddhists and followers of the old religion—Bön, particularly the 'evil' works of Bön ministers. No doubt, the supporters of the old religion may have plotted to oust the king and thereby stop the unreasonable privileges enjoyed by the Buddhist clergy. In order to do so successfully, it was thought that those who supported the king had to be eliminated first. Thus, it was decided that the king's brother Tsangma, who would ascend the throne in the absence of Tri Ralpachen, had to be got rid of. According to the standard story, the supporters of Bön bribed the renowned astrologers of the country to exclaim unanimously that if Prince Tsangma were to remain in Tibet, a great calamity would befall the nation. This forced the king to send Tsangma into exile and Tsangma, as a pious figure, may have happily accepted the proposal.

This is not the only case of a major Tibetan event being decided through false use of astrology and divination. Exploitation of astrologers and fortune-tellers figure prominently in ancient Tibet. During Tri Songdetsen's minority, when the Bön ministers had the upper hand over those favouring Buddhism, the Buddhist minister Zhang Nyazang is said to have bribed the astrologers and diviners to suggest that the most important minister would have to sacrifice his life to clear obstacles for the king. He then offered his own life with the intention of provoking his rival Mazhang Drompake, the minister favouring Bön and responsible for the persecution of Buddhist culture. Mazhang Drompake did not know this was a ruse. He certainly did not like the public to see Zhang Nyazang as either the most important minister or as the most loyal. He thus offered to be sacrificed. The two ministers were both put in a dungeon and sealed but only Zhang Nyazang had plans to escape. Astrology and divination, and occasionally false prognostications, played a great part in Tibet's history and continue to do so even today in the exile government under the Dalai Lama. Divine intervention on controversial issues is a very handy method to use to make difficult decisions and also win popular support for them. More importantly, if the plans fail, no one has to take the blame and the astrologers and soothsayers always find a way to explain the course of events.

Prince Tsangma was thus banished from Tibet using the ruse that his presence was unpropitious for Tibet and the king. We shall return to subsequent events in the Tibetan court in a moment. He was sent off, according to some accounts, with a large following and gifts, all of which he sent back when he crossed the Tsangpo river. Others, however, talk about how he took with him a great number of Buddhist texts. There is also no general consensus among the sources on where exactly he was exiled to and what happened to him. Many Tibetan sources talk about his exile to Lhodrak, Bumthang or thereabouts and the subsequent death through poisoning. Some, however, mention that he went on to modern Bhutan and left a family line there. Nyangral Nyima Özer tell us about how Tsangma brought a lot of Buddhist texts from Tibet and buried them in remote places around Paro for posterity.[24] Both the accounts of his assassination and the burial of religious texts also bear close resemblance to the accounts of his uncle Murum Tsenpo's death and the burial of Bönpo texts narrated in Bönpo sources. Both Michael Aris and John Ardussi have discussed the stories in these various sources at length.[25] We shall here focus on the Bhutanese accounts which mention his arrival in Bhutan with a small group of attendants and the political ramifications for Bhutan in the subsequent centuries.

The main source for the Bhutanese version of Tsangma's story is a genealogical text written by a monk named Ngawang. Aris dated this text to 1728 but Ardussi has put it to 1668, which is much more likely inferring from the milieu of the author. The text entitled *The Clear Lamp which Illuminates the History of Royal Clans* (རྒྱལ་རིགས་བྱུང་ཁུངས་གསལ་བའི་སྒྲོན་མེ་) is prose writing mainly aimed at recording the family histories which were until then transmitted orally or in fragmentary chronicles. The author claims to be from the Jar (ཇར་) clan which is said to have descended from Prince Tsangma. According to this genealogy, Prince Tsangma was asked by his brother King Tri Ralpachen to travel along the southern Mon corridors on a tour when the soothsayers proclaimed that he had to be banished. He entered Bhutan via the Chumbi valley with five attendants. While at Namthong Karpo in Paro, he cohabited with a local lady who gave birth to a son. This gave rise to two ancient aristocratic clans in Paro and Thimphu, which today seem to have ceased to exist.

Tsangma continued on his journey, which took him eastward through the Thimphu and Punakha valleys, then via Khothangkha and over the mountains to Mangdechu valley, from where he headed downstream to the Kheng region and finally upstream along the Kurichu valley. Obstructed by the Kurichu river from travelling further, he made a wish: 'If I am destined to settle in the region and rule it, may there be a bridge.' A tall tree was felled and it effectively became the bridge over the river. He continued on his journey eastward through Ngatshang, Wageng, Brahmi, Halong to Jamkhar. According to oral sources, he built a castle and resided here for some time. He moved further to Palkhar in La-og Yulsum, which is in modern Arunachal Pradesh. Hearing of the bad times in Tibet under his brother who persecuted Buddhism, he decided to leave Palkhar due to its proximity to Tibet. He then seems to have journeyed westward until he reached Tsenkhar, where he found Mizimpa to be a favourable place to settle.

At Mizimpa, he met Ami Dhondup Gyal, a Tibetan from the Lang clan who had left Tibet due to family disputes. Tsangma took Ami Dhondup Gyal's daughter as his wife, and two sons, Trimi Lhayi Wangchuk and Chebu Thonglegtsun, were born to them. Trimi was sent as the ruler for La-og Yulsum in the modern Tawang region. The Jowo clan, the line of kings of this area, according to Ngawang, descended from him. Chebu inherited the castle of Mizimpa and had three sons: Triten Pel, Gongkar Gyal and Palkye Dar. The first was based in Mizimpa and gave rise to the Je clan and the latter two became the progenitors of the Jar clan. The clan was called Jar (ཕྱར་/སྦྱར་) or 'attached' because they were born attached to one another. If we are to believe Ngawang, as the news of new royal line began to spread, people from various regions approached Mizimpa to seek male descendants of Tsangma as their rulers. It must be remembered that by then the royal lineage in Tibet had broken down with the assassination of the last king and the fierce contestation over the legitimacy of his heirs.

In the midst of strife, many Tibetan people are said to have moved to the southern valleys of Bhutan. Tsangma's grandson Gongkar Gyal had four sons among whom three gave rise to the clans of Yede, Tungde and Wangma. Ngawang gives a fairly detailed genealogy of these different lines which spread out across the eastern Bhutan and Tawang regions. Nearly all leading elites in the eastern region belonged to one of the Je, Jar, Jowo, Yede, Tungde and Wangma clans. The numerous ruling elites created their own fiefdoms and ruled them often from their bases in fortified houses on hilltops generally known as *khar* (མཁར་) or castle. Such a distributed polity of hereditary rules based on the notion of Tibetan kingship continued in eastern Bhutan until the seventeenth-century unification of Bhutan under the leadership of Zhabdrung Ngawang Namgyal. Ngawang also gives a very insightful account of Migyur Tenpa's campaign for the accession of the eastern region to the Drukpa state which was being formed in western Bhutan in the middle of the seventeenth century. We shall return to this later but for now let's turn to the Tibetan political troubles and the second batch of prominent refugees to arrive in Bhutan in the ninth century.

After Prince Tsangma was banished, the anti-Buddhist ministers in Tri Ralpachen's court focused their plot against Drenka Palgyi Yontan, the strong Buddhist minister supporting the king. They are said to have spread a rumour that Drenka was having an affair with Queen Ngangtshulma. The king ordered them to be punished but the queen committed suicide. Aware of the plot, the minister went into hiding but was found and, according to one later Tibetan source, executed by removing his skin to make a mount. With all his strong allies removed, the plotters then attacked the king. King Tri Ralpachen was strangled to death in his Meldro palace around 841. His brother Udum Tsenpo or Lang Darma succeeded him to the throne. The later Tibetan histories would describe him as the apostate king who sided with the followers of the old religion and brought down the Buddhist civilization of Tibet. His rule is associated in these sources with the systematic destruction of the Buddhist system through demolishing temple, removing statues, destroying texts and persecuting monks.

Modern historians however contend that he was not such an 'evil' king. He is believed to have been a Buddhist himself but perhaps against the undue privileges his brother showered on the Buddhist monastics at the expense of the state and public funds. It is highly likely that the fiscal troubles which the court faced as a result of various entitlements the Buddhist clerics enjoyed provoked strong opposition from members of the court, including Prince Darma and his supporters who favoured the old religion. Whatever be the case, one thing we can be certain of is that under Udum Tsenpo's rule, the policy towards the Buddhist clergy shifted radically. Monks are said to have been disrobed, sent to hunt, and forcibly married or to do things which were contrary to those allowed by the Buddhist monastic code of conduct, the Vinaya.

This suppression of Buddhist monastic practice and destruction of the Buddhist tradition is what is said to have led the Buddhist monk Lhalung Palgyi Dorji to the course of action which was to change Tibet's future forever. Standard accounts have it that Palgyi Dorji was a monk meditating in a cave when he became alarmed by the widespread persecution of Buddhism. Instigated by a Buddhist goddess, he disguised himself in a spectacular costume of a sorcerer with very broad sleeves, in which he hid his bow and arrow. He wore a black hat and a black gown with a white inner lining and rode a white steed, painted black with charcoal. In such a disguise, he approached the king, who stood in the open studying the inscriptions on a stone pillar, to perform a dazzling dance for the king in his honour. In the course of his dance, he shot the arrow from his broad sleeves and killed the apostate king. As he escaped, he rode through the river washing the black colour off his steed and reversed the robe he wore. When the king's men came looking for a black rider, people could only report seeing a white rider on white horse. To this day, the Buddhists in the Himalayas remember Palgyi Dorji's assassination of King Lang Darma as a great act defending the faith and as a victory of good over evil. It is seen as a case of the use of the tantric ritual of liberation (སྒྲོལ་བ་) in which an extremely unruly and evil character has to be stopped from committing further negative actions by slaying him and his mind consummated in a state of enlightenment by the psychic power of the slayer. The very common black-hat dances performed across Bhutan are often believed to be an enactment of this tantric ritual of liberation performed by Palgyi Dorji, who, most historical sources agree, ran away to far eastern Tibet after the murder.

The Bhutanese versions, particularly the oral ones, however, have a much more interesting story, filled with wit and suspense, to tell about the aftermath of the murderer. After the assassination, Palgyi Dorji rushes back to his hermitage and goes into seclusion, miraculously creating bird droppings, cobwebs and dust along the entrance to pretend that he has not stepped out of his seclusion for a long time. He was considered as one of the prime suspects and the king's men duly arrived to investigate but his trick worked to make them think that he had not left his seclusion. Then, his sister, who was also one of the queens of the dead king, arrived to find out the truth. When asked by her, he denied any involvement in the assassination. Women being more intuitive, she put her palm on his chest to feel his heart, which was no doubt pulsating strongly out of fear. Sure of his hand in the regicide, she quietly advised him to escape from Tibet as soon as possible and also informed her other brothers to clandestinely leave Tibet at the earliest opportunity. Palgyi Dorji fled to eastern Tibet and his six brothers, known as the Dorji brothers, are said to have come southward to Bhutan.

According to Ngawang, the first three brothers entered Bhutan from the west along the Chumbi and Paro valleys. With no reception or even large settlements on their way, they travelled eastward and eventually settled in Bumthang. The first one, Lawa Dorji, became the chieftain of Tang; the second, Treu Dorji, became the chieftain of Chokhor and the third, Kheu Dorji, settled around the border between Tibet and Bhutan in order to control the trade mart and he became the progenitor of the aristocratic pastoralists of Tshampa. It must be noted that another Bhutanese source, however, mentions these three brothers in a very different context, which we will see below. The other three of the six Dorji brothers made their escape from Tibet through Lhodrak and reached the Kurichu valley. They agreed to split up and go in separate directions to build their own fiefdoms. Leki Dorji settled in Tongphu Zhangtshang and gradually extended his dominion over the communities in this region. His presence in this area is supposed to have led to a brief confrontation with the incumbent of Mizimpa castle. The chieftains of this area are said to be his descendants. Drakpa Dorji extended his control along the Kurichu river valley and the aristocrats in the Kurelung area are said to originate from him. Changrig Dorji went on to rule the Molpalung area around present-day Mongar and gave rise to the clan called Khengpo.

If we are to believe the genealogist Ngawang who wrote down these accounts in the seventeenth century, most of the early ruling nobilities of the eastern districts and some in central Bhutan by the end of the first millennium descended from Tsangma and the six Dorji brothers. The clans which arose from these figures are said to have formed their principalities and ruled the locals, with their authority and legitimacy almost entirely based on their Tibetan royal and aristocratic roots. The argument of the Tibetan royal or aristocratic ancestry was important for the people and for Ngawang because their view of civilization was not one of egalitarianism but of a social order with a well-defined hierarchical structure. 'To have no lord above and subject below' is equivalent to being uncivilized and anarchic. Besides, the Tibetan royal connection gave the nobilities some kind of a divine ancestry, which justified their rule and gave the subjects a reason to submit themselves to the ruler. It must have also been the case that the figures who came into exile were clever and experienced in political and administrative affairs given their exposure to and experience in Tibetan court life. Thus, there is no reason to generally doubt Ngawang's claim about the rule of these clans in the eastern region. Oral stories, which are still vibrant, support his account and family pedigrees based on these ancient clans still play a very important part in Bhutanese social practices, particularly in forming nuptial ties. There is also a lot of evidence for such a structure of principalities and polities in the local toponyms, especially those ending in the word *khar* (མཁར་) or castle.

As noted in the previous chapter, Ngawang also makes a very interesting claim with regard to the origin of the commoners, which is quite different from the claims made by the later Bhutanese monk-historians. Not only are the eastern Bhutanese nobilities descendents of the Tibetan elites, he claims that the commoners are also descended from Tibetan clans. Ngawang no doubt uses the standard Tibetan story of how the Tibetan race started from the Bodhisattva monkey and the clans which descended from his offspring. Linking the eastern Bhutanese to these clans, he lists some twenty-six different clans or groups of common people which are supposed to have made up the demography of eastern Bhutan. It is very difficult, if not impossible, to determine if the early eastern Bhutanese are indeed of Tibetan stock as Ngawang claims or when they would have migrated to the eastern regions. The numerous clans he mentioned seem to have already ceased to exist as distinct groups by his own time. However, one can safely assert the theory that most of their rulers and nobilities did descend from Tibetan figures who came into exile. The genealogical accounts he provided and other evidences present a persuasive case for it. In the subsequent centuries, this stratum of the eastern Bhutanese nobilities was further enriched by the new lines of religious elites which rose from lines of important religious figures and intermarried with the former nobilities. It is to this later part of the ancient era of the rise of many religious sects and elites that we shall turn to now.

Early Historic Period:
Later Diffusion of Buddhism

IF THE SOCIAL AND POLITICAL narratives concerning events in the first millennium are largely mythical, there is very little of even such mythical narratives about the political and social structure of the Bhutanese societies in the second millennium until about the middle of the seventeenth century. The paucity of credible written records and material evidence for the sociopolitical landscape of this period of Bhutan's history makes it very difficult to say anything comprehensive. The sparse information on society and politics in this period comes mainly from very scattered and embellished folklore passed down orally. Even written records such as Ngawang's seventeenth-century genealogical account and the political histories written in the twentieth century mainly draw on the oral stories found in the local traditions.

To these oral accounts, one may add the scanty information which can be gleaned from Tibetan histories and the hagiographies of religious figures from this period. Thus, our knowledge of the social and political structure before the seventeenth century is far from clear and comprehensive. Beyond a very general point that the country was divided into many principalities ruled by their own chieftains, we are unable historically to say anything substantial on the dates, families, lives and domains of the rulers, the geopolitical make-up, their vicissitudes and the socioeconomic conditions of the people.

However, the religious history, in contrast, is fairly well documented in the form of hagiographies (རྣམ་ཐར), religious histories (ཆོས་འབྱུང), spiritual narratives (རྟོགས་བརྗོད), study records (གསན་ཡིག), guide books (གནས་ཡིག) and catalogues (དཀར་ཆག). There is ample historical information on Bhutan in the accounts and writings of both Bhutanese and Tibetan religious hierarchs. Through the lives of these hierarchs, we can gauge a relatively accurate picture of the religious landscape. Because many such religious figures were also the ruling elites and the life of the populace was largely influenced by such religious persons and practices, the religious sources also make up, to some degree, for the lacuna left by the lack of secular records in giving a partial understanding of the contemporary sociopolitical state of Bhutan. Given this predominance of religious records, the history of Bhutan for this era, which I call the Later Diffusion of the Early Historic Period, is normally told, in both traditional and Western sources, through the stories of the various Buddhist schools and traditions. We shall generally adopt the same framework but before we do so, let's turn to briefly discuss the legendary stories of the secular lineages of *dung* (གདུང).

The dung lineages

In the Bhutanese sociopolitical context, the term *dung* refers to an important group of secular family lines. It is an honorific term for the 'bone' and generally designates the paternal bone line as opposed to the maternal bloodline. A great number of ruling elites in traditional Bhutan, particularly in the central region, belonged to the *dung* families, who ruled their local fiefdoms from their castles or large manor houses. The other very important lines of nobilities are the *lam chöje* (བླམ་ཆོས་རྗེ) or lamas and lords of religion, who are normally descendents of religious figures and perform a religious role in the community. Most of the *lam chöje* families begin in this period of Bhutan's history and we shall return to them later. Like the patriarchal *lam chöje* but unlike the mainstream populace, who practised a matrilineal system, the *dung* families were (and some of them still are) patrilineal, passing the family line and property from father to son.

The *dung* were mostly powerful landlords who directly ruled their principalities before their domains were integrated into the new state of Bhutan in the seventeenth century. Except for a very few cases, the *dung* leaders were perceived as secular rulers and did not play a religious role although they also have stories of divine origin as we shall see. They are mostly found in areas where the related languages of Bumthangkha and Khengkha are spoken. This may suggest their ancient roots in the region although some of their origin myths trace their origin to Tibet. We have only sparse information available to us, leaving us unable to say anything in detail or definite about their origins, succession, role and influence. Perhaps the earliest comprehensive written piece about the *dung* lines is Ngawang's genealogical records which we have seen earlier. Some scattered information can also be gleaned from the other literatures such as religious hagiographies. However, much of the story is passed down even today in embellished oral stories. There is also material evidence in the form of castle ruins and toponyms which support the existence of *dung* rulers.

Based on the available sources, stories and other indicators, we can perhaps best approach the study of *dung* families by asking the questions: who were the Ura *dung* discussed by Ngawang, the Ngang *dung* mentioned by Tenzin Lekpai Dhondup, the *dung reng* about whom we hear in Tibetan sources and the *dung drok,* who lived south of Paro? Historians have so far not found a convincing answer to explain the origins, dates, domains and interrelations of these *dung*. With no further written information likely to be found on them and the fast decline of oral traditions, it is now highly improbable that we will ever know clearly about the *dung*, which appear to be a unique local Bhutanese social institution. I have put the period of the *dung* rulers between the tenth and seventeenth centuries. It is unlikely that they existed before the tenth century and their existence as autonomous rulers generally ceased around the middle of the seventeenth century.

The Ura dung

The *dung* of Ura in central Bhutan, according to Ngawang and oral accounts, is the primary source from which all other *dung* families have spread. The story begins with the people of Bumthang praying to the god Ode Gungyal (ཨོ་དེ་གུང་རྒྱལ་), a well-known Tibetan mountain deity. They ask for a leader as they did not have a qualified leader after the death of Prince Khikha Rathö. In response to their prayers, Ode Gungyal sends the celestial prince Guse Langling (གུ་སེ་ལང་ལིང་) to be their leader. Using a procedure, which is reminiscent of the ancient myths of Tibet's old religion of Bön, Guse Langling descends from heaven using a *mū* rope (རྨུ་ཐག་) and then dissolves into light to enter the womb of a special Ura lady named Sonam Peldren. His arrival is announced by a loud voice from the sky saying: 'This child is a celestial prince and will become the ruler of mankind for many generations.' The child was named Lhagon Palchen and he grew up to be the ruler of the region.

Locals even today identify a place called Lhababteng (ལྷ་བབ་སྟེང་) or the spot where the god descended. His son was Lhazang Gyal, and Lhazang's son Drakpa Wangchuk. Drakpa Wangchuk fell seriously ill before producing an heir. Before he passed away, he instructed his people to go in search of their leader to Yarlung in Tibet when they begin to miss him. 'Take a lot of good

Bhutanese pears and throw them to the children in the main town of Yarlung. The one who collects the most will be an emanation of the god. Fetch him and make him your lord.' Some years after his death, five Ura men went to Yarlung in search of their leader as instructed. They gave Bhutanese pears to Tibetan children but only one knew what they were and took them all. Using more pears, they enticed this child out of sight of other Tibetans. They put him in a yak-hair sack and carried him to Ura. At the Zhangmaya pass, above Ura, they opened the sack and the handsome and happy boy, readers are to believe, jumped out of the sack with a beaming smile. With the boy came, accidentally, a cluster of Tibetan grass, which grew roots on the pass. Ngawang reports this Tibetan grass growing on Zhangmaya but nowhere else in Bhutan in his days, but a visitor today cannot find any such unusual Tibetan grass.

The boy grew up to be *dung* Lhawang Drakpa and a ruler of the people in the region. During his rule, he sent a team to find out about his own ancestry. It was discovered that he was the fourth son of Jowo Kuenga Drakpa and Pelmo Zom, his father being a direct descendant of the Yarlung kings through the line of Odsrung, son of Lang Darma. He took a certain lady Dronzom from the neighbouring Chokhor valley as his wife and had three sons. These sons gradually gave rise to the *dung* families in Chume, Gyatsa, Domkhar, Dur and other places in Bumthang. Their influence and family also began to spread in the Kheng and Mongar regions. Lhawang Drakpa's grandson Nyima Wangchuk gave rise to the Tunglabi, Goshing, Pangkhar, Kalamti and Nyakhar dung families in the Kheng region. The Yonglam Je families in the Molpalung in the current Mongar districts are said to be descendents of the Ura *dung*.

In a different version of the origin myth of the *dung* and Yonglam Je families, which Ngawang provides based on a Bönpo source and oral stories known in the far-eastern part of Bhutan, the story takes a highly mythical twist. The celestial Prince Guse Langling is sent by Indra to help the people of Merak and Sakteng, who were then fleeing into exile after killing a despotic ruler in Tibet. This god-prince subsequently settles in the Mukulung Lake and becomes the guardian of both the human and non-human worlds. When a beautiful bride for the Dungsamkhar family spends the night on the banks of the Mukulung lake on the way to her future husband, she is miraculously impregnated by a white snake which slithers over her in her dream. The snake, we are to understand, is the god Guse Langling. Soon after she arrived in Dungsamkhar, she gives birth to a son, who was called Barkye. Barkye grows up and sets out on a journey to the Indian trade mart but is obstructed at Ngetsang Longpa by the *lu* or *nāga* spirit of that lake. Barkye is perplexed and asks his mother about his paternity. His mother tells him that he is a son of a *tsen* (བཙན་) god of Mukulung lake and that the *tsen* gods and *lu* spirits do not get along.

Barkye then goes to Mukulung and calls out to his non-human father asking for help to get past Ngetsang Longpa. His father appears in the form of a flourishing youth dressed in white silk and gives him a bamboo tube containing an army, with the admonition to open it only when he reaches the Ngetsang Longpa lake. Halfway to the lake, Barkye gets curious and opens the tube slightly and a few snakes slither out of the tube. When he reaches the lake, he throws the tube open and numerous snakes come out of it and miraculously drain the lake of its water, leaving it bare with sand. In the centre of dried lake, Barkye sees a huge copper vessel turned upside down and when he turns it over, a maidservant of the *lu* hiding in it hits him with a large ladle on the head thus killing him on the spot. After all, the forces of the *lu* spirits were not fully overcome as he lost, through his curiosity, some of the serpentine army his father gave him on the way.

However, due to his non-human paternity, he is able to transfer his consciousness into the fish which ate his brain. In the body of the fish, he journeys along the Drangmechu, Kurichu and finally along the Changkhö river where he gets trapped in a fishing net. The man, who set the net, keeps the fish in a trough and goes off to work in the fields. When he returns in the evening from work, to his great surprise, he finds his meals ready for him. The same thing keeps happening until one day he pretends to go to work and hides nearby to see who is doing the work. To his utter amazement, he sees a handsome young boy creep out of the fish skin and do the chores. Hoping to keep the young boy as his adopted son, he throws the fish skin into the fire. The young boy grows up to become a very strong and powerful man and rules the Molpalung and Ura regions, with his base in a strategic place called Itungla and takes on the new name of Ralpa Tobchen. The old Zhongar dzong, of which ruins can still be seen across the river from the motor road to Mongar, is said to be built on this spot.

However, power beguiles Ralpa Tobchen and he demands his subjects demolish a hill so that he could get a direct view of his in-laws in Chali. In the course of the forced labour to demolish the hill, an astute woman conspires by spreading the word that it is easier to cut off the lofty man than the lofty hill. Ralpa Tobchen's subjects revolt and he is killed but before he dies he advises his subject to look for his rebirth in the Yarlung valley. Ngawang says that from this point the story concurs with the one we saw above about the Ura *dung*, except for the use of cowry shells instead of Bhutanese pears. In the local oral stories, some toponyms in this area are still explained through events leading to Ralpa Tobchen's death. Whether the toponyms preserve traces of historical events from the distant past or merely represent the case of a folk story being superimposed on the local landscape is difficult to say.

The story of Barkye and Ralpa Tobchen no doubt takes us into the realm of fairytales. However, the story is a good case with which to study the transmission and adaptation of common sociocultural themes from place to place. The story of a handsome boy or girl emerging out of fish or some other animal form is a common trope in the Himalayan region as is the descent of a godly figure on a rope or ladder of some kind. The concept of gods descending from and also ascending to heaven using a rope is also a very well-known theme in Tibetan historical literature as all Tibet's monarchs until Drigum Tsenpo are said to have descended from heaven on the *mū* rope and also returned on the same rope following their demise without leaving corporeal remains. Similarly, the story of a woman challenging the despotic ruler is found in different variations in several places in Bhutan. We already touched on almost an identical plot of a poor but sharp woman instigating a rebellion against a tyrannical ruler in the legends of the people of Merak and Sakteng. Thus, these stories provide us with some wonderful glimpses of the dissemination of sociocultural ideas.

Pema Tshewang presents yet another account which is found in the hymns of a certain lama Karma Thinley of Bumthang.[1] According to this version, a son of Tri Songdetsen, who was ruling from Ura, passed away to be reborn in heaven as Prince Drime Özer. From there, he descended again to Ura on the *mū* rope and ruled his subjects. When he was recalled to heaven, his wife cut the *mū* rope. So, he lived a full life on earth and, before his death, instructed his subjects to find his rebirth in Yarlung. After five years, seven Ura men went to Yarlung in search of the rebirth and found the child in the line of Yarlung dynasty. From this point, the story concurs with the first account about his journey to Ura and the subsequent royal lineage he gives rise to. However, Karma Thinley's version adds that the prince was brought with full consent from his parents. The author claims that he was born in the family of Danlungpa, a branch of this *dung* lineage of Tibet's religious kings.

To return to the historical inquiry into the Ura *dung*, apart from the mythical and legendary embellishments found in the accounts, there is generally no doubt about the historicity of the Ura *dung*. Structural remains in Ura point to the existence of a powerful chieftain and local traditions also explain the toponyms and social organization in and around the village in association with a *dung* institution. The traditional claim that the Ura *dung* line descended from the ancient royal line of Tibet certainly also has some substance. Nyangral Nyima Özer (1136–1204) in his history of Buddhism mentions that the descendents of Tashi Gön and Degön, who were the great-great-grandsons of Lang Darma, have spread in the Mon region.[2] Although Nyangral's Mon area is vague and can refer to the entire stretch of the southern Himalayas, we have good reason to believe that the descendents of the royal line have spread in Bhutan, particularly in Ura. Guru Chöwang (1212–70), who visited the valley in the thirteenth century, records meeting in Ura a *tsedpo* (བཙད་པོ་) or king who claimed to be a descendant of Tri Songdetsen.[3] Similarly, Longchenpa who travelled through the place in the fourteenth century writes about the presence of the ancient royal lineage in Ura whether or not this is in reference to the *dung* family.[4] Pema Lingpa in the following century mentions a certain lord Lhawang of Ura although he uses the title Jowo (ཇོ་བོ་) or lord rather than *dung*. The two titles appear to be generally synonymous but somehow the title of Jowo seems to have gone out of fashion in later centuries.

Ngawang reports that the Ura *dung* had great control over the districts of Kheng and Molpalung and the *dung* chieftain came each year to collect taxes from his subjects in these districts. The migration and landownership patterns continuing to this day strongly affirm this point. Even today, large stretches of land in these districts are owned by the people of Ura as pastures for their cattle. The Ura people still take their cattle to these districts in the winter and still cultivate rice and maize, which Ura as a high valley cannot grow. There are also monoliths said to have been erected by the *dung* rulers to demarcate territorial boundaries. Many large stone-slab bridges over the streams in Ura are also attributed to one *dung* Nagpo, a leader remembered for his Herculean strength. The ruins on the hilltop near Pangkhar village are believed to be of his castle. It is however not clear if *dung* Nagpo was one individual or a title adopted by a line of the later Ura *dung* rulers. The last ruling Ura *dung* resisted the Drukpa forces led by Migyur Tenpa in the middle of the seventeenth century and escaped to Tibet when he was not able to withstand the Drukpa invasion. Like all other Bhutanese principalities, the domain of the Ura *dung* fell under the power of Zhabdrung's new government and the final takeover is recorded on a stone slab on a *mani* wall in Ura, carved at the behest of Migyur Tenpa.[5]

Ura in Bumthang, said to be the origin of *dung* rulers

Ngang Lhakhang, the home of the Ngang dung
(courtesy: Bhutan Cultural Atlas)

The household and line of the *dung* in Ura seems to have continued for most of the medieval period but we do not know anything about any power or position they might have held under the new Drukpa government. It is quite unlikely that they played an important role in the new political and administrative structure introduced by Zhabdrung. Some time in the nineteenth century or at the turn of the twentieth century, the Ura *dung* finally ceased to exist even as a distinct family line. Today, no trace is left to be found except for the name—*dung*'s house. Some *dung* families in Bumthang and Kheng still continue although they no longer enjoy any special positions and privileges in society. With unprecedented sociocultural and political changes sweeping across the country, it seems certain that these last remnants of *dung* rulers will disappear into oblivion in a generation or two.

The Ngang dung

In the biographies of the second Gangteng Trulku Tenzin Lekpai Dhondup (1645–1725) and his grandnephew Mipham Wangpo (1709–38), we find another line of the *dung* associated with the Ngang village in upper Chokhor. These two lamas were both born in the family of Bönbji Chöje, who were descendents of *dung* Lhadar of Ngang. The line is believed to have originated in a son of the Tibetan King Tri Songdetsen named Dechung Dhondup, who was born out of wedlock. The king is said to have granted to this son the area of Lhodrak as his private domain and this line, also referred to as the Demel Dechung line, became known in the local area as the line of the religious kings of Layak, which, Ardussi argues, seems to have been at one point an independent territory between Bhutan and Lhodrak.[6] It is not clear if Demel Dechung is another name of Dechung Dhondup or one or two of his descendents. Both Aris and Ardussi treat Demel Dechung as two persons.

According to this account, the line later produced the three Dorji brothers, who we have seen in the accounts about the six Dorji brothers. The three brothers came southward to Bhutan; the eldest Lawa Dorji settled in Tshampa, a place close to the Tibetan border; the youngest Treu Dorji settled in the Tang valley and gave rise to the chieftains there and the middle brother Kheu Dorji stayed in the area of Ngang and Dur and started the Ngang *dung* lineage. A certain *dung* Lhadar of this line in the sixteenth century followed a religious life as a disciple of Thugse Dawa Gyaltshen (1499–1592?), the son of Pema Lingpa. Dawa Gyaltshen advised him to move westward and settle in Bönbji. It seems that from this point, the secular *dung* line got converted to a religious line of a *chöje* family. This family rose to prominence in medieval Bhutan, producing a number of important religious incarnations and civil rulers, who played leading political roles.

This account is, however, not without historical problems in terms of both chronology and corroboration. Except for the two biographies mentioned above, written in the eighteenth century, we find no mention of a son named Dechung Dhondup of Tri Songdetsen or any other king of the early dynasty. However, some Tibetan histories do mention two persons named Depo and Dechung who were born some twelve generations later in the twelfth century in the royal line continuing from Ösrung, the son of Lang Darma. Depo ruled Yarlung from his Bantsig palace but Dechung died young.[7] Another possibility is Dechung Dhondup in the Bhutanese biographies is a minister of Tri Songdetsen named Deman Gurzher Dechung, who is reported by the Tibetan historian Khepa Deu. This is further corroborated by rock inscriptions in Lhodrak which contain the royal order that the descendents of Deman Dechung shall enjoy the land tenure for perpetuity without decrease and that his tomb shall be protected and rites of the tomb performed by a higher authority.[8] Without further evidence, it is impossible to tell if Demal Dechung refers to two persons, the Depo and Dechung of the twelfth century, or simply refers to the minister Deman Dechung of Tri Songdetsen.

The story of the descent becomes even more complicated with the mention of the three Dorji brothers. In the genealogy of Ngawang, we have already seen the three names given to the brothers of Lhalung Palgyi Dorji, who entered Bhutan via Chumbi and not Lhodrak. They were not really of a royal descent but only brothers of the famous assassin, Lhalung Palgyi Dorji. It appears that the two narratives were later conflated. Whatever their origins, the three brothers settled in the Bumthang area and gave rise to three aristocratic families. The descendents of the *dung* Lhadar continue to flourish to this day in the house of Bönbji Chöje.

Dung/dung reng

Despite the traditional lore tracing the ancestry of the *dung* families in the ancient Tibetan royal family, historians have begun to ask if the *dung* are in fact clans or tribes who may have old local roots. This question was raised particularly in connection to the *dung* or *dung reng* groups who posed a serious threat to Tibetans in the north in the first half of the fourteenth century, according to some Tibetan sources. These sources are the *Sino-*

Tibetan Records of the Sakya government, which discusses the way in which the Sakya government dealt with these groups called *dung reng* or obstinate *dung*, and a couple Tibetan biographies. The account is repeated later in Tibetan histories such as the *Religious History of Nyang* and Tibetan history by the fifth Dalai Lama.[9] The Tibetan sources talk about two groups of *shar* or eastern *dung* and *lho* or southern *dung* and historians differ in identifying them and their exact locations. These *dung/dung reng* people are said to be active in the border area between Tibet and Lhomon, extending from Phari to Lhodrak but they raided the Tibetan areas to the north as far as Shang and Uyug valleys. Alarmed by the frequent raids involving 'looting castles, killing herds of domestic animals, and committing acts of arson',[10] the Sakya government sent Khampa Gedun Gyaltshen and six other leaders who established military posts to protect people from the raids but their attempts to suppress the *dung reng* did not succeed. One Tibetan lama, Jamyang Kuenga Senge of Druk Ralung (1314–47), who had some religious influence on the Bhutanese valleys, was asked to appease the southern *dung*. The Drukpa hierarch acted about three times to persuade his southern patrons to stop the *dung reng*. His calls, however, could not end the *dung reng* raids entirely although he claims to have pacified them even during his first trip.

The Sakya government finally decided to use proactive military force to eliminate the *dung reng* power. Phagpa Palzang (1320–70), the official from whom the Gyantse kings descended, was appointed to put down the *dung reng* hordes. First the *shar dung* faction was defeated in Lhodrak and brought under control after one of its leaders Dondrub Dar submitted to Phagpa Palzang. Their forts were demolished and many of them were relocated in Nyangtö and their leaders given new posts under the Sakya rule. Then, to subjugate the *lho dung*, Phagpa Palzang resorted to a cunning military ploy. He first enticed the chieftain Tag Odzer of Paro Banthrang with gifts and gradually managed to invite some 160 important figures of Paro, Haa and other parts of western Bhutan to a great feast in Phari Rinchengang. In the course of the feast, the chieftains were attacked and slaughtered. Their vital parts were buried under the floor and the threshold of the chamber for the protective deity.

The historian John Ardussi argues that those who did not want to submit to the Sakya rule must have escaped southward to Bumthang or eastward to Tawang, where they settled to give rise to the respective *dung* families and their associated myths. This, he argues, also helps explain the discontinuities in the origin myths of *dung* we have seen above. Thus, he identifies the southern *dung* with the group from western Bhutan, most of whom were killed at the feast in Phari, and the eastern *dung* with a group in Lhodrak, who either submitted to Sakya rule or escaped to central Bhutan and the Tawang area.[11] If his hypothesis is true, the *dung* of central Bhutan we discussed earlier would have only started as late as the fourteenth century. Yet, it is difficult to think that historically vibrant places such as Bumthang had a political vacuum with no *dung* or similar power-holders while places in western Bhutan such as Haa and Paro were rife with feuding *dung* chieftains.

Michael Aris, on the other hand, takes the southern and eastern *dung* defeated by the Sakya forces to be the indigenous *dung* groups of central Bhutan and Tawang respectively. He argues the *dung* of Bumthang 'must at one time have been powerful enough in this region of the Himalayas to be capable of foreign invasion'.[12] Thus, according to his hypothesis, the southern and eastern *dung* had been around for some time before the Sakya assault and all the Sakya forces did was to stop their northward raids and drive them out of Tibetan areas which they have invaded. The group of *dung* who were killed in Phari must then represent a group of the southern *dung* based in western Bhutan, whose political presence, after that tragic event, drastically declined. The traditional Bhutanese historians are silent on this apart from some citations by Pema Tshewang.

The identity of the *dung reng* certainly arouses further curiosity. Both the above speculations, which follow Tibetan historical accounts, unhesitatingly identify the *dung reng* with the chieftains of Bhutan. Yet, with closer scrutiny, it seems that the *dung reng* cannot be conflated with the ruling chieftains of Bhutan although there may have been some link. Perhaps a more accurate understanding of the *dung reng* can be obtained through a close reading of the biographies of Jamyang Kuenga Senge and Barawa Gyaltshen Palzang (1310–91), both of whom worked to overcome the political turmoil in the northwestern parts of Bhutan in the fourteenth century. Their biographies, which are contemporary accounts, provide us many interesting glimpses of the political conflicts of this period. Jamyang Kuenga Senge was asked by the Sakya ruler to use his position as the spiritual teacher of the rulers of south (Bhutan) to persuade them to bring down the *dung reng*[13] while Barawa was requested by Kuenga Phagpa, son of Phagpa Palzang (b.1320), to appease the feuding chieftains in the south.[14] Jamyang Kuenga Senge's biography uses the term *dung reng* but the chieftains in Bhutan are not described or addressed anywhere as *dung/dung reng*; only the titles *lopön* and *zhalngo* are used for them. The term *dung/dung reng* is not found in Barawa's autobiography.

Neither is there any account of mass marauders but his biography is full of accounts of internal feuds and conflicts in western Bhutan. He also uses the term *lopön* for the many chieftains who were his patrons and whose conflicts he stopped successfully many times. As we shall see below, one of his main contributions was mediation between warring factions.

The biography of Jamyang Kuenga Senge describes the *dung reng* as gangs of unruly and fierce men who inflicted suffering on many beings and despoiled many lands. The Tibetan authorities requested him to ask his patrons, the rulers of the south (Bhutan), Lhodrak and Yardrok to drive out (འདོན་) and bring down (བབ་) the *dung reng*. Jamyang Kuenga Senge thus travelled to the south, where he was received with much pomp by large gatherings led by the local chieftains. He toured the western valleys, delivering religious sermons to the public and also using material incentives to settle some of the *dung reng* marauders and have them take an oath to stop their raids. The biographical account written in 1350 clearly does not treat the chieftains of western Bhutan as the much-feared *dung reng* marauders but rather as pious and civilized rulers. No doubt, there were numerous internal feuds and conflicts among the chieftains, which may have slackened the rule of law among their subjects and consequently led to unabated brigandage along the border.

Barawa Gyaltshen, who visited Bhutan in 1355 and eventually died in Paro in 1391, spent much of his time mediating between local chieftains and stopping internal feuds. It seems that there were many conflicts, many of which would have entailed plundering. However, the conflicts were mostly results of political and territorial disputes and proper battles rather than anarchical pillage. It is clear that the prominent rulers of western Bhutan of his time were not lawless raiders of the *dung reng* type. The *lopön*s who patronized Barawa were very spiritually inclined, had a sophisticated culture and a well-developed sense of moral integrity. This we can infer from their interaction and exchanges with him.

It is further intriguing that Barawa does not mention the Phari event in 1352 in which some 160 leaders are alleged to have been killed. Could this have been simply because the event took place a few years before his arrival in Paro? More interesting, however, is the fact that Paro and other western valleys appear to have had a plethora of chieftains and leaders. There is no indication that the place had just suffered an enormous elimination of its leaders. We may, thus, ask if the event in Phari involved many important figures and if it was politically significant. It is likely that the Sakya account of the massacre is exaggerated and the people killed in Phari were the ringleaders of the marauders, who were tricked with the incentive to settle down. We have seen above how Dhondup Dar and some of the *shar dung* leaders were settled and given official posts. The leaders of *lho dung* may have hoped for a similar deal.

At any rate, it is very clear that the chieftains of Bhutan cannot be fully identified with the *dung reng* discussed in the Tibetan histories. It is highly plausible that the *dung reng* is a term used by the Tibetans to refer to strong bands of lawless marauders roaming freely along the border, albeit with some coordination. Such a culture of brigandage and robbery was quite common along the border, especially where there were trade routes, until modern times. There are many oral accounts of depredations caused by hordes of brigands, who would roam in the highlands and raid villages and settlements, particularly in Tibet. The same sort of brigandry and marauding became the cause of Anglo-Bhutanese wars to the south in the eighteenth and nineteenth centuries. The *dung reng* marauders operated from the south (Bhutan), Lhodrak and Yardrok areas, where they had their base. They may have been mostly people of these areas, thus, under the jurisdiction of local principalities. As Bhutanese valleys fell outside of the Tibetan jurisdiction, a fact which the *Sino-Tibetan Records* clearly states, the Tibetan government deputed Jamyang Kuenga Senge to persuade his southern patrons to drive out the *dung reng*.

To return to the question of *dung,* we may safely surmise based on the above observations that the *dung reng* discussed in Tibetan histories were bands of roaming marauders and cannot be directly linked to any particular ethnic group or locality, let alone the *dung* clans or other mainstream leaders of Bhutan then. While some of them were settled in the Nyangtö area in Tibet by the Sakya government and many were killed, many others may have fled and settled in various places. Dung Langmar, the chieftain of Haa, whom Thangtong Gyalpo met in 1433–34, may have descended from one of them. Similarly, the places such as Dungyulzhi and Dungdrok mentioned in later written records are perhaps places where they settled.

A group of people, mostly jungle dwellers, living far south of Paro were known as *dung nag* even in modern times. Could it be possible they descended from *dung reng* who started a settled life? Although they fell under the jurisdiction of the *pönlop* or governor of Paro after Bhutan was unified and the governor appointed a minor chieftain, people were said to have remained more faithful to their own chieftain. A story goes that when the Paro *pönlop* arrived with a decree showing his own seal to collect the annual tax, the people refused to accept the *pönlop*'s *thiu* (ཐེའུ་ non-honorific for seal) but demanded that he show the *chagdam* (ཕྱག་དམ་ honorific for seal) of their chieftain, quite oblivious of the fact that he was the boss of the chieftain.

However, if, based on these vestiges, we are to assume that the *dung* presence in western Bhutan was in the past similar to what it was in central Bhutan, it is almost certainly the Phari massacre and constant feuds which must have caused the rapid decline of their powerful presence. It may be also due to this that we rarely find the *dung* title for chieftains in western Bhutan. Whatever the case, the death of many leaders and the constant feuds and wars among chieftains must have gradually diminished the power of the rulers and created a major power vacuum which was quickly filled by the rising religious groups. We know from the reliable historical sources that even as early as the thirteenth century, the various religious groups were not only expanding their religious works but building their economic and political bases in western Bhutan in the form of monastic estates and associated privileges and titles. In addition to the political rivalry and feuds among the secular leaders, we see also a lot of religious rivalry and contests between lamas and priests mainly in winning patronage, studentship and control over land and trade routes. It is to the introduction of these religious factions and their vicissitudes that we shall turn now.

The religious lines

To understand the religious developments in Bhutan we must briefly explore the religious history of Tibet during the Later Diffusion of Buddhism. The assassination of Tri Ralpachen followed by that of Lang Darma some years later effectively ended the Tibetan dynastic era of the first millennium. The great Tibetan empire fell into disarray as the two claimants to the throne, Odsrung and Yumten, started to compete for power. With no central authority, the country splintered into numerous fiefdoms with a series of peasant's revolt. The Buddhist religion which suffered serious decline during Lang Darma's short reign remained neglected with no support and Tibet is traditionally understood to have gone through some 137 years of 'dark ages' with no popular cultural or religious activities. However, some Tibetan sources claim that although Buddhism had no institutional support and popular presence, the Buddhist message and its practice were secretly carried on by the hidden yogis in remote hermitages or ordinary homes. Most of the translations and transmissions from the Early Diffusion were certainly preserved to become the building blocks of the resurgence from the eleventh century. Modern academic findings also generally point out that in spite of the lack of centralized state support for Buddhist activities and decline of open monastic culture, other Buddhist activities continued through this period.

The revival of Buddhism in Tibet at the beginning of the second millennium took place in two principal forms. One group championed the revival of the old by promoting particularly tantric texts and teachings claimed to have been passed down from the Early Diffusion while the other promoted new tantric teachings brought in from north India and Nepal. The former gradually formed the Nyingma (ཉིང་མ་) or old school, following the Early Translation (སྔ་འགྱུར), and the latter the Sarma (གསར་མ་) or new schools, following the Later Translation (ཕྱི་འགྱུར). The new schools based on the Later Translation included, among many others, the Kadampa, Sakya and Kagyu schools. These schools further branched out into many subschools producing the colourful and sectarianized world of Tibetan Buddhism. The schools were primarily distinguished on the basis of their lines of transmission, core texts and essential practices. There was very little or no doctrinal or philosophical difference between them and they also shared most of their ritual practices.

The twelfth and thirteenth centuries saw the rise of many Tibetan Buddhist sects and subsects and with them the proliferation of religious establishments and institutions. The growth of these establishments and institutions led to some strain on resources and consequently to sectarian competition for religious estates, patronages and conversion of the people to the individual sects. As the religious institutions grew in size and number, they looked for support and expansion further afield. It was in search of opportunities for growth and expansion beyond Tibet that many Tibetan teachers of the new Buddhist schools made their journey to Bhutan on their religious missions. While socioeconomic concerns may have driven many religious missions, one must not, however, overlook the spiritual zest of some of these missionaries to convert people to their righteous religious tradition or their belief in a divine call to tame the barbarians of the borderlands. Many figures came with such a conviction and sociopolitical benefits naturally followed as a byproduct. A great number of mystics belonging to the Bön religion and the old school of Buddhism also came in search of treasures and hidden lands which they believed were to be discovered by destined persons. Among the Tibetan visitors, one also finds truly spiritually inclined masters who journeyed to Bhutan in order to find a favourable spiritual environment and to escape the political and sectarian turmoil of Tibet, which began especially with the invasion of Tibet by Mongol warlords.

The series of the religious missions from Tibet were the defining events of history, especially of western Bhutan. The accounts of life and works of the religious visitors from Tibet and their successors mainly make up the known history of Bhutan during the first half of the second millennium. Our records for this period are mostly religious histories and hagiographies associated with these religious schools. Thus, the best way to look at this period of Bhutan's history is to look at the introduction of the various religious schools. We have very little or no information about the secular power structures in Bhutan in this period. Power in western Bhutan gradually slipped from secular chieftains into the hands of religious families between 1000 and 1600 CE.

In eastern Bhutan, the descendents of the Tsangma and Dorji brothers are said to have ruled the region but no details are known about the society and political settings. In addition to Tibetan visitors, there were also a number of native Bhutanese religious figures around the middle of the second millennium, most of who belonged to the Nyingma school. The most important and famous one among them is Pema Lingpa, about whom we shall learn more below. Biographies and religious writings also give some sporadic idea about the society and political conditions of Bhutan in those times. Here, I shall adopt the same scheme as most traditional and modern historians do to discuss this stage of Bhutan's history through the various religious traditions and schools.

Bön religion

The term Bön has two different designations in the Tibetan and Bhutanese world when used in reference to a religious tradition. The word Bön is used to refer to the form of religion which is thought to have arrived in Tibet before Buddhism was introduced and which co-existed with Buddhism to some extent after the introduction of Buddhism despite periodic tensions and conflicts between the adherents of the two religions. This Bön was then considered to have been Tibet's old religion. It took a highly institutional and Buddhicized form during the time of the Later Diffusion and exists to this day with very sophisticated doctrinal and practice systems. It shares a great deal of similarity with the Buddhist traditions of Tibet and is today often termed as the fifth religious tradition of Tibet in addition to the four Buddhist schools. The term Bön is also often employed, inaccurately, to designate the numerous pre-Buddhist practices across the Himalayas. A wide variety of local rituals and practices found in Bhutan which are shamanistic, animistic or paganistic are often mistakenly branded as Bön practices for the simple reason of being pre- or non-Buddhist. In this use, it designates what R.A. Stein called 'the nameless religion', comprising the diverse folk beliefs and rituals found in their localized variations with or without some influence of the institutional Bön and/or Buddhist practices.

The Bön tradition we are concerned with here is the organized Bön religion of Tibet, which has not managed to take proper roots in Bhutan as a religious tradition in spite of various activities in the country. Nonetheless, Bhutan was a major centre of Bön treasure rediscovery in the eleventh and twelfth centuries. Places such as Paro and Bumthang were frequented by the early treasure-discoverers from the Bön tradition. Some of these the Bön treasure-discoverers also adopted the Buddhist tradition and moved freely between the two without any qualms. The earliest discoverer with Bönpo name in Bhutan is perhaps Bönpo Dragtsal who discovered texts on the teachings of the Great Perfection from the Tsilung temple in Bumthang and Namthong Karpo in Paro. However, the first important real Bönpo figure is Khutsa Dayod alias Kusa Menpa, who discovered at Chalkha in Paro many Bön texts which were later collectively known as *Padroma* (སྤ་སྒྲོམ་). He is said to have discovered four boxes containing Bön, Buddhist, medical and astrological texts.[15] These Bönpo texts were believed to have been buried by Murum Tsenpo and Khyungpo Gyerdame while Buddhist texts discovered on the same site were said to have been hidden by Prince Tsangma.

Many other treasure-discoverers associated with Bön worked in Bhutan but the single most important figure respected by both Bönpo and Buddhist circles was Dorji Lingpa. A number of Bönpo centres were also established in Bhutan but they did not last long as purely Bönpo establishments. Like the case of the Kubum temple in Gangteng, they were gradually converted into Buddhist temples although they still retain Bönpo characteristics, such as propitiation of the Bönpo-protecting deity Sridpa Gyalmo. Traces of influence from the institutional Bön of ancient Tibet can be also found across the country in the names of certain deities, ritual texts and religious rites but the overall role of Bön in the history of Bhutan is of little significance, if at all.

The Lhapa Kagyu School

One of the earliest and most important Tibetan Buddhist schools to arrive in Bhutan is the Kagyu, particularly its Lhapa and Drukpa subschools. Followers of these schools had the religious and political control of western Bhutan and the Drukpa school in later times came out victorious to become the ruling power and state religion. The Kagyu tradition begins with Marpa Chökyi Lodoe, the master of meditation and translator during the period of the Later Diffusion of Buddhism into Tibet. Marpa travelled to India and Nepal to receive teachings from his Indian teachers, including Naropa and Maitripa but was later based in Drowolung in Lhodrak, just across the border from central Bhutan. Marpa's reputation in Tibet was, however, surpassed by his famous disciple Milarepa, the most celebrated and exemplary hermit-saint of the entire Himalayan Buddhist world. The mainstream Kagyu tradition of Marpa passed through Milerepa although Marpa's teachings were also transmitted through other disciples, including Ngog Chöku Dorji. This master is said to have come to Bhutan and established a religious centre in Bumthang.

Milarepa is said to have visited the Taktshang site and spent some time in meditation. A cave in Phunying is also associated with him but there is no particular place attributed to him in Bhutan. His strong presence and influence in Bhutan, like in many other parts of the Tibetan Buddhist world, is an outcome of his fascinating and dramatic biography told through a collection of spiritual songs. The hymns are arguably one of the most popular and celebrated literary compositions in the entire Buddhist world. The collection was first printed in 1495 by Tsangnyon Heruka but the hymns must have been in wide circulation long before that. It is these hymns, the iconic portrayal of him as cotton-clad hermit in art and the semi-operatic enactment of his miraculous conversion of a hunter to religion, which have made Milarepa a popular name across Bhutan.

Milarepa's student Gampopa Sonam Rinchen, a monk-physician, is the last one of the trio (Marpa, Milarepa and Gampopa) seen as founding fathers of the Kagyu tradition. The Kagyu subschools which were to start from the four major students of Gampopa are commonly known as the four major ones (ཆེ་བཞི་). Those that started from the students of Phagdru Dorji Gyalpo, who was one of the main students of Gampopa, are known as the eight minor ones (ཆུང་བརྒྱད་), as shown in the following diagram. Their difference is not based on size of membership or religious importance but merely on temporal proximity to the founding fathers.

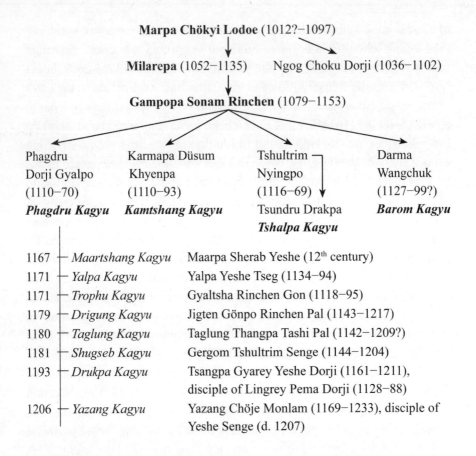

Marpa Chökyi Lodoe (1012?–1097)

Milarepa (1052–1135)   Ngog Choku Dorji (1036–1102)

Gampopa Sonam Rinchen (1079–1153)

Phagdru	Karmapa Düsum	Tshultrim ┐	Darma
Dorji Gyalpo	Khyenpa	Nyingpo	Wangchuk
(1110–70)	(1110–93)	(1116–69) ↓	(1127–99?)
Phagdru Kagyu	*Kamtshang Kagyu*	Tsundru Drakpa	*Barom Kagyu*
		Tshalpa Kagyu	

1167	*Maartshang Kagyu*	Maarpa Sherab Yeshe (12th century)
1171	*Yalpa Kagyu*	Yalpa Yeshe Tseg (1134–94)
1171	*Trophu Kagyu*	Gyaltsha Rinchen Gon (1118–95)
1179	*Drigung Kagyu*	Jigten Gönpo Rinchen Pal (1143–1217)
1180	*Taglung Kagyu*	Taglung Thangpa Tashi Pal (1142–1209?)
1181	*Shugseb Kagyu*	Gergom Tshultrim Senge (1144–1204)
1193	*Drukpa Kagyu*	Tsangpa Gyarey Yeshe Dorji (1161–1211), disciple of Lingrey Pema Dorji (1128–88)
1206	*Yazang Kagyu*	Yazang Chöje Monlam (1169–1233), disciple of Yeshe Senge (d. 1207)

As amply indicated by the proliferation of the subschools, the Kagyu school perhaps saw the most rapid growth among the new schools of the Later Diffusion. The school clearly claimed special access to the esoteric pronouncements of the Buddha through a line of unbroken transmission as reflected by its name Kagyu (བཀའ་བརྒྱུད), which literally stands for the lineage of pronouncements or teachings. Some adherents of this school, such as the Drukpa scholar Pema Karpo, however, preferred to use the alternate rendering of Kargyu (དཀར་བརྒྱུད), literally 'the white lineage'. This designation was derived from the appearance of some of its main patriarchs who were dressed in simple white clothes. Whether seen as an unbroken line of sacred pronouncements or as a lineage of cotton-clad recluses, the school gained great popularity in twelfth-century Tibet, mainly for its uninterrupted transmission of profound esoteric instructions and expedient hermetic practices and it rapidly spread across the Himalayas.

The Lhapa school is perhaps the earliest organized Tibetan religious group to gain significant religious and political power in Bhutan. It was a branch of the Drigung Kagyu, which was started by Jigten Gönpo Rinchen Pal in 1179 with the foundation of the Drigung Thil monastery. The Drigungpas were a major player in Tibetan politics, becoming the main rival of the Sakyapas who ruled Tibet through Mongol intervention. The Lhapa school was founded by Lhanangpa Zijid Palbar (1164–1224), who was a student of Jigten Gönpo. The term Lhapa is an abbreviation of Lhanangpa but the Lhapa school did not gain any prominence in Tibet. At the behest of his teacher and following his own visions, Lhanangpa travelled to western Bhutan in 1193 and based himself in Chalkha in Paro but established a number of other religious centres, including the Do-ngon *dzong* which was supplanted by Tashichödzong in the seventeenth century. The Lhapa school had significant control over the Thimphu, Paro and Haa areas of western Bhutan and imposed both taxes in kind and labour on the local people. It appears that the local chieftains owed allegiance to them until the Drukpa hierarchs won these chieftains over.

However, the influence of the Lhapa school on western Bhutan was not merely due to the works of Lhanangpa himself. Lhanangpa inherited the control over Bhutan from one of his ancestors. In the eighth century, Tri Songdetsen is said to have granted a large tract of land as an appanage to one minister Gö, perhaps Gö Trizang Yablha. The tract, known as Phagri of Gö (མགོས་ཀྱི་ཕག་རི), stretched across upper Tsang region extending as far as Kyerchu in Paro to the south. It is perhaps for this reason the area next to Kyerchu is called Satsham (ས་མཚམས་) or border and known by this name even today. The area was owned by the two clans of Gö and Gya, this last one being the clan to which the founder of Bhutan belonged. Some time in the beginning of the second millennium, a portion of this appanage was given to Nyö Yonten Drakpa (b.973), a priest and translator from the Nyö clan, in return for the tantric initiation and teachings Yonten Drakpa bestowed on one of the members of the Gya clan. Thus, the area around the Chumbi valley coming as far south as the Kyerchu temple in Paro, known as Lhokhazhi, came under the control of Nyö Yonten Drakpa. This figure from the Nyö is remembered, in Kagyu hagiographies, as a jealous colleague of Marpo Chökyi Lodoe, the founder of the Marpa Kagyu tradition. He went to India with Marpa to study Buddhism but coming from a rich family, is said to have been less hardworking than Marpa and hence jealous of the latter's success. He is said to have ordered his servant to throw Marpa's books into the river on their return to Tibet.

Lhanangpa was a descendent of Nyö Yonten Drakpa and he inherited the area which was offered to this ancestor. Thus, his control over the place was not merely due to his religious works. It was a result of a secular appanage. Lhanangpa is said to have ruled the areas as both a religious lama and a secular ruler. In Bhutan, he appears to have succeeded in expanding his territory. The previous domain which stopped at the upper ends of the Paro valley was extended using his religious influence. The Lhapa school seems to have gained a clear authority over the whole of Paro, the adjoining valley of Thimphu and perhaps even further east. John Ardussi argues that the application of the term Lhokhazhi also shifted in accordance with the extension of the domain. Over 1700 monks are reported to have assembled in Chalkha for religious sermons which Lhanangpa gave. Lhanangpa is also said to have made a series of large-scale offerings to his teachers and the monks of Drigung in Tibet with the tax he collected. 'Inferring from over tens of thousands of loads of gifts he made to Drigung, the Bhutanese public apparently suffered,' laments Bhutanese historian Pema Tshewang.[16] After about eleven years, Lhanangpa himself returned to Tibet to set up his base there. He was worried that the trade marts of Phari and Lhokhazhi would distract his monks from spiritual practice although these places were good for material resources. His descendents and students continued to control these areas. However, as early as the beginning of the thirteenth century, the Lhapa School began to face a serious challenge from the Drukpa Kagyu hierarch, Phajo Drukgom Zhigpo. The fight for religiopolitical control over western Bhutan locked the two Kagyu traditions in a contest from which eventually, the Drukpa came out victorious and the Lhapa school was eradicated from Bhutanese soil.

Although the Lhapa school of Lhanangpa suffered at the hands of the Drukpa Kagyu lamas and were finally uprooted from Bhutan, the Nyö clan began to grow only deeper roots in central Bhutan. With a mythical origin and long history, this clan is one of the oldest and most respected clans of Tibet. A certain scion of Nyö named Nyötön Demchog or Thrulzhig Chöje (1179–1265), considered to be the son of Lhanangpa, arrived in Ura from Tibet and began to settle in 1228. Local stories have it that following his guru Jigten Gönpo's instructions he sent a flying drum to find the spot of his destiny and he followed. The drum is today preserved in Somthrang as one of its main relics. Nyötön Demchong is said to have first built the centre near the village of Shingkhar, where he came across a number of obstructions. He then moved to Somthrang and built his centre on a strategic spot marked by a pillar called the cosmic megalith (བསྐལ་པའི་རྡོ་རིང་) and with a swastika-shaped rocky slope to the east, a milky brook to the west, a conch shell-like mound to the south and a cliff resembling book stacks to the north. The centre specialized in Vajrakīla practice and may have originally been affiliated to the Drigung Kagyu tradition but it later became a largely Nyingma centre. Thrulzhig Chöje left a leading hereditary religious line in Ura known as the Somthrang Chöje, which continues to this day and is recorded in the detailed genealogy of Lama Sa-ngag.[17] The father of Pema Lingpa, Bhutan's foremost religious figure, came from this family. Through Pema Lingpa and his scions, the Somthrang Chöje family has today spread all over Bhutan.

The Drukpa Kagyu school

Another Kagyu school to thrive in Bhutan is the Drukpa Kagyu or the Dragon Kagyu. It is from this Tibetan Buddhist school that Bhutan got its name in the later centuries. The Drukpa Kagyu school started as a successor to Lingrey Kagyu, a minor Kagyu school started by Lingrey Pema Dorji, a yogi who claimed to have obtained great learning through his meditative power. When others questioned his scholarship, he is said to have even dressed up as a book and challenged his doubters to an open debate. Lingrepa was one of the prominent students of Phagdru Dorji Gyalpo but is perhaps best remembered for being the master of Tsangpa Gyarey Yeshe Dorji. It was under the leadership of this very illustrious and influential disciple of Lingrey that his school acquired the new name, Drukpa Kagyu.

The Drukpa Kagyu school, which was begun by Tsangpa Gyarey in a valley south of Lhasa, gained popularity rapidly. We have already discussed in Chapter 1 how the temple of Druk got its name. After its beginnings in Namdruk, the Drukpa tradition moved its centre to the Ralung monastery, due north of western Bhutan. From here Tsangpa Gyarey is said to have sent forth large waves of thousands of his disciples at least three times in order to spread his teachings. There is little doubt that the Drukpa school attracted a large following if we are to even remotely imagine the exaggerated claim that 'half of the world is followers of Drukpa; half of the Drukpa are paupers and half of them saints with spiritual accomplishments'. The Drukpa tradition is supposed to have spread as far as a vulture can fly in eighteen days. This is an interesting metaphor as one could not have known then how far a vulture can really fly in eighteen days. An oral explanation of this metaphor connects to a beautiful story. Tsangpa Gyarey's master is said to have given his three favourite students three items to choose from in order to foretell the prospects of their religious influence: a drum, a conch shell and a bell. The first one chose the drum and began beating it. The master foretold that his influence would go as far as the sound of the drum. The second one blew the conch shell and he was told his spiritual impact would spread as far as its sound. The last disciple, who got the bell, tied it to a vulture which, alarmed by the noise, flew until it finally got worn out after eighteen days. The master predicted that the spiritual influence of this last disciple, Tsangpa Gyarey, would spread as far as the sound of the bell.

As the Drukpa tradition expanded in the generation of Tsangpa Gyarey's students, it was divided into three groups of the Töedruk (སྟོད་འབྲུག) or Upper Drukpa, who were as numerous as stars in the sky, the Bardruk (བར་འབྲུག) or Middle Drukpa, who were as many as particles of dust in the air, and the Meydruk (སྨད་འབྲུག) or Lower Drukpa, who were countless like the dust on the earth. From among the large following, the Drukpa tradition produced a great number of spiritual adepts and it gained a great reputation of being the school of rigorous 'white-clothed' meditators. Its main centre in Ralung, associated mainly with the Middle Drukpa line, was run by the descendents and incarnations of Tsangpa Gyarey. We shall see in the next chapter how this seat was initially passed from uncle to nephew as the chief hierarchs were celibate but, after a few generations, it became a hereditary line being passed from father to son with interception of incarnate figures, who were sometimes born within the family.

In the generation after its founder, the Drukpa school began to spread southward into the western valleys of Bhutan. This diffusion took place under the stewardship of an eastern Tibetan man named Phajo Drukgom Zhigpo (1184?–1251?). According to his only biography, he was born in Kham, known as Tharpa Gyaltshen and was undergoing his religious training under a Nyingma master called Tharpa Lingpa when Tsangpa Gyarey's reputation reached his village. The name Tsangpa Gyarey filled Tharpa Gyaltshen with an unknown sense of devotion and awakening. He immediately set off for Central Tibet to study with Tsangpa Gyarey. The journey took nearly a year and when he reached Druk, Tsangpa Gyarey had already passed away. Tsangpa Gyarey's spiritual heir and nephew Sangay Onre took Tharpa Gyaltshen under his wing and gave him instructions on meditation. Tharpa Gyaltshen excelled in meditation, earning himself the new name Drukgom Zhigpo or the liberated meditator of Druk. Sangay Onre then revealed to Drukgom Zhigpo that the great Tsangpa Gyarey before his demise had predicted the arrival of a young man from Kham and left a prophecy. The prophecy indicated that Drukgom Zhigpo should head southward to spread the teachings of the Drukpa school. Thus, Sangay Onre prepared a farewell ceremony and saw off Phajo Drukgom Zhigpo on his destined mission with advice, prayers and a few presents, including two religious books.

Phajo Drukgom Zhigpo arrived in Bhutan in 1222. He started his mission by staying in retreat in a number of places, including Taktshang. While in retreat in Taktshang, he is said to have had a vision of Padmasambhava, who prophesied that he would establish many retreat centres in the region and also meet the consort of his destiny. Following this prophecy, he travelled across the mountains and valleys of Paro, Lingshi, Thimphu and Punakha setting up new centres for meditation. While meditating above the village of Wang Chudo, he met a group of local women and appears to have fathered his first son, Dampa, with one of them. His biography only records this in a highly allegorical account of giving one of the girls 'five pills' to prepare the 'right circumstances' for her to give birth to a holy child.[18] Giving 'the pill', quite contrary to the English idiom of our time, was perhaps a metaphor for spiritual or biological insemination as we also find this metaphor used in the story of Thangtong Gyalpo, which we shall see below.

Not long after giving the pills to the first lady, he met her sister and his consort of destiny, Sonam Peldren, and they settled in Dodena, a confluence north of Thimphu. From here, Drukgom Zhigpo began to spread his religious influence in the region. He and Sonam Peldren also produced a daughter and four sons while in Dodena. His biography, however, has an even more fascinating account about his sons. Sonam Peldren gave birth to a lump of flesh out of which emerged seven sons. The boys grew abnormally fast. One good day, Drukgom Zhigpo sent Sonam Peldren and his daughter on an errand and, while they were gone, he took his sons to the bridge and threw them into the river saying:

O masters and deities of Kagyu! Save them if they are going to be custodians of the Buddha's teachings. Let them cast their body and be reborn in the Buddha's world if they are not. May those who are incarnations of holy beings survive and may those who are incarnations of evil forces die and be reborn in a Buddha's realm.[19]

Four of them returned unharmed, proving that they were sons of destiny with supernatural powers, the other three perished and their minds were transferred to the pure land of Sukhavāti by the miraculous power of their father. The news of the four babies surviving the river ordeal spread swiftly across the region and enhanced the spiritual stature of Drukgom Zhigpo as a miracle maker. The biography makes it quite clear that Drukgom Zhigpo's authority was rapidly growing through his spiritual achievements at Dodena and Tango.

The rise of Drukgom Zhigpo's reputation and influence vexed the Lhapa lamas in Paro who had until then held full control over the western valleys. They were the religious kings of Lhokhazhi then. In a harsh letter sent to Drukgom Zhigpo, he was reprimanded for living in an area under their jurisdiction without their permission and was given the options of either taking care of one of the Lhapa centres or looking after their horses. Drukgom Zhigpo defied their command, warning them to restrain their own despotic rule and the suffering they inflicted on the people. The Lhapa lamas, according to the biography, imposed on the people heavy taxes including large amounts of rice, textiles, silk and iron. No doubt, his defiance provoked their anger and consequently armed assaults, which he is said to have repelled through his magical powers. Although he used his occult power to scare away many assailants sent by the Lhapa lamas, his main tactic in winning the support of the local people seems to have been the issue of taxation. He objected to the heavy taxation imposed by the Lhapa group and thereby gained the sympathy of the local people. Not long after his open opposition to the Lhapa authority, some of the local chieftains approached him secretly and pledged their support to him if he did not distress them with similar taxation.

The magical and armed conflicts between Drukgom Zhigpo and the Lhapa school eventually ended with Drukgom Zhigpo coming out victorious and the Lhapa school reduced to a symbolic religious presence in a few centres. They lost the political control of the area to Drukgom Zhigpo, who appointed his sons as chiefs of the various valleys. This effectively started the era of Drukpa political control over valleys of western Bhutan. Word of his domination of the western Bhutanese valleys even reached the Kamāta king in Assam who sent gifts to him. Drukgom Zhigpa, however, did not live long to enjoy the glory of the Drukpa influence as he succumbed to a poisoning, which the Lhapa lamas are said to have arranged. Phajo Drukgom Zhigpa died at the age of sixty-eight, leaving behind a daughter, five sons, a profound religious influence and a loose control over the principalities of western Bhutan. We do not have the name of his daughter but his sons were Dampa, Gartön, Nyima, Wangchuk and Lama.

Before his death, his son Dampa was appointed to take care of his seat in

Tango and oversee Paro. Dampa's great-grandsons gave rise to the *zhalngo* nobilities of Hungral Drungdrung and Lama Gangtagpa in Paro. Gartön became the chieftain of the Dung, Hed and Dong groups and the trade route in the east. His descendents started the *zhalngo* of Wachen, which branched out into other *zhalngo* nobilities in the valleys to the east. Nyima was given the Chang and Gung communities around Thimphu and his descendants became the *zhalngo* of Changangkha. The family provided a bride for Zhabdrung Ngawang Namgyal in the seventeenth century. Wangchuk went to rule over the areas of Punakha and Gön and left behind the *zhalngo* line of Sangma in Gön. The priestly family of Ura Gaden also claims direct descent from him. Lama appears to have had no particular principality to rule. He is said to have inherited Phajo's seat in Dodena and also given rise to some *zhalngo* families in Paro. It is clear from this distribution and later records that Phajo Drukgom's sons had a structured control over the entire area of western Bhutan, including its trade routes.

Phajo Drukgom Zhigpo was, however, not the first promoter of the Drukpa Kagyu school on Bhutanese soil as claimed by standard history books according to the historian Sangay Dorji.[20] Even before Drukgom Zhigpo met his teacher in Druk, Rinchen Drakpa Paldan, also known as Drubthob Terkhungpa, is said to have founded the Obtsho and Dechenchöding monasteries around 1212 in the Gönyul region, north of Punakha. Terkhungpa was a disciple of Tsangpa Gyarey and most well known in Bhutan for his subjugation of the deity Gomo. These centres and their later branches became affiliates of the main Drukpa centre in Ralung and were run by a line of religious elites originating from the nephew of Terkhungpa, whom he appointed to take care of the establishments. Unlike the Drukgom Zhigpo line, the Obtsho family did not grow to wield much influence in Bhutan until much later times. Through the centuries, it maintained close links with Ralung, with which it also shared marital ties. The sons of the Obtsho family were sent to Ralung for training and one of them in the seventeenth century was Tenzin Drukgyal (1591–1656). He rose through the ranks to become the *umze* (དབུ་མཛད་) or monastic precentor and was crucial in inviting Zhabdrung Ngawang Namgyal to Bhutan in 1616. Subsequent to the centralization of political power in Bhutan, he became the 1st Desi ruler of Bhutan. Another prominent son of Obtsho was Ngawang Gyaltshen (1647–1732), the monk-diplomat who was Bhutan's ambassador to the kingdoms of Ladakh and Derge in the later half of the seventeenth century.

The Drukpa Kagyu also reached Bhutan through Lorepa (1187–1250), one of the students of Tsangpa Gyarey. He is credited with the founding of the Lower Drukpa subschool and became famous as a wandering yogi after his arduous retreat at the Namtsho lake. Like Thangtong Gyalpo, whom we will discuss later, Lorepa is said to have vowed to not 'cross the threshold' of a house in the true spirit of a homeless mendicant. Due to this oath, he had to be brought into the house through the attic using two ladders when he visited his mother's rebirth, who was gravely ill.[21] He came to Bumthang at least twice and is said to have founded Tharpaling in Chumey, which we must identify with the Tharpaling in the lower Chumey valley. The foundation of the Chödrak temple above the famous Tharpaling monastery is also attributed to him. Some 2800 monks were supposed to have gathered in Bumthang for his teachings during his first trip. It appears that his works in Bhutan and elsewhere generally ceased after his death. Similarly, Chilkarwa of the Upper Drukpa subschool came to Paro and established Chilkarkha but left no major following. Six generations later, two brothers who were his descendents are said to have come to Paro and established the two centres of Zarchen Samten Chöling and Kyila Dechen Yangtse. The *chöje* family of Zarchen in Paro are said to have originated from the younger one of the two brothers.[22]

Throughout the thirteenth to the seventeenth centuries, the descendents of Drukgom Zhigpo's sons would host a number of prominent Drukpa religious visitors from Ralung. An important figure is Jamyang Kuenga Senge (1314–47), the chief hierarch of Ralung, who made his journeys to the southern valleys in order to appease the *dung reng* at the behest of Tibetan authorities. Although he did not quite succeed in permanently stopping the marauders, he had successful tours across western Bhutan performing religious services. He was received and looked after by the descendents of Drukgom Zhigpo, among others, and even took a consort from Gön from among the descendents of Phajo Drukgom. She became the mother of the next chief hierarch of Ralung.[23] His biography, written by one of his students, is full of praises for the places he visited, including Dechenphu and Changangkha. Even the name Thimphu is said to have been coined during one of his visits to Dechenphug where the local deity Jagpa Melan appeared before him before dissolving into a rock; in the name Thimphu, the *phu* (ཕུ), or high ground, is where the deity got dissolved, or *thim* (ཐིམ), into a rock. Whether or not this is the etymological origin of Thimphu, the name was current by the time Dorji Lingpa visited Bhutan in the second half of the fourteenth century.

Another important figure is Kuenga Paljor (1428–76), the 13th chief hierarch of Ralung. He visited Bhutan about three times and became the main teacher of Drukgom Zhigpo's descendent Drungdrung Gyalchog, who started the Hungral Drungdrung family mentioned above. A translation of some verses from the colophon of the *Kanjur* collection written in Hungral Drungdrung's memory immediately after his death is provided below to get a glimpse of Paro at the end of sixteenth century. The master is said to have established a great number of religious centres as a method of Drukpa expansion and his disciple Drungdrung to have built numerous dykes, perhaps for both irrigation and embankment. Thus, a popular saying went: 'Don't raise your knees [when sitting cross-legged], Drukpa lamas will build a temple [on the space]. Don't let your nose run, Drungdrung will build a dyke [over the mucus].'

The visitors from Ralung continued in the fifteenth and sixteenth centuries and the Drukpa mission started to spread further east toward central Bhutan. Among the main figures who visited Bhutan in this period were Ngawang Chögyal (1465–1540) and Ngagi Wangchuk (1517–54), the 14th and 15th holders of the Ralung throne, who travelled widely and established numerous centres in Bhutan. While the former has many temples, including the temple in the middle of Paro town and the famous Khyime temple in Lobesa, to his credit, the latter is commonly attributed the foundation of religious centres at locations where the Tongsa, Jakar and Lhuntse *dzongs* were later built. The list of the names of the numerous temples they founded can be found in traditional histories.[24] Ngagi Wangchuk was followed by his son, Mipham Chogyal (1543–1604) who visited Bhutan about five times since 1567 and he was followed by his son Tanpai Nyima (1567–1619). Both these figures travelled east to Bumthang, Kurtoe and Shongar, thus expanding the Drukpa influence further east.

However, the figure who is most loved and remembered by the Bhutanese today among the Drukpa lamas from Tibet is undoubtedly Drukpa Kunley (1455–1529?), the 'divine madman' who was a close relation of the main Ralung line. Drukpa Kunley gained great fame in western and central Bhutan so much so that many Bhutanese think he was a native Bhutanese and some foreigners even think he is the patron saint of Bhutan.[25] Drukpa Kunley was neither of these but his popularity among the populace was and continues to be unsurpassed.

Born in a collateral line of the Drukpa family in Ralung, he pursued a religious life some time in his late teens. He was disillusioned with the worldly life by the death of his father in a feud and thus became a monk. However, he soon lost interest in institutionalized religion and a monastic career and began to roam as a carefree mendicant. He quickly gained a reputation as the 'Madman of Druk', one of the three famous madmen of his time. Styled on the *mahāsiddha* figures of India, the 'madmen movement' perhaps reached its climax during Drukpa Kunley's time but it remained only in the periphery of mainstream religious traditions.

The holy madmen were, however, hardly mad. They were spiritual adepts known for their unprejudiced and uninhibited wisdom. In fact, from their enlightened perspective, the rest of world was utterly mad and intoxicated by bewildering thoughts and emotions. Drukpa Kunley is believed to have reached the great heights of spiritual realization to see through the vanity of life and the meaninglessness of worldly pursuits of happiness. He was seen as a spiritual man who was free of worldly concerns (ཇ་འབངs་) and had fully realized the uncontrived, open and empty nature of all things. Thus, at the core of his maverick personality is the realization of ultimate reality of all things. This unrestrained awareness of reality, which defies all worldly logic and conventions, is put in the modern idiom as crazy wisdom.

To the Bhutanese, Drukpa Kunley was a crazy-wisdom master *par excellence*. In the Bhutanese legends about him, he roamed the country, carrying a bow and arrows and wielding a phallus, the 'flaming thunderbolt', with which he subjugated many demons. We find a recurring theme of subjugation of natural forces in the form of demons in stories about Drukpa Kunley, just like the legends of Padmasambhava's taming of malevolent spirits. Like Padmasambhava, he was a master of magical deeds. Another common thread in the legends of Padmasambhava and Drukpa Kunley is their relationship with women. Padmasambhava's engagements with his consorts are generally portrayed as solemn spiritual affairs. In contrast, Drukpa Kunley is remembered for his jovial and lewd lifestyle, and for travelling from place to place, enjoying local liquor, singing licentious songs and seducing adult women of every age group. Drukpa Kunley was said to have been a handsome and well-endowed priest who could charm any girl. Sex and alcohol were used as means for building spiritual connections and as catalysts for speeding up the process of enlightenment. Bawdy songs and jokes were used to undo the fetters of social inhibitions and cultural taboos.

In the true fashion of the crazy-wisdom master, he used uninhibited and provocative methods to free people from ordinary perceptions, prejudices, conventions and sociocultural constrictions. Through his humorous and satirical songs and behaviour, he attacked the hypocrisy, corruption and self-aggrandisement of established institutions. The stories of his life are full of humour, mischief and mockery of orthodoxy but these acts were clearly intended to convey a deeper message and purpose. His character epitomized at once both frivolity of conduct and seriousness of religious purpose. That is roughly the persona of Drukpa Kunley perpetuated in the Bhutanese imagination. The historical person may have been less colourful and more sober. He was definitely a very learned scholar and an unparalleled critic of the corrupt and hypocritical elements of Tibetan Buddhist practices. He was an itinerant traveller and an inspiring poet and humourist. Above all, he was a spiritual figure who genuinely saw through the ritualistic and materialistic trappings.

In Bhutan, he traversed western Bhutan and also fathered a son from a local lady. This son, Ngawang Tenzin was the father of Tshewang Tenzin of Tango, who became an important host and patron of Zhabdrung Ngawang Namgyal. Tshewang Tenzin's son Tenzin Rabgay became an eminent student of Zhabdrung and eventually the 4th Desi of Bhutan. Drukpa Kunley thus left an important family line in Bhutan. Although the family line has ceased a long time ago, the line of incarnation of his great-grandson Tenzin Rabgay continues to this day. Drukpa Kunley also visited Bumthang, approaching it directly from Tibet and had interesting encounters with Pema Lingpa (1450–1521), who, in some ways, must have shared his spiritual sophistication and maverick character. In iconographic forms, Drukpa Kunley is portrayed as a wandering yogi, holding an arrow and bow and accompanied by a dog. Although he was an anti-institutional figure and founded no centres of his own, he came to be associated with Khyime lhakhang, which was founded by his cousin Ngawang Chogyal. Today, people primarily know this temple in connection to Drukpa Kunley and tour guides often introduce it to foreign guests as the fertility temple. Its name suggests that the temple was built on the spot where a demoness, who was running away in the form of dog, was subdued by Drukpa Kunley. A phallus and a bow and arrow are kept in this temple to bless visitors.

Drukpa Kunley left hardly any legacy in terms of institutional establishments or religious doctrine or practices. Yet, his influence on the Bhutanese religious and cultural consciousness is far-reaching. For one, the figure of Drukpa Kunley can be given much credit, though not all, for the libertine sexual character of the Bhutanese man and woman. Much of the traditional sexual laxity and openness, including the ubiquity of sexual symbols, can be said to be an influence of his maverick behaviour and the concepts of uninhibited wisdom. Drukpa Kunley was, to the Bhutanese, a role model who had no hang-ups with sex and sexuality. The Bhutanese love of alcohol and leniency towards social problems caused by it must also partially spring from the place of alcohol in tantric religion and the lives of tantric masters. Above all, the impact of Drukpa Kunley is seen in the easygoing attitude to life and the robust sense of humour, found abundantly in traditional Bhutanese society. His biography and the many oral anecdotes about his travels and religious missions are today some of the most entertaining stories one can hear in western and central Bhutan.

Drukpa Kunley thus stands out as a unique case among the religious visitors from Tibet. Even among the Drukpa lamas from Ralung, who visited Bhutan in the successive generations, there was no one of his category or calibre. However, in the four centuries since Drukgom Zhigpo started his mission, the Drukpa lamas succeeded in establishing their tradition in most parts of western Bhutan. A large number of western Bhutanese appears to have become patrons of the Drukpa school and many of them went to Ralung to receive religious training. A very close and solemn connection, which may be described as the priest–patron relationship, was firmly built between the hierarchs of Ralung and the people of Bhutan. It was such a cordial relationship which would eventually attract Zhabdrung Ngawang Namgyal to Bhutan in exile and lead to the formation of the state of Bhutan as we know it today. We shall return to this in the next chapter but now turn to the discussion of other religious traditions of the Later Diffusion.

The Nyingma school

We have seen above that the Buddhist renaissance in Tibet during the period of the Later Diffusion consisted of the two main processes of (1) reviving the earlier teachings and (2) introducing new ones from India and Nepal. The two processes respectively correspond to (1) the Nyingma (རྙིང་མ་) or old school of those who were primarily occupied with the revival of the teachings transmitted during the Tibetan dynastic period and (2) the Sarma (གསར་མ་) or new schools, which were mostly engaged in new imports. There was generally no difference between these two groups concerning the acceptance of texts, which fall in the category of exoteric Buddhist philosophy and practice known as 'the philosophical vehicle of sūtra' (མདོའི་མཚན་ཉིད་ཐེག་པ་). The bulk of the Buddhist corpus translated during the Early Diffusion, which consisted of large sūtras, were accepted mutually and used by both. Their primary difference lay in the esoteric tantric teachings, also known as secret mantra (གསང་སྔགས་) which often formed the core texts for the schools' spiritual practice. The Sakya school, for instance, focused on the *Lamdre* (ལམ་འབྲས་) teachings while the Kagyu specialized in Mahāmudrā, six yogas of Naropa and tantras such as *Hevajra* and *Cakrasaṃvara*, which were newly transmitted to Tibet during the Later Diffusion.

The adherents of the Nyingma school championed the cause of recovering and promoting tantric teachings which were transmitted during the Early Diffusion. At the wake of the Buddhist revival in the tenth and eleventh centuries, they brought to light a large collection of tantric teachings which they claimed were translated from Indic or Chinese originals during the Early Diffusion and passed down in an unbroken transmission. Some of their Sarma counterparts, however, contested such claims and alleged that many of the Nyingma tantras were composed by Tibetans and not authentic Indian works. As a result, most of these tantric texts did not make it into the standard Tibetan Buddhist canon of *Kanjur* (བཀའ་འགྱུར་) or the *Translations of the Words [of the Buddha]* but were separately compiled by the Nyingma masters as the *Collection of Nyingma tantras* (རྙིང་མ་རྒྱུད་འབུམ་). This tantric collection and the numerous other teachings, which were passed down from master to disciple, became the class of Nyingma teachings known as *kama* (བཀའ་མ་) or transmitted precepts. However, the *kama* collection, which exists in its fourth edition today, does not include all the tantras. It is a large body of literature which includes some tantras but is mainly made up of commentarial and auxiliary texts related to the three tantric cycles of the Nyingma school known as *Dogyusemsum* (མདོ་སྒྱུ་སེམས་གསུམ་) and the nine vehicles for enlightenment (ཐེག་པ་རིམ་དགུ་) in the Nyingma soteriology.

It was not just the 'received teachings' of *kama* which constituted the literary wealth of the Nyingma tradition. During the renaissance in the eleventh century, the Nyingma school also saw the emergence of 'revealed knowledge' in the form of *terma* (གཏེར་མ་) or rediscovered treasures. The treasures were mostly texts, but also included artefacts, which were believed to have been concealed by Padmasambhava or other figures during the dynastic period in order to be revealed when the time is ripe by individuals destined to do so. This skilful technique of religious preservation and regeneration perhaps started as a simple practice of burying texts for safety during troubled times and having them recovered when the sociopolitical situation became conducive for their use. A great number of texts and objects may have been buried for safekeeping when the Tibetan empire crumbled, the state support to Buddhism was lost and political chaos ensued after the peasant revolts. Thus, it is likely that a lot of the early treasure discoveries involved only ordinary human procedures of retrieving the texts or artefacts, although the acts of retrieval may have been accompanied by some religious prayers and rituals.

However, as the practice developed, the treasure culture appears to have gone through an accretive process of sacralization and ritualistic systematization. It evolved into a complex mystical and transcendental process involving sacred sites, secret codes, guides, rituals, miracles and, above all, treasure-discoverers with special connections to Padmasambhava and the figures of the dynastic period. It was not merely an ordinary practice of hiding and retrieving things but a transcendental revelation of religious knowledge and objects using superhuman and prophetic abilities. The treasure culture also expanded in terms of what was discovered. In addition to texts (ཆོས་གཏེར་), religious artefacts and holy substances, (རྫས་གཏེར་), the treasures also included visionary (དག་སྣང་) and psychic revelations (དགོངས་གཏེར་). The locus of the treasures also expanded with treasures discovered not only from the earth but from lakes, cliffs, space and even the inner depths of the human psyche. Similarly, as the treasure culture and its influence began to spread, it was no longer limited to the Nyingma school. So we find in the seventeenth century, both the 5th Dalai Lama, who was the chief Gelug hierarch and ruling over Tibet, and Zhabdrung Ngawang Namgyal, who was the chief Drukpa hierarch and ruling over Bhutan, involved in their acts of treasure discovery.

This fascinating and problematic practice of religious regeneration and revelation had a substantial impact on the course of Bhutan's history as the country saw a great number of *tertön* (གཏེར་སྟོན་) or treasure-discoverers from the very early days of treasure culture. The following table shows the list of Tibetan and native Bhutanese *tertön*s who were active in Bhutan from the eleventh century until the end of the twentieth century.

Tertöns in rough chronological order

Tibetan tertöns active in Bhutan

Bonpo Dragtsal
Raksha Chobar
Setön Ringmo
Gya Phurbu
Gyaton Tsundru Senge
Drugu Yangwang

Chogden Gönpo
Tenyi Lingpa/Tshewang Gyalpo
Drime Kuenga
Jatson Mebar
Gönpo Rinchen
Drodul Lethro Lingpa
Jangchub Lingpa

Balpo Ahum Bar
Ajo Walbo
Latod / Dampa Marpo
Lama Drum
Phajo Drukgom Zhigpo
Sarpo Jaugon
Kusa Manpa
Gurung Chowang
Ugpa Lingpa
Ogyen Lingpa
Yungton Dorji Pel
Gönpo Dorji
Sherab Mebar
Longchenpa Drime Özer
Drubthob Gönpo Dorji
Gyalwangje Kuenga Paljor
Ratna Lingpa
Dorji Lingpa
Thangtong Gyalpo

Ngari Rigzin Legden Dorji
Nyima Drakpa
Khyungpo Pelge
Drime Lingpa
Yebonpa Phurbu Gonpo
Sa-ngag Lingpa
Ngawang Namgyal
Dudul Lingpa/ Dorji Drolöd
Zhigpo Lingpa
Drukdra Dorji
Jigme Lingpa
Zilnon Namkha Dorji
Serkong Tshultrim Donden
Dudjom Lingpa
Zurmang Drungpa
Jigme Phuntsho
Dilgo Khyentse
Pelgyal Lingpa
Ganor

*Local Bhutanese tertön*s

Tsetan Gyaltshen
Sarben Chogme
Padropa Nagpo Kharwa
Ugyen Zangpo
Pema Lingpa
Dawa Gyaltshen

Kuenga Wangpo
Ngawang Drakpa
Tsering Dorji
Zhanda Gyaltshen
Yongdrak Gyatsho
Ngawang Tenzin

Unlike the Kagyu institutions discussed above, these treasure-discoverers did not originate from one establishment or institution or even from one school although most of them belonged to the Nyingma tradition. They did not function as part of an organized religious movement or group although they loosely shared goals and stratagems. The *tertön*s of the Early Historic Period were mostly individual mystics, seeking religious treasures and hidden lands following the cryptic prophecies and guides which came to their hands or their own prognostic dreams. Besides, they shared the link to Padmasambhava and the claim to be his destined spiritual heirs. Most *tertön*s associated with Bhutan also shared two beliefs; that the hidden lands conducive for spiritual practice lay mostly in the borderlands south of Tibet and that these places were filled with treasures buried by Padmasambhava and his disciples to be revealed when the propitious time came. With these beliefs, they set out on their journeys mainly to find and extract treasures but also subsequently, to spread the teachings which they have rediscovered.

These religious explorers traversed the entire country either in search of treasures or on their missions to promote their treasures. They attracted large following as they were believed to be the incarnations of the important persons who received the teachings directly from Padmasambhava and their teachings and techniques to be spiritually more fresh and effective than other forms of teachings, which have become stale due to gradual transmission through the ages. The teachings they discovered and propagated often became the trendy religious practices of their times. Thus, their religious works left a substantial impact on the lives of people. Many, however, failed to leave any significant legacy for posterity and passed into oblivion. In the case of many of the minor *tertön*s, we do not even know when they lived and what they did apart from a sparse mention of their acts of treasure discovery. A great many of these *tertön*s were from Tibetan areas not far from Bhutan although some, like Sherab Mebar and Jigme Phuntsho, came from places as far as Kham and Golok in eastern Tibet. While some stayed for long periods and established centres and institutions in Bhutan, others were merely passing pilgrims and treasure-hunters who returned to Tibet as quickly as they came.

Due to the Bhutanese faith in Padmasambhava and treasure tradition, almost all of them would have enjoyed a very good reception, hospitality and even devotion from local patrons, followers and the Bhutanese public but an unfortunate few may have faced scepticism and utter rejection like the case of a recent Tibetan *tertön* whose discoveries were examined and declared to be forgeries by the Bhutanese state and the person seen off unceremoniously. Today, the proliferation of clinical scientific thinking has placed the belief in ancient treasure under intense scrutiny. There are perhaps fewer persons who claim to be *tertön*s today than in any of the last ten centuries. Nevertheless, it is still not very hard to find Tibetan religious visitors travelling across Bhutan on pilgrimage to imbibe blessings from the powerful places and also extract a treasure if it comes their way.

The Bhutanese religious culture is heavily influenced by the *tertön*s and their rediscovered treasures. Notwithstanding their importance in Bhutanese history and religion, it will be beyond the scope of this book to deal with the concept, practice and significance of treasure tradition in any detail. Only the sociohistorical and political ramifications of their lives and works in Bhutan will be pointed out here. One such ramification is the family lines several of the Tibetan *tertön*s left in Bhutan. Like the descendents of the exiled princes in the first millennium and the families of other Tibetan hierarchs, the descendents of the important treasure-discoverers also obtained high social and political standing in their regions. The families of Lukchu and Nyalam in Kurtöe descending from Guru Chöwang (1212–70) and Ogyen Chöling descending from Dorji Lingpa (1346–1405) are good examples. These families, known as *dung* or *chöje* in their areas, have risen to the ranks of local nobilities.

The same can be said of the descendents of Sherab Mebar (fourteenth century) in Paro. This treasure-discoverer from eastern Tibet, whose dates are not clear, is said to have spent some time in Bumthang first and subsequently in Paro, where he founded the temple of Pangpisa. Unfortunately, he is perhaps remembered more for his failures than successes. In Bumthang, he is said to have extracted a treasure under the duress of a local ruler which was not intended to be found by him. The action led to the death of the ruler and his own untimely death. In Haa, he is said to have also failed in recovering the treasure from Nubtshona Patra, leading to the death of some thirty people. Another well-known Tibetan treasure-discoverer who built at least two temples in the Kurtoe area is Ratna Lingpa (1403–79). His treasure text on the practices of the wrathful deity Vajrakīlaya is still very popular in Bhutan. Ogyen Lingpa (b.1323), the treasure-discoverer famous for his discovery of Padmasambhava's biography, also visited Bhutan and perhaps opened the hidden valleys of Monkha Shridzong and Aja Nye in eastern Bhutan.

One of the most prestigious Tibetan treasure-discoverers, who left both family lines and widespread religious legacies in Bhutan, is Dorji Lingpa, one of the five 'king' *tertön*s (གཏེར་སྟོན་རྒྱལ་པོ་ལྔ་). Considered to be the incarnation of the learned translator Vairocana, Dorji Lingpa was well known for his learning. However, the most remarkable trait of Dorji Lingpa is perhaps his eminent stature in both the Buddhist and Bönpo circles. Only very few figures in Tibetan history were able to claim religious authority in both traditions. Dorji Lingpa moved between the two traditions seamlessly and spent a great deal of time travelling to Bhutan from his base in southern Tibet. He left a direct family line in the Menlog region of western Bhutan through his son. The *lama* families of Jakar Lhakhang, Buli and Chagkhar and the *chöje* family of Ogyen Chöling, who are among religious elites in Bumthang, are said to have also descended from this treasure-discoverer although this was not clear at the time of his second reincarnation, Chogden Gönpo. Dorji Lingpa founded many centres in western and central Bhutan and had a large following, to whom he wrote beautiful homiletic letters from Tibet. Not only did he visit his patrons and devotees in the south, he also had them come frequently to Tibet. A number of places in Wangdi, Tongsa and Bumthang district still carry on his tradition and his treasure texts and writings have recently been updated and published.

His second reincarnation, Chogden Gönpo, also became very active in Bhutan. Chogden Gönpo was born in Tibet but he spent a lot of time in Bhutan visiting the descendents and devotees of his previous incarnation. Chogden appears to have started his religious career with some hardship and controversy over the authenticity of his claim as the reincarnation of Dorji Lingpa. However, he found a stalwart endorser of his claim in the person of the famous Pema Lingpa, who became his main spiritual mentor. Coincidentally, Drukpa Kunley, the madman whom we discussed above, was also in Bumthang when young Chogden Gönpa got his endorsement and spiritual recognition from Pema Lingpa. Drukpa Kunley is said to have, perhaps teasingly, questioned Chogden Gönpo's candidacy and challenged him to a contest in miracles to test his authenticity. Pema Lingpa heard about the challenge and jumped to defend Chogden Gönpo, saying the latter was merely a child and that any contest to verify the authenticity of what he approved must be with him.[26] There is, of course, no account of a contest having taken place but Chogden Gönpo grew up to be the undisputed incarnation of Dorji Lingpa. Thus, in spite of much demand for his religious services, particularly for repelling Mongolian invasions, in the court of Tibetan rulers, Chogden Gönpo travelled across central and western Bhutan many times and carried out many religious activities. Today, one can find many statues attributed to Chogden Gönpo in Bumthang although his autobiography gives no hint of him being a sculptor or artist.

Longchen Rabjam alias Drime Özer (1306–64), who visited Bhutan a generation before Dorji Lingpa, stands out as another prominent visitor to Bhutan among the Tibetan treasure discoverers. Although a senior treasure-discoverer, he is not known to have extracted any treasure in Bhutan. The discovery of treasures was not on the agenda for his journey to Bhutan. A scholar and religious person of great reputation, Longchenpa came to Bhutan to escape the political turmoil of Tibet. He attracted a large following in Bhutan and established several centres across the country, which are often enumerated as 'the eight spiritual sanctuaries' of Tharpaling in Chume,

Dechenling in Ura Shingkhar, Ogyen Chöling in Tang, Drechagling in Ngenlung, Rinchenling in Khothangkha, Kunzangling in Shar, Samtenling in Paro and Kunzangling in Kurtoe. Longchenpa was the discoverer of the teachings known as Nyingthig (སྙིང་ཐིག་) or Seminal Quintessence but he became more renowned for his writings on the philosophy of Dzogchen (རྫོགས་ ཆེན་) or 'Great Perfection'. He was a scholar and poet of phenomenal learning and talent, and a spiritual master of a quality rarely seen in history. It was for this vast erudition that the Tibetan ruler of his time, Tai Situ Jangchub Gyaltshen, gave him the honorary title Longchen (ཀློང་ཆེན་) or 'Vast One'.

His synthesis of Buddhist teachings in general and the Dzogchen tradition in particular earned Longchenpa a place among the very greatest thinkers and writers of Tibet. Perhaps the words of Gene Smith, one of the greatest scholars on Tibet, best describe him:

> The figure of Longchen Rabjampa was for the Dzogchen school what St. Thomas Aquinas was for Christian scholastic philosophy. In a number of magnificently original treatises like the Seven Treasuries (*Mdzod bdun*) Longchen ordered the philosophical and psychological truths and corollaries of Dzogchen into a cohesive system. For stylistic lucidity and structural organisation Longchen has seldom been equalled in Tibetan literature; Nyingma philosophy *is* Longchen Rabjampa.[27]

Longchenpa wrote some of these famous treatises while he was in Bhutan. His works, including the *Seven Treasures, Trilogy of Self-Liberation, Trilogy of Relaxation* and *Seminal Quintessence in Four Parts* are today the classics of the Nyingma school and widely studied in Bhutan. A very interesting piece is his eulogy to Bumthang entitled *The Flower Garden: A Profile of the Celestial Hidden Land of Bumthang* which contains very useful information on the region. Translation of some verses from this piece is provided below. His teachings, which his students such as Paljor Gyaltshen and Drakpa Özer continued to promote after him, spread in many parts of Bhutan and were known as the Nyingthig Gongma or Higher Seminal Quintessence.

Longchenpa's own time in Bhutan, however, finished with a messy and controversial story. Although a monk, he is said to have had sexual relations with a Bhutanese girl who was the sister of one of his disciples. When she gave birth to a daughter, Longchenpa advised her to conceal the relationship and asked one of the monks who was serving him as an attendant to act as the child's father. Five years later, the girl became pregnant again.

The monk attendant was once again asked to act as the father. When other monks complained about the unsightly pregnancy in the monastery and had the couple expelled to give birth in a nearby forest, the girl finally spilled the beans. This must have caused a scandal among the monks and the local patrons. Disappointed with the sad turn of events, Longchenpa returned to Tibet and soon after that passed away in Samye Chimphu.[28] His family line continued in Bhutan through his children. The two religious nobilities of Samtenling in Chumey and Shingkhar in Ura are said to have descended from Longchenpa although the lines were ruptured in later centuries.

Longchenpa's spiritual legacies in Bhutan continued through his direct disciples but his stature and influence in Bhutan was to reach new heights through the works of two separate later treasure-discoverers, both of whom claimed to be incarnations of Longchenpa albeit in different forms and in different times. One is the foremost Bhutanese saint Pema Lingpa (1450–1521), who claimed to be his rebirth and to whom we shall return later in detail.

The other figure is the seventeenth-century mystic and poet Jigme Lingpa (1730–98), whose 'person' is believed to have been spiritually impregnated by Longchenpa. During his meditation at Samye, Jigme Lingpa had visions of Longchenpa three times and received his teachings in their entirety. Jigme Lingpa was a lay Buddhist priest with no formal education but said to have turned phenomenally learned and prolific by 'unleashing' his intelligence through meditation. The result was a corpus of extremely beautiful verse compositions covering a wide range of subjects, including the Dzogchen tradition. Among his works on Dzogchen is a collection of highly inspirational texts known as Longchen Nyingthig (ཀློང་ཆེན་སྙིང་ཐིག་) or Longchen's Seminal Quintessence. As this cycle of ritual and meditation texts spread across the Tibetan world, the figure of Longchenpa found new life. Jigme Lingpa's Longchen Nyingthig cycle elevated Longchenpa from a great master to a divine object of worship and revitalized the whole Nyingthig tradition. Jigme Lingpa's texts are today the most popular ritual texts used by the Nyingma tradition. His teachings gained their highest respect and popularity in eastern Tibet, where they significantly transformed the existent traditions of religious practice, but they also spread quickly to Bhutan, particularly through the works of his student, Jigme Kundrol alias Jangchub Gyaltshen (b.1717?). Although Jigme Lingpa visited Bhutan, it seems his visit had been a short one and with no major religious impact in Bhutan. He came to Ura to conduct the funerary ceremonies for the grandfather of his disciple, Lhawang Chojin Zangpo (1748–1808) of Somthrang.

His student, Jangchub Gyaltshen, however, played an important role in propagating the Longchen Nyingthig tradition. Jangchub Gyaltshen was a young officer from the lower part of the Thimphu valley. He first became a novice in the Pagar monastery and then joined the court to gradually rise through the ranks of the medieval government to the official post of meat in-charge in the Tongsa dzong. Disgusted by the bloody task of collecting meat, he ran away to Tibet to pursue a religious life and became a close disciple of Jigme Lingpa. Later, he returned to Bhutan as an accomplished religious master and established his seat in Yongla in eastern Bhutan after trying the solitudes of Thowodrak in Tang and Wangthang in Ura. He also acted as a Bhutanese envoy to the British in Calcutta and it was perhaps based on his personal accounts that Jigme Lingpa even wrote an account of contemporary India.[29] Today, the teachings of both Longchenpa and Jigme Lingpa flourish in Bhutan having been taken up by many Nyingma monasteries and their Nyingthig system of tantric meditation and liturgy is one of the most popular religious traditions.

Mention may be also made of two other Nyingma masters who were treasure-discoverers but also strong propagators of the *kama* or received teachings. They both followed the Nyingma masters of the Zur lineage. The Zur line represented one of the two main schools of Nyingma tantric scholarship in Tibet; the other one being that of Longchenpa and his followers. The two groups comprise two parallel schools of thought for understanding the tantric philosophy of the Nyingma, particularly in relation to the classic text, *Guhyagarbhatantra*. Yungtön Dorji Pal (1284–1365) was an acclaimed master of *Guhyagarbhatantra* and is said to have lived in Paro. He built a meditation centre in Namthong Karpo and also extracted a treasure from the spot. Similarly, Ugpa Lingpa, a treasure-discoverer and a descendant of Nyingma masters of the Zur lineage, settled in Nyizergang in the Shar valley. He propagated both the *kama* teachings and his own *terma*, or revealed teachings. The line of his incarnations continued his legacy and built more temples in the region but they gradually adopted the Drukpa Kagyu school in the medieval period. The most recent incarnation in this line was the 67th Je Khenpo of Bhutan, who passed away in 2005. Both these Nyingma masters employed the deity Rahula as their tutelary protector but the latter came to be known for his ability to command this deity in his service.

Pema Lingpa and other local Bhutanese tertöns

Bhutan was not merely a ground for Tibetan treasure-discoverers. The country produced a very interesting group of native *tertön*s. The first one, according to Kongtrul's biographies of treasure-discoverers, is Sarben Chogme, a lay priest from Paro, who extracted texts for meditation on Mañjuśrī, the Buddha of wisdom. Another one is Tsheten Gyaltshen, a learned scholar and a monk, also from western Bhutan. He extracted many treasures from the Chumphu cliff in Paro. Sarben probably lived in the thirteenth century and Tsheten Gyaltshen in the early part of the fourteenth century. Another Bhutanese treasure-discoverer, Ugyen Zangpo, lived roughly a generation after Tsheten Gyaltshen. He is said to have been born in Bumthang and he extracted a treasure text known as the *Clear Mirror of Great Perfection* from the cliff in the Kurjey temple. We have already discussed the very little we know about his brief and mythical life. Yet, despite being an obscure figure, Ugyen Zangpo's importance in Bhutanese history cannot be underestimated. The whole story of the Bumthang King Sindharāja and Padmasambhava's visit to Bhutan from India, which are treated as established fact in all later history books, is based on his treasure text. It is the earliest local account explaining the significance of the important religious cave site of Kurjey.

However, the most eminent of treasure-discoverers born in the land which roughly constitutes the modern state of Bhutan is Pema Lingpa (1450–1521), Bhutan's foremost religious figure. For both his high religious stature in the Himalayan Buddhist world and the pervasive impact he left through his teachings and institutions, Pema Lingpa is arguably the most well-known and influential person produced by Bhutan in its entire history. Pema Lingpa's life and works continue to shape Bhutan's sociopolitical landscape and define the cultural identity of the Bhutanese people. His teachings spread across the Himalayas even in his own days and are studied and followed by people in many parts of the world today. In Bhutan itself, Pema Lingpa is now viewed as the spiritual father of the country and a cultural hero. It is, therefore, important that he is discussed in some detail and I partially reproduce here what was written as part of an introduction to his autobiography.[30]

Pema Lingpa's prominent stature as a spiritual figure was mainly due to his work as a *tertön* although he was also an artist, writer, teacher, traveller and a public figure. He was the fourth and the only Bhutanese among the five 'king *tertön*s' (གཏེར་སྟོན་རྒྱལ་པོ་ལྔ་), with a sizeable following of minor *tertön*s. Pema Lingpa was born above Chel village in Tang to Pema Drolma, who

Pema Lingpa (1450–1521), Bhutan's home-grown saint and cultural hero

was a cowherder. His father, Dhondup Zangpo, was a son of the Somthrang *chöje* family, which we have discussed earlier. A year after his birth, his mother gave birth to a younger brother and he was taken under the care of his grandfather, who ran a smithy in Mani Gönpa. Pema Lingpa was very bright but a difficult, wilful and frivolous boy with a sturdy, average physique and a number of uncomplimentary nicknames. During his youth, he learnt smithery, sewing, masonry and carpentry under his grandfather and received no formal religious training. His aptitude for self-learning is perhaps one of his most outstanding qualities, which he asserts with pride. His followers attribute this to the spiritual and intellectual achievements in his previous rebirths, particularly the immediate one as the great philosopher-saint, Longchenpa.

Pema Lingpa discovered his first treasure, the text entitled *The Quintessence of the Secrets of Clear Expanse* (ཀློང་གསལ་གསང་བ་སྙིང་བཅུད་), in a state of trance, from the riverine pool below the cliff of Naringdra on a full-moon night in 1476. This was followed by a public exposition of the text and performance of rituals, for which he also received instructions in a dream from Yeshe Tshogyal (consort of Padmasambhava), on the manner of chanting and the ritual dance. His second act of treasure extraction also took place at the same riverine pool in the presence of a large crowd, partly in order to establish the authenticity of his first discovery. In a spectacular act witnessed by a huge crowd, Pema Lingpa plunged into the deep pool with a butter lamp in his hand, swearing the oath: 'If I am an emanation of a devil, may I die in this river. If I am the heart-son of Guru [Padmasambhava], may I return with the required treasure and not even this lamp be extinguished.'[31] He emerged from the pool with a statue of the Buddha and a sealed skull, the lamp purportedly still burning. It is for this feat of extracting treasure in public (ཐོབ་གཏེར་), to convince the crowd, that Pema Lingpa is best remembered by posterity and the riverine pool perhaps got its name Mebartsho or the Burning Lake (མེ་འབར་མཚོ་).

These acts of treasure discovery near his birthplace initiated for Pema Lingpa a life of pursuing religious treasures, which were first concentrated in his local area but gradually extended to places beyond his native country of Bumthang. He traversed the region which is now Bumthang and Kurtoe in earnest quests for treasures he was destined to reveal, according to the list of treasure locations (གཏེར་བྱང་) he had received. A significant number of his later discoveries were also made in Lhodrak, which today forms part of the southern border region of the Tibet Autonomous Region (TAR). The culmination to his treasure discovery, however, took place in Samye, the epicentre of the early Buddhist propagation in the days of Padmasambhava, in 1487. It was at Samye, according to Pema Lingpa's own accounts, that he was ordained to be a treasure-discoverer by Padmasambhava when Pema Lingpa was born as Princess Pema Sel in the eighth-century court of Tri Songdetsen.

Much of Pema Lingpa's time from his first discovery at Naringdra in 1476 to his last discovery at Samye in 1513 was occupied by revealing treasures, performing placatory rites for the treasure guardians (གཏེར་བདག་) or spirits who guard the treasures, transcribing the symbolic *dākinī script* (མཁའ་འགྲོའི་ བརྡ་ཡིག་) of the yellow papers into a standard Tibetan script, and delivering religious sermons on his revelations. The treasure discoveries became less frequent in the latter part of his life, much of which he spent travelling to meet his patrons and students and propagating his treasure teachings. Pema Lingpa's discoveries generally belong to the class of earth treasures (ས་གཏེར་), that is, treasure buried in and rediscovered from the physical world, such as a cliff, temple or lake. His treasures mainly consist of cycles of religious rituals and meditation instructions, which traditionally fall under the category of religious treasures (ཆོས་གཏེར་). Beside the religious teachings, which form the main bulk of his treasures, he also revealed objects (རྫས་གཏེར་) such as the Buddha statue and the skull he extracted from Naringdra during his second hunt. One finds today in many places in Bhutan a great number of statues and other religious artefacts which are deemed to be hidden treasures discovered by Pema Lingpa. Many of Pema Lingpa's revelations also fall within the class of pure visions (དག་སྣང་) and mind treasures (དགོངས་གཏེར་). These latter categories are spontaneous and dynamic projections and expressions of the enlightened mind. Pema Lingpa's visionary revelations consist mostly of experiences occurring in the state of dreams and trances. His life as a treasure-discoverer was interspersed with such episodes of mystical visions, dreams and trances. In addition to his revealed teachings, Pema Lingpa also composed a number of biographical and exegetical works for which he claimed personal authorship. His teachings, including both his revelations and writings, currently make up the twenty-one volumes of the Pema Lingpa cycle of teachings (པདྨ་གླིང་ཆོས་སྐོར་) but it is expected this will increase significantly when the project to update this corpus under the present author is completed.

His quest for new treasures and mission to promote those he already discovered took Pema Lingpa on long and frequent journeys. His autobiography, which records his travels and activities, is in effect a travelogue and shows us that he was an enthusiastic public figure, a charismatic leader and a caring spiritual guide for his followers. During his travels, he met his patrons and disciples, who held him in high esteem, to bestow blessings on them, to impart teachings and to perform religious rituals. Such events ranged from sessions with a single individual to a public sermon attended by huge crowds. There is no doubt that Pema Lingpa in his final years was one of the most respected and prestigious lamas in 'proto-Bhutan' and southern Tibet. His lay supporters included the chieftain of Ura, Dung Lhawang, the regents of Chokhor, Thubpa Tashi and Chokyi Tashi and Jowo Namgyal Rabten (perhaps the chieftain of Ura after Dung Lhawang).

In Tibet, Pema Lingpa enjoyed the strong patronage of the prefects (དཔོན) of Lhalung, Sonam Gyalpo and Gyalwa Dhondup. It was to visit them that Pema Lingpa made most of his two dozen journeys northward. Pema Lingpa was also received by other prominent families of southern Tibet, including the Depa Yargyabpa family, the Depa Kyidshodpa, the Ngakartsepa and Taglung Nangso, during his travels. Other eminent supporters and disciples of Pema Lingpa included Tashi Dargye, myriarch of the Ja clan in southeast Tibet, and Dakchen Dondrup Phakpa, hereditary governor of Gyantse. Pema Lingpa was also invited and attended by King Jophak Darma of Shar Dongkha, in today's Arunachal Pradesh. He became a faithful follower and it was at his court that Pema Lingpa met an exiled Indian prince, who Aris has identified to be Nilāmbar, the last ruler of Kāmatā before its conquest by the nawab of Bengal.[32]

Just like the speedy rise in Pema Lingpa's physical mobility which took him out of his quiet village to many distant lands as an itinerant religious teacher, there was an ascending change in his social mobility. Within a few years of his treasure discovery, Pema Lingpa had already established himself as a respected lama with a large following. In the accounts of his early travels, we can see Pema Lingpa make a lot of effort to reach people, especially the important ones, and also notice him being very conscious of his status, recording even the number of layers of mats stacked for his seats. Such tendencies, however, diminished in the later years, perhaps as a consequence of age, spiritual maturity and growing fatigue of attention. Towards the end of his career, he wilfully declined invitations from several important families in Tibet and instead of going to see his disciples, he would summon them to a place of his convenience. We can see this shift especially in his relationship with the prefect of Lhodrak and King Darma of Monyul. In the years before Pema Lingpa's death, he made these two statesmen travel long distances to meet him.

This social ascent in Pema Lingpa's life reached its zenith in the last few years of his life, when grand receptions were arranged for his visits and thousands of devotees flocked to him to receive his blessing. During his last trip to Tibet, 9000 people are reported to have attended a ceremony which he conducted in Ney. On two occasions, he was put on elevated thrones under which people filed through to receive his blessing. A hilarious anecdote which demonstrates both his popularity as a high spiritual master and the odd character of Tibetan spirituality is the passing record Pema Lingpa made about an invitation he received from Nedong, the house of the Phagmodru rulers of Tibet. The Phagmodrupas had by then lost their control over Tibet but were nonetheless a very important family. Pema Lingpa politely declined the invitation saying that his friends from Mon wanted to hastily return to Bhutan. Perhaps this was an ostensible reason to avoid any misunderstanding with Depa Yargyabpa, who sacked the Phagmodrupas from Lhundrupling and whose hospitality and support Pema Lingpa enjoyed in that establishment. Unable to see the lama himself, the Nedong ruler sent a special silverware asking Pema Lingpa for his faeces as a blessing. Pema Lingpa was most obliged.

Pema Lingpa's religious tours to Tibet and other places also without doubt contributed a great deal to the local economy. His autobiography provides lists of the various gifts offered to him after his religious sessions, thereby giving us a good insight into the economy, gift culture and religious piety of the people in his days. For instance, it is interesting to see how the ironware known as *tro* (ཙྲོ), which is no longer produced and indeed is a rare antique today, was in great currency. Pema Lingpa received eighteen of these as an offering at the end of one sermon. The total he collected in the course of his travels is easily in the excess of a hundred, according to the list in his biography. While returning from Tibet in 1483, he mentions bringing with him forty horse-loads (རྟ་ཁལ་) of gifts from Tibet. We can guess that this increased in size and value in subsequent years as he became more and more popular and met more important people. Pema Lingpa was the first and perhaps the only Bhutanese figure, who effectively reversed the flow of religious offerings from Bhutan to Tibet.

Pema Lingpa's autobiography gives a very clear picture of his religious stature and also his social and political position but there are only sparse hints of the general sociopolitical set-up of the region in his days. Pema Lingpa's native land of Bumthang and the other valleys, which are referred to as Mon, were certainly perceived as a very different country from Tibet. Except for

Gyalwa Dhondup's remark at the end of the biography, which suggests that the Chokhor chieftain was paying some kind of tax to the *nangso* of Lhalung, there is no mention of any Tibetan political influence on the Bhutanese valleys. On the other hand, the biography mentions wars and disputes among the various Bhutanese rulers and Pema Lingpa, as an influential figure, was frequently involved as a mediator in such disputes and conflicts.

Pema Lingpa also encountered important religious characters of his time, including the 7th Black Hat Karmapa Chödrak Gyatsho, and the 4th Red Hat Zhamarpa Chökyi Drakpa, both powerful and popular churchmen of Tibet. Tshultrim Paljor, the abbot of Ney, was one of his strong religious supporters, as was Karpo Kuenga Drakpa of Kongpo. Pema Lingpa also enjoyed cordial relations with Drukpa Kunley, whom he probably met several times although the biography only mentions twice. Stories of their brief encounters reveal their shared spiritual sophistication and maverick characters. In addition to the above persons, his autobiography also mentions, in a long appended list, a wide range of religious leaders and lamas, who came to receive religious teachings from him from all parts of the Buddhist Himalayas. Many, such as Tertön Jangchub Lingpa, Lethro Lingpa, Jetsun Dechen Karmo and Chogden Gönpo, the incarnation of Dorji Lingpa, also became close disciples of Pema Lingpa.

Despite his prestige and popularity, Pema Lingpa's high religious profile and treasure discoveries did not go unquestioned. Both of his staunch patrons in Bhutan and Tibet, the Chökhor Deb and the Lhalung Nangso were said to have begun as doubters. A serious dissenter and rival was a certain Namkha Samdrub of Nyemo in Tibet. The lama arrived in Pemaling to request teachings from Pema Lingpa but, for a bad start, he mistook a dumb attendant for Pema Lingpa and made prostrations to the attendant. When that was rectified, he requested teachings in an offhand manner: 'I myself have dharma. If you impart your teachings, I will receive them. If you don't, perhaps you don't have anything more than what I have.'[33] The lama stayed for three years, only to leave in an outrage at having been asked if he had found the missing pages of the yellow papers on which Pema Lingpa was then working. He went to Kurelung and Kharchu, spreading malicious gossip about Pema Lingpa.

The full conflict between Pema Lingpa and Namkha Samdrub, however, unfolded when Pema Lingpa was invited to teach by some ladies of Zhamling in Kurelung in around 1484. Namkha Samdrub interfered, demanding that equal thrones be installed for both of them and that people receive teachings from both of them in turns. When no such arrangements were forthcoming from Pema Lingpa and the locals, he challenged Pema Lingpa to a debate and harassed his party. After unsuccessful attempts on the part of Pema Lingpa and his hosts to resolve the issue amicably, he challenged Namkha Samdrub to an ordeal by fire, where both of them would leap into the flames. Unable to face the challenge, Namkha Samdrub fled to Tibet the next day and, according to Pema Lingpa's accounts, soon succumbed to a terrible leprosy. Pema Lingpa also faced challenges from other persons, including ordinary people. When he extracted treasure from Nai in the Kurelung region, the people of Nai attacked his group for taking away the spiritual wealth of their land.[34] Similarly in 1490, when he had already become a well-known figure as a treasure-discover, the people of Chokhor accused him of duly extracting a turquoise from the Vairocana statue in Chokhor Lhakhang which he renovated in 1479 and 1480. Pema Lingpa had to go to the temple and take an oath that he did not take the turquoise.

Pema Lingpa's religious and social life as an acclaimed treasure-discoverer and influential high priest was no doubt rich, active and intriguing. It is also the facet of his life that is well documented. On the other hand, we have sparse information on his personal and family life. What we can glean from his autobiography and other sources seems to suggest a varied and complex love life. His first marriage to the daughter of the Lama of Rimochen neither lasted long nor produced any heir. But, according the genealogist Lama Sa-ngag, in the latter half of his life, Pema Lingpa went on to beget six sons and a daughter from his three wives.[35] We know from this biography that he had two wives at the time of his death and he was having a sexual relationship with a third woman before that. Among his sons, the biography attests Köncho Zangpo, Dawa Gyaltsen, Drakpa Gyalpo, Kuenga Wangpo and Sangdag, the last one perhaps born in 1509. The biography also mentions a sister (ཨ་ཅེ) in Pema Lingpa's admonition to Drakpa Gyalpo from his death bed but it is unclear whether this refers to Drakpa Gyalpo's sister, his sister-in-law or Pema Lingpa's sister.

It is generally clear that Pema Lingpa's love life extended beyond the nuptial bonds. Compounded with the belief that female consorts are expedient for esoteric Buddhist practice and that *tertön*s may have to rely on destined consorts for their successful discovery of treasures, Pema Lingpa, like many other *tertön*s and his later followers, seems to have enjoyed a lax sex life. A hint of this libertine attitude surfaces in an apologetic joke he tells his patron, Lhalung Nangso: 'The people of Lhodrak have no understanding, the people

of Mön have no vows [of chastity].'[36] Another example is the anecdote of
Pema Lingpa's first meeting with Karpo Kuenga Drakpa of Kongpo who
was a master of magic. Upon being told by Kuenga Drakpa that he is good at
black magic, Pema Lingpa says: 'Is black magic what makes a good Kongpo
lama?' To this Kuenga Drakpa retorted: 'Is having a wife what makes a good
Monpa lama?' It is not surprising that Pema Lingpa as a treasure-discoverer
in the Nyingma tradition may have been frivolous in his sexual relationships.
However, it is ironical and surprising that such a relationship with 'an
incarnation of a demoness', in fact the cousin of his wife Bumdren, became
allegedly the cause of Pema Lingpa's final illness and death.[37]

On the third day of the first month, Iron Snake year, 1521, Pema Lingpa
passed away at his seat of Tamshing, in the posture of meditation, with his
hands resting on his sons, Dawa and Drakgyal. He had gathered his family
and patrons and delivered instructions as to how they should live and carry
on their religious and worldly pursuits in his absence. It is in his last words
that we also find a curious remark that he will not be born again but live in
the celestial realms of enlightened beings. This has certainly stimulated some
thoughts and hermeneutics in the times of his incarnations. Gyalwa Dhondup
tells us how, despite his failing health and a wailing family, Pema Lingpa
faced death with full control and composure in an undisturbed meditative
state. In the end, his was a great Buddhist death, accompanied by many
positive signs, like his birth.

If Pema Lingpa can be said to have lived a successful life and died an
exemplary death, the traditions and legacies that ensued from him have
certainly secured him a distinguished place in Himalayan Buddhist history.
Not only was he respected in his lifetime, but Pema Lingpa's reputation and
religious influence kept increasing in the centuries after him. His teachings and
rituals, which had spread widely in his own days, were studied and practised
in many monasteries across the Himalayas in the subsequent centuries. The
Lhalung temple—founded by Karmapa Dusum Khyenpa (1110–93), and seat
of the hereditary prefects and administrative headquarters of the Lhodrak
region—later became the main base for his tradition in Tibet and even the
subsequent incarnations of Pema Lingpa came to be known as Lhalung
Sungtrul, the speech incarnations of Lhalung. Today, there are several religious
centres focusing on Pema Lingpa's teachings even in Europe and America.

In Bhutan, Pema Lingpa remained an outstanding home-grown figure
and a religious hierarch unparalleled for his influence in the country. He
became, to use his own metaphors, 'the pillar of the house and the handle

of the parasol'[38] for his own tradition and community, through his teachings, works of art, establishments, institutions and family lines. The teachings and rituals originating in Pema Lingpa form the main religious texts for rituals and practices in numerous monasteries. His tradition flourished concurrently with the vigorous expansion of Drukpa Kagyu, which took place under Zhabdrung Ngawang Namgyal (1594–1651) in the seventeenth century. While almost all non-Drukpa schools were disbanded or eliminated during the unification of Bhutan, Pema Lingpa's tradition thrived with support from the new power in Punakha and his religous rituals were incorporated into the ritual cycle of the State Monk Body.

Beside his literary legacy, Pema Lingpa also composed and taught religious arts, including dances, hymns and fine arts. The sacred dances, known as *peling tercham* (པད་གླིང་གཏེར་འཆམ་) are performed throughout Bhutan during festivals and ceremonial occasions. The most popular ones are the *ḍākiṇi* dance mentioned above, the three *ging* dances (པད་གླིང་གི་ང་གསུམ་) signifying the identification and subjugation of evil and the subsequent celebration, and the *ging* and *tsholing* (གིང་ཚོགས་ལིང་) dance. Pema Lingpa is also proudly remembered for his metalwork, which is viewed with deep religious awe. Flat-iron plates (གོ་སྲང་) for making buckwheat pancakes are still used in Bhutanese homes with the belief that all those eating the pancakes will escape rebirths in the lower realms. The plates and long swords attributed to Pema Lingpa, called *Bumthang tsendri* (བུམ་ཐང་བཙན་དྲི་) are believed to bear his thumbprint as a trademark and are treasured as priceless heirlooms. These artefacts, and the ones he revealed as hidden treasures, constitute the sacred spiritual relics and rare cultural items of Bhutan.

The most salient legacies of Pema Lingpa, however, are the numerous establishments and institutions founded by him and his spiritual and physical descendents. These establishments and institutions which rose from him had major ramifications for the religious and social structure of Bhutanese society. Pema Lingpa spent most of the gifts and alms he received on the construction and renovation of religious centres, sites and objects in central and eastern Bhutan. Among them, the first temple he built was Pemaling in his native village, but the most important and grandest is perhaps the Tamshing monastery, his main seat in Bumthang, finished in 1505. He also renovated numerous sites and objects, including his grandfather's temple at Mani Gönpa, Chel Lhakhang, Chokhor Lhakhang and Langmathil Lhakhang in Bumthang. He also built a number of *stūpas* in the Kurelung and Mangde districts. After him, his sons and disciples went on to found many other monasteries and temples. These establishments served as the centres of Pema Lingpa's tradition and became premier Buddhist institutions in Bhutan and southern Tibet.

In conjunction with the physical establishments were the three socioreligious institutions that have sprung from Pema Lingpa: the family line, the reincarnation line and the transmission/disciple line. These three lineages mostly owned or ran the centres and establishments. Pema Lingpa's family, since his time, emerged as a leading class of religious aristocrats and gave rise to the largest network of religious nobilities in Bhutan, many of whom intermarried with the existent religious *chöje* and secular *dung, khoche* and *pönche* elites. The Tamshing *chöje* family in his main seat in Bumthang began with his son Drakpa Gyalpo but he appears to have died without leaving an heir and the family line continued through Pema Lingpa's youngest son Sangda. Sangda's descendents branched off to start the *chöje* families in Tsakaling, Drophu, Drametse and Yagang in Mongar. Pema Lingpa's son Dawa Gyaltshen started the Prakhar *zhalngo* family in Chumey while Kuenga Wangpo started the Khochung and Bidung *chöje* families, the first of which branched off to Kheri and Dungkar. Based on their religious authority and holy ancestry, these *chöje* families and their agnates became leading households in their areas and enjoyed a great deal of power and privileges. At the beginning of the twentieth century, the Dungkar *chöje* family took the political status of Pema Lingpa's descendents to a new level when one of its charismatic scions became the first King of Bhutan. Today, it is this ancestral connection to Pema Lingpa which some royal historians use to construct a divine origin and legitimacy for Bhutan's monarchy.

While his descendents only gradually rose to positions of power, Pema Lingpa's incarnations and the incarnations of his son, Dawa Gyaltshen, and grandson, Pema Thinley, had great influence over the pious Bhutanese people throughout the centuries through their religious stature. These three incarnation lines, who were often known as the father–son trio (པ་སྲས་ཡབ་ སྲས་གསུམ་), made up the supreme hierarchs of Pema Lingpa's tradition and carried on his spiritual legacies. His incarnation, the Lhalung Sungtrul, is in its eleventh reincarnation, and those of his son, Thugse Dawa Gyaltshen, and grandson, Gyalse Pema Thinley (1564–1642), are in their tenth and ninth respectively. These incarnations originating in Pema Lingpa also led to an extraordinary religiopolitical relationship with southern Tibet. Building on the support Pema Lingpa enjoyed from local Tibetan leaders, the main centre for Pema Lingpa's tradition was established in Lhalung in Tibet as mentioned above. His successive incarnations and those of his son Dawa Gyaltshen based themselves in Lhalung and had an interesting and mutually useful relationship with the descendents and followers of Pema Lingpa across the border in Bhutan.

The religious teachings, rituals, arts, establishments and the sociopolitical institutions which originated in Pema Lingpa today form part of the core of Bhutan's mainstream culture and artistic tradition. While many of Bhutan's cultural expressions are derived from Pema Lingpa, many later developments were inspired by his works. The spirit of Pema Lingpa today permeates many aspects of Bhutan's religious, cultural, social and political spheres. Thus, it is no surprise that many Bhutanese see Pema Lingpa as a spiritual father and a cultural hero. He was undoubtedly the first and foremost Bhutanese person to gain the stature of a high lama in the entire Buddhist Himalayas stretching from Amdo to Ladakh. While the lines of the family and reincarnation have remained concentrated in the region that one can call Pema Lingpa's world, the transmission of his teachings has spread far and wide today, making the Pema Lingpa tradition more dynamic and widespread, and the master himself ever more famous.

Pema Lingpa certainly took the Nyingma tradition in Bhutan to a new level of prominence and popularity. He was the only figure to leave behind an endogenous spiritual tradition, which became important within Bhutan and was also followed by many people in other parts of the Himalayan Buddhist world. In the centuries after him, his disciples and descendents, who spread his teachings and rituals, made up most of the important Nyingma masters in Bhutan. Bhutanese *tertön*s and Nyingma masters after Pema Lingpa included his own sons. Among them, his chief spiritual heir, Dawa Gyaltshen (1499–1592?), enjoyed enormous popularity among religious and political leaders of his day. Although his religious stature was partly due to his great father, Dawa Gyaltshen was a *tertön* in his own right. He discovered treasures from the same area in Naringdrak and Lhodrak Mendo, from where Pema Lingpa extracted treasures some decades earlier. Among his treasures were a special ritual and substances for the repulsion of a Mongol invasion and interference, a problem which had plagued Tibet since the days of Chenghis Khan. Dawa Gyaltshen was vigorously sought by the Tibetan rulers for this ritual and he made most of his journey northward in order to perform these rituals. He also toured the area of modern Bhutan in order to visit his and his father's patrons and disciples with his base in Prakhar in Chumey, where he left behind a religious family line.

Pema Lingpa's son, Drakpa Gyalpo, inherited the establishment of Tamshing from his father but perhaps did not gain as high a religious stature as his brother Dawa Gyaltshen did. Nevertheless, he was active as a religious figure throughout his life. We know nothing about the religious positions and activities of Köncho Zangpo and Sandag but Kuenga Wangpo, the son who settled in the district of Kurtoe, appears to have had a rich spiritual life. We have today a collection of his spiritual hymns and accounts of visionary experiences. The choreography and customs of the famous Drametse Ngacham (དྲ་མེ་རྩེ་ང་འཆམ་) or drum dance of Drametse, which is performed all over Bhutan now, is commonly said to have been introduced by him after he saw it being performed in the heaven of Padmasambhava in one of his visionary experiences.

The Nyingma school and the associated treasure culture was not only prevalent in central and eastern Bhutan as we may assume today; it was also thriving in Paro and other western valleys around the time of Pema Lingpa and his sons. The Kathogpa lamas, as we shall see later, were active in the Taktshang complex and many of Pema Lingpa's disciples were also prominent religious figures in the region. Among them, Drubwang Rinchen Chödor was a great meditation master who combined Nyingma and Kagyu teachings and attracted a great number of students to his rigorous training in meditation. He held these trainings and retreats in his seats of Medri, Dongkarla and Bodmori, all three of them in the lower Paro valley. Rinchen Chödor is known to us through his two prominent students, who were *tertön*s and followers of Pema Lingpa's teachings.

Tertön Tshering Dorji was from lower Paro and grew up as an ill-tempered and unruly young man, who was often up to a lot of mischief. Even his parents disliked him. When he was sent herding animals, many of the animals had their limbs and horns broken due to his terrible temper. No herder would want to be in his company. He went hunting, fishing and also 'maruading if he managed, and stealing if he didn't', according to his autobiography. On one occasion, he and two of his friends stole a cow and slaughtered it for meat but as they opened the carcass, he found the calf which was about to be born. This sight, which moved him to tears, along with the sudden death of his mother soon after while her loved ones were away, and some religious experiences that had turned his mind to religion. Tshering Dorji excelled at meditation and religious practice under Drubwang Rinchen Chödor and was appointed as the tantric master for the Medri centre by Thugse Dawa Gyaltshen and Rinchen Chödor. In fact, his autobiography claims that he was the rebirth of Princess Saley Ödron, the daughter of King Tri Songdetsen from his queen from Paro called Menday Zangmo. We have no other sources to corroborate the existence of a Bhutanese queen of Tri Songdetsen but the account effectively connects Tshering Dorji to Padmasambhava and his career as a *tertön,* which was soon to unfold.

After this appointment, he took the initiative to establish the temple in Dongkarla and move the meditation centre from Medri to the new temple. This would become his primary seat. Following the prophetic instructions and vision, he made a few journeys to Sikkim and Tibet and also revealed treasures from a number of places in Tibet. His *chiti* (ཤྲི་ཏི) cycle of Dzogchen teachings was rediscovered from Drakmar near Gyantse. Unlike his teacher, Dawa Gyaltshen, whose tradition he followed ardently, he did not enjoy a great reception from Tibetan leaders although individual devotees offered hospitality on his trips to Tibet. His religious stature in Paro and the adjacent areas was, however, well established and he presided over many public rituals and had many local chieftains as his patrons.

This was also the case with his junior colleague, Ngawang Drakpa. However, unlike Tshering Dorji, Ngawang Drakpa was born in the well-respected family of lamas of Kunzangling in Shar, where the great scholar–saint Longchenpa established one of his spiritual sanctuaries. Ngawang Drakpa was inclined to religion from his early youth and he left home to train under Drubwang Rinchen Chödor in Paro. Soon after his arrival, his master started the hermitage of Bodmori, where Ngawang Drakpa would go through most of his meditation and spiritual training. Like Tshering Dorji, he also sailed through the stages of meditation and was soon made to teach other students who flocked to his master. In his autobiography, Ngawang Drakpa claimed to be the incarnation of the monk-scholar Yesheyang at the time of Padmasambhava's mission in Tibet. He was considered to be a destined *tertön* and received several scrolls which guided him to the treasures. Ngawang Drakpa's treasure discovery took place mostly in his locality of Paro except for one instance of discovery in southern Tibet. He extracted treasures from the Kyerchu, Chumuphu and Taktshang sites.

Both Tshering Dorji and Ngawang Drakpa were closely connected to their master, Drubwang Rinchen Chödor, who held both of them with affection and respect. They were also closely connected to the sons of Pema Lingpa, particularly to Thugse Dawa Gyaltshen whom they visited in Bumthang and also invited to Paro many times. They shared connections to the Tibetan *tertön* Tenyi Lingpa and the monk-abbot Lodoe Rabyang, two well-known contemporary masters across the border in southern Tibet. Both these *tertöns* had the support of many of the local chieftains in the Paro and Wang (Thimphu) valleys, who often sponsored the grand rituals of making sacred pills known as *kedun rildrub* (སྐྱེ་བདུན་རིལ་སྒྲུབ་) and the recitation of the mantra *oṃ maṇi padme huṃ* ten billion times (ལ་ཆེ་དུང་སྒྲུབ་). The valleys of Paro and Thimphu, from the sparse information we can glean from their biographies, were regularly rocked by internal feuds among the *chipön*s and *chukpo*s. During one such conflict, even the Bodmori religious centre and Ngawang Drakpa were attacked by the men of a chieftain called Drakwang. His disciples, however, punished Drakwang using their occult powers. The institutions started by Drubwang Rinchen Chödor and his two *tertön* disciples continue to this day.

Another figure who was also a treasure-discoverer although not many Bhutanese remember him as one is Zhanda Gyaltshen from the family of Hungral Drungdrung. According the genealogical accounts of the Hungral Drungdrung family, he discovered two turquoises as sacred treasures from Mebartsho, the deep river pool from where Pema Lingpa discovered his first treasure.[39] Similarly, Yongdrak Gyatsho of Dolpo Shaladrak is said to have jumped into a lake with a burning butterlamp and come out with a treasure and the lamp still burning.[40] There are also many other figures who are not generally thought of as treasure-discoverers but who were involved in supernatural experiences such as visions and extemporary revelations, which are often associated with treasure-discoverers. We have already seen how Pema Lingpa's son Kuenga Wangpo had a vision through which he received the choreography for the famous drum dance of Drametse. Jamyang Drakpa Özer (1382–1442) of Somthrang also composed the the unique horse dance of Draktsen performed in Somthrang village in Ura after such a vision.[41] This master, who lived in the fourteenth century about a generation before Pema Lingpa, also had a large following in central Bhutan. It was in his time that the Somthrang *chöje* family gained great popularity and reached the height of its influence in Bhutan. Among more recent Bhutanese figures, the late Je Khenpo Gedun Rinchen (1926–97) can be considered a modern treasure-discoverer for his visionary revelation of a ritual pertaining to Zhabdrung Ngawang Namgyal.

The treasure culture slowed down after the unification of Bhutan as a nation. Although the unification cannot be the main cause, it is possible that the political changes contributed to this decline. It is arguable that the country, which then came to be regulated by a centralized authority, was no more seen as a conducive area for free-spirited treasure-discoverers to conduct their treasure hunts. A more compelling explanation, however, is perhaps to be found in the general trend of religious activities in the region, including the neighbouring regions of Tibet. In the last half of the second millennium, the focus of activity of treasure discovery generally shifted from central and southern Tibet to the eastern Tibetan regions of Kham and Amdo. It is difficult to provide convincing socioreligious reasons for this shift here without digressing from the main story. We can perhaps simply use the analogy of geographic explorers. As explorers, including botanists and zoologists, move on to uncharted territory once a place is unravelled and all its secrets discovered, the southern valleys perhaps ran out of fashion and the new uncharted world of Kham and Amdo appealed to the treasure-discoverers. There is no doubt that the rise of the Nyingma tradition, which took place through the influence of the great master, Jigme Lingpa, in the eighteenth century, also had a part to play. This Nyingma renaissance initiated by him took place through his disciples mainly in the Kham region, turning Kham into a fertile ground for the proliferation of the treasure culture. We must remember that the treasure culture was mainly a Nyingma enterprise although members of other schools did take part in it.

Interestingly, the mode of treasure discovery also saw a slight shift from what were earlier largely discoveries of *sater* (ས་གཏེར་) or earth treasures buried in physical space to revelations of *gongter* (དགོངས་གཏེར་), or mind treasures, and *dagnang* (དག་སྣང་), or pure visions. This makes our analogy of explorers even more compelling. Perhaps, with fewer external treasures or clues for them left, it was only practical for treasure-discoverers to turn to the internal human psyche or mind, which is after all, an inexhaustible treasury of Buddha's wisdom and skilful means if one knew how to unlock it. Even the hidden valleys and power spots, with which the discovery of earth treasures were connected formerly, were to become mere catalysts and conditions which could inspire or provoke spiritual realization. Such spiritual experience would then lead to the revelation of treasures in the form of extemporary compositions or extraordinary visions. Thus, most of the modern Tibetan treasure-discoverers such as Dudjom Rinpoche, Jigme Phuntsho, Dilgo Khyentse and Chogyam Trungpa, who visited Bhutan, were known to have mainly discovered their mind treasures.

Lhomon Kathogpa

The Kathogpa represent the other mainstream group under the Nyingma school, which is distinct from the treasure-discoverers we have discussed above. They come from a strong institutional base carrying on the tradition of *kama* (བཀའ་རྫས་) or transmitted teachings rather than promoting new revelations. The monastery of Kathog was established in 1159 in Kham by Dampa Desheg (1122–92) and became the first of the six great monasteries of the Nyingma school in Tibet. It is situated in the far eastern part of Tibet and was once a great centre for the study and tradition of the transmitted teachings before the treasure culture grew popular and overshadowed the transmitted teachings, particularly in the case of rituals and practice. One abbot of the Kathog monastery, Zhagla Yeshe Bumpa,[42] came to Bhutan and Sikkim towards the end of the fifteenth century to spread the Kathogpa tradition in Bhutan. Although not known as a treasure-discoverer, this hierarch followed the trend promoted by the treasure culture and left his monastery in eastern Tibet on a quest to open the hidden valley of Dremojong or Sikkim. He was followed by his nephew and another master of the Kathog monastery, Sonam Gyaltshen (1466–1540) in 1493.

It was while Sonam Gyaltshen was in Sikkim carrying out the funerary ceremony for Zhagla Yeshe Bumpa that the former received a request to come to Paro from Lama Ngangju Gyalpo. Sonam Gyaltshen toured the western valleys of Bhutan and, in 1508, following the wishes of his uncle and the requests made by the local deities in his dream, he established the centre of Ogyen Tsemo on the hilltop overlooking Taktshang. When he was hindered by the lack of stone for construction and the need to carry water uphill, he had dreams showing where to find them in the proximity. The temple became the centre of Kathogpa activity and Sonam Gyaltshen gained the status of a leading religious figure in the country. As the followers of the Kathogpa tradition increased, the tradition even acquired a separate name, Lhomon Kathogpa. Centres were also established in other areas, particularly in the Shar and Khothang regions. Sonam Gyaltshen visited these areas about seven times and gave teachings, particularly in Longchenpa's centre of Kunzangling. He made one trip to Bumthang and gave teachings in Ura Tangsibi but regretted not being able to effectively link with Pema Lingpa.

Descendents of the Kathogpa lamas also gave rise to a local *chöje* line in Dolpo Shaladrak in Paro with some social standing in western Bhutan. Like the line in Ralung, this one also had a mixture of hereditary family lines interspersed with incarnations. One of their eminent members is Yongdrak Gyatsho, who we discussed above briefly. He is said to have discovered a treasure in Drakye Phangtsho Lake and emerged out of it carrying a butter lamp burning in the fashion of the great Pema Lingpa. The Lhomon Kathogpa school controlled the famous hermitage of Taktshang until it was taken over by Zhabdrung Ngawang Namgyal in the seventeenth century. Their presence and influence declined after the Drukpa school came to power in the seventeenth century.

Chagzampa tradition

To return to the proliferation of religious schools, a figure who was both a treasure-discoverer and a founder of a religious tradition well known in Bhutanese history is Thangtong Gyalpo (1385−1464/85?). Thangtong Gyalpo was a true renaissance man and an unusual figure in the history of Tibetan Buddhism. He was a great spiritual adept, who is commonly described as a *drubthob* (གྲུབ་ཐོབ་) or a master who has reached great spiritual heights. For his maverick character and nonconformist practices, he was also known as a *myonpa* (སྨྱོན་པ་) or a madman, like the divine madman, Drukpa Kunley. Yet, like many other eminent religious persons of Tibet, he was a leading public figure revered by the highest rulers and churchmen of Tibet in his time. Thangtong Gyalpo also had a large following and founded many establishments and institutions. His religious role was very colourful and his interests very broad and eclectic. He was both a fully ordained monk and a non-institutional mystic, a promoter of the most basic Buddhist principles and a master of the most advanced and esoteric tantric practices. He followed teachers from many traditions and his own religious tradition turned out to be an eclectic synthesis of the Nyingma, Kagyu and Sakya traditions.

However, it is his engineering, architectural and artistic productions for which he is best remembered by the Tibetan people. Besides being a prominent religious master, he was also an exceptional artist, architect, engineer, blacksmith, physician and a profuse traveller. His architectural distinction is seen in the temples he built in the shape of a *stūpa*. The Dumtse *stūpa* temple, which he built at the end of the ridge line between the main Paro valley and Dolpo Shari in order to subdue the spirit associated with the ridge, is an example of his architectural talent although it is quite likely he based his design on similar shrines in Jonang and Gyang Bumoche, with which he was familiar.

The most celebrated of his contributions is undoubtedly his work of bridge-building. Even in his own lifetime, he was given the name Chagzampa or the iron-bridge man. Thangtong Gyalpo is said to have built about fifty-eight iron chain-bridges and over 100 ferry crossings across the Himalayas to make people's travel for pilgrimage and trade easier and faster. His biography recounts that he, while an itinerant mendicant, was once kicked out of a boat while crossing the Kyichu river in Lhasa to make room for someone wealthy. This incident extremely saddened him and made him resolve to undertake the unprecedented project of building iron bridges to facilitate easy travel and pilgrimage. To him, bridge-building was not merely social work. It was a religious practice. He called his iron bridges 'the highway to enlightenment'. Even in iconographic representation, he is portrayed holding an iron chain for this contribution, which had the greatest socioeconomic impact. Tibetans also popularly believe that he set up an opera team of seven sisters to raise resources for the bridge-building project although his biographers are silent on this. Thus, he is also remembered as the father of the Tibetan opera tradition known as Ache Lhamo (ཨ་ལྕེ་ལྷ་མོ).

Whether or not he started the Tibetan opera, it was his quest for iron for his bridges which brought him to the southern land of Mon. Thangtong Gyalpo visited Bhutan at least three times. His first trip brought him to Paro via Phari in the Chumbi valley where he was invited, according to the Bhutanese biography,[43] by the guardian deities of Paro and Haa to visit the southern country of four approaches. In Paro, he extracted a ten-yard-long scroll from the Taktshang cave, where he was invited by five *ḍākinīs*, and founded the *stūpa* structure of Dumtse lhakhang. He then proceeded southward, having visions at Phurdo and spending three nights in Tachogang at the end of the Paro valley. According to a local legend, he gave three pills to a local lady in this place and sowed the seeds for his family line. His chief Bhutanese disciple and biographer, Monpa Dewa Zangpo, was from this place and considered to be his son. Dewa Zangpo gave rise to the *chöje* family of Tachogang, who claim to be his descendants. From here, he visited a rich family in Wang and also a lama named Gyaltshen. The rich man, Olag, offered him a turquoise to extract water for the village and at Lama Gyaltshen's place, he miraculously opened a rock and liberated a swarm of scorpions, who were rebirths of the ancestors of the lama trapped in the rock. Thangtong Gyalpo seems to have then gone southward along the Thimphu river and turned west to visit lower and upper Haa. He returned to Paro, where he left the iron he had collected from his rounds and continued further east to Thimphu and

Thed. He continued to the Shar district and met the contemporary incumbent at Kunzangling, one of the centres founded by Longchenpa. In many of the places he visited, he built religious monuments and iron-chain bridges. He gathered the blacksmiths of the region in Paro and prepared some 7000 iron chains from the iron he collected. When he left for Tibet, he had the Bhutanese deliver some 1400 loads of chains and iron rods and 700 loads of other goods to Phari, from where the ruler of Gyantse helped him carry them to Chuwori on the banks of Tsangpo river.

On his second trip, he came directly from Lhodrak to Bumthang and travelled through Bumthang, Mangde, Kheng and Tashigang. Although his biographers make no mention, local tradition holds that he left a physical heir named Gyalwa Zangpo in eastern Bhutan. The daughter of Somthrang Chöje, Drubthob Zangmo, who was also the aunt of Pema Lingpa is said to have been his consort and he is said to have lived in the village of Pangkhar in Ura. He made his third trip to Bhutan on his way to the Indian plains to visit one of the kings of Kāmatā. At the court of one Durug Naran, he is said to have encouraged the king to stop the practice of human- and animal-blood sacrifice and the Indian tradition of *sati*, the burning of widows with their husband's corpse. The account is too heavily laden with legendary stories to glean much about what may have really happened.

Thangtong Gyalpo lived an interesting and active life, travelling great distances, building bridges, religious monuments and producing artistic work wherever he went. According to the list provided by Dewa Zangpo, he is said to have created or commissioned hundreds of statues and religious artefacts, including huge bowls and butter-lamp chalices out of pure gold for use in the Jokhang chapel in Lhasa, ten sets of *kanjur* and thirteen sets of *tanjur* scriptures, in addition to the numerous iron-chain bridges, ferry crossings and temples. He also lived a very long life, perhaps from 1385 to 1485, although there is no consensus on how long he lived. He was also well known for his magical power to keep away the Mongolian invaders and it is to this effect that his death was concealed for over a dozen years.

His main centres were Chung Riwoche, where he built the grand *stūpa* temple, and Chagzam Chuwori, which was run with the toll collected from his longest iron-bridge over the Tsangpo in Chusul. Long before his death, he appointed Nima Zangpo, who was his heart son, as his spiritual successor in Tibet and this disciple continued Thangtong Gyalpo's work of bridge-building. In Bhutan, he is associated with a number of places including Tachogang, where the *chöje* family claiming descent from him is based.

Dewa Zangpo, who is believed by some to be a physical heir, was his closest Bhutanese disciple and appears also to be his main link between him and the Kāmatā king. Nothing is known about his son Gyalwa Zangpo, whose body is still preserved in Merak in eastern Bhutan. Thangtong Gyalpo is said to have built eight iron-chain bridges in Bhutan, of which the last one to survive was in Doksum in Tashi Yangtse. The bridge in Tachogang has recently been renovated using chains from various sources. Otherwise, his chains from his bridges remain largely scattered having been appropriated by people as a religious relic.

Thangtong Gyalpo's religious teachings have spread widely even in his own lifetime and are today carried on by masters in many traditions. His rituals for long life, in particular, gained much popularity. In Tibet, his eclectic religious tradition came to be known as Thanglug. It was also known as the Chagzampa school although this appellation seems to have gained more currency in Bhutan than in Tibet. The Chagzampa school gained a separate identity in Bhutan and thrived until the seventeenth century. It is often listed among the five infamous schools that opposed the rise of Zhabdrung Ngawang Namgyal in western Bhutan. The school suffered a serious setback for this opposition. Today, the tradition does not exist as a separate school but the teachings are taken up by various other traditions. The *chöje* family and followers of Chagzampa tradition continued through the centuries but with no significant roles. The foundation of a nunnery in Thimphu by Rikey Jadral, an incarnation of Thangtong Gyalpo, has recently rekindled the interest in this saint in Bhutan. At the turn of the twenty-first century, there were as many as three Bhutanese claimants to the throne of the ancient iron-bridge builder.

Nenyingpa

The Nenying tradition has an ancient beginning according to its religious histories.[44] It is located in the Nyangtö region, 15 km south of the Gyantse town in Tibet and is said to have been founded in the ninth century. We have already seen above how the tract of upper Tsang stretching as far south as Kyerchu Lhakhang in Paro was granted as an appanage by Tri Songdetsen to his minister from the Gö clan. The Nenying temple was established by one of the sons of the minister, Trizang Yablha of the Gö clan and his spiritual teacher Jampal Sangwa of the Gya clan and run by the families of the two clans. The historian John Ardussi presents a succinct account:

For two hundred years thereafter, Nenying was administered and supported by members of these two clans, the Gya descendents of Jampal Sangba serving as abbots and the Gö as their formal lay patrons. The monastery became a regional center of religious activity within the districts bordering western Bhutan. Over time, successive abbots expanded its reach through a growing network of subsidiary monasteries, including several in Paro valley. Nenying's early religious practices represented a mixture of Nyingma, Bön, and other traditions. But with the advent of the reformer Atisha to Tibet during the 11th century, his disciples from the local Yol clan of Nyang Tö were able to wrest control of Nenying and reorient it to the Kadampa sect, an affiliation that gradually strengthened at Nenying until its full absorption into the Gelugpa system during the 17th century.[45]

Like many establishments from the early part of the Later Diffusion, Nenying appears to have gone through many changes to its religious affiliation in tune with the changing Tibetan religious landscape. Its list of abbots included masters from the Kadam, Sakya and Kagyu schools but during the time of one Chime Rabgye, the monastery seems to have come into the fold of the new Gelugpa school. By the time it spread its influence to Bhutan, the Nenying monastery probably adopted a mixture of Tibetan Buddhist traditions. Ardussi, however, considers the Nenyingpa tradition a minor Kagyu sect,[46] perhaps based on Gedun Rinchen's report that the two masters of the Upper Drukpa school occupied the seat of Nenying.

The first spread of the influence from the Nenying monastery to Bhutan, if we are follow the history of the Nenying monastery, start with a certain Gönpo Dorji, who was sent with religious relics and prophecy by Rinchen Samten Palzang (1262–1311), an abbot of Nenying, to open the sacred space of Dzongdrakha.[47] Dzongdrakha, as Aris puts it, is a spectacular temple complex built on steep cliff 'second only to Taktshang for the beauty of its location and architecture'.[48] Gönpo Dorji arrived in Paro, opened the sacred spot of Dzongdrakha and discovered as treasure a crystal stūpa, which was enshrined in a larger stūpa. Gönpo Dorji settled here with people from the neighbourhood as his patrons thus establishing a link between Nenying monastery and Bhutan. A line from one of his incarnations is said to have started the *chöje* family of Dzongdrakha.

Gönpo Dorji was followed by series of Nenying lamas including the master who sent him southward, Rinchen Samten Palzang. A generation later, the son of this master, Jamyang Rinchen Gyaltshen (1304–62) sent one Rinchen Darpo with many gifts to Bhutan to set up as many centres as he could. Rinchen Darpo was followed by Rinchen Drubpa (1403–52) and Gyaltshen Rinchen (1405?–68?), both of whom had large followings in Bhutan.[49] They travelled through western Bhutan, extending the Nenying domain deeper into the Bhutanese valleys. Through generations, the Nenyingpas established a large number of centres and their expansion continued even after the Nenying monastery began to follow the new Gelug school in the fifteenth century. The reformed Nenying school spread in many parts of Bhutan until they were fully replaced by Drukpa Kagyu in the seventeenth century. The Nenying school, which is listed among the five lamaist factions who opposed Zhabdrung Ngawang Namgyal, would have been mainly the reformed Nenying school.

Barawa of Kagyu school

The Barawa school is an offshoot of the Drukpa Kagyu started by Barawa Gyaltshen Palzang (1310–91), who we discussed earlier. Gyaltshen Palzang got the title of Barawa after founding his monastery in Baradrak in Tibet. He was also known as Shang Barawa because he was from the Shang valley but this title should not be confused with the Shangpa Kagyu tradition, which is an independent school from the Marpa Kagyu schools we have discussed so far. Barawa was a student of Rinchen Palzang (b.1263) who followed the Upper Drukpa tradition of Götshang Gönpo Dorji (1189–1258). He also studied with many other great teachers of his time and became a very respected scholar. Gyaltshen Palzang was also recognized as the incarnation of Yangönpa Gyaltshen Pal (1213–58), the disciple of Gönpo Dorji and teacher of Gyaltshen Palzang's own teacher's teacher and the line of Barawa incarnations continued from him.

Like Longchenpa, Barawa came to Bhutan to escape from the political turmoil of Tibet. He sent a disciple named Tsariwa to find a place in the southern lands and this disciple talked a local chieftain named Lopen Kuenga in Paro into becoming a patron for Gyaltshen Palzang. Lopen Kuenga's family thus received Gyaltshen Palzang and introduced him to another chieftain named Sakhar Dorji. After a tour of Paro and a brief stay, he returned to Tibet, as insisted on by Tsariwa. However, conflicts soon broke out in his own area of Shang and he was inclined to accept the invitation of his patrons in Paro to return to the south. This time, another chieftain named Trogyal also joined Sakhar in supporting him. These chieftains are referred to with the title *lopen*

(སློབ་དཔོན་). They sent escorts to Phari to protect Gyaltshen Palzang on his way to Paro. In his second visit, his patrons offered him land and helped him build his seat of Drangyekha in Paro. This became his primary base from where he travelled across western Bhutan to give teachings, stay in retreats or perform religious services. On one such trip to perform the near-death and funerary rituals for a chieftain, he stopped the locals from a customary slaughter of animals after the death of an important person.

In his three years in Bhutan, Barawa is said to have acted as a mediator to resolve many conflicts including those between his two main patrons, Sakhar Dorji and Trögyal. He recounts three major conflicts he successfully diffused. In one case, his chief patrons, *lopön* Sakhar Dorji and *lopön* Trögyal of Paro, who were leading chieftains in the area and once close friends, were locked in a feud. The discord between the two friends was maliciously caused by some people who feared that they would be unbeatable if they remained united. In another case, the nephew of a chieftain called Azang was mistakenly murdered by the people of Tsenthang, present-day Tsento, which provoked the wrath of chieftains in the area led by Sakhar Dorji and Trögyal for revenge. In yet another dispute, the people of upper and lower Tsenthang led by Sakhar Dorji and Trögyal respectively were about to wage a war when he intervened. Conflict resolution was a major occupation for him. He mediated between warring parties, bestowing upon them Buddhist teaching and making them take sacred oaths to live amicably.

We saw such a role played by Jamyang Kuenga Senge earlier and also find a similar role played by Pema Lingpa over a century later. The Sakyapa lamas and Panchen Lama also played the role of mediators in seventeenth- and eighteenth-century conflicts between the Bhutanese and Tibetans, and Bhutanese and the British respectively. We also see senior religious hierarch being actively engaged to settle internal conflicts during the medieval period. As a respected figure with substantial influence on rival parties, it was common for a lama to be asked to act as a mediator or use his influence to stop conflicts. Barawa certainly used his religious stature for this purpose and successfully averted many armed conflicts and invasions. Apparently, it was after such a hectic life mediating between feuding parties in the Paro, Gönyul and Shar regions that he finally passed away in Drangyekha. The seat was taken over by one of his brothers, and his descendants and incarnations also carried on Barawa's reputed role of mediating between parties in dispute. In the seventeenth century, the Barawa school and Drangyekha monastery suffered a major setback during the unification of Bhutan under Zhabdrung

Ngawang Namgyal. Even at such times, the reincarnation of Barawa tried to mediate between Zhabdrung Ngawang Namgyal and the ruler of Tibet but without any success. The seat was taken over by the Drukpa forces and the Barawa school found new support in the neighbouring kingdom of Sikkim.[50]

Sakyapa

One other Tibetan Buddhist school that made its way into Bhutan is the Sakya. Founded by Khon Könchog Gyalpo (1034–1102) in 1073, their principal monastery is located near Lhatse in the Tsang region of Tibet. The Sakya lamas ruled Tibet from about 1264 to 1350 through the support of the Mongol Yuan dynasty in China. The Sakya theocratic rule brought Tibet together for the first time since its break-up in the ninth century after Lang Darma's death. During this period, they also vanquished the *dung reng* hordes, whom we have already discussed. Their arrival in Bhutan is late and their presence marginal compared to other Buddhist schools we have discussed so far although the Sakya centre itself is geographically not very far from western Bhutan. It is very surprising that Sakya cultivated neither any secular presence nor any large religious influence in Bhutan at the time of the proliferation of centres of other Buddhist schools in the country. Gedun Rinchen recounts that a certain Drubthob Pawo Tagsham and his consort, who is a daughter of the Sakya family, came to Bhutan and founded the Lhading temple in Paro in the fifth sexagenary cycle (1325–85). The statue in the temple is also said to have been brought from Sakya.[51]

Proper Sakya monasteries however started with a figure named Thinley Rabyang, who belonged to the Ngor branch of the Sakya school. Gedun Rinchen dates him in the eighth sexagenary cycle (1505–65). He established Chizhing Gönpa in Wang, Shalmar Gönpo in Chapcha and Nepa Gönpa in Shelngana, Punakha. Another figure of the same branch named Nyarong Dondrub founded temples in Gönyul. Panchen Drapa, a follower of the mainstream Sakya school, founded Pagar Gönpa in the Thimphu valley and a couple of others in the Shar region. Unlike some of the schools we have discussed above, the Sakya school and monasteries did not face any threat from Zhabdrung Ngawang Namgyal, given the cordial relationship he and his Drukpa school enjoyed with the Sakya establishment. A daughter of the Sakya family was even sought as a bride for Zhabdrung's son, Jampal Dorji. Thus, Sakya, it appears, was not one of the lamaist factions, who were considered as enemies of the Drukpa school. Yet, the Sakya school did not flourish as much as it could have and gradually declined with most of the monasteries taken over by Drukpa centres. Today, some of the places associated with Sakya in the past do not even retain the memory of their Sakya origins. Among them Chizhing is perhaps an exception with its original Sakya affiliation being popularly remembered by the humourous anecdotes about the pranks played by a Bhutanese attendant, Tashi, on his master, the lama of Chizhing. In these humorous stories, the lama of Chizhing is portrayed as a naïve and trusting character, always being fooled by his own smart and witty attendant.

Shingtapa of Gelug school

The Gelug or Gedan school, to which the Dalai Lama officially belongs, is the latest one to appear among the major Tibetan Buddhist schools. It was founded by Tsongkhapa (1357−1419) with the establishment of his Ganden monastery in 1409 some thirty miles upstream from Lhasa. Tsongkhapa was undoubtedly one of the most renowned and influential figures of his time. A great monk-scholar, meditation master, reformist thinker and spiritual leader, Tsongkhapa changed the Tibetan religious landscape. His Ganden school, later known as the Gelug school, rose by leaps and bounds to become perhaps the most popular Tibetan Buddhist school in Tibet by the time of his disciples. With rapid growth in its religious prestige, it also soon became a major sociopolitical player. Two centuries later, when the 5th Dalai Lama was made the supreme leader of Tibet through Mongol support, the Gelug school formally became the political power to rule Tibet through a theocratic government for the next 400 years.

Its influence in Bhutan, however, was marginal. Even the Gelugpa lamas who had a minor following and influence on the northern frontiers of Bhutan appear to have come not from the mainstream Gelug line but from a rare line, which was not even known in Tibet. The Shingtapa line starts with a certain lama Palden Dorji of Phanyul, who was a student of Tsongkhapa and counted among the three Dorjis who have reached great spiritual heights. Later, he is said to have been 'blessed' by Padmasambhava and spent time in meditation around Mt Jomolhari. Some of his followers established a centre in Lingshi and the Shingta temple in Gasa, from which the group got its name. This is almost the only case of the Gelug or New Kadampa presence in western Bhutan, despite their roaring success in Tibet. In the seventeenth century, Lama Dechog Gönpo of this temple and his patrons opposed Zhabdrung Ngawang Namgyal and consequently fled to Tibet.

In far eastern Bhutan, Lobzang Tanpai Dronme, a student of the 1st Dalai Lama, established a few centres. However, they were also taken over by the forces of the Drukpa school during the campaign to integrate eastern regions under Drukpa rule in the seventeenth century.[52] Some Gelug influence continued over the centuries in the eastern highlands of Merak and Sakteng, which are contiguous to the Gelug-dominated areas of Tawang in Arunchal Pradesh.

Kamtshang of Kagyu school

The Kamtshang or Karma Kagyu school was started by Düsum Khyenpa (1110–93), a student of Gampopa, with the foundation of Tshurphu in the Tölung area of Central Tibet. It gradually grew to become the most popular Kagyu school by the middle of the first millennium. The 2nd Karmapa Pakshi (1204–83) and his successor, the 3rd Karmapa Rangjung Dorji (1284–1339) took the Kamtshang Kagyu to new heights by becoming preceptors in the Mongol imperial court in China. The 3rd Karmapa also became well known as the first popular case of a lama who was formally recognized as the reincarnation of an earlier person. This led to the rise of the widespread religious institution of incarnations or *trulku* (སྤྲུལ་སྐུ). Several of the Karmapa hierarchs including the 1st, 12th and 16th visited Bhutan to see places such as Taktshang and Kurjey, and a student of the 3rd Karmapa Rangjung Dorji lived in Bhutan, as we shall see below, but the school did not extend its institutional influence in Bhutan until the fifteenth century. Its activities in the southern Mon area were focused further to the east in the modern Tawang region. The 7th Karmapa Chödrak Gyatsho (1454–1506) met Pema Lingpa and received blessings from him in Tibet.[53]

The first known instance of institutional establishment by the Kamtshang school in Bhutan took place in the fifteenth century through the 4th Zhamarpa Chökyi Drakpa (1453–1524). According to Pema Lingpa's report, Zhamarpa Chökyi Drakpa arrived in Bumthang in 1479 with the intention to build a meditation centre for his school and consulted the local lamas, including Pema Lingpa, on where it might be built.[54] Pema Lingpa suggested a spot between Jampa Lhakhang and Chokhor Lhakhang but other lamas and chieftains suggested Thangbi where a centre was finally built. In course of the construction at Thangbi, the Jowo brothers of Ura fell into the disfavour of the Zhamarpa hierarch and the latter, through the support of other Bumthang lamas and chieftains, sent an army to Ura but the army was disgracefully defeated. Thangbi, however, became a centre of the Kamtshang Kagyu and continues to this day.

The 5th Zhamarpa hierarch, Konchog Yanlag (1526–83) also visited Bumthang and the Kurichu valley, where he established some centres. He is said to have travelled from the Kurichu valley to Bumthang via Ngala Kharchung. Many spots on this route are marked by stories about his journey. At the end of the journey, he is said to have briefly stayed in Wangthang Gönpa in Ura. Despite the importance of the Karmapa institution in Tibet and their growing influence in the subsequent centuries, the school did not develop further in Bhutan. Perhaps, the Karmapa school reached its highest point in Bhutan in the twentieth century during the life of the 16th Karmapa Rigpai Dorji (1924–81), who came to Bhutan during the Tibetan exodus in 1959 and enjoyed the patronage and support of the royal family.

Drigung of Kagyu school

The Drigung Kagyu school, which we have already seen above, was started by Jigten Gönpo Rinchen Pal in 1179 and its main base was the Drigung Thil monastery. It rose to be a major player in the Tibetan political arena during the period of Mongolian suzerainty over Tibet, especially after gaining the support of Hülegü Khan, the Mongol ruler of Persia. However, like the Sakyapas and Karmapas we have seen above, its presence in Bhutan was insignificant despite its importance in Tibet. One Öthön Sangay, a Drigungpa hierarch from the Kyura clan, was sent from Drigung to the southern valleys by his teacher to spread the tradition. He arrived in Bhutan and started a hermetic life on the cusp of the Dakarla mountain range. Soon after that, he also took a local consort, who produced a son. Eventually, he settled next to a cliff and founded the hermitage of Tshamdra on the western slope of the Dakarla mountain. This was the beginning of the *chöje* family of Tshamdra. From here, his descendants gradually spread among the local population and even started the village of Metem.

Instead of spreading the Drigung tradition, the descendents soon took up the Nyingma and Drukpa Kagyu schools, which were dominant in the area. One scion became the disciple of Tashi Dorji, who was a master of the neighbouring Dongkarla monastery, and attracted some following. The most popular descendants of this Drigung master were Ngawang Drukpa (1682–1748) and Yonten Thaye (1724–83). Ngawang Drukpa, who started the line of Tshamdra incarnate lamas, became a disciple of the 2nd

Gangteng Trulku and the fourth Je Khenpo Damchö Pekar and thus followed a combination of the Nyingma and Drukpa Kagyu tradition while Yonten Thaye took up Drukpa Kagyu and became the 13th Je Khenpo of Bhutan.

Other prominent religious visitors

The groups mentioned so far represent the important religious traditions which Bhutan witnessed during the period I call the Later Diffusion. Most of them were promoted by the representatives of the schools already well established in Tibet while some, like the Chazampa and Pema Lingpa traditions, were just emerging. The schools mentioned above generally had some sort of communal structure and continuing existence as a tradition in Bhutan. Most left a significant impact on the Bhutanese society and religious consciousness. However, these schools or groups are not the only ones to arrive in Bhutan. There were many others about whom we know very little and some who left no significant institutional legacy in the form of a continued religious tradition or family line. Given the prevalence of a self-effacing and elusive character among Buddhist recluses, it is quite plausible that many more spiritual men and women may have roamed the Bhutanese country than revealed by the list of names we can glean from textual and oral sources.

Among them, in the early part of the Later Diffusion, Machig Labdron (1055–1145), the great teacher of Chöd practice, is said to have stayed in Paro and Haa. The Machigphug cave and spring in Taktshang, Bumdra in Paro and Jungnedra in Haa are associated with her. In the centuries after her, the Chöd practice was gradually incorporated into other Buddhist traditions and her legacy did not exist as separate school. It flourished in Bhutan among both the Nyingma and Drukpa Kagyu followers. The master Zhang Debai Dorji, whom Gedun Rinchen places in the third sexagenary cycle (1147–1207), visited Bumthang and Kheng. He established Pangshong temple in Punakha but left no major impact. According to Gedun Rinchen, one Jonangpa master named Kuenga Lodöe is said to have built his seat in the Gön area north of Punakha. The Jonangpas in Tibet represented the proponents of an absolutist Buddhist philosophy arguing that all sentient beings are primordially enlightenment Buddhas but incapable of recognizing that nature through the influence of temporary delusion. This philosophical thought was suppressed in Tibet during the reign of the 5th Dalai Lama but it survived in Bhutan. The Jonangpa seat in Gön declined by the seventeenth century but Tenzin Rabgay is said to have renovated it.

Indian visitors

The period of the Later Diffusion in Tibet was marked by the resurgent flow of Buddhist teachings from India. In most histories, it begins with Rinchen Zangpo (958–1055) and stops by the time of Vanaratna (1384–1468), who was known as 'the last Indian pundit' to visit Tibet. In contrast, the Later Diffusion in Bhutan's history is almost entirely about the diffusion of Buddhist teachings from Tibet. Unlike the period of the Early Diffusion, for which the main credit is given to the Indian master Padmasambhava, the Later Diffusion is characterized by the spread of Tibetan religious schools or development of Bhutan's own spiritual tradition. One finds only two Indian names among the hundreds of religious figures who are said to have visited Bhutan in this period. The first one is Pha Dampa Sangay (d.1117), the master of meditation practice known as *zhijed* (ཞི་བྱེད) or pacifier. He is said to have visited Tibet about five times and, according to one oral tradition, eventually to have gone to China under the name Bodhidharma, the founding patriarch of Chan Buddhism. In Tibet, he spent time in Dingri near Mt Everest and is today best remembered for the inspirational piece he composed as advice for the people of Dingri. During his visit to Bhutan, Pha Dampa is said to have meditated in Taktshang and left behind a footprint and created a holy spring. He also spent time near Kyerchu in a place now known as Damkhang Gönpa.

The second illustrious Indian name in Bhutan during this period is Vanaratna, the Bengali scholar and yogi described as 'the last Indian pundit'. Born a prince in eastern Bangladesh, he left the royal life to become a monk and pursue religion. As a peripatetic scholar and spiritual master, he travelled across South Asia and made three trips to Tibet in the fifteenth century to teach many important religious figures. He was particularly known for promoting the six-part yoga of the Kālacakra system in Tibet. It was during his first trip, according to Kongtrul, that he visited Taktshang on the way.[55] He is said to have found Taktshang as special as holy places in India and to have a vision of Padmasambhava. During his meditation there, he saw a *dākinī* who led him into a cave, which turned out to be a mansion with Padmasambhava seated on a throne in the centre. He received from Padmasambhava the instructions for a long life, which he later passed on to the Drukpa Kagyu hierarch, Kuenga Paljor.

Local sources based on oral stories also attribute three temples in Punakha to him. He is said to have come searching for his mother's rebirth, which, he discovered through his meditative clairvoyance, was trapped in a large rock.

He magically spilt the rock to release the rebirth of his mother. The rock, with the temple, is today remembered as *dojagarlam* (རྡོ་རྒྱ་གར་བླམ་) or the rock of the Indian guru. The foundation of the first shrine on the confluence, where the Punakha *dzong* was built later, is also attributed to him and now marked by a smaller temple called Dzongchung. His own biographies composed by his Tibetan students are silent on his trip to Punakha, making scholars cast a doubt on the historicity of his trip to Punakha and the foundation of the temple. The journeys of Pha Dampa and Vanaratna to Bhutan are not found in any contemporary or early sources. Moreover, the visionary experience of Vanaratna at Taktshang and the magical act of liberating his parental rebirth trapped in a rock, as we have seen, also appears in the accounts of Thangtong Gyalpo. It is possible that the two were conflated or the stories about one superimposed on the other. Thus, there is nothing definite one can say about either of these famous Indian visitors to Bhutan.

A sketch of society and polity

Although we lack reliable dates and detailed information for many of the important historical figures and also have no comprehensive historical writings from this period, it is still possible to construct a rough but convincing picture of the sociopolitical circumstances in the period of the Later Diffusion. Unlike the Prehistoric and Early Diffusion Periods for which we have only much later records, we have a variety of scattered historical sources which help us gain a very good understanding of the religion, society and polity in Bhutan in this period. Bhutan during the first half of the second millennium clearly seems to have been spiritually fertile and dynamic, socially cohesive and structured, economically independent and prosperous but politically fragmented and unstable. Apart from the political system which has changed a few times since then, the five centuries from 1000 to 1600 CE were perhaps the most formative period for the Bhutanese religious, social and cultural identity, which we call 'traditional' today.

We have already seen above the religious fervour and activities of this period. In terms of sects and denominations, Bhutan was far more diverse and open during this period than it ever was after the political unification. The political unification in the seventeenth century under the Drukpa Kagyu banner resulted in both direct expulsion of some groups, gradual decline of others and the homogenization and syncretization of yet others. The religious developments of this period can be placed in two categories: the exogenous reintroduction of religious schools and teachings from Tibet and the endogenous development of religious traditions within Bhutan. The latter was mainly a work of the native treasure-discoverers, with Pema Lingpa at the helm of the group. The former, however, was more widespread and persistent, and had much more bearing on Bhutan. These Tibetan religious missions to Bhutan, then known as the Lho (ཇོ) or Lhomon (ཇོ་མོན), took place for a number of reasons.

   Like most religious missions in world history, the primary motive of the Tibetan missions was religious conversion. Often, it was to dispel the darkness of the barbaric country of Mon by lighting the lamp of *dharma* or *chö* (ཆོས) that Tibetan missionaries embarked on their journey southward. Perhaps many of the visitors may have truly believed in this mission. Yet, their religious forays into the southern valleys were not merely for bringing *dharma* and the southern Mon was not a barbaric land. One can notice in their accounts that the phrases such as 'darkness of the Mon' and 'barbaric people of the borderland' were empty clichés, which they bandied merely to justify their missions to their own conscience. For instance, the author of Lorepa's biography, Götshang Repa writes: 'Then, he went to Lhomon. When he arrived in Mon Bumthang, about 2800 monks gathered. He gave teachings on *karma* ... to these barbaric people, who were like animals, without the dispensation of *dharma*.'[56] The statement is self-contradicting. Who were the 2800 monks if there was truly no dispensation of the *dharma*? The fact that there was a large number of monks among the audience of a visiting Tibetan master in Bumthang in the thirteenth century is strong evidence that religion had taken deep roots. It is a large group even by today's standards.

   Like Götshang Repa's portrayal, the presentation of the southern Mon as barbaric country by the Tibetan authors is generally a casual and hollow description, which they used rhetorically. It may have been used meaningfully in the earlier times before the Buddhist tradition had taken proper roots in Bhutan[57] but by the thirteenth century the country was certainly no more a backwater as Götshang presents it to be. Surprisingly, we find even some of the Bhutanese emulating the Tibetans in using these phrases. So, we find Lama Ngangjud Gyalpo of Taktshang writing to Sonam Gyaltshen in 1494: 'Like animals, we are ignorant beings [in] a barbaric land of Mon where *dharma* has not spread. Please hold us with great affection and, in particular, establish one meditation centre here at Taktshang Senge Samdrub, the major site of the great Padmasambhava.'[58]

   Ngangjud Gyalpo perhaps used the Tibetan stereotypical description of

Bhutan as barbaric and the people as ignorant only to make a self-effacing and effective plea to Sonam Gyaltshen to come to Paro so he could fulfil his own wish of having a meditation centre at Taktshang. His world, particularly Taktshang and the Paro valley, was far from being the land where *dharma* had not spread. By the fifteenth century when he wrote this invitation, Paro was thoroughly foraged by a series of religious missions from Tibet. One of its own great sons, Drubwang Rinchen Chödor was also at the height of his religious career and his two *tertön* disciples, Ngawang Drakpa and Tsering Dorji, were both active then. To the east, the tradition Pema Lingpa started had gained full momentum and was spreading across the Himalayas. Thus, the use of such description is at the best an exaggeration and most likely a simple ruse to attract the Tibetan master. Like the name Mon we have discussed in the chapter on name, it is certainly a case of internalization and adoption of a perception, designation and descriptions which were used by Tibetans. However, it is quite possible that many Tibetans who have never been to or heard much about Bhutan thought of it as a barbaric land. Thus, some would have ventured with a genuine conviction of a religious missionary to spread the light of enlightenment. The majority of the visitors used this reason only as an excuse for many other things they pursued as we shall see below.

The main reasons for the Tibetan visitors to travel to the south were concerned with the religious, social and political situations in Tibet itself. There was a paradigmatic shift in the Tibetan religious thought and structure in the twelfth and thirteenth centuries with the rise of many new religious schools. The proliferation of the monastic centres and their sustenance weighed heavily on the Tibetan economy. This led to a constant competition and rivalry among them to sustain and expand their individual religious establishments and schools. It was thus partly economic pressure, and not purely missionary zeal as we are made to believe, which led the Tibetan religious hierarchs to seek opportunities further afield in areas such as Lhomon, which, in both literal and metaphoric senses, was considered to be beyond the pale. The religious missions to the south were efforts to find new patrons and estates. They resulted in a *chöyön* (མཆོད་ཡོན་) or priest–patron relationship between the Tibetan lamas and Bhutanese laities and exchanges of various offerings, including grains, textiles and metals for religious services.

We see in the biography of Lhanangpa how he collected goods from Bhutan and made at least three mass distribution of offerings in the Drigung Thil, the monastic centre of his teacher.[59] His biographer reports that there were over 55,000 clerics receiving his gifts. On one of the trips from Chalka in Paro to Drigung, he made the famous offering of 'one hundred of a hundred items' (བརྒྱ་འབུལ་རིགས་མི་འདྲ་བ་བརྒྱ་). The list included among other things, a hundred novices on a hundred horses, a hundred measures of gold, a hundred large tents, a hundred parasols made of peacock tails, a hundred copper vessels, a hundred ironware, a hundred golden vases, a hundred tiger skins,[60] a hundred leopard skin, a hundred elephant tusks, a hundred bundles of textiles, a hundred bags of raw sugar, a hundred sacks of dyes, a hundred sacks of medicinal herbs, a hundred sets of decoctions and innumerable cookware, food and clothes. The file of people carrying these goods is said to have stretched more than 100 km from Tshalgungthang to Drigung Thil.

When Thangtong Gyalpo returned to Tibet after his first trip, he had 1400 loads made out of 7000 iron chains and rods and 700 loads of other goods according to his Bhutanese biographer.[61] Similarly, Dorji Lingpa received a great deal of offerings from his Bhutanese patrons for his religious services as did Barawa Gyaltshen Palzang. Chogden Gönpo, Dorji Lingpa's incarnation, was amazed by offering he received even at the point of his entry to Bhutan. He was met at the border by the students of Dorji Lingpa with many riches, including an embellished horse, clothes, bedding, food, servants so much so that he remarked that he 'arrived a pauper but was instantly turned into a king.'[62] The waves of lamas who visited Bhutan from Ralung also returned to their centre with vast amounts of offerings collected during their tours. Needless to say, these offerings were largely perceived by both the givers and recipients as righteous transactions with high spiritual benefits. Thus, it was not generally perceived as an extraction of religious tribute or imposition of taxes although they were at times exactly that. Pema Lingpa is the only figure who effectively reversed this trend. During some two dozen trips he made to Tibet, he returned to Bumthang with a large amount of gifts given by his Tibetan patrons and devotees. He records returning from his tour in 1483 with forty horse-loads of offerings. One can safely conclude that these increased in size and value in the subsequent years as he became more popular and met more important people.

This economic factor in the Tibetan missions and their endeavours to meet the increasing institutional needs in Tibet must not, however, totally blind us from seeing the good works they frequently carried out in expanding and sustaining the Buddhist teachings in Bhutan. Most leading Tibetan visitors, as we have seen above, have established many centres and promoted the Buddhist civilization. The Tibetan master, Karpo Kuenga Drakpa, even bitterly complained about Tibetan lamas neglecting Tibetan welfare and flocking to Lhomon when Chogden Gönpo informed him about his impending trip to Bumthang.[63] Nevertheless, many of their activities had an implicit economic and political agenda. The religious centres were domain markers as much as holy shrines for worship. Some lamas such as Nenyingpa Rinchen Darpo and the Drukpa hierarch Ngawang Chögyal built as many temples as they could. The Bhutanese mountains were dotted with temples; a majority of the temples and centres we have today initially started in this period. Despite their deep religious piety, the local people must have also felt some displeasure as all these temples were built with voluntary labour or corvee. We have already seen above the satirical remark on the Drukpa's temple and Hungral Drungdrung's numerous dyke projects. Drawing on this,[64] we find, in the Shar district, a slightly different oral version: 'Don't raise your knees, Nenyingpas will build a centre. Don't let your nose run, Kathogpas will build a dyke.'

The lamas reciprocated the contribution of both material and human resources by their devotees with religious teachings. It was common practice in traditional Bhutan for lamas to go on tours of villages to provide religious services in return for offerings in kind and voluntary labour to build their centres. Hungral Drungdrung, for instance, would frequently interrupt his building activities with religious teachings. Thus, it was mischievously remarked: 'O patrons of Wang, Chang and Dolpo! Hungral Drungdrung is giving empowerment. Come to receive it with panniers and backpad.'[65] The lamas were also quite ingenious in their methods of spreading their influence. While religious teachings and services were the main methods, they also employed a number of other means. Thangtong Gyalpo built bridges, Hungral Drungdrung was well known for his irrigation channels and dykes and Barawa used his diplomatic and negotiating skills.

In addition to the religious cause and pursuit of economic gains, we must also add two other developments in Tibet which increased the flow of visitors to the southern borderlands. Simultaneously with the monastic and institutional expansion, Tibet saw two very important developments: a political and a religious one. The rise of the Mongols through Chenghis Khan (1167?–1227) brought about a great political upheaval in central and inner Asia. By the middle of the thirteenth century, Tibet was seriously ravaged by Mongolian invasions. The Tibetan Buddhist schools cultivated ties with Mongol warlords, drastically increasing the Mongol influence on Tibetan affairs. The Tibetan–Mongol alliance culminated in the Sakya leadership over the whole of Tibet in 1264 through the support of Kubilai Khan, grandson of Chenghis Khan. This subsequently brought a lot of political turmoil triggered by sectarian rivalry, especially between the Sakyapas supported by Kubilai and the Drigungpas patronized by Hülegü Khan. Tibet saw an increased sectarian strife in the competition for political control.

Roughly coinciding with these changes, Tibet also saw the rise of the treasure culture. Numerous spiritual men and a few women brought out texts and artefacts, which are said to have been buried in the eighth century to be revealed in the future by a destined person when the right time has come. Some of these rediscovered texts even predicted the Mongol invasions and many offered ways to avert the invasion or escape the resultant turmoil. With nostalgia for the imperial past, these treasure texts portrayed contemporary Tibet as a strife-striken land. They encouraged those seriously interested in spirituality and wishing to enjoy peace and tranquillity to journey southward to the hidden lands. Many of these spiritual men also simultaneously ventured southward to seek and open these hidden lands. Many areas bordering Tibet from Nepal to Yunan were identified and promoted as hidden lands. The whole country of Bhutan was generally viewed as a hidden land although a number of places within Bhutan became well known as such in the later times.

Thus, the primary reason for the Tibetan treasure-discoverers to journey to Bhutan was to find hidden lands and reveal hidden treasures, which were believed to have been buried in these lands in plenty. It was considered the time for the sons of Padmasambhava to journey southward in search of hidden lands and treasures and escape from the Mongol hordes. Talking about this era, Thangtong Gyalpo said it is the time when 'Mongols arrive in Tibet, Tibetans escape to the frontiers and the frontiersmen are pushed to India'.[66] Many visitors such as Longchenpa and Barawa would come to Bhutan to flee from the political strife in Tibet. There were also many others who visited Bhutan on pilgrimage, particularly the famous caves of Taktshang and Kurjey.

Whatever their motives and reasons, the Tibetan visitors contributed the lion's share to the making of Bhutan's religious indentity. The religious history of Bhutan between 1000 and 1600 CE is primarily a story of a proliferation of Tibetan Buddhist schools. Except for the tradition which started with Pema Lingpa, all of the Buddhist traditions of Bhutan originated in Tibet. The people, we can surmise, were very pious and devoted to religion and thus contributed a significant per cent of their time and resources to religious causes. There were certainly no major centres of higher learning as in Tibet but religious study and practice were widespread. The number of people who gathered when Lorepa and Lhanangpa gave sermons in the thirteenth century and Pema Lingpa and Chogden Gönpo taught in the sixteenth century indicate that most of the population was devoutly Buddhist and there were large numbers of Buddhist clerics. The religious culture among the masses in this period seems very much like that existing even today in some remote villages. The Bhutanese reception of and devotion to visiting Tibetan lamas appear to have also continued through the centuries and have not changed much even today.

The people in this period however seem to have generally considered themselves as distinct from Tibetans. Unlike some cis-Himalayan ethnic groups such as the Sherpas who trace their origin to Tibet, the ancient Bhutanese appear to have distinguished themselves from the Tibetans. Though they look up to Tibet as the hub of Buddhist civilization and had most of their religious masters and nobilities coming from Tibet, they seem to construe themselves as a culturally different stock. Bö (བོད་) and Mon (མོན་) are presented as two separate geographic and cultural realms. This difference was certainly reinforced by the Tibetans of this period, especially by those with a missionary zeal. The Bhutanese valleys were uncharted barbaric hinterland beyond the civilized Tibetan realm. Geographically, Bhutan was obviously different. While some Tibetan visitors such as Jamyang Kuenga Senge and Longchenpa cherished the tranquillity and greenery of Bhutan, others loathed its dense vegetation and dreaded the subtropical climate. Thus we find the students and attendants of Jamyang Kuenga Senge pleading him not to leave for Bhutan saying:

> The land of Lhomon has high humidity and narrow paths. There are many fierce beasts and unruly people. With poison and intense heat, the land is terrifying, hair raising and hazardous to one's life. The humidity and poison will destroy the bodily strength. It is a place filled with snakes, flies and frogs. The poison of heat and fierce beasts will cause harm. It is well known as a difficult place for travel.[67]

Chogden Gönpo nearly died from a 'heat' disease immediately after his first trip to Bumthang and lost one of his attendants to 'heat' as did Barawa Gyaltshen Palzang. Dorji Lingpa postponed his journeys to winter months as Bhutanese summers are considered dangerous for health. Many Tibetans from the barren and dry plateau of Tibet could not cope with the warm and humid climate and forested landscape of Bhutan and many succumbed to subtropical diseases, particularly malaria. Many lamas however loved the freshness of the greenery and floral beauty. Paro was often eulogized as the land of medicinal herbs, an epithet later applied to the whole country. Similarly, Chogden Gönpo and his predecessor Dorji Lingpa praised the Punakha region as a land of the cypress, a simile which also was later used for the whole country. Perhaps the best praise of Bhutan is found in Longchenpa's eulogy of Bumthang. He writes:

> The valleys are wide and filled with flowers and fruits. The villages are enchanting filled with many 'lotuses'. In all directions, the land shines with splendor and excellent beauty, as if in a contest with the heavenly realm of gods.[68]

The Bhutanese also clearly had a different dress, sometimes called a *lhochey* (ལྷོ་ཆས་) or southern costume. Lhanangpa had a vision of people in a 'strange' dress in Drigung and later remarks that the people in his vision were his patrons in Paro wearing a 'strange' dress. Pema Lingpa's biographer, Gyalwa Dhondrup of Tibet, mentions being given by Pema Lingpa a 'dress of Mon tradition.' It is not clear what these dresses looked like but it is quite likely that they were prototypes of today's *kira* and *gho*. Or could they have been the tunics, which were worn in central Bhutan over a century ago and which resemble the tunics worn by people of Merak and Sakteng today? The Bhutanese also had a very different range of cuisine and some unique food culture. Gyalwa Dhondrup gives a long list of dishes and snacks laid out by the Bumthang ladies when he visited Tamshing in 1521.[69] Many of the names are unrecognizable today but most still survive and were popular until recent times.

There is no doubt that agriculture was flourishing and the backbone of the ancient economy. Cereals such as rice, buckwheat, wheat, barley, millet and peas were commonly cultivated and a wide variety of fruits and vegetable were also grown. We have already come across Longchenpa's mention of tea. When popular religious figures visited the villages, the bulk of the offering was grains, heaped as high as houses on some occasions. It was also very common for monks and priests to go on alms gathering rounds during the harvest season. This practice continues in some places but has generally stopped today. The cultural behaviour of the people seem not so different from what was prevalent in early twentieth-century Bhutan. The spread of Buddhism perhaps changed some of the unorthodox rituals and practices which were not compatible with its basic principles. For instance, the biographies of Lhanangpa and Barawa both mention killing of livestock as part of funerary practice. This practice continued in some parts of Bhutan even as late as the twentieth century. Known as *tangsha* (གཏང་ཤ) or sacrificial meat, as soon as someone dies, one cow or bull belonging to the family would be let loose to graze anywhere, including gardens or fields. The animal would be slaughtered a few weeks later for the final funerary rites. With meat readily available from India and the persistent Buddhist influence, this practice has today completely stopped.

Longchenpa notes that the architecture in the Bhutan was also distinct. Built of wood, the houses had raised slanting roofs, much like the houses still commonly seen across the country. There were also houses built of bamboo. It is difficult to gauge the linguistic map of Bhutan in this period. It is not clear if the country was as linguistically diverse and divided as it was in the middle of the twentieth century. However, it is very clear that the language spoken in the Bumthang valley was unintelligible to the Tibetan spoken in neighbouring Lhodrak. When Chogden Gönpo visited Tamshing in the beginning of the fifteenth century, Pema Lingpa had to make his introduction of the reincarnate lama twice: first in local vernacular for people who assembled for the reception and then in Tibetan for Chogden Gönpo and his entourage.

The economy of this period was certainly simple, self-contained and stable. Agricultural and pastoral farming were certainly the driving force. Without any significant bureaucratic, bourgeois or professional culture, most people were either active farmers working on their land or clerics committed to religious life. Inferring from the amount of farm products offered to the religious visitors, it is clear that people produced surplus food. People appear to have also produced surplus textiles which were given as gifts as Pema Lingpa did to the large gathering during one of his last sermons at Tshampa, the border settlement north of Chökhor. The surplus food and textiles were also exchanged with other goods. Trade was perhaps a profession some people took up, at least seasonally, in this period. The occurance of the terms *lego* (ལས་གོ) or trade marts in the early accounts of the Nenying and Lhapa schools and Phajo Drugom's biography suggests that there was some trade. Tononyms such as *tsongdu* and *hey* (ཧེ or ཧེས) or market also show that these place were once trade centres. The appointment of Phajo Drukgom's sons as overseers of the trade marts also shows that control over the trade marts and routes was important for economic and political gain.

Like the general movement of people, trade was largely of a north–south orientation. One vibrant route was along Paro and Haa to Tibet via Phari in the north and India to the south. Another route was along Bumthang/Kurtoe to Lhodrak in the north and Kheng and India to the south. A third would have existed along Tashigang and Tashi Yangtse to Tawang and Tibet in the north and India in the south. Longchenpa adds that a visitor could find goods from all directions even in places such as Tang in Bumthang. The trade, we can surmise, was mainly the barter of goods as there was certainly no monetary currency then although Barawa does mention receiving silver coins.[70]

Inferring from the items lamas received as gifts, among the goods and merchandise for trade would have been cereals, dairy products, raw sugar, salt, textiles, silk, cotton, jewellery, including gold, silver and turquoise, silverware, woodwork, cookware, peacock tails, animal skins, dyes, herbs and paper. Horses must have been very valuable and common items of trade while other forms of livestock may have also been traded. The lamas certainly prized offering of horses. Chogden Gönpo was elated when Karpo Kuenga Drakpa told him that he would receive as many superb Mon horses as he liked when he reached Mon. The Tibetan lamas' love of horses is betrayed in a joke the divine madman uses to tease his cousin Ngawang Chögyal. 'Ngawang Chögyal likes ponies and Drukpa Kunley likes pussies. May there be beneficence for the lovers of ponies and pussies'.[71]

The colophon of the Kanjur manuscript which is partially cited below states that 'from the market of Phari, flow like a river gold, turquoise, silk and other goods and from the holy land of India, rise like steam from the ground, gold, silver, silk and cloths'.[72] The exchange with India was also perhaps very vibrant but it was very poorly documented. Dewa Zangpo mentions his trip to the King of Kāmatā and also the one made by his master Thangtong Gyalpo. Before that, Phajo Drukgom also received gifts from one Kāmatā ruler and Barawa mentions some of his Bhutanese devotees leaving for India.[73] These suggest that there were some movements southward.

The proliferation of religious schools certainly led to many significant social changes. One obvious result is the rise of a new class of religious elites, who also assumed a lot of political and economic control. Although ancient Bhutan was relatively an egalitarian society with no strong aristocracy or a deeply entrenched social disparity like Tibet or India, this period saw a significant increase in social stratification. We have already seen how many Tibetan visitors in the ancient period started families who became ruling nobilities in their individual principalities. The Tibetans effectively introduced a hierarchical social structure in the Bhutanese valleys. Among the religious elites in the western valleys, we see first the scions of the Nyö clan and then descendents of Phajo Drukgom. The *zhalngo* and *chöje* nobilities of western Bhutan mostly begin in this period from a host of religious personalities. Similarly, in the central and eastern parts, we see the rise of the descendents of Nyötön Thrulzhig, Guru Chöwang, Dorji Lingpa and Pema Lingpa making up most of the *chöje, lama, zhalngo* and *khoche* families. The latter gained popularity and predominance in the medieval and modern period. The growth of the religious aristocracy also consequently led to the emergence of serfs known as *draap* (སྒྲ་པ). The class of *draap* generally evolved from the groups of students and followers who flocked around a religious master and settled around a religious establishment.

Bhutanese society in this era and early medieval times roughly comprised three tiers: On the top were the secular and religious nobilities including the *dung, jowo, lam, lopön, chipön, chöje, khoche, ponche* and *zhalngo,* who owned large areas of land, exercised some control over their domain and extracted tributes and taxes from the people. Below them were the middle-class majority, who were common citizens with their own property and lived independently but paid taxes and occasional corvee to their rulers. Some of the wealthy families in this class known as *chup* (ཕྱུག་པ) or rich households enjoyed similar privileges as the nobilities. At the bottom were two kinds of serfs. The *draap*, like the Villiens of medieval Europe, had some land often given to them by the religious master, and lived with some freedom but were required to provide various services to the master. They were almost always attached to a religious establishement. The *zap,* who were inhouse servants and labourers of the nobilities and wealthy middle class, had no property and worked fully for the house which owned them. Guessing from the marital practices in medieval times, social mobility across the two top tiers was perhaps common but less so between the two top classes and serfs. However, religion frequently provided the opportunity to break the social barrier. We shall return to the social stratification once again in the chapter on Early Modern Period.

Despite the rise of religious nobilities, there was also a large number of temporal rulers, many of whom had control over the people and patronized the religious figures. However, the actual political domains, roles and prerogatives of these temporal rulers are most elusive and difficult to capture. All we can say with certainty is that the country was fragmented into many principalities with constant conflicts between them. Eastern Bhutan was largely controlled by the chieftains belonging to the six clans descending from Prince Tsangma. Based on their links to ancient Tibetan kingship, they ruled the country from their *khar* (སྨཁར་) or fortified castles. In central Bhutan, we know that the *dung* chieftains, who purportedly started in Ura and Ngang, had spread across the districts of Mangde, Kheng, Kurtöe and Mongar. There were also others such as the Chökhor Pönpo. When Bhutan was unified in the seventeenth century, there were about two dozen major regional chieftains controlling the valleys of central and eastern Bhutan, who resisted the Drukpa domination.[74]

The scenario of secular rulers in western Bhutan is far more sketchy and scattered. The northern part of Paro was part of the Gö appanage and was perhaps controlled by the Gö and Gya clan until it was given to the family of Nyö Yonten Drakpa in the early decades of the second millennium. The appanage called the Lhokhazhi was perhaps then gradually extended to most of what is now western Bhutan. It appears that when Phajo Drukgom Zhigpo arrived in early thirteenth century, there were many local chieftains in the western valleys, who paid heavy tributes to the Lhapa establishment in Chalkha. According to Drukgom Zhigpo's biographer, seven such *chipön* of the Dung, Gongthru, He, Chang, Wang, Karbi and Dong communities met him secretly and revealed that each *tsho* (ཚོ) or section paid annually a hundred sacks of rice, a hundred bags of raw sugar, a hundred bundles of raw silk and a hundred sacks of iron to the Lhapa or risked being punished in the Tibetan style. It appears that their allegiance soon shifted to Drukgom Zhigpo and his descendents and the Lhapa school lost control.

In the fourteenth century, however, we come across numerous *lopön*s or masters in the biographical accounts of Jamyang Kuenga Senge and Barawa Gyaltshen Palzang. We do not exactly know what kind of relationship they had with the religious figures and the descendants of Drukgom Zhigpo. Only some of these *lopön*s seem to be Drukgom Zhigpo's descendents. Many people with the *lopön* title were killed in the Phari massacre which we have discussed above. Yet, there were certainly many *lopön*s both in Paro and Gön in Punakha who Barawa met toward the end of his life. Thus, neither the *lopön* chieftains ceased after the event in Phari, nor did their conflicts completely stop after Barawa's days. There are reports of conflicts in the sixteenth century in the biographies of Pema Lingpa, Tshering Dorji and Ngawang Drakpa and the history of the Hungral Drungdrung line. Pema Lingpa complained about spending a whole year of 1510 acting as a mediator for conflicts in western Bhutan and again having to mediate between the Chokhor Pönpo and Ngalong in 1520.

Despite the lack of political stability and cohesion, the areas in Bhutan appear to have been generally organized and structured according to some administrative and geographic features. In the western valleys, we see administrative groups, such as six sanctuaries of Tsanthang (ཚན་ཐང་གླིང་དྲུག), six middle sections of Paro (སྤ་གྲོ་བར་སྐོར་ཚོ་དྲུག) and eight great sections of Wang (ཝང་ཚོ་ཆེན་བརྒྱད) to give a few examples. There are also rare occurences of terms such as *tongpön* (སྟོང་དཔོན) or ruler of a thousand and *gyapön* (བརྒྱ་དཔོན) or ruler of a hundred. It is not clear if these posts worked like the *tripön* (ཁྲི་དཔོན) or myriarchs, who ruled over 10,000 households during the Sakya rule in Tibet. In any case, notwithstanding the fragmentary and chaotic appearance of the political situation, people had a clear concept of the political and administrative divisions and the general lay of the land. This understanding of political distinction is particularly true in the case of Bhutan's relation to Tibet. Even along the Paro and Bumthang valleys, the places best connected to Tibet, the Bhutanese and Tibetans clearly saw the land on either side of the Himalayan watershed as distinct countries and were aware of the exact border. When Thangtong Gyalpo returned from Bhutan with many thousands of his iron chains, the Bhutanese patrons transferred it up to Phari and the Tibetans took over the loads from there. Similarly, when Barawa visited his patrons in Paro at turbulent times, his patrons in Paro sent escorts for him as far as Phari. Thus, Tibetan control in this region effectively ended in Phari. Along the route north of Bumthang, the border was clearly the Monla pass. The pass separated the two countries and Pema Lingpa and his patron, the Nangso (ནང་སོ) or Prefect of Lhalung met at the border several times. Although the Nangso of Lhalung was entitled to some tributes from the ruler of Chokhor, his actual power did not stretch beyond the Monla pass. The places on two sides of the pass were categorically treated as two different countries by both the Tibetan and Bhutanese of the time. The *Sino-Tibetan Records*, which we cited earlier, also explicitly mentions that Lhomon was not under the Sakya domination.[75] Thus, the valleys of Bhutan, as the land of Lhomon, in some sense already formed a contiguous country even before the unification in the seventeenth century. Despite their political fragmentation, they had a shared family resemblance and sociocultural continuity, which distinguished them from Tibet to the north and India to the south. There was already by the middle of the sixteenth century a vague sense of conceptual, cultural and geographical unity and cohesion. Even the word Lhomonkhazhi appears to have gained a new range of reference, extending from Dromo in the west to Khaling in the east, as we see in the colophon of the *kanjur* cited below. However, it was in the seventeenth century under the leadership of Zhabdrung Ngawang Namgyal that this conceptual or cultural affinity was cast into a concrete political and territorial unity. It is to this emergence of Bhutan as a medieval nation state that we shall turn now.

***

Excerpts from Longchenpa's *The Flower Garden: A Profile of Bumthang, the Celestial Hidden Land*, composed in 1355 in Tharpaling, which describe Bumthang in central Bhutan:

> O hear this profile of the celestial hidden land of Bumthang,
> A land visited by the great ancient kings and ministers,
> A land where there are wondrous temples,
> A land where scholars and saints have continually come.
> In the four directions, as in the centre,
> This country is pristine and wide,
> Round like a round of a vase
> And beautiful like a burgeoning lotus.
> It is nothing like a human world.
> It is like a celestial land transported here.
> The mountains are delightful, green and lush,
> And their summit a chain of bright white snowy peaks.
> They stand in equal heights and form a circle,
> As if to form a circular fence of jewels.
> The valleys are wide filled with flowers and fruits.
> The villages are enchanting filled with many lotuses.
> In all directions, the land shines with splendor and excellent beauty,
> As if in a contest with the heavenly realm of gods.
> ...
> In Bumthang, the prized celestial hidden land,
> The mountains are broad and there are no erosive ravines.
> The villages are pleasant with a constant temperate autumnal season.
> The people are righteous; they abide by the ancient laws.
> The pleasant settlements have semi-raised roofs.
> There are also many houses made of bamboo.

The castles and houses with wooden roofs
Look like celestial mansions from a distance.
Here, the people are naturally righteous.
They do not hunt and there are no highway brigands.
Theft is rare as are violence and injury to others.
They are soft-natured and congenial for company.

Excerpts from the colophon of a *kanjur*, written in the sixteenth century as a funerary rite for Hungral Drungdrung,[76] which describe Paro in western Bhutan:

Some leagues from there [Tibet], to the south,
Is the land of Lokhazhi where reading and writing flourishes.
The outstanding country is Paro, the land of medicinal herbs.
Perched on the immutable cliff protruding from Chongla,
Is Heap of Jewels, the palace of victory.
The mountain behind resembles a majestic elephant.
On it thrive forests of plants such as cypresses
And divine birds sing melodious songs.
The mountain to the front is like a bowing queen.
The ridge to the right is like a curtain of white silk unfurled.
The ridge to the left is like a pile of the seven royal jewels.
In the upper reaches abide the great and glorious gods.
In the lower reaches, the celestial river of water with eight qualities
Flow like *yönchab* offering and go on to swirl in the sea.
The wealthy mermaid makes her offering of gems;
The various water birds beat the bell of their throats.
In the surrounding meadows resembling a turquoise tub,
Many sorts of animals flaunt their peaceful plays.
In the middle, where low fields spread out like Chinese silk,
Bloom many kinds of harvests which are satiating.
At all times, this joyous mind is bewitched
To wonder if this land is a heaven transposed on earth.
From the market of Phari, the source of all pleasant things,
Flow like a river, gold, turquoise, silk and other goods
From the holy land of India, the source of all pleasant things,
Rise like steam from the ground, gold, silver, silk and cloths.
In particular, this centre of spiritual accomplishment,

This new temple of Hungral is like Gaden transposed on earth.
From Thed, Thim, Ngenlung and as far as Khaling to the east,
From Wang, Dong, Ödü and as far as India to the south,
From Hey, Dromo and as far as Mönlhog to the west,
From Naljor, Tsendong and as far as Phari to the north,
From others such as Wang, Chang and Dolpa in between,
This is where the haves make their offerings to
And the have-nots seek their basic support from.
This is where the men compete in their skills
This is where the girls show off their looks.
In this seat, which is like Bodh Gaya,
The king of southern lands, Drungdrung and his sons
And his disciples, monks and subjects, like an assembly of stars,
Enjoy peace and happiness of a virtuous religious life.

Excerpts from the catalogue of *rNying ma rgyud 'bum* written in 1647 which describe Khaling in eastern Bhutan:[77]

The valley of Khaling, where religion flourishes,
This land blessed with wealth on the frontiers of southern Mon,
Is the meeting point of Indian and Tibetan trade.
From Tibet pours down horses, gold, salt and so forth like rain.
From India ensues commodities such as dyes, cloth and rice.
Whatever varieties of grains are sown grow in this land.

Zhabdrung Ngawang Namgyal (1594–1651), the founder of Bhutan

The Medieval Period:
The Unification of the Dragon Country

THE EMERGENCE OF BHUTAN as a nation state in the middle of the seventeenth century was the culmination of the successive socioreligious developments we have seen above. Though it could not have happened without the figure of Zhabdrung Ngawang Namgyal at its helm, it was certainly not the work of one generation, let alone a single man. It was an outcome of a cumulative process, which began as early as the introduction of Buddhism in the eighth century by Padmasambhava. In fact, many Bhutanese believe that it was a tryst with destiny set long ago with Padmasambhava's prediction that Ngawang Namgyal will come to found the country. Beside the evolution within the country, it was a process in which the politics of neighbouring Tibet had an important role to play. So, we must once again turn to Tibet and its historical and political vicissitudes in order to fully understand the unfolding of major events in Bhutan which led to the formation of the state.

The historical conditions

The Tibetan empire which was chaotically splintered after the assassination of King Lang Darma around 842 CE was roughly reunited in the twelfth century through Mongol intervention. The Sakya lamas became the first new rulers of Tibet in 1264 when Kubilai Khan offered Chögyal Phagpa (1235–80), a Sakya hierarch, the authority to rule over Tibet in return for the tantric initiation he gave the Yuan emperor. Tibet was then divided into thirteen myriarchies or clusters of 10,000 households for the sake of easy administration and tax control. The Sakya–Mongol alliance continued for nearly a century but, with problems of both lack of male heirs on some occasions and too many claimants at other times, the regime was ridden with internecine conflict. Eventually, the Sakya rulers lost the power to one its own officers, Jangchub Gyaltshen of the Phagmodrupa sect, an order belonging to the Kagyu school. Jangchub Gyaltshen was given the position of Tai Situ or chief minister by Togon Temür, the last ruler of the great Mongolian empire in 1354, thus formally ending the Sakya rule.

Tai Situ Jangchub Gyaltshen re-energized Tibetan politics by orienting it to its imperial antiquity and even reintroduced ancient official dress codes. He also introduced new legal codes and the governance of the country through the system of district administration, in which the districts were governed by a *dzongpön* (ཛོང་དཔོན་) or district governor from a *dzong* or fort. The height of Phagmodrupa rule was particularly well known for the peace and security it brought across Tibet that it was said an old woman could travel perfectly safely through the country with a basket of gold. This allegory of an old woman carrying gold (རྒན་མོ་གསེར་ཁུར་) would be used by both Tibetans and Bhutanese to describe similar eras of peace and security. The district administration introduced in Bhutan during the medieval and subsequent periods was also certainly based on the Phagmodrupa model. The Phagmodrupa rule was in any case not without the problem of inheritance. When Drakpa Gyaltshen (r.1385–1432), the immediate successor to Jangchub Gyaltshen passed away after a long propitious reign, the seat was supposed to go to his brother's son. But his brother was bent on having the power himself thus leading to a protracted conflict between the father and son. The Phagmodrupa gradually lost power to the princes of Rinpung, who based themselves in Shigasamdruptse. By 1500, the Rinpung Prince Donyö Dorji (r. 1479–1512) became the *de facto* ruler of Tibet and Phagmodrupa merely persisted as a leader in name. The Rinpungpa rulers supported the Karma Kagyu school and were embroiled in a long sectarian conflict against their opponents, who were patrons of the new rising Gelug school, but ironically, they were defeated by one of their own officers, Shingshagpa Tseten Dorji (r.1565?–82?) in an internal conflict. The political power thus slipped from the Rinpungpas into the hands of the family of this officer.

Known as the Depa Tsangpa or rulers from Tsang after their main base in the Tsang province, the Tsangpa rulers, like their predecessor, showed support to Karmapa's school and relentlessly campaigned against the Gelugpas. This family, however, only managed to consolidate control over most of Tibet by 1618 and lost it in 1642 to the new government under the 5th Dalai Lama. The founder Tseten Dorji was succeeded by his son, Lhawang Dorji. He was followed by his brother Karma Tensung until 1611. The infamous dispute between the Tsangpa government and Zhabdrung Ngawang Namgyal, the incumbent of Ralung, over the reincarnation of Tibet's most illustrious Drukpa scholar and saint, Pema Karpo (1527–92) began during his reign. However, it was during the time of Karma Tensung's successor and Lhawang Dorji's son, Phuntsho Namgyal (1586?–1921), that the dispute became vehement. The events which were to unfold from this dispute consequently led to the emergence of Bhutan as a distinct political entity.

The main bone of contention between the Tibetan ruler and the founder of Bhutan was a tricky matter of religious politics, which requires further explanation. Many Tibetan monastic establishments which began in the Later Diffusion were associated with leading families and clans. The Sakya monastery was directly associated with the Khön clan, the Ralung establishment with the Gya clan, the Phagmodrupa school with the Lang clan, the Drigung with the Kyura clan and so forth. As can be seen in the chart of Ralung hierarchs below, the abbatial posts in most of these establishments were initially passed from uncle to nephew. However, with the unreliability of this procedure and the growing desire to retain power in the immediate family, the uncle–nephew lineage switched to a hereditary line. Given the social, political and economic stakes, there were many hierarchs who believed in the virtue of preserving the family line rather than following the Buddha's example as a celibate monk. Many, of course, fulfilled their secular role as progenitor first and then became celibate monks.

The hereditary transmission of position and power was, however, not free of problems. We see this in the case of the Sakya line mentioned above. The direct line ceased with the untimely death of the only male heir two generations after the first ruler, Chögyal Phagpa. A cousin, who was even alleged to be illegitimate, was brought in and groomed to save the line. He married six wives and produced thirteen children, giving rise to the opposite problem of having too many claimants to the seat and a consequent outburst of internecine conflict. The uncle–nephew transmission of the Phagmodrupa had their share of the problem when both the brother and nephew contended for the seat of power. Thus, the Tibetan uncle–nephew and the hereditary systems were seriously burdened with the problem of continuity. This problem, as we will see later, also seriously troubled the new Bhutanese state. Moreover, the family's control of monastic assets and spiritual affairs led to increasing tension between the family and the followers of the school.

It was this tension and, above all, the desire on the part of the monks to retain power and economic assets and entitlements out of the familial control which gave rise to the ingenuous Tibetan solution to the problem: the tradition of finding the *trulku* (སྤྲུལ་སྐུ) or reincarnation of the deceased person and passing down the monastic establishment and all associated entitlements and assets through the successive incarnations. The belief in reincarnation came from India through Buddhism and has a sound theological base. Informal recognition of a person as the rebirth of someone from the past existed long before the beginning of the *trulku* institutions in the thirteenth century. The *trulku* institution was novel in officially claiming the child to be the spiritual successor and thus the legal heir to properties, rights and entitlements of the deceased person. Some Tibetan scholars say that the first child to be officially recognized as a *trulku* was the incarnation of the 3rd Karmapa, which was done with the intention of retaining the position of power the 3rd Karmapa enjoyed in the Mongol court of Togon Temür.[1] In any case, the rise of the *trulku* institution reformed the Tibetan system of ecclesiastical succession but it did not easily resolve the problem imposed by the family's control of the monastic establishment. Instead, many of the families of important religious personalities identified one of their own members as the *trulku* thus using both the spiritual incarnation line and the physical family line to reinforce their power over the religious establishments.

The Gya family of Ralung is a very good example for such institutional adaptation and accommodation in order to strengthen its position. The Ralung monastery was founded by Tsangpa Gyarey in 1180 and has since become one of the most important centres of the Drukpa Kagyu school. Located in southern Tibet within the present-day Gyantse county and in a special place according to geomantic considerations, it was the principal establishment of the Middle Drukpa tradition starting from Onre Dharma Sengey, Tsangpa Gyarey's nephew who succeeded him as the abbot of the monastery. The Gya family in Ralung was one of the prominent families of princely abbots in Tibet. It started with uncle–nephew transmission and after a few generations turned into a hereditary line. Then, in the fifteenth century, perhaps in tune with changing practices, Kuenga Paljor, a male scion was also recognized as the *trulku* of the founding father, Tsangpa Gyarey, more than two centuries after his death. This would have certainly reinforced the strength of the Ralung family to combine both the family line and spiritual embodiment in the same scion.

However, the *trulku* system proved as unpredictable and unreliable as the hereditary transmission. It was based on the notion that certain religious procedures after or before the death of a religious master would lead to the identification of the child reincarnate but there was no certainty. The procedures were highly unclear and flexible and they often left the process of ecclesiastical succession prone to abuse and manipulation. After all, how could lamas conclusively prove that a child is a rebirth of a certain figure in the past when they could not even effectively prove rebirth itself? The 5th Dalai Lama's account of how he was chosen on the basis of lies and exaggerations amply demonstrates this. When Tshawa Kachupa, who led the search party, showed him a statue and rosary of the previous Dalai Lama, he did not recognize them but Kachupa walked out of the room and announced that he clearly did. Then, he was indirectly briefed about Panchen Lama's late arrival and when he later blurted out 'Panchen, you took time', the remark was interpreted as recognition of the Panchen Lama. Getting momentarily distracted by the long queue of people at the reception at Drepung, the five-year-old Dalai Lama forgot to bless Gedun Gyatsho, an attendant of the previous Dalai Lama, by touching the latter's head, and they claimed that this was an act from clear memory of the previous life. He is said to have recognized this monk who had displeased the previous Dalai Lama. 'Let alone Gedun Gyatsho, there was not a single person I recognized that day,' the 5th Dalai Lama later remarked. Similarly, when as a child he played with drums, this was interpreted as a habit from his previous life. He said: 'If all those who play such games are incarnate lamas, there would be indeed numerous of them.'[2]

The *trulku* system was thus open to abuse and a highly fallible one as far as genuine succession was concerned. Yet, one interesting thing the *trulku* system did was to throw the door of succession wide open beyond family, class and region. It is no surprise then that Kuenga Paljor's immediate reincarnation, Chökyi Drakpa, was found not in the Gya family in Ralung but in the house of Tashi Dargay, the ruler of the Ja province to the southeast. Chökyi Drakpa's reincarnation, Pema Karpo was also born in the southeastern region of Kongpo. Both of these incarnate hierarchs built their own monasteries in the southeast thereby lessening the significance of Ralung as the central seat of the Drukpa Kagyu tradition. In particular, Pema Karpo became one of the most illustrious scholars and saints of his time. He wrote over a dozen volumes of books on history, philosophy, ritual, meditation and astrology and founded many centres. It would have been certainly to the advantage of the Ralung establishment to have his reincarnation born in the family.

Zhabdrung's Pedigree

Tsangpa Gyarey belongs to the Gya line started by two Chinese men who came to Tibet in the seventh century. They pulled the cart on which the Jowo statue was transported.

Arrows indicate trulku *incarnations.*
Jamyang Chökyi Drakpa (1478–1522)

Padma Karpo (1527–92)

1. **Tsangpa Gyarey** (1161–1211)
2. Önrey Dharma Sengey (1177–1237), nephew of 1
3. Zhönnu Sengey (1200–66), nephew of 2
4. Nyima Sengey (1251–87), nephew of 3
5. Sengey Rinchen (1258–1313), cousin of 4
6. Sengey Gyalpo (1289–1326), son of 5
7. Jamyang Kuenga Sengey (1314–1347), son of 5/rebirth of 1?
8. Lodrö Senge (1345–90), son of 7 (Bhutanese mother)
9. Sherab Senge (1371–92), son of 8/rebirth of 7
10. Yeshe Rinchen (1364–1413), son of 8
11. Sherab Zangpo (1400–38), son of 10
12. **Kuenga Paljor** (1428–76), son of 11
13. Ngawang Chögyal (1465–1540), nephew of 12
14. Ngagi Wangchuk (1517–54), son of 13
15. Mipham Chögyal (1543–1604), son of 14
16. Mipham Tanpai Nyima (1567–1619), son of 15
17. **Ngawang Namgyal** (1594–1651), son of 16
18. Jampal Dorji (1631–80/81), son of 17
19. Tshokye Dorji (1681-1697), daughter of 18

Zhabdrung's dispute in Tibet

Zhabdrung Ngawang Namgyal was born in 1594 in central Tibet to Mipham Tanpai Nyima, the sixteenth incumbent of Ralung and holder of Gya lineage.[3] His mother, Sonam Palgyi Buthri, was a daughter of the Kyishö Depa, a rising noble and patron of the Gelug school. She was first married to Phuntsho Namgyal of Dagpo Kurag but after the birth of a daughter, the marriage fell apart and she turned to religion. It was while she was staying in a nunnery near the Drukpa estate of Zhika Gardrong that Mipham Tanpai Nyima met her and took her as a consort.[4] Zhabdrung, according his biographers, was an exceptional child and both his father and grandfather took full notice of his potential. Even his conception was marked by several auspicious omens according to his biographers. Later, historians and followers would rank him among the many incarnations of Avalokiteśvara, the Buddha of compassion.

His education is said to have begun by the age of four or five and he was a fast learner, grasping things effortlessly. Lhawang Lodoe, the eminent Drukpa scholar and master of astrology, was appointed as his personal tutor. At eight, he took his lay Buddhist vows and at about this time, the Sakya hierarch, Sonam Wangpo, conferred on him the religious title of Zhabdrung (ཞབས་དྲུང་), which may be rendered as 'at whose feet one submits'. By thirteen, Zhabdrung had finished much of his training and a ceremony was organized to formally install him on the throne of Ralung as the head of the establishment. Many Tibetan figures representing the major monasteries and ruling families of Tibet were present at this event bearing gifts and prayers for Zhabdrung's long life. However, it is not clear if this event was also considered as the installation of Zhabdrung as the reincarnation of Pema Karpo, but we can be sure that this was a move to confirm his authority and pre-eminence over his rivals. The disagreement over the recognition of the incarnation of the famous Pema Karpo must have become well known by then. Zhabdrung's rival Pagsam Wangpo was already born in 1593 and endorsed as the incarnation of Pema Karpo by Lhatsewa Ngawang Zangpo, who was a major student and attendant of Pema Karpo.

An interesting and colourful story with the ambiguity and vagueness typical of the *trulku* recognition process is found in a recently discovered Bhutanese biography of Zhabdrung. According to this account, the great Pema Karpo visited Ralung in the last days of his life but Dechen Gyalmo, the wife of Mipham Chögyal and the lady of the Ralung establishment did not serve the master well. Displeased by the poor reception in Ralung, Pema Karpo went to the house of the governor of Chongye. While there, Pema Karpo gave the lady of Chongye a cup of yogurt 'to indicate' that he may incarnate as her child. Unfortunately, the lady did not understand the symbolism and instead of eating it herself, she gave the yogurt to her maid. Another account says that she gave it to the governor who ate the yogurt and threw away the cup derisively remarking that the present from an eminent lama was merely a cup of yogurt. The story continues that the Chongye ruler then had an illicit affair with the maid and an illegitimate child was born. The child was informally proclaimed to be the incarnation of Pema Karpo by Lhatse Ngawang Zangpo, who was a relation of the Chongye governor. However, the ultimate authentication had to be sought from the hierarchs of the central establishment of the Drukpa school in Ralung. Thus, a request was finally made to the main hierarchs of Ralung to come and examine the child in 1596.

To verify the authenticity, Mipham Chögyal and Mipham Tanpai Nyima first performed a divination before the holiest relic of Ralung, the vertebra of Tsangpa Gyarey which has miraculously turned into an image of the Buddha Khasarpaṇi. The result came out negative. Then, Tanpai Nyima set off for the house of Chongye governor with three artefacts, which Pema Karpo entrusted him to be used in the verification of the reincarnation. The child failed to recognize the objects. When Tanpai Nyima held the child's hand and invited the child to his lap, saying 'Come, my lama, come here', the child only retreated and wailed. Slightly embarrassed, Tanpai Nyima left Chongye declaring that the true incarnation of his teacher, Pema Karpo, was apparently his own son, Zhabdrung Ngawang Namgyal. It was later said by the child's family that Tanpai Nyima frightened the child with his serious demeanour and dress. Having just come out of a three-year retreat, he was said to have been wearing long tresses and a frightful tantric costume. Zhabdrung in a later rebuttal denied that his father presented himself in such demeanour and dress. However, Lhatsewa and the Chongye governor persisted with their requests for his endorsement of Pagsam Wangpo to which Tanpai Nyima is said to have bluntly replied: 'We the incumbents of Drukpa establishment cannot speak falsely that someone is a *trulku* when he is not.'

The rejection of Pagsam Wangpo by the Ralung hierarchs as the incarnation of Pema Karpo split the Drukpa followers into two camps. While the Ralung establishment and its followers promoted Zhabdrung as the incarnation of Pema Karpo based on prophecies which the late master is said to have left behind, the Chongye group ignored Ralung's rejection and formally installed Pagsam Wangpo as the successor of Pema Karpo at Tashi Thongmon monastery. The relationship between the two groups turned sour. In 1605, the leader of the Ja myriarchy attempted to reconcile the two incarnates when Zhabdrung was visiting the Ja province but Zhabdrung's party declined to meet his rival after discovering that the meeting was to take place with the Zhabdrung seating on a slightly lower seat than his rival. By 1610, the Chongye governor appealed to the Tsangpa ruler of Tibet to intervene in the dispute, which the ruler promptly did. Being an important political ally, the Tsangpa ruler understandably sided with the Chongye governor. Tanpai Nyima, however, solemnly stood his ground saying the Drukpa deities will decide who the true incarnation is.

Meanwhile the enthusiastic Zhabdrung openly challenged Pagsam Wangpo to a spiritual duel. 'Pagsam Wangpo, if you are the true incarnation, bring the myrobalan tree from India with its fruits and branches intact. If you cannot, I will do so. Or bring the goddess Palden Lhamo holding the rein of her riding mule. If you cannot, I will do so. Alternately, let's stir each other's intestines.'[5] Of course, no such contests ever took place but the Tsangpa ruler, being wary of the power of Drukpa deities and advised by his famous teacher Tāranātha, did send an invitation to Zhabdrung to visit his court. It appears that tension between the ruler and Ralung also developed after the ruler cast a blind eye to Ralung's complaint about the forced conversion of a Drukpa centre to a Karmapa school. Such conversion of centres belonging to other schools into those of the Karmapa school was occuring rampantly during the rule of Rinpung and Tsangpa princes.

Zhabdrung visited the Tsangpa court in modern-day Shigatse in 1614. The ruler came at the gate to receive Zhabdrung but the proud young Zhabdrung continued on his horse through the gate all the way to the steps, causing the ruler some discomfiture. Although Zhabdrung and his party were received with great respect and hospitality and the meeting was cordial, it failed to yield any positive result. Both leaders, Tsangpa ruler Phuntsho Namgyal, aged twenty-eight and Zhabdrung, aged twenty, were said to have been impressive but uncompromising and sharp. On their way back to Ralung, Zhabdrung and his entourage encountered by chance Pawo Tsuglag Gyatsho (1568–1633), a lama of the Karmapa school, and his attendants at the Tagdrukha ferry crossing. Pawo Tsuglag's group was in a bit of hurry, and in their rush, the attendants of Pawo Tsuglag dragged out Zhabdrung who was already in the ferry. This enraged the attendants of Zhabdrung and in the ensuing skirmish, two of Pawo's attendants were stabbed and the ferry turned upside down. Zhabdrung was very infuriated by Pawo's attendants but he ordered his attendants to save the followers of Pawo Tsuglag from drowning. Locals would later remark that 'the drukpa *trulku* has both intense anger and compassion'. Leaving the ferry crossing, Zhabdrung and his team were on the way when they came across another incident in Rongtsathang. A woman who was alone was being robbed of her jewellery by some soldiers. Zhabdrung's attendants went to her rescue and thrashed the soldiers who happened to be men under a general of the Tsangpa ruler.

The incident at the ferry crossing almost irreparably damaged the relationship between Zhabdrung and the Tsangpa ruler, which was already heavily strained from the dispute over the incarnation. The Bhutanese would later humourously add that they should be grateful to Pawo Tsuglag for without the incident Zhabdrung may have never left Tibet. The Tsangpa ruler, who was a staunch patron of the Karmapa school, seized this opportunity to put down Zhabdrung. After his return to Ralung, Zhabdrung received a letter from the Tsangpa ruler commanding him to pay a fine for homicide (མི་སྟོང་) to Pawo Tsuglag. Zhabdrung explained that he was not guilty of the charge and requested a fair investigation. The Tsangpa ruler reprimanded Zhabdrung for disobeying him and demanded all important relics, including the vertebra relic (an image which had miraculously formed from Tsangpa Gyarey's vertebra), to be submitted to him or face serious reprisals. This image was the holiest relic of the Drukpa school and its possession came with a great deal of authority and legitimacy.

Zhabdrung refused to comply with the order and sent a stern reply: 'The self-born Khasarpani image is as vast as space or as minute as a mustard seed. No one can be even certain of its existence or nonexistence. Even if it exists, I cannot submit it to you. If you wish to be so determined to harm a hermetic adept like me with a small monastic establishment, do what you wish just as you have done so far. I have no reason to be attached to a small monastery if you are not attached to your kingship.'[6] He then amplified his supplication to the protecting deities and cultivated occult powers and warned the Tsangpa ruler of facing the wrath of Mahākāla, the chief of his tutelary deities.

The wrath of Mahākāla came soon indeed. The palace of the Tsangpa ruler was surrounded by many disturbing omens leading to rituals of protection and repulsion being conducted. The governor of Chongye was stabbed to death using his own sword and Lhatsewa Ngawang Zangpo died from a stroke. Confronted with the fear of the invisible, the Tsangpa ruler decided to swiftly eliminate Zhabdrung before he used more of his occult powers. A secret army was to be despatched to Ralung. Fortunately for Zhabdrung, a minister in the court, who was well disposed to the Drukpa establishment and who owed his father a favour, secretly sent intelligence of the imminent attack. It was about this time that Sithar, a Bhutanese patron from Gön, also arrived in Ralung. In an intimate conversion, Zhabdrung confided to him that he may go via Tagtse to Mongolia to seek Mongol support and return to annihilate the Tsangpa power. The Bhutanese patron, however, suggested an alternative option of fleeing to the south, where, he assured the Zhabdrung, there was plenty of land and support and the need for a unifying leadership. That night, Zhabdrung went to sleep with this thought and had a clear dream in which he followed a large raven southward and arrived at an unknown place. The raven was understood to be his tutelary deity, the Raven-headed Mahākāla. The next morning, Tanpai Nyima and Zhabdrung carried out a divination in front of the holy vertebra image and the indication was unequivocally to go southward. Thus, the decision was reached about 'turning the horse southward' (ཆིབས་ཁ་ལྷོ་ལ་བསྒྱུར), as the later accounts would put it metaphorically, and a message was sent to the Bhutanese patrons to send escorts to meet the party at the border.

While Zhabdrung concentrated on prayers to the tutelary deities for guidance and protection throughout his last day in Ralung, his father packed the important relics and organized the people who would accompany him. Some thirty Bhutanese monks at Ralung, including Tenzin Drukgyal of the Obtsho family in Gön, who was Zhabdrung's steward, were selected for the journey. When darkness fell, the party quietly loaded the ponies and set off on the arduous journey. Zhabdrung was twenty-two (twenty-three by Tibetan reckoning), the year 1616 according the standard version. We do not know the day and the month. A similar journey into exile would take place 343 years later in 1959 when the 14th Dalai Lama fled from the Chinese forces in Tibet. The party took two days to reach the border and were then stranded in a cave at the border for a number of days under heavy snow and blizzard until, according to the narratives, a fox finally showed the way over the pass. Soon after they crossed the pass, they were received by the Bhutanese party composed of many lamas and chieftains from the Gasa region who were waiting for them on the Bhutanese side of the watershed.

Zhabdrung arrives in Bhutan

From the border, Zhabdrung travelled through the Gön and Gasa area, blessing local patrons and devotees, and gradually made his way to Thimphu via Lingshi. When he reached Pangrizampa in Thimphu at the monastery established by his ancestor, Ngawang Chögyal, he found the 'unknown place' he saw in his dream at Ralung. It was to this place that the raven-headed protector led him in his prognostic dream. Zhabdrung's southward journey into exile or the act of 'turning the horse southward' was thus seen as an course of destiny. Later biographers and historians would interpret this fateful journey as a preordained course of history, which was predicted by no less a figure than Padmasambhava in the eighth century. The saga would become a major theme of Bhutanese cultural creations. Many songs, ballads and proverbs are related to this journey as are many toponyms along the route. The social identity of many families of his patrons and followers in this area was also shaped by this event. The journey thus transformed the cultural and religious stature and significance of the land and people he encountered.

Above all, the arrival of Zhabdrung in Bhutan became a historical and political milestone. However, the exact date for his journey still remains a moot point. While most historians following Zhabdrung's Tibetan biographer, Palden Gyatsho, agree that he left at the age of twenty-three by Tibetan reckoning, the Bhutanese biographer, Ngawang Pekar, states that he had the incident at the ferry crossing at eighteen and left the same year.[7] Moreover, we do not have the day or month of his departure, which Sangay Dorji speculates could have happened in the first two months of Fire Dragon.[8] If it was however in the last months of that year, the journey may well fall in 1617 CE.

In Thimphu, Zhabdrung enjoyed a very good reception from the followers of the Drukpa Kagyu school in the area. The patrons of Kabji, Chang and Wang and various lamas including Tshewang Tenzin of Tango and descendants of Phajo Drukgom flocked to see him. During his rest in Pangrizampa, he also conducted ceremonies of thanksgiving to the protector deities of the school and visited Dechenphu hermitage. From Thimphu, he travelled to Paro, visiting various Drukpa establishments on the way. He was again received by prominent persons, including the scions of Hungral Drungdrung and Zarchen Chöje. While he was in Drukchöding, another centre founded by Ngawang Chögyal in Paro town, he received a letter from the Tsangpa ruler informing him that all of Zhabdrung's estates in Tibet had been seized and that he should return to Tibet with the vertebra relic and surrender. Zhabdrung wrote back a long rejoinder to the ruler with a stern warning: 'You have inflicted on me all the damages you possibly could. On my part, if I fail to eliminate you and your family line, you may then decide that the Drukpa school does not have protecting deities and I am not the true incarnation of the omniscient Pema Karpo.'[9]

The Tsangpa ruler retaliated with a sudden attack organized in collaboration with the Lhapa hierarchs who were vexed by Zhabdrung's growing popularity in western Bhutan. The soldiers stormed Drukchöding while Zhabdrung and his retinue were busy conducting a grand ceremony. Zhabdrung had to flee in his undergarments across the river to the Hungral *dzong,* leaving behind even his personal effects but the *dzong* was also soon surrounded by the Tibetan and Lhapa soldiers. Zhabdrung escaped further uphill to

Damchen and Drela. Moved by the sight of the beleaguered Zhabdrung and his group, the Bhutanese chieftains led by Zarchen Chöje and the scions of Phajo Drukgom raised a local militia and came to Zhabdrung's aid. A full war ensued between the Tibetan invaders and the Bhutanese fighting for Zhabdrung. Zhabdrung himself continued on his way to Thimphu escorted by some Bhutanese patrons. On the pass above Paro, he is said to have had a vision of Mahākāla, the chief protector, who, in the vision, offered the whole of the southern land to him and ensured him victory over the Tibetan forces. However, Zhabdrung seems to have been in inner turmoil. At Tshaluna, he had a sudden urge to renounce everything and follow a hermetic life in the style of Milarepa. He blew his ritual trumpet three times in the direction of Ralung calling out the names of his father and predecessors out of exasperation and lamented about the difficulty to maintain the Drukpa order. That night, he had a dream of four *ḍākiṇis* who told him that he was the second of the nine great personalities to come in the family line and that he should strive to promote the Drukpa tradition in the southern lands. Psychologically, this was a defining point in Zhabdrung's career. It seems he resolved from that night to gather support and build a strong base in Bhutan.

From Tsaluna, he travelled through the Thimphu valley, where there was even an attempt on his life but the arrow shot at him hit the saddle of his steward's horse. He then went as far as the Shar valley, visiting Drukpa centres and patrons on a campaign to raise support but perhaps also to get further away from the invaders. While in Wachen in Shar, he received the news that the Tibetan forces were thoroughly vanquished, their general Laguney killed and his organs offered to the protecting deities. Laguney's head was clearly hanging in Cheri even in the eighteenth century.[10] A celebration followed in Shar. Zhabdrung then returned to Thimphu, visiting places in the Punakha valley on his way. He then proceeded to Tango, which was offered to him by his relative, Tshewang Tenzin, the grandson of Drukpa Kunley. At the holy cliff in Tango, he went into a retreat to cultivate further magical powers.

Zhabdrung's mastery over occult power, according to traditional accounts, became manifest when his enemy, the Tsangpa ruler, and some members of the ruler's family suddenly contracted smallpox and died in 1621 in the midst of war with the Gelugpa and Mongolian forces in central Tibet. The Tsangpa court, however, kept this death a secret until 1624. When the news was out, the Tibetans attributed the ruler's death to Zhabdrung's magical power and it was commonly said: 'Do not compete with the Drigungpa in wealth, do not compete with the Sakyapas in manpower and do not compete with the Drukpa in magical power.'[11] In Bhutan, Tsangpa's death was seen as a testimony of Zhabdrung's invincible power and the support of the protector gods. He assumed the title of *thuchen* (མཐུ་ཆེན་) or the one with great magical power and composed the famous emblematic document called the Ngachudruma (ང་བཅུ་དྲུག་མ་) or Sixteen Is, shown below. In subsequent iconographic representation, Zhabdrung was also shown with the apparels of a tantric priest performing wrathful activities of subjugation and liberation or ritual murder.

This poetic statement of 16 I/me is used as a seal and emblem.

1. I turn the wheel of the dual systems (of secular and spiritual).
2. I am a good refuge for all.
3. I hold the teachings of the glorious Drukpa.
4. I destroy those who feign to be Drukpa.
5. I have become Sarasvatī in composition.
6. I am the pure source of moral aphorisms.
7. I am the master of views free from extremes.
8. I refute those with wrong views.
9. I am the master of power and strength in debates.
10. Who is the rival that does not tremble before me?
11. I am the hero who destroys hosts of demons.
12. Who is the powerful one that can repulse my power?
13. I am the lord of speech in expounding religion.
14. I am learned in all sciences.
15. I am the incarnation prophesied by the patriarchs.
16. I am the eliminator of deviant incarnations.

The Tsangpa court is said to have gathered powerful priests in Tibet to repel Zhabdrung's magical offensives. The first major result of such an endeavour, according to the historians, was a major earthquake in Tango, when the walls of the cave in which Zhabdrung was meditating, crumbled but Zhabdrung escaped unhurt. A large boulder is said to have been held miraculously over his head by a thin canopy. Such accounts of magical feats fill his biography and certainly must also have spread in the region, attracting increasing admiration and support.

In 1619, Zhabdrung's father had passed away in Tibet; his death was perhaps seen as the outcome of the magical exchanges. The circumstances

Ngachudruma—Zhabdrung's seal containing the Sixteen Is

around his death remain unknown but we know he was under constant duress by the Tsangpa leader. His body was secretly smuggled out of Tibet and cremated in Tango. In order to house his remains and to accommodate the growing number of followers, Zhabdrung embarked on building Cheri, his first seat in Bhutan, in 1620. Just before the foundation of Cheri, Zhabdrung visited Chapcha at the invitation of the local patrons of the Drukpa tradition. It was through one wealthy patron, Darchug Gyaltshen, that he was also introduced to the ruler of Cooch Behar, Rāja Padma Nārāyaṇ, who sent him numerous gifts, including a manuscript of *Perfection of Wisdom Sūtra* in 1,00,000 verses. This Padma Nārāyaṇ in Bhutanese sources must be either Lakṣmi Nārāyaṇ (r. 1587–1621) or Bīr Nārāyaṇ (r.1621–26) and the exchange was certainly the first instance of Zhabdrung's international diplomacy. The Bhutanese biographers may have confused the name with Prāṇ Nārāyaṇ (r.1626–65), who ruled later and had direct contact with the Bhutanese rulers as Damchö Pekar's biography clearly shows. At this time, Zhabdrung's popularity was evidently rising and he enjoyed ample support from the local populace. Much of the resources and labour for building Cheri were provided for free by his patrons and devotees. Tshewang Tenzin supervised the construction and five Nepalese craftsmen were brought in to build the gilded silver reliquary for the remains of Zhabdrung's father. Zhabdrung also sent forth messengers to Tibet in order to invite his tutor, Lhawang Lodoe. Immediately after his arrival, this master clarified Zhabdrung's doubts on mensuration for the reliquary stūpa which Zhabdrung was in the process of designing.

The foundation of Cheri began a new chapter in the history of the Drukpa school. As soon as the temple was finished and the reliquary stūpa installed in it, Zhabdrung instituted a monastic community composed of some thirty monks and regulated by the constitutional and procedural framework he had drawn for his first monastic community in Ralung. These monks and the lay devotees, who gathered in Cheri, were then taught by Lhawang Lodoe, who passed down the Drukpa teachings transmitted to him by Pema Karpo. Whenever time permitted, Zhabdrung would join to either receive teachings or give sermons himself. This was the beginning of his religious tradition which would become known as the Lhodruk (ལྷོ་འབྲུག) or southern Drukpa order. Zhabdrung also requested his master Lhawang Lodoe to compose astrological commentaries based on the interpretations of the famous Pema Karpo. Lhawang Lodoe's writings on astrology later became the main source for the unique Bhutanese calendrical system, of which one distinct feature is the calculation of a day twenty-four hours earlier than in other systems. So, it is Monday associated with the moon in Bhutan while it is Sunday in the rest of the world.

In 1623, Zhabdrung went into a three-year-long retreat to finish his spiritual training. The accounts of his diligence and concentration in his spiritual practices give us a clear picture of Zhabdrung's personality. He placed a written warning 'Be mindful Ngawang Namgyal!' before him and submerged into his practice with very little sleep and rest. He made 6000 prostrations a day when he heard Pagsam Wangpo did 5000. Later, he remarked that this hard work turned him into a skeleton.[12] We can surmise that his spiritual stature improved when he came out of his seclusion after three years. Hundreds of devotees flocked to celebrate the conclusion of his retreat. It was also after this retreat that Zhabdrung kept the long beard which is presented in the standard iconographic portrayals of Zhabdrung and described in both Bhutanese and Western sources.[13] His hair was also nearly a metre and half long after this retreat but he must have cut it off when he became a monk later. However, a much more significant change was to occur to the general purpose and direction of his life. It was when he contemplated on returning to another long session of meditation that he had several extraordinary experiences and visions, including one of his father. The visionary experiences unanimously directed him to build his Drukpa state by securing both spiritual and political power over the southern lands. It was a turning point in his career and even some of his spiritual endeavours after this were directed towards this goal of state-building.

At the age of thirty-three, in a very bold and interesting move, he sent out edicts with his emblem of Ngachudruma declaring 'all gods, humans and spirits of the Lhomonkhazhi, from this day, fall under the dominion of the great magician Ngawang Namgyal and everyone must heed to his words'.[14] The edicts, with the accompanying tokens of gifts, were sent across the country to be placed on strategic spots at mountain passes, riverbanks, cliffs, forests, monuments and castles. Although ostensibly despatched to the non-human denizens of the land, the edicts had a palpable impact on psychology of the human citizenry. It was Zhabdrung's first proclamation of his ambition to become the spiritual and temporal ruler of Bhutan and to rule over the many religious leaders and chieftains in the country. It must have aroused a great deal of excitement among some people and a furore among others. We will see later that while the lamas of the Sakya and Nyingma schools accepted this political domination, lamas of other schools did not. This decree was followed by a number of strategic programmes. Zhabdrung gave many series of religious sermons to large gatherings of devotees. Such religious teachings were in those days the most effective way to garner support and allegiance. Not only did the people come to Zhabdrung for the teachings, he also went on long tours, meeting patrons and devotees and bringing teachings and sermons to their own areas. Meanwhile, he also took a consort in order to produce an heir to the line. One other programme of which we have vivid reminders to this day was his construction of fortified monastic edifices or *dzongs* (རྫོང་) which dot the Bhutanese landscape.

The Portuguese guests

It is certainly at the time of one of his regional tours in 1627 that Zhabdrung Rinpoche first met the Portuguese Jesuits, Estevao Cacella and Joao Cabral. In a report Cacella wrote on 4 October 1627 from Cheri to his superiors in south India, he mentions meeting Zhabdrung, who was camping in a 'tent well decorated with silk—he was sitting in a high platform dressed in red silk trimmed with gold; to his right and quite close to him, in a corresponding position, there was an image of his father with a lamp in front which was always kept burning'.[15] The Jesuits were the first known Westerners to visit the territory of Bhutan and Cacella's report the first eyewitness account of Zhabdrung's personality, activities and control over the area. His description of Zhabdrung and the life around him are almost entirely corroborated by the Bhutanese accounts. He writes:

> The King received us with great affability, showing that he was happy to meet us—he wanted to know where we came from, from which kingdom or nation and asked us many other questions as is usual on a first encounter; we told him that we were Portuguese, and as strangers never to come to these mountains, no one could remember ever having seen or heard that similar people had passed through that land, and therefore had never heard the word Franguis which is the name the Portuguese are known by, throughout the East . . .
>
> This King known as Dharma Rajah [Shabdrung], is 33 years old; he is both King and highest lama of this kingdom of Cambirasi [Bhutan], the first kingdom of Bhotanta [Bhutan/Tibet] in these parts—it is very large and well populated; the King prides himself in his gentleness for which

he is very much esteemed rather than feared . . . The King is also famous for his abstinence as he never eats rice, meat or fish, sustaining himself only with milk and fruit; he is also renowned for the three-year retreat he went on before we arrived here, having lived in a tiny hut he built above a rock on a high mountain, without seeing or being seen by any one; he got his food by sending down two ropes from his little hut linked to two others below which he then pulled up, never talking to anyone during all that time; he told us he occupied himself praying, and in his spare time carved some pieces—he showed us one which was his best, an image of God in white sandalwood, small but exquisitely made—he is very proud of this piece of art, and he is also a good painter—he showed us some of his paintings; . . . This King is also well known as a man of letters and is revered as such by all the other high lamas—kings send him gifts and he is very much sought out by people around this area, being host to lamas from far away kingdoms. The reason for finding him living in a tent on this mountain is that the people from each village ask him to visit and so he camps at some place where he is near to all of them; they give him many presents of horses, cattle, rice, cloth and other goods which are his principal revenue, and those people that do not invite him to their villages because they are very far away, come themselves to him with their offerings. It was for this reason that he was in that mountain with his lama school which always accompanies him; the school has more than a hundred lamas who apply themselves to their studies and perform ceremonies . . . .

The lamas do not carry weapons and shave their heads; some, but not many let their beards grow; the King has a long one which reaches to his waist, and he normally keeps it wrapped in silk, except during festivals when it is uncovered as when we first met him; the hair on his head is nearly one and half metres long; it seems he is very proud of it and wears it thus as a mark of greatness; however he told us that he planned to cut it when he had a son who would be his successor, and that he would then go into retirement and leave the world because he did not want death to come upon him while he had his hair long, as had happened to another King, his ancestor, who had caused a scandal for not having cut his hair before his death. The dress of the lamas is a short tunic which covers the chest leaving the arms bare; the rest of their body down to the feet is well covered with a large cloth over which is another cloth worn as a cape; they never wear anything else nor do they go about naked.[16]

Talking about the feasibility of missionary work he and Cabral had come to carry out, he continues:

> ... the freedom that exists in this fairly large and well populated kingdom will greatly help us to achieve our ends, as the people willingly submit to the King, without feeling any obligation to defer to him or follow his doctrine, nor does he have the power to force anyone to do anything; rather, his main revenues come from what the people voluntarily give him—he does not wish anyone to be unhappy and everyone is free to do what he wants, as the King himself told us many times when speaking of his lamas who are the group most dependent on him.[17]

The Bhutanese sources corroborate the arrival of the visitors from Purdhukha (Portugal), the likes of whom had never been seen before. They are said to have travelled a long distance by land and sea through many countries, including 'the land of cannibals' and brought to Zhabdrung gifts of firearms, ammunition, telescopes and other wondrous objects. Although there is no mention of their missionary work, Zhabdrung's biographer reports that the visitors offered to bring military support from their country if needed, which Zhabdrung declined as it is against Buddhist principles to resort to 'barbaric forces'. The biographer also adds that the technology of making bombs and ammunition can be found in the tantric texts but the guns, which were unknown until then, could cause fear among the enemies with its mere sound.[18] No doubt, these gifts must have come handy in Zhabdrung's direct confrontation with his enemies.

Cacella's report makes no mention of the arms and ammunition or offer of military support. However, his description aptly captures not only the personality and religious devotion of Zhabdrung but also the prevailing religious and political situation in which Zhabdrung was manoeuvring. The southern land did not have a centralized political authority and people were largely left to fend for themselves. Meanwhile, Zhabdrung's religious stature in western Bhutan had certainly become unrivalled and his political influence was growing rapidly. This growth was largely due to Zhabdrung's spiritual authority and personal charisma but it was also actively cultivated through his constant religious tours and services. The Jesuits found Zhabdrung's peripatetic life quite cumbersome for their own work but their presence in his company was very advantageous to Zhabdrung. It was in order to gain political mileage and prestige that Zhabdrung strongly encouraged the Jesuits to stay on and even allowed them to use a room in Cheri as a chapel, granted land in Paro to build a church and sent some of his own attendants to join the congregation. With no success in conversion and despite much discouragement from Zhabdrung against their departure, the Jesuits eventually left for Tibet.

Zhabdrung's first *dzong* and the second Tibetan invasion

Zhabdrung's political domination however increased and it was to consolidate his political sway over the people of the western valleys by strengthening his defence position that he embarked on the construction of his first *dzong* in Semtokha. The site already had a small shrine on it built by Lama Pangkha Shongpa, which was offered to Zhabdrung. In 1629, Zhabdrung laid the foundation of the new structure, including a central temple with twelve corners and surrounding quarters and walls.[19] The design was based on Gyalje Tshal, the tantric college founded by Pema Karpo in Tsang. His students from Tibet and local areas carried out the building works at daytime and received teachings from Zhabdrung in the evening. The construction of the large *dzong* undoubtedly aroused the fear of Zhabdrung's rising influence among his religious rivals. Presented as the five lamaist factions in standard Bhutanese histories, these lamas joined hands to combat Zhabdrung's dominance. I shall discuss later who the five lamaist factions were. These groups not only harassed the people who were supporting Zhabdrung but launched a direct assault on Zhabdrung's party during the construction of the Semtokha *dzong* killing many devotees from Tibet. Zhabdrung's forces retaliated and a full battle broke out. It was only after their leader, Lama Palden, was killed that the enemies retreated and dispersed. The *dzong* was finished successfully and consecrated by Zhabdrung's tutor, Lhawang Lodoe in 1631.

Around the time the Semtokha *dzong* was completed, Zhabdrung also saw the birth of his son, Jampal Dorji (1631–81). Jampal Dorji was born to Tricham Gökar Drolma, Zhabdrung's second consort. Like the first consort, she was following Zhabdrung as a religious disciple when Lhawang Lodoe had a visionary experience in which he saw Zhabdrung's father seeking to be reborn as Gökar Drolma's child. Gökar Drolma was thus presented to Zhabdrung as a consort after going through rituals of purification. Despite the injunction normally placed on matchmaking for Buddhist monks, Lhawang Lodoe did not seem to have any compunction in arranging this matrimonial link to sustain the Ralung line. When the relationship finally resulted in the birth of Jampal Dorji, he was considered to be the rebirth of Zhabdrung's father Tanpai Nyima based on Lhawang Lodoe's visionary experience.

Meanwhile Zhabdrung's relationship with his first consort Damchö Tenzin (1606–60) had become strained. Damchö Tenzin was a daughter of the *chöje* family of Changangkha descending from Phajo Drukgom Zhigpo. She became Zhabdrung's consort around 1626 and had already given birth to a daughter. By 1630, her relationship with Zhabdrung was not going well, perhaps due to the arrival of the new consort and the pressure to produce a male heir. Damchö Tenzin left Bhutan and wandered in western Tibet for many years until her brother Kuenga Pekar went in search of her to bring her back. When she eventually returned to Bhutan in 1634, Zhabdrung had already taken the full ordination of a monk and she was passed on as a wife to Tshewang Tenzin of Tango. Her second conjugal relationship to Tshewang Tenzin was to produce one of Zhabdrung's most prestigious successors, Tenzin Rabgay, who we shall meet later.

In 1632, Zhabdrung renewed his former connection with the Sakya establishment in Tibet when the Sakyapa hierarch Thutob Wangchuk (1588–1637) toured the Sakyapa centres in western Bhutan. This would later lead to a marital alliance with the Sakya family from which a bride was brought for Jampal Dorji. However, for now, Jampal Dorji was just a baby and there was another pressing spiritual duty Zhabdrung wanted to fulfil. If he were to carry on the transmission of monastic vows from Pema Karpo, he had to receive it quickly as his master Lhawang Lodoe was already quite old. Thus, in 1633, two years after he produced a male heir to carry on the line, Zhabdrung took the ordination of a full-fledged monk from Lhawang Lodoe, who died the following year aged eighty-four, a satisfied master.

Meanwhile, the challenges posed by the internal rivals and Tibetan enemies were far from over. Tenkyong Wangpo (r.1619–42) had succeeded his father Phuntsho Namgyal as the ruler of Tibet and he was instigated by Zhabdrung's rivals in Bhutan to send his army to attack Zhabdrung. The coalition planned a major assault on Bhutan. The second Tibetan invasion took place in 1634 with as many as four battalions sent down via Paro, Gasa and Bumthang. Although Bumthang had not yet come under Zhabdrung's dominion, the Tibetans perhaps thought it had. These armies were aided by the local militia of the five lamaist factions and the valleys were filled with warfare. Zhabdrung deputed all his duties to Tenzin Drukgyal, entrusted some of the important relics in Shar Wachen and escaped with some relics to Jarogang in Khothangkha. If the situation got too difficult for him to remain in Bhutan, it was Zhabdrung's intention to escape to India. The invaders appear to have overcome the local resistance without great difficulty and occupied the Semtokha *dzong*, Zhabdrung's new seat. However, they were not to enjoy the final victory very long as the ammunition stored in the *dzong* caught fire, perhaps accidentally, and the *dzong* collapsed on the invaders who were busy looting. Bhutanese historians would claim this to be a work of the protecting deities. The Tibetan invaders, who knew nothing about the explosives, were utterly puzzled and frightened. The few who survived, returned to Tibet with the news of a terrible defeat.

It is not clear what the actual mission of the Tibetan forces was. If it was to capture Zhabdrung or obtain the vertebra relic, 'the bone from his late father' which Zhabdrung told his Portuguese visitors was what we might call the main bone of contention between him and the Tsangpa ruler, the military invasion failed as they found neither Zhabdrung nor the vertebra relic. The relic was confidentially kept in Wachen and Zhabdrung found sanctuary in Jarogang. If their objective, as the lamaist factions may have wished, was to destabilize Zhabdrung's rising power by taking over his new fortified base of Semtokha, they partially succeeded. If not for the fire from the ammunition, Zhabdrung may not have managed to regain control of the *dzong* and the adjacent valleys. Thanks to the fire, the invaders were routed but barely four years after its consecration, the new edifice of Semtokha was reduced to rubbles. It was renovated only some thirty-seven years later in 1671.

The Palace of Great Bliss and the third Tibetan invasion

Zhabdrung bounced back with undiminished determination to carry on his task of state-building. As soon as he received the news of victory, he returned to Cheri, where he performed prayers for those who died in the battles. Then, he resumed his tour of the western valleys, this time partly in search of a venue for a new fortified centre. He travelled through the Punakha valley and in the process took over some places which belonged to the opposing lamas, particularly one at Gön Tshephu which was owned by the Barawa school. It was while he was residing at the small shrine founded by Vanaratna at the confluence of the two rivers in Punakha that he decided to build a larger and grander *dzong* than the one destroyed. For the later Bhutanese, the construction of a fortified centre between the male and female rivers, Phochu and Mochu, was a prophetic choice. It was the fulfilment of a prediction supposedly made long ago by Padmasambhava that 'between the two rivers, a Drukpa fortress will be established' and that 'someone named Namgyal will come to [reside] on the trunk of the mountain which resembles a haughty elephant'.[20]

The account of Zhabdrung's construction of the Punakha *dzong* is full of magical elements. The timber and stone needed for the *dzong* were offered by the local deities. The local mermaid 'offered' seasoned wood, which was used for making the pillars. One deity 'brought' timber floating down the river and another 'revealed' by causing a landslide to show a quarry of excellent stones for the construction. The architect was a local man from the village of Balingkha, who was thought to be 'an emanational architect' (སྤྲུལ་ པའི་བཟོ་བོ་) or a divine being who had taken the incarnation of an architect. When Zhabdrung summoned him, he came with a bucket of milk and basket of red berries, which Zhabdrung thought was highly auspicious, heralding the growth of the red-robed monastic community. According to the narrative, he was made to sleep in Zhabdrung's presence for three consecutive nights when, through Zhabdrung's spiritual power, he was taken to Ralung and the Copper-coloured Mountain paradise of Padmasambhava in his dream in order to see the architectural designs of these sites. Zhabdrung then instructed him to build the Punakha *dzong* in the image of the temple in Ralung.

We have no contemporary accounts beside these mythical narratives and can say very little about the actual process of construction. The foundation for the Punakha *dzong* was laid in 1637 and the work carried out by the local devotees under the supervision of Pekar Rabgay. We can assume that the size of the *dzong* was approximately equal to what exists today with the *utse* tower structure in the centre, multiple shrines and courtyards, battlements in four corners and monastic quarters on four sides but with only one of the two main assembly halls we find today.[21] Zhabdrung, with great foresight, designed the assembly hall to be large enough to house over 600 monks although there were only about a hundred monks then. His followers, including the chief architect Balingpa, at the time complained that it was too large but respectfully complied with Zhabdrung's wishes. Zhabdrung's farsightedness was to prove right as the population of monks increased to 300 in his own lifetime and to over 800 by the time of Tenzin Rabgay, some fifty years after the completion of the *dzong*.

At the height of the construction of the Punakha *dzong*, Zhabdrung laid the foundation of another *dzong* further downstream on the ridge of a mountain which resembles a sleeping elephant. This second *dzong*, which was named Wangdiphodrang, was intended to subdue the enemies to the south.

The awesome location, where three waterways, three ridges and three skies converge and where the wind and rivers roar like a thousand thunder dragons, was considered to be very powerful according to traditional geomancy. He is said to have received prophecies to build a *dzong* on this strategic location between the Punatsangchu and Dangchu rivers many years earlier but it was while he was in meditation in Khyime Lhakhang, the seat of his predecessors, that he received the decisive prognostication. After a dark figure instructed him in his dream to meditate on the strategic ridge, he sent his attendants to check the place. The attendants saw on the ridge four ravens, which flew away towards four cardinal directions as they approached. Zhabdrung understood the four ravens to be the four raven-headed protecting deities and the spot to be the point from where he could subjugate the country in four directions. This is how the *dzong* got its name Wangdiphodrang (དབང་འདུས་ཕོ་བྲང་) or 'the Palace of Subjugation' according to most sources. An oral account has it that when Zhabdrung approached the site, he saw a young boy named Wangdi playing in the sand. Upon being asked what he was doing, the boy replied that he was building a palace. Zhabdrung saw this as an auspicious omen, and named his new dzong, Wangdiphodrang or 'the Palace of Wangdi'.

Whatever the origin of the name may be, Zhabdrung's initiative to build the Wangdiphodrang *dzong* must have actually come about after a wealthy local patron offered a large stretch of land in the area. The foundation was laid in 1638 and one *pönlop*, Nyama Kukye, was appointed as supervisor while Zhabdrung continued on his tour of the valleys. We have no accounts about the size, structure and process of its construction except that it had a central edifice with many floors and its roof tied with metal chains, several shrines for deities, jingling bells and decorations of sun and moon-shaped icons called 'mirrors' and surrounding high walls with parapets and a large entrance.[22] We can again safely assume that the initial structure was roughly the same size as it is now.

Of the two *dzongs* which were built simultaneously and known then as the upper and lower seats, the one at Punakha was finished first and a great celebration took place when Zhabdrung's patrons from all directions came with heaps of offerings. Historians comment that Punakha was hence rendered as Pungthangkha (སྤུངས་ཐང་ཁ་) or 'the ground of heaps' and the *dzong* called Dewachenpoi Phodrang (བདེ་བ་ཆེན་པོའི་ཕོ་བྲང་) or 'the Palace of Great Bliss'. There is no doubt that Zhabdrung conceived Punakha as his central seat and the substitute for his seat of Ralung in Tibet. As soon as it was completed, the relics including the vertebra image were brought to the Punakha *dzong* and the monastic community at Cheri and his son, Jampal Dorji, were also moved there. He also initiated his dual system of governance, in which the spiritual and secular affairs were conjointly housed within the walls of the *dzong*. While he presided as the overall lord of religion and political affairs, he delegated various tasks through new appointments. Pekar Rabgay was appointment as the governor or *dzongpön* (རྫོང་དཔོན་) of Punakha, Damchö Gyaltshen as the caretaker of the ecclesiastical community, Tenzin Drukgyal as main person responsible for secular affairs and Jatang Pekar Tashi as the first *pönlop* of Dungyul. Another person was sent as the *pönlop* of Jarogang.

Peace times were however cut short with another invasion from Tibet. The third Tibetan invasion of 1639 was also instigated by the lamaist factions and a large army was again sent by the Tsangpa ruler through Paro and Gasa mainly to destabilize Zhabdrung by striking at his new fortresses of Punakha and Wangdiphodrang. At this point, the Tsangpa ruler, Tenkyong Wangpo, was more eager to settle the dispute and reach a peaceful agreement than to wage a protracted war. A great deal of political changes had taken place in Tibet by then. The Tsangpa ruler was caught up in a fierce war with the Mongol forces of Gushri Khan, who came to the support of the beleaguered Gelugpa school. Thus, it was in the Tsangpa ruler's interest to settle disputes with minor enemies so that he could commit more soldiers against the great Mongolian threat from the east. For this reason, the Tsangpa ruler is said to have reached a settlement with King Singye Namgyal of Ladakh at about this time. Moreover, the Tsangpa alliance with the Chongye family, in which Zhabdrung's rival Pagsam Wangpo was born, had also fallen apart by then. This fall out deteriorated further as a son of the Chongye ruler and Pagsam Wangpo's nephew was recognized as the 5th Dalai Lama, a leading figure of the Gelugpa school. Thus, the Chongye family, which was once a close ally of the Tsangpa ruler, was now at the head of the party opposing the Tsangpa rule.

The Tibetan fear of Zhabdrung's magical prowess cannot be understated either. As much as the Bhutanese attributed their victories to Zhabdrung's occult power and command over the protecting deities, the Tibetans feared Zhabdrung for his power in black magic. The Tibetan court and the family of the ruler were said to have witnessed many frightening omens each time Zhabdrung exercised his magical prowess. Even the rival incarnate Pagsam Wangpo is said to have suffered from the serious repercussions of Zhabdrung's sorcery. The Tsangpa ruler was repeatedly advised by his teacher Tāranātha to seek a reconciliation with Zhabdrung in order to avoid the unwanted consequences of black magic or the wrath of Drukpa deities. In the light of such religious and political scenario, the Tsangpa ruler was only keen to see the end of the conflict with Zhabdrung which his predecessors had started. Thus, the invaders were sent primarily with the hope of bringing Zhabdrung to the negotiating table rather than to cause real harm. The generals were in fact instructed to use the occasion to bring about conciliation and avoid unnecessary violence.

At the wake of the war, Zhabdrung was secretly ushered to Cheri from where he is said to have once again used his power of magic to defeat the Tibetan troops. Despite the Bhutanese resistance, the Tibetan troops managed to surround the two new *dzongs* but they failed to enter them. Except for some minor damages inflicted on both sides, the war seemed to have soon turned into a stalemate with Tibetan troops stationed around the *dzongs*. Meanwhile, the negotiation between the Tsangpa ruler and Zhabdrung was in full swing with the Sakya hierarch as the mediator. The Sakya hierarch had the Tsangpa ruler order his general Gölungpa to withdraw the troops from Bhutan and also despatched messengers to Zhabdrung. It seems probable that efforts for negotiation have been going on for some time by then. Zhabdrung received letters and presents from the Sakya hierarch, the Tsangpa ruler and even the rival incarnate Pagsam Wangpo, who appears to have expressed an interest in meeting Zhabdrung personally to resolve the dispute. We do not exactly know the content and tone of the letters received by Zhabdrung but we have two of the several rejoinders sent by him preserved in his biography written by Palden Gyatsho. They give us a general idea of what the letters to which he was responding may have contained.

The first letter recounts the controversy in some detail starting from the final days of Pema Karpo. Zhabdrung argues that Pagsam Wangpo was wrongly identified as the incarnate of Pema Karpo by Lhatsewa Ngawang Zangpo and the Tsangpa rulers misguidedly supported this candidate and unjustly mistreated him and the Ralung establishment. He insists that a definite conclusion be reached as to who is right and who is wrong. In addition to the exchange of letters, it seems that some meetings also took place to discuss a solution to the dispute. In the course of the exchanges, some of the mediators acting on Pagsam Wangpo's behalf made sharp and outrageous remarks including the innuendo that if Pagsam Wangpo were not an incarnate of Pema Karpo, Zhabdrung could not be a scion of the Ralung line.

In the second letter, Zhabdrung dismisses such silly remarks as counterproductive to the settlement of disputes. While in favour of a resolution, Zhabdrung was unrelenting in his position with regard to the issue of the incarnation. This letter contains a number of very interesting points and demands. Firstly, he clarifies that he had no ill feeling toward the young ruler, Tenkyong Wangpo. The new ruler was not a target of his sorcery. If Tenkyong Wangpo suffered repercussions of the sorcery aimed at the former ruler due to the close relationship the two of them enjoyed, Zhabdrung indicates that amendments were being made through prayers and confessions to the protecting deities. He also instructed how a magical talisman previously planted in the Tsangpa palace must be removed. We can conclude from this that in the hope of reconciliation Zhabdrung had stopped his work of magic against the Tsangpa ruler by this time.

However, he persisted with his request for a clear cut verdict for the Drukpa controversy. He gives a long account of how the Ralung family played an important role in Tibetan history, indicating that the reputation of the family must be restored. Earlier he was asked if he was willing to go through the ordeal of 'picking pebbles from boiling oil'. This traditional Tibetan method of verifying truth from falsity is an ordeal in which a white and black pebble would be put in a pot of boiling oil and the two disputing parties made to blindly pick one each. One who picks the white pebble claims the truth and becomes the winner. Zhabdrung agreed to this ordeal as the best solution. However, if the dispute was to be resolved through negotiation without such a contest, he demanded that Pagsam Wangpo must revoke the claim of being Pema Karpo's incarnation and receive no entitlements connected to such a claim. If Pagsam Wangpo wished to meet Zhabdrung, he should expect to be treated as no more than an ordinary priest of Chongye. Zhabdrung also demanded that all appointments in Drukpa monasteries should be made by him from Bhutan and that the manuscripts and woodblocks for the collection of Pema Karpo's writings be delivered to him.

The dispute over the incarnation was never fully resolved. The Tsangpa government on its part is said to have officially acknowledged both Zhabdrung and Pagsam Wangpo as legitimate incarnations of Pema Karpo. While Zhabdrung was to control Ralung, the Druk monastery and many other affiliates in central and southern Tibet, Pagsam Wangpo was given Sangag Chöling, a monastery founded by Pema Karpo in southeastern Tibet. Such arrangements would not have been acceptable to Zhabdrung. Earlier when his teacher Lhawang Lodoe, soon after the latter's arrival from Tibet, tried to bring about a reconciliation by suggesting that Pema Karpo could come in multiple incarnations and that Zhabdrung could be the emanation of the body and Pagsam Wangpo of speech, Zhabdrung sharply replied:

'I alone am the emanation of body, speech and mind.'[23] Throughout his life, Zhabdrung relentlessly maintained his position and refused to accept Pagsam Wangpo as an incarnation of Pema Karpo. Acceptance of a false incarnation, according to him, was perjury about supernatural things (མི་ཆོས་ཀླ་མའི་རྫུན), one of the most serious offences in Buddhism. Thus, there was no sight of a proper reconciliation between the two candidates which Pagsam Wangpo and many other followers of Drukpa school hoped for. In 1641, Pagsam Wangpo suddenly passed away at the age of forty-seven (forty-eight by Tibetan reckoning), thus bringing a natural but only temporary closure to the dispute.

As for the status of the five lamaist factions in Bhutan, it was, as far as Zhabdrung was concerned, an issue in which the Tibetan authorities had no say. The area of Lho, as Bhutan was known then, fell outside the Tibetan jurisdiction. It was beyond the Pümula pass and whoever won local support had the right to establish their religious centres. Zhabdrung made it quite clear that he was not creating a sectarian state unable to tolerate multiple religious traditions. As long as the leaders of other religious schools were willing to pledge their political allegiance to him, they would be allowed to carry on their religious work freely in the country. It was their refusal to submit to the political authority he was striving to establish and their persistent confrontations which resulted in their complete banishment or temporary decline. The lamas who opposed Zhabdrung are generally described as the five lamaist factions (བླ་ཁག་ལྔ) although there is no agreement as to who exactly the five were as there were normally more than five groups enumerated including the Lhapa, Nyenyingpa, Gedan Shingtapa (Gelug), Barawa, Chagzampa, Kathogpa and sometimes even Sakyapa. We can be sure that the Sakyapa was not part of this group as Zhabdrung enjoyed an amicable relationship with them and their monastic centres thrived throughout Zhabdrung's period.

The letter preserved in Zhabdrung's biography by Palden Gyatsho refers to the Lhapa, Nenyingpa, two Kathogpas and Chagzampa as the five lamas but does not include Barawa and Gedan Shingtapa, who certainly challenged Zhabdrung and were consequently removed from Bhutan. In his analysis of the list, Gedun Rinchen argues that the five lamaist factions included Lhapa, Nenyingpa, Gedan Shingtapa, Barawa and Chagzampa, the latter two being only minor opponents. He excludes Kathogpas based on the evidence that their centres continued to flourish under Zhabdrung.[24] Pema Tshewang, however, includes the Kathogpas among the five lamas and identifies the lama who died while attacking Semtokha as a Kathogpa scion.[25] Sangay Dorji, following Ngawang Pekar, excludes Gelugpas from the list of lamas who opposed Zhabdrung during his conflict with the Tsangpa rulers. Zhabdrung is said to have even made offerings to the Gelugpa monasteries before he fell out with the new Gelugpa government in Tibet when the Gelugpas were expelled from Bhutan.[26] Most scholars provide a partial enumeration while also holding this to be an all-inclusive list of dissenting lamas. It is plausible that the five lamas mentioned in Zhabdrung's letter were the lamas about whom the Tibetan ruler raised issues and the list is not be construed as one which includes all lamaist groups opposed to Zhabdrung. The terminology of five lamaist factions as a standard list covering all groups of dissenting lamas is perhaps a later development.

At any rate, with consecutive defeats in wars and the withdrawal of Tibetan support, the coalition of rival lamas had no chance of combating Zhabdrung's growing influence and military successes. By the end of the third war, most followers of the Lhapa, Nenyingpa, Shingtapa and Barawa schools had left Bhutan while some, such as the followers of Chagzampa school, were stripped of their power and forced into submission to the Drukpa authority. It must, however, be remembered that many other lamas who cooperated with the Zhabdrung and accepted his political supremacy continued to thrive under Zhabdrung's rule. Among them were the lamas of the Sakyapa school and the followers of many different forms of Nyingma school. Hierarchs from the Pema Lingpa tradition such as Pema Lingpa's grandson, Pema Thinley, and Pema Lingpa's incarnation, Tshultrim Dorji, were later even received by Zhabdrung at the Punakha *dzong* with great honour. Based on these examples and Cacella's report, we can generally confirm that Zhabdrung showed good respect and tolerance for sectarian differences as long as they did not impinge on his political project of state-building. The lamas who were evicted from Bhutan challenged his push for political supremacy and thus earned his disfavour.

The 1639 war thus did not bring the desired outcome for the lamas who opposed Zhabdrung or for the Tibetan authorities who wanted Zhabdrung to slacken his position. Instead, the opening of negotiations elevated Zhabdrung to a playing field equal to the Tibetan ruler and established Zhabdrung as the indisputable leader of Bhutan although we must remember his power at this point is limited to the western valleys. His biographers are quick to point out that after the failure of the third invasion, Zhabdrung was recognized as the supreme ruler of Bhutan not only by the Tsangpa ruler but also by many Tibetan leaders, including the Karmapa, Sakyapa and Gelukpa figures. Zhabdrung's connection with King Singye Namgyal of Ladakh had also been well established by then. One prince of Ladakh was receiving his training in Bhutan and later became the *dzongpön* of Wangdiphodrang and another became the chief abbot. Zhabdrung had also already been offered several temples in western Tibet. In the following decades the number of temples given to Zhabdrung's care outside Bhutan would increase in number. Recognition and presents also came from Indian princes to the south and from kings of the Kathmandu valley. Zhabdrung indubitably emerged as the supreme head of a new state. Meanwhile, the Tsangpa government in Tibetan was on the verge of collapse under the pressure of Mongol–Gelugpa forces. Zhabdrung must have been aware of this situation when he declined an invitation from the Tsangpa ruler to come to Tibet some time in 1640. He said the Druk or dragon year is unpropitious for the Drukpa and he had a lot of work to do to renovate a temple in Paro.

In the years following the third invasion, Zhabdrung amplified his efforts to strengthen his power base in Bhutan. In 1641, he took over the Do-ngon *dzong*, at the current location of Dechenphodrang, in Thimphu from the followers of the Lhapa school. He renamed it Tashichödzong and made it the summer seat of his government and monastic community and introduced the practice of seasonal migration between Thimphu and Punakha. This tradition of the migration of monks between the summer and winter seats following the ancient transhumance pattern continues to this day. As his domain expanded and material resources became increasingly available, Zhabdrung also felt the acute need for human capital, particularly of educated religious figures to occupy important posts. Thus, he went on another tour of the valleys accompanied by his steward Tenzin Drugyal to enlist candidates for monkhood. Although the term 'monk-tax' or *tsunthrel* (བཙུན་ཁྲལ་) was used, we do not know exactly if such a tax was imposed on the families, as was the case in later times, or young men were encouraged to join the monkhood voluntarily. Such a custom of monk tax also known as *drathrel* (གྲྭ་ཁྲལ་) was practised in central Bhutan by Pema Thinley, a contemporary of Zhabdrung.[27] In any case, the outcome was beyond Zhabdrung's expectation of about 300 monks. Some 360 postulants joined the monastic community, which Zhabdrung insisted must follow a very rigorous discipline and routine of life. A scholastic department was also established in order to promote the study of Buddhist philosophy and Pema Karpo's scholarly writings. A Tibetan teacher named Khukhu Lopön, who was one of his colleagues at Serdog

College in Tibet, was invited to teach the scholastic classes. Meanwhile, Zhabdrung also continually gave religious sermons to the monks and lay devotees or presided over religious ceremonies. His educational programme was to pay off well when many of his monks became competent to take up important posts including the abbotship of temples offered to Zhabdrung in various places abroad.

The Dalai Lama's rule and Zhabdrung's victory

While Zhabdrung was busy strengthening his base in Bhutan, Tibet was going through a tumultuous political period. At the invitation of the Gelugpas, who suffered immense damages at the hands of the Tsangpa government and their Kagyupa allies, the forces of Gushri Khan of the Khoshot Mongols swept through Tibet taking full control of the country and putting the Tsangpa ruler Tenkyong Wangpo under arrest. Stripping the Tsangpa ruler of political power, Gushri Khan offered the supreme leadership of Tibet to his spiritual master, the 5th Dalai Lama in much the same way as Kubilai Khan offered to Chögyal Phagpa in the thirteenth century. This event in 1642 began the rule of the Dalai Lamas in Tibet, and Ganden Phodrang or Ganden Palace, the private residence of the Dalai Lamas in Drepung, formally became the name of the Tibetan government. This system of the Dalai Lama rule was to continue officially until 1959. The Gelugpa ascension to power was followed by a series of widespread sectarian persecutions. The Kagyupas, particularly of the Karmapa group, and Jonangpas who were closely associated with the former rulers and previously at the forefront of sectarian campaigns against the Gelugpa school now faced serious reprisals from the Gelugpas. Their monasteries were converted to Gelugpa centres and their properties expropriated. The situation got worse when one of Karmapa's officers was caught carrying a letter with Karmapa's seal on it mentioning how the Gelugpas must be exterminated without a trace. The Karmapa had to flee into exile and the Tsangpa ruler is said to have been put in a cowhide and thrown into the river. In addition to the ravages of political strife, Tibet also suffered years of bad weather and severe famine.

In the midst of such problems in Tibet, Bhutan was once again, as it was often in the past, a safe haven and place of refuge for some Tibetans. Zhabdrung's biographer and Karma Kagyu monk, Palden Gyatsho, and his sister journeyed to Bhutan from Tsang in order to escape the sectarian strife under the new Gelugpa rule. The Tibetan country, he noted as he crossed the border, was an expanse of grey and dusty land swept by the cold wind and run down by the Mongol hordes. In contrast, the lush green Bhutanese country covered with forests and bestrewn with flowers spread out before him in a great view and filled him with immense joy.[28] It was to him, as to many before him, a southward journey to the wholesome and peaceful hidden lands prophesied by the great Padmasambhava. However, there was one evident difference by this time. Tibetan refugees or travellers could not freely enter the southern valleys. While Palden Gyatsho and his sister, who were children of a longstanding patron of the Ralung establishment, were allowed to enter, their travelling partner and a treasure discoverer, Ngadag Tagsham, was refused entry to Bhutan by Zhabdrung. He thus went to Sikkim.

When the Gelugpas came to power in Tibet, some members of Zhabdrung's inner circle became hopeful of finding a close ally in the new the Gelugpa government. They saw the fall of Tsangpa rule and the rise of Gelugpa government as a positive development in their relation to the north. Zhabdrung, however, was doubtful, perhaps partly because the 5th Dalai Lama was a close relative of his rival, late Pagsam Wangpo. Notwithstanding his reservations, at the request of his coterie Zhabdrung sent an envoy led by his half-brother Tenzin Drukdra to congratulate the new power in Tibet with a letter and gifts of rice, textiles and horses. Now that the common enemy, the Tsangpa ruler, was fully vanquished, his letter sought friendship between the Gelug and Drukpa schools for the sake of a peaceful Bhutan and Tibet (ཀྲོ་བདེ་བོད་འབྲུག). Tenzin Drukdra showed Zhabdrung's letter to the 5th Dalai Lama's secretary Sonam Chöphel alias Awu, before making the formal presentation of gifts to the Dalai Lama. This shrewd and bellicose secretary was the main agent who brought the Gelugpa to power by advancing his military ploys, either keeping the Dalai Lama in the dark or openly ignoring his religious concerns. Peace, which Tenzin Drukdra hoped for, was unfortunately not to be. While supporting Zhabdrung's proposal for Gelug–Drukpa friendship, Sonam Chöphel demanded that Zhabdrung return to Ralung, give back the estates of the five lamaist factions in Bhutan and that both Zhabdrung and his enemies submit to the new Gelugpa hegemony. If these conditions were not fulfilled, he said that his Mongol king (Gushri Khan) would not accept any such deal. Sonam Chöphel's brash response sent the brief chance for good relations between the two new governments down the drain. In fact, a Lhapa scion was already in the court of the 5th Dalai Lama in 1642 begging for military support according to the 5th Dalai Lama's autobiography.[29]

When Tenzin Drukdra sought Zhabdrung's advice on what to do next,

Zhabdrung instructed him to donate the rice to a Sakya monastery and return with other goods and horses. Tenzin Drukda immediately returned to Bhutan and the congratulatory gifts to the Dalai Lama were never made. Infuriated by the snub, Sonam Chöphel despatched a message to Zhabdrung demanding that the conditions previously stated to his half-brother be fulfilled or otherwise risk suffering the wrath of his Mongol king. With a message was sent a bag of mustard seeds and word that there are as many Mongol warriors as the seeds, ready to attack. The account of the exchanges between Zhabdrung and the Tibetan ruler gets even more thrilling. Zhabdrung pounded the mustard seeds to a mash and sent it back with the message: 'If your Mongol king would not listen, my protecting deity Mahākāla would not listen either.'[30] If the mustard seeds symbolized Mongol soldiers, Zhabdrung indicated that they can be pulverized. With his message, Zhabdrung also sent a rock and a needle agreeing to accept Sonam Chöphel's demands if the latter could pierce the rock with the needle and return them to him. Following this reply, Zhabdrung actively raised a local militia from the western valleys and had them gathered in Punakha. He also expelled the followers of the Gelugpa school, who were previously on good terms with him, from Bhutan. In response, the Tibetan government expelled many lamas of the Drukpa school from Tibet.

The invasion of the Gelug–Mongol forces from Tibet took place in the autumn of 1644 through Paro. According to the 5th Dalai Lama's records, 700 Mongolian and Tibetan soldiers were deployed, perhaps in addition to the militia of the lamas who sought their help. Zhabdrung had by then assembled and prepared his warriors or *pazap*s (དཔའ་རྩལ་པ་) at the Druk Chöding monastery in Paro. The first battle was fought on the grounds where the current Paro town is located. With no immediate signs of victory on either side, the war seems to have been protracted well into the spring in the following year with the invaders still camped in the area. It was perhaps a Bhutanese ploy to wait for the hot and humid climate of spring, in which Mongolian and Tibetan soldiers would be susceptible to many health problems. In any case, the Tibetan forces were soon thoroughly vanquished and their leaders, including three Tibetan commanders, arrested. The Dalai Lama blamed the defeat on the small size of the contingent and we will see his regent sending larger troops in subsequent attacks. The Tibetan historian Shakabpa argues that it was the ineptitude of the Mongolian and Tibetan highlanders to deal with the Bhutanese jungle terrain that led to their defeat. He writes:

The troops were accustomed to fighting on the high mountains and plateaus of Tibet and had no experience with the dense forests and high temperatures of Bhutan. They marched too far south, lost their bearings, and were surrounded by the Bhutanese. Three prominent officers, Nangso Dondup, Drongtsenas, and Dujungnas, were captured. Their troops scattered and fled, most of them finding their way back to Tibet. This defeat shattered the myth of an invincible Mongol army and, in the future, Mongols were unwilling to fight in the humid southern regions.[31]

The Bhutanese allowed the ordinary Tibetan soldiers to return to Tibet after being disarmed. Their arms and armour were brought to the Punakha *dzong* to decorate the new deity's chamber (མགོན་ཁང་) which was being built to honour the protecting deities. The leaders including the three commanders were held as hostages in Punakha. When they were brought to Punakha before Zhabdrung and made to voluntarily disarm, the governor Drongtsenas is said to have remarked: 'Were it not before a lama, I cannot bear to offer my armour to the enemy.' To this, Zhabdrung bluntly added: 'It is not you who offers the armour but my deity Mahākāla.' The three commanders and other hostages were released a couple years later. During his time in Bhutan, governor Nidup is said to have found salt in Bhutan of such very poor quality that he offered to send much better salt from Tibet when he was released. This, he did later as promised.

In Punakha, a grand celebration took place after the first victory over the Gelug–Mongol coalition. The shrine dedicated to the protecting deities was completed and named Yulgyal Gönkhang (གཡུལ་རྒྱལ་མགོན་ཁང་) or 'the shrine of the protectors who are victorious in war'. A Karma Kagyu artist named Trulku Zing was invited from Tibet to work on the art works under Zhabdrung's supervision. In the festivities which followed, Zhabdrung himself took the role of the lead dancer for the sacred mask dances. Meanwhile in Tibet, the defeat became a topic of popular mockery for the new Gelugpa regime. Sonam Chöphel, who has assumed the title of the regent of Tibet, was not convinced and sent his nephew Norbu to find out the facts. The latter came as far as Phari and returned to confirm the defeat and arrests. Thus, a satirical song punning on words went around in Tibet among the supporters of Drukpa:

ཧྲ་མ་སྟོ་ར་བཞུགས་འདུག །འབྲལ་བ་སྟོ་ར་རྒྱབ་སོང་། །
དངོས་གྲུབ་འབྲུག་པས་བསྒུས་འདུག །ནོར་བུ་ཕྱུ་ར་བྱས་སོང་། །

The lama must be residing in the south
For all offerings (armour, etc.) were made to the south.
The Drukpas have captured Nidup (spiritual bounties);
Norbu (gem, i.e. vertebra relic) has worked as a spy (protector).

Around this time, Zhabdrung was also busy with the construction of
the Paro *dzong* and the heavy schedule of teachings bestowed by Rigzin
Nyingpo, a visiting Nyingma lama. It appears that in the wake of the invasion,
Zhabdrung realized the urgent need for both these projects in order to ensure
the long-term security of his state. Paro's physical proximity to and easy
access from Tibet made it often the first and main target for Tibetan invaders.
Zhabdrung learnt that it was vital to have a strongly fortified place in Paro to
withstand future attacks. While on his tour of Paro following the expulsion
of the Mongol–Tibetan army from the valley, Zhabdrung was looking for the
right spot to build a *dzong*. The scions of Phajo Drukgom in Paro approached
Zhabdrung while he was staying in Druk Chöding to offer the Rinpung *dzong*
which was built by their ancestor, Hungral Drungdrung. It appears the family
was having some difficulty maintaining the *dzong* and was also trying to win
Zhabdrung's favour. The Hungral family at that time was in a conflict with
the *chöje* family of Zarchen, with whom they were connected by marriage.
The head of the Zarchen family once even took over the *dzong* after a feud.
As both families were Zhabdrung's staunch supporters, he mediated between
the two families and harmoniously united them. He also happily accepted the
dzong from the Hungral family, demolished the five-storeyed old structure
and laid foundations for the new *dzong* in 1646. We do not know how long
it took to complete the new *dzong*. Neither do we know anything about its
process of construction but the *dzong* was probably completed by 1648 when
a second Gelugpa invasion took place.

The other activity which occupied Zhabdrung during and after the
1644 war was attendance at various teaching programmes and ceremonies
conducted by the Nyingma master, Rigzin Nyingpo. Zhabdrung firmly
believed in the importance of close links with the Nyingma school, through
which the teachings of Padmasambhava are mainly passed down. His
predecessors, including his ancestors and former incarnations enjoyed a
close relationship with the Nyingma masters. It was crucial that he carried
on this tradition and benefited from the religious wealth of the Nyingma.
We may recollect that his initial journey into exile and the successes in
Bhutan were seen as the fulfilment of Padmasambhava's ancient prophecy.

Padmasambhava's blessings were indispensible for a successful life in the lands associated with and so deeply impregnated by the presence of Padmasambhava. Moreover, the Nyingma school specialized in religious rituals particularly designed to avert Mongol and other foreign invasions, which Zhabdrung needed in plenty. It was primarily for these reasons that Zhabdrung sought Pema Thinley, the grandson of Pema Lingpa and the first Gangteng Trulku, and received him in Punakha with great respect in the summer of 1642. Besides being a leading Nyingma figure, Pema Thinley was also a native of central Bhutan, where a close ally would have been certainly useful for him. Zhabdrung requested Pema Thinley to return in the winter, when the temperature is favourable, to give him teachings but sadly, Pema Thinley passed away that autumn.

Zhabdrung thus turned to Rigzin Nyingpo, the seventh in line of descendents of Sangay Lingpa, from the Kongpo region in Tibet. By the time of Rigzin Nyingpo's arrival in 1644, Zhabdrung had also taken control of the famous hermitage of Taktshang from the Kathogpa lamas. Zhabdrung and his guest spent some time in Taktsang and conducted many esoteric religious ceremonies. In the fashion of a treasure-discoverer, Zhabdrung is also said to have come across some treasure guides, directing him to scrolls hidden under the reliquary stūpa of Langchen Pelgyi Senge. Zhabdrung, however, did not reveal the scrolls but he had a profound experience of being blessed by Padmasambhava. After finishing the esoteric rituals in Taktshang, they moved to Punakha, where Rigzin Nyingpo gave, among many other teachings, the transmission of Sangay Lingpa's *Guru Practice: A Gathering of Enlightened Intent,* a tantric meditation ritual which was later incorporated into the liturgical curriculum of Zhabdrung's monk body. Zhabdrung's biographers provide a long list of Nyingma teachings which Zhabdrung received from Rigzin Nyingpo before the latter returned to Tibet in 1646.

Religious practices were, however, not the only form of influence he had on Zhabdrung. Just before Rinzin Nyingpo left, Zhabdrung received an envoy from Sonam Chöphel requesting the release of the hostages, who were still held in Punakha. Both Rinzin Nyingpo and the Sakya hierarch, Ngawang Kunga Sonam, used their good connections to persuade Zhabdrung to release twenty-five leaders held in prison. Zhabdrung gladly freed the prisoners with gifts after the envoy agreed to respect the existent boundaries and send no further Tibetan troops. Unfortunately, the militant regent Sonam Chöphel had other plans. He was probably bent on revenge and recovering the shattered image of his Mongol–Tibetan coalition. In 1647, he first took over the control of Ralung monastery, which at that point was run by a lama appointed by Zhabdrung. Nidup, the commander who had just returned from Bhutan after being released, was sent to confiscate the properties of Ralung. Coinciding with the Tibetan New Year in 1647, Mipham Wangpo (1642–1717), the new incarnation of Pagsam Wangpo, was brought to Lhasa for the tonsure ceremony before the Dalai Lama by Yongzin Kuenga Lhendup (1617–76), the incarnation of Lhatsewa. The occasion was observed with some pomp and attended by many prominent Tibetan and Mongolian figures. The recognition of the incarnations of Zhabdrung's archenemies was clearly seen as a ploy to undermine him.

This ceremony for Mipham Wangpo formally started the line of Druk Thamche Khyenpa incarnations, which continues to this day. It also ossified the Drukpa divide which began with the rivalry between Zhabdrung and Pagsam Wangpo. The Drukpa school was subsequently split into the southern Drukpa or Lhodruk school of Bhutan and the northern Drukpa or Jangdruk school of Tibet. The Ralung establishment, which was under the care of Zhabdrung, was officially given to Mipham Wangpo by the Tibetan regent, thus ending the age-old ownership of the Ralung establishment by the scions of the Gya family descending from its founder, Tsangpa Gyarey. This must have also finally ended Zhabdrung's hope of returning to Ralung, a hope which he cherished for a long time. After giving away Zhabdrung's ancestral home to the incarnation of his rival, Sonam Chöphel planned another Tibetan invasion to Bhutan.

Gaden Phodrang's second defeat and Zhabdrung's celebrations

A much larger army composed of many Tibetan troops was sent in the winter of 1648 in what was supposed to be a carefully planned invasion. The armies of central Tibet, according to the 5th Dalai Lama, were sent toward Punakha and the army from Tsang province sent down to attack the Hungral *dzong* in Paro via Phari.[32] It appears that the armies marched through the valleys and succeeded in surrounding the dzongs in Paro and Punakha. They also managed to occupy a fort known as Kawang *dzong*, which we cannot identify today but was probably a *dzong* in the Thimphu valley. The Tibetan troops under Depa Norbu, the nephew of the Tibetan regent, camped in the area of the current Paro town and attacked the new *dzong*. However, Sonam Chöphel was not to see the victory he expected. The Bhutanese militia under Tenzin Drukdra in Paro launched a surprise attack at night sending the Tibetan invaders into a panic. Depa Norbu, the commander of Tibetan troops in Paro, took flight to Phari followed by his soldiers, leaving behind all their possessions. The Tibetan historian Shakabpa gives this account:

> The Tibetan troops came as far as Paro, via Phari, capturing a Bhutanese fort on the way. They camped a few miles out of Paro; but at night, Bhutanese troops took them by surprise and the Tibetans had to leave their tents and supplies behind in their hasty retreat to Phari. The Tibetan commander had to manage with a very common tent; his elaborate and costly one had been captured. That defeat went down as a disgraceful one in Tibetan history.[33]

Tibetans rebuked Depa Norbu's cowardice and made a mockery of Depa Norbu's flight as the Dalai Lama later noted. Soon after this retreat, the Sakya hierarch once again tried to find a peaceful settlement and travelled to Paro via Phari to negotiate. But his efforts to end the war and withdraw the Tibetan troops from Paro were in vain as two strong contingents of reorganized Tibetan cavalry and infantry secretly entered Paro. The Bhutanese seems to have retaliated with an ambush and over a thousand Tibetan soldiers were said to have been caught and nearly put to death when once again the Sakyapa hierarch intervened to beg for their lives. On the site of this victory, a *dzong* was built and named Drukgyal *dzong* or 'fort of Drukpa victory'.

Meanwhile the Tibetan troops in Punakha, unable to penetrate the *dzong*, were stationed on the Jiligang hill facing the *dzong*. Some of the Bhutanese in the *dzong* were certainly disturbed by the sheer size of the Tibetan army and even suggested to Zhabdrung that a truce may be a wiser option than war. Zhabdrung replied that his deities would not fail. He opened two of the *dzong*'s gates and made his soldiers file out of one and come back through the other. This deceived the Tibetans, who were spying from the distance, into thinking that Zhabdrung had a very large contingent in the *dzong*. It seems he might have also laid out dummies in rice fields and gardens to give the Tibetans a false impression of the number of his troops. In any case, the Bhutanese accounts generally claim that due to the power of the protecting deities, the Tibetans saw many more soldiers during the battles than there really were. When the Tibetans descended the hill to attack, they could not even gain a good footing. It was mid-winter, when the floors of the Bhutanese

Drugyal *dzong* by John Claude White in 1905

Tashichödzong with Wangditse on the ridge in 1905

forests is covered with dry pine needles. The ground was dangerously slippery for the Tibetans, who were not familiar with the vegetation.

Furthermore, when the news of their commander Norbu's flight to Phari reached the Tibetan troops in Punakha, they lost hope. Finally, a fire along the hill where they were stationed sent them running in a panic, leaving behind their possessions. The Bhutanese obtained a great number of Tibetan arms and armour. Later, when Zhabdrung was asked if the Tibetans would attack again, he is said to have joked: 'Tibetans have no prudence. They will come again but they cannot do any harm. We have sufficient arms and armour now. We may even ask them to bring clothes and silk next time.'

The invasion, indeed, ended in a disgraceful defeat for Tibet as the Tibetan historian Shakabpa noted. However, this was not to be the last one although it was the fifth Tibetan offensive and second under the Dalai Lama's government. Tibetan military incursions were to occur again in 1656–57, 1668, 1675–76, 1714, 1729 and 1732. However, for now, Zhabdrung and his subjects turned to their mind to a festival to celebrate the victory and to honour the protecting deities. This festival involving the religious ritual showing appreciation to the deities came to be known as Punakha Drubchö and was repeated every year since then. The famous dance of the four Mahākālas was also introduced at that time as was the grand procession feigning the disposal of the gem (vertebra relic) into the river. Some unsuspecting Tibetans are said to have really believed that the 'stupid' Bhutanese threw away the relic, the primary bone of contention between Zhabdrung and the Tibetan rulers.

After successive victories over the invading foreign forces, Zhabdrung's attention then turned to the consolidation and expansion of his power within the southern valleys. Among them, the southern frontiers of Dagana were one of the first areas to come under Zhabdrung's control. Many marauders and robbers are said to have harassed the people in the region and travellers along the trade route to India. In 1650, Zhabdrung despatched Druk Namgyal, who was appointed as *zhung dronyer* (མཞུང་མགྲོན་གཉེར་) or state chief of protocol in Punakha after his removal from Ralung, with a battalion of western Bhutanese troops to subjugate the unruly marauders of Dagana. After the successful domination of the people, a *dzong* was built in 1651 and named Tashi Yangtse and Tenpa Thinley appointed the first *pönlop* or governor of Dagana. Zhabdrung had also by then fully secured the frontiers to the north and built two *dzongs* of Lingshi and Gasa, although we do not exactly know when they were built. Throughout this period and since the first war with Tibet, the core and perhaps the main bulk of Zhabdrung's militia consisted of trusted followers from six great groups of Wang (ཝང་ཚོ་ཆེན་བཅུད་) corresponding to the valleys of Thimphu and Punakha. To the *pazap*s or heroic warriors of Wang were added those from Paro and Shar valleys. The three regions of Shar, Wang and Paro (ཤར་ཝང་སྤ་གསུམ་) were the primary dominion of Zhabdrung. This dominion was however gradually expanding as we have seen with the southward and northward consolidation of power.

A major chapter in the unification of Bhutan is the expansion of Zhabdrung's power eastward. By 1646, Zhabdrung had already posted one of his trusted followers, Migyur Tenpa, to Tongsa as the overseer of the religious establishment which was founded by his great-grandfather Ngagi Wangchuk. Before this appointment, he served as the head of Dargay Chöling in the Shar district. He was one of Zhabdrung's dedicated and able monks who combined monastic life with military roles and later became the first *pönlop* of Tongsa and the 3rd Desi ruler of Bhutan. He built a strong base at Tongsa and sent forth military campaigns across eastern Bhutan. The opposition which the Drukpa forces faced in central and eastern Bhutan was quite different from what they faced initially in the western valleys. Although religious figures exercised great influence, actual political power in central and eastern Bhutan lay mostly in the hands of secular chieftains. These chieftains were often at war with each other or with their Tibetan neighbours, a political scenario which was advantageous for the Drukpa power wishing to extend its domain. Furthermore, if religious piety played an important role in determining political allegiance in medieval Bhutan, Zhabdrung also had it in the bag. With close links to the lamas of Pema Lingpa tradition, who were influential in the central and eastern valleys, and the widespread network of Drukpa centres in the region, Zhabdrung did not face any religious rivalry as he did during his early days in western Bhutan.

It was around the time Zhabdrung was contemplating the extension of his power toward the east that a certain lama named Namsey from far-eastern Bhutan arrived in his court with Migyur Tenpa. Lama Namsey was the son of the Drukpa lama and involved as an interpreter in a judicial case between King Dewa of Khaling and his opponent Drukgyal, who were engaged in a dispute over trade routes to India. The two chieftains sought help from the Gelugpa government in Tibet, who sent two officials to adjudicate and Lama Namsey was appointed as the spokesperson for Drukgyal. In a drunken brawl at night caused by King Dewa in order to discredit Lama Namsey, one of the Tibetan officials and Namsey got into a fight. The Tibetan official and his party killed two companions of Lama Namsey and in the exchange, Lama

Namsey stabbed the Tibetan official with a knife. Fearing reprisal from the Tibetan government and King Dewa of Khaling, he then took flight and arrived in Tongsa to take refuge with Migyur Tenpa. Migyur Tenpa led him to Punakha to meet the Zhabdrung, who took Namsey into his fold, gave various religious teachings and blessings and instructed him to return to Tongsa and play an active role in the programme of propagating the teachings of the Drukpa school in the eastern region. Although Zhabdrung did not live to see the accession of the eastern valleys under Drukpa rule, it seems he was already planning on it and Namsey, with the internal knowledge of power structure in eastern Bhutan was a handy person to have. The Drukpa forces led by Druk Namgyal as commander and Lama Namsey as guide would later sweep through central and eastern Bhutan.

Zhabdrung's retreat and expansion of the state

Zhabdrung increasingly turned to spiritual activities after the celebrations, which followed the victory over Tibetan forces in 1649. First, as an absolution of the negativities of successive wars and as funerary rites for many people who died on both sides, Zhabdrung engaged in the creation of 1,15,00,000 miniature statues of 115 different Buddhas. He would personally work with some monks into the very late hours on this. He also conducted various religious ceremonies in the main Drukpa centres in Thimphu. We begin to notice that he was going through poor health by this time. After working late into the night, he casually complained of eye strain.[34] In the last year of his life, Zhabdrung also went twice to the hot water springs of Chuphu for treatment and recuperation. It was during his second stay at the hot springs in Chuphu, following an illness in the beginning of 1651, that he received the grave news of the death of his only granddaughter. The news saddened Zhabdrung and certainly had a bad effect on Zhabdrung's spirit. This time, he even called off the customary ceremonial reception, which he received whenever he returned to Punakha. Zhabdrung soon fell ill during a religious ritual in the second month of Iron Hare, 1651 and 'entered into a retreat' on the tenth day of the following month.

Although the death was not announced for some fifty-eight years, he must have passed away on the tenth day of the third Bhutanese month, 30 April 1651, when he 'entered into a strict retreat'. His death anniversary is observed on this day annually now. Although we know very little about the last days or hours of Zhabdrung's life, he is said to have entrusted all secular responsibilities to Tenzin Drukgyal and all ecclesiastical duties and personal matters to his chamberlain, Drung Damchö Gyaltshen. The death was strictly concealed, perhaps known only to a very few members of his inner circle. Every effort was made to pretend that Zhabdrung was alive. His food was served on time, ritual instruments were played frequently and in about 1653 when the young incarnation of Pema Thinley was brought to Punakha for a tonsure, there was even someone, perhaps acting as Zhabdrung, who received the gifts and tonsured the young incarnate from behind the door. This was also repeated in 1662 when young Ngawang Gyaltshen was tonsured.[35] Orders were made out on wooden boards in his name. During the monastic migration between the summer and winter residence, a lookalike statue created by Trulku Zing of Zhabdrung was carried at the head of the procession although this was probably done as a mark of respect than to feign his presence.

We do not know if it was Zhabdrung's final wish or a canny move on the part of his two trusted attendants, Tenzin Drukgyal and Drung Damchö, to keep his death a secret. However, we can be sure that the intention to do so was to retain the popular support for Zhabdrung even in his absence, to hold the new state together and give no hopes to the enemies in the north. The Tibetans understandably suspected Zhabdrung's long retreat and are said to have posted spies to verify it. Although they could not really be certain about Zhabdrung's death until much later, when they did so, the 5th Dalai Lama claimed that Zhabdrung's death was a result of sorcery conducted in Tibet.[36] He even elaborated that Zhabdrung was struck with a fatal disease at the hot spring and secretly rushed back to Punakha on a stretcher barely alive. The local Bhutanese, however, were not aware of such events. They generally bought the story of strict retreat which Tenzin Drukgyal and Drung Damchö presented with all persuasion. They were told that Zhabdrung took the initiative of entering a strict retreat after receiving a prophecy from Padmasambhava to do so and at the behest of the deities for the greater good of the sentient beings and Buddhist doctrine. Tenzin Drukgyal explained that Zhabdrung put him and Drung Damchö under strict orders not to disturb the retreat and that the retreat would be terminated only on the basis of omens Zhabdrung saw.

For one, the pretext of the retreat certainly helped to sustain the campaign to extend Drukpa dominion eastward as both Migyur Tenpa and Druk Namgyal, who were at the helm of this campaign, believed that Zhabdrung was still alive. By the time Zhabdrung entered into 'retreat', Migyur Tenpa had already built a strong base in Tongsa. He had built in about 1652 the core part of what was to grow into the large Tongsa *dzong* on the spot where a small shrine built by Ngagi Wangchuk in 1543 stood. The new *dzong* was named partially after him as Druk Migyur Chökhor Rabtentse and was extensively enlarged in 1667 when he became the ruler of Bhutan. From Tongsa, his first military quest was directed at Bumthang, where local chieftains, including the Chökhor Depa and *dung* of Ura, ruled. After a number of failed military attempts to take over Chökhor, Migyur Tenpa managed to win over some minor chieftains of Bumthang to his side. With local support and intelligence provided by dissenters, he invaded Chökhor with the combined forces of western Bhutan and Mangde led by Druk Namgyal and guided by Lama Namsey. We do not know exactly when this happened but the Chökhor Depa's palace fort of Yuwashing was stormed and the Chökhor Depa fled to Tibet. We know from one contemporary source that the Chökhor Depa entertained the second incarnation of Pema Lingpa in his seat of Draphey dzong in 1651. Thus, the defeat of Chökhor Depa by Migyur Tenpa's forces must have taken place after 1651.[37]

One of the prized booties of the invasion and an item of cultural and political significance was the the reliquary stūpa containing the remains of the famous saint Pema Lingpa, which they claimed to have transferred from Tamshing to Punakha. This, they may not have achieved however. According to another account, the *chöje* of Tamshing is said to have tricked the commanders into thinking that the remains of Pema Lingpa's son Drakpa Gyalpo were that of Pema Lingpa's.[38] When asked to identify the relics of the famous saint, *chöje* Köncho Tenzin inserted a small statue of Pema Lingpa at the end of his sleeve and, pointing his finger at this statue but standing in front of the remains of Pema Lingpa's son, he swore that he may vomit blood and die if this was not the relic of Pema Lingpa. Convinced by his oath, the invaders are said to have taken the reliquary containing Drakpa Gyalpo's remains to Punakha, where it remains to this day side by side with Zhabdrung's remains. The *chöje* then carried the remains of Pema Lingpa out of harm's way to Tama in Kheng from where it was brought to Yungdrung Chöling in the nineteenth century.

To return to Migyur Tenpa's campaign, it is quite likely that he and his army also took over the other Bumthang valleys, including Ura, which was clearly under the control of a local king until then.[39] Migyur Tenpa based his rule of Bumthang at Jakar, where there was also a religious centre founded by Ngagi Wangchuk in the sixteenth century. This spot would later become the site of Jakar *dzong*. He appointed Nyerpa Longwa, the steward who was partially blind, as the first *dzongpön* but the locals rejected him on account of his disability. Migyur Tenpa, however, impressed upon them that it was the fulfilment of Padmasambhava's prophecy that the King Sindhurāja of the Iron Castle would return to rule over Bumthang as a lame or blind person.[40] After they took control of Bumthang, the large army marched onto Kurtoe at the invitation of the widow of Lhabu Dar, a chieftain of Kurelung who was killed by his rivals, Darma of Kyidlung and Gawa of Phagdung. The two chieftains put up resistance but were eventually defeated and captured by the invading forces. Their domains were annexed to the Drukpa state and, at a site called Lengleng, where another one of Ngagi Wangchuk's shrines stood, the foundation for the Lhuntse *dzong* was laid in 1654. Druk Phuntsho was appointed as the governor. From Kurtoe, the forces went eastward to the modern district of Tashi Yangtse where they faced no opposition. The *dzong* of Tashi Yangtse is said to have been built at this time in Dongti where there was formerly a structure attributed to both a descendent of Prince Tsangma and Pema Lingpa. The troops then marched back westward to the Kurichu valley and took over the local fiefdoms of Zhongar and Tongphu including the old Zhongar *dzong*, which is today in ruins. These two principalities were embroiled in a dispute and the Zhongar faction solicited the support of Drukpa troops. Then, going eastward again towards Tashigang, the forces conquered King Darjam of Ngatshang, King Dawla of Chitshang and King Dorey of Brahmi, Halong and Wagrom.

While the commanders stayed in Zhongar to build the *dzong*, Lama Namsey led a detachment of the troops eastward. The chieftains of Uzurong and Tsengmi submitted to the Drukpa forces but other local chieftains showed signs of reluctance to submit to the invading forces. Among them were King Dewa of Khaling, who earlier plotted against Lama Namsey, King Achi of Kanglung and Lama Nakseng of Merak. These rulers had a significant army and enjoyed close ties with the Gelugpa government in Tibet. However, by then the reputation of the unassailable might of the Drukpa forces was widespread and most of these petty chieftains had no alternative but to submit to the Drukpa rule and seek its favour. Needless to say, the distrust and constant feuds between the numerous chieftains also greatly helped the conquest of these fiefdoms by the Drukpa forces. Thus, much of eastern Bhutan was annexed to Zhabdrung's new state without any substantial warfare and in a short span of time although no proper system of administration and control was set up during this campaign. On their way back from the east, the forces went southward at the invitation of a minor chieftain to annex the Kheng region which was under the rule of Nyakhar Dung. Having subjugated Nyakhar Dung and all the other petty chieftains of Kheng, they came up along the Mangdechu valley, where they eliminated Lama Gyaltshen of Rephay who was resisting submission to the Drukpa power. When the troops arrived in Tongsa after a successful campaign, Migyur Tenpa threw a big party to celebrate. He rewarded the soldiers with many gifts.

However, apart from a nominal submission through verbal oath, no clear system of administration and political control over the eastern districts was yet put in place. The chieftains were still largely left to their own devices and when Lama Namsey returned to Tashigang in the following year and tried to collect taxes and corvee, a faction of rulers including the kings of Khaling, Tsenkhar and Chenkhar put up an armed resistance. Lama Namsey brought in a military contingent raised from other principalities under the command of Damchö Rabgay. The dissenters were crushed and Lama Namsey and Damchö Rabgay took over the main castles of both Wengkhar in Tashigang and Jirizor in Khaling. The local supporters requested Lama Namsey to use Wengkhar as the main base and build a proper fort. Perhaps with knowledge from an earlier visit to the region, Migyur Tenpa is said to have favoured the establishment of a strong fort at Wengkhar for the benefit of securing Drukpa power in the eastern region. Lama Namsey, however, kept Damchö Rabgay in Wengkhar and chose to base himself in Khaling due to the favourable climate and terrain of this place. He called a meeting of all chieftains in the region and started having taxes delivered to Khaling. But his authority was short-lived as a rebellion supported by the Tibetan government and Mon soldiers from the east laid siege to the castle in Khaling. Lama Namsey was subsequently captured and taken to Tibet, where he is said to have been killed in an attempt to escape. The eastern region of Tashigang was taken over by the Gelugpa forces and Damchö Rabgay rushed to Tongsa to seek reinforcement.

The Drukpa reinforcement was quick to come under the leadership of Pekar Chöphel and Nyerpa Longwa. The considerable size of troops, composed of the entire armies of Wangdiphodrang and Mangde and some soldiers from Wang, marched across Bhutan to easily defeat the feeble resistance put up by the coliation of eastern Bhutanese dissenters and their Tibetan, Dvagpa and Monpa supporters. The easy victory is once again attributed to the work of the protecting deities and the new technology of muskets and firearms which the Drukpa forces used against enemies that had no knowledge of their power. Word was then sent out that local chieftains should come to show their allegiance or face being invaded. The commanders thus received a stream of local chieftains in Wengkhar, who were all made to take an oath that their allegiance lay to the Drukpa power in Bhutan and not the Gelugpa government in Tibet. Pekar Chöphel stayed in Tashigang to supervise the construction of the new fort of Tashigang on the spot of the castle of Wengkhar. The *dzong*, with its central tower and the surrounding walls was completed in 1659 and a *tadzong* or watch tower was also probably finished by that time. Simultaneously, some rough system of control and taxation were also put in place. This fully secured the eastern Bhutanese districts under the Drukpa rule although the bounderies would remain unclear and variable for several centuries.

The victory of Pekar Chöphel and Nyerpa Longwa officially brought 'the eight spokes of the wheel of the east' under Drukpa rule (ཤར་ཕྱོགས་འཁོར་ལོ་རྩིབས་བརྒྱད). The eight spokes were (1) the four sections of Mangde, (2) the four sections of Bumthang, (3) three areas of Kheng, (4) the seven sections of Zhongar, (5) the four blocks of Kurtoe, (6) the ten sections of Tashigang, (7) the five sections of Tashi Yangtse and (8) the three blocks of Dungsam, all of which fall east of the Pelela pass. Thus, in medieval administration, the Pelela range separated the western centre of power and the eastern provinces. The accession of 'the eight spokes of the wheel of the east' to Drukpa rule for the first time brought about the territorial integrity of Bhutan roughly as we know it today. In the metaphoric medieval description, this unified territory included 'the eight auspicious signs of the south' (ལྷོ་བཀྲ་ཤིས་རྟགས་བརྒྱད) and 'the seven precious jewels of the west' (ནུབ་རིན་ཆེན་རྒྱལ་བདུན) and 'the eight spokes of the wheel of the east' in addition to the central valleys of Shar, Thed and Thimphu.

Zhabdrung's Legacy and the
Early Monk Rulers

WE HAVE SEEN AT THE END of the previous chapter that already in the middle of the sixteenth century there was a vague sense of conceptual, cultural and geographical unity extending from western Haa to Khaling. During his early days in Bhutan, Zhabdrung also received gifts and tributes from many local chieftains of principalities covering roughly the area of modern Bhutan (although this account might have been retrospectively adjusted to align to the actual extent of unified territory at the time of writing). The territorial unification changed the prevalent conceptual and cultural affinity or semblance into a political unity. In any case, by the end of the 1650s, the area corresponding roughly to Bhutan was clearly unified as the Drukpa state.

The term Drukyul or land of the Drukpas was not used yet but the name Lhokhazhi, which had been in use for many centuries by then, soon came to be an official denotation referring to the southern country with four *kha* or entrances including, as we have seen, Dungsamkha to the east, Dalingkha to the west, Tagtsherkha to the north and Pasakha to the south. Punakha became its political centre. All Bhutanese historians later would explain the terms Lhokhazhi and Lhomonkhazhi through these references. In fact, the modern territorial limits to the north and south had generally been reached during Zhabdrung's final days and were circumscribed by the topographical features of the snowy watershed to the north and terai tropical foothills to the south. But with no distinct natural boundaries, the extents of the new Drukpa state to the east and west were not as fixed and those boundaries would keep shifting slightly in the subsequent decades as consequences of military skirmishes. Nevertheless, apart from the small changes at the border, the state of Bhutan was almost fully consolidated by the end of the 1650s.

Zhabdrung's legacy of a religious state

State-building, however, was not merely about territorial expansion. Territorial conquest occurred concurrently with the cultivation of a national political identity. In addition to the territorial unification, Zhabdrung also promoted a political unity under the banner of Drukpa religious hegemony. The entire stretch of southern land after all was believed to have been 'offered to him' by the protecting deities as his field of spiritual subjugation (གདུལ་ཞིང་). The country was perceived to be a realm for religious rule, which he was destined to introduce. This political unity and identity based on religious justification was enhanced through numerous activities, including the construction of *dzong*s, institution of monastic communities, cultural and religious practices and the introduction of a dual system of governance. Zhabdrung's legacy of the state, thus, extended beyond a mere domination of local principalities and control of the territory.

The most visible of his legacies, which to this day marks the Bhutanese landscape, are his *dzong*s, which house within the fortified walls both the political and religious bodies of state. They were not merely structural edifices with obvious functions of defence, accommodation, administration, public worship, etc. but loud political statements to mark his dominion and supremacy not only over the human inhabitants but also over the natural landscape and non-human denizens. Within the *dzong*, he established his dual system of 'the religious law which gets tighter like a silken knot' (ཆོས་ཁྲིམས་དར་གྱི་མདུད་པ་) and 'the secular law which gets heavier like a golden yoke' (རྒྱལ་ཁྲིམས་གསེར་གྱི་གཉའ་ཤིང་). By introducing these two systems, he brought, to put it in the idiomatic phrase of the time, 'law to the lawless south and handle to the handleless pot' (ལྷོ་ཁྲིམས་མེད་ལ་ཁྲིམས་དང་ཟྭ་ཡུང་མེད་ལ་ཡུང་). In other words, Zhabdrung brought to the southern valleys law and order through both religious conversion and exertion of political control. It is difficult to say how far his law and social order spread in the country but some historians of this era tell us that lawless brigandry, robbery, desecration of holy monuments and senseless violence were all suppressed and peace and a sense of security prevailed alike the era when an old woman could travel unharmed carrying a basket of gold.[1] This Tibetan metaphor of the old woman carrying gold (རྒན་མོ་གསེར་ཁུར་) is used by many traditional historians to describe Zhabdrung's introduction of law and order across the country and the resultant peace and security it brought. One thing we can say with some certainty is that violence and harassment connected with local feuds and warring fiefdoms must have decreased as the valleys were subsumed under Drukpa rule, although these local struggles were replaced by a series of bigger wars with Tibet.

Whether or not Zhabdrung's work of state-building led to nationwide peace and order, his initiatives did leave behind a legal legacy and administrative and organizational structures, which were quite innovative. The religious law, as codified in the monastic code of etiquette or *chayig* (བཅའ་ཡིག་) and developed primarily as in-house rules for clerics, was generally based on the Buddhist monastic discipline found in the *vinaya* corpus of Buddhist scriptures. Zhabdrung strongly believed in the importance of discipline in spiritual life and had already written one regulatory document for monks while he was in Tibet. This document became the core of the religious law and ecclesiastical rules and regulations in his new state. Zhabdrung's secular law, following the example of Songtsen Gampo's legal codes, was based on 'the sixteen pure laws of man' (མི་ཆོས་གཙང་མ་བཅུ་དྲུག) and 'the ten virtuous laws of gods' (ལྷ་ཆོས་དགེ་བ་བཅུ) we have seen earlier. However, no separate legal document seems to have been written until 1729 and the law was enforced through unwritten understanding and through edicts, ordinances and regulations on the behaviour of officers, taxation, etc.

His dual system was partially styled on Tibetan precedents of hereditary religious families, including the Gya establishment in Ralung. In fact, it was the system at Ralung, which Zhabdrung initially aspired to establish in Bhutan albeit in a heavily modified form. A prototype of the dual system also existed before Zhabdrung in western Bhutan which was largely ruled by priestly families combining both the roles of a religious lama and civil ruler (བླ་དཔོན་འཛིན་མ). Zhabdrung amplified this synthesis of religious and secular rule (ཆོས་སྲིད་ཟུང་འབྲེལ) and applied it to the governance of his new state. In his own days, the religious and political rule coalesced into a natural union with the person of Zhabdrung as its ultimate arbiter. The office of Zhabdrung, who the British later called the Dharmarāja, was known as the *tse* (རྩེ) or 'apex' and immediately under him were the branch offices of 'inner' ecclesiastical affairs and 'outer' secular administration. The 'apex' office resembled a modern royal secretariat and consisted of the chamberlain, advisors and some other household officers and functionaries. It was the private office of the supreme leader, originally intended to be passed down in a hereditary line. Both the term and functions of this office were later adopted by the office of the Dalai Lamas in Tibet. Zhabdrung appointed Drung Damchö Gyaltshen as the chief of his staff. He was one of the officials closest to Zhabdrung and was responsible for the welfare of Zhabdrung and his heirs. As such, he must have been present during Zhabdrung's last hours and it was he and Tenzin Drukgyal who effectively concealed Zhabdrung's demise.

The office of the 'inner' ecclesiastical affair took care of the monks and religious heritage. Zhabdrung delegated this task as well to Drung Damchö Gyaltshen although after the demise of Zhabdrung this office was passed to Pekar Jungney, who became the first Je Khenpo (རྗེ་མཁན་པོ་) or chief abbot. The Je Khenpo, who was appointed on merit, then became the head of the State Monk Body and continues to be even today. However, Zhabdrung was seen as the overall spiritual leader and the Je Khenpos only as his spiritual subordinate. The Je Khenpo was assisted by *lopön* (སློབ་དཔོན་) or masters in various departments of ecclesiastical activities, of which the number has generally come to be four including one each in esoteric tantric practices, in monastic ritual and music, in scholastic study and in linguistics.[2] In addition, there were also three disciplinarians and one precentor who made up the ecclesiastical officials.

By far the most important office under Zhabdrung was the post of chief administrator responsible for the 'outer' civil administration. Tenzin Drukgyal was appointed as the chief administrator by Zhabdrung quite early in his time in Bhutan. The Portuguese Jesuits described him as the 'lama who is the whole government of the King'.[3] After Zhabdrung's death, he became the first Desi (སྡེ་སྲིད་) or regent, whom the British would later call Deb Raja. Under him were three regional governors known as *chila* (སྤྱི་བླ་) based in Paro for the western region, Dagana for the southern region and Tongsa for the eastern region. The term *chila* or lama overlord denoted a minor priestly ruler and was in common use in early days of the state but later the term was largely replaced by *pönlop* (དཔོན་སློབ་) or master-ruler. Zhabdrung appointed Tenzin Drukdra as the governor of Paro, Migyur Tenpa as governor of Tongsa and Tenpa Thinley as governor of Dagana.

Also under the Desi were the three *dzongpön* (རྫོང་དཔོན་) or *dzong* rulers of the central seats of Punakha, Wangdiphodrang and Thimphu. Pekar Rabgay was appointed the *dzongpön* of Punakha, Au Tshering of Thimphu and Namkha Rinchen of Wangdiphodrang. Another very important post was that of *zhung drönyer* or state chief of protocol, to which Druk Namgyal was appointed following his escape from Tibet after the usurpation of Ralung by the Gelugpa government. The three *dzongpön*s, three *chila*s and the *zhung drönyer* with the Desi at their head constituted the cabinet of executive leaders, which ruled the country. Below them was a plethora of officials including stewards, protocol officers, chamberlains, secretaries, clerks and retainers in the *dzong*s. Across the country, there were also *dzongpön*s in all other dzongs and village heads and local officials known as *drungpa* or *gup*. Although not all official positions of medieval administration have started during Zhabdrung's lifetime, his vision of an administrative framework and a system of governance set the ground for the political structure and civil organization which came to dominate Bhutan until the middle of the twentieth century.

The state which Zhabdrung built was inherently a religious state. One main purpose was to preserve and promote the Drukpa religious heritage. Thus, Zhabdrung's political and cultural programmes were driven by a deeply religious ethos, which was manifest in all facets of Zhabdrung's project of nation-building. If the laws were heavily impregnated by Buddhist religious values, almost all of the civil administrators who put them in force were also monks. The rich cultural and artistic traditions which Zhabdrung started were also religious in content and style. These include the monastic rituals, music, sacred dances, sculpture, painting, embroidery, etc. In some cases, certain new features are said to have been improvised to develop a tradition which is distinct from their Tibetan origins. The same can be said for architecture. The *dzong*s, which are marked by their red stripes and generous space for monastic congregation and worship, were mainly fortified monasteries. The whole enterprise of state-building was thus a religious project at the heart of which was the sacrosanct person of Zhabdrung and his Gya family line. The state existed for the line and vice versa. It was the need to find a succession to the lineage and to keep the state going which would seriously tax the ingenuity of Zhabdrung's main followers and administrators.

Sustaining Zhabdrung's legacy

Zhabdrung's curious retreat must have left his court in disarray although its chief players made it look as orderly as possible. Whether Zhabdrung advised his two confidantes, Tenzin Drukgyal and Drung Damchö, to conceal his death as a 'strict meditation retreat' until the next in the line of succession is confirmed or whether Zhabdrung passed away abruptly and his attendants contrived the strategy is not clear. We will never know the details about Zhabdrung's death and what transpired before as only a very few members of his inner circle had access to him in his final days. Even the contemporary reports, including the biographies we have of him, come from people who were kept in the dark about his actual demise and thought he was in a long retreat. By the time his death was in the open, the few members who attended him during his last days were already dead. Thus, nothing is known apart from the story that Zhabdrung entered into a retreat on the tenth day of the third Bhutanese month, 30 April 1651 after leaving his final testament with Tenzin Drukgyal. The testament said:

> At this point, I have no choice but to undertake a strict retreat. The time of the conclusion of the retreat will depend entirely on the signs I receive. As no big or small officers, leaders, monks and patrons including you, Umze, can persuade me to stop, don't make any pleas and requests which could turn into obstacles for the retreat. Please instruct everyone to show genuine dedication to their responsibilities, cherishing my teachings in their heart.[4]

Whether or not these words are Zhabdrung's, Tenzin Drukgyal called a meeting of all important figures about three months after Zhabdrung 'entered the retreat' and made an official announcement that Zhabdrung had entered a strict retreat for the benefit of all sentient beings after issuing this instruction. He added that the announcement had been deferred with the hope that Zhabdrung might accept his plea to have a slightly open retreat but it now seemed that the retreat would last longer. He requested everyone to show unquestioned faith and commitment to the Drukpa cause and carry on their duties with pure intentions of solidarity, like passengers sharing the same boat. Meanwhile, he was to assume the full position of a regent and oversee the state and execute the orders from Zhabdrung.

The 1st Desi or regent Tenzin Drukgyal (1591–1656) was one of the most trusted and senior Bhutanese disciples of Zhabdrung. His family of Obtsho in the Gön area north of Punakha was a longstanding patron of Ralung, having started from Terkhungpa's nephew as we have already seen. Tenzin Drukgyal became a monk in Ralung at the age of eleven and a close disciple of both Zhabdrung and his father. He rose through the ranks of precentor and steward in Ralung and thus came to be known as Umze (དབུ་མཛད་) or precentor for the rest of his life. When Zhabdrung was planning to go into exile, he and his family played a major role in inviting Zhabdrung to Bhutan. In Bhutan, Umze took charge of the administration under Zhabdrung and was well known for his rigour of discipline and knowledge of divinational science to prepare for war. As Zhabdrung's chief of staff, he was no doubt involved in planning the five successful wars against Tibetan invaders and also in building the *dzong*s but he was particularly renowned for his promulgation and enforcement of the code of law and discipline. By the end of his life, the eastern parts of Bhutan had also effectively come under the Drukpa rule, thus making him the first ruler of unified Bhutan and indeed the first native ruler. With his experience as precentor, the 1st Desi is also attributed with the composition of the unique Bhutanese styles of performing monastic music and liturgy. After serving for five years as the regent, Tenzin Drukgyal passed away in the middle of a seasonal ceremony in Cheri. The 5th Dalai Lama in Tibet was prompt to claim Tenzin Drukgyal's sudden death as a result of his occult power aimed particularly at the latter, much like the Bhutanese claim that Gushri Khan died as a result of Bhutanese works of magic.[5] His body was cremated in 1681 by Tenzin Rabgay.

La-ngonpa Tenzin Drukdra (1602–67) succeeded Tenzin Drukgyal as the 2nd Desi of Bhutan. Tenzin Drukdra was considered to be a half-brother of Zhabdrung from their father's extranuptial liaison with a girl from Yuling village above Tongsa. He bore a physical resemblance to Zhabdrung and from an early age was admitted to Ralung, where he had his education. His first major position was as the first governor of Paro in 1646. Well known for his skills in military strategy, he was given the main credit for the astounding victory in Paro over the second Gelugpa invasion involving many large contingents of forces. The defence fort of the Drukgyal *dzong* built at the upper end of Paro valley is thought to be his work. If military planning was one of his skills, it would come in handy as barely months after his appointment as Desi, there was a major Tibetan offensive—the sixth Tibetan invasion and the third one under the Gelugpa government.

The reasons for the invasion are unclear and the 5th Dalai Lama, who wrote about this, does not tell us why the extensive military offensive was undertaken. The Bhutanese assumed that it was mainly an act of revenge by the Tibetan ruler Sonam Chöphel for the disgraceful defeat he suffered in 1649. Tibet is said to have been rife with rumours that the armies of all thirteen myriarchies of Tibet were no match in combat with a single Drukpa hierarch due to his occult power. The Bhutanese also believed that the 5th Dalai Lama and his regent nurtured desires to put Bhutan under Tibetan Gelugpa hegemony. The real causes were perhaps more complex and a mixture of a desire for vengeance, territorial expansion and fear of occult powers. The belief in and fear of occult power was strong and serious in the Himalayan world then, as it is to some extent even today, and huge investments were made towards cultivating magical powers or averting them. To this, one may add also the instigation by some groups such as the Lhapa and Nenyingpa who were still disgruntled with Bhutan.

The invasion was carefully planned, involving Mongol forces and Tibetan armies from the Ue, Tsang, Kham and Kongpo regions under the chief commandership of Depa Norbu. Two major Tibetan oracles and the 5th Dalai Lama were consulted but only the Nechung oracle appears to have predicted the war would be successful. The 5th Dalai Lama, however, gave his blessings to some of the generals leading the troops. In the seventh month of 1656, troops were sent down towards Paro, Gön and Bumthang but the Tibetans were yet again to lose sight of their expected victory. Although there are no clear details about the war, it appears from the Dalai Lama's account that the troops coming via Bumthang did not even succeed in penetrating into Bhutan. Meanwhile, all supporting armies were sent to Paro, where the forces were being led by Depa Norbu. Depa Norbu's slow and cautious move however protracted the invasion well into the summer of 1657. The Neychung oracle later blamed Depa Norbu's slackened approach and poor strategy for the failure of the invasion.

With the onset of summer, the Mongol and Tibetan soldiers found themselves in an inhospitable climate and began to succumb to various health problems. We have already seen how the heavily forested terrain and subtropical climate often was to the advantage of the Bhutanese locals in war. According to oral accounts, Bhutanese also ingeniously used their knowledge of nature to upset the invading forces. In one story, the Bhutanese carried beehives captured in a sack and let them out at the marching Tibetan and Mongolian army, who knew nothing about bees. 'If even the bite with the butt (sting) of this horrible Bhutanese fly is so painful, what need to mention the bite with its teeth?' one ignoble Tibetan is said to have remarked. In another story, the invaders were tricked with a welcome feast laid amid strange flowers and herbs, which made the invaders ill with allergies. It is also quite possible that the Bhutanese adopted tactics of a guerrilla war in addition to open battles.

In any case, the invaders suffered a defeat and retreated to Phari, where they deliberated plans for a complete withdrawal or another attack. The two Mongol generals Machig Taiji and Dalai Pathur objected to the withdrawal, adding that they 'could not show their faces to other Mongols' returning from a terrible defeat. This exacerbated the tension already growing between them and Depa Norbu when Machig Taiji suddenly died, supposedly from fever but some Tibetans suspected he was poisoned by Depa Norbu. It appears that the invaders had a sour internal conflict and the Bhutanese once again proved, according to the Dalai Lama, 'invincible even if all of the Tibetans were sent'.[6] A treaty was finally drawn up between Bhutan and Tibet through mediation by the Panchen Lama of Tashilhunpo, the Ngor hierarch of Sakya and the ruler of Kyidshod.[7] The two parties agreed to maintain peace for four or five years and free all prisoners, including some who had been kept from earlier conflicts. Among the prisoners released was Nenying Jetsun, a scion of the Nenying family who opposed Zhabdrung. An interesting piece of information revealed in the Dalai Lama's account of post-war events is the defection of Namkha Rinchen, the *dzongpön* of Wangdiphodrang, to the Tibetan side although we do not know the reasons for it. This suggests that there were dissidents among the Drukpa party. Tenzin Drukdra is said to have executed some twenty relations of Namkha Rinchen for his treason.[8]

Yet outside of the war period, Tenzin Drukdra was not a strong character with a bellicose proclivity. Compared to the strict and high-handed rule of his forerunner, Tenzin Drukdra's reign is said to have been relaxed and liberating. With much love for philosophy and medical science, he started a vibrant college for the study of philosophy and created quite a large collection of medicinal substances and herbs. He is said to have twice made substantial offerings of medicinal herbs to all physicians of Tibet. During his regency, Tenzin Drukdra also successfully completed the construction of the second monastic hall, the *kunra* (ཀུན་ར་), in Punakha along with its murals. In 1662, he began the work of building the eight large silver stūpas as a commemorative tribute to Zhabdrung although Zhabdrung's death was still kept a secret. Similarly in 1665, he started the workshop for building the stūpas from sandalwood and in 1666 he launched the project of writing the manuscript of the *kanjur* canon in gold. Despite the turbulence of war in the early years of his reign, Tenzin Drukdra left a remarkable legacy in terms of artistic and intellectual creations but he passed away in 1667 before all of his projects were completed.

A notable event during his reign concerning Bhutan's relations to the south was the escape of the King of Cooch Behar as a refugee to Bhutan in 1661 in the wake of the Mughal invasion of his kingdom by Mīr Jumla, the governor of Bengal. The kingdom of Cooch Behar had been a vassal of Mughal power in Delhi since its King Lakṣmi Nārāyaṇ (r.1587–1621) accepted Mughal suzerainty in 1596. However, by 1658, Emperor Shah Jahan was ill and the Mughal empire was about to break down with war among his sons. Prāṇ Nārāyaṇ, the King of Cooch Behar, took the advantage of this fratricidal conflict to wrest full control over his kingdom from Mughal rule, as did the Ahom rulers in Assam. He was temporarily successful but when Aurangzeb took over the Mughal throne, having defeated his brothers and arrested his father, he sent troops under Mīr Jumla to punish Prāṇ Nārāyaṇ and reclaim the territory. We learn from Indian sources that Prāṇ Nārāyaṇ escaped to Bhutan. A Bhutanese was captured and sent to the Desi asking for the arrest and return of the Cooch King. The Desi politely replied that he could not drive away a guest. The Bhutanese captive is said to have told Mīr Jumla that the Dharmarāja of Bhutan was an ascetic over 120 years old who ate only bananas and drank only milk. This story of Zhabdrung's retreat and righteous rule may have surprised the Mughal governor but no political exchange of any consequence seems to have taken place between the Mughals and Bhutan. Prāṇ Nārāyaṇ's asylum, however, commenced Bhutan's involvement in the affairs of Cooch Behar leading to various developments in the years to come.[9]

Following the death of the 2nd Desi, Drung Damchö produced a written order on a wooden tablet, claimed to be from Zhabdrung, appointing Migyur Tenpa (1613–81), the governor of Tongsa, as the 3rd Desi in 1667. This appointment must have been mainly on the basis of his successes in the unification of eastern districts. He was originally from the village of Minchud in Tibet but nothing is known about his youth. A trusted follower of Zhabdrung, he was appointed as the head of the Dargay monastery in Shar before he was promoted to the position of the Tongsa *chila* some time around 1646. Migyur Tenpa was a strong leader and differed from his predecessors in his tenacious and undiplomatic approach to problems. For one, he was unsatisfied with the indirect instructions produced on a small wooden board from Zhabdrung. Soon after his appointment, he demanded direct access to the supreme leader and his heir to consult them on important matters of the state. What he discovered following this request must have certainly at least surprised him for much of the campaign for territorial extension in eastern Bhutan under his leadership was conducted with the belief that Zhabdrung was still alive and head of the state. Perhaps alarmed by the seriousness of the problem of succession, we see Migyur Tenpa immediately taking measures to secure the hereditary succession, to which we shall return soon. This revelation and the fact that he was kept out of the inner circle soured his relations with Drung Damchö, the only surviving member behind the 'retreat' hoax. With this resentment, Migyur Tenpa is said to have later mistreated Drung Damchö who, despite being a prominent player in the foundation of

Bhutan and longstanding chamberlain of Zhabdrung, died a sad death in Wangdiphodrang following his retirement.

Migyur Tenpa completed the silver stūpa and gold *kanjur* projects, which his predecessor started. He also undertook the reconstruction of the Semtokha *dzong*, which was destroyed during the second Tibetan invasion when the explosives stored in the *dzong* caught fire. The structure was brought to its initial grandeur and Migyur Tenpa added to it a very rich collection of images, paintings and carvings, which were consecrated by Tenzin Rabgay. Migyur Tenpa also enlarged the central tower of Punakha and built the *dzong* of Lingshi in the north and of Dalingkha in the far-western frontier. He also undertook a nationwide project of building stūpas and stone walls with prayers on them. These walls known as *mani dangrim* and stūpas were built on roadsides, high passes, riverbanks, crossroads and village outskirts to give protection to people from evil spirits. They were also stark markers of his domain. Later, some of his opponents blamed him for the suffering he brought to the Bhutanese populace through forced labour to build these monuments. We must remember that the construction of six *dzong*s in eastern Bhutan, including the Tongsa, Jakar, Lhuntse, Tashi Yangtse, Tashigang and Zhemgang *dzong*s also took place under his command as the governor of Tongsa.

Cultural creations, however, did not feature as high on his list as did territorial expansion. He was perhaps one of the few Drukpa protagonists who dreamed of a greater Drukpa hegemony and wished to extend it across the Himalayan region. Tshewang Tenzin of Tango and the 2nd Desi Tenzin Drukdra appear to have shared such a wish.[10] In any case, Migyur Tenpa was, according to the historian John Ardussi, 'a monk ill-disposed by nature or habit to passive administration'.[11] Soon after his ascension to the throne of Desi, Migyur Tenpa was dealing with the extension of the state westward, just like his extension eastward while he was the governor of Tongsa. The expansion eastward had, as it were, reached its feasible and necessary limits. The forested areas of what is now Arunachal Pradesh were mostly populated by intractable tribal people and there was also perhaps, a strong Gelugpa presence in some areas. Thus, there was probably neither sufficient political will nor missionary zeal to go further east. In any case, it was too far away for Migyur Tenpa to manage from Punakha. In contrast, the western frontiers were vibrant with sectarian and political activities. Places such as the Chumbi valley were strategic areas not only for its agricultural riches and commercial role as a trade corridor but it was also a playground of sectarian control and contestation. The Lhapa and Barawa schools, which have been uprooted from Bhutan, were established there under a loose Gelugpa control. A little south of Chumbi, the state of Sikkim had just been founded with the installation of Phuntsho Namgyal as the 1st Chögyal of Sikkim in 1642. Based on Tibetan ancestry, this ruling family developed very close ties with the Tibetan government of the 5th Dalai Lama and was naturally wary of the Bhutanese power to the east.

Going further west to the kingdoms of Nepal, Mustang and Ladakh, which are geographically removed from Bhutanese territory, the Drukpa government saw a growing stake. The struggles between Tibet and Bhutan, argues Ardussi, were not merely of territorial matters but fundamentally of religious orientation.[12] Thus, wherever the Drukpa and Gelugpa religious schools met, there was a potential for affecting their own national interests. The southern borders of the Himalayas have been grounds for competition between the Gelugpa and Drukpa schools and the Gelugpa influence in some of them was rapidly growing after the Gelugpa rose to power in Tibet. The Bhutanese, by the time of Migyur Tenpa's regency, had already secured a good standing in Ladakh and Mustang and it was important for them to continue their presence. Several monasteries in these countries were under Bhutanese care and lamas were appointed from Bhutan. We have already seen how two princes of Ladakh had been trained in Bhutan and occupied important posts. Bhutan enjoyed a similar relationship but to a lesser degree with Mustang.

Connection with the kingdoms in Kathmandu and Jumla before Migyur Tenpa was not known but Migyur Tenpa actively cultivated a close link with Kathmandu hoping to leverage it against Lhasa's influence. He sent a mission of twenty-one people led by Damchö Pekar to Kathmandu. Damchö Pekar met the King of Yambu (Kantipur), probably Pratāpamalla, and had even established a temple or two when news of their presence in the Nepali court reached Tibet.[13] The Gelugpas were then bent on diminishing Bhutanese influence in all areas west of Bhutan extending from Chumbi to Ladakh. According to Damchö Pekar's biography, the Tibetans instigated people against them in the Yambu court by bribing the Nepali ministers. In the end, the friendly king died and Damchö Pekar and his entourage had to flee from Kathmandu under difficult circumstances. Their initial efforts were thus unsuccessful but Migyur Tenpa must have persisted with his aim as one Bhutanese record of Bhutan's relationship with Nepal shows. The document contains a long list of lamas sent to Nepal after Damchö Pekar's mission and the areas granted to them for their support by the Nepali rulers.

An interesting development of religious diplomacy under Migyur Tenpa was the presence of Bhutanese lamas in the court of the Gorkha kings, who were Hindus, long before the Gorkhas unified the modern state of Nepal. It is unlikely that the Bhutanese foresaw the rise of the Gorkhas but, fortuitously for Bhutan, the Gorkhas took control of entire Nepal a century later during the time of Pṛthivī Nārāyaṇ Śāḥ (1723–25). By then, the Gorkha court had a longstanding tradition of keeping a Drukpa court priest to whom were entrusted several religious establishments. However, Drukpa presence in Nepal during Migyur Tenpa's rule was only beginning and there were serious political obstacles.

It was in such a political climate and the peak of sectarian rivalry that Migyur sent his army to vanquish Achog, a recalcitrant leader of the Monpa people living around modern-day Darjeeling. Achog was a local chieftain with some control over the area when he ran into conflict with the Bhutanese who were in the process of consolidating frontier territories under the Drukpa rule. Sikkimese history also mentions one Achog but places him much later during the rule of Chagdor Namgyal (r.1700–15). He is said to have allied with Bhutanese against the Sikkimese king.[14] Whether or not they are the same person, the Achog with whom we are concerned here appears to be a local ruler who managed to play off the larger powers against each other. Unable to resist the Bhutanese forces, Achog went to Lhasa to seek support from the 5th Dalai Lama, who considered him to be a subject of Tibet. The Dalai Lama notes that in their first meeting, while Achog was making prostrations to him, Achog slipped and nearly fell to the floor. This, the Dalai Lama remarked, was an ominous sign of the insecure future he was to face. Insecure indeed was his future to be though the Dalai Lama's government sent Tibetan troops to back him.[15] Some time at the end of 1668 or the beginning of 1669, three divisions of Tibetan troops were sent toward eastern, central and western Bhutan. As they marched, the Dalai Lama sent gifts and supplications to different protecting deities of Tibet to seek their help.[16] In four supplicatory poems he composed, he urged the deities 'to put the enemies to death, to pulverize them to dust and to eat their flesh, blood and life'. He referred to Zhabdrung as the enemy of peace bearing the dress and name of a meditating priest.[17]

According to the Dalai Lama's accounts, the Tibetan division entering eastern Bhutan and Bumthang had successfully entered Bhutan but the main forces led by the three generals toward western Bhutan did not go as planned and led to the withdrawal of the two other divisions.[18] With the expedition proving difficult and urgent requests from the officials of Sakya, Tashilhunpo and Kyishod for a peaceful settlement, the Dalai Lama quickly turned to negotiations. In any case, there was perhaps very little fighting and the Bhutanese records do not even mention divisions from Bumthang and eastern Bhutan. However, it is not clear what kind of arrangement was reached through the negotiations. Both the Tibetan and Bhutanese sides claimed Achog's area, which was under dispute, to be their territory. Thus, both sides considered this war as a defence against foreign invasion into state territory. We do not know the terms of the treaty but a peace deal was agreed to be observed until 1675.

Peace did generally prevail between the two nations for some years during which Migyur Tenpa was occupied with the cultural project we have seen above. However, just as the treaty was nearing its expiry, fresh war broke out again in early 1675. The Dalai Lama was informed by Achog that the Bhutanese were preparing an offensive. Whether or not this was true, the Dalai Lama made a preemptive attack, burning down a Bhutanese border fort in Tendung, northwest of modern Samtse. This early offensive, he argued, was to beat the Bhutanese to the action as the Tibetan proverb goes 'the father acts while the child talks'.[19] The Bhutanese retaliated with vengeance; the Dalai Lama commissioned prayers for out- manoeuvring the Bhutanese. By the middle of 1675, negotiations were once again under way to avoid further bloodshed but the Bhutanese stood their ground relentlessly. They demanded that Achog should be treated as their subject and Sikkim should be a common ground with equal influence. The Dalai Lama found the Bhutanese demands totally one-sided but, in the absence of a civil regent and giving his altruistic inclination as a reason, he appears to have conceded to the terms so as to avoid further strife.

However, things took a different turn when his new regent Lobzang Jinpa, who was installed in the autumn of 1675, came into the picture. Lobzang Jinpa was the 4th of the five regents to serve under the 5th Dalai Lama. His predecessors, Sonam Chöphel and Thinley Gyatsho, died in office and Lobzang Thutob was removed from office as the 4th one would be four years later. With the 5th Dalai Lama as the spiritual supremo, Tibet was at that time juggling with a precarious system of power sharing between the Tibetan regents and male descendents of the Mongol warlord Gushri Khan. This delicate balance would fall through after the Dalai Lama's death during the time of his 5th regent Sangay Gyatsho. Meanwhile, Lobzang Jinpa found the terms of agreement with Bhutan completely unacceptable. 'It is not a treaty if there is no reciprocal compromise and we agree to whatever the Bhutanese say,' he remarked.[20] He ordered all trade routes for salt and wool to be closed and border patrols to be stationed along the whole of northern frontier. A full-scale assault on Bhutan was planned. By government order, all religious centres in Tibet were made to perform various rituals to support the assault. The Dalai Lama gives a three-page list of the various 'strategic' rituals performed to support the war. They mainly composed of rituals for exorcism and repulsion.

Meanwhile in Bhutan, even as the negotiations in Phari were in process, the Bhutanese forces under Au Tshering and Drönyer Dorleg pushed the invaders and recovered the fort of Dalingkha. They captured the rebel leader Achog and put him to death and his head and arms were carried to Punakha as a trophy. Following this temporary victory, there were celebrations and ceremonies of thanksgiving to the protecting deities. It is not clear if the Bhutanese were aware of the drastic change of Tibetan policy for a full war after Lobzang Jinpa came to power. Migyur Tenpa and Tenzin Rabgay, two of the leading figures, spent the summer travelling across the country in what looked like a familiarization tour for young Tenzin Rabgay, who was then being groomed to be the leader.

Within weeks of their return from their tour, Bhutan was besieged with the largest Tibetan army ever sent against Bhutan. There were five forces with some fifteen generals: one from Paro led by Gamponey, Tashi Tsegpa and Garpon Dogonpa, one from Lingshi led by Gongkar Drungyig, Tshagurney and Depa Kyishodpa, one from Bumthang led by Sonam Wangyal and Yardrok Depa, one from Tashigang led by Lhagyari, Tadongney and Depa Japa, and another from Phari led by general Kyagurney. Among the generals were also Bhutanese dissidents including Gön Lama Dechog Gönpo and Chokhor Depa. Dung Nagpo of Ura, who had paid a visit to the Dalai Lama's court in 1675 and again in 1679, was also said to be among the group but there were conflicting reports and it was not confirmed.

On the Bhutanese front, the main leaders were Gedun Chöphel of Kabji, Ngawang Rabten and his son Ngawang Phuntsho, both of the Obtsho family in Gasa and close relations of the 1st Desi. We know nothing about the general forces but the 3rd Desi Migyur Tenpa was himself behind the whole operation, certainly throwing in the best of his military skills. Among those to lead the prayers to the deities for aid and the rituals to repel the enemies were Tenzin Rabgay and the 2nd Je Khenpo Sonam Özer. The 1st Je Khenpo Pekar Jungney had passed away by then due to a fatal accident caused by his riding pony in

Changlimethang. Tenzin Rabgay was asked to do an esoteric tantric ritual in which effigies of the leading Tibetans were ritually slain. Among the list was also Dung Nagpo of Ura, but when Migyur Tenpa heard he was not among the invaders, his effigy was taken out and thrown into the river. Yet some time later, Migyur Tenpa was told that Dung Nagpo was colluding with the enemies. The perplexed Desi remarked that Dung Nagpo must have a strong deity to protect him from being slain in the ritual.

The entire stretch of northern Bhutan was filled with the terror of war.[21] As an early win, the invaders occupied the Jakar *dzong* in Bumthang and Migyur Tenpa had to divert some troops from western Bhutan to Bumthang under the commandership of Ngawang Rabten. He and his men succeeded in taking back the *dzong*. However, the battle continued and, according to local accounts, the Tibetan army camped on the slope and plain across the river, opposite current Wangdichöling, where they also built a defence post called Thobgyal *dzong*, after a fort with the same name in Tibet. Recently, some underground structures dating from around this period were accidently discovered during a construction and some archaeological works were carried out by a Swiss team.[22] The turning point in the war in Bumthang was the shooting of a Tibetan general. An embellished oral account has it that at the climax of the invocation to Mahākāla, a shot was taken at the Tibetan general through the opening of a window which hit him on the forehead. We can assume that the use of firearms and psychological confidence gained from belief in Mahākāla's intervention must have played a big role in the Bhutanese victory. The Tibetan camp was certainly routed and the area is to this day known as Bodpalagthang or 'ground where Tibetans were destroyed' and until recently the victory was commemorated with a procession from this battlefield to the Jakar *dzong*, enacting the victorious return of the soldiers.

With the Tibetans repelled and the *dzong* secured in Bumthang, Ngawang Rabten and his troops were called back to join forces in Gön, where the Bhutanese have also lost their positions due to strategic blunders made by the leader, Gedun Chöphel. Gedun Chöphel is said to have nearly lost his own life which was only saved by brave assistance from Ngawang Phuntsho. Soon after Ngawang Rabten joined the forces in the northwestern front, the Lingshi *dzong*, which was totally besieged by the Tibetans, was fully recovered. A recurring theme in the Bhutanese sources is the delusion caused by Bhutan's deities in the minds of the invaders, who saw innumerable Bhutanese soldiers inundate the valley. Seeing such an illusion, the Tibetans are said to have panicked and fled. In the final event, the Tibetan general Gamponey and the renegade Gön Lama were killed, several other leaders taken hostage and hundreds of ordinary soldiers were also captured but sent back to Tibet. To memorialize the victory, the two *dzong*s of Jakar and Lingshi were both named Yulgyal *dzong*—'the *dzong* of victory in war'.

The Bhutanese accounts are muddled and very patchy and it is difficult to use them to construct a clear account of the war. They are also too onesided to gain from them a complete and objective picture of the war, but Tibetan sources are almost non-existent. The 5th Dalai Lama, who gave a cryptic but substantial report of Tibet–Bhutan issues until the repudiation of the treaty in the autumn of 1675, goes into a curious silence and gives us no clue as to what the Tibetans thought about the war. He only returns to talk about Bhutan when he hears the news of the death of Migyur Tenpa and the internal strife in the seventh month of 1680, which became an occasion for celebration in Lhasa.[23] There is no claim either of victory or defeat in his records while Bhutanese historians boast of another victory. Why was the Dalai Lama silent although he continued to keep an extensive journal of his activities during this period? Did he or the editors of his autobiography intentionally evade the episode of another embarrassing defeat? The historian John Ardussi thinks we may gauge the failure of Tibet's Bhutan policy more from their deeds than words. Lobzang Jinpa, the regent who took Tibet to war against Bhutan, resigned from the post in the year of the defeat and the Dalai Lama changed his tactic from military confrontation to religious consolidation in strategic areas by renovating Gelugpa temples and building new ones.[24]

Large Tibetan contingents remained along the border and sporadic skirmishes continued until the end of 1678. In the final month of the Earth Horse year or early 1679 a treaty was signed through mediation by officials from Sakya, Tashilhunpo and Depa Kyishodpa. The Bhutanese team was lead by Gedun Chöphel and the Tibetan team by Kyagurney.[25] Although we do not know the full terms of the treaty, it is clear that the Tibetans recognized a border line, which generally corresponded to the current boundaries of Bhutan with a bit more to southwest, now under India. This war and the subsequent treaty was followed by a period of peace between the two countries, which lasted about three and half decades. However, Tibet was by then locked in war with Ladakh, another state following the Drukpa school, and Bhutan was just beginning to see the internal strife, which would frequently batter the country during the next two centuries.

Before we delve into the internal conflicts, let us briefly turn to the developments of Bhutan's relations to the south with Cooch Behar. Migyur

Tenpa's policy of territorial expansion and the Drukpa influence was not merely limited to the high Himalayan countries. His reign saw an increasing Bhutanese involvement in the southern plains, particularly in the affairs of Cooch Behar, although the Bhutanese sources are curiously silent on these events. We only find a passing mention of Darchuk Gyaltshen's presence in the court of Cooch Behar when Damchö Pekar and his team passed through Cooch Behar on their return from Nepal.[26] It is not clear if he was posted there by the state or was there by his own accord. This Bhutanese merchant from Chapcha definitely shared close ties with the rulers of Cooch Behar. We may recollect that he was the person who put Zhabdrung in touch with Lakṣmi Nārāyaṇ (r. 1587–1621). The silence in Bhutanese sources is however compensated for by Indian sources, which attribute a significant role to Bhutanese power in the politics of Cooch Behar.[27]

King Lakṣmi Nārāyaṇ appointed his son Mahi Nārāyaṇ as the first Nazir Dev, a post akin to a prime ministerial office, but was succeeded by his son Bīr Nārāyaṇ (r.1621–26), who ruled only for a short period. Bīr was followed by his son Prāṇ Nārāyaṇ (r.1627–64/65), who escaped to the Bhutanese mountains in 1661 at the time of the Mughal invasion. When Prāṇ Nārāyaṇ died in 1665/66, the sons of Mahi Nārāyaṇ, the Nazir Dev, intrigued for the throne, which was passed down to Mod Nārāyaṇ, the very young son of Prāṇ Nārāyaṇ. Mahi Nārāyaṇ held reins of power in his hands and kept young Mod Nārāyaṇ as a puppet but the king gradually managed to wrest power from his great-granduncle by winning the trust of the army. He crushed the contenders, killed Mahi Nārāyaṇ and banished his supporters. According to Indian sources, the sons of Mahi Nārāyaṇ retaliated with the military help of the Bhutanese. This help must have been despatched during the reign of Migyur Tenpa although the Bhutanese sources make no mention of it.

The Desi forced King Mod Nārāyaṇ to accept Yajña Nārāyaṇ, son of Mahi Nārāyaṇ, as the new Nazir Dev. King Mod Nārāyaṇ died childless in 1680 and Yajña Nārāyaṇ again designed to take the throne with Bhutanese support when the Raikat brothers of the Baikunthapur line, a royal line sharing the same ancestry as the Cooch Behar kings, who ruled the Jalpaiguri region, intervened. They defeated Yajña Nārāyaṇ and his Bhutanese allies and installed the late king's brother Vasudev Nārāyaṇ as the new king. But as soon as the Raikat brothers left, Yajña Nārāyaṇ attacked the capital again, killed the king and claimed the throne. The Raikat brothers returned again, crushed Yajña and installed Mahendra Nārāyaṇ, the great-grandson of Prāṇ Nārāyaṇ, on the throne. The Bhutanese, the Indian sources allege, were involved in supporting this collateral royal from Mahi Nārāyaṇ and were against the main line of Prāṇ Nārāyaṇ. The Bhutanese monk-historians, however, present a different story. They tell us that the Bhutanese rulers valued the good relations with the line of Prāṇ Nārāyaṇ, which began in the days of Zhabdrung. The real Bhutanese political policy, however, may have been different as the course of Cooch Behar's history reveals. For now, let's return to the serious matters which were brewing at home.

The pressing question of succession

Despite repeated victories against Tibet, Bhutan was stirring with its own political crisis by 1680. At the heart of the crisis was the question of succession to the throne of Zhabdrung, who had 'entered retreat' without leaving a capable heir. The tension caused by the issue of succession can be gleaned from the Bhutanese biographies and histories from that period and somewhat later but, hidden in the accounts of religious piety and miracles, the real story is not very obvious. The best account of this issue is still the dissertation of John Ardussi in English written in 1977 for those who are interested in more detail.[28] Here, I provide the story in brief.

The issue of succession is inextricably linked to Zhabdrung's position as the leader of the Drukpa school and the ruler of the new state. Zhabdrung's authority as a leader and ruler was based on a number of religious and sociopolitical factors. Foremost among them was Zhabdrung's status as the principal legitimate heir to the divine line of Ralung, which originated from Tsangpa Gyarey. This social position gave him the special legitimacy to be the leader of the Drukpas. In addition, he was seen as a manifestation of a Buddha who had come to save the world. He was, after all, the genuine incarnation of the great Pema Karpo and thereby of Tsangpa Gyarey and of Avalokiteśvara, the Buddha of compassion. Like the Dalai Lamas who later became known as kingly manifestations of Avalokiteśvara, Zhabdrung was also seen as an embodiment of this Buddha, who was destined to rule and care for the land of snows.

As for the new state of Bhutan, Zhabdrung was undoubtedly its chief architect. It was principally his position, power, charisma and vision which led the formation of the new state of Bhutan. Moreover, many verses attributed to Padmasambhava clearly connected Zhabdrung's fate to the foundation of Bhutan. Thus, he was viewed as the predestined founder and ruler of the land, which the divine deities offered to him as his field of spiritual subjugation

(གདུལ་ཞིང་). For these reasons, Zhabdrung was the uncontested leader of Bhutan and his authority and leadership was fundamental to its existence. In the event of his absence, it was critical that there was a legitimate and capable successor to carry on his legacy. The posts of the Desi and Je Khenpo, who carried out the secular and ecclesiastical duties, were only subordinates in service of the office of the apex, that is, the seat of Zhabdrung or Dharmarāja as the British would call it later. These posts were not constituted to replace Zhabdrung but only intended to be two arms which would support the office at the apex, that of the supreme head of the state, which was to be passed down through a divine succession. This divine succession was planned to occur through a male hereditary line, as it was in Ralung. At least, this was the preferred choice for the time being. We must remember the formation of Bhutan came about largely as a result of Zhabdrung's initial efforts to replicate the establishment of Ralung. Succession by the incarnation line, such as the one in the institutions of the Dalai Lama and Karmapa hierarchs, was at that point not under consideration.

Seen in this light, the untimely death of Zhabdrung without an able successor was a great blow to the new state and the subsequent hoax of a 'strict retreat' and the various shams of taking meals on time, playing musical instruments, issuing orders and tonsuring acolytes were merely expedient ploys to keep official order and buy more time to find an acceptable solution to the problem of succession. The obvious answer to the problem of succession was Zhabdrung's son Jampal Dorji, who was born in 1631 and was trained under Drung Damchö. He was the heir apparent, or at least that was the case until he was struck by a serious illness when he was around eight years old.[29] Just before that, he was in Cheri and active as we know he gave a name for the newly born Tenzin Rabgay. Soon after that he moved to Punakha and fell ill but we do not know exactly what the problem was. The Bhutanese sources describe the illness as *ledrib* (ལས་སྒྲིབ་) or 'karmic impurities'. According to one source, his throat was blocked, leaving him without the ability to speak.[30] In all probability, he must have had something like a stroke which seriously handicapped him for the post of a ruler. If he was indeed seriously disabled, which it seems he was, popular superstition against having a handicapped ruler may have further prevented him from taking any public office.

Following this illness, Jampal Dorji remained secluded from the public eye, purportedly in deep meditation. Unfortunately, Zhabdrung had by then taken the full ordination of a celibate monk and could not produce another heir without doing damage to his spiritual credibility. Thus, all hopes were placed on Jampal Dorji's ability to produce an able heir. In spite of his handicap and debilitation, we are told he was able to perform the duties of a procreator. A daughter was born to him some time before 1651 about whom we know nothing except that she died young in 1651 causing great distress to Zhabdrung.[31] We do not either know who the mother was or what became of her. It is also not clear why no other efforts were made to help Jampal Dorji produce an heir between 1651 and 1678. Perhaps, there was some hope of Jampal Dorji's own recovery or there was no real hope for another heir in the main line and the attention instead turned to the alternate line, which we shall discuss below.

Interestingly, another attempt was made in 1678 when a bride for Jampal Dorji was brought from the venerable family of Sakya, arranged by the lama of the Chizhing monastery. The girl was a daughter of Ngor Zhabdrung Luding and she was brought from Tibet. Tenzin Rabgay's sister was asked to give her company in Punakha and she was soon installed as *tsei dagmo* (ཙེའི་ བདག་མོ་) or 'the lady of the apex' after the auguries were found to be positive.[32] Then in 1680, news spread that the royal lady was pregnant and there was certainly much excitement in the capital. The incumbent Desi Migyur Tenpa was jubilant that at last the direct lineage would survive and he could retire happily after the heir was born.[33] There was also a prophetic claim circulating that the child is going to be a boy. The 2nd Je Khenpo Sonam Özer even had a silk robe especially prepared for the new heir. Though he had no attachment to any material possession, he is said to have cherished this silk robe waiting eagerly for the birth of the baby boy.[34] However, history had a different plan. To everyone's utter dismay, a girl was born in the following summer. This must have caused much disappointment and consternation, especially as Jampal Dorji was no more in the position to father another child. He died in the same year although his death was also kept a secret. Notwithstanding the shock, the birth of the daughter was celebrated and congratulatory greetings and presents were received from various places.[35] The daughter was given the name Tshokye Dorji, a very masculine name.

By the time Tshokye Dorji was born, the 3rd Desi Migyur Tenpa had been already toppled following Bhutan's first episode of violent internal conflict. One scholar blamed this internal conflict for spoiling Bhutan's common fortune and causing the birth of a daughter who really should have been, according to the prophecy, a son. He underlined his point with the proverb: An internal leak is more detrimental than the external rain.[36] Another scholar argued that this mishap was a result of the wrath of the protecting deities who were confused by Zhabdrung's inconsistent orders. He first ordered them to eliminate the Tsangpa ruler's line but later adopted a conciliatory approach and even exchanged gifts. This scholar argued that from a strict tantric religious perspective, it is wrong to associate with anyone who has once become the target of one's tantric rituals of killing through magic.[37] This breach of tantric rule brought about for Zhabdrung the unfortunate termination of the male line. Whether or not the reader gives credence to such esoteric explanation, it was a common practice among the Bhutanese to find such spiritual and karmic answers to explain the turn of events. It is true to some extent even today.

The downfall of Migyur Tenpa was also explained as an outcome of the excesses he committed during his campaigns in eastern Bhutan. He is said to have mistreated and killed people, destroyed their properties and offended their gods with blatant disrespect. As a result of his militant and highhanded dealings, he is said to have turned more and more unreasonable and uncompromising towards the end of his life. It appears that Migyur Tenpa through his rather aggressive policies and ambitious projects had made many internal enemies during his tenure as the Desi. Early on in his regency, he is said to have mistreated the elder figure Drung Damchö Gyaltshen, who retired in Wangdiphodrang and passed away in 1672. This trusted chamberlain of Zhabdrung was a prominent member of Zhabdrung's team and largely responsible for the smooth running of internal court and ecclesiastical affairs around the time of Zhabdrung's 'retreat'. A dedicated monk, an incorruptible steward and versatile religious artist, he is said to have enjoyed good health through a disciplined vegetarian diet. His eyesight was particularly good allowing him to carry on intricate embroidery even at the age of seventy-one. He was also one of the masterminds of the 'retreat' hoax and Migyur Tenpa was his choice for the regency. Ironically, he received ignominious treatment from Migyur Tenpa, who was scorned by people for his outrageous ingratitude.

One event which certainly contributed to the final debacle of Migyur Tenpa's strong authority was the execution of three servants of Wangdiphodrang. The victims appealed to Migyur Tenpa's own protégé and successor, Tenzin Rabgay, for help and Tenzin Rabgay tried every means to change Migyur Tenpa's mind but in vain. The men were consequently thrown into the river and Tenzin Rabgay felt bitterly offended. Gedun Chöphel, who was the *dzongpön* of Wangdiphodrang and thus perhaps the master of the executed men, was outraged by the sentence. This event certainly threw apart the widening rift between Gedun Chöphel and Migyur Tenpa and his allies of the Obtsho family. We may recall that during the last war with Tibet, Gedun Chöphel made serious military blunders and the Desi reprimanded him harshly while his rivals, Ngawang Rabten and his son Ngawang Phuntsho, came out of the war as heroes, partly at the cost of Gedun Chöphel's reputation. As a mark of recognition, Migyur Tenpa promoted Ngawang Rabten of Obtsho to a ministerial position in Punakha. This exacerbated the rivalry between the Obtsho family of Ngawang Rabten and the Kabji family of Gedun Chöphel and there was growing jealousy and enmity between them.

The first assault of Gedun Chöphel on Migyur Tenpa and the Obtsho party took place in Punakha when they killed Ngawang Drukdra, Ngawang Rabten's brother who was serving as chamberlain to Jampal Dorji. Then at the end of 1680, in a *coup d'etat*, Gedun Chöphel's men cornered Desi Migyur Tenpa in Jampal Dorji's residence in the Punakha *dzong*. The Desi ran and sought refuge in the shrine room where the vertebra relic was kept and from behind the slammed door, he confronted the dissidents. He said:

If you, the beings of the southern land, can have peace and happiness, it matters not for an old Tibetan like me to either die tomorrow or the day after. Your wanton and inconsiderate actions such as this will not augur well for the welfare of Drukpa state in the long run.[38]

But the crowd outside rebuked him for the misery he brought to the people of the southern land through taxes and corvée for his numerous projects of *dzong* and stūpa constructions.

Before leaving, the assailants captured his chief ally, Ngawang Rabten and the latter's son, Dondrub and had them imprisoned in Wangdiphodrang. Ngawang Rabten's wife and daughter were also arrested in Gön and brought to Wangdiphodrang but later sent into exile to Uma, a remote village to the south. Subsequently, Ngawang Rabten was put to death and his other sons Ngawang Phuntsho and Thinley were also imprisoned. The only member of the Obtsho family excluded from this ruthless abuse and depredation was Ngawang Gyaltshen, who was then a rising star among the monks and whose career we shall review very briefly later. Following the revolt of Gedun Chöphel and his men, Migyur Tenpa stood down from the post of the Desi in the beginning of 1681 and retired in Cheri, where he died in the following summer, five days after the birth of Tshokye Dorji. The news of the birth may have devastated the retired ruler as it quashed the last hope of a direct male line from Zhabdrung. In contrast, when the news of the bloody internal conflict and his death reached Lhasa some months later, the 5th Dalai Lama greeted it with three days of celebratory and thanksgiving rituals to his deities and composed two short texts to mark the event.[39]

The same month Migyur Tenpa stood down from the regency, the illustrious Tenzin Rabgay (1638–96) was installed as the 4th Desi as well as the first holder of the golden throne in Punakha. The grand enthronement of Tenzin Rabgay as the Gyaltshab (རྒྱལ་ཚབ་) or royal regent was attended by representatives from all corners of the country and abroad bearing all kinds of precious gifts. The ceremony was perhaps the most luxurious Bhutan has seen until then. The 2nd Je Khenpo Sonam Özer led the offering of congratulatory gifts followed by the three district rulers or *dzongpön*s of Punakha, Wangdiphodrang and Thimphu, three regional governors or *chila*s of Paro, Dagana and Tongsa, Tenzin Rabgay's sister from Tango, half-brother from Taktshang and many other heads of dzongs, monasteries, communities and prominent families. Beside the Drukpa Kagyu religious establishments, the Nyingma and Sakya schools were also very well represented, although understandably eastern Bhutan was not represented as much as western Bhutan. From abroad, there were delegates from Sakya monastery in Tibet, from the King of Ladakh, from the Princess of Cooch Behar and from the lama of Kailash bearing many riches. The ceremony was also marked by a generous distribution of coins and other gifts to all the tax-paying citizens of Bhutan and special gifts for the brave warriors of eight sections of Wang.

Tenzin Rabgay's installation as prince regent marked a different direction in Bhutan's programme of succession. With no male heir in Zhabdrung's line, the court now took recourse to the alternate line of the Gya family descending from the madman Drukpa Kuenley and his son who was Tenzin Rabgay's grandfather. This was nothing seriously anomalous as the ancient Tibetan system of the uncle–nephew transmission through the lateral line was a familiar practice in the Ralung establishment. In fact, Tenzin Rabgay had been already treated as a possible heir ever since the illness of Jampal Dorji. He was not only born in the august male line of the Gya family, his father Tshewang Tenzin was a stalwart supporter of Zhabdrung in Bhutan. His mother Damcho Tenzin was from the *chöje* family of Changangkha descending from Phajo Drukgom and was the ex-consort of Zhabdrung. In fact, there were even some rumours, according to oral sources, that Tenzin Rabgay might be Zhabdrung's own child. Zhabdrung had paid special attention to Tenzin Rabgay and, at the time of his death, he is said to have instructed the 1st Desi to groom Tenzin Rabgay with special care. This is particularly interesting because Tenzin Rabgay's brother, Jinpa Gyaltshen and the latter's son, as far we know, were never considered for the continuation of the hereditary line.

Tenzin Rabgay was indeed the back-up plan and extra care was given to his upbringing and education. All requirements for his upkeep were provided from the state treasury and his training was closely supervised by Zhabdrung and by the Desis after the former's death. Tenzin Rabgay received a thorough training in all aspects of Buddhist studies, language, astrology, monastic rituals, religious arts, meditation and even medicine under the leading master of his day. When he joined the monastic community at eight, Tenzin Drukgyal suggested that he be allowed to remain without the vow of celibacy but Zhabdrung did not consent to this for practical reasons. As a direct descendent of the Drukpa line, Tenzin Rabgay could not be placed towards the end of the row in the seating layout and it would be wrong according to the monastic code of ethics for a non-celibate person to sit higher than the celibate monks. So, he was given the ordination of a novice.

The first two Desis monitored Tenzin Rabgay's education very closely and generally contemplated on plans to find a consort for him to sustain the male line but nothing had eventuated before they passed away. The unpredictable condition of Jampal Dorji may have been a reason for the indecision and delay, and the Buddhist monastic injunction against matchmaking may have deterred their spirits. In any case, the question of succession was becoming more pressing and no stones could be left unturned to find a solution. This forced the 3rd Desi Migyur Tenpa to take a decisive action as soon as he got into office in 1667. Migyur Tenpa took Tenzin Rabgay, who was then thirty by Bhutanese reckoning, out of the monastic community in an open effort to exhort him to produce heirs. The following summer when the monks moved to Thimphu, he was kept in Punakha to perform 'the task of producing an heir' according to his biography. The biography does not give any more information. We can guess that dates were set for him and he had sexual relationships with either one or many consorts but unfortunately there was no news of any child coming yet. He did not particularly like the heat in Punakha but benefited from teachings he received from Drung Damchö and his own half-brother Jinpa Gyaltshen. By 1680, Migyur Tenpa must have become desperate. Tenzin Rabgay was unable to produce a child in over a dozen years and Jampal Dorji was getting old. Migyur Tenpa perhaps arranged the bride from Sakya for Jampal Dorji in a last attempt to gain an heir from the main line of descent.

While these attempts at sustaining the line were going on, Migyur Tenpa had also placed on Tenzin Rabgay's shoulders the full responsibility for making decisions concerning religious matters. He was to preside over religious ceremonies, give sermons and play the role of the spiritual head of Bhutan. The Desi also consulted him on the matters of state administration thus actively grooming Tenzin Rabgay for the supreme post of the ruler. Tenzin Rabgay indeed benefited from his guidance and support and eventually rose to be an illustrious holder of the post but Migyur Tenpa was to take no part in it when it finally happened in the 1681. Virtually days before the installation of Tenzin Rabgay as the Gyaltshab, Migyur Tenpa retired to Cheri and was not even present during the enthronement of his protégé in whom he had placed such high hopes.

The position of the Gyaltshab was a new creation and its constitutional bearings were vague. Tenzin Rabgay was not installed merely as another Desi although later historians generally recorded him as the 4th Desi. He was installed as the supreme head of the state and incumbent of Zhabdrung's throne until there was a better replacement. He was the Gyaltshab, literally, a substitute for the king. The best English term we can use to describe this post is perhaps 'prince regent'. The word 'regent' is commonly used to translate Desi or Depa or similar positions. In this new position, Tenzin Rabgay combined the roles of the apex or Dharmarāja and the Desi, an arrangement which occurred rarely with the future holders of this post. Had Tenzin Rabgay produced a male line, the whole system could have turned into a hereditary line descending from him.

In this role of the supreme spiritual hierarch, Tenzin Rabgay launched many projects aimed at consolidating the political and religious spheres of the new state. He was more concerned with strengthening and promoting the existent statehood rather than expanding it. Tenzin Rabgay's reign was the first glorious era for Bhutan under a native ruler. It was largely marked by exuberant cultural advancement, compassionate governance, astute diplomacy and abiding peace. One of his first projects was to strengthen the monastic community, the main custodians of high culture. So, he went on a tour of the western valleys to recruit new monks through a monk tax. One son, normally the middle one, from every family with three sons was recruited to join the central monastic order. Nearly a hundred candidates from the Thimphu valley alone were tonsured on the tenth day of the seventh Bhutanese month, 23 August 1681 and a difference worth noting is that Tenzin Rabgay, as the spiritual leader, tonsured them. There was no need for someone behind closed doors posing as Zhabdrung to do this. He elaborated and codified the state religious rituals and ceremonies and injected extra rigour to monastic discipline and academic studies, which were already introduced by his predecessors. The code of monastic discipline, which originated with Zhabdrung and was codified by the 1st Desi, was to be seriously followed and unbecoming practices such as consumption of alcohol were harshly put down. The monastic community was to have a separate scholastic section where studies of both exoteric and esoteric forms of Buddhism and traditional sciences were to be conducted. The full list of his initiatives is too long to be included here and can be found in his wonderfully informative biography by Ngawang Lhundup.

If Tenzin Rabgay was ardent in cultivating a strong cultural ethos through the promotion of intellectual studies and practice, he was more so in making such an ethos manifest in various forms of cultural expressions. He was a great patron of Bhutanese high culture ranging from architectural edifices to music and dances. Special schools were set up for painting, sculpture, carving, embroidery, gilding, silver smithy, calligraphy, medicine, astrology, music and dance. The new gilded cupola of the *dzong* and the three-dimensional maṇḍala in Punakha finished in 1691 were commissioned by Tenzin Rabgay as was the set of golden *kanjur* manuscripts in Thimphu finished in 1686 as well as many other canonical scriptures. Nepali artisans were invited to create many statues, including the statues of Zhabdrung distributed across the country. The grand appliqué *thongdrol* (མཐོང་གྲོལ་) wall hangings of Punakha depicting the Buddha and sixteen elders and of Thimphu depicting Padmasmabhava and his eight characters were also produced under his guidance and elaborate celebration held to unfurl them for public view. Seeing these magnificent religious works of art is said to have helped some people even regain their eyesight. Tenzin Rabgay was himself talented in this art and created a set of embroidered wall hangings, which one Tibetan master remarked was unparalleled in its style and beauty in the entire Himalayan world. Many aspects of Bhutanese cultural pageantry including the grand *tshechu* festivals involving spectacular mask dances and *thongdrol* wall hangings begin from his reign although observance of *tshechu* holy days existed long before him. Most dances including the Rigma Chudrug, Tshamchöd, Tum-ngam, Guru Tshengye and Khadro De-nga were introduced during his time by sending one Ugyen Tshering to Tibet to learn these dances from a number of places. Ugyen Tshering rigorously learnt the Tibetan choreographies, modified them or blended them with existent local dances to develop a unique Bhutanese style.

Tenzin Rabgay ordered the expansion of the small Jakar *dzong* to its current size and the construction of the *dzong* in Tango, his birthplace and main seat. The Tongsa *chila* Nganlungpa Sherab Lhundup and Thimphu *dzongpön* Norbu were respectively responsible for the actual construction of the *dzong*s. As a measure of state defence, he had shrines of protecting deities in some major *dzong*s either newly built or improved with the inclusion of special ritual artefacts. The Damtshang *dzong* in Dalingkha was also renovated. Tenzin Rabgay also commissioned the building of a temple in Taktshang and the renovation of the Kyerchu temple, the Chökhortse temple of Jamyang Kuenga Senge, the Jabar temple of Sherab Mebar, a stūpa at Chuzom and the Drangye, the seat of the Barawa school. The temple of Tachogang temple, the seat of the Chazampa school, was also rebuilt and Thimphu *dzongpön* Au Tshering, who was responsible for the fire which destroyed it during Zhabdrung's conflict with the non-compliant lamas, was made to undertake the project as an act of karmic absolution. Toward the end of his career, Tenzin Rabgay also enlarged Tashichödzong and built an extensive two-storeyed congregation hall with some fifty-six pillars and a spacious walkway around it covered with stone slabs.

The cultural exuberance of Tenzin Rabgay's reign was matched by his compassionate rule and sustained peace and prosperity. His overall policy for internal and external affairs was one of reconciliation and friendship. Throughout his reign, there was only one occasion, when he undertook the religious ritual to destroy an enemy, unlike earlier decades when such rituals were conducted continually. The sectarian conflicts which were rampant in early days of the Drukpa state were generally over and the internal dispute which immediately preceded his coronation as the Gyaltshab had subsided for the time being. Although there were sustained efforts to spread the Drukpa influence through appointment of lamas or construction of temples, the approach was one of open dissemination rather than aggressive conversion. Tachogang of the Chagzampa school, as we have already seen, was even reinstated. Tenzin Rabgay generally promoted a policy of religious tolerance and ecumenism. Following the example of Zhabdrung, Tenzin Rabgay particularly cultivated the friendship of the Nyingmapa hierarchs who still exercised a dominant influence in the central and eastern regions of Bhutan. A special mention must be made of the close friendship between him and the second Gangteng Trulku Tenzin Lekpai Dhondup (1645–1725). They enjoyed profound respect and affection for each other and Gangteng Trulku was rewarded with the winter residence of Chitokha and its estates.

Tenzin Rabgay's conciliatory approach can also be seen in his dealings with the local conflict between the Kabji faction of Gedun Chöphel and the Obtsho family. John Ardussi strenuously conjectures that there may have been a divide between the 'loyalists' who favoured the main line from Zhabdrung and the 'nationalists' who held anti-Tibetan sentiments and wanted a native Bhutanese leadership.[40] The 3rd Desi Migyur Tenpa and the Obtsho family would belong to the first camp and Gedun Chöphel and his allies to the second. No hint of such ethnic and nationalist tension can be found in the contemporary texts although it is quite possible that some tension along ethnic lines existed. What is quite clear is that there were rivalries among Bhutanese families, particularly between the well-known house of Obtsho and Gedun Chöphel of Kabji, and Tenzin Rabgay had to play a delicate role between the two. He reinstated the estates of Obtsho which were confiscated by Gedun Chöphel on behalf of the state and also supported the slow rise of one of the sons of Obtsho, Ngawang Gyaltshen. Meanwhile, he also kept a good relationship with the faction of Gedun Chöphel, who served as the *dzongpön* of Punakha until his temporary retirement from politics. Several other names from Kabji held important posts.

Tenzin Rabgay also made special efforts to show his unflagging dedication to the office and family of Zhabdrung, mostly out of his profound respect for Zhabdrung. The threshold over which Zhabdrung had trod, for instance, was removed and venerated. But these efforts were perhaps also intended to prove his unwavering support to the main line and dispel any doubts, if there were any, of him acting willingly to supersede the main line. One exemplary effort right at the beginning of his reign was the repatriation of Jampal Dorji's mother and Zhabdrung's consort Gökar Drolma from Tibet. This lady had curiously left for Tibet around the time her son Jampal Dorji fell ill and Tenzin Rabgay was born in 1638. There might have been some vilification or tension based on superstition or some other important reason, which we do not know but which took her away from Bhutan and kept her in Tibet for so long. She is said to have gone through much hardship in Tibet, spending some of her time in prison. Nothing is known of her until Tenzin Rabgay sent one courtier in disguise to find her in 1680 with some money. The lady was deeply touched by Tenzin Rabgay's gesture, more so because the previous Desis made no attempts to reach her.

In 1682, when the Tibetan government repeatedly requested Bhutan to extradite Bodong Chime Trulku, a lama who had escaped to Bhutan, Tenzin Rabgay took the opportunity to bring her back home. If the Tibetan lama was spared of any punishment after his return, Tenzin Rabgay agreed to deliver him in return for Gökar Drolma. The Tibetan government accepted the conditions and the two were exchanged at the border, where Gökar Drolma was received by Bhutanese officers with great respect in a lavish reception, which surprised the Tibetan escorts as they seemed to be unaware of her identity. She proceeded to Punakha, where she was again showered with much respect and very generous provisions from the state treasury by Tenzin Rabgay. Her son Jampal Dorji had died by then and she herself died in 1684, thoroughly imbued by Tenzin Rabgay's magnanimity.

Apart from this exchange, there was no change of policy towards the north and Bhutan's relationship with Tibet was still tense. The 5th Dalai Lama had died in 1682 and his death, like Zhabdrung's, was kept secret by his new regent Sangay Gyatsho, who was allegedly ordered by him to do so. Bhutan and Tibet were thus mysteriously ruled by two dead spiritual leaders, both of whom were believed to be alive. Occasional skirmishes at the northwestern border continued throughout Tenzin Rabgay's reign with two notable incidents. In the first case, a petty chieftain named Sergyi Jichung of Nenang defected from Bhutan to join the Sikkim/Tibetan hegemony. Against the militant tendency of the regional officer of Daling to regain control of Nenang, Tenzin Rabgay showed restraint in military deployment arguing that only abiding peace could help the ultimate Drukpa goal of propagating the Buddha's teachings.

In the second case, a chieftain called Azin defected from the Tibetans to join Bhutan and his domain of Chiding became the bone of contention. A major negotiation between Tibetan and Bhutanese representatives took place in Chumbi to resolve the disagreement but the meeting hardly resulted in a clear-cut border, and territorial disputes continued. However, there was no ardour for military intervention on the Bhutanese side under Tenzin Rabgay's leadership. Tibet, similarly, was preoccupied with its own political problems vis-à-vis both China and Mongolia in the absence of the 5th Dalai Lama. The rift between the Tibetan regent and descendents of Gushri Khan was widening. Eventually, the regent Sangay Gyatsho, who was also rumoured to the 5th Dalai Lama's son, was beheaded by the wife of Gushri Khan's grandson Lhajang Khan and the young 6th Dalai Lama arrested and subsequently killed by Mongol soldiers but we will come to that later.

To the south, Bhutan was playing a vigorous role in the affairs of Cooch Behar as we have seen above. We have noted the friendly exchanges between Zhabdrung and Lakṣmi Nārāyaṇ, the escape of Prāṇ Nārāyaṇ to

Bhutan during the Mughal invasion of Cooch Behar in 1661 and the visit of Prāṇ Nārāyaṇ's daughter to Tenzin Rabgay's coronation in 1681, which are clearly recorded in Bhutanese sources. But Bhutanese involvement in Cooch Behar by Tenzin Rabgay's time was far more serious than just exchanges of diplomatic niceties. According to the Indian sources, the Bhutanese supported Yajna Nārāyaṇ, the Nazir Dev, from the collateral line originating in Mahi Nārāyaṇ and fought to depose kings from the main line of Prāṇ Nārāyaṇ. We have seen above how the Raikat brother of the Baikunthapur line, Jaga Dev and Bhuja Dev, came to the rescue of the main line and installed Mahendra Nārāyaṇ, the great-grandson of Prāṇ Nārāyaṇ after the assassination of Vasudev Nārāyaṇ, Mahendra's uncle.

Mahendra Nārāyaṇ was barely five years old when he was installed on the throne in 1682. Without a strong ruler, the kingdom began to fall apart as different factions continued to fight. This time, the Raikat brothers were unable to help, perhaps being occupied with problems in their own area or due to poor health. Many zamindars, or landlords, defected to the Mughal rule to become direct tributaries of the Mughal governors in Bengal. Taking advantage of this anarchic situation, the Mughal forces under Edabat Khan invaded Cooch Behar and began to occupy parts of it. In the face of a common external threat, the warring princes briefly united to oppose the Mughal invasion and also sought help from Bhutan. Tenzin Rabgay's biographer tells us that the King of Cooch Behar requested Tenzin Rabgay to send his chamberlain Norbu as an ambassador. The primary motive was to have Norbu conduct negotiations between the King of Cooch Behar and the Mughal invader but the negotiations must have not taken place or failed as Tenzin Rabgay was soon asked to send military support. Tenzin Rabgay reluctantly sent two contingents led by the chief of protocol of Paro and the officer of Dalingkha to support Cooch Behar against the Mughal forces. The outcome of the campaign, Indian sources record, came out in favour of the Mughals and Cooch Behar lost control of several territories. On the contrary, Tenzin Rabgay's biographer, probably compounding this one with a later invasion under Ali Khan, states that the Mughal leader escaped to Nepal.

The conflict with the Mughal forces may have been barely over when the family disputes erupted again. In 1683, Tenzin Rabgay was again asked to send his chamberlain Norbu to mediate in a dispute between the king and a certain minister, Kungkuri Joki Dheva. This Joki Dheva must be Jaga Dev, one of the Raikat brothers of the Baikunthapur line as he is identified as a descendent of Sishu, who started the Baikunthapur line. It appears that the

Bhutanese perceived the line from Mahi Nārāyaṇ as legitimate and objected to the interference from the Raikat brothers. The negotiation failed and the king once again sought military assistance from Bhutan. Tenzin Rabgay was very wary of getting involved in an internal conflict and of sending troops but unable to deny support to a close friend, Tenzin Rabgay, against his own Buddhist disposition, sent some Bhutanese troops. He repeatedly instructed Norbu and the generals to find a peaceful solution and to use military force only as a last resort, to merely suppress the opposition and to avoid bloodshed at all costs. Tenzin Rabgay's decision to assist the ruler also had an economic consideration as many goods were annually received from Pasakha in the form of taxes which Bhutan was allowed to collect from Cooch Behari territory. The outcome of the intervention, regrettably for Tenzin Rabgay, turned out to be quite violent although his biographer does not give any details.

The subsequent fighting among the princes may have resulted in the death of the Raikat brothers and Yajña Nārāyaṇ and his brother Jagat Nārāyaṇ. With their death, Yajña's son Shānta Nārāyaṇ was made the Nazir Dev and his nephew Rūp Nārāyaṇ became the commander of the army. It was perhaps in his capacity as the commander of army that Rūp Nārāyaṇ paid a visit to Punakha in 1690 carrying many gifts. In return, he was given a grand reception and entertained in the highly decorated hall of the Punakha *dzong* with mask dances and other luxuries during his stay. When he left, he was sent off with numerous presents but it is not clear what the main purpose of the visit was and what he might have achieved. The Bhutanese sources sound quite oblivious of the fact that he was the son of a rival royal line, and not from the main line of Prāṇ Nārāyaṇ. Did they already know where Cooch Behar's politics was heading and were they playing in tune with the changing times? Or, even more importantly, did they intentionally change the course of Cooch Behar's politics? Whichever it may be, the visit was propitious for Bhutan. Their wonderful reception and hospitality would be paid off well in 1693 when the young King Mahendra Nārāyaṇ of the main line died at the age of sixteen and Rūp Nārāyaṇ emerged as the undisputed new King of Cooch Behar. Mahendra Nārāyaṇ's death ended the main line of the Cooch Behar kings and, with the enthronement of Rūp Nārāyaṇ, the throne was passed to the line from Mahi Nārāyaṇ, the line which the Bhutanese are said to have supported throughout.

Bhutan also saw a vigorous growth of spiritual and diplomatic ties with countries who were not immediate neighbours. Tenzin Rabgay sent at least two missions to the Kathmandu valley, primarily to invite Newari artisans from Bhaktapur. The first one in 1691 was obstructed by the rulers of Nenang who, at this point sided with the Tibetans. Disguised as robbers, they attacked the mission, killing people and horses and looting their belongings. The second, led by a monk from western Tibet, managed to reach Bhaktapur and return with several Newari artists but neither seems to have attempted to establish formal diplomatic ties or spiritual links as did Damchö Pekar's mission a decade earlier. Spiritual and diplomatic links were, however, forged with the Derge kingdom in eastern Tibet. After receiving repeated requests from King Sangay Tenpa of Derge (r.1675?–1710) for a Drukpa preceptor, Tenzin Rabgay sent Ngawang Gyaltshen of Obtsho with eighteen horses and nine attendants including a Tibetan guide. The party left for Kham in 1688, travelling through Tibet incognito as there were no formal diplomatic relations with Tibet and such a mission would have been obstructed by the Tibetan regime. Even the ceremony for appointing Ngawang Gyaltshen as Bhutanese ambassador to Derge was conducted secretly at night in Punakha in order to avoid arousing any Tibetan suspicion.

After successfully evading Tibetan authorities, the mission arrived in Chamdo beyond which they did not have to remain incognito. Soon, they were formally received by the welcoming party sent by their host. The Derge king and his court found Ngawang Gyaltshen not only a very gracious person but also a learned, versatile and accomplished master. During his time in Derge from 1688 to 1695, Ngawang Gyaltshen gave numerous teachings and performed various religious services for the king and his family. He won the faith and devotion of the royal family and the people of Derge. He also visited important religious centres and met some prominent religious figures of Kham. The Derge royal household, we learn from his report, treated all religious persons with great respect and hospitality irrespective of the religious tradition. It is for such impartial and ecumenical patronage of religious activities that the royal house would became renowned in the following centuries. In Ngawang Gyaltshen, they found both a great teacher and powerful court priest. He so deeply impressed the Derge king that the latter was in great despair when Ngawang Gyaltshen announced that he was summoned back to Bhutan. 'We cannot find a Lama like you even by searching with a torch lit during daytime; now that we have finally found you, how can we possibly let you leave? You must stay here until I die,' the King pleaded.[41]

It is no surprise that the Derge king was thoroughly imbued by Ngawang

Gyaltshen's qualities. Ngawang Gyaltshen was indeed a consummate Drukpa master with exceptional learning and experience in traditional sciences and religious matters. Born in the Obtsho family as a grandnephew of the 1st Desi Tenzin Drukgyal, he was blessed by Zhabdrung at childhood. After being tonsured by the 'imposter' at the door of Zhabdrung's meditation cell in 1662, he was trained under many great masters and had the opportunity to work on many state-sponsored artistic projects to hone his skills. He was a learned scholar in all aspects of Buddhism, an experienced master of meditation, an expert in monastic ritual and a versatile artist with talents in fine arts, sculpture and mask dances. No one in his days could have filled the post of a Bhutanese spiritual and cultural ambassador better than he did. Thus, the success of Bhutan's first and only mission to Derge was primarily due to the personality and merits of Ngawang Gyaltshen. The riches he brought from Derge on his return, it was alleged, filled the Desi's treasury. Back in Bhutan, Ngawang Gyaltshen had to sadly go through the tribulations of his family's tragedy one more time under the new Desi Gedun Chöphel, before he was sent away again as Bhutan's spiritual ambassador to Ladakh, at the other end of the Himalayan world.

The glorious reign of Tenzin Rabgay had ended in a bitter conflict by the time Ngawang Gyaltshen returned from Derge. Despite all efforts Tenzin Rabgay had not succeeded in producing a male heir. We may recall that since 1667, when he was twenty-nine and Migyur Tenpa came to power, Tenzin Rabgay was strongly urged to produce an heir. However, there is no report of anything happening until 1686 when we hear of a consort named Wangdi Lhamo from Kabji Dashing, who produced two daughters from him. Unfortunately, both were girls and both died at birth or quite young. Depressed by the loss, their efforts to produce an heir were weakened and Tenzin Rabgay and Wangdi Lhamo seem to have got separated. In 1689, the second Je Khenpo Sonam Özer was on his death bed but still holding on to the silk robe he made and still waiting for a male heir. To a group of prominent hierarchs who gathered around him, he made his last plea to save the Drukpa line by finding around three wives to be placed in the different residences of Tenzin Rabgay. 'You must put this message to the lord's ear,' he said. 'For the welfare of the sentient beings and the Buddha's teachings, I pray to him that he ensure at all costs the glorious Drukpa hereditary line is not terminated.'[42]

The master passed away making this last wish, a sign of his immense affection for the Drukpa hereditary line, but his wish would not become a reality. In 1690, a girl named Deleg was officially brought to Tango as Tenzin Rabgay's new wife. She came from the *chöje* family of Changangkha and was thus a cousin of Tenzin Rabgay on his mother's side. Her arrival coincided with the celebrations for the consecration of Tango and this was not merely a coincidence because Tenzin Rabgay believed that this place was blessed to be the home of the Drukpa line by a series of masters, including Drukpa Kunley, Zhabdrung, and his own father and grandfather. If there was any place for the Drukpa line to survive, it had to be here at Tango and Deleg made the ideal mother in terms of her ancestry. But things did not turn out as wished. In 1691, the new wife gave birth to a beautiful daughter, who was named Kunley. She was an adorable child and Tenzin Rabgay loved her very much despite his frustrations of not getting a son. Lhacham Kunley (1691–1732/33) grew up to be an exceptional woman, like her aunt Jetsun Drung (1634–1708). Both she and her aunt became highly respected figures in their own right as deeply committed and accomplished religious figures. Considered as reincarnates, both women dedicated their life to religion and occupied a special position among the male-dominated religious world of the Drukpa school.

There may have been also other girls with whom Tenzin Rabgay had relationships but no one, we can be sure, produced a son. As years passed by, Tenzin Rabgay's hope of producing a male heir was gradually slipping away from him. Tenzin Rabgay was, by temperament, a deeply spiritual man inclined to be a recluse rather than a ruler and family man. This may have significantly reduced his efforts to produce an heir. Why his elder brother Jinpa Gyaltshen, who appears to have also produced a son, was not considered for continuing the collateral line from Tshewang Tenzin is still a mystery.[43] Although Jinpa Gyaltshen did not share the same mother as Tenzin Rabgay and his sister, he was a legitimate son of Tshewang Tenzin of Tango and thus from a male scion of the Ralung line. Perhaps, the issue of succession from the collateral line was not yet acutely felt when he died. Yet, we hear nothing about his son Damchö Tenzin even when the hereditary line was in a critical state. Could he have also died very young?

By 1693, Tenzin Rabgay's chances of fathering a son were indeed very slim as he fell seriously ill. Although he temporarily recovered, he was far from the health his duties as a ruler and procreator would have required. When he stood at the head of congregation to read the code of monastic discipline during the New Year celebrations in 1694, the monks noticed that his eyesight was failing as he struggled to read it. The senior monks wept as they listened to him, their hearts soaked in sadness. Then, during the ceremonies which followed in that year, he had to use a prop to stand and a monk had to help him lift the cymbals he played. In the summer of 1694, the monks and the state undertook a plethora of rituals and prayers for his recovery and long life but his health only deteriorated. Offerings were sent to all religious centres for prayers and a nationwide distribution of salt was undertaken to dispel obstacles to his life. There was an outpouring of ceremonial supplications from his subjects asking him to live long for the welfare of the world. Gangteng Trulku, his close friend, was by his side in Tashichödzong conducting many rituals for recovery. There was frenzy and a lot of apprehension and misgivings about the nation's future.

With no improvement in his health, Tenzin Rabgay decided to retire and go into a retreat. He believed that his illness involving pressing lethargy as well as his failure to sustain the hereditary line resulted from the sorcery and occult attacks his enemies had targeted against him and Zhabdrung. A retreat to repel the effect was the most appropriate remedy. He delegated the ecclesiastical duties to the 3rd Je Khenpo Pekar Lhundup and secular affairs to three persons, including his chamberlain Norbu. He was planning to leave Tashichödzong for his ancestral home of Tango, when suddenly the *dzong* was surrounded by the army of rebels led by Gedun Chöphel, the monk who deposed the previous Desi.

The reason for the revolt is unclear and most historians think it was an act of sheer jealousy. Gedun Chöphel, the *dzongpön* of Punakha, had already been relieved from office following his requests for retirement from office in 1689. Instead of retiring to his home in Seula, Tenzin Rabgay advised him to retire in Wangdiphodrang under the care of his faithful friend, Druk Tenzin, so that he remained at a distance from his enemies of Obtsho. Gedun Chöphel, however, was far from retired in spirit. When Norbu was given the joint post of Tenzin Rabgay's private chamberlain and *dzongpön* of Thimphu, Gedun Chöphel had already expressed some annoyance. It may be recalled that Norbu was a courtier under Gedun Chöphel and given by him to Tenzin Rabgay as a private attendant when Tenzin Rabgay stayed in Punakha during the summer of 1667, having moved out of the monastic community to produce an heir. Now, Norbu was made to fill the post of a ruler. If Gedun Chöphel did not like the unabated rise of his former courtier, the circumstances under which it happened were certainly suspicious. By the summer of 1694, only a few people had direct access to Tenzin Rabgay and rumours were rife that Tenzin Rabgay had also entered retreat. Zhabdrung and his son Jampal Dorji were officially still in retreat, their meals served on time, but most people by now had guessed that they were no more alive and that 'retreat' was a convenient euphemism for being deceased. To proclaim that Tenzin Rabgay was in retreat sent the wrong signal, even if it were really true. In the midst of anxiety and fear of the uncertain future, people wondered if Tenzin Rabgay were alive or already dead.

Gedun Chöphel may have feared that Tenzin Rabgay was dead or close to dying and that real power was being usurped by chamberlain Norbu and his coterie. He may have wished to occupy the post of the Desi himself or simply wanted to get rid of Norbu. Whatever his motive, his army surrounded Tashichödzong and stopped anyone from leaving the *dzong*. The rebels clearly used the name of the members of Zhabdrung's family which then included Tshokye Dorji, Zhabdrung's granddaughter and her mother from Sakya. Tshokye Dorji and her mother may have been completely ignorant of the plot and merely used as pawns. We do not know either what the rebels demanded, but Tenzin Rabgay was only too willing to step down and pass the throne of Gyaltshab to the mother and daughter (ཡུམ་སྲས་) if they wished to take charge.

Steadfast with his commitment to peace and non-violence, Tenzin Rabgay advised his men against any confrontation. He also advised his chamberlain Norbu to forsake any political ambition and relinquish his post. His sister Jetsun Drung made arrangements for Norbu to be taken to Dochöten in Paro for safety while he undertook negotiations but Norbu was soon assassinated by the rebels on the way. Tenzin Rabgay consequently retired to Tango, where he briefly got better. Gedun Chöphel requested him to return to the office of Gyaltshab but he declined and passed away in 1696 after placing statues of Padmasambhava and Zhabdrung on his head and chanting 'Ogyen Pema Khyen, Ngawang Namgyal Khyen!—I beseech Padmasambhava, I beseech Zhabdrung!'

The following verses translated by John Ardussi captures his two moods.[44]

With the mind of a monk long accustomed to the peace of nonattachment,
'Til now have I resided in the solitudes of snow and forest.
But I must also possess the glorious karmic legacy of a Universal Emperor,
a Cakravartin,
For, if not, then why do I so love to travel throughout the many districts
of the land?
To serve as foremost the needs of others, is the Bodhisattva vow, taken
in my past (lives).

With no attachment to my own happiness,
Dedication to the needs of sentient beings is the sacred path.
…
Like the (rolling) clouds of Autumn
Are dear friendships in this ever changing artificial world.
When first we meet our prayers are answered,
Yet soon does the force of Karma separate us.
Exactly the same are all artificial constructs of the Four Extremes.
Sentient beings take what is impermanent to be permanent,
And once there is mutual attachment, separation becomes unbearable.
Forever after they remember it. Yet this is but a residue in the mind.
For that reason, having abandoned friendships far behind,
Alone with my shadow in the mountain retreat,
In complete concentration of body, speech and mind …
To dwell thus, one pointedly, unwavering, that is Bliss.

The beginning of internal strife

If history, like a drama, has to have a hero and a villain, Bhutanese historians
are quick at identifying them. The only difference is that this drama of real
history did not end with the righteous prince defeating the villain and living
happily ever after. Tenzin Rabgay represented the best of Zhabdrung's legacy,
and his righteous rule and peaceful reign was not matched by any ruler in
pre-modern Bhutan. A man of deep piety and great concern for his subjects,
Tenzin Rabgay was an enlightened ruler and Bhutan enjoyed relative peace,
security and prosperity under him. He was always wary of burdening his
subjects with excessive taxation as he was with fighting unnecessary wars.
Even the peace in Tibet was in some part attributed to his anti-war sentiments.
His only failure—one which would cost Bhutan dearly—was his inability to
produce a male heir. But this was in a way beyond his control.

Gedun Chöphel, on the other hand, is depicted by the traditional historians
as the unrelenting power-hungry villain. He was a monk with no discomfiture
in ruthlessly murdering his foes. By the time he installed himself as the
5th Desi, he had killed two prominent ministers and toppled two prominent
Desis. His regency is generally remembered by historians as a time of
epidemics and strife. Some historians even considered him a devil incarnate.
Foreboding prophecies were circulating, though only after he had come
to power, that he was the rebirth of an evil spirit whom Zhabdrung forgot

to subdue. The famous Minling Terchen, who was also court priest of the 5th Dalai Lama, is said to have compared Gedun Chöphel to 'a worm which ate the lion from within'.[45]

Historians and contemporary reports are almost unanimous in portraying a negative picture of Gedun Chöphel's actions and rule. With no records giving us his side of the story, it would be difficult to tell a completely objective story and understand the motives for his actions. However, his actions do sufficiently indicate that he was a man of militant tendency and unforgiving temperament. Originally from Kabji Gongma in Punakha, he was a staunch follower of Zhabdrung before he rose to the position of the Wangdiphodrang *dzongpön* in 1670. During his tenure in Wangdiphodrang, he renovated the *dzong* and built the iconic cantilever bridge below the dzong, records of which we now have in the British paintings. He also served as a hostage during negotiations with Tibet. In the war of 1675, he was leading the troops against the Tibetan invaders in Gön when he committed a strategic blunder leading to the loss of many lives. He nearly lost his own life then but was saved by the brave intervention of Ngawang Phuntsho of Obtsho, a family he, ironically, antagonized throughout his time in power.

As we have already seen above, he was the chief dissident who deposed Migyur Tenpa from the office of the Desi. His armed men chased Migyur Tenpa in Punakha and after the Desi agreed to step down, they arrested Migyur Tenpa's chief ally and minister Ngawang Rabten of Obtsho. Ngawang Rabten was subsequently killed and his family of Obtsho subjected to serious injustice and misery. Gedun Chöphel officially retired in 1689 after Tenzin Rabgay gave him the permission to do so in Wangdiphodrang. It must be here that his political ambition was once again aroused when he heard of Tenzin Rabgay's retreat and the delegation of the leader's secular duties to Norbu. He sent a secret army to Thimphu overnight and laid siege to Tenzin Rabgay's party in Tashichödzong. It is clear that Gedun Chöphel used the name and possibly even the support of Zhabdrung's granddaughter Tshokye Dorji to justify his actions. It appears that his main intention for the revolt was to eliminate Norbu and not necessarily to depose Tenzin Rabgay and to take the post of Desi for himself for soon after Norbu's death, he sent a party inviting Tenzin Rabgay to Punakha to resume his role as the head of the state. By then, the damage has been done and Tenzin Rabgay declined to return although their strained relationship continued until he died in 1696.

Immediately after Norbu's death and Tenzin Rabgay's departure from office in 1694, Gedun Chöphel assumed full power as the 5th Desi of Bhutan.

He installed Tshokye Dorji, the daughter of Jampal Dorji, on the throne of the Gyaltshab or prince-regent (or should we say 'princess-regent' to get the gender right). Later historians would recount that she was even dressed as a man for the enthronement and one biographer described her as a prince, betraying the unwillingness of Drukpa hierarchs to appoint a female heir even under desperate circumstances.[46] She was merely a puppet in the hands of Gedun Chöphel. With no notable event or achievement, her short reign as Gyaltshab is passed over in silence in the annals of history. Most historians do not even include her in the list of Gyaltshab post-holders and blame Gedun Chöphel for the inauspicious act of installing her on the throne, which is said to have provoked the wrath of the deities.

The divine wrath came in the form of an epidemic of smallpox in the 1695–96 when even the monastic body had to break up and escape to solitude. Many lives were lost and 'Prince' Tshokye Dorji was not spared. Stuck by smallpox, she retreated to Cheri, where we hear about her urging Damchö Pekar to take the post of Je Khenpo as the 3rd Je Khenpo Pekar Lhundup had resigned.[47] Damchö Pekar (1639–1708), we may recollect, led the first Bhutanese mission to Kathmandu and managed to establish a couple of centres there. Since then, he had served as the lama of the Chöjedrag temple in Bumthang and Taktshang in Paro. His appointment as Je Khenpo came with blessings of both Tshokye Dorji and the outgoing Je Khenpo Pekar Lhundup, who apparently resigned being displeased with the turn of events.[48] When Damchö Pekar returned from Punakha where he was formally enthroned, Tshokye Dorji came out of her seclusion in Cheri to join him in Tashichödzong thinking she had fully recovered.[49]

In the summer of 1697, Tshokye Dorji had a relapse and succumbed to smallpox thus ending the direct line from Zhabdrung. With Tshokye Dorji's death, Zhabdrung's dream of re-establishing the direct line of Ralung in Bhutan came to its final end. He had succeeded in creating a state and in giving it a political identity and a unique cultural and religious trait but nothing could save his own family line. The collateral Gya line, however, continued for another thirty five years or so through Tenzin Rabgay's sister, Jetsun Drung, and daughter, Lhacham Kunley, both of whom became even more popular and influential in the absence of any male members of the Gya clan. But upon Lhacham Kunley's death in 1732/33, the Gya line in Bhutan reached its final terminus. The plan for hereditary succession was thus permanently closed.

The alternate line of succession

With no male heir left, attention soon turned to the alternate mode of succession through incarnations. We have already seen how this mode of succession had widely spread in Tibet since the fourteenth century and was replacing in many places the ancient system of succession through the uncle–nephew or hereditary lines. When Zhabdrung died without an able heir and an issue from Jampal Dorji was not forthcoming, some members of the inner circle of Zhabdrung's court may have been already contemplating an incarnation taking over. The system of succession through reincarnation, as I have noted earlier, is an open and egalitarian one in that it gives the opportunity of choosing the successor from a wide range of candidates but it also opens, as Ardussi puts it, 'a floodgate of pretenders to the throne'.[50] Thus, the preferable option for the old members associated with Ralung was to continue the hereditary line in the tradition of that establishment. They would have preferred a hereditary line as the head of the establishment and for an incarnation to play a spiritual role, just as it was with the Drukpa school in Tibet before Zhabdrung. The best possible option would have been another case like that of Zhabdrung where the incarnation and family lines were combined in a single capable person.

Unfortunately, the new state of Bhutan did not have the luxury of any of these when Zhabdrung passed away abruptly without leaving a capable heir. Given the precarious political situation and war with Tibet, the best move was to conceal Zhabdrung's death in the hope of obtaining a capable heir from Jampal Dorji or/and Tenzin Rabgay and in the meantime do whatever was necessary to hold the country together. Given the circumstances, an open search for an incarnation was not really possible but some members of the inner circle who knew about Zhabdrung's death have already started to clandestinely seek Zhabdrung's reincarnation. The eminent historian Shakya Rinchen, in his biography of the 7th Je Khenpo, reveals that attempts at locating Zhabdrung's incarnation had already begun before Tenzin Rabgay came to the throne in 1681.[51] Although we do not know how the incarnate was found and confirmed, Zhabdrung's reincarnation was discovered in a Tibetan territory called Göyul near the Tibet–Bhutan border north of Paro. Being at the height of hostilities with Tibet, attempts to secretly bring the incarnation to Bhutan were unsuccessful and open negotiation with the Tibetans on this was out of question as the fiction of Zhabdrung's retreat was still maintained as a major defence tactic. After Tenzin Rabgay became Gyaltshab, he is said

296 • Karma Phuntsho

to have also tried unsuccessfully to clandestinely bring the incarnation from Göyul. Subsequently, the boy was allegedly taken to Tibet from where he is said to have gone to China and died.

Apart from this lone source, no other Bhutanese sources available to us talk openly about Zhabdrung's incarnation before his death was revealed in 1708. Tenzin Rabgay ruefully remarked in 1695 in the presence of a few people that it was the shared misfortune of the world which kept an incarnate of Zhabdrung from manifesting.[52] Was he talking about the incarnate discussed above or lamenting about the general absence of an incarnation? John Ardussi interprets this as a proposal from Tenzin Rabgay to solve the problem of succession by recourse to the incarnation line.[53] If that were the case, Tenzin Rabgay would not have been alone in having this thought. It seems there were by then a lot of people who strongly believed that the throne should be passed to the incarnation rather than the physical heir. The lack of a male heir and the epidemics which killed the only female heir were seen as sure signs of divine direction as well as displeasure at the insistence on the family line. But no one seemed to have quite dared to break the silence about Zhabdrung's death and go for the incarnation openly. Meanwhile in Tibet, the regent Sangay Gyatsho announced the death of the 5th Dalai Lama in 1696 after thirteen years of concealment, and the following year he brought the fourteen-year-old incarnate lama to Lhasa. This was Tshangyang Gyatsho, the amorous 6th Dalai Lama, whose love songs to this day churn Tibetan emotions.

Pressure was building on the Bhutanese side. While uncertainty about Zhabdrung's incarnation continued, efforts were underway to groom other incarnates who could fill the gap. One such candidate was Drukdra Gyatsho (1665–1701), the reincarnation of Tenzin Rabgay's father, Tshewang Tenzin and thus indirectly of Phajo Drukgom, the pioneer of the Drukpa school in Bhutan. Tshewang Tenzin, we must recall was holder of the collateral Gya line in Bhutan and a stalwart supporter of Zhabdrung. His rebirth, Drukdra Gyatsho, was born in the Chang area of Thimphu but in a family which descended from the Bhutanese saint, Pema Lingpa. Thus, he could in his person combine the two main religious lines of Bhutan. He entered the state monastery in 1681 and was trained by a number of important figures, including Tenzin Rabgay. Tenzin Rabgay took Drukdra Gyatsho with him during his religious rounds and always accorded the latter a prominent place. Sadly for Tenzin Rabgay, when Gedun Chöphel rebelled against him in 1694, Drukdra Gyatsho was also involved in some way in conceiving the plot.

Drukpa Gyatsho had to atone for this before Tenzin Rabgay in the following year but it was at the beginning of eighteenth century that we see Drukdra Gyatsho come briefly to the centrestage of Bhutan's politics.

Another incarnation who was definitely admitted to the state monastery and groomed to fill the succession gap was Kuenga Gyaltshen (1689–1714). He was also born in what was traditionally eastern Bhutan. He gives the village name of Tashichöling and was discovered as a reincarnate lama when he was seven. Drukdra Gyatsho initially recognized him and the 4th Je Khenpo Damchö Pekar confirmed the recognition. When Damchö Pekar announced the news of the child incarnation to Desi Gedun Chöphel, the latter was full of jubilation. The country had had no spiritual head since the death of Tshokye Dorji and such a figurehead was fundamental to legitimize his rule. After being installed as an incarnate lama, Kuenga Gyaltshen received most of his training from the 4th Je Khenpo and the two enjoyed a wonderful master–disciple relationship until the master's death in 1708.

Kuenga Gyaltshen emerged as the leading religious figure of his time but it is not clear from contemporary sources, including his own writings, whose incarnation he was supposed to be. In his biography of Damchö Pekar, he seems to hint that he is Zhabdrung himself. When the Desi showed him a painting of sixteen arhats and asked what it was, the seven-year-old Kuenga Gyaltshen replied: 'Hey hey, these are figures of the sixteen arhats. I have given this as an amulet to Ngawang Jampal Dorji.'[54] It was indeed Zhabdrung who gave the paintings to Jampal Dorji. The personal accounts of his process of recognition and enthronement are also very vague and do not explicitly identify him with either Zhabdrung or his son. Was he, then, implicitly presenting himself as an incarnation of Zhabdrung when he wrote his master's biography? Whatever it may be, later historians consensually recorded him as the first rebirth of Zhabdrung's son, Jampal Dorji. He was accorded the title Gyalse Trulku (རྒྱལ་སྲས་སྤྲུལ་སྐུ་) or prince incarnate and he also became the third person to hold the post of Gyaltshab or prince regent. We shall later come across the brief political career of this incarnate lama, his untimely death and the unfolding of the reincarnation lines but let's first return to the story of Gedun Chöphel's reign.

Gedun Chöphel's highhanded rule continued in the absence of a religious figurehead after Tshokye Dorji's death. Interspersed with a few positive acts, his reign was generally judged as an era of warfare, epidemics and other calamities. There was neither subsidence to his militant character and hot temper, nor retraction of his earlier grudges. His days in power were just as violent and turbulent as his initial journey to power. One victim to suffer from his reckless action under the influence of prejudiced advisors was Tenzin Lekpai Dhondup, the second Gangteng Trulku. This hierarch was kept under a detention in Wangdiphodrang for three months but, fortunately, one of Gedun Chöphel's trusted officer in Wangdiphodrang happened to be a devotee of the hierarch. Thus, he was cleared of all blame and allowed to return to his monastery. It is not clear what led to this incident but it seems his detention was triggered by a passing spate of sectarian discrimination against the Nyingmapas, to whom Tenzin Rabgay showed zealous support just as Zhabdrung did before him. Musing on this sad incident, Gangteng Trulku's biographer, the 10th Je Khenpo, wrote a long discourse on how Drukpa Kagyu and Nyingma were essentially the same and sectarian discrimination should be shunned.[55] Surely, Gangteng Trulku's detention may have also been connected to the close friendship he enjoyed with Tenzin Rabgay, who was ousted. Under good advice, the Desi did change his attitude and the brief flare of sectarianism passed but peace was not to prevail as Gedun Chöphel began to set old scores. It seems Bhutan's relationship with Tibet had slightly loosened at this time as Gangteng Trulku was allowed to resume direct interactions with the hierarchs of his tradition in Tibet. Visits to and from Tibet were also allowed without prior permission and Gedun Chöphel even made contributions toward the construction of the reliquary for Thugse Tenzin Gyurme's remains.[56]

Not long after coming to power, Gedun Chöphel resumed his old hatred against the Obtsho family. This family was on constant alert to avoid any excuses for the ruler to harass them. But for the ruler, the opportunity for pursuing the vendetta came in 1700 when a marriage dispute arose in the locality of the Obtsho family. Gedun Chöphel arrived in the village to investigate the case and in the process trumped up charges against Ngawang Phuntsho of Obtsho, who had no role in the dispute. Ngawang Phuntsho was consequently imprisoned but the whole community in the locality united behind him to explain to Gedun Chöphel that he was innocent. As a result, Ngawang Phuntsho was released but soon for no reason his son, Druk Dargyal, was arrested and imprisoned. Lama Tenzin, the brother of Ngawang Phuntsho, went to meet his nephew in prison in Punakha and appears to have planned a rebellion against Gedun Chöphel. However, when the critical moment to strike the Desi came, he panicked and he and his nephew fled to their village. There they waited with anxiety as the rebellion continued in Punakha.

The rebellion was finally put down, filling the courtyard with blood and litter. The Desi's men followed Lama Tenzin to Obtsho, where the family including the old mother was arrested, their big family home put to flame, their properties looted and many of their supporters killed. Lama Tenzin and Druk Dargyal were once again imprisoned and eventually killed and the rest of the family banished to the southern frontiers of Dagana.[57] Ngawang Gyaltshen remained unmoved and outwardly unaffected by his family's tribulations but he may have endured a great deal of internal torment which his biographer chose not to record. He soon sought a posting of a lama to a remote temple in the Khothangkha region, perhaps to escape from the troubles. His family was allowed to return from their exile after Gedun Chöphel died but their return was further hampered when the new Desi who sanctioned the return also died. The family arrived in Amorimu eventually, during the 7th Desi's time only to find their ancestral home in ruins.

It is certainly his aggressive character and the vendetta that he rekindled, which led Gedun Chöphel to his final downfall. We do not exactly know what happened but the rebellion appears to have continued even after defeating the Obtsho family. Gedun Chöphel appears to have made new enemies with his hot temper and bellicose temperament. We get a glimpse of this in the biography of the 4th Je Khenpo Damchö Pekar. On one occasion, the precentor and assembly got the chants of a ritual slightly out of tune and the Desi scolded the entire congregation with invectives. On another occasion, three men were about to be executed when the pious Je Khenpo asked them to be forgiven. With his hand holding the sword, the Desi threatened the hierarch to mind his own business or meet the same fate. Finally, one night at the end of 1700, the Je Khenpo was woken up by a commotion and when he checked what it was, from above the assembly hall, he saw crowds of people scurrying with arms and weapons. He had no idea that the incarnate Lama Drukdra Gyatsho and his comrade *pönlop* Damchö had just killed the Desi. He returned to his room with a lot of worry that something terrible may be happening. Some moments later a man came to ask him to come to Drukdra Gyatsho's room. 'Where is the old ruler?' he asked. 'He has been separated from life,' said the man. 'Well then, I am not going. You do whatever pleases you,' he retorted. Then, *pönlop* Damchö came to request the Je Khenpo again to come. This time he came and he delivered a diatribe against Drukdra Gyatsho for the awful action he committed for a religious preacher. Drukdra Gyatsho and his allies stood sullen and unable to respond to the master.[58]

We know neither the motive nor the mode of Drukdra Gyatsho's assassination of Gedun Chöphel. It was a late night *coup* and perhaps Gedun Chöphel did not see it coming from a senior hierarch with whom he worked closely. There are no known records of any conflict between them. If Drukdra Gyatsho harboured a hidden ambition to occupy the seat of power himself, that was not to be as Gedun Chöphel's faction retaliated with an unforgiving vengeance. Drukdra Gyatsho appears to have held the ruler's post unofficially for a short period although none of the historians put him among the list of Desis. In the spring of 1701, Gedun Chöphel's men attacked Drukdra Gyatsho and his team at Punakha. The Je Khenpo and monastic community had by then left for Tashichödzong, which was rebuilt after a fire in 1698. Receiving the news of a fresh outbreak of violence when he reached Semtokha, the Je Khenpo hurried back to Punakha with about a hundred monks to stop another carnage but many people were already killed by the time they got there. Drukdra Gyatsho had fled toward eastern Bhutan but was caught somewhere near Gangteng and put to death by his opponents.

After bringing the two factions to a truce, the *dzongpön* of Wangdiphodrang, Ngawang Tshering was formally enthroned as the 6th Desi of Bhutan in 1701. Most senior officials were probably present at this investiture. Gangteng Trulku, we are told, presented him many gifts including two horses. After installing the new Desi, the Je Khenpo turned to undertake purification and confession rituals in Thimphu but he was soon summoned to Wangdiphodrang to cremate Gedun Chöphel's corpse which was found on the riverbank there. Ngawang Tshering was a man of letters and for his work as secretary for rulers in the past, he was commonly known as *drungyig* (དྲུང་ཡིག) or secretary. Originally from Kabji Gonga, he was well respected for his upright and kind personality and this came in handy for him to appease his warring subjects. The government's relationship with Gangteng Trulku was reinstated to the state it was during Tenzin Rabgay's time and Ngawang Tshering also ordered the repatriation of Obtsho family. His three-year reign generally passed with peace and no major upheaval. He commissioned illuminated *kanjur* manuscripts in Tashichödzong to replace the one lost to fire and a gilded copper statue of Amitayus in Punakha. In the early spring of 1702, Kuenga Gyaltshen, the reincarnate lama we discussed earlier, was enthroned as Gyaltshab in Punakha in a ceremony attended probably by most prominent officials. He became officially the second holder of the golden throne.

The following year, Ngawang Tshering died in office after a sudden illness and some monk-historians are quick to point out that his untimely death was caused by deities who were upset with his mistreatment of Kuenga

Gyaltshen. Whatever the cause of his death, it is quite clear from Kuenga Gyaltshen's writings that they did not get along well and there was a growing tension between him and the Desi. We have already seen how conflict erupted between the incarnate Drukdra Gyatsho and Desi Gedun Chöphel ending in their tragic deaths. These were, however, only the beginning of a series of conflicts that Bhutan would see between the incarnate hierarchs and the rulers. Such frictions resulting from a tension in their sensitive power sharing would plague Bhutan's politics throughout the following centuries. Thus, the hope of resolving the succession problem and bringing peace and security to the country through the installation of Zhabdrung's incarnation line proved to be a failure right from the outset. Yet, the institution of the incarnations only multiplied as we shall see.

The Umze (དབུ་མཛད་) or precentor Paljor alias Samten Tenzin of the state monastery was appointed as the 7th Desi following the death of Ngawang Tshering in 1703. He was surely skilled at monastic rituals but he had virtually none of the qualities required for the post of Desi. The historian Tenzin Chögyal thus called his reign 'a joke' and 'enjoyment of entitlements for almost three years'.[59] Pema Tshewang however dismissed such remarks as biased and portrayed him as an easygoing and peaceful character, who ruled righteously.[60] There is little doubt that he was a mild character and had no real grip on power. This we see as Kuenga Gyaltshen, the incarnate who was the Gyaltshab, began to exercise more and more power so that by 1705, Paljor and Kuenga Gyaltshen were practically sharing the prerogatives of Desi. However, the real challenge to the two politically naïve monks acting as Desi and Gyaltshab came from the *dzonpön*s of Thimphu and Punakha, who were both strong and shrewd politicians and locked against each other in a contest. Unable to deal with such ruckus, Paljor retired to Cheri, some time in 1705 although he remained nominally as Desi until his death in 1707. Meanwhile, Kuenga Gyaltshen became the *de facto* ruler although he too was a spiritual recluse by disposition and would eventually be destroyed by the political imbroglio.

Overture to Ladakh and disclosure of the 'open secret'

Two notable events took place under Kuenga Gyaltshen as Gyaltshab and *de facto* ruler. The first is the delegation of Ngawang Gyaltshen of Obtsho to Ladakh as a Bhutanese spiritual ambassador in 1705. When the Ladakh King Nyima Namgyal (r.1694–1729) asked for a Drukpa lama, Ngawang

Gyaltshen was the obvious choice with his record of a successful mission to Derge. Moreover, it was important to send a representative of good standing and ability to Ladakh. Not only did Bhutan and Ladakh enjoy a strong and old connection, the Gelugpa and Northern Drukpa schools had began successive campaigns to gain control of Ladakh and undermine Bhutanese influence there. However, Ngawang Gyaltshen was far from happy to set out on such a long journey. He made requests to be replaced, stating that he was old and unfit for a journey across the treacherous desert-like terrain. The Ladakhi messenger persisted saying the king would not accept anyone other than him. Thus, Ngawang Gyaltshen was once again made to leave Bhutan and his ageing mother and embark on a long and arduous journey through enemy territory. He requested all prisoners in Bhutan to be freed to make his journey propitious.[61]

This time, he and his group could get a travel permit albeit only as ordinary travellers. When the Tibetan officer asked his name for the permit, he made up one and gave Tenpa Dargay, literally, profusion of teachings. This, he thought, would be an auspicious name for the mission. Just as wished, his mission to Ladakh was as successful as the earlier one to Derge. He won the respect and devotion of the king and his court and succeeded in spreading the Drukpa influence. During his stay, he was known for bringing rain during droughts, subduing spirits, extracting water from the ground and effectively ending epidemics although he lost one of his attendants to smallpox. He and his attendants also took the opportunity to tour the ancient Buddhist sites in Kashmir and went as far as Taxila and Lahore and also had exchanges with various non-Buddhist priests. When the time came for him to leave, the Ladakhi king begged him to stay longer but after deferring twice, he insisted he must return for the sake of his ageing mother. On his part, he persuaded the king to send one prince to Bhutan for training. Thus, Prince Tenzin Norbu came to Bhutan and later even took the position of Je Khenpo.

Ngawang Gyaltshen's own return turned out to be full of problems. Soon after his party set off, a Mongol officer working for the Tibetan government harassed them. They managed to get past him but were then diverted by many people wanting to see Ngawang Gyaltshen on the way. The journey was further impeded by a short illness he had. When they reached Phari in the summer of 1711, the border patrols have been alerted to his arrival and he was detained for about eight months. The Tibetans were upset at not detecting the Ladakhi prince who entered Bhutan. With poor facilities in detention, Ngawang Gyaltshen fell ill. The animals and goods they brought with them were all looted and the Tibetan officers even nearly found the letter to the Desi from the Ladakhi king. The Bhutanese in Paro planned to secretly get him out but he rejected the plan saying he would not risk provoking a war for his own sake. The Sakya hierarchs negotiated his release in the spring of 1712 but Ngawang Gyaltshen was not able to see his old mother. Tragically, she passed away shortly before his return to Bhutan.[62]

The second significant development during Kuenga Gyaltshen's time was the official announcement of Zhabdrung's death some time at the beginning of 1708. Although most people in court must have by then already believed that Zhabdrung had long since passed away, his death was officially still a secret and he was claimed to still be in meditation. The practice of appointing a private chamberlain of Zhabdrung and serving meals on time, which were initially carried out for the purpose of hiding his death, had by then become routinized and these rituals continue even today. Kuenga Gyaltshen opened the retreat chamber and allowed people such as his master, the 4th Je Khenpo, to see and pay homage to Zhabdrung's corpse. Perhaps, the same was done to Jampal Dorji's corpse. Only after this, did it become officially known that Zhabdrung had passed away.

It is unclear why Kuenga Gyaltshen decided to disclose the 'open secret' and declare Zhabdrung's death. Could it be another indication of his implicit claim that he was the incarnation of the Zhabdrung? Was he trying to show that there was no need for further concealment as he had already reincarnated? In any case, some of his contemporaries and later historians disproved of his action. They seem to have believed that Zhabdrung's meditative state should not have been disturbed but sustained as long as possible. Kuenga Gyaltshen's own downfall is explained as a retribution for disturbing the meditation. However, in later sources, we hear that when he prayed before Zhabdrung's corpse having revealed the secret, Zhabdrung 'woke up' from his deep meditation and three rays of light emitted out of his body and travelled to Sikkim, Dagana and Tibet leading to the birth of three incarnations of his body, speech and mind. This is undoubtedly a later hermeneutic effort to retrospectively explain the multiple claimants to Zhabdrung's rebirth. Nonetheless, such explanation is theologically quite sound and convincing. According to the theories of death accepted by most Tibetan Buddhist traditions, a person at the time of death goes through a series of experiential stages, some of which can be turned into a catalyst for the process of enlightenment by an experienced meditation master. One such stage is the final moment of psychosomatic dissolution called Clear Light, a state of luminous emptiness in which all cognitive and existential processes come to a halt. If a lama can remain in this state, then the lama is said to be in a state of deep meditation called *thugdam* (ཐུགས་དམ་) and his body does not disintegrate in spite of the biological death. Zhabdrung was believed to have been in this state until he was implored to rise out of his meditation.

Whether Kuenga Gyaltshen's reasons to reveal the secret were out of a theological or a political consideration or both, we do not know, but it did formally open the gate for many aspirants to Zhabdrung's throne. These multiple contenders were in theory seen as complementary and were easily accommodated giving these sound theological explanations. But in real life, such accommodation and acceptance were hard to come by as their lives were overshadowed by ordinary religious or political rivalry. The incarnation system also became a useful political tool for some and one did not have to wait long for an example of such use. Soon after Kuenga Gyaltshen lifted the veil of secrecy over Zhabdrung's death, his own opponents began to use the expedience of the system to find a Zhabdrung incarnation in order to replace him. It is to this story and the reign of the first lay ruler that we shall turn now.

Nyötön Demchog (1179–1265),
who established Somthrang
temple and started the Chöje
family

Phajo Drukgom Zhigpo
(1184?–1251?), the master who
introduced the Drukpa Kagyu
school to valleys of western Bhutan
(courtesy: Yonten Dargye)

Drukpa Kunley (1455–1529?),
the Divine Madman (courtesy:
Yonten Dargye)

Dorji Lingpa (1346–1405), a king
treasure-discoverer and ancestor of
many Bhutanese religious elites

Longchenpa (1306–64), the Dzogchen master who founded
the eight spiritual sanctuaries

Dumtse Lhakhang, the round temple built by Thangtong Gyalpo (1385–1464 or
1485?) to subdue the serpent-like landscape in Paro

Cheri Dorjeden, Zhabdrung's first monastic seat on a steep slope.
The remains of Zhabdrung's father were kept here in receptacle. (This is also
the first monastery the author joined as a monk.)

Semtokha, Zhabdrung's first *dzong* structure in Bhutan, built on
the spot of an earlier establishment

Punakha *dzong*, the Fortress of Great Bliss, built at the confluence
of the Phochu and Mochu rivers in 1637, was the first capital of Bhutan.

Wangdiphodrang *dzong* and bridge before the *dzong* was destroyed
by fire in 2012 (with permission from Felicity Shaw)

Dechenphodrang—this was the original site of Tashichödzong
before Zhidar relocated it (with permission from Serindia Publications).

Dechenphodrang today: The structure has not changed much since 1783,
apart from the surrounding quarters and archery range which is now a car park
and volley court for monks.

Paro *dzong*, the Heap of Jewels, with its watchtower behind
paddy fields ready for harvest. The *dzong* was rebuilt soon after
it was destroyed by fire in 1907.

The temple of Tango, where Zhabdrung cultivated magical powers.
This was the home of the 4th ruler Tenzin Rabgay's family.

Tongsa *dzong*, the seat of Tongsa pönlop from where eastern
Bhutan was ruled

Jakar Yulgyal *dzong* in Bumthang, built to celebrate Bhutanese
victory in 1675

Migyur Tenpa, the 3rd Desi ruler. He brought eastern Bhutan under Zhabdrung's rule.

Tenzin Rabgay, the 4th Desi ruler. Bhutan saw the first spell of glorious rule during his reign (courtesy: Yonten Dargye).

Monks at a religious ceremony

Multiple Incarnations and the Rise of Lay Rulers

THE FORMAL DECLARATION of Zhabdrung's death threw the door wide open for the politics of reincarnation. The founding father had woken up, as it were, from his meditative absorption to reappear in multiple forms simultaneously. In the days to follow, the politics of Bhutan would become deeply intertwined with the institution of reincarnations. It also marked the beginning of the rise of non-monastic power. In the absence of the great founder himself, lay persons began to vie for political leadership, which was until that time viewed almost as a sacrosanct prerogative of the monastic figures close to the founder.

The Shaman of Wang and the rise of the first lay ruler

Kuenga Gyaltshen loosely held the reins of power after Umze Paljor took the back seat in Cheri but Kuenga Gyaltshen was not a strong leader. He spent more time in meditation than running the state and the feuding *dzongpön*s of Thimphu and Punakha soon began to rock his rule. Kuenga Gyaltshen even summoned the two *dzongpön*s to the congregation hall and reproached them harshly in the presence of the monks but this did not abate their militancy. The cause for conflict between the two *dzongpön*s, Druk Rabgay of Thimphu and Tenpa Wangchuk of Punakha, is not clear. They were perhaps both competing for the post of the Desi, which was practically vacant.

Druk Rabgay, who was from Wang Sinmo, started his career as a court retainer and slowly rose to become the in-charge of meat (ཤ་གཉེར་) in Gasa before he was appointed as *dzongpön* of Thimphu. He was a forceful character and even during his time as a *dzongpön* of Thimphu, he had gained some notoriety according to one source, although this is doubtful.[1]

He was blamed for the death of Lama Zhang, an eminent master from Kheng Gongphu and incarnation of Shakya Özer of Beyul. This lama is said to have learnt about the misdeeds of Druk Rabgay and secretly sent a letter of complaint to the Je Khenpo while also sending a pleasant letter to him but the messenger made a tragic mistake of delivering the letter of complaint to Druk Rabgay himself. Enraged by the treachery, the *dzongpön* secretly ordered the villagers in Zhemgang to kill the lama on the way to his village. The assailants assassinated the lama when he reached the village of Trong, literally meaning 'killed', and he was pointed out by people of Dagapa, literally meaning 'who pointed out'. According to the locals, this is how the toponyms Trong and Dagapa came about.

Locals of Zhemgang tell us an even more repugnant story. Lama Zhang, after whom Zhemgang was named, had a brother in Thimphu serving the ruler, who was actually a cannibal. The ruler secretly killed his courtiers one by one and ate them; Lama Zhang saw this through his clairvoyance. When the turn of the lama's brother was approaching, he sent one letter to his brother explaining the situation and asking him to escape and another to the ruler feigning illness and requesting for his brother to be sent home. The messenger, however, delivered the wrong letters and the ruler meted out his fury by ordering the villagers to kill the lama. The story, as we hear it, is a good example of a true historical event which may have become gradually embellished and exaggerated simply to appeal to its audience. The locals perhaps resented the assassination of their lama as well as the authoritarian rule of Thimphu to the extent that they demonized the ruler as a cannibal, similar to the Tibetan demonization of the Lang Darma, the 'apostate' king we have discussed above.

Druk Rabgay was most likely not a cannibal as conceived by the pious villagers of Zhemgang but he was certainly a very shrewd and unrelenting politician. To gain Kuenga Gyaltshen's support for his candidacy for the post of Desi, he first worked on winning the backing of the hierarch's mother, who had a strong influence on the hierarch. He feigned genuine and deep devotion to the hierarch and pampered her with generous gifts and sweet speech. Eventually, Kuenga Gyaltshen and his mother were beguiled by Druk Rabgay's ingratiation, which must have also included slander against his rival Tenpa Wangchuk, and to the displeasure of many senior figures of the state, Druk Rabgay was appointed the 8th Desi in 1707. For his beardy countenance, he came to be known as the Desi Jawu (ཪྗེ་སྲིད་ཅུ་རྒྱོ) or Bearded Desi. He was also the shaman for his village, thus called Desi Phajo (ཪྗེ་སྲིད་དཔའ

ཨ) or Shaman Desi. Druk Rabgay became the first non-monastic official to occupy the post of Desi.

As soon as he got into power, the Bearded Desi began the process of eliminating his rival, Tenpa Wangchuk, who had already gone into hiding in the mountains. Soldiers were dispatched to find Tenpa Wangchuk and many people were killed in course of the pursuit. Tenpa Wangchuk eventually offered himself up to avoid further loss of life. Consequently, he was brutally murdered by Druk Rabgay. In a visionary experience, Kuenga Gyaltshen saw Tenpa Wangchuk approach him for refuge with a white scarf, which he interpreted as a sign of pure devotion. By then, the hierarch realized the blunder he had made with his appointment of Druk Rabgay as the Desi. When Druk Rabgay heard of the visionary experience and Kuenga Gyaltshen's take on it, he was obviously offended and a rift began to develop between Kuenga Gyaltshen and Druk Rabgay. One historian also adds that Druk Rabgay was offended by Kuenga Gyaltshen's disclosure of the secret of Zhabdrung's death in 1708.[2]

Frustrated by the turn of events, Kuenga Gyaltshen went into a three-year retreat in Tashichödzong some time in 1710. Meanwhile, the Desi Druk Rabgay set himself to the task of engineering Kuenga Gyaltshen's downfall. First, a child, who claimed to be Zhabdrung, was found in Nyidukha in Dagana. According to his biography, he is supposed to have remembered a lot of things from his days as Zhabdrung.[3] Some time in 1713, at the age of six, he was brought to Punakha and installed on the throne as the incarnation of Zhabdrung. He would later become known as the first Sungtrul (གསུང་སྤྲུལ་) or speech incarnation Chogley Namgyal (1708–36) although his exact status as Zhabdrung appears to have remained controversial until the end of his life. When Kuenga Gyaltshen emerged from his long retreat and came to Punakha in 1713, the Desi had already made plans for him to step down and to install young Chogley Namgyal on the golden throne. Kuenga Gyaltshen may have approved the recognition of Chogley Namgyal but he certainly did not see this coming so soon and without consultation. This may have led to some conflict between the camps of the two incarnates but we do not know. At any case, Druk Rabgay forced Kuenga Gyaltshen to step down and retire in Wangdiphodrang, where he was subjected to constant harassment including threats to his life. Chogley Namgyal became the 3rd holder of the golden throne.

On the ninth day of the seventh Bhutanese month, 30 August 1713, at the first call of the rooster, Kuenga Gyaltshen escaped from his captivity in

Wangdiphodrang without even a pair of shoes. He ran along the Dangchu river and arrived at daybreak in Lamdo village, where he hid in the forest to resume his flight after dark. Kuenga Gyaltshen spent some months in solitude with hermits before he was hunted down by Druk Rabgay's men who scanned the forests. After his arrest, his attendant was killed and he was harshly denounced and finally poisoned to death some time in the beginning of 1714. In his final words, he warned, according to his biographer, that Bhutan would see terrible calamities in between the Snake and Horse years (1713–14).[4] The calamities did come whether or not they were divine punishments for unjust atrocities committed against Kuenga Gyaltshen.

First, on the twentieth of the third Bhutanese month, 4 May 1714, a major earthquake wrecked the country, causing a great deal of death and destruction of property. The earth shook about thirty times that day alone. The grand new temple of Gangteng, which Tenzin Lekpai Dondup had just then completed, was one of the prominent casualties as it was nearly reduced to rubbles. The dzongs generally survived with serious cracks. As the aftershocks continued for about a month, people across the country were stuck in fear. The state monks including young Chogley Namgyal had to sleep in a tent outside the *dzong*.

Just as the people were beginning to settle to normal life, the second calamity struck in the form of war as Lhazang Khan's Tibetan and Mongolian army invaded Bhutan. Lhazang Khan was the grandson of Gushri Khan, the Mongol warlord who made the 5th Dalai Lama the supreme head of Tibet. Ever since the new Gelugpa government came to power in 1642, the country was ruled through a delicate power sharing between the Tibetan regent and the Mongol descendants of Gushri Khan. This alliance had, however, ended in a bloody conflict in 1705 with the execution of the regent Sangay Gyatsho. At the core of this tragedy which unfolded in the early years of the eighteenth century in Tibet was also a problem of the incarnation system, albeit of a different kind from that of Bhutan. A child born in a family connected to the Bhutanese hierarch Pema Lingpa in the Mon area of modern Arunachal Pradesh was recognized as the reincarnation of the 5th Dalai Lama and thus enthroned in Lhasa as the 6th Dalai Lama Tshangyang Gyatsho (1683–706). This charming and talented young incarnate, however, did not have much interest in the austere life and position of a lama-king and frolicked in Lhasa taverns with his girlfriends much to the displeasure of his regent, the Mongol warlord and the Manchu emperor in China, all of whom had a part to play in Tibetan affairs. The songs, through which

Tibetans affectionately remember him today, perhaps aptly evoke his frolic romance and maverick life.

> While residing in the Potala,
> I am sublime Tsangyang Gyatsho.
> While I linger in the Shol village
> I am the promiscuous Lustrous Lord.

> I went seeking my love at night.
> The snow has fallen in the morning.
> There was no point in concealing my flight,
> Footprints have been found on the snow.

> The face of the lama I visualized
> Would not come to my mind.
> The face of beloved without meditation
> Comes so quickly and clearly.

> If my mind were to turn to religion
> As it turns to her,
> In one lifetime and one body
> I would become a Buddha.

The controversy around the romantic and libertine conduct of the young Dalai Lama precipitated the political tensions between the Tibetan and Mongol factions into a full military conflict. The outcome was tragic for Tibet. The Tibetan regent Sangay Gyatsho, his mentor, was defeated by Lhazang Khan, who wanted to depose him. Sangay Gyatsho was executed and the 6th Dalai Lama Tshangyang Gyatsho taken in captivity to Qinghai where he died. The Mongol ruler Lhazang Khan became the King of Tibet and even installed his son as the 6th Dalai Lama.

The immediate cause of Lhazang's invasion of Bhutan appears to be a sharp letter which the conceited Desi Druk Rabgay despatched in response to the former's patronizing reprimand concerning a dispute over a temple along the eastern border of Bhutan.[5] The Mongol king arrogantly warned Bhutan of the dire consequences of facing his large army if existent border lines were not respected. Druk Rabgay defied him by quickly pointing out that there was not a single instance of Tibetan victory over Bhutan whatever size of army they sent. Anyone invading Bhutan, he argued, is comparable to an insect entering a spider's net in an attempt to destroy it. 'Bring all heavens with you for support and still it will not so much as stir a hair of the Bhutanese under Mahākāla's care,' he boasted. However, this exchange was not the only cause. Tensions were growing due to other reasons, such as the diplomatic connections Bhutan built with Ladakh through Tibetan territory without their notice. John Ardussi adds that Lhazang may have had scores to set against Bhutan also for hosting a Tibetan *tertön* who spread prophecies in Tibet about the rise of a Mongol devil named Lhazang.[6] The *tertön* in question, Dorji Drolöd, was popular in western Bhutan during the reign of the 6th and 7th Desis but later returned to Tibet, where he is said to have been captured and imprisoned.

Bhutan's engagement in Sikkim may have also been another reason. Although the Bhutanese sources are generally quiet, it seems that the Bhutanese occupied large stretches of eastern Sikkim including the capital, Rabtentse, by 1700. One Sikkimese source reports that Panding Wangmo, the daughter of the 2nd Sikkimese King Tensung Namgyal (b.1644) from a Bhutanese queen, invited the Bhutanese forces with the intention of wresting power for herself during the minority of her half-brother, Chagdor Namgyal (1686–1715).[7] Bhutanese activity along the western frontier seems to have generally continued throughout early decades of eighteenth century. Some time in 1725–26, we find the religious figure of Ngawang Gyaltshen lamenting the terror and havoc the war with Sikkim was causing to many people.[8] Moreover, Tibet was also keen on maintaining its grip over Sikkim. We can clearly see this when Lhazang Khan fined the Sikkimese king for not promptly showing up with troops to support his impending campaign against Bhutan.[9] The Sikkimese were delayed because King Chagdor Namgyal had died suddenly in 1715 and his death was being kept a secret.

Lhazang Khan certainly had no shortage of reasons to invade Bhutan. In the eighth Bhutanese month of 1714, Lhazang Khan ordered armies along three routes. Lhazang himself led the main troops towards Paro while the future Tibetan ruler Pholhaney Sonam Tobgay and Erkhe Daiching led the troops toward Bumthang and Baring Taiji and three Tibetan generals commanded the troops to eastern Bhutan. We do not know anything about the Bhutanese defence apart from the information that the Desi invoked the deities in earnest. The 2nd Gangteng Tulku and the monks were asked to undertake rituals of repulsion and Ngawang Gyaltshen was appointed, against his wish, as *chila* of Paro perhaps to garner support among the public. The Tibetan advance towards Bumthang is recorded in some detail in the biography of the Pholhaney Sonam Tobgay (1689–1747), who later became the King of Tibet.[10] As soon as the Tibetans and Mongols crossed the Monlakarchung pass, they were confronted by the Bhutanese resistance. Nonetheless, according to the biographer, they advanced without much difficulty killing people, burning settlements and pillaging goods on their way. Houses on the route, save the holy shrine of Kurjey, were all set on fire. However, victory was far from sight when they faced the formidable fortress of Jakar, which Nelungpa Sherab Lhundrup and Kudrung Phuntsho had cleverly designed under Tenzin Rabgay's guidance. The invaders tried every tactic for weeks to penetrate the fort but in vain. Meanwhile, Lhazang Khan did not have a successful campaign in the west and ordered all troops to withdraw. It might again be the case that the invaders in Paro found the vegetation and climate of Bhutan's summer to their disadvantage. Whatever the reason, the invasion ended at the whim of the Mongol ruler just as it began and brought no changes, apart from the senseless destruction and looting in some areas.

We do not exactly know what role Druk Rabgay played in the war but he certainly emerged as the obvious winner. Like his predecessors, he celebrated the repulsion of the invasion and embarked on a series of religious activities. In 1615, he built on the ridge above Tashichödzong the hermitage of Wangditse, also known as Zabdön Lhuntse. Beautiful sets of statues, books and stūpas were created as its relics. During its consecration in 1717, all prominent religious and secular figures of Bhutan gathered there to congratulate him and make offerings. The young Chogley Namgyal, who had just recently got ordained as a novice, gave his first religious sermon on the occasion. The Desi himself made generous offerings to the state monks including coins, clothes and a sheepskin each for a mattress. He also distributed coins to the all households across the country. Through the advice of the eminent master Ngawang Gyaltshen, he promulgated some legal policies, which advanced the values of the ten virtuous actions we have seen above. The implementation of the monastic code of ethics was also reinforced. In fact, when the Desi asked for a way to avoid earthquakes, Ngawang Gyaltshen recommended these measures to enhance communal merit and avert natural calamities. He also revoked the policy of confiscating properties of families without any children, a law which was in force until then. His work of piety extended also to neighbouring Indian plains where he is said to have stopped the Indian practice of *sati*. It is plausible that Bhutan's control over the plains was growing by then.

In 1717, Tibet was enveloped in a new war between Mongol factions. In a tragic story of love leading to war, a son of Lhazang Khan fell in love with the daughter of Tshewang Rabten, the chieftain of the Zhungar tribe. The Zhungar chieftain saw this as an opportunity to take over Tibet from Lhazang Khan, who was of the Khoshot tribe. When he sent his daughter to Lhasa in marriage, he also despatched some 5000 soldiers under the guise of being the bride's escorts. The bridegroom, Lhazang's son, had been secretly killed on the way. Needless to say, this aroused fear in Lhazang and a war broke out in which Lhazang Khan was defeated. The Zhungars took control of Tibet during which time they ruthlessly persecuted the followers of the Nyingma school. Worried that the Zhungar menace may spill over to Bhutan, the Desi asked the state monks and Gangteng Trulku to carry out elaborate rituals for averting war. A stūpa for suppressing evil forces was also built in Kurjey in Bumthang. At the height of the persecution, the hierarchs of the Pema Lingpa tradition in southern Tibet took refuge in the northeastern frontier of Khenpalung in Bhutan and priests from Gangteng were sent to help them build new shelters. The Zhungar forces were soon defeated by the Tibetan–Manchu coalition in 1720 and did not reach Bhutan.

In 1719, the Bearded Desi Druk Rabgay retired from the throne of Desi to his new temple of Wangditse purportedly to pursue a more spiritual life. However, this would be too good an ending for a ruler whom monk-historians portrayed as a ruthless and evil character and some villagers viewed as a cannibal. We must also remember that despite his good works Druk Rabgay was not very popular among the people for his opposition to Kuenga Gyaltshen, the incarnate hierarch whose blood lay mainly on his hands. There were already prophecies of a *tertön* named Drukdra Dorji circulating in Bhutan that were explicitly identifying Druk Rabgay as an evil character.

It may be noted here that the prophetic words of the *tertön*s or treasure-discoverers attributed to Padmasambhava played a great role in swinging popular sentiments. Through these prophecies, the *tertön*s played a highly political role. We have already seen how Zhabdrung was predicted by such prophecies, helping him legitimize his new rule over Bhutan. However, not all these so-called prophecies are straightforward cases of ancient predictions. We can often find figures such as Zhabdrung prophesied as saintly persons by one *tertön* and as an evil character by another depending on their religious and political ties. Sometimes, the same *tertön* changed his opinion over time with change of political affiliations. The 5th Dalai Lama dismissed Pawo Düdul Dorji as a spurious *tertön* for exactly doing that.[11] He produced a prophecy praising the Karmapa and Zhabdrung and condemning Tsongkhapa, the founder of the Gelugpa school, when the Gelugpa school was still a weak force. After the Dalai Lama came to power, he produced another prophecy which put the Dalai Lama in a positive light and the Karmapa and Zhabdrung in very negative terms. In this respect, prophecies often reflect their contemporary situations rather than predict the future. Thus, for us, these prophecies are useful historical tools in gauging the spiritual standing of the political players in popular opinion and instances of political dissent and vicissitudes during the time of the *tertön*.

Druk Rabgay became the subject of prophecies by two *tertön*s: Dorji Drolöd from Tsang and Drukdra Dorji from Kham who were both busy in Bhutan around the time he came to power although the first one probably came slightly earlier than the second. Dorji Drolöd alias Düdul Lingpa, we have seen earlier, depicted Lhazang Khan as an evil character and was thus imprisoned in Tibet.[12] But he was much more diplomatic in Bhutan. The *tertön* predicted the rise of Druk Rabgay and the fall of his opponent, Tenpa Wangchuk, which may have influenced popular support and individual spirit. In contrast, Drukdra Dorji demonized Druk Rabgay by identifying him with an anti-Buddhist minister during Padmasambhava's time. For this bold claim, Drukdra Dorji lost his life. Kuenga Gyaltshen, according to Drukdra Dorji, was Kawa Paltseg, an eminent translator of Buddhist texts during the Early Diffusion and Druk Rabgay was Lhazang Lüpal, an evil minister supporting the Bön religion in Tri Songdetsen's court. He argued that Kuenga Gyaltshen's fate would have been different if the hierarch had succeeded in building a strong connection with *tertön* Dorji Drolöd, a representative of Padmasambhava. Failing this, Kuenga Gyaltshen was left open to abuse by Druk Rabgay, the incarnation of an anti-Buddhist minister. Thus, their antagonism was traced back to their former lives in eighth-century Tibet.

Drukdra Dorji predicted that Druk Rabgay will 'in the beginning honour Kuenga Gyaltshen like a hat, in middle use him like clothes and in the end take him off like shoes'. The similes appropriately described Druk Rabgay's changing relationship with Kuenga Gyaltshen. The ancient karmic enmity between them revealed by Drukdra Dorji was further reinforced by the identification of Druk Rabgay with another enemy figure, namely Nenying Jetsun, the Nenyingpa lama who opposed Zhabdrung and was imprisoned until 1657. Nenying Jetsun is said to have died with a fervent prayer to take rebirth as someone who could take revenge on Zhabdrung. Druk Rabgay fitted this role and was considered to be the immediate rebirth of Nenying Jetsun.

Thus, Kuenga Gyaltshen, in his last word before he was poisoned to death, explained to one of his disciples that his ordeal was a karmic retribution for the damages done to the Nenying school by Zhabdrung and the fulfilment of malicious prayers made by Nenying Jetsun.

From these beliefs in former connections and the prominent role played by incarnations and *tertön*s, we can see how medieval Bhutanese politics was strongly influenced by religious faith in various ways. Religion was still the dominant factor of statehood as it was when the nation was founded as a Drukpa state. Rulers were judged by their religious accomplishments and service to the Drukpa church more than by anything else. Thus, as the first non-monastic ruler, Druk Rabgay must have faced an immense difficulty in attempting to take politics out of the monastic fold. We might even wonder if he tried to set up a structure of civil authority, which did not go down well with the monastic hierarchs. His opposition to Kuenga Gyaltshen and subsequently, to the latter's reincarnation certainly added fuel to the fire and brought his final downfall. Thus, the portrayal of Druk Rabgay as a diabolic figure by the *tertön*s and monk-historians must be seen in the light of such tensions between religion and secular power. Druk Rabgay was not anti-religious or anti-monastic. In fact, he even took the full ordination of a monk in the final year of his life. But it was his unquenchable thirst for political power, which lay so thoroughly enmeshed in religious faith, belief and institutions, that became the main cause of the ensuing imbroglio and of the first serious rupture in Bhutan's unity.

The proliferation of incarnations and the fall of Bearded Desi

A few years before Druk Rabgay's official resignation as the Desi, another incarnation appeared in the scene. This was Mipham Wangpo, the second incarnation of Tenzin Rabgay. The first one was born in Dagana and once brought to Tango but died as a child. Mipham Wangpo was born in 1709 in the eminent *chöje* family of Bönbji whose ancestral roots we have already discussed. His granduncle Tenzin Lekpai Dondup, the second Gangteng Trulku, initially confirmed him as the incarnation of Tenzin Rabgay after the child showed various signs. This was followed by a party from Tango who investigated him and subsequently took him to Tango where he was placed on Tenzin Rabgay's seat at the age of seven by the latter's daughter, Lhacham Kunley. This line of incarnations originating from Tenzin Rabgay would be known as Tritrul (ཁྲི་སྤྲུལ་) or incarnation of throne-holders although they were also referred to as Gyalse Trulku (རྒྱལ་སྲས་སྤྲུལ་སྐུ་) or incarnations of a royal prince. This led to two lines of Gyalse Trulku in the subsequent periods of Bhutanese history: one originating from Prince Jampal Dorji of Ralung and the other from Prince Tenzin Rabgay of Tango.

The year after he arrived in Tango, Mipham Wangpo went to see Desi Druk Rabgay in Tashichödzong. He also saw the Zhabdrung incarnate Chogley Namgyal, who presided over his tonsuring ceremony and gave him a new name. After this, Mipham Wangpo was admitted to the state monastery to begin his formal training. Meanwhile Druk Rabgay retired in 1719 after installing his own nephew, Ngawang Gyatsho, as the 9th Desi of Bhutan. He did not, however, relinquish all his control over the affairs of state. Instead, he ruled from his hermitage with his nephew largely as a puppet ruler. Ngawang Gyatsho, the new Desi, was a monk of good stature and profound learning with special expertise in linguistics. He was known as *geshe* (དགེ་བཤེས་) or a scholarly master and served as the personal tutor of Chogley Namgyal. One of the main achievements of the first few years of his peaceful reign was the institution of a separate school for linguistics and grammar. He also commissioned numerous artistic projects including production of statues, books and *thangka* wall hangings. Respected for his gracious personality, he even briefly got the title of a righteous Bodhisattva king (ཆོས་རྒྱལ་བྱང་ཆུབ་སེམས་དཔའ་). His peaceful reign regulated by his uncle was, however, to see its end with the appearance of another incarnate lama in the scene.

This lama was Jigme Norbu, the incarnation of Kuenga Gyaltshen whom Druk Rabgay eliminated. He was born as the younger brother of Mipham Wangpo in the family of Bönbji in 1717 and was recognized as the incarnation of Zhabdrung's son based on his own recollection. It is quite possible that his granduncle Tenzin Lekpai Dondup was involved in the verification but our sources are silent and no separate biography of Jigme Norbu is available. Tenzin Chögyal, who wrote the biography of Tenzin Lekpai Dondup, reports the presence of the child in Gangteng in his early youth. Even at this time, it is not clear if Jigme Norbu and his former reincarnation Kuenga Gyaltshen were considered as rebirths of Zhabdrung or his son. Chogley Namgyal, who wrote about them at this time, hardly makes that distinction. Only about a generation later, biographers clearly considered him and Kuenga Gyaltshen as reincarnations of the son and referred to them as Gyalse Trulku or prince incarnate although this title, as I have noted earlier, can be used for Mipham Wangpo and other incarnations of Tenzin Rabgay as well.

Nothing definite can be said about the cause of the conflict, which followed Jigme Norbu's recognition. It appears that Druk Rabgay harboured an unrelenting hostility against Kuenga Gyaltshen, and the latter's return as Jigme Norbu from a prominent family only provoked his displeasure and objection. Yet it is difficult to see why Druk Rabgay felt so strongly against Jigme Norbu. One probable reason is Druk Rabgay's fear of losing the power which he gained through legitimacy granted by his close association to Chogley Namgyal. We must remember that before Jigme Norbu's entry to the scene, the only incarnate claimant to the main line of Zhabdrung was Chogley Namgyal. The return of Kuenga Gyaltshen as Jigme Norbu inevitably brought a new contender to the golden throne. Mipham Wangpo, being the incarnation of Tenzin Rabgay of Tango line, was not seen as a real rival or threat compared to his brother, Jigme Norbu. Nevertheless, at this time, Chogley Namgyal was well established and the most senior incarnate and the young Jigme Norbu could not have been a strong rival to the throne. So, could it be that the Desi Druk Rabgay did not even recognize Kuenga Gyaltshen as the authentic incarnation of Jampal Dorji and he rejected Jigme Norbu as well on such grounds?

If Chogley Namgyal, as later historians record, was an incarnation of Zhabdrung and Jigme Norbu was considered as an incarnation of Jampal Dorji, it is also difficult to see why the leaders could not accommodate both the incarnations amicably. Chogley Namgyal would surely have some prominence over Jigme Norbu due to the difference in stature of their former lives but as incarnations of Zhabdrung and his son both would have been acceptable. Thus, we may wonder if both Kuenga Gyaltshen and Jigme Norbu in their days were thought to be incarnations of Zhabdrung himself and thus seen as direct rivals of Chogley Namgyal. This is at least what the contemporary Tibetan minister Tshering Wangyal, who took part in the negotiations with Bhutan, thought. He wrote that the conflict was essentially about the legitimacy of the two contenders to Zhabdrung's throne and Druk Rabgay alias Wang Phajo supported Chogley Namgyal, whom others rejected. The opposition, he wrote, was composed of some rowdy monks who rejected Chogley Namgyal.[13] Perhaps, this is true and only after the terrible conflict and the death of Jigme Norbu, with the benefit of hindsight, had the religious hierarchs decided to identify Kuenga Gyaltshen and Jigme Norbu as incarnations of Zhabdrung's son and not of Zhabdrung himself. This could have partly resolved the differences and avoided any future problem. Whatever the reasons, our sources give no clear account apart from putting the blame on Druk Rabgay's resilient grudge. Occupied by their religious duties, the three incarnate lamas seem quite innocent politically and appear to play no active role in the conflicts. The warring officials, however, used the incarnates for advancing their own political career and this was most likely what Druk Rabgay feared right from the outset when Jigme Norbu entered the scene. In any case, the factional divide among the Bhutanese court officials along the reincarnation lines brought the most serious rupture in Bhutan's unity and the first major civil war.

Even before Jigme Norbu had made his debut in the political centres of western Bhutan in 1730, it appears that the Bhutanese court had already been split into two groups. One faction, led by the retired Desi Druk Rabgay and his chief of protocol, Kabji Dondrub, seemed to have openly opposed Jigme Norbu's legitimacy and backed Chogley Namgyal, who was then occupying the golden throne. The other faction mainly consisted of students of Kuenga Gyaltshen, who had suffered grievances under the Druk Rabgay and now promoted Jigme Norbu, the new incarnation of their master. Druk Rabgay even expelled some 200 monks of this group, which included the future Desi Sherab Wangchuk, from the state monastery.[14] The incarnate lamas themselves, from what we know, were not directly involved and were used merely as pawns. The main agenda for the conflict, we can assume, was competition for power among the officials although people generally must have also been divided on the incarnation lines. The historian Pema Tshewang argues that it was the incumbent Desi Ngawang Gyatsho and the state monks on one side and former Druk Rabgay and his friends on the other. This seems unlikely as the senior monks acted as mediators and were not partisan. Desi Ngawang Gyatsho was also too close to his uncle Druk Rabgay to be openly against him and was killed after the Druk Rabgay's party were defeated.

Western Bhutan was torn with internal war and bloodshed between 1729 and 1735. In the words of Shakya Tenzin, 'both inside and outside, the noise of "kill him! hit him!" filled the earth and sky. The powerless fainted. The country turned into a land of demons filled the constant cries like shrills from the depth of hell.'[15] However, we were once again left with such poeotic allegories and only patchy information about actual events, making it difficult to gain a clear picture about this complex and protracted conflict. The monk-historians, who are our only sources, are excruciatingly sparse with details on these sad and inauspicious events. They mention the conflict in passing as 'misfortunes of the state' or 'works of evil' and choose to focus on their grand religious narratives. The best account, by far, is again John Ardussi's thesis, which analyses the conflict using even Tibetan and Chinese sources. I shall present here only a brief account of the conflict.

The tension between the two factions erupted into an open conflict some time around the beginning of 1729. Druk Rabgay was in his hermitage of Wangditse in Thimphu, having become a fully ordained monk in the preceding summer. A windstorm blew off the cupola of his new temple, presaging bad times for him. Chogley Namgyal was also in Wangditse having entered a retreat in autumn. Mipham Wangpo was in Gangteng where he had been appointed as regent since 1625. After the death of Tenzin Lekpai Dondup in 1725, he spent much of his time as regent in Gangteng supervising religious works as part of the funerary rites for this master. In 1729, Mipham Wangpo went briefly to Bumthang in disguise to see the black-hat and red-hat Karmapa hierarchs who were then in Thangbi. They were on an eighteen-month tour of eastern Bhutan. The conflicts in Punakha had already made Mipham Wangpo's travels to and from Bumthang difficult and risky. Jigme Norbu, still a young boy, was either in his village in Bönbji or in Gangteng.

At Punakha, the conflict took a bloody turn and numerous officials including most ministers in office were killed. The *dzong* was littered with corpses and the temples filled with stench of fresh blood, according to Shakya Tenzin. The ruling Desi Ngawang Gyatsho was put under arrest but not killed yet. We have no information on who were killed or which faction was winning. We can only infer from the outcome that the faction opposing Druk Rabgay was winning. The strife soon spread to Thimphu. The senior monk figures led by the 6th Je Khenpo Ngawang Lhundup, Ngawang Gyaltshen and Ngawang Thinley began their efforts to mediate between the factions but in vain. As enemy soldiers arrived in Thimphu, Druk Rabgay moved from Wangditse to Tashichödzong for better security, taking Chogley Namgyal with him. As the fighting escalated, it was too dangerous for them to remain even in Tashichödzong. Thus, Druk Rabgay and Chogley Namgyal escaped at night in secrecy for the border, but they were captured by the pursuers when they reached Haa Langchu. In great terror, the group was brought back to the Paro *dzong*, where Chogley Namgyal was separated from Druk Rabgay. When Druk Rabgay clung to Chogley Namgyal's robes in desperation, the latter burst into tears and wailed. This was the end for Druk Rabgay. The Bearded Desi was thrown into the river and two of his nephews and a servant were also executed. Chogley Namgyal was kept in the Paro *dzong* for the time being.

Two incarnate brothers and the last Tibetan invasion

With the death of Druk Rabgay, the conflict temporarily came to a halt. Now that the main opposition has been removed, Mipham Wangpo and his brother, Jigme Norbu, were formally brought to Punakha. They were received with a grand welcome and both enthroned at the same time in 1729: Jigme Norbu as the 4th holder of the golden throne or the spiritual firgurehead and Mipham Wangpo as the 10th Desi. Ngawang Gyatsho apparently was removed from the post of Desi and subsequently killed although it is difficult to tell who did this and which faction this scholarly monk was associated with. Pema Tshewang claims that he was killed by his uncle's faction. We know he was involved in the installation of Jigme Norbu and Mipham Wangpo, either through coercion or willingly. It is possible that the supporters of Druk Rabgay killed him to punish him for defection.

Immediately after their installation, Jigme Norbu and Mipham Wangpo began to receive teachings from the Je Khenpo and other senior hierarchs. Curiously, Jigme Norbu was only tonsured in the following year by Ngawang Gyaltshen who also ordained him as a monk, perhaps because the hierarch was not well. Ngawang Gyaltshen and the Je Khenpo Ngawang Lhundup were certainly the two most respected and dominant monk statesmen of this time although their abstention from use of force on religious and moral grounds did not make them the most powerful. In a bold move to reconcile the incarnate lamas, the Je Khenpo in consultation with Mipham Wangpo invited Chogley Namgyal to Punakha. This was perhaps a tactical move to ensure Chogley Namgyal's security but also to avoid the growth of a separate power base in Paro. The Je Khenpo had already appointed the respected monk, Ngawang Pekar, as Chogley Namgyal's guardian and, when they received the order to come to Punakha, Chogley Namgyal and Ngawang Pekar set out with some attendants full of anxiety wondering what might happen. During their stop in Thinleygang, Ngawang Pekar gathered his courage to raise the sensitive question; he asked Chogley Namgyal if he truly believed he was Zhabdrung or if there is a possibility that he was rebirth of the 3rd Je Khenpo as some people thought. If it were the second case, now would be a time to announce this so that all tensions would be diffused. Chogley Namgyal stood his ground and gave a categorical reply that he fully believed he was Zhabdrung. Ngawang Pekar still insisted that Chogley Namgyal bow down to the lama brothers when they met the incarnate brothers. This, Chogley had no option but to accept. The two arrived in Punakha safely with their small party but there was no ceremonial reception or fanfare, which Chogley Namgyal was used to having in the past. After this, Chogley Namgyal mostly stayed in Punakha and Wangdiphodrang in the shadow of the two brothers and under the harassment of some court officials although the monastic hierarchs and Mipham Wangpo did what they could to support Chogley Namgyal.

Despite his reluctance, Mipham Wangpo in the meantime attended to the duties of the Desi but the conflict was far from over. In an ironic move, Druk Rabgay had sent for Tibetan support in 1729 although he did not live to see the response. Pholhaney Sonam Tobgay (1689–1747), who was now the *de facto* King of Tibet, must have found such a request amusing and ironic, coming from the man who fifteen years ago challenged and defeated his master, Lhazang Khan. His biographer says Pholhaney was a wise leader who understood such vagaries of political life and, instead of taking advantage of the situation, he politely offered to help without any strong commitment. He did, however, collect information to understand the exact political situation in Bhutan. The Karmapa hierarchs, who were travelling in Bhutan and were in regular touch with him, were probably important sources of his intelligence.

In 1730, Kabji Dondrub, who served Druk Rabgay as chief of protocol, resumed the conflict and led an insurrection against Punakha from his base in Paro. The rebel group led by Kabji Dondrub and the government forces led by one Sithub were said to have camped in the Jungshi and Kudrong areas of Thimphu and engaged in a bloody contest. On the verge of defeat, Dondrub sought help from Tibet. The Tibetan ruler Pholhaney, according to his biographer, was once again noncommittal but he sent a letter which Tibetan generals at the border allegedly misunderstood as an order to grasp the opportunity provided by the disunity in Bhutan to bring the whole country under Tibetan rule. Thus, Tibetan troops entered Paro and occupied the Drukgyal and Paro *dzong*s with the help of Kabji Dondrub's men but they soon found themselves cornered by the Bhutanese forces. These soldiers sent for support from Tibet and Pholhaney, his biographer would have us believe, launched a military campaign against Bhutan in order to rescue his men. But this was perhaps an ostensible reason and, in reality, Pholhaney may have carefully and shrewdly engineered the whole invasion. John Ardussi warns us that the Tibetan sources cannot be trusted and 'there is every reason to suspect that the Tibetan government's long-cherished design to gain a tighter hold on Bhutan was shared by Pholhaney also. Tibetan armies had never fared well against united Bhutanese resistance; divided, the country would be more easily dominated'.[16]

In the spring of 1730, Pholhaney ordered a coalition of Tibetan and Mongolian troops under four generals to invade Bhutan. There were no divisions sent toward Bumthang or eastern Bhutan this time. The Tibetan troops all entered through Paro and were soon in Thimphu. By the time the monks moved from Punakha to their summer residence, there was such widespread fighting in Thimphu that they had to go back and instead proceed to Wangdiphodrang for the summer. Shakya Rinchen, who was then twenty years old, later reminisced:

> At that time, the great army of the enemies filled Thimphu region leaving no space. Weapons clashed in holy shrines in the presence of oceans of sacred objects. Stūpas and meditation huts were demolished and religious practitioners assaulted and enslaved. Even the innocent animals were slaughtered out of severe bigotry. In brief, it was as if the Mongol breath of evil times has touched all of the southern land, this grove of happiness, taking away from it its state of peace.[17]

We have neither any information on Bhutan's defence strategy nor on who were fighting on the Bhutanese side apart from Ngawang Gyaltshen, the *dzongpön* of Thimphu and future Desi and a chief of protocol called Sithub. It is likely that Tshering Wangchen and Paljor of Bönbji, uncles of the incarnate brothers, played crucial roles. Unlike other occasions, there is no account of even state rituals being performed to repel the invaders. We can gauge that the state was severely divided and in serious chaos. By the autumn of 1730, Paro was fully controlled by Kabji Dondrub and the Tibetan invaders. It had practically seceded from Bhutanese rule but before the invaders managed to gain full control beyond Paro, the Panchen Lama, the Sakya Trichen and Karmapa lamas requested Pholhaney to stop the violence and open negotiations. Thugse Chogdrub Palbar spent a whole month in Lhasa in 1730 trying to persuade Pholhaney to pull out the Tibetan troops.[18]

Pholhaney readily agreed to this and pulled the forces out of Thimphu; in fact he had already posted Tshering Wangyal, his minister and biographer, to Gyantse to prepare for the negotiations. The Karmapa lamas, who left Bhutan earlier that year, returned via Phari and Paro. Negotiations began in earnest between the Tibetan generals and the Bhutanese officials. The meeting was attended by the two Karmapa lamas, several Tibetan generals and many Bhutanese hierarchs, including the Desi and Je Khenpo. In the tenth Bhutanese month of 1730, a treaty was drafted and endorsed in

Tashichödzong but we do not know the details of the treaty. Our sources loosely state that the forces of Kabji Dondrub were not to revolt against the state and the state not to attack or suppress the rebels, who had now secured Paro as their stronghold. It appears that one of the terms was also to give deference to Chogley Namgyal because soon after this treaty was signed, Chogley Namgyal was allowed to sit on the throne and preside over some state ceremonies. The Karmapa lamas remained in Bhutan through that winter attending festivals in Punakha but perhaps also making sure that terms of treaty are carried out. The treaty must have also required the two Bhutanese factions to send hostages to Lhasa. Tshering Wangchen, the uncle and chamberlain of the two reigning incarnates, was sent to Lhasa as hostage on behalf of the government. He arrived in Lhasa with attendants from Gangteng and many riches. Kabji Dondrub went on behalf of the rebels. In Lhasa, the Chinese Amban and Pholhaney interrogated them about the dispute in order to prepare memorials to the Emperor of China. Tshering Wangchen was later remembered as the first Bhutanese *lochag* (ལོ་ཕྱག) or representative to Lhasa.

Unfortunately, the treaty did its work only for a short period as fighting broke out again in the spring of 1731. From the quick resurgence of fighting, we may surmise that the conflict was not merely between leaders over political power. The people and the monastics seemed to be divided over the incarnation line to the extent that foreign intervention and a treaty could not easily close the gap. Tibetans troops once again returned to Thimphu and there was a lot of fighting, plundering and pillaging. The state monks for the second consecutive year turned toward Wangdiphodrang for their summer residence, which they found in the Khothang area. There were further negotiations involving Tibetan officials while fighting continued but there are no clear details. The Tibetan troops appear to have continued their campaign until they were thoroughly worn out and forced to return. The Bhutanese accounts generally state the Tibetan forces gradually dispersed, not being able to overcome the Bhutanese. It is quite likely that the protracted nature of the campaign in an unfamiliar terrain and unfavourable climate took its toll on the Tibetan men, forcing them to retreat. When Thugse Chogdrub Palbar returned to Tibet from Bhutan in the early months of 1732, he came across sporadic fighting along the Tibetan border north of Bumthang. By then, the Tibetan troops may have retreated from the central valleys. The Bhutanese government on its part had to accept the secession of Paro to the rebel factions with the terms that the area shall be returned to the state at the death of Kabji Dondrub. With these terms, the Tibetan forces appear to have left Bhutan by the middle of 1732 and the civil war began to subside.

In Punakha, Chogley Namgyal's position was still precarious in spite of the friendly relations he had with the two incarnate brothers. There were court officials who continued to harass him and there was even an attempt on his life. Thus, on the ninth of the eleventh Bhutanese month, 25 December 1732, he made a desperate move to escape. He, his guardian Ngawang Pekar and two attendants climbed down from the window of the *dzong* using a rope. The bridge was closed and they were forced to wade through the river in dark when Ngawang Pekar was nearly swept away by the currents. Having crossed the river, they then headed upstream, Chogley Namgyal being carried by his attendants in turn until they were received by Kabji Dondrub's men and via a northerly route taken to Paro, where Kabji Dondrub welcomed them. Chogley Namgyal spent the rest of his life in Paro, from where he corresponded with the Tibetan ruler Pholhaney and even received a gift of a set of *kanjur*, which the Tibetan ruler must have printed from the blocks he commissioned some years earlier. The incarnate hierarch thanked Pholhaney for the gift with a beautiful poem.

Mipham Wangpo was going through hard times when Chogley Namgyal escaped. The leading monastic gurus, Ngawang Lhundup and Ngawang Gyaltshen, who guided him, had both died and he had not been able to unite his subjects. On the contrary, Kabji Dondrub had successfully carved out a separate principality in Paro and tension between the factions remained undiminished. Beside, there was a strong presence of Tibetan forces in the country. Given this situation, Chogley Namgyal's defection must have come as a strong blow. Although they continued to remain on good terms and exchanged letters, their relation was strained and Mipham Wangpo felt dejected. Perhaps to recuperate from this low spirit and to turn to divine help, Mipham Wangpo went into a short retreat at the end of 1732 and his spirit may have been briefly excited by the visit of Thugse Chogdrub Palbar and the young incarnate of Gangteng Trulku that winter. In the spring of 1733, he moved with the monks to Thimphu, where he presided over the funerals for Lhacham Kunley, his sister from his previous rebirth, but was soon taken seriously ill, allegedly due to 'breaches in spiritual bonds'. This 'breach' probably refers to Chogley Namgyal's abscondment.

Mipham Wangpo did recover quickly from the illness and resumed his duties and also carried out a number of religious projects, including the production of several large gilded copper statues for which he probably employed the Newari artisans he had invited while he was in Gangteng. In

1733, things took a more positive turn for him. The Tibetan troops had largely left Bhutan and the people of the Kabji area, who supported the insurrection, now asked for forgiveness and rejoined the state. Paro was still outside his jurisdiction but fighting seems to have significantly subsided. Toward the end of 1733, the Tibetan ruler Pholhaney made his last intervention, perhaps to use the opportunity presented by Bhutanese disunity for one last time to please his Chinese masters before the political situation in Bhutan changed. An envoy composed of the Tibetan ministers Drongtsepa and Manchu Major Hoshang were sent to Bhutan. According to Ardussi, they arrived in Wangdiphodrang, where an agreement between the two factions was signed and the sealed copy of the agreement and memorials from the two factions were taken to Lhasa with their emissaries. The emissary on behalf of the state was one monk called Barchungpa but we do not know who represented the Paro faction. From there, the emissaries were sent to China by the Chinese Amban in Lhasa to submit the memorials to the emperor.

The successive Tibetan negotiations resulted in an agreement, which stipulated the state was to refrain from offences against the rebels and the rebels to stop further acts of revolt. Paro was to remain under Kabji Dondrub until his death, when it would be returned to the state. Chogley Namgyal acted as the spiritual figurehead and Kabji Dondrub was officially the independent *pönlop* of Paro. This stalemate continued but in the early months of 1734, Chogley Namgyal passed away in Paro. His death was attributed to an illness deriving from his poor diet as he had been a strict vegetarian. Before his death, he was requested to take rebirth in the family of Kabji Dondrub, which, according to his biographer, he agreed to. The Paro faction kept his death a secret for about a year and cremated his body only in the beginning of 1735. Around this time, Kabji Dondrub also passed away and, following the mutual agreement, the territory under the control of the Paro faction was returned to the state under Mipham Wangpo. Just as this transfer of power was in process, a child was born in the family of Kabji Dondrub and identified by Ngawang Pekar to be the rebirth of Chogley Namgyal. This child became the 2nd Sungtrul Shakya Tenzin (1735–80) but as Pholhoney agreed to provide protection to some leaders of Paro faction, the young incarnate, his mother and the old guardian, Ngawang Pekar, quickly moved via Phari to Dalingdzong on the frontiers of western Bhutan, where Shakya Tenzin spent his first few years.[19]

Meanwhile in Tashichödzong, the monk Barchungpa returned from China in the summer of 1735 with an imperial letter and seal and many other gifts for Mipham Wangpo. His long trip to the imperial court of China was hailed as a success and a great service to the Drukpa state. He was perhaps the first or one of the few Bhutanese who had travelled as far as Beijing at that time. By the time he returned, Paro was also reunited with the rest of Bhutan and rituals of celebration and thanksgiving to the deities were performed. The celebrations were, however, cut short as Jigme Norbu passed away tragically in the summer of 1735 at the age of eighteen. The golden throne, which had two occupants a few years ago, was left without a single occupant now. The country was without a spiritual figurehead. To make things worse, an epidemic of smallpox of struck the country, killing at least sixty monks in the state monastery alone. Monks had to be dispersed to remote places. The monastery of Cheri was destroyed by fire. Saddened by his brother's untimely death and exhausted by the burden of managing a war and disease-torn state, Mipham Wangpo, at the annual meeting to appoint monastic disciplinarians, proposed to retire to a hermitage, giving a host of reasons.[20] However, his proposal to retire fell on deaf ears and he was begged to continue, which he did for another year.

The 1729–33 war and Sino-Tibetan intervention is striking for a number of reasons. Internally, it was the first major conflict which led to a brief territorial and political disintegration. Paro was practically seceded as a separate polity outside the jurisdiction of the central government but heavily controlled by Tibet. Driven by political motives and religious affiliations, the conflict caused a serious rupture in Bhutan's unity. The country had two contenders for the supreme post at the beginning of the conflict but none at the end though their deaths were not directly linked to the war. It was also a period when Bhutan was ruled by two brothers as its religious and secular heads. The state monks were diverted from Thimphu for two consecutive summers due to military turbulence. It was also the first conflict in which some of the major players were from outside the western valleys of Bhutan.

Externally, the division left Bhutan without an outward united front. It was not the only time Bhutanese dissidents sought Tibetan support and Tibetans interfered but it was certainly the only time Tibetans came out with some success. The conflict resulted in a victory of sorts for the Tibetan invaders. It gave them loose control over the polity of Paro for a stipulated period and left them in a better position to negotiate with the central authorities in Thimphu and Punakha. The Tibetans, however, saw it slightly differently. According to the Tibetan historian and minister Tshering Wangyal, the invasion of 1730–32 was an unprecedented victory for Tibet. Past Tibetan approaches to Bhutan, he comments, had sometimes been aggressive, throwing at Bhutan all its military force, but sometimes conciliatory and yet other times indifferent. None of these approached had given the Tibetans an upper hand. All military aggressions in the past failed due to the hostile terrain including deep ravines, narrow pathways and thick forest infested with beasts.[21] The campaign under Pholhaney was successful in winning Bhutanese submission mainly through 'power of merits' of the great leader without much military investment. At least, this is the account of Tshering Wangyal, who wrote a panegyric praise to his master, Pholhaney.

There is no doubt Pholhaney was a shrewd and wise ruler and he indeed made the most out of the conflict. He exploited the factionalized political situation in Bhutan to gain a symbolic victory without harbouring any long-term colonial desires which would have been unwise and unviable anyway. Although his initial assessment of the problem was superficial and imperceptive and the treaty he had the parties sign in 1731 fell through almost as soon as the negotiators left, he and the Chinese Amban in Lhasa managed to make the Bhutanese factions submit peace agreements and memorials to the Chinese emperor. With this, Pholhaney duly pleased the emperor and got his promotion to the rank of Beile (Lord). He also succeeded in keeping a Bhutanese representative in Lhasa and started the *lochag* tradition, which some Tibetan interpret as the practice of paying tribute and the Bhutanese as a diplomatic representation. Whichever way one may take it, a Bhutanese representative was present in Lhasa to pay respects to the Dalai Lama at Tibetan New Year festivals.

The memorials and submission to Peking and the Chinese emperor was another one of his symbolic gains. Although Bhutan would have been of very little significance to distant Peking and Chinese imperial concerns, peace with Bhutan was important for peace in Tibet, one of the empire's prized territories. For Pholhaney, whose rise as *de facto* ruler of Tibet was largely due to Manchu imperial support, he was doing a proud service to the emperor by sending submissive emissaries from a foreign country, however small and distant. The Bhutanese appear to have also seen the link and exchanges with the Chinese emperor as a great achievement. To them, the mission was not about submission to a suzerain power as the memorials drafted in Lhasa for them may make it seem. Nothing in the political process and state administration in Bhutan at that time or later even remotely indicate any submission to the China. Instead, the Bhutanese saw the official link as a proof of China's recognition of Bhutan's status. This was very important at a time of persistent Tibetan interference in Bhutanese politics. The imperial letter and seal granted by the emperor to Mipham Wangpo were thus largely symbolic and had no real use. There is no record of Mipham Wangpo or later hierarchs having ever used the seal and even the link to China dissipated as quickly as it began and no official connection between Bhutan and China has existed since.

Mipham Wangpo's escape and the continuation of Bönbji rule

One of the best outcomes of the conflict was Bhutan's new phase of warm relations with Tibet. Perhaps due to the imperial intervention or maybe because Tibet had now at last succeeded in punishing the irritable neighbour, which it had desperately wanted to do for a long time, Tibet's approach to Bhutan turned more conciliatory and friendly. The credit for this development of cordial relations must to some extent go to the Tibetan ruler Pholhaney. He did not approach Bhutan with the same patronizing and supercilious attitude as his predecessors did. The antagonism between the Gelugpa and Drukpa governments and between the Northern and Southern Drukpa schools also began to disappear as they undertook some joint religious projects and exchange of religious hierarchs. This change in Tibet's Bhutan policy marked the end of over a century of wars between the two countries and the beginning of a whole new neighbourly relationship.

Despite easing the tension with Tibet, the internal tensions in Punakha were far from over. We don't know exactly what triggered it but on the twenty-fifth of the first Bhutanese month, 8 March 1736, Mipham Wangpo with a number of attendants sneaked out of the Punakha *dzong* at midnight and made their way to Tibet. It is not even clear if Mipham Wangpo was running away or simply setting out secretly on a tour of Tibet. John Ardussi states that political opposition to Mipham Wangpo had reached its peak, his biography merely says he made the journey due to 'other circumstances' and Gedun Rinchen adds that he went on a pilgrimage in order to carry out funerary rites for his deceased brother.[22] Whichever it may be, the departure was sudden and his flight left the court in disarray and the Je Khenpo extremely worried. Some monks pursued them but before they could catch up, Mipham Wangpo's team managed to cross the border over Wakyela to Tibet despite being very poorly equipped for the snow and blizzard.

When Pholhaney heard of his arrival in Tibet, the ruler sent supplies and ordered local officials on the route to offer him service. On his way, Mipham Wangpo spent a night in Ralung and when he reached Nyethang, he was received by his uncle, Tshering Wangchen, the Bhutanese representative in Lhasa. When he reached Lhasa, the Tibetan officials extended Mipham Wangpo a grand reception. Pholhaney, according to the Bhutanese biographer, was extremely courteous to Mipham Wangpo and he and Mipham Wangpo found each other congenial as if they have already known other. Mipham Wangpo's time in Lhasa was filled with formal receptions and dinners with the Lhasa officials, Chinese Amban and lamas. He also met the 7th Dalai Lama Kelzang Gyatsho (1708–57), who had just been reinstated in Lhasa. The Bhutanese team also went on pilgrimage to the major religious sites in Kyichu and Yarlung valleys and Tshurphu. Mipham Wangpo also met many senior religious hierarchs, including the incarnation of Drukpa Kunley, who later visited Bhutan.

We don't know if Mipham Wangpo carried out any political discussions during his stay in Lhasa. While the biographer gives a detailed account of the pilgrimage and religious activities, he is generally silent on the content of Mipham Wangpo's conversation with the officials. One also wonders what the Tibetan officials may have thought of his arrival into exile, as he was the first ruler of the country to do so. However, the warm hospitality and high respect which were shown to him in Tibet must have surely sent a strong signal to his opponents in Bhutan and helped curbed the rise of any opposition, if that was what forced him to exile. It is difficult to get a clear picture of the public opinion in Bhutan on Mipham Wangpo's sudden departure. According to their biographies, the contemporary hierarchs were saddened by the departure and very sympathetic to Mipham Wangpo. However, the officials in power may have taken a stronger stance. We know at least that the *dzongpön* of Thimphu, Ngawang Gyaltshen, who later became the 12th Desi, ordered the border patrol to stop anyone following Mipham Wangpo to Tibet. The illustrious scholar, Shakya Rinchen, who was then twenty-seven and on his way to Tibet in quest of spiritual teachings, was taken for a political fugitive and imprisoned in Lingshi. He was then led with his hands tied together to Chapcha and detained there while some of his friends were exiled to the south. The Je Khenpo Ngawang Thinley, who was still in tears and worried about the affairs of the state, sent a letter pleading Mipham Wangpo to return and also sent a petition to Pholhaney to allow him to do so. This seemed, of course, to be the wish of the vast majority of the people as well. Thus, unable to refuse the entreaties, Mipham Wangpo returned to

Bhutan. He was seen off with lavish gifts and escorts by the Tibetans and received by the Bhutanese with much jubilation and ceremony along his route to Thimphu via Paro.

Back in Bhutan, Mipham Wangpo was installed in the place of his late brother as the 5th holder of the golden throne. His uncle Paljor from Bönbji had already been appointed as the 11th Desi in early 1736 following Mipham Wangpo's escape to Tibet. Thus, the power continued to remain in the hands of Bönbji family. The temple of Cheri, which had earlier been destroyed by fire, was rebuilt during their reign. Mipham Wangpo also carried out other religious projects while moving between Thimphu, Punakha and Tango but he suffered increasingly from poor health as a result of an attempted poisoning. In the middle of 1738, he passed away in Tango but his death was concealed for many months with orders and responses issued on a wooden board. Even a high-ranking mission from Derge court of the deceased King Tenpa Tshering (1678–1738), who could not be refused an audience, was given one from behind a thin curtain by his disciple and biographer, Shakya Rinchen. The Bhutanese, who were quite familiar with such ploys, soon found out his death and monastic and secular officials led by the new Je Khenpo Tenzin Norbu and the Desi converged at Tango to perform the rituals of cremation and other funerary rites. Soon after the cremation in 1739, Desi Paljor also resigned from the office of the Desi after three years and retired to a small hermitage above his home in Bönbji. This formally ended a decade of rule by the Bönbji family.

The 12th Desi was Ngawang Gyaltshen from Wang Dramdo in Thimphu. He was a lay officer well known for his military valour and skill. His outstanding military service during the last Tibetan invasion earned him the post of the *dzongpön* of Daling and subsequently of Thimphu before he became the Desi. Following Paljor's resignation, Ngawang Gyaltshen was installed as the Desi in 1740 through some sort of a consensus. His rule continued Mipham Wangpo's legacy of friendly ties with Tibet. Right at the beginning of his tenure as the Desi, Yungön Dorji, the incarnation of the divine madman, Drukpa Kunley, visited Bhutan. This incarnate lama, whom Mipham Wangpo met during his trip to Tibet, was an important Drukpa hierarch, being the incarnation of one of its celebrated masters. He was trained in a Gelugpa monastery and his eclectic religious approach combined Drukpa, Nyingma and Kadampa teachings and practices. Although his presence in Bhutan seems to have been controversial as many high-ranking officials and monks may have still distrusted anyone with close ties to the Tibetan government, he became an important link between Bhutan and the Tibetan government. Thus, it was him and the former Je Khenpo Ngawang Thinley who consecrated the large gilt statue of Avalokiteśvara in Punakha. This project was started by Mipham Wangpo but could not be finished in his lifetime. Ngawang Gyaltshen also allowed religious hierarchs to go to Tibet. So, Shakya Rinchen, the monk scholar whom he earlier stopped in his capacity as the Thimphu *dzongpön*, was now allowed to go to Tibet. In fact, by this time, Ngawang Gyaltshen had already apologized to Shakya Rinchen for the mistreatment and mended their relationship. In a programme to educate young Bhutanese at Tibetan centres of learning, monks were also sent to study in Loseling college of the Drepung monastery. In 1741, Ngawang Gyaltshen sent envoys to congratulate the new Panchen Lama Palden Yeshe (1738–80) and from Tibet, the 7th Dalai Lama sent donations for the renovation of the Kyerchu and Tagtshang temples in Paro, which Ngawang Gyaltshen carried out.

Ngawang Gyaltshen's relationship with Sikkim to west was not as smooth as with Tibet to the north. The Sikkimese King Gyurme Namgyal (1707–33) died leaving only an illegitimate son from a nun. This boy was not accepted as a genuine heir by Tandin, one of the powerful ministers, who assumed the power and the title of the king. The royalist who supported this boy, Sikkim's 5th King Namgyal Phuntsho, waged a protracted war against Tandin. Finally in 1740, Tandin was defeated with the help of the Bhutanese, who also gave protection to the prince. Sungtrul Shakya Tenzin, who spent his early youth in the Daling area, reminisces in the biography of his teacher about the constant skirmishes along the border and Bhutanese forays into Sikkim. The Bhutanese military support was perhaps not very large but their contribution to the overthrow of the usurper was significant. This assistance to the royal line during the civil war of Sikkim earned Bhutan the right to keep a small military garrison in Gangtok and also collect taxes from some 143 households. Many families of Sikkimese refugees, who were removed by the war, were also allowed to settle in Bhutan by the *pönlop* of Paro.

The early days of Ngawang Gyaltshen's rule also saw the arrival of the child incarnation of Jigme Norbu. He was born in 1737 in Kurtoe in the *chöje* family of Dungkar, who are descendents of the Bhutanese saint Pema Lingpa. The child was brought to Punakha and installed as the 6th holder of the golden throne in 1740. He was tonsured by the former Je Khenpo Ngawang Thinley and given the name Drukdra Namgyal. He received his training under the incumbent Je Khenpo Tenzin Norbu, the prince of Ladakh, and the prominent scholars Shakya Rinchen and Tenzin Chögyal. While Drukdra Namgyal enjoyed a cordial relationship with the Desi, the other incarnate, Sungtrul Shakya Tenzin, was not so lucky. Shakya Tenzin and his guardian Ngawang Pekar left the country when Paro was reunited with the rest of Bhutan. They spent many years in the frontier area of Daling, from where they moved back to Paro some time in 1740. However, almost immediately after their return to Paro, they were summoned to Punakha and subjected to ill treatment by the Desi. Ngawang Gyaltshen was unforgiving with those from Kabji Dondrub's faction, against whom he fought during Bhutan's civil war. Thus, the incarnate lama and his old mentor became targets of his old grudge. After episodes of rebuke and harassment by the Desi, they were finally made to live separately. Shakya Tenzin was left without much support in Paro while Ngawang Pekar was banished to Dagana. Fortunately for these religious hierarchs, the Desi died from a stroke in 1744. His sudden death was presaged by the windstorm which blew away the roof of his residence and black ravens which flew at him. These, according to the traditional historians, were signs of the wrath of the protecting deities for his ill treatment of the Zhabdrung incarnate and his teacher.

The glorious days of Sherab Wangchuk

Ngawang Gyaltshen was succeeded by one of the most celebrated rulers of medieval Bhutan. He was Sherab Wangchuk (1697–1767), undoubtedly the most popular and able stateman of his time. His childhood name was Sithub and he was the last of eight siblings born in Khasarkha village in the Thimphu district. He joined the state monastery at the age of fourteen and spent eighteen years in the monastery until he was posted some time in 1729 as chief of protocol to Tongsa first and then to Wangdiphodrang. His last post before becoming the Desi was as the governor of the Paro at the time this region was being reunited with the rest of Bhutan. It was in his capacity as Paro *pönlop* that he welcomed the Zhabdrung incarnate Shakya Tenzin and his teacher Ngawang Pekar and the Sikkimese refugees, we saw earlier. He also built the large gilded copula of the *dzong* and copper statues of the Buddha, Padmasambhava and Zhabdrung.

Sherab Wangchuk had temporarily retired from politics when Ngawang Gyaltshen suddenly passed away, leaving the post of the Desi vacant. Although Sherab Wangchuk might have had no desire to occupy the post, he was certainly the most popular candidate for it. Thus, soon after his predecessor's death, Sherab Wangchuk was unanimously appointed as the 13th Desi. The popular choice of his candidacy was perhaps also reinforced by some prophecies and prognostications, which vaguely hinted that he was the destined ruler. At least, that is how historians, including his contemporaries, presented it.

Sherab Wangchuk ruled the country with a refreshing benevolence, sagacity and diplomacy, which would make his twenty-year reign a medieval golden era in more than one sense of the word. The country enjoyed political stability and unprecedented friendly relations with its neighbours; it was economically prosperous and flourishing in cultural and literary activities. It was a period marked with the use of gold and silver as he carried out nationwide gilding projects and silver coin distribution. His biography contains interesting information about his benevolent activities, especially of his repeated distribution of wealth from the state treasury to all households in the country. These accounts indirectly provide a rough census of the people and record of the administrative hierarchy in the eighteenth century.

The first notable event of his enlightened rule is his installation as the Desi in 1744. Words about it were sent to all neighbouring countries and congratulatory messages were received from the 7th Dalai Lama, Pholhaney, the Emperor of China, the chief Drukpa hierarch of Tibet Kagyu Thinley Shingta, the Sakya hierarch and from Kings of Kāmarūpa, Ladakh, Zanskar, Nepal and Sikkim. The investiture was presided over by the incarnate Lama Drukdra Namgyal and attended by all important figures of Bhutan. The celebrations lasted for many days. Throughout his long reign, Sherab Wangchuk would continue his zest for such celebrations and the cordial relationship with all neighbours exchanging large amounts of gifts with them. We shall return to them shortly.

One of the most remarkable and exciting works of Sherab Wangchuk was his policy of religious inclusivism for an amicable accommodation and integration of the multiple incarnation lines and harmony between different schools. Such a reconciliatory approach was crucial as most conflicts in the past were results of sectarian discrimination or rivalry of factions supporting different religious lines. The issue of incarnation lines following Zhabdrung's death is highly complex. It has taxed the minds of Tibetan and Chinese rulers and later of the British, none of whom understood it properly. Even historians on Bhutan are sometimes confused. To appreciate the problems of competing incarnates and Bhutanese attempts to bring them to a harmonious relationship, we must list the main lines. The first line to start was the one from the hierarch

Kuenga Gyaltshen, which ran through his two subsequent incarnations, Jigme Norbu and Drukdra Namgyal. Drukdra Namgyal was occupying the golden throne when Sherab Wangchuk became the Desi. Sherab Wangchuk received his name from the first one and supported the second one during the civil war. The second line consisted of Chogle Namgyal and his rebirth, Shakya Tenzin, who were associated with the faction of Druk Rabgay and Kabji Dondup. The third line consisted of Tenzin Rabgay's incarnations, Mipham Wangpo and Jigme Senge.

To these, we must now add a new line with the arrival of Jigme Drakpa (1725–61). I have mentioned earlier that some members of Zhabdrung's inner circle were already aware of a Zhabdrung incarnate, who was born in Göyul across the border from Paro, by the time Tenzin Rabgay became the Desi in 1681. However, they could not openly proclaim this as Zhabdrung's death was still a secret. Neither could they bring the incarnate to Bhutan due to strong hostilities with Tibet at that time particularly around that area. Subsequently, the incarnate is said to have been taken to central Tibet and, from there, to China, where he died. Many years later another child was found in central Tibet and claimed to be his reincarnation and therefore of Zhabdrung. The child was born in a family of Drukpa patrons and was predicted by the 12th Karmapa Jangchub Dorji (1703–32). This child was Jigme Drakpa and his appearance as a contender to the golden throne complicated matters in Punakha. He was held in Tibet under state protection and only allowed to travel to Bhutan in 1746 although several attempts were made by Bhutanese leaders to bring him to Bhutan. Mipham Wangpo, during his time in Tibet, is said to have met this Jigme Drakpa but his attempts to bring the incarnate with him were not successful. The Tibetan government did not allow it, perhaps unwilling to part with their most prized political pawn. They might have also been genuinely worried about Jigme Drakpa's safety in Bhutan. Bhutanese efforts persisted and two crucial players in bringing this incarnate to Bhutan were the retired Je Khenpo Ngawang Thinley and his counterpart, Yungön Dorji, the incarnation of Drukpa Kunley on the Tibetan side. These two hierarchs enjoyed mutual respect and a warm relationship but Ngawang Pekar did not live to see the arrival of Jigme Drakpa, who was finally granted leave to go to Bhutan in 1746.

There were four incarnation lines with political significance when Sherab Wangchuk became Desi. Of the four, one was clearly traced to Tenzin Rabgay, whose incarnations Mipham Wangpo and Jigme Senge did not face any rival claimants. Thus, this line was theoretically without any problem. In later sources, they were called Tritrul (ཁྲི་སྤྲུལ་) or incarnates of throne-holders and sometime Gyalse Trulku (རྒྱལ་སྲས་སྤྲུལ་སྐུ་) or prince incarnates although this last title was shared by another line. Their direct link was to the Tango line of Tenzin Rabgay and they were subordinate to incarnates who claimed a direct connection to Zhabdrung or his son. The other three lines appear to have all initially traced their origin to Zhabdrung himself thereby leading to a great deal of tension and rivalry. The tension was particularly palpable between the two lines starting in Bhutan with Kuenga Gyaltshen and Chogley Namgyal, which consequently triggered the conflict that temporarily even divided Bhutan.

It is quite clear that Sherab Wangchuk and the prominent religious figures with whom he worked closely made a concerted effort to reconcile these two rival lines. The key players must have been the illustrious monk scholars, Shakya Rinchen and Tenzin Chögyal, whom I shall introduce a little later. They were the leading religious figures, both of them serving as Je Khenpos during Sherab Wangchuk's reign. They seem to have formally come up with the convenient and crafty institutional and theological arrangements to accommodate all incarnations. The theories and interpretations which they applied retrospectively may have existed earlier in informal oral versions but from their time, these became standard history. One clear solution to the rivalry was to distinguish the contenders as two separate lines. Shakya Rinchen's spiritual stature was particularly commanding to make such a distinction. Thus, it is in his writings that we first find Kuenga Gyaltshen being considered as the incarnation of Zhabdrung's son Jampal Dorji and not of Zhabdrung himself.

In Kuenga Gyaltshen's own accounts and Chogley Namgyal's description of him and his reincarnation, this is not clear and there are many hints that Kuenga Gyaltshan and his incarnation Jigme Norbu were perceived to be incarnations of Zhabdrung himself. The incarnate lamas from both lines were described vaguely as Chogtrul (མཆོག་སྤྲུལ་) or supreme incarnates and there is no indication of Kuenga Gyaltshen being an incarnation of Jampal Dorji in the historical records before Shakya Rinchen's biography of Kuenga Gyaltshen. It is this biography among the known sources, which clearly and for the first time identified Kuenga Gyaltshen as Jampal Dorji's incarnation although this source too contains earlier allusions about Kuenga Gyaltshen being an incarnation of Zhabdrung.[23] If Kuenga Gyaltshen was considered to be Zhabdrung as our textual evidences suggest, we can clearly see why the supporters of Kuenga Gyaltshen and those supporting Chogley Namgyal came into direct confrontation. They were both contenders to the same throne. The rivalry and subsequent conflict may not have occurred if Kuenga Gyaltshen was considered as the incarnation of Jampal Dorji right from the start. Sherab Wangchuk and his monastic prelates saw this strategy as a way forward to solve the contentions. For later histories, Kuenga Gyaltshen and successors would be consistently presented as incarnations of Jampal Dorji and addressed as Gyalse Trulku or prince incarnates.

However, with the newcomer Jigme Drakpa in the picture, Chogley Namgyal's line found another contender to Zhabdrung's throne. Although Jigme Drakpa had just arrived and Shakya Tenzin, the rebirth of Chogley Namgyal, kept only a low profile at that time and no immediate conflict arose between them, the scenario presented a potential for dispute in the future. There was no way to reconcile these two lines or other prospective lines originating in Zhabdrung other than to turn to a theological strategy, which was being used in Tibet by then to resolve problems concerning multiple incarnations. Thus, the tantric Buddhist framework of body, speech and mind emanations was applied to the Zhabdrung incarnations. Tenzin Chögyal recounts that when Zhabdrung was woken up from his meditative state, three rays of light representing his enlightened body, speech and mind went forth to Sikkim, Dagana and Tibet. As a result, the bodily incarnation was born as a prince of Sikkim. The speech incarnation was Chogley Namgyal born in Dagana and the mind incarnation Jigme Drakpa from Tibet.[24] We have no further information on this bodily incarnation from either Sikkimese or Bhutanese sources apart from what Tenzin Chögyal heard from a Bhutanese officer who served on the Bhutan–Sikkim border. However, what is clear is that there were multiple claimants and there was also some vague prophecy attributed to Drukdra Dorji justifying the multiplicity of Zhabdrung's incarnations. Sherab Wangchuk and his monk historians seem to have formalized this theological possibility and conveniently accommodated the two rival incarnates. Chogley Namgyal and his rebirth Shakya Tenzin were referred to as the Zhabdrung Sungrul (གསུང་སྤྲུལ་) or speech incarnation and Jigme Drakpa and his successors became the Zhabdrung Thugtrul (ཐུགས་སྤྲུལ་) or mind incarnation. Both lines became legitimate but the Thugtrul incarnates assumed a slightly superior position.

Sherab Wangchuk's endeavours to recognize and accommodate all incarnation lines were certainly not in vain. Although tension persisted among supporters of different incarnation lines, they did not erupt into political conflicts, as they did before. This must be largely due to the high stature and authority Sherab Wangchuk held even among religious circles.

In a unique move for cooperation, Drukdra Namgyal and Jigme Drakpa even jointly occupied the seat of the Gyaltshab after 1746 and were both officially recorded as the 6th holders of the golden throne. However, in practice, they did not hold the office simultaneously for any significant time with both of them going into long retreats in turn. The retreats certainly helped suppress the tension temporarily but before long strains began to appear in their relationship. Jigme Drakpa, as a latecomer and foreigner, felt sidelined and mistreated by some partisan officials. Consequently, he moved out of the two seats of the Punakha and Thimphu *dzong*s and spent time in Semtokha and Wangditse without the privileges of the post until he went to Bumthang, where he is said to have been poisoned to death in 1761. Mysteriously, Drukdra Namgyal, the other head of state also died the following year. Thus, Jigme Senge, the incarnation of Mipham Wangpo, was installed as the 7th holder of the golden throne in 1763. Meanwhile, Shakya Tenzin, the incarnation of Chogley Namgyal, remained without any key position despite his seniority and the general recognition of him as the speech incarnation of Zhabdrung. His association with the Kabji faction during the civil war seems to have affected his popularity in the court although he did gain widespread respect toward the end of his life. He traversed the country on pilgrimage, performed numerous religious services and founded the Sa-ngag Chökhor monastery in Paro before his death in 1780.

Sherab Wangchuk was successful not only in his project of bringing the leading hierarchs together. He also brought the whole country together through his grand festivities and the acts of mass distributions of wealth known as *mangyed* (མང་འགྱེད་). He is said to have carried out some eight such distributions. The first occasion when he made a mass distribution of wealth was to celebrate the conclusion of some large religious projects. His biography contains a detailed account of the offering made to religious and secular members. Offerings were first made to the shrines containing Zhabdrung's remains and that of his son, Jampal Dorji, followed by Drukdra Namgyal, the throne-holder, Jigme Drakpa, the mind incarnation and Jigme Senge, the incarnation of Mipham Wangpo. They were followed by the Je Khenpo Shakya Rinchen, Shakya Tenzin, the speech incarnation and retired Desi Paljor of Bönbji. All these figures received a long list of items and hundreds of silver coins. There were some 661 monks in the state monastery and 1149 civil functionaries under nine ministerial officials, who received offerings taking the total value of gifts to 14546 silver coins.

A nationwide distribution of coins was also carried out at this time to coincide with the enthronement of Jigme Drakpa. Coins or goods were distributed to some 140 subdistrict polities known as *drungwog* (དྲུང་འོག་) in 1747, most of which are preserved today in the form of administrative blocks or *gewog* (དགེ་འོག་). Ardussi and Karma Ura have calculated that there were about 27,223 tax-paying households. They estimated Bhutan's population to be around 2,61,340 including about twenty per cent who may have fallen outside the tax payer's class. This is not far from the 3,12,500 which the Chinese Amban in Lhasa gave for Bhutan in 1796. Sherab Wangchuk distributed coins in the excess of 47,000 to all tax-paying households of Bhutan.[25] He repeated this nationwide distribution about seven times: in 1753 to celebrate the completion of large appliqué hanging of Padmasambhava in Punakha and in 1756 to celebrate the completing of gilt cupola of Punakha, in 1760 to celebrate the renovation and extension of Tashichödzong, in 1761 on the sad occasion of Jigme Drakpa's demise, in 1763 to celebrate Jigme Senge's enthronement as the Gyaltshab, again in 1763 to gild statues in temples across the country and in 1765 to simply empty his remaining coffers. The last two were carried out after he had already resigned from the post of the Desi in 1763.

Sherab Wangchuk was a ruler with an unusual sense of giving in the whole of Bhutanese history. In addition to the above distributions, he also sent donations and offerings to temple establishments of which there were about 250 in his days. He also distributed medicinal herbs and substances to the physicians across the country and made two separate mass distributions to the people of Thimphu and Punakha. The monastics and the state functionaries, of course, received offerings on many other occasions as was the custom. He was a great patron of religious projects, including artistic creations and ritual chanting. The large appliqué of Padmasambhava and the 1000 Buddha wall hangings in Punakha, the large silver statue of Zhabdrung in Thimphu, the large copper statue of the Buddha and eight Bodhisattvas, Songtsen Gampo and his retinue and the illuminated *kanjur* manuscripts are some examples. He believed in creating spiritual power in temples and thus built many gilded cupolas on many *dzongs* and temples and filled them with sacred and precious objects. He re-energized the *gönkhang* (མགོན་ཁང་) or chapels of protecting deities by supplying them with symbols of power including guns, some of which were ironically received as gifts from the Dalai Lama in Tibet.

His two major projects were the extension of Tashichödzong and the construction of the gilded cupola on the Punakha *dzong*. The last one alone costs the state coffers 142,886 silver coins. He also built the Phajoding temple, where Shakya Rinchen retired, and Kuensel Phodrang in Thimphu and Baling Rinchen Khangzang in Punakha where he retired and spent his summer and winter respectively. Sherab Wangchuk used what John Ardussi calls his 'temple diplomacy' to promote close ties with the 7th Dalai Lama in Tibet, who shared his passion for temple renovation and artistic creations. One area of Tibet–Bhutan cooperation was the renovation of the Ralung monastery in Tibet. The Tibetan government contributed free labour and Sherab Wangchuk provided funding to complete the project which had started some years earlier. The leading Drukpa hierarch in Tibet acknowledged Sherab Wangchuk's staunch support by including his portrait among the wall paintings of Ralung. Thus, Sherab Wangchuk's diplomacy also effectively closed the rift between the Northern and Southern Drukpa schools. Meanwhile, Sherab Wangchuk received large grants from the 7th Dalai Lama to renovate the ancient temples in Bhutan. The Tibetan leader, who had assumed full power by 1751, ran a programme to renovate and develop all 108 temples believed to have been built by the Tibetan Emperor Songtsen Gampo.

With their truly open and enlightened outlook and shared interests in religious works, the 7th Dalai Lama and Sherab Wangchuk enjoyed a very close relationship showing mutual appreciation and exchanging of expensive gifts. In a letter of praise written to Sherab Wangchuk, the Dalai Lama called him 'the wish-fulfilling tree blooming in the southern grove'. Sherab Wangchuk's diplomacy with Tibet was not limited to the Dalai Lama. When the Tibetan court was torn apart with internal conflict among Pholhaney's sons, Sherab Wangchuk sent a mission to mediate between them with gifts to all major Tibetan figures. The mission was led by the Dagana *pönlop*, who was accompanied by 300 soldiers. Although the Bhutanese intervention did not yield any result and the conflict ended in bloodshed, it was a noble initiative out of genuine concern and accrued significant political mileage for Bhutan as an important player in the region.

A similar mission with presents was also sent to Ladakh in 1751 led by Zhidar when the Ladakhi royal court was gripped with an internal dispute. Sherab Wangchuk's diplomatic rapproachement was as vigorous towards the south as to the north. Some of his nationwide distributions also covered citizens of the north Assam and Bengal plains. He also sent large gifts to the Prince of Cooch Behar and exchanged presents with the King of Assam. Thus, under Sherab Wangchuk, Bhutan assumed an unprecedented position of regional importance. His astute assertion of political significance and friendly overtures were particularly important and timely because the political landscape in the region was beginning to change drastically with the increased Manchu control of Tibet, the Gorkha takeover of Nepal and the growing British presence in India. Sherab Wangchuk's assertion of Bhutanese nationhood and its significance was underscored by the publication of Bhutan's first history by Tenzin Chögyal completed in 1759 and widely distributed in Bhutan and Tibet. For generations to come, this would serve as the official account of the first hundred years of Bhutan's existence. Other social achievements during Sherab Wangchuk's rule included his ban on state confiscation of private property from families without children and on the *sati* practice among the lowland Hindu people on whom Bhutan exercised some control. These were earlier enforced by the 8th Desi Druk Rabgay but had fallen into a lapse. His changes in monastic rules allowed monks over sixty years old to be free from daily monastic chores and over seventy to enjoy the privileges of a senior civil functionary.

Sherab Wangchuk's rule was certainly the highlight of medieval Bhutan, a heyday of cultural and literary creations and a spell of peace and prosperity amid the chapter of history marred with foreign invasions and civil strife. It was, as contemporaries described and posterity remembered, a just and enlightened rule. To crown it all, his glorious reign had a graceful end. After twenty years in power, Sherab Wangchuk voluntarily stepped down from the post of the Desi to pursue a life of religion in the fashion of noble Buddhist rulers. He turned to serious Buddhist practice under the guidance of Tenzin Chögyal and emptied his personal treasury with further spates of large-scale giving. This, he continued until his death in 1767 at the age of seventy-one.

Sherab Wangchuk's reign also saw the rise of a number of important Bhutanese religious and literary figures, who must have had an immense influence on his political outlook and the general atmosphere in the country. Among them, Shakya Rinchen (1710−59) and Tenzin Chögyal (1701−66/67) stand out as the leading luminaries of this period for both their spiritual stature and literary legacies. Shakya Rinchen was from the district of Shar and trained mainly under the famous master Ngawang Gyaltshen. He was a very bright student and committed practitioner who excelled in his religious training. When he was twenty-seven, he had a mystical experience, purportedly of his previous rebirths, which inspired him to embark on a journey to Tibet with a few friends. This, he did just after the time Desi Mipham Wangpo had escaped to Tibet, when the border was heavily patrolled to stop political fugitives leaving the country. Shakya Rinchen and his mates were wrongly caught and incarcerated first in Lingshi and then in Chapcha. He was only released at the request of the state monastery but some years later, he managed to visit Lhasa officially with Yungön Dorji. Shakya Rinchen was selected to be the 9th Je Khenpo in 1744 at an unusually young age of thirty-five. In 1755, he stepped down to retire in his new monastery of Phajoding.

His successor, the 10th Je Khenpo Tenzin Chögyal was from Nenying Yulsar in Shar district. Tenzin Chögyal entered the state monastery at twelve and received his training from many teachers including Gangteng Trulku Tenzin Lekpai Dondup. As a young monk, he was devoted to Padmasambhava and would diligently chant the *vajraguru* mantra earning him the nickname Bazaguru. Overcome by an urge to spend his life in such prayer, young Tenzin Chögyal once ran away from the monastery. Looking back at punakha *dzong*, he made three prostrations wondering if he would ever see it again in his life. But the following day, monastic pursuers apprehended him and he was brought back. He joked that 'it took him only a night to see the dzong which he thought he may not see again in his whole life.' Fearing punishment, he prayed to Padmasambhava but 'even Padmasambhava could not save him from the punishment' as he amusingly noted later.[26] He was stripped naked, hung from a beam with ropes around his wrist in front of the congregation and lashed with willow whips until his body was covered with wounds and blood. Whether or not this gave the impetus, Tenzin Chögyal became well known for his learning, which earned him yet another epithet, this time the prestigious title, *paṇchen* (པཎ་ཆེན་) or great scholar. One of his remarkable achievements as the Je Khenpo was his establishment of the monastery in Tongsa, the first state monastic community in the area which was then considered eastern Bhutan. He served as the 10th Je Khenpo from 1755 to 1762 and retired due to poor health.

Like Ngawang Gyaltshen before them, Shakya Rinchen and Tenzin Chögyal were no doubt religious figures of sublime spiritual stature. What we may specifically note here is the crucial role they played in the formation and formulation of Bhutan's historical narratives and national identity. In addition to their religious works, Shakya Rinchen wrote numerous biographical accounts and Tenzin Chögyal authored the first history of the Bhutanese state in addition to a few biographies. There were also many other religious and historical authors during this period but Shakya Rinchen and Tenzin Chögyal stand out for their widespread influence. Their writings have largely shaped the Bhutanese historical consciousness and continue to do so in our own times. It is in their writings that we find the first wave of literary and intellectual expression and formulation of a distinct Bhutanese religious and national discourse and identity. The religious and cultural exuberance during twenty years of Sherab Wangchuk's rule was also largely due to their work and inspiration.

Sherab Wangchuk was succeeded by Druk Phuntsho, a figure from upper Thimphu, as the 14th Desi in 1763. Druk Phuntsho was a man of reputed intelligence and served as the *chila* of Tongsa, *dzongpön* of Thimphu and *pönlop* of Paro consecutively before becoming the Desi. While at Tongsa, he was largely responsible for the installation of the gilded cupola of the *dzong* and as *dzongpön* of Thimphu, he supervised the extension of the *dzong* under Sherab Wangchuk's leadership. He received full ordination as a monk from Tenzin Chögyal when he was the *pönlop* of Paro and was soon appointed as the Desi following Sherab Wangchuk's resignation. However, he did not remain long on the Desi's throne as he succumbed to an unknown illness in 1765. The ministers and the state monks requested Sherab Wangchuk to take the throne again but he declined, giving his age as a reason but throughout these years Sherab Wangchuk remained the most influential person in Bhutan. It appears that the Desi appointees were mainly his choice and the incarnate hierarchs also danced to his tunes and had no real power besides taking up religious roles in state ceremonies and monastic gatherings.

After Druk Phuntsho's death, Druk Tenzin, a figure from lower Thimphu, was appointed as the 15th Desi in 1765. Like the reign of his immediate predecessor, his reign was short and without great significance. He completed the stūpa project which Druk Phuntsho started and celebrated the completion with a nationwide distribution of gifts. Another important project of his reign was the production of the finest *kanjur* manscript in Bhutan based on an exemplar from Derge in eastern Tibet. He completed this and a few statues in 1767 and passed away in 1768. He was succeeded by the forceful ruler Zhidar or Sonam Lhendup, another figure from the Wang region.

The Rise of Southward Relations and Internal Strife

AFTER THE FIRST FEW DECADES of rule by the inner circle of Zhabdrung, it appears that regionalism and familial connections came to play an increasingly important role in Bhutan's politics. First, power was in the hands of Kabji men, the 5th and 6th and probably even the 7th Desi being from Kabji. Then, power was wrested by 8th Desi and his nephew the 9th Desi from Wang. This was followed by the reign of the 10th Desi and his uncle, the 11th Desi from Bönbji. After Bönbji, the power reverted to rulers from Wang with five consecutive rulers from this area.

Zhidar and Bhutan's affairs with Cooch Behar

Zhidar was an orphan and as a child he lived in abject poverty, even sleeping in the cowshed next to a bull to keep himself warm in winter. He started his career as a servant of the border patrol officer in Tsirang, whom he subsequently succeeded. When Mipham Wangpo escaped to Tibet, Zhidar was one of the servants among the escape party. This early Tibetan connection would come handy in the last stage of his life. From his humble beginnings, he gradually rose to be the *pönlop* of Tongsa, where he invited Tenzin Chögyal and started the monastic community. Monk tax was perhaps imposed for the first time in the Mangde and Bumthang valleys to recruit monks for the new community. On this occasion, Zhidar himself received the ordination of a novice and the name Sonam Lhendup. He then served as the *dzongpön* of Wangdiphodrang, when he led the mission under Sherab Wangchuk's orders to Ladakh in order to mediate between the king and a dissident minister who is said to have invited the Kashmiri force to dislodge the king. We have no information about the outcome of the mission but Zhidar was appointed as the 16th Desi in 1768 upon the death of Druk Tenzin. His candidacy for the post of the Desi must have been supported by his former master Sherab Wangchuk, who also passed away in 1768 after Zhidar was installed as the Desi.

Zhidar alias Sonam Lhendup undertook a number of cultural projects in the early part of his rule. These include the production of a set of wall hangings of Zhabdrung's spiritual lineage depicting his former lives, cast images of 1000 Buddhas and of eight manifestations of Padmasambhava, gold and silver reliquary stūpas and a set of illuminated *kanjur* manuscripts. He also built the Zamling Gatshel temple on the spot where Vanaratna meditated in the fifteenth century. In 1772, Tashichödzong was devasted by fire and he earnestly undertook its swift reconstruction in a new location in the rice fields near the river, which he acquired from local farmers. A contemporary witness marvels that 'like a magical feat, an outstanding monastic edifice with all interior relics and excellent facilities for the monastic community and state treasury was completed in just over a year and followed by celebrations worthy of pleasing men and gods'.[1] But to accomplish this feat, he is also said to have imposed intensive labour demands on the populace thereby earning himself much dislike and notoriety as a despotic ruler. He named the new *dzong* after himself as Sonamphodrang but the name did not gain currency. The old name Tashichödzong was used for the new *dzong* and when the ruins of old *dzong* on the hill were renovated later, it became known as Dechenphodrang. Zhidar's authoritarian attitude extended even to the non-human denizens. He sacked the existent protecting deity of Tashichödzong, Düdrakpa, for failing to guard the dzong from fire and appointed Dorji Draktsan as the new protector. He also openly issued edicts to the protecting deities and spirits in the country commanding them to bring timely rain or carry out such other superhuman duties.

The first cracks in his highhanded rule, however, appeared when he showed his displeasure of Jigme Sengay, the incarnation of Mipham Wangpo and the head of the state since 1763. The political division through religious favouritism along incarnation lines, which Sherab Wangchuk so dextrously suppressed, began to surface again. Zhidar had little respect for Jigme Sengay and even took the reins of religious affairs in his own hands. When the senior religious members of clergy complained, he reproached and punished them by sending them to remote postings. In contrast, Zhidar openly supported Chökyi Gyaltshen (1762–88), the rebirth of Jigme Drakpa, due to their earlier connection. Zhidar was the *dzongpön* of Wangdiphodrang when

Jigme Drakpa passed through the place in 1761 upset by the mistreatment he received from some state officials. Zhidar requested Jigme Drakpa to use Wangdiphodrang as his base in winter and Khothangkha as his base in summer, and pledged to provide all necessary resources. Jigme Drakpa declined the offer but predicted that Zhidar would become the Desi and also get an opportunity to support him in his next life. Soon after this, Jigme Drakpa died from poisoning and his reincarnation Chökyi Gyaltshen was found in Central Tibet. Fully aware of the prediction, Zhidar promptly brought the child to Bhutan and installed him on the throne. Unlike Sherab Wangchuk, Zhidar openly adopted a partisan approach to the issue of multiple incarnations. His disapproval of Jigme Sengay and the resentment he had provoked by forcing the construction of Tashichödzong in one year would eventually contribute to his downfall but the immediate cause of his fall lay in the military clashes with the new enemy to the south.

We have already seen the vigorous development of Bhutanese influence on the politics of Cooch Behar toward the end of the seventeenth century. By 1768, when Zhidar became the Desi, Cooch Behar was virtually ruled by the Desi through a frontier official known as Pagsam *drungpa* (དཔག་བསམ་དྲུང་པ་) or chief of Pasakha, later known to the British as Buxa Subah. Let me here briefly recount the events leading to Bhutanese control of Cooch Behar. Rūp Nārāyaṇ (r.1793−14), who visited Punakha and whom we dicussed earlier, ruled Cooch Behar until 1714 under Mughal supremacy. During his reign, Bhutan controlled some parts of the northern plains but did not exercise much control of Cooch Behar proper. This changed during the long reign of his son Upendra Nārāyaṇ (r.1714−63). Upendra failed to produce a male heir on time and thus groomed Dina Nārāyaṇ, his second cousin and son of his Dewan Deo or finance minister, as a potential successor. He continued to hope for a son, which he eventually fathered late in his life. Meanwhile, his prospective heir demanded a written promise of succession before he produced a male child. This he declined to give and the angry Dina Nārāyaṇ colluded with the Mughal military officer at Rangpur to bring in Mughal forces to occupy Cooch Behar in return for making him a puppet ruler under Mughal supremacy. In the face of the Mughal invasion, Upendra turned to his northern neighbour for military support. Although Bhutanese histories do not mention this, Bhutanese troops were sent and the joint forces of Cooch Behar and Bhutan successfully repelled the Mughal forces and eliminated Dina Nārāyaṇ. The trouble for Upendra, however, was only beginning as the Bhutanese soldiers stayed and increasingly took control of his state. By then much of northern plains adjacent to Bhutan were fully under Bhutanese control governed by the Pagsam *drungpa* with an annual tribute extracted each year in Chichakotta. The Dewan Deo was responsible for the rovision of requisites for the Bhutanese officers in Cooch Behar.

The next king Devendra Nārāyaṇ (r.1764–65) was barely four years when his father Upendra Nārāyaṇ died in 1763. The queen installed the young prince on the throne and immolated herself on the pyre of her husband's cremation in order to observe the religious rite of *sati*. With only a nominal king, the Bhutanese became *de facto* rulers and practically all decisions were taken by the Pagsam *drungpa* in consultation with the Desi. The Pagsam *drungpa* at this time was probably Samten, one of the patrons of Shakya Tenzin.[2] The political situation for Cooch Behar got even worse when the infant king, after over a year on the throne, was beheaded in 1765 by a Brahmin while playing with his friends. The murderer was apprehended and killed and the mastermind of the plot, a court priest Ramananda Goswari, was brought to Punakha and put to death. The Nazir Dev was found to be involved in the plot and a fight broke out between the Nazir Dev and Dewan Deo, the two leading ministers, but a settlement was reached and the throne was passed to Dewan Deo's son, the late king's cousin Dhairjendra Nārāyaṇ (1765–70). He appointed his trusted brother Ram Nārāyaṇ to the post of Dewan Deo, married six queens and produced two heirs. Nevertheless, peace was not to prevail.

Some time around 1770, Bhutan invaded Vijayapur, the capital of the Limbu kingdom in the eastern part of modern Nepal and western part of Sikkim and Bihar. The Bhutanese invasion, according to Bhutanese sources, took place in order to punish the Limbuwan king, who failed to pay the annual tribute. The King of Cooch Behar was asked to send his army to support the Bhutanese forces, which he did under the commandership of Dewan Deo Ram Nārāyaṇ. We do not have any detail about the invasion and the concurrent internal conflict in Vijayapur but in the turmoil that ensued, the Limbuwan King Kāmadatta Sena was killed and his prime minister Buddhikarṇa Rayaṇ grabbed power and became king. The Bhutanese and Cooch Behari troops returned home but this incursion led to two significant outcomes for Bhutan.

First, the dead Limbu King Kāmadatta was a cousin of the rising Gorkha King Pṛthivī Nārāyaṇ, who had by then taken over the Kathmandu valley and was vigorously expanding his domain. Kāmadatta's death and replacement by Buddhikarṇa Raya provoked the Gorkha king, who sent his troops eastward to incorporate Limbuwan into his Gorkha kingdom. Pṛthivī Nārāyaṇ, who was on friendly terms with Desi Zhidar of Bhutan, sent a message to the Desi asking him not to send any military support to the new Limbu king. Bhutan may have been obliged to provide military protection for Vijayapur as this country was considered a tributary annex of Bhutan. In exchange for relinquishing Vijayapur and in lieu of tributes collected from there, Pṛthvī Nārāyaṇ offered Bhutan the temple establishments at Swayambhūnāth and two other places. The Lumbi kingdom was subsequently invaded by Pṛthvī Nārāyaṇ and acceded to his new kingdom of Nepal and Bhutan obtained the custodial right of the temples in Nepal, which continued even in the twentieth century.

The second outcome was far more serious and damaging for Bhutan. When the Dewan Deo returned from Vijayapur with booty, he delivered only some to King Dhairjendra and kept most of it for himself. This annoyed the king, who was already uncomfortable with the Dewan's growing influence. In addition, some court officers maliciously instigated the king against the Dewan Deo, resulting in his dismissal from the court and confiscation of properties by the king. The Dewan Deo turned to his Bhutanese allies for support and forced his way back to the court. But he was eventually killed by his brother, the king, in 1769 while he was waiting on the king unarmed. In addition to such court intrigues, a severe famine stuck the region of Bengal in 1770 killing one-third of the population but we do not know how much harm was done to Cooch Behar. The news of the assassination of the Dewan Deo aroused serious concerns in Bhutan about the stability of Cooch Behar. On the occasion of the annual feast which was organized for the Bhutanese and Cooch Behari officials, the Bhutanese invited King Dhairjendra to the party. Fearing reprisal, the king initially declined but when the Bhutanese threatened him with a total boycott of the annual feast, he was forced to attend. At the feast, the Bhutanese forces arrested King Dhairjendra and his new Dewan Deo and took them captive to Punakha. He was the second King of Cooch Behar to set foot in central Bhutan, the first being his grandfather Rūp Nārāyaṇ. The Bhutanese appointed his brother Rajendra Nārāyaṇ (r.1770–72) as the new puppet ruler and the Pagsam *drungpa* exercised even greater control on the state and the royal household. He kept the new king and queen mother on a meagre allowance and took possession of the royal regalia, including the sceptre and umbrella.

The tragedies to fall on Cooch Behar's royal house were far from over. Rajendra died in 1772, five days after his own wedding. The successive tragedies brought together the Cooch Behari officials for a short period to revolt against the Pagsam *drungpa*. Through a sudden attack on the Bhutanese guards, they regained possession of the royal insignias, and Dhairjendra's son Dharenda Nārāyaṇ (r. 1772–75), who was earlier kept in hiding, was now crowned king. New coins were quickly minted, as was the custom, to announce his reign. The Bhutanese were fully dislodged and the Pagsam *drungpa* fled to the hills. Their victory, however, was short-lived. When the Pagsam *drungpa* returned with some 4000 fresh troops, a full war broke out between Bhutan and Cooch Behar. The united forces of Cooch Behar succeeded in resisting the Bhutanese until more troops arrived from Bhutan. In the fighting which ensued, the Cooch Behar troops stood no chance and Nazir Deo and other leaders fled with the young king. The Cooch Behar historian Jadunath Ghose later described the Bhutanese forces in the following words:

> The soldiers were able-bodied men, and they were all mad for battle. Some of them wore iron-helmets, called by them *luyā*s. Over their clothes of many colours they also wore chain armour; and each man had two Bhutia knives suspended from his waist. In their hands they carried bows and arrows. Some of them also had muskets, but they were not skilled in the use of this weapon. They could fight well, when at a distance, with bows and arrows. At close quarters, they could fight incomparably with their knives. No nation could equal them in the use of short weapons. Besides this, each man held in his hand a wooden spike six cubit long, pointed at one end. These spikes were, at night, planted round the place of encampment, and served as a defence. In the morning, on breaking ground, each man carried away his own spike.[3]

The Bhutanese once again occupied the capital, built many forts and installed Bijendra Nārāyaṇ (r.1772), the son of the late Dewan Deo Ram Nārāyaṇ as the new king. To keep close watch, they made the new puppet king rule the country from a Bhutanese fort in the foothills but he too died soon after arriving in this new place allegedly due to the change in climate. Meanwhile, the Nazir Deo who escaped with Dharendra Nārāyaṇ, turned to the British East India Company (EIC) for military support. The EIC had by then replaced the Mughal power in Bengal.

The opportunistic EIC

Set up originally in 1600 as a company to trade with the East Indies using the sea route around Africa, the EIC arrived in the mainland of India a few years after that. In 1615, the company obtained the Mughal imperial writ to trade with the Indian subcontinent, which became its main base and throughout the seventeenth century set up fortified trading posts known as factories in several places, including Bombay, Madras and Calcutta. The EIC was well armed to protect the company's interests, its merchants and local patrons against European and local rivals and the EIC influence rose as the Mughal power declined. The victory of the EIC forces under Robert Clive in June 1757 over the Nawāb of Bengal was a defining point when the EIC wrested direct control over Bengal. This was reinforced by the victory over the Mughal emperor and the Nawāb of Oudh at Buxar in 1764, after which the EIC obtained the right to collect tax and became the *de facto* ruler of much of India.

The EIC was at the height of its relentless expansion across India when the unsolicited invitation for military intervention came from Cooch Behar. At the head of the EIC in Calcutta at that time was the remarkable figure, Warren Hastings, described by many as the greatest Governor-General of India. Even before the appeal from Cooch Behar arrived, Hastings had anticipated the need to pay more attention northward as the Bhutanese invaders and the gangs of *sannyasin*s ravaged territories already under British control. The Bhutanese invaders were most probably frontier strongmen and officials who abused their power during the periods of a weak central authority. The *sannyasin*s, contrary to what the term originally designated, were militant bodies who had quasi-religious affiliations and wandered freely committing rampant raids. They used the power vacuum left by the crumbling Mughal rule and the poorly regulated border regions to carry out their dacoity. The company managed to suppress them in some central areas but their movement remained unabated along the frontiers. For all these reasons, Hastings readily agreed to send the British troops to Cooch Behar when the appeal for military support reached him through Charles Purling, the collector at Rangpur. A treaty was signed between King Dharendra Nārāyan of Cooch Behar and Warren Hastings on 5 April 1773 in which the king agreed to pay all the military expenses and half of Cooch Behar's annual revenue, the other half to be kept only if Cooch Behar remained loyal to the company.

This was a heavy price to pay for the King of Cooch Behar but even as the details of the treaty was being discussed, the British troops arrived under Captain Jones and started their assault on the resistance put up by a combination of the Bhutanese forces, some local resisters including Darpa Dev, the Raikat of Baikunthapur who was aligned with the Bhutanese, and some *sannyasin*s. The Bhutanese troops were pushed out of Cooch Behar town but victory proved far more difficult than was expected and company troops incurred severe losses. Captain Jones was himself wounded and later succumbed to malaria in the course of the conflict. Meanwhile in Thimphu, the Desi launched a vigorous campaign to fight the new enemy by conscripting men for the army and making the monks conduct rituals of repulsion as they did in the past during wars against Tibet. One of the religious hierarchs actively engaged in performing such rituals was Shakya Tenzin, the speech incarnation of Zhabdrung, who was at that time the lama of Taktshang. He conducted tantric rituals of repulsion at Taktshang. Unlike the wars with Tibet, this one did not actually take place in Bhutan proper. Still, the disturbances were palpable and the atmosphere was rife with the fear of war that Ngawang Chökyi Gyatsho who lived in Thimphu reports: 'Due to the intense war in India, there was no peace in this southern land [Bhutan] under even a single tree.'[4]

We may recollect that Zhidar had already become quite unpopular for his ill treatment of the reigning incarnate hierarch Jigme Sengay and for his harsh imposition of labour to complete Tashichödzong in one year. To these, we may add Zhidar's self-serving overtures toward the north. He was very active in bringing Chökyi Gyaltshen (1762–88), the Tibetan reincarnate of Jigme Drakpa, to Bhutan partly to legitimize and stabilize his own position. He also forged a strong but an unequal relationship with the 6th Panchen Lama in Tashilhunpo and the regent in Lhasa. His submissive relation to Tibet in order to reinforce his own political standing in Bhutan was scorned by most Bhutanese, for whom the numerous wars with Tibet and concomitant enmity were still lingering in their memory. Furthermore, Zhidar is said to have sought a seal from the Chinese emperor to enhance his authority. For patriotic Bhutanese, this amounted to an act of high treachery against the sovereignty of the Bhutanese state which he was supposed to protect. Thus, his campaign for war in the south was certainly not appreciated by many in the court and monastic circles.

When Zhidar approached Kuenga Rinchen, the master of dialectical studies (མཚན་ཉིད་སློབ་དཔོན་), for his advice and support, the latter took the opportunity to remove Zhidar from power with lip service. Kuenga Rinchen and Zhidar were previously very good friends, the former aspiring to be the Je Khenpo and the latter to be the Desi. They were said to have even pledged to each other that if Kuenga Rinchen became Je Khenpo first, he would support Zhidar to attain the post of the Desi and if Zhidar became the Desi first, he would support Kuenga Rinchen to become the Je Khenpo. However,

Zhidar became the Desi and Kuenga Rinchen did not see any support from his friend.[5] Embittered by this, Kuenga Rinchen treacherously persuaded Zhidar to lead the army himself, adding that there was no one more able. Zhidar was quite oblivious to the fact that his old friend was now on the side of Jigme Sengay and the clergy and conniving towards his downfall. They decided that it was best to consult the protecting deities on this through a divination. The form of divination chosen was a traditional lucky dip in which the supplicant picked one of the two tiny paper rolls or balls of dough which contain the answers: one saying 'good' and the other 'bad'. Zhidar was made to pick one for obtaining a divine answer to the grave question of whether it was 'good' or 'bad' for him to lead the troops. The answer was an unequivocal 'good' and Zhidar was now obliged to lead the troops. What Zhidar did not know was that the divination was a ruse to trick him. The monks had put 'good' in both options.

With divine instruction to lead the troops, Zhidar raised a large army and descended to the plains, leaving the conniver Kuenga Rinchen as the acting Desi. He is said to have also solicited military help from Nepal, Assam and Tibet but we do not know how much came, if at all.[6] Majamdar tells us that Darpa Dev and his troop of *sannyasin*s were fighting side by side against the British.[7] The Cooch Behari sources state that there were some 4000 Bhutanese men in the first detachment and some 17,500 in the second one under a Zimpön (གཟིམ་དཔོན་) or chamberlain but do not mention Zhidar's own engagement at the battlefront. It is clear that most young men were recruited through a nationwide programme of conscription if we were to extrapolate from the words of Ngawang Chökyi Gyatsho, who saw the events unfold. 'Through strong hatred and arrogance born from discontentment,' the hierarch lamented, talking about Zhidar, 'he led all beloved sons of Bhutan as his troops to make a sacrifice of human flesh to the Indian foxes, wolves, dogs and vultures.'[8] A human sacrifice it was in one sense as Bhutanese soldiers fell in hundreds to superior British firepower and the British under Purling advanced to occupy all the plains. Some 600 Bhutanese soldiers were killed in the first encounter on 22 December 1772 alone when the British ousted them from the fort of Cooch Behar.[9] The British also suffered serious casualties with a large number of sepoys killed and the death of at least three captains. Forty British sepoys were killed on 11 March 1773 just by the boulders the Bhutanese sent rolling down the hill on the British troops.

The Bhutanese fought gallantly and left a remarkable impression of their military courage and skills on the British. The bravery of their commander, one *zimpön*, probably Ngawang Tenzin from Paro,[10] was specifically noted by a Cooch Behari source. Ngawang Tenzin, who was a devotee of Shakya Tenzin, had already distributed most of his wealth and possessions for various religious works. He even set aside funds for his funerary rites before he set off to the war. He was ready to die and die he did in the fearless way of a hero. According to this source, he led an army 'from the northern portion of Bootan, who were half as tall again as ordinary men, and were of very fair complexion, and spoke a dialect unintelligible to the southern Bhutias [Bhutanese]'. Unwilling to submit even at the final point of defeat and cornered in a fort by hundreds of sepoys armed with guns, he and a few of his men pounced on the sepoys with the last dash of valour. Our source narrates:

The sepoys using the bayonet succeeded now and again in slaying an enemy; but the Bhutias fired their muskets with their left hands, and attacked the sepoys with the small swords which they held in their right . . . Jimpé [*zimpön*] received twenty wounds in various parts of his body, and even after he had fallen to the ground, he kept waving his sword in the air. An English officer went up and offered to help him by procuring surgical aid, but all that Jimpé asked for, was some spirits to drink. The officer at once gave him some brandy, and Jimpé drank it and expired.[11]

The English, our source says, measured the height and size of this gigantic man for there had never been seen such powerful man before. He may have been one of the *nyagö* (གཉའ་གོང་) or strongmen, who were popular in traditional Bhutan. Ngawang Tenzin, whether or not he can be identified with this warrior, certainly died during the war and his funerary rites were carried out by his guru Shakya Tenzin,[12] who, like many other lamas at that time, was occupied by the funerary prayers and rituals for the men lost in war.

The loss of many lives in the war against the British was not the only tragedy to befall Bhutan by the end of 1773. This war was barely over when internal conflict erupted in Bhutan. The deprivations of war in the south must have exacerbated the seething tension between Zhidar's faction and his opponents. The reigning hierarch Jigme Sengay officially removed Zhidar from the Desi's office and appointed Kuenga Rinchen as the 17th Desi. Following this, those who opposed Zhidar openly attacked the supporters of Zhidar and some of his family members barely escaped death by taking refuge in the residence of Je Khenpo Yontan Thaye. When the war in the south was finally over, the new government blamed Zhidar for the losses and banned him from returning to the capital. All checkpoints were ordered to arrest or shoot him if he tried to return. Zhidar, however, managed to sneak into Paro and take refuge with the Neten (གནས་བརྟན་) or monastic elder of the Paro *dzong* but before long, his opponents found out and came for him. The biographer of contemporary hierarch, Shakya Tenzin, who lived in Paro reports that 'members of Zhidar's faction were yoked to misery, Paro dzong surrounded by the armed forces and the noise of firearms and battle reverberated day and night'.[13]

Zhidar escaped from Paro and, according to most Bhutanese sources,[14] was killed in 1773. However, this, we know from the 6th Panchen Lama's biography, was not the case. Zhidar made his way to Tashilhunpo in Tibet to seek refuge in the court of the 6th Panchen Lama Palden Yeshe (1738–80), who was at that time the most powerful figure in Tibet, the 8th Dalai Lama being in his minority. Zhidar had a good relationship with the 6th Panchen Lama as we have seen above. Earlier in 1772, as the Desi, he even sent a mission to the Panchen Lama to offer him New Year greetings. Now, Zhidar arrived as a refugee and the Panchen Lama took care of him, providing him requisites and advices. Zhidar must have arrived in Tashilhunpo some time at the beginning of 1774, by which time, the Panchen Lama was fully aware of the Anglo-Bhutanese conflict. The envoys from the new Gorkha king of Nepal, who visited him in the middle of 1773, already briefed him about the war and requested him to mediate. Then, there were the Tibetan monk, Pema and the Indian priest, Gosain Pūran Giri, who travelled between India and Tibet carrying news and messages for the Panchen Lama. However, it was probably only after Zhidar's arrival and at his request that the Panchen Lama decided to write an official letter of mediation to Warren Hastings in very poetic and hyperbolic language typical of the Tibetan art of letter writing. In the letter, he wrote after the customary praises:

> I have been repeatedly informed that you have been engaged in hostilities against the Deb Jadhur [Desi Zhidar], to which, it is said, the Deb's own criminal conduct, in conducting ravages and other outrages on your frontiers, has given rise. As he is of a rude and ignorant race (past times are not destitute of instances of the like misconduct, which his own avarice tempted him to commit), it is not unlikely that he has now renewed those instances; and the ravages and plunder which he may have committed on the skirts of the Bengal and [Cooch] Behar provinces have given you provocation to send your vindictive army against him. However, his party

has been defeated, many of his people have been killed, three forts have been taken from him, and he has met with the punishment he deserved; and it is as evident as the sun your army has been victorious, and that, if you had been desirous of it, you might, in the space of two days, have entirely extirpated him, for he had not power to resist your efforts. But now I take upon me to be his mediator, and to represent to you that, as the said Deb Rajah is dependent upon the Dalai Lama, who rules in this country with unlimited sway (but on account of his being in his minority, the charge of the government and administration for the present is committed to me), should you persist in offering further molestation to the Deb's country, it will irritate both the Lama and all his subjects against you. Therefore, from a regard to our religion and customs, I request you will cease all hostilities against him, and in doing this you will confer the greatest favour and friendship upon me.[15]

The letter ends with customary remarks of humility. Delivered by Gosain Pūraṇ Giri, this letter was the first case of Tibetan official correspondence with the British and thus with the Western world. It started a series of fascinating but brief exchanges between two progressive and eminent figures in the region at that time: Warren Hastings and the 6th Panchen Lama. Perhaps carried away by such fascination, most of today's writers on this exchange easily overlook the fact that the letter was not written by the Panchen Lama to mediate at the request of the Bhutanese state. The Bhutanese, except perhaps Zhidar, were unaware of the Panchen Lama's mediation. It is, one can clearly see, a Tibetan story claiming that Bhutan is a dependency of the Dalai Lama, which Bhutanese at that time would have denied and the British soon discovered was not the case, even as a remote tributary as the Dalai Lama was to the Chinese emperor. Also, we have only access to the English translation which may not have exactly captured the mood and connotations of the original letter which the Panchen Lama wrote in Persian. The 6th Panchen Lama knew this language through his mother who was from a place in the western Himalayas, where Persian was spoken. Anyway, we know for sure that the letter was received in Calcutta on 29 March 1774.

By then, fighting had fully stopped and the EIC and the new government of Kuenga Rinchen had already negotiated a ten-point treaty, which was signed by the Bhutanese some time in March 1774 and by Warren Hastings on 25 April 1774. The main official representing Bhutan in the negotiation of the treaty was perhaps Sangay Gyatsho, who spent the hot spring of

1774 in India, although he may not have gone as far as Calcutta.[16] He later became the *pönlop* of Dagana, most likely as a reward for his service. As Purling found the occupied territory inhospitable, he recommended Hastings to restore all areas occupied by them after the war in exchange for five Tangun horses. The British, like the Indian and Tibetans, as we saw in the chapter on ancient Bhutan, admired these sure-footed Bhutanese horses. Thus, the former border of control was restored, and the Bhutanese agreed to return King Dhairjendra and the Dewan Deo, which they did with gifts. This king, however, did not experience any joy of release when he reached his kingdom. Instead, he was flabbergasted by the agreement his Nazir had reached with the British in order to get military support. Dejected by the idea of being a king under a foreign overlord, he made his son Dharendra occupy the throne until the latter's death in 1775. The treaty also granted the Bhutanese merchants right to trade in the Company's territory without duties and the Company to cut timber from Bhutan's forests without duties. The two parties also agreed to a mutual release of prisoners and expulsion and extradition of criminals and offenders, especially *sannyasins* who had been a menace to the EIC territories.

Bogle and the first British Mission to Bhutan

Hastings' overtures for friendly relations with Bhutan and Tibet, which he did not yet know were two different countries, had farsighted economic considerations. Beside the fiscal benefit the EIC could reap from trade with the immediate Tibet/Bhutan to the north, he envisioned that the link might provide a new trade route to China or contact with the Chinese emperor via the Himalayas. This would have been highly significant as the Company's trade with China was highly lucrative and substantial and the business through the existent route of Canton (Guangzhou) was proving to be difficult. The EIC was still intrinsically a commercial entity although it was running parts of India like a government and its profit-bearing interests were of paramount importance to the concerns of its Court of Directors. Tibet/Bhutan provided a new and prospective avenue for such commercial gains. Moreover, Hastings, living in the final years of the European Enlightenment, had an enormous interest in the exploration of knowledge and cultures of far away places. Given these reasons, when Hastings received the friendly letter from the Panchen Lama and had the treaty signed with the Bhutanese, he was only too willing to pursue further communications. Merely two months after the treaty was signed, Hastings despatched the first and perhaps most interesting British mission to Bhutan/Tibet led by a young Scotsman named George Bogle.

Besides trading opportunities, Bogle was to find out the geography, agriculture, livestock, culture, governance and, in fact, everything. He was told 'to keep a diary, inserting whatever passes before your observation which shall be characteristic of the people, the country, the climate, or the road, their manners, customs, buildings, cookery, & c., or interesting to the trade of this country, carrying with you a pencil and a pocket-book for the purpose of minuting short notes of every fact or remark as it occurs, and putting them in order at your leisure while they are fresh in your memory'.[17] With these instructions, thirty-five servants and twenty-two porters, George Bogle and his attendant surgeon, Alexander Hamilton, set off in the heat of May 1774 from Calcutta. He entered Bhutan's territory on 9 June and arrived in Thimphu on 28 June 1774.

Bogle complied with Hastings' wishes by keeping a detailed journal and writing reports and letters about his trip. His journal, which Hastings considered was equal to the standard accounts of Captain Cook's travels, is one of the earliest and most informative records of Bhutan by a European visitor although the honour of the first European visitor to Bhutan goes to the two Portuguese priests who visited Zhabdrung in 1627. Bogle and the other British visitors who followed him in the subsequent decades kept quite detailed records of the country and people of Bhutan so that we are relatively rich in observations and accounts of Bhutan in the English language after this period although most of them did not sufficiently understand the significance and symbolism of many things they came across. This is sadly true with most Western travelogues even in our own times despite partially overcoming the difficult language barrier, which taxed the pre-modern visitors to Bhutan. Most of their journals and reports have been published and are easily available. These, combined with the local Bhutanese accounts of the time, make up the comparatively rich historical literature on medieval Bhutan.

The British mission was received by the new Desi Kuenga Rinchen and his court on 5 July 1774 at the Tashichödzong, which Bogle described as a palace, in a formal ceremony involving several rounds of tea. Curiously, Bogle was even dressed in a silk *gho* and blessed by the Desi with a statue of the Buddha. After this formal reception, the Desi and Bogle met several times without formalities, the main topic of their discussion being the permission for Bogle's journey to Tibet. The Panchen Lama sent letters and presents to Bogle asking him to return to Bengal. He reasoned that by letting Bogle into Tibet, he risked annoying the Chinese emperor, whom he considered as his ultimate overlord. Bogle persisted with his wish, supported by his Bhutanese hosts, and finally got the consent to enter Tibet in the beginning of October 1774. He was ready to embark on the journey, having taken leave of both the Desi and reigning hierarch, Jigme Sengay, when fighting broke out between the government and the people supporting Zhidar in Thimphu. The insurgents attacked the capital but soon retreated to find a base in Semtokha, which the state troops put under siege. After their access to basic resources including water was cut off, the insurgents gave up their position and fled in moonlight on 12 October 1774 and escaped to Tibet. Bogle then left Thimphu the following day via Paro to make a gruelling and cold journey to Tashilhunpo. He saw the aftermaths of some of the skirmishes and extirpation of rebels and their supporters on his way. The tale of Bogle's successful mission to Tibet and striking friendship with the 6th Panchen Lama shall not be told here. There are already a number of published materials on this. Bogle returned to Bhutan on his way to Calcutta the following year arriving in Thimphu on 8 May 1775.

The two most significant achievements of Kuenga Rinchen's short rule as the Desi were the successful suppression of the rebellion of Zhidar's faction and the opening of good relations with the British. The insurrection by Zhidar's faction could have easily spiralled out into a full-scale civil war, as in the past, if it was not suppressed quickly or if the Tibetans or Chinese gave Zhidar active support. Zhidar is said to have sought military support from the Tibetan regent and even from China by offering them, in return, to keep two Chinese officials in Bhutan, like the Ambans in Lhasa, and to pay regular annual tributes.[18] Were Zhidar's design to succeed, Bhutan could have faced another invasion from the north and have risked no more being, what Bogle called, 'this state, naturally free and independent'.[19] Fortunately for Bhutan, the Panchen Lama, the most influential figure in Tibet, took a conciliatory approach as a mediator between Bhutan and the ousted Desi, maintaining a good relationship with Bhutan and a close and caring watch over Zhidar and his faction. Zhidar was in the Panchen Lama's monastery until just a day or two before Bogle's arrival on 9 November 1774,[20] when he moved to Gyantse from where he must have continued his unsuccessful campaign. On 26 May 1775, an envoy from the Panchen Lama and the Tibetan regent arrived in Thimphu requesting the Desi's government to allow some eighty insurgents to return to their homes in Bhutan and also to grant Zhidar a regional governorship or some other post in the government[21] but the requests seem to have fallen on deaf ears and Zhidar's insurgency would continue for some more years although Zhidar almost certainly died by the end of 1775, probably executed after being caught by Bhutanese troops. Hamilton gives two accounts, one of which states that Zhidar's head was brought back fixed on a pole to Punakha.[22]

The opening of relations with the British was indeed a very tricky issue, mainly due to the fear of the unknown. The Bhutanese leaders did not clearly know who the British or *philing* (ཕི་ལིང་), as they called them, were or where they came from and what they wanted. Bogle wrote that 'some of them look upon the Company as a great Rajah; others say it is a woman; and most did not know what to make of it'.[23] Strangely, for an envoy assigned to start friendly relations, Bogle thought it was no business of his to teach them and their poor understanding of the British only hindered Bogle's endeavour for a trade agreement. The conservative clergies saw the British as the barbaric strangers who have not yet seen the light of the Buddha's wisdom. The regent Jigme Sengay, whom Bogle described as someone with 'more curiosity than any man I have seen in the country', met Bogle many times but he was harshly rebuked by the former Je Khenpo Yontan Thaye for interacting with the British and being enamoured of their goods.[24] From a strict tantric religious perspective, it was wrong to associate and develop ties with someone who has been formerly identified as a target of tantric ritual killing.[25] An enduring view of the English which the orthodox clergy held until very recent times was as barbaric people and heretical outsiders bereft of higher Buddhist morality and understanding.

In the eyes of a politician with some information, the British were foreigners who had come under the masquerade of trade and commerce and now controlled Bengal, their immediate neighbour to the south and were forcing their way deeper into the Himalayan hills. They were aware of the EIC's beginning as a commercial venture and its gradual domination of the Indian lands politically. Thus, they had every reason to be suspicious and cautious. Some officials such as the *zhung dronyer* (གཞུང་མགྲོན་གཉེར་) or state chief of protocol were politically astute and knew only too well that trade was followed by a takeover in many places. It is thus astonishing that a mission and an exchange were allowed at all. Much of the credit for the successful mission and good relations must go to the forward-thinking and congenial character of the people involved. Perhaps influenced by ethos of the age of Enlightenment, Warren Hastings and George Bogle were adventurous, open-minded and accommodating persons, characteristics which were shared by the

6th Panchen Lama and to some extent also by the Desi. Bogle, in particular, was a good-humoured and gentle person who believed in adapting himself to the custom of the country as far as possible. Desi Kuenga Rinchen was highly cultured and composed and not a strong and forceful character as was his precursor. However, for his mildness, he was also indecisive and dependent on many other officials. The ministers and leading officials around him were also approachable and friendly people although some of them were politically very astute. Jigme Sengay, the reigning Gyaltshab was also a very inquisitive and sociable person as we shall see later.

The thrust of the mission was to establish a trade route to Tibet via Bhutan as it was no longer easily manageable through the Kathmandu valley which was now under the Gorkhas. The Bhutanese strongly resisted this, giving a host of reasons but Bogle insisted that it was fundamental to the new relations between Bhutan and the EIC, a relationship which has been initiated by the signing of the post-war treaty. The Bhutanese stood their ground and Bogle had to diplomatically request the free access of only local Hindu and Muslim traders and the exclusion of any European. The Bhutanese still resisted, arguing that it could lead to further misunderstanding between Bhutan and the Company if, for example, some of these merchants became victims of banditry or theft. They argued that the Bhutanese country is rugged, the routes unsafe, there was no proper trade mart and too many traders could burden the local population. Bogle persisted in getting past these objections but was more often than expected outmanoeuvred by the negotiating skills of the sharp and tenacious *zhung dronyer*, who advised the Desi and was, in Bogle's words, 'by far the cleverest man at Tashichödzong'.[26]

Bogle was repeatedly surprised by the demands of this officer in return for allowing access of trade through Bhutan. The officer's demands included free trading rights and protection for Bhutanese merchants in Rangpur and Bengal (which the Company happily provided), monopoly over various trade items (the Company gave exclusive rights for indigo), reduction of the prices of fish and oil which had gone up since the war (Bogle promised to redress this), return of some villages in the Baikunthapur appanage which were formerly tributaries of Bhutan and even the complete return of the Cooch Behar territory as the king was finding it difficult to pay the hefty tribute to the British and had even appealed to Bhutan for loans. Bogle suggested submitting a petition to the governor on the last two as he had no mandate to deliberate on territorial issues. Bogle was in fact exasperated by the points raised and demands made by the shrewd *dronyer* or chief of protocol, he conceded upfront: 'you are far too able a negotiator for me.'[27]

After negotiating and lobbying with the *dzongpön* of Thimphu, the *pönlop* of Paro, the *zhung kalön* and above all the *dronyer*, Bogle finally received an affirmative response from the Desi on 28 May 1775 allowing Hindu and Muslim merchants to travel via Bhutan between Bengal and Tibet. The question of whether Tibetan merchants would be allowed through Bhutan was a sensitive question, which Bogle did not dare to raise. Insurgents against Bhutan were still at work from their base in Tibet. But Bogle felt the mission was accomplished with the permission for Indian merchants to travel via Bhutan. Thus, after taking leave from all important officials, Bogle finally set off for Calcutta on 30 May 1775 with a Bhutanese official to present Bhutan's demands to the governor; Alexander Hamilton had already left for India directly from Tibet. The Bhutanese official, we may assume, was Jangchub Gyaltshen, the student of Jigme Lingpa, whom we have discussed above under religious schools.[28] A religious master in his own right, Jangchub Gyaltshen alias Jigme Kundrol is said to have spent about three years in Calcutta and other parts of Bengal as the Bhutanese *vakil* or authorized representative. Samuel Turner adds that he was the first Bhutanese to arrive in Calcutta, where he was present at one of Hastings's concerts.[29] He may have also been the Bhutanese official who, along with the Indian officer for the EIC, fixed the boundaries between Bhutan and areas under the EIC control although one Dawa Tashi was sent to recover tributes from areas near Vijayapur.[30]

Bogle's return from Bhutan was not as eventful as his journey to Bhutan but he left Bhutan with a deep liking for the country and its people. He wrote:

> The more I see of the Bhutanese the more I am pleased with them. The common people are good-humoured, downright, and, I think, thoroughly trusty. The statesmen have some of the art which belongs to their profession. They are the best-built race I ever saw; many of them very handsome, with complexions as fair as the French. I have sometimes been tempted to wish I could substitute their portrait in the place of my friend Padma's.[31]

Four years later, when he was posted as the collector at Rangpur, he fondly wrote to his sister: '. . . although not in my Bhutan hills, I am within sight of them'. He also wrote to his brother saying he wished to spend a month in the north, 'but shall regret the absence of my friend the Teshu [Panchen] Lama, for whom I have a hearty liking, and should be happy again to have his fat hand on my head'. The Panchen Lama was then visiting Peking, where he subsequently died in 1780. Bogle himself died in Calcutta in 1781 aged only thirty-four just as he was planning to return to Bhutan and Tibet.

Bogle's much-cherished wish to return to Tibet and Bhutan was not to be and the trade link he initiated also did not take off as expected. While Bhutan remained partially open to British missions, Tibet sealed its southern borders by the end of the eighteenth century, thus triggering the myth about it as a closed and mysterious country. However, it was Bogle's legacy that the two countries of Bhutan and Tibet were known, if at all, by the Western world in the subsequent decades and by these specific names. Before Bogle's journey, the names Tibet and Bhutan were used interchangeably and very vaguely to refer to the uncharted highlands north of Bengal stretching as far as Mongolia. European cartographers showed Tibet and Bhutan in various spellings as the same country, different countries or one within the other. There was no clear knowledge of the geopolitical structure beyond the Himalayan foothills. It was Bogle's report to Hastings written on 30 September 1775, which finalized once and for all the political distinction between the two countries and application of the two names. 'This country,' Bogle wrote referring to Bhutan, 'which I shall distinguish by the name of Bhutan, is said to have united under one government by Noanumgay [Ngawang Namgyal] . . . The kingdom of Tibet lies to the northward of Bhutan.'[32] Thus, the name Bhutan, which derives from the word *bod* (བོད་) for Tibet, was with some arbitrariness, applied by Bogle to the kingdom of Druk founded by Zhabdrung.

Bogle's legacies also include potatoes, which he planted along his route according to Hastings' instructions. The tuber grew fairly easily and the Bhutanese took an immediate liking to it so that in 1776 the *dzongpön* of Punakha even requested Bogle to send some more as they had eaten all of them without leaving any seed.[33] He sent Bhutanese pears to Bogle as his gift. Hastings and Bogle also tried to grow tea in Bhutan although the project was not successful. When Bogle showed the tea seeds to the Pagsam *drungpa* in 1780, the Bhutanese official got up and danced around them out of sheer joy as this could save the huge amount of money that left Bhutan for tea brought overland from China.'[34] It was a remarkable foresight of Hastings to attempt this some fifty years before tea plantation in India actually took off. Tea was one of the most important items of merchandise for the EIC and sending seeds to Bhutan not only gained favour with Bhutan but could potentially free the EIC from its dependence on Chinese tea.

In order to consolidate the emerging relations, Hastings sent Dr Hamilton to Bhutan in April 1776. He was the first European to arrive in Punakha, where the Desi's government was based in the six winter months. In May, he moved to Thimphu with the court but, unlike other British visitors, Hamilton did not keep a descriptive journal. Hamilton was sent to continue the trade negotiations and to adjudicate the claims Bhutan made over districts in the plains bordering Cooch Behar, including Chichakotta, Paugula Hat, Luckeeduar, Kyranty and Maraghat districts extending roughly from current Buxa to Siliguri. The Bhutanese complained that the Cooch Behari king and the Raikat of Baikunthapur, who were now both under the British, obstructed the reoccupation of these districts as per the terms of the 1774 treaty. Without a clear action on the return of these areas to Bhutan, Bhutan was not willing to open the trade route and some Indian merchants who came from Tibet to Bhutan were sent back. Hamilton requested Hastings, who was only too eager to win the favour of the Bhutanese in order to open a trade route, to officially return these areas to Bhutan. This, the Dinajpur Council did officially on 28 May 1777 and Bhutan received all the places it laid claim to. Hamilton planned to return to Bhutan again in 1777 to congratulate the new Desi Jigme Sengay but it is not clear if he ever did. He may have made it both to Bhutan and Tibet but he did not live to see the final results of his journeys as he died in October 1777 in Buxa duar.[35]

The Bogle–Hamilton mission and their negotiations resulted in a trade agreement between Bhutan and the British signed in 1778. The agreement allowed Hindu and Muslim merchants to pass freely through Bhutan, but restricted any European. Trade in sandalwood, indigo, gogul, skins, paan and betel nut through Bhutan were reserved exclusively for the Bhutanese merchants. This must have helped some of the Bhutanese leaders retain the monopoly they had over trade of some goods from India and Tibet. All Bhutanese were allowed to trade in Bengal without duties, which led to what Bogle, then the collector of Rangpur, described as 'a great concourse' of the Bhutanese, who had come to Rangpur. Bhutanese merchants enjoyed the free trade and security provided by the successive collectors of Rangpur.

The reign of Jigme Sengay and more white men

We can safely infer that the fulfilment of the trade agreement between Bhutan and the EIC was also to a great extent due to the new leadership in Bhutan. Jigme Sengay (1742–89), who was the Gyaltshab or prince-regent on the golden throne, took over the post of the Desi in 1777. He was the second Gyaltshab hierarch to also occupy the secular position of the Desi, after his previous rebirth as Tenzin Rabgay a century earlier. Jigme Sengay was born in the same family of the Bönbji *chöje*, in which his precursor Mipham Wangpo was born. At an early age, he was brought to Punakha and trained under religious luminaries such as Shakya Rinchen, Tenzin Chögyal and Yontan Thaye. When the 6th throne-holders, Jigme Drakpa and Drukdra Namgyal, passed away in 1761 and 1762 respectively, Jigme Sengay was enthroned as the 7th holder of the golden throne but he was largely under the influence of the successive Desis and Je Khenpos. His engagement in real politics perhaps started when the infamous 16th Desi Zhidar tried to undermine him as we saw before, by wresting religious power from him and promoting the rival incarnate figure, Chökyi Gyaltshen, the rebirth of Jigme Drakpa. Whatever be the case, Jigme Sengay was still merely a figurehead with only limited political authority when Bogle visited Tashichödzong. This changed with the death of the 17th Desi Kuenga Rinchen in office; Jigme Sengay took the reins of state as both incarnate prince regent and the 18th Desi.

Jigme Sengay was an unusually open-minded and adventurous character for his milieu and his orthodox upbringing. Unfortunately, we do not have a biography of him but we can draw a clear portrait of him from the British sources. Bogle, we saw earlier, described him as the most curious man in the whole country. This is corroborated by the Turner's account, which applauds 'the versatility of genius, and a spirit of enquiry' he possessed.[36] According to Samuel Turner, 'he was tall, and muscular in his make . . . with dignity and good humour; he was grave, but animated; his behaviour collected and composed. He spoke rather in a low tone of voice, but very articulately; his delivery was accompanied with moderate action; and . . . exhibited a degree of urbanity.'[37] Jigme Sengay was a vegetarian with a deep respect for life. 'My food,' he told Turner, 'consists of the simplest articles; grains, roots of the earth, and fruits. I never eat of anything that has had breath; for so I should be the indirect cause of putting an end to the existence of animal life, which, by our religion, is strictly forbidden.'[38] Turner was deeply impressed by Jigme Sengay's sentiments and described them as 'highly honourable to the humane spirit of their religious faith'.[39]

For a monastic hierarch occupying the highest office in the country, Jigme Sengay also had unrestrained sense of free and adventurous spirit, which can be inferred from his travels to Tibet. He travelled to Tibet twice, first when he was the reigning hierarch and next when he relinquished the post of the

Desi. Jigme Sengay was already installed as the Gyaltshab when he is said to have gone to Tibet on pilgrimage in the disguise of a mendicant. Jigme Sengay made his second journey to Tibet in 1788, after he felt thoroughly saddened by the court intrigues and insurrections. He first proposed to stand down from the post of the Desi but the state clergy and leading officials implored him to remain. Then in the winter of 1788, he repeated exactly what his predecessor Mipham Wangpo did some decades earlier. He suddenly fled from Wangdiphodrang eastward to go on pilgrimage to Tsari in Tibet and then continued from there to Central Tibet. Despite requests to return and resume his post, he remained in Samye Chimphu in Tibet and seems to have died there in 1789.

Although his reign is not marked by any outstanding developments, the spirit of religious, literary and artistic creations, which flourished during the time of Sherab Wangchuk and Shakya Rinchen, continued during Jigme Sengay's time. The main religious figures included the 12th Je Khenpo Kuenga Gyatsho (1722–72), the 13th Je Khenpo Yontan Thaye (1724–84), Pagar Geshe Kuenga Gyatsho (1702–76) and Chökyi Gyatsho (1759–1812). Of them, the 13th Je Khenpo Yontan Thaye, the founder of Dodedra, was certainly one of the towering religious figures of his generation. Born in the religious *chöje* lineage of Tshamdrak and trained both in Bhutan and Tibet, he was a leading personality in Bhutan.

Jigme Sengay finished a number of building projects during the twelve years of his rule. He is said to have built the Kabji Soral *dzong*, the Namdrol Khachödling temple in Tango, Chöten Nyingpo in Punakha and the Sa-ngag Chöling temple in Talo. He also expanded the prayer hall in Tashichödzong and carved woodblocks for Pema Karpo's writings. However, the most significant project during his reign was the reconstruction of the Punakha *dzong* after it was destroyed by a tragic fire in 1780. This was the first fire which burnt down the Punakha *dzong* since it was built by Zhabdrung in 1637 and the first of the three which would take place in less than a quarter of a century. Ngawang Chökyi Gyatsho, an eyewitness, reports the incident:

> Flames spread like a canopy inside, outside and in between the doors. The wooden frame of the central tower was engulfed by patterns of flames with roaring and cracking sounds. It was like the realm of death; we ran out in rush with no attachment to anything. In an instant, the palace of Cakrasaṃvara was reduced to ashes by the fire of people's misfortunes.[40]

Jigme Sengay immediately began rebuilding the *dzong* and its interior shrines and relics. The renovation was most likely completed by 1783 when Samuel Turner and his friends arrived in Thimphu on 1 June 1783.

The Turner mission was the second effort made by Hastings to fully establish trade links with Bhutan and Tibet and gain access to China. The 6th Panchen Lama, who died in China in 1780, was now reborn and an eighteen-month-old child had been recognized as his incarnation. Hastings took the opportunity to send a party ostensibly to congratulate the young incarnate and to resume the links left by the previous Panchen Lama and Bogle. Thus, the mission composed of Captain Samuel Turner, Samuel Davis, who was to act as draughtsman and surveyor, and Robert Saunders, a surgeon, set off from Calcutta in January 1783. They were to strengthen trade links with Tibet and Bhutan and also to resolve some of the recurring territorial issues with Bhutan. Turner was instructed by Hastings, who followed Hamilton's suggestion, to fully cede the districts of Jalpaish and Fallakotta to the Bhutanese in the hope of furthering trade relations. These areas were officially already under Bhutanese control but, in reality, Bhutan had difficulties holding control over them.

Taking the same route as the Bogle mission, they came via Buxa duar, making even more detailed observations and reports of what they encountered during their journey. Turner's mission was in many ways a re-enactment of the first mission under Bogle. Like Bogle's mission, Turner's mission also produced very positive and glowing reports of Bhutan. Instead of summarizing them here, readers are directed to the fascinating reports and diaries of George Bogle, Samuel Turner and Samuel Davis for more information. In addition, Robert Saunders kept a detailed record of the flora, fauna and agricultural produces and minerals in Bhutan and Samuel Davis produced the earliest set of drawings of the places and architecture in Bhutan. These and the letters they wrote from Bhutan make the best English-language sources on eighteenth-century Bhutan.[41]

Desi Jigme Sengay formally received the Turner mission on 3 June 1783 after they were comfortably settled in a house near Tashichödzong, probably the same place where Bogle and Hamilton were put up. Turner and his friends mostly stayed in Thimphu, waiting for permits to travel to Tibet as Bogle and Hamilton did in 1774. They travelled around Thimphu observing Bhutanese nature and culture. They marvelled at the irrigation technology of bringing mountain springs through aqueducts made of hollowed tree trunks. They frequently met Jigme Sengay as Bogle did during his trip. After the first one,

Bhutanese men by the riverside—by Samuel Davis (courtesy: Serindia Publications)

Bhutanese warriors armed with bows and arrows—by Samuel Davis (courtesy: Serindia Publications)

The new Thimphu *dzong* in 1783—then about ten years old (courtesy: Serindia Publications)

Wangdiphodrang *dzong* in 1783—then 145 years old. The dzong was destroyed by fire in 1838 and again in 2012. (courtesy: Serindia Publications)

the meetings were mostly without formalities and they talked about various things, including the similarities and differences of their cultures. They exchanged gifts and dined together. With Robert Saunders, Jigme Sengay shared local medical knowledge and herbs and, in return, the English surgeon shared his skills and drugs. Samuel Davis showed his artistic works in return for an exhibition of local artistic talents.

One of the curios which Turner showed him was an electric apparatus, which they used to inject a brief electric jolt. This became a great source of entertainment for the Desi and his courtiers and was eventually gifted to the Desi. We may recall that Alexander Hamilton showed him a pair of binoculars during the Bogle mission. It is perhaps for his indulgence in such worldly contrivances and his keen interest in and association with European people and goods that he was even scolded by his teacher, the former Je Khenpo Yontan Thaye, as we have seen above.

The missions, though seven years apart, also both witnessed a local insurrection by the disgruntled people who belonged to Zhidar's faction. The main actor in the insurgency of 1783 was the *dzongpön* of Wangdiphodrang, who took sides with Zhidar's supporters most of whom were still banned from Bhutan. He made appeals to the state monks and the court to allow them to return but both Je Khenpo and the Desi's court appear to have rejected the appeal. The infuriated *dzongpön* may have then taken arms against the government. At any case, fighting broke out in Thimphu in July 1783 when the British mission was still there. The rebels took over three villages around Tashichödzong. However, after some skirmishes, the government troops regained control over Thimphu. We have detailed and reliable account about this fighting written by Samuel Turner. The rebels retreated to Wangdiphodrang, where they were also defeated and forced to eventually flee. After expelling the rebels from Wangdiphodrang, the Desi soon visited the place and his foreign guests were also invited to join him there.

Turner and his friends were the first Europeans to arrive in Wangdiphodrang where they spent some nights. Turner gives an interesting account of the *dzong* and the conflict. From there, they visited Punakha without the Desi but a zealous guard did not allow them inside the newly built dzong. They returned to Thimphu and in September 1783; the permit to Tibet finally came but only Turner and Saunders could proceed to Tibet as the Tibetans gave permit only for two Europeans, no more than the number of Europeans in the first mission. Davis remained in Bhutan for some more time making his drawings and watercolours which have today become the most valuable portrayals of medieval Bhutanese.[42] Samuel Turner and Robert Saunders returned from Tibet in December 1783 and visited the Desi in Punakha. Thoroughly imbued by the Desi's trust and friendship and refreshed by the temperate climate and bountiful garden in Punakha, they departed for Bengal on 30 December 1783.

During Jigme Sengay's reign, Bhutan's political relations with the EIC to the south were very cordial. However, the political situation to the west of Bhutan remained as effervescent during his rule as it was before his time. Border incursions into Sikkim continued throughout the eighteenth century. Moreover, the new Gorkha state of Nepal was continually expanding its domain although its campaign had slightly slackened after the death of Pṛthivī Nārāyaṇ in 1775. Pṛthivī Nārāyaṇ's son Pratāp Singh ruled Nepal from 1775 to 1777 and when he died leaving behind only an infant heir, his Queen Rajendra Lakṣmi acted as the regent until her death in 1785. She was followed by Pratāp's brother Bahadur Shah as regent until 1794, when Prince Rana Bahadur Shah, the son of Pratāp Singh came of age. Throughout this period, Nepal did not stop its territorial expansion toward Sikkim but under the militant and ambitious regent Bahadur Shah, Nepal's expansionist approach found a fresh and vigorous champion. In Sikkim, the 5th King Namgyal Phuntsho (1733–80), the child born to a nun and proclaimed to be the son of King Gyurme Namgyal, had succeeded to the throne after the dissident forces within the kingdom were vanquished with the help of Bhutan and Tibet. He ascended the throne and consolidated his rule over his subjects but his reign was marred with a foreign menace both from the Gorkha power to the west and Bhutan to the east. When he died, he was succeeded by his son Tenzin Namgyal (1769–93), who had to even flee from Sikkim with his infant son Tsugphud Namgyal (1785–1861) in the wake of the Gorkha invasion of his capital.

Strangely, Bhutan happily allied with the Hindu Nepal right from the beginning of the rise of Gorkha power under Pṛthivī Nārāyaṇ and the days of the infamous Desi Zhidar. This was largely because of almost incessant border conflicts Bhutan had with the Buddhist neighbour, Sikkim but in part also due to the personal rapport between Bhutanese and Nepali leaders. We have seen how Bhutan had relinquished the claim it had over Vijayapur in about 1772 in exchange for some establishments in Kathmandu, when the Gorkhas invaded and took control of this kingdom. The Nepal–Bhutan alliance persisted and a deal was again struck with regard to Sikkim, which they both frequently battered with military incursions. Although Sikkim closely aligned itself with Tibet and remained as its protectorate, Bhutan held an historical claim of suzerainty over Sikkim. Thus, when Bahadur Shah made plans to launch a full invasion of Sikkim, he thought it wise to first approach the Desi of Bhutan and request him not to intervene on behalf of Sikkim. Bahadur Shah sent Tenzin Drugay, the Bhutanese court priest in Kathmandu, to Thimphu to ask the Desi to relinquish Bhutan's claims over Sikkim and provide no military support to Sikkim. In return, he offered Bhutan several religious estates in Nepal. Having likewise appeased Bhutan, the Gorkha troops invaded Sikkim and occupied the capital in 1788 forcing its king and royal family into exile. The royal entourage escaped to southern Tibet, where they went through a serious ordeal, not even having enough food to eat. The Bhutanese sent a humanitarian aid of rice, tea and 1200 silver coins, which temporarily eased the difficulties of the Sikkimese royal entourage and healed the deep wounds caused by Bhutan's alliance with Nepal. However, some Sikkimese officials are said to have blamed the Bhutanese as the chief instigator of the Gorkha occupation and they vowed never to treat the Bhutanese hospitably.[43]

About the same time as the occupation of Sikkim, the Gorkha expansionist movement was also wrecking havoc on Tibet to the north. The reasons for the Nepal–Tibet war of 1788–92 are numerous. One was the reluctance of Tibetans to use silver coins minted by the Gorkha government although they were in terms of silver content superior to the coins minted for Tibet by Newari rulers before them. There were also the issues concerning trade. The Gorkhas felt that the Nepalese merchants were mistreated in Tibet and duties on Nepalese goods entering Tibet have been raised. Tibetans scorned the territorial expansion of the Gorkhas, particularly with regard to Sikkim, which they considered as their vassal state. To crown it all was a political imbroglio involving the high incarnate figure of the Zhamarpa Chödrup Gyatsho (1741–91), who was the brother of the late 6th Panchen Lama. He allied with the Gorkhas, allegedly to claim his share of the inheritance, which he was denied when the Panchen Lama passed away in China.

The Gorkhas, along with Zhamarpa's supporters, invaded Tibet in 1788 and took over Tashilhunpo. The young Panchen Lama incarnate and the regent of Tashilhunpo had to flee to Lhasa. The regent of Tashilhunpo even clandestinely wrote to the EIC for help but the new Governor-General Lord Cornwallis declined to send any military help against the Gorkhas. Negotiations between the Tibetan and Gorkhas began in earnest and brought a fleeting settlement but the invasion took a more dangerous turn in 1791 when the Dalai Lama refused to pay the tribute to the Gorkhas as previously agreed. Before this second invasion was launched, Bahadur Shah again sent a messenger to Bhutan, as in the past, asking the Desi not to extend any military support to Tibet. The new Desi immediately sent a response to Bahadur Shah trying to dissuade the Gorkha ruler from invading Tibet but the Gorkha ruler did not heed his words and Tashilhunpo was occupied and looted. In the course of the war, the men from Kyidrong in Tibet were surrounded by Gorkha soldiers and about to be executed when the Bhutanese court priest in Kathmandu came across them. The Bhutanese lama used the influence of his office to save the men. In reciprocation, the men started a tradition of sending annual gifts of gratitude to Bhutan from Kyidrong. Meanwhile, the news of Gorkha pillaging reached Peking and 17,000 Chinese troops were despatched under a Manchu officer to remove the Gorkhas. There was also an order for the Sikkimese to join the assault on the Gorkha, which they did with great enthusiasm. The Chinese pursued the retreating Gorkhas as far as some twenty miles outside Kathmandu, when the Gorkhas sued for peace. The two Bhutanese envoys, Lama Thinley Drukgay and Drakgo Chöje, were also sent to mediate between the Chinese and Nepalese but we do not have details about their contribution, if any.[44]

The Nepal–Tibet war of 1788–92 and the Chinese intervention had many implications for the political situation of the region. First, Nepal was made a tributary of China and it remained so for some period. The issue of coins minted in Nepal was dropped as Tibetan coins then began to be minted in China. The defeat at the hands of the Chinese also severely curbed Nepal's expansionist policy, particularly toward Sikkim. The Gorkha troops were dislodged from that country and the young Prince Tsugphud Namgyal was installed on the throne. The exiled King Tenzin Namgyal died in Lhasa in 1793 before he could return to Sikkim. With the northern and eastern borders formally fixed by the Tibetans for them, the Gorkha territorial intrigues would now turn westward and southward bringing them into conflict with the British. In Tibet, the Chinese military intervention led to a tighter control of Tibet by Peking. Tashilhunpo and Lhasa lost the autonomy from Peking which they enjoyed in the past. Moreover, the Chinese and Tibetan had suspicions, albeit unfounded, that the British may have actively supported the Gorkha invasion. Thus, they resolved to stop all diplomatic communication with EIC in India. This sealed the fate of the British aspirations to open a robust trade with Tibet and a link to China via the high Himalayas. The British cultivation of a good relationship with Bhutan in order to gain access to Tibet via Bhutan was no longer as important and worthwhile as it seemed before the war.

The war also had a curious consequence for Tibetan Buddhist culture, as it involved an eminent incarnate lama, the 10th Zhamarpa. His monastery and assets were impounded by the Tibetan government and the recognition of his reincarnation in the future was officially banned. Emperor Qianlong of China saw the war partly as a result of nepotism in selection of *trulku* and incarnate lamas because the 10th Zhamarpa and the 6th Panchen Lama were brothers. It was common to see high lamas born in prominent families. Thus, the emperor sent a golden urn to Tibet with the imperial instruction that 'whenever a *khubilghan* [incarnate lama] is to be elected, the names of all eligible persons shall be written and placed in the urn. (The person to be appointed) shall be determined by the lot.'[45] This imperial rule of spiritual lottery was enforced and practised in Tibet to some extent but with much resentment among the people. The recognition and appointment of incarnate lamas in Bhutan and places outside the Chinese domain continued in the traditional way composed of a number of mysterious, unreliable, dubious techniques which were always open to abuse.

Factional fighting and the imbroglio of incarnations

By the time the Tibet–Nepal war ended, the post of the Desi had changed twice in Bhutan. Exasperated by court intrigues, Jigme Sengay abruptly left Bhutan on pilgrimage for Tsari in eastern Tibet, from where he proceeded to Central Tibet and subsequently died there in 1789. Sporadic conflict between the government and the dissidents who sided with Desi Zhidar and the *dzongpön* of Wangdiphodrang continued after the armed rebellion which took place during the Bogle's mission in 1775 and Turner's in 1783. The dissidents also persistently lobbied with state monastic hierarchs but the Je Khenpo and the leading monks maintained their neutrality. Around 1789, an epidemic of smallpox seems to have also struck the state monks, forcing them to disperse in small groups to remote places. The vacuum which Jigme Sengay left in 1788 was filled by the appointment of Druk Tenzin from Wang Sisina as the 19th Desi. He was a respectable figure and a candidate acceptable to the two dissenting parties. The historian Tshering Dorji, however, states that he was unpopular with the clergy and soon forced out of office. Pema Tshewang, on the contrary, recounts Druk Tenzin's short reign as righteous and popular. He cites Ngawang Chökyi Gyatsho, a contemporary of this Desi, to argue that Druk Tenzin was a zealous patron of religious projects and had he lived longer, his rule could have resembled the glorious reign of the 13th Desi Sherab Wangchuk.[46]

During his short reign, Desi Druk Tenzin built the second temple in Phajoding for the fourteenth Je Khenpo Sherab Sengay (1724–93) and built a copper image of the Buddha at Dodedra equivalent to the height of his teacher, the thirteenth Je Khenpo Yontan Thaye. The 19th Desi also introduced changes in monastic regulations and allowed senior monks to retire to hermitages in their old age. A number of illuminated sets of *kanjur* manuscripts were also completed in his time. He passed away in 1792 due to an illness and was immediately succeeded by his nephew, the 20th Desi Sonam Gyaltshen alias Tashi Namgyal. Sonam Gyaltshen's rule was, however, quickly disrupted by court intrigues and he had to share the post of the Desi with Umze Chapkhrapa, who is enumerated as the 20th Desi in Nyerchen Drepa's history. There is no information about this Umze Chapthrapa apart from a brief mention in the biography of the 18th Je Khenpo Jamyang Gyaltshen.[47] The joint rule appears to have persisted for nearly six years before it collapsed and Sonam Gyaltshen was perhaps pushed out of office leaving only Umze Chapthrapa in the post. However, Umze soon became ill and passed away in 1796.

Upon Umze Chapthrapa's death, Druk Namgyal was appointed as the 21st Desi. Described as intelligent, brave, charismatic, wise, articulate and composed, Druk Namgyal's most outstanding legacies were the wood blocks he commissioned for a great number of books. The last quarter of the eighteenth century saw a thriving culture of book production, primarily in the Thimphu region. Besides creating numerous illuminated manuscripts and wood blocks in Bhutan, vast quantities of paper were also sent to Tibet to print Buddhist canons from the wood blocks in Tibet. Druk Namgyal's rule however was not to be a peaceful and prosperous one. The omen of evil times came some time in the early part of 1798 in the form of a very heavy snow; even the roofs broke under its weight. The 18th Je Khenpo Jamyang Gyaltshen warned the Desi of an impending disaster if prayers and rituals were not conducted. The Desi earnestly sponsored prayer services but sadly they were not sufficient to avert the calamity.

The Punakha *dzong*, which was rebuilt by Jigme Sengay after the first fire in 1780, was once again reduced to rubble in 1798. The monks ran out in a panic leaving behind most of the relics. After evacuating the monks, the incumbent Je Khenpo Jamyang Gyaltshen rushed out of the blazing *dzong* with whatever he could lay his hands on. All he found in his hand when he reached safety was a piece of a monastic robe. But the abbot sighed with relief; to him the robe was a comforting sign that the precious Buddhist tradition would survive. Although most relics were lost, the body of the Zhabdrung was successfully rescued. It was placed in the gardens near the *dzong*, where the ritual of offering regular meals was duly resumed. The reconstruction of the *dzong* began in earnest under the supervision of the former Desi Sonam Gyaltshen, the incumbent Desi Druk Namgyal and the Je Khenpo Jamyang Gyaltshen. Funded by the two Desis, the Je Khenpo undertook an intensive production of religious objects including wall paintings, wall hangings, statues and ritual artefacts. The *dzong* was rebuilt in just over a year and replenished with relics and ritual objects in four years.[48]

The cultural enterprise to rebuild and restock the Punakha *dzong* was barely over when fresh internal disputes broke out. The most damaging one was the conflict between the former and the incumbent Desis, which the Je Khenpo Jamyang Gyaltshen worked hard to resolve. The main cause of the conflict may have been rivalry for power between the Desis but it was triggered by the installation of Sungtrul Yeshe Gyaltshen on the golden throne by Druk Namgyal. The influential Je Khenpo managed to initially suppress the discord between the parties of the two leaders. However, a violent clash erupted between the parties on the concluding day of the annual Drubchö festival in Punakha in 1803. For two days, fighting continued non-stop, causing much bloodshed both inside and outside the *dzong*, according to a biographer.[49] Finally, Desi Druk Namgyal was shot dead by his opponents with a gun and his supporters dispersed in a panic. Following the death of Druk Namgyal, the former Desi Sonam Gyaltshen reoccupied the post of Desi and became the 22nd Desi. The internal strife, however, was far from over. The supporters of Desi Druk Namgyal retaliated with unforgiving vengeance and on 29 April, 1803, they set fire to the Punakha *dzong*, which had just been finished.[50]

As the flames engulfed the edifice, the young incarnate Jigme Drakpa II was carried out of the *dzong* on the back by a servant of his chamberlain. He and his teacher were about to get past the fire when they were confronted by the armed rebels. They had to flee along another route and struggle through a pile of corpses to reach the grounds outside the *dzong*.[51] The venerable Je Khenpo Jamyang Gyaltshen was, however, not as lucky. When the fire raged through the *dzong*, he called out three times to the remains of Zhabdrung, overcome by the ruin and intense anguish. Residing in the upper floors of the *dzong* and with all routes blocked by fire, he resorted to the window and attempted to slide down the tall wall using a rope. Tragically, his old hands lost their grip; he fell to the ground and passed away on that day.[52] For the third time in a quarter of a century, the Palace of Great Bliss was reduced to ashes.

The main reason for this devastating conflict seems to be the rivalry for power between the two Desis. Such worldly desires for political power, however, were often mixed with or masqueraded as a spiritual cause in order to gain popular support. To do so, the civil leaders usually supported and used one of the four pre-eminent incarnate hierarchs: Zhabdrung's mind incarnation, Zhabdrung's speech incarnation, Jampal Dorji's incarnation and Tenzin Rabgay's incarnation. We shall refer to these incarnate hierarchs as regal incarnations as they are directly connected to the institution and family of Zhabdrung, the founding ruler. The British used the Indian term Dharmarāja. The allegiance to one of the regal incarnations gave the civil rulers the legitimacy to rule as guardians of the Drukpa system and also helped them garner support from a large section of the populace in the name of religion. Desi Zhidar, we saw earlier, supported Thugtrul Chökyi Gyaltshen, the second mind incarnation and Kuenga Rinchen supported Jigme Sengay, the second incarnation of Tenzin Rabgay. When Zhidar was ousted, Thugtrul Chökyi Gyaltshen also suffered ill treatment in the hands of Zhidar's opponents. This mistreatment or neglect appears to have continued during the reign of Jigme Sengay. Jigme Sengay was himself a regal incarnation as well as the Desi. However, long before his retirement, Jigme Sengay appointed his relation Gyalse Trulku Jigme Namgyal (1763–95), the fourth incarnation of Jampal Dorji, as the holder of the golden throne.[53] It was around the time of the installation of Gyalse Trulku Jigme Namgyal on the golden throne that Thugtrul Chökyi Gyaltshen was also poisoned to death in 1785, most likely by the supporters of Gyalse Trulku Jigme Namgyal. It is quite likely that Chökyi Gyaltshen's faction have objected to the enthronement of Gyalse Trulku Jigme Namgyal.

Just before his death, Thugtrul Chökyi Gyaltshen was requested by the 16th Je Khenpo Sherab Sengay to take his rebirth in Bhutan as it became difficult to bring the incarnations to Bhutan when they were born in Tibet. Both the 1st and 2nd Thugtruls or mind incarnations were born in Tibet and it has proved very difficult for the Bhutanese authorities to bring them to

Bhutan.[54] Thugtrul Chökyi Gyaltshen was, however, too ill to discuss the issue. He accepted the request with a nod of his head from his death bed and his rebirth was subsequently found in Bumdeling in eastern Bhutan. The young incarnate hierarch Jigme Drakpa II, the 3rd Thugtrul, was born in 1791 and brought to Thimphu at the age of three. Gyalse Trulku Jigme Namgyal passed away in 1795 in Cheri and that same year, Jigme Drakpa II was installed on the golden throne by the 20th Desi Sonam Gyaltshen and the 17th Je Khenpo Yeshe Dorji. Offerings were made by the state monks and government officers. Gifts were received from the estimated 60,000 households in the country through the various governors and regional officers.

When Desi Sonam Gyaltshen was ousted from the office of the Desi and Druk Namgyal took the office in 1796, there was also a change in the holder of the golden throne. It appears that Druk Namgyal supported as his choice of regal incarnation, Yeshe Gyaltshen (1781–1830), the 3rd Sungtrul. Thus, Druk Namgyal placed the 3rd Sungtrul on the golden throne. This immediately triggered a dispute between him and the former Desi Sonam Gyaltshen, who had installed the 3rd Thugtrul on the golden throne in 1795. Although the dispute was temporarily appeased by the 18th Je Khenpo Jamyang Gyaltshen, it resurfaced in 1803, when Druk Namgyal was shot dead by Sonam Gyaltshen's supporters as we saw earlier. With Druk Namgyal's death, the 3rd Sungtrul lost his patron. He had to flee from the enemies of his patron and seek refuge in the quarters of Je Khenpo Jamyang Gyaltshen. Sungtrul Yeshe Gyaltshen temporarily lost all his position and privileges and retreated to Sa-ngag Chökhor. The former Desi Sonam Gyaltshen once again came to power and Thugtrul Jigme Drakpa II, whom he supported, returned to the golden throne. When the supporters of Druk Namgyal resorted to arson and destroyed the Punakha *dzong*, Jigme Drakpa II, then only thirteen years old, nearly lost his life to the arsonists while being carried out of the *dzong*.

It is very clear from the pattern of conflicts and the association of state rulers with their incarnate hierarchs that the nominal leadership and blessings of the regal incarnations were vital to the secular authority of the Desis. Whether or not the incarnate hierarchs were themselves active in politics and affairs of state, the Desis used the regal incarnations as their figureheads in order to garner public support. The parties contending for power were mostly formed along allegiances to incarnation and family lines rather than being based on principles or policies. The civil wars of Bhutan throughout the eighteenth and nineteenth centuries were mostly fought between political factions who pledged their allegiance to one of the four regal incarnations. Consequently, such political use of the regal incarnations also led to their short lives and tragic deaths, mostly through poisoning. It is no surprise that all food served to an important official in medieval Bhutan was first confirmed to be poison-free by the courtier who served it by consuming a portion of it first. The British visitors clearly noted this practice during the official ceremonies. However, such measures did not fully stop the treacherous method of assassination by poisoning and poison continued to be the most commonly suspected cause of the untimely death of the regal incarnations.

By the end of the eighteenth century, real power lay almost entirely in the hands of lay rulers, and the regal incarnations, whom the British called Dharmarājas, performed merely nominal and figurehead roles. All three regal incarnations at the turn of the nineteenth century were in their minority and puppet-leaders controlled by strong lay figures. As time passed, the position of the Desi overshadowed the position of the Gyaltshab or prince-regent so much so that soon even the incarnate hierarchs vied for the post of the Desi. Due to their religious status, the incarnate hierarchs did win the post of the Desi but the uneducated or ill-trained incarnations were inept for the executive post and real power slipped into the hands of their lay supporters. The office of the Desi was also increasingly being called the 'golden throne', a term which was initially reserved for the position of the Zhabdrung occupied by one of his Gyaltshab or prince-regents. After Tenzin Chögyal's enumeration of successive holders of the golden throne stopped in 1759 with the two 6th throne-holders, Mipham Wangpo and Jigme Drakpa, no effort was made to continue the list.

Thus, the power, prestige and authority associated with the post of the Gyaltshab were gradually taken over by the office of the Desi. The holder of the golden throne was no longer as significant or powerful as the occupant of the Desi's seat. Concurrently, the post of the Desi was also occupied increasingly by lay figures. Since Druk Rabgay's time, many Desis were lay officials who climbed to the country's highest position through family connections. As pious and cultivated monks lost their control over the affairs of state and more and more lay officials, who had less or no inhibitions to use military force to grab power, took over political positions, Bhutan began to see an era of constant civil strife.

An admirable institution in the midst of such chaotic changes and political strife was the office of the Je Khenpo, almost always occupied by a highly educated and enlightened personage. The appointees normally

started their spiritual career as ordinary novices and gradually rose through
the monastic ranks with hard work and religious commitment. Thus, they
were thoroughly trained in monastic education and immensely well versed
in the rituals, doctrines and meditation practices of the Drukpa school. They
were dedicated monks, skilled masters of meditation and above all, mostly
humane, sagacious and compassionate persons. Appointed purely on the
basis of spiritual merit and authority through an informal consensus, they
generally remained untouched by partisan conflicts and wisely used their
position and spiritual power to avert many disasters. Moreover, they were
the real custodians of the Drukpa spiritual and cultural heritage, passing it
down to the next generation in the midst of constant political turbulence.

After the Punakha *dzong* was burnt down by the arsonists in 1803, Desi
Sonam Gyaltshen began in earnest to rebuild the *dzong*, for the second
time under his supervision. Sherab Gyaltshen, who later became the 25th Je
Khenpo, was the main cultural expert to design the interior arts and ritual
artefacts. The *dzong* was roughly finished in about a year but Desi Sonam
Gyaltshen was by then exhausted by the enormous task and political tumult.
He finally resigned from the post of the Desi and entrusted the affairs of
the state to the fifteen-year-old Jigme Drakpa II in 1805. Jigme Drakpa II
seems to have unofficially held the reins of government for a brief period
at the request of Sonam Gyaltshen, but soon after Sonam Gyaltshen's death
that year, he passed the position of the Desi to Sonam Gyaltshen's nephew,
Sangay Tenzin, who was officially declared as the 23rd Desi in 1805.

The clash of incarnations and the first pressure from the east

Sangay Tenzin, like his uncle and precursor Sonam Gyaltshen, was from
Wang Sisina in the lower Thimphu valley. He started his career as an ordinary
courtier and had risen to the rank of the Thimphu *dzongpön* before he became
the Desi in the middle of 1805. His short rule as the Desi was, however,
thoroughly unremarkable. In the year he became the Desi, Tshaphu Dorji,
the *pönlop* of Tsongsa, staged a rebellion to overthrow him. The forces under
the Tongsa *pönlop* arrived in Punakha in 1805 and reached Thimphu in the
following year. This was the first instance of a military campaign against
the central power in western Bhutan by forces under Tongsa *pönlop*, who
ruled the areas traditionally considered as eastern Bhutan. It is not fully clear
what caused the Tongsa *pönlop* to revolt but his rebellion was substantial
enough to wreck havoc in the capitals. Pema Tshewang states that the Tongsa

pönlop harboured intentions to gain the post of the Desi for himself and led the rebellion.[55] The situation, however, may have been more complex.

It seems the *pönlop* of Tongsa supported Sungtrul Yeshe Gyaltshen, who was ousted from the golden throne by Desi Sonam Gyaltshen. He may have also backed Tritrul Tshultrim Drakpa (1790–1830), the rebirth of Jigme Sengay and a member of the Bönbji family, which was based some miles north of Tongsa. These two reincarnations were close to each other and even travelled to Tibet on pilgrimage together. They certainly allied together as one group patronized earlier by Druk Namgyal and later by Tshaphu Dorji, the *pönlop* of Tongsa. Jigme Drakpa II, on the other hand, was supported by the former Desi Sonam Gyaltshen and his nephew Sangay Tenzin. With the death of Druk Namgyal, Sungtrul Yeshe Gyaltshen was forced out of the golden throne of Gyaltshab, on which Jigme Drakpa II was reinstated. This probably incensed Sungtrul's patron Tshaphu Dorji and led him to rise in rebellion.

Whatever the motives, the revolt was significant and to stop the revolt, the senior monastic hierarchs mediated between the Desi and the Tongsa *pönlop*. Their negotiations resulted in the resignation of Sangay Tenzin from the post of the Desi, barely a year after he took up the post, and the appointment of Umze Yeshe Gyaltshen from Paro as the 24th Desi. Umze Yeshe Gyaltshen was from Dolphu in Paro. He had gone through the rigorous monastic training and reached the position of the precentor of the State Monk Body when he was appointed as the Desi in 1806. He seems, however, to have been totally inept at running the temporal affairs of the state. During his short period in office, he presented Talo Sa-nga Chöling, the temple establishment above Punakha, to Jigme Drakpa II. This meditation site was started by a hermit called Ngawang Rabgay and was officially established by Jigme Sengay. Many important figures used the place as a spot for meditation. Following the normal pattern of inheritance, Talo Sa-ngag Chöling should have been passed down to Tshultrim Drakpa, the incarnation of Jigme Sengay. Umze, however, presented the place to Jigme Drakpa II.

This irregular gift of the religious estate may have exacerbated the displeasure of Tshaphu Dorji, the *pönlop* of Tongsa, against the central government and caused him to once again revolt. By the time Tshaphu Dorji marched on Punakha for the second time perhaps at the end of 1806, the state militia was reportedly in a very poor state. The monastic hierarchs, including the 19th Je Khenpo Ngawang Chögyal, immediately took recourse to negotiations. In the negotiating team was also Pema Chodrak, also known as Bodpa or Tibetan Chodrak (because he lived in Tibet perhaps as the *lochag* representative). He was considered the rebirth of Tshering Wangchen, the first *lochag* and uncle of Mipham Wangpo and was also a relation of Tritrul Jigme Sengay from Bönbji. He came from Tibet with Sungtrul Yeshe Gyaltshen and Tritrul Tshultrim Drakpa, when these two incarnate hierarchs returned from their pilgrimage to Tibet.

The negotiations resulted in two major outcomes: Tritrul Tshultrim Drakpa, the reincarnation of Jigme Sengay, who was not officially enthroned until then, was installed on the golden throne as Gyaltshab, and the Desi Umze was made to share the office with Pema Chodrak, who was by then the personal advisor of Tritrul Tshultrim Drakpa. During their brief joint rule, they commissioned new records of the country's landholdings. A new shrine for Pehar Gyalpo, the protecting deity of Samye temple in Tibet, was built in Punakha under Jigme Drakpa II's supervision. After its completion, the deity was invited and installed in the shrine.[56] Pema Chödrak also undertook other religious works including the gilding of the assembly hall of Tashichödzong, the construction of the Samarzingkha temple, the installation of the gilded cupola of Dodedra and the murals of Phajoding. Monastic artists and cultural experts such as Sherab Gyaltshen, who later became the Je Khenpo, were very active building cultural artefacts and monuments during this period. That winter, Bhutan felt the tremors of a major earthquake but no serious damage was done.

Peace times, which are conducive for cultural creations, however, did not last long. On the fifteenth of the first Bhutanese month, 22 February 1807, trouble broke out again in Punakha. The Je Khenpo and the clergy promptly negotiated and Desi Umze was eventually asked to retire leaving only Pema Chodrak in the post of the Desi.[57] Pema Chodrak thus became the 25th Desi in the early part of 1807. With Tshultrim Drakpa on the golden throne and Pema Chodrak as Desi, the Bönbji group was once again in charge of the country. Their ally, Sungtrul Yeshe Gyaltshen, was also by then appointed as the 20th Je Khenpo although he did not remain long in the post. During the supremacy of this group, the rival hierarch, Jigme Drakpa II, spent his time in Talo Sa-ngag Chöling and Semtokha or travelling in various places conducting religious services. He rarely came to the two capital seats and strains began to appear in the relationship between him and Desi Pema Chödrak. To make things worse, Norbu Rinchen from Tsamang, an officer waiting on Jigme Drakpa II, is said to have craftily slandered the Desi Chödrak, reporting that the Desi was disparaging Jigme Drakpa II in the midst of court and state monks.

According to Jigme Drakpa II's biographer, Norbu Rinchen ingratiatingly informed Jigme Drakpa II that the Desi spoke ill about Jigme Drakpa II to the congregation of state monks and Desi's court:

> Formerly, I had plans to offer the office of the political leader to the incarnation of Zhabdrung [i.e. Jigme Drakpa II] but this Zhabdrung incarnation, as if corrupted by an evil spirit, is not staying in one place. Instead, he is misbehaving and not maintaining the ways of a lama. Now, I shall not offer the political office to this incarnation.[58]

He added that Desi Chödrak was an enemy of the guru and such an evil person must be eliminated through sorcery and that devotees like him are ready to die for their spiritual master. These words of instigation Norbu Rinchen is said to have spoken with the hope of attaining for himself the post of the chief of protocol of the state, if Desi Chödrak were eliminated and Jigme Drakpa II were to come to power. Jigme Drakpa II neither listened to Norbu Rinchen nor made efforts to reconcile with the Desi. Instead, he went into a retreat when he saw a terrible vision portending the things to come. First the Mochu river dried up leaving all fishes struggling. Then in its place, a sea of blood was formed and some armed men appeared to sprinkle, drink and wash in it. He interpreted the drying of the Mochu as the impending death of the Desi and the sea of blood as the strife which was to follow.[59] There were also other ominous signs indicating the calamities to come. Unnerved by the vision, Jigme Drakpa II came out of the retreat and conducted a series of esoteric rituals, purportedly to avert the calamities and in self-defence. As predicted, a conflict soon erupted between the Desi and Jigme Drakpa II's party and Desi Pema Chödrak was killed some time in the winter of 1809.[60] The state monks and the leading officials installed the reigning hierarch Tshultrim Drakpa, the third incarnation of Tenzin Rabgay, as the 26th Desi, placing in his hands the reins of both the secular and spiritual affairs. As this political transition took place, Jigme Drakpa II embarked on a pilgrimage to Tibet.

Tshultrim Drakpa (1790–1830), a member of the Bönbji family and relation of his previous incarnations, Mipham Wangpo and Jigme Sengay, was not a strong leader. He did not possess the political will to rule. Besides, he is said to have cultivated a genuine respect for and a benign relationship with Jigme Drakpa II. Thus, it was perhaps at his behest that the court and state monks sent a team of messengers led by two prominent persons to invite Jigme Drakpa II, who was then in retreat having returned from Tibet. Jigme Drakpa II initially declined to come to Punakha giving as a reason the importance of his spiritual retreat. The messengers persisted saying that he should, if at all possible, return to live with the court and monks in the two capitals, or otherwise come to Punakha for a few nights when he could give advice to the court and monks. At the least, they pleaded him to visit Punakha on a day trip. After consulting the protecting deities through divination, he eventually accepted a visit to Punakha from Talo Sa-ngag Chöling on a day trip.

When Jigme Drakpa II arrived in Punakha in the third Bhutanese month of 1809, Tshultrim Drakpa asked him to take over the post of the Desi. Tshultrim Drakpa admitted that he was neither interested nor capable of running a country and wished Jigme Drakpa II to take over the office. Jigme Drakpa II politely declined but the same petition was made again in the afternoon by a group of senior members of the court and clergy. Jigme Drakpa held his ground and insisted on returning to his base before it got late but they implored him at least to stay in Punakha for the night and return the following day if he so wished. Jigme Drakpa II relented to this request and decided to spend the night in Punakha. In the evening, the group approached him once again with many presents to supplicate Jigme Drakpa II to take the post of Desi, even reminding him that it was his responsibility as an incarnation of Zhabdrung to take care of the country. Jigme Drakpa II was furious and terribly upset by the imposition but he very reluctantly accepted to assume the post. Immediately, there was a rush of preparation for the investiture and the news that Jigme Drakpa II was going to be enthroned as Desi the following morning began to spread. In and around the *dzong*, there was much activity as courtiers and monks made preparations for the ceremony of enthronement.

However, when the morning came, there was no bustle and the *dzong* was quiet and calm. The monks finished their morning prayers and breakfast and yet there was no sign that an enthronement was going to take place. Some local villagers arrived to watch the ceremony but returned to their work when nothing happened. By mid-morning, Jigme Drakpa II's attendant even saddled the horse, pretending to get ready for their return to Sa-ngag Chöling but there was no sign of any activity. No officer or monastic leader either came to see Jigme Drakpa II or inform the party. Jigme Drakpa II and his party waited for something to happen, utterly perplexed and offended.

What they did not know was that the plan for the enthronement ceremony was aborted late in the night after a few powerful supporters of Tshultrim

Drakpa protested against the transfer of power to Jigme Drakpa II. These men were not among the group who decided on the power transfer and entreated Jigme Drakpa II to become the Desi earlier in the afternoon. They challenged the decision to replace Tshultrim Drakpa by Jigme Drakpa II adding that the court and clergy were acting like children to unanimously request Tshultrim Drakpa to be the Desi a few months ago and then to remove him for no reason. They defied the plan to remove Tshultrim Drakpa from the office of the Desi and vowed to fight against such actions. The Je Khenpo and the monastic and court officials had no option but to suspend the preparation for enthronement in order to avoid any bloodshed.

By mid-afternoon of the day the enthronement was due to happen, Jigme Drakpa II and his party had resigned themselves to the opinion that the whole fuss was a hoax to ridicule and dishonour him. The enthronement never took place. Embarrassed and insulted, they now prolonged their stay in Punakha by pretending that Jigme Drakpa II was ill. They contemplated what course of action they could take to punish their opponents. Open confrontation was not an option as they were only about forty men in total. Beside, Jigme Drakpa II discouraged his attendants from any untoward actions. His supporters insisted upon actions, whether in the form of religious sorcery or real attack, to wreck vengeance on the opponents, who snubbed the enthronement. By the following morning, the opponents, on their part, had also posted guards around the *dzong* to pre-empt any attack. The news of rising tension and imminent war between the parties of the two incarnate hierarchs spread in the region.

At this point, Chudra Gopön and Katama Palbar, the *dzongpön* of Punakha, along with their men pledged their allegiance to Jigme Drakpa II. The *dzongpön* of Wangdiphodrang was also summoned but he dissuaded Jigme Drakpa II from engaging in an armed conflict. Taking this advice, Jigme Drakpa II also decided to return to Sa-ngag Chöling without stirring any trouble. But before he could do so, his attendants led by Chudra Gopön and Katama Palbar launched an attack on the government at night. These two officials feared that if Jigme Drakpa II returned to his reclusive life in Sa-ngag Chöling and the Wangdi *dzongpön* to his base in Wangdiphodrang, they would have neither an ally nor any cause left. The attackers managed to take over the central tower of the *dzong*, where Jigme Drakpa II was now taken to conduct prayers to the protecting deities. In middle of the turmoil, Tshultrim Drakpa, the incumbent Desi managed to climb out of the window along a rope. He sought refuge in the residence of the Je Khenpo.

In this manner, Jigme Drakpa II's party gained control of the *dzong* for some time and took over the government in the spring of 1809 but this did not last long. The Dagana *pönlop*, who harboured a dislike of the *dzongpön* of Punakha, went to Thimphu and raised the support of both the Paro *pönlop* and Thimphu *dzongpön*. He also despatched a message to the Tongsa *pönlop*, who we saw earlier was not in favour of Jigme Drakpa II. Thus, the warriors of Bhutan converged in Punakha, where a full-scale war erupted between the forces faithful to Jigme Drakpa II led by the *dzongpön*s of Punakha and Wangdi on one side and the troops faithful to Tritrul Tshultrim Drakpa and Sungtrul Yeshe Gyaltshen led by the *dzongpön* of Thimphu and the three *pönlop*s of Tongsa, Paro and Dagana on the other.

The fighting did not last very long as it was already the middle of spring and the state monks and the government moved to Thimphu. The government forces also moved with the government and monks to Thimphu, where Sungtrul Yeshe Gyaltshen was installed as the new Desi in the fourth Bhutanese month. Tshultrim Drakpa retired to Tango. Sungtrul Yeshe Gyaltshen was born in Khasarkha in the Thimphu valley and as a young boy recognized as the third speech incarnation of Zhabdrung. He received his training under senior masters of his day and was appointed as Je Khenpo in 1807. In the spring of 1809, he was made to resign from the post of Je Khenpo and installed as the 27th Desi when Tshultrim Drakpa retired. After the government and monks moved to Thimphu, Jigme Drakpa II left Punakha for Wangdiphodrang where his men continued to fight with the men of Tongsa *pönlop* in the Shar valley. Among the men fighting for Jigme Drakpa II were Pala and Pila, the two brothers from Dungkar who were cousins of his sister's husband. Pila's grandson would later become the first King of Bhutan. Some of his forces marched to Thimphu and managed to capture Semtokha, which Jigme Drakpa II used as his summer residence. Although the control over the rest of the country was in the hands of the government under Sungtrul Yeshe Gyaltshen in Tashichödzong, Jigme Drakpa II and his team operated a rival court based in Semtokha.

The summer of 1809 passed with no major confrontation between the two factions led by the two regal incarnates. When it was time for harvest, Jigme Drakpa's faction demanded that some portions of the *wangyön* (དབང་ཡོན་) or grain tax be given to the dissident group based in Semtokha. The Tashichödzong faction refused to share the offering saying 'the offering of grains for Semtokha faction has yet to be planted'. However, the forces of Jigme Drakpa II successfully ambushed some people carrying the tax to

Tashichödzong and managed to appropriate some of it. With the onset of autumn, Jigme Drakpa II returned to Wangdiphodrang and from there to Punakha. The state monks and governing court also soon arrived in Punakha accompanied by the troops. Men fighting on both side once again converged in Punakha and fighting broke out leaving no one in peace.

In a concerted effort to end the violence, the elders and chieftains of the western valleys gathered to request the clergy to mediate between the warring parties and bring an end to the conflict. The 17th and 19th Je Khenpos, who were retired, and the incumbent 21st Je Khenpo Jampal Drakpa led the negotiations between the two factions. It was agreed that both Sungtrul Yeshe Gyaltshen and Jigme Drakpa II were to rule jointly as Desi. Jigme Drakpa II, thus, became the 28th Desi but the joint rule did not last long. By the spring of 1810, the two hierarchs decided to occupy the post independently and they consulted the protecting deities on who should remain on the throne as the Desi, using the common device of a 'divining by lot'. It is not clear if they wanted to relinquish the post or hold the position but it looks more likely that they were both tired of the power sharing and wished to return to their easy and quiet hermetic life. The 'lucky dip' came out in favour of Yeshe Gyaltshen as the ruler. Jigme Drakpa II's biographer, however, curiously suggests that the lucky dip came out in favour of Jigme Drakpa II but that he deliberately hid the actual result and pretended that the divine verdict was for Yeshe Gyaltshen to rule so that he could renounce the political burden as well as make his enemies happy. Whether this is true or not, Yeshe Gyaltshen continued as the Desi following the outcome of divine lucky dip. Jigme Drakpa II retired to Semtokha, where he started to compose the biography of his teacher, Jamyang Gyaltshen. But soon, he fell ill and was carried to Talo Sa-ngag Chöling on a stretcher.

Yeshe Gyaltshen ruled the country peacefully during the summer of 1810 but when the government and state monks returned to Punakha in autumn, Katama Palbar, the *dzongpön* of Punakha, reignited the factional fighting. He killed the chamberlain of Yeshe Gyaltshen and arrested several important monastic and civil hierarchs. This time, however, Katama Palbar was on his own as even Jigme Drakpa II chastised him for rekindling the troubles. He was consequently driven out of the Punakha *dzong*. One of his important allies was thrown into the river and many others banished by the government. Katama Palbar sought refuge in Baling temple, where the 17th Je Khenpo was residing. On the concluding day of the Punakha Drubchö festival, the state forces laid siege to the temple and set flames to it with

Katama Palbar, his wife and his son trapped within it. The 17th Je Khenpo was distraught with anguish for failing to protect the fugitives who sought refuge with him.

It may be mentioned here that the Drubchö festival of Punakha was a major event when the *dzongpöns, pönlops, zimpön*s and many other senior officers gathered in Punakha for the annual council. Begun as a celebration of victory over Tibetans and a ritual of thanksgiving to the protecting deities in 1649 by Zhabdrung, it was the most important event in the medieval state calendar. The festival was also an occasion when the appointments and removals of important officers were made, as Krishna Kanta Bose noted in 1815, and national issues were discussed by the clergy and civil leaders. Consequently, much of the contestation and conflicts concerning the claim to power also took place on this occasion and ironically, the Buddhist festival became probably the most turbulent and bloodiest events in Bhutan's national calendar. Like many others before him, the fate of Katama Palbar and his family was sealed as the concluding prayers of the Buddhist festival were being said.

Yeshe Gyaltshen did not enjoy the post of Desi although his chief enemy was eliminated. He retired in 1811 and returned to his seat of Sa-ngag Chökhor in Paro. In the following years, both he and Jigme Drakpa II would spend time performing religious rituals, patronizing religious projects and developing their monastic seats: Sa-ngag Chökhor for Yeshe Gyaltshen and Talo Sa-ngag Chöling for Jigme Drakpa II. The *pönlop* of Tongsa, Tshaphu Dorji, was installed as the 29th Desi. We may recall that he started the rebellion from the east against the government of the 23rd Desi in 1805. Apart from his active involvement in the conflicts between the two factions supporting the different incarnate hierarchs, we know nothing about him. If his military campaigns were aimed at wresting the office of the Desi for himself, as Pema Tshewang claims, he accomplished this mission but he was not to enjoy the fruits of his hard work for long. A few months after he became Desi, he died in office, most probably killed by the forces of Sonam Drukgay, the *dzongpön* of Thimphu. It was perhaps during his short reign that Thomas Manning, the first Englishman to enter Lhasa, passed through Paro on his way. He was the first European to visit Bhutan in the nineteenth century although his passage through Paro was of no consequence to Bhutan.[61]

Sonam Drukgay succeeded Tshaphu Dorji as the 30th Desi in the summer of 1812. He was from Wang Sikhod but he grew up in Bumthang and served as the Tongsa *pönlop* and Thimphu *dzongpön* before becoming the Desi. His ascension, as one can imagine, was not without contention and the eastern

Bhutanese supporters of the late Desi Tshaphu Dorji and the attendants of Yeshe Gyaltshen and the incumbent Je Khenpo began to stir an upheaval. Fortunately, Sonam Drukgay managed to win the favour of Jigme Drakpa II and diffuse the tension using the latter's supporters.[62] He disbanded the various contingents of militia, which had assembled in Punakha under the warring chieftains, and sent the men back to their villages. With the forces largely dispersed, the country had under him a brief respite from the endless internal conflicts. Some sources state that one Shakya Özer co-ruled with Sonam Drukgay but we have no information on this ruler.[63]

Bhutan's stake in British expansion

Sonam Drukgay ruled as the Desi for five years during which Bhutan enjoyed some calm and peace. His rule saw neither serious turbulence nor remarkable achievements. The most notable proceedings during his rule were the exchanges he had with the British and Nepal, who were then at war. The Gorkha War or the Anglo-Nepalese War (1814–16) took place as a result of border tension, mutual suspicion and expansionist ambitions and resulted in the loss of about one third of Nepal's territory around the Terai region to the British. During the conflict, the British suspected Nepal of persuading its neighbours to join the war and particularly of instigating China against the British. China, which had established a firm base in Tibet since the Gorkha invasion of 1788–92, was wary of British expansion into the Himalayas. Thus, in order to remove China's fear, the British needed a way to reach China via Lhasa, for which Bhutan and Sikkim were the best channels.

Moreover, the British were fully aware of the close ties between the Gorkha rulers of Nepal and Bhutan. The patron–priest relationship between Gorkha rulers and Bhutanese lamas, which began over 150 years ago, was still continuing. We see in the last year of Sonam Drukgay's rule, the Bhutanese lama Sangay Norbu, who was sent to Nepal in 1813 to restore the Swayambhunath stūpa, return from Nepal having fulfilled the mission. Engaged in a protracted war with Nepal, the last thing the British wanted was for the anti-British intrigues to spread across the sub-Himalayas. It was very important for them to maintain good ties with Bhutan and they even openly requested the Desi to not take side with Nepal. The Desi gave an assurance of Bhutan's neutrality in the war and confirmed that its friendship with the British was like one 'between milk and water'.[64] Bhutan was enjoying a brief respite from the constant internal strife and a military campaign of a scale required to join Nepal and challenge the British would have been the last thing in the mind of the Bhutanese authorities.

However, there were minor territorial disputes with the British along the southern border. With British military support, the ruler of Cooch Behar took control over Maraghat, an area in the southwest clearly ceded to Bhutan in the treaty of 1774. The ruler of Cooch Behar produced a decree by Purling, the collector of Rangpur, which gave Cooch Behar the right over Maraghat but differed from terms of the treaty signed by Warren Hastings. The Bhutanese failed to provide any written evidence that Maraghat was under their jurisdiction, the papers perhaps being lost in one of the fires. They insisted that the area be reinstated given the cordial relationship the British and Bhutan enjoyed. They used the regional political situation to leverage this. Simultaneously, there was also a suspicion among the British that the ruler of Cooch Behar may be seeking military support from Bhutan to oust the British from his country in exchange for Maraghat. There were rumours of an exchange of letters between Bhutan and the ruler of Cooch Behar and of the latter even having sent his brother-in-law to Bhutan on such a mission. It was never fully established whether or not this was true but it certainly incited the British to make a concerted effort to gain Bhutan's favour and strengthen the political alliance. In the midst of war with Nepal, the British could not afford to have a conflict with the coalition of Cooch Behar and Bhutan.

It is partially to allay these fears of Bhutan's dealings with Nepal and Cooch Behar and to resolve the Maraghat dispute and strengthen the existent relations that the British sent the Indian official, Krishna Kanta Bose, to Bhutan in 1814. He was accompanied, according to Majamdar, by Ram Mohan Roy, the Hindu social reformer and activist who was a luminary of the Bengali renaissance in the nineteenth century.[65] Krishna Kanta Bose approached Bhutan from Bijnee and travelled via Sarpang, Tsirang, Khothangkha and Wangdiphodrang to Punakha. We do not know the political outcome of the mission, if there was any, but he left behind a very interesting account of Bhutan's state organization, administrative hierarchy, people's lifestyle, economy and natural environment of this time although one cannot take everything in his accounts without a pinch of salt. Whether it was due to a communication gap or driven by a political motive, or perhaps because of sheer ethnographic naïvety, his accounts are largely distorted and at times preposterous as the samples here demonstrate. Perhaps, his informants enjoyed pulling the legs of a credulous visitor.

When they fight with a Deb Raja, or the Pillos [*pönlop*s] amongst themselves, they stand at a distance and fire arrows at each other, and if one of them is killed, both parties rush forward and struggle for the dead body; whichever of them succeed in getting it, they take out liver and eat it with butter and sugar; they also mix the fat and blood with turpentine, and making candles thereof, burn them before the shrine of the deity.[66]

They eat the flesh of every sort of animal except that of the pigeon; but if any one should eat even that he will not lose caste, but will merely be exposed to ridicule.[67]

There was no obvious outcome of Krishna Kanta's mission but the routes he took and the report he wrote suggest that he was primarily sent to gather information about Bhutan's position vis-a-vis the Anglo-Nepalese war, relationship to Tibet and about Bhutan itself, if there were to be a military offensive against Bhutan. The exchanges between Bhutan and the British concerning Maraghat continued even after his visit but eventually ended in Bhutan's favour. Maraghat was officially returned to Bhutan on 14 June 1817 by the British authorities in Calcutta. Sonam Drukgay resigned from the office of the Desi in the same year due to ill health and Tenzin Drukdra became the 31st Desi. He was also from the Wang region and served as the Punakha *dzongpön* and *gongzim* (གོང་གཟིམ་) or chamberlain to the Desi before he was appointed to the office of the Desi by the clergy and senior officers. Tenzin Drukdra enjoyed a close relationship with Jigme Drakpa II, who had assumed the role of the Je Khenpo after the 21st Je Khenpo Jampal Drakpa resigned from the post in the summer of 1817. Jigme Drakpa II, however, did not remain long in this office as the problem he had in his foot deteriorated; Jigme Gyaltshen was appointed as the succeeding Je Khenpo. Later historians do not even list Jigme Drakpa II among the Je Khenpos.

Soon after Tenzin Drukdra came to power, there was a rebellion led by Trelwa, the *pönlop* of Tongsa. We do not know what instigated the rebels but the eastern Bhutanese forces once again reached Thimphu. The senior members of the clergy were yet again asked to mediate but even before negotiations started, Trelwa was stabbed to death. The elders of the clergy switched from conducting negotiations to funerary services, these being the two major occupations of the monastic hierarchs during the times of strife. In 1822, after five years on the throne, Tenzin Drukdra resigned from the post of the Desi and settled in Semtokha to pursue a religious life. He was succeeded by Chökyi Gyaltshen from Wang Sikhod.

Chökyi Gyaltshen started his career as a monk and was the *dzongpön* of Thimphu when he was selected to be the 32nd Desi. He carried out a number of cultural and religous projects, including installing the large gilded copula over the tower and main gate of Tashichödzong using 5872 measures of gold and 23,348 measures of mercury. He also plated the *rabsel* wooden frames of the Dechenphug temple in Thimphu with copper and made a large distribution of wealth to the citizens in the country. Many other religious projects also took place around the time of his rule although they were not directly his initiative. The rising monk scholar Sherab Gyaltshen renovated Dumtse, Zarchen, Khagu and Kyerchu temples in Paro and Jigme Drakpa II expanded his seat in Sa-ngag Chöling and introduced its annual festival with five days of entertainment. The dance known as Chözhe and the mask dance-drama of the Stag and the Hound were introduced at the festival along with the Rakṣha dance of Dorlungpa and the Ngonpa dance of Nyizergangpa.

Chökyi Gyaltshen's reign also witnessed an important change in Bhutan's geopolitical situation with the takeover of Assam by British India in 1826. This event does not appear to have featured as a major issue for the Bhutanese government at that time. Perhaps, because the seats of government were on the other end of the country, the troubles in Assam were not felt acutely. However, the change of power in Assam would lead to major political ramifications in the subsequent decades and centuries as we shall see. The British takeover of Assam was a result of the First Anglo-Burmese War (1824–26), allegedly the longest and most expensive war in British Indian history and the first event leading to the end of Burmese independence. Ironically, it was a direct outcome of Burma's own expansionist policy which brought it in direct military conflict with British India.

As early as 1784, Burma began invading the areas of today's north Indian states and its conquest reached Assam by 1817. The Burmese soldiers caused devastations in the occupied areas leading to the rise of large groups of rebels and refugees, which spilled over to the British Indian territory. Furthermore, the Burmese forces pursued these rebels and refugees into the British territory and provoked a full-scale war with the British in 1824. A war was waged for two years and in 1826 the Burmese army was defeated, the King of Burma forced to sign the treaty of Yangdabo and Burma made to pay Rs 10 million as indemnity for expenses of the war. Consequently, the British took formal control of Assam and other states in the region after thrusting out the Burmese invaders.

The British takeover of Assam in 1826 ended the six centuries of Ahom rule in Assam and for the first time made Bhutan share a contiguous border to the south with British India. Prior to the British control, Bhutan is said to have had a very active trade link with Assam but nothing much is known about its relationship with the Ahom rulers. Most likely, a lot of Bhutanese traders and pilgrims went to Assamese towns including Hajo, a pilgrimage site widely considered at that time to be the place where the Buddha passed away. British archaeologists were to prove only around 1862 that Kusinara in modern-day Uttar Pradesh was the spot for the final act of the Buddha. We shall return to the ramifications of the new territorial situation in the next chapter.

Death, destruction and reappearance

The final year of Chökyi Gyaltshen's rule saw the death of four leading incarnations. Firstly, the 17th Je Khenpo Yeshe Dorji, the incarnation of Seula Jamgön, passed away on the nineteenth of the fourth Bhutanese month, 10 June 1830. Considered as an embodiment of the future Buddha, Yeshe Dorji was one of the most respected religious figures of his time. His death was followed by the demise of Tritrul Tshultrim Drakpa in the sixth Bhutanese month. This hierarch had retired to Tango, the seat of his earlier incarnation, Tenzin Rabgay, after the supporters of Jigme Drakpa II took over Punakha and ousted him in 1809. Two months after Tshultrim Drakpa's demise, on the thirtieth of the eighth Bhutanese month, 16 October 1830, Jigme Drakpa II passed away in Talo Sa-ngag Chöling after having finished the new annual Tshechu festival in this centre. He instructed his disciples to keep his body embalmed for the sake of posterity. It was later enshrined in a silver reliquary stūpa.

Barely a month after the death of Jigme Drakpa II, on the twenty-seventh of the ninth Bhutanese month, 12 November 1830, Sungtrul Yeshe Gyaltshen passed away in Sa-ngag Chökhor in Paro. By then, he had completed his works of expansion and refurbishment of the Sa-ngag Chökhor. With the death of Tritrul, Thugtrul and Sungtrul, only one of the four regal incarnations was left behind. This was Gyalse Trulku Jampal Dorji II[68] (1798–1833), about whom we know very little. He was recognized as the fifth incarnation of Zhabdrung's son Jampal Dorji and after the death of three older regal incarnations, he ascended the golden throne of Gyaltshab in the eleventh month of 1831 without any dispute.

Chökyi Gyaltshen, however, did not last in the post of the Desi to see the installation of Jampal Dorji II on the golden throne. In 1830, Dorji Namgyal, the *pönlop* of Tongsa led a rebellion against the Desi with a desire to win the office of the Desi for himself, according to Pema Tshewang.[69] Chökyi Gyaltshen may have initially succeeded in resisting the rebellion but Dorji Namgyal allegedly sought military support from the Ambans in Lhasa. The Ambans were Chinese representatives stationed in Lhasa by the Qing rulers of China with significant military support. A small contingent of Chinese soldiers probably arrived in Bhutan to assist Dorji Namgyal, who eventually managed to defeat the Desi's forces. Following his defeat, Chökyi Gyaltshen stood down from the post of Desi in 1831 and Dorji Namgyal became the 33rd Desi.

Dorji Namgyal was from the Wang valley and a nephew of the 30th Desi. He was thus groomed from his early youth for a court life but his term as the Desi was far from smooth and peaceful. Soon after he took office, a fight erupted in 1832 in Punakha during the death anniversary of Zhabdrung between his forces and those who supported the previous Desi. In the turmoil that ensued, Punakha *dzong* was once again reduced to cinders and the monk body had to move to Thimphu.[70] This was the fourth fire of Punakha in less than half a century. Desi Dorji Namgyal immediately launched the project to rebuild the *dzong* and Sherab Gyaltshen, now a leading monastic figure, was once again put in charge of the interior art designs. Meanwhile, the forces of Dorji Namgyal marched into Thimphu in pursuit of the previous Desi, who had retired there. The previous Desi fled further to Paro, where his ally, Agay Haapa, the *pönlop* of Paro, gave him protection and support. Dorji Namgyal pursued his enemy to Paro, where his forces came into direct confrontation with the men of the *pönlop* of Paro and the previous Desi.

An all-out war had already started at Chewakha when the incumbent and previous Je Khenpos and the retired Desi Tenzin Drukdra intervened at the request of local elders to mediate between the two warring parties. We know that one of the senior figures who accompanied the three leaders in mediation was Sherab Gyaltshen.[71] The efforts of the monastic elders resulted in a peaceful settlement and the previous Desi Chökyi Gyaltshen was allowed to retire in Wangditse in Thimphu. Dorji Namgyal returned to Punakha to continue the reconstruction of the *dzong*, which was finished and consecrated in the winter of 1832. Zhabdrung's body, which was temporarily housed in Wangdiphodrang, was reinstated but not all was to go well.

Firstly, the incarnate prince-regent Jampal Dorji II passed away on the seventeenth of the third Bhutanese month, 5 May 1833, leaving the Bhutanese state without any of the four regal incarnations. Unlike previous decades when several of them were often simultaneously vying for the golden throne, Bhutan was now without a single one of them. The death of all four incarnations must have left the political leaders and aspirants without a religious figurehead, whom they often used as a puppet to further their political ambitions and actions. It must have also left the pious Bhutanese public with much uncertainty as the most important institutional post of the reigning hierarch remained vacant. Given the importance of a spiritual figurehead, the absence of a regal incarnation may have left a vacuum in the Bhutanese psyche. However, this did not take much time to change as three of the incarnations were soon found and once again used as pawns of political games.

Secondly, the tension between Dorji Namgyal and his opponents was still fermenting and far from over. Inevitably, a fight erupted on the thirteenth of the eleventh Bhutanese month, 24 December 1833, in which Dorji Namgyal was fatally stabbed. It seems Athang Thinley, the *gongzim* or chamberlain of the Desi was appointed as acting regent while Dorji Namgyal lay ill with the stab wound.[72] With most of his cultural projects unfinished, Dorji Namgyal eventually succumbed to his wound and Athang Thinley became the 34th Desi on the eleventh of the twelfth Bhutanese month, 21 January 1834.[73] The cultural projects started by Dorji Namgyal were later finished by the rising religious hierarch, Sherab Gyaltshen.

Athang Thinley was a pious man and one of the main projects he undertook as the Desi was the recruitment of some 320 new monks for the state monk body as monastic membership had fallen very low. The new recruits came to be known as the Athang Thinley's sixteen scores of monastics. However, in the summer of 1835, the Desi Athang Thinley died in Thimphu from an incurable disease and an internecine conflict broke out immediately after his death among the people of Wang as officials vied for the position of power. Tashichödzong 'was turned into a hell' according to a contemporary account[74] and the former Desi Chökyi Gyaltshen once again came to power as the 35th Desi. Despite being ousted by Dorji Namgyal in 1831, he remained politically active, sharing close ties with the *pönlop* of Paro and many other senior hierarchs.

Chökyi Gyaltshen's second term as Desi, just like his first one, was marked by developments pertaining to the regal incarnations and relations with the British. If his first term saw the death of the three main reigning incarnates, his second term now witnessed the reappearance of all three of them. Firstly, a boy from Drametse in eastern Bhutan was recognized as the 4th Thugtrul or mind incarnation of Zhabdrung. The child's mother, Druk Gyalmo, was the sister of the previous incarnation, Jigme Drakpa II. Thus, in a canny familial scheme only possible in a system based on reincarnation, her late brother returned as her son. The boy's father was the *chöje* master of Drametse, who held the post of the chief official of Mongar. The child was verified using traditional methods and brought to the seat of his former incarnation in Talo, given the name Jigme Norbu and installed on the golden throne in Punakha in the winter of 1834.

About the time Jigme Norbu (1831–61) was elevated as Thugtrul or the mind incarnation of Zhabdrung, Jigme Dorji (1831–50) from Tang in Bumthang was also proclaimed to be the immediate incarnation of Yeshey Gyaltshen and thus the 4th Sungtrul or speech incarnation and installed in the seat of the previous incarnations in Paro. We also know that Thinley Gyatsho (1835–51), the rebirth of Tshultrim Drakpa and thus the 4th Tritrul or incarnation of Tenzin Rabgay, was also born in 1835 in Bumthang and soon afterwards recognized and invited to his seat in Tango. The emergence of the three leading incarnates was certainly a significant development for Bhutan in terms of both religion and politics although they did not exercise as much political power as some of their precursors did. However, we see in these three incarnations repetitions of the general patterns of political alignment which we have seen with the incarnations before. When Bhutan got divided into two political camps in 1838, Thugtrul was put at the helm of the faction at Thimphu while the other two incarnates allied together with the power in Punakha. In spite of being religious firgureheads for the rival courts, they seem to have enjoyed among themselves a cordial relationship, being more inclined toward religion than state politics and studying under the same renowned teachers.

Another notable series of events around the beginning of Chökyi Gyaltshen's second term concerns the office of the Je Khenpos. The Je Khenpos and other senior religious hierarchs played an important role as the social–political cement to hold the state together during civil wars. As political leaders engaged in ruthless and violent battles for selfish gains, it was often these enlightened monastic elders to whom the nation turned with the plea to mediate and settle the conflicts and heal the wounds of hatred. Both in their capacity as mediators and spiritual advisors and as masters of religious rituals and prayers, which the pious populace believed would help solve the political problems, they worked tirelessly, sometimes risking their own lives. They used the power of their office and their spiritual stature to advise, admonish and suppress the pugnacious politicians, to negotiate between warring parties, to rebuild and salvage the damages of war and to organize and conduct numerous religious ceremonies to remedy the social ruptures and avert them in the future.

One such figure was Jampal Drakpa (1766–1835), the 21st and 23rd Je Khenpo, who occupied the office twice in 1811–16 and 1826–31. This luminary passed away in the wake of the conflict in 1835 followed by the 24th Je Khenpo Shakya Gyaltshen in 1836. A month after the latter's demise, Sherab Gyaltshen (1772–1847), a leading figure and renaissance man, whom we have come across many times earlier, was appointed as the 25th Je Khenpo on the first of the seventh Bhutanese month, 13 August 1836. Throughout his life, this hierarch carried out numerous religious projects and countless religious ceremonies for the welfare of the state, some of which he funded by giving up everything he possessed. He was mainly responsible for the redevelopment of interior art works in the Punakha *dzong* following the last three fires and some of the art work in the Wangdiphodrang *dzong* after the fire in 1838. Other works included the renovation of temples of Dumtse, Kyerchu, Khangu, Zarchen, Drangay, Langma, Samarzingkha, Drukchöding and the establishment of the Kila hermitage and Gorina monastery in Paro.

He was indisputably the most renowned religious master in western Bhutan at the time he was appointed Je Khenpo. Both the clergy and laity held him in great esteem. All incarnate lamas of western Bhutan, who lived around that time, received teachings from him and he was deeply respected by most political leaders. He was certainly revered by Desi Chökyi Gyaltshen and later by Desi Tashi Dorji with whom he struck a good rapport. His biography, which is today a rare and rich source of information, gives us not only a detailed account of his impressive life and works but also an accurate picture of Bhutan's religious and cultural atmosphere, economic condition and political vicissitudes around the first half of the nineteenth century.[75]

The existence of saintly figures such as Sherab Gyaltshen was, however, sadly counteracted by the growth of power-hungry and pugnacious officialdom across the country. Civil strife was far from over and Chökyi Gyaltshen's second term would end as violently as the first term with a rebellion once again from the east. But before we discuss his final fall, we shall turn to the events along the southern border of Bhutan which were beginning to damage the economic lifeline of the state.

Civil Wars and Frontier Troubles

BY 1826, THE BHUTANESE border with British India and the British protectorate of Cooch Behar extended from the Teesta river on the west to the Dhansiri river, which flows through the Darrang district of Assam today (not be confused with the river of the same name flowing out of Nagaland), on the east. This stretch of borderland, ranging in breadth from ten to twenty miles, was composed of plains and Himalayan foothills, which are extremely fertile and conducive for cultivation. The tract was administratively divided into eighteen duars or passes and under the control of provincial governors known as *dzongpön* or *drungpa* whom the British called Soubah. Seven of these duars between the Dhansiri and Manas rivers fell within Bhutan's border with Assam, thus called the Assam duars, and eleven of them, between the Manas and Teesta rivers, fell within the border with Bengal, thus called the Bengal duars. Despite the remote and itinerant Bhutanese control, the duars were generally run by local officers, who were not ethnic Bhutanese but appointed by the Bhutanese authorities, particularly by one of the three *pönlop*s under whose jurisdictions the duars fell.

While Bhutan generally enjoyed absolute possession of the eleven Bengal duars, its control over the seven Assam duars was not straightforward. Even during the Ahom rule, the Bhutanese did not gain full possession of the duar tracts. As a result, they are said to have harassed the population along the Assam frontiers with persistent incursions and raids. In order to avoid these violent attacks, the Ahom rulers gave possession of the five duar tracts along the Kamrup district to Bhutan in exchange for an annual payment. The payment included about thirty-seven *tola* of gold, thirty-seven bags of musk, thirty-seven yak tails, thirty-seven daggers, thirty-seven blankets, fifty-seven ponies and about 4785 Narrainee rupees in cash in total. Two duars of Khaling and Buri Guma along the Darrang district were occupied by the

Ahoms from 15 July to 15 November and by the Bhutanese for the rest of the year. This arrangement between Bhutan and Ahom rulers of control over the seven Assam duars continued with the British after their annexation of Assam in 1826. However, there were complications in its implementation, and problems soon began to erupt in Anglo-Bhutanese relations, leading to serious consequences.

First clash with the British in the east

In the years following the British annexation of Assam, the relationship with the British along the southern border became difficult. To begin with, the British were dissatisfied with the payments they received from Bhutan for the duars although Bhutan paid exactly the same amount as they did previously to the Ahom rulers. Cash payment was deposited in the local treasury and payment in kind such as daggers and blankets sold in a public auction to convert to cash. But each year there was a discrepancy between what the British expected and received in cash. The discrepancy was mainly due to the mischief of the officers the British employed to collect the payments, Sezawals, who changed articles they received with substitutes of inferior quality for the auction.[1] The alternating control of the two duars in Darrang district also proved too complicated for the British officers, who may have wished for a complete control of the territory.

To make things worse, there were frequent cross-border raids and counter-raids from both sides, often clandestinely sanctioned by the local officers, who shared the booty with the perpetrators. The raids were not only aimed at plundering property but also kidnapping people, including women and children, many of whom were employed as slaves. A great number of medieval Bhutanese serfs, one can safely surmise, originated in the Indian captives of such raids. No doubt, the unending civil wars in Bhutan led to the lack of a strong central government and unregulated peripheral administration, which in turn rendered the situation along the borders conducive to such outrages. The border officials were able to exercise a great degree of freedom and autonomy in governing the duars to their own benefit without consideration of the greater good of the nation.

One such incident which sparked off some territorial conflict between Bhutan and the British was a skirmish in 1828 between a Bhutanese border official and a British agent for the Northeastern Frontiers. The *drungpa* or provincial official responsible for the Buri Gumar duar pursued some

Bhutanese fugitives into British territory and had them brought back but in their stride also carried off the British subject who gave refuge to the fugitives. David Scott, the British agent in the area, demanded the release of the British subject and sent a small contingent of eight sepoys to the frontier post, perhaps to enforce the demand. The *drungpa*, aided by one Nakpola and some 280 men attacked the British contingent killing some and carrying away many British subjects into captivity. David Scott retaliated with greater force and took full possession of the Buri Gumar duar. He demanded the release of all captives and the surrender of the *drungpa* and his associates who committed the outrage before any negotiation could take place.

However, the letters and demands the British submitted from the eastern end of Bhutan perhaps never reached the rulers in Punakha or even Tongsa. Even if they did, Bhutanese officials were meanwhile occupied by internal disputes and no negotiation took place with the British. The British managed to rescue most of their subjects in captivity but the *drungpa* or his associates were never caught or surrendered. The stalemate continued with the British occupying Buri Gumar until Bhutan made its first request to the British in 1831, three years after the occupation, to return the duar. Bhutan claimed the perpetrators of the offence were dead but the British were not convinced. A similar request was made again in 1832 and then in 1834 by Desi Athang Thinley when Buri Gumar was fully reinstated after Bhutan paid a compensation of Rs 2000 and reaffirmed that the *drungpa* and his main accomplice Nagpola were both dead.

Whether it was a fact or a ruse to quell British doubts, Bhutan claimed that the said *drungpa* was confined in chains in the Punakha *dzong* when the *dzong* was burnt down in 1832 and that Nagpola was sent to build a chain bridge near Punakha when one of the chains he was standing on accidentally snapped and he fell off to the torrents below and drowned. Two *zingup* officers were sent to the new British agent, F. Jenkins, to give evidence of the deaths and Jenkins, satisfied with their testimony, returned Buri Gumar to Bhutan at the end of July 1834. As was the case with most duars, Bhutan put it under the management of a local Assamese officer.

This truce, however, did not bring a total end to the episodes of raids and depredations along the duars but the lawless marauders, harboured by petty officials, continued the incursions across the border to plunder and kidnap. The ordinary people along the border, particularly those in the duars with alternating jurisdiction, remained oppressed from both sides. The tight control and smooth administration of the duars, which Bhutan direly needed to make the most out of these fertile plains and to maintain a cordial relationship with the British, would remain beyond Bhutan's grasp as political stability broke down at the capital.

Barely ten months after the settlement with the British over the Buri Gumar duar, there were reports of fresh outrages on British subjects by marauders under Bhutanese protection in the Bijni and Khaling duars. In May 1835, F. Jenkins, the British agent, reported some fifty armed men entering British territory from the Bijni duar and carrying off ten people. The British responded by sending a small detachment of infantry but this only provoked more incursions and a total of some twenty-two people were said to have been carried away in this area alone. The British stormed the Bhutanese stockade and captured the *drungpa* official responsible for the Bijni duar. They rescued some of the captives while others were released by the Bhutanese officer but many had already been taken northward to be enslaved by Bhutanese officials. The *drungpa* even confessed that some of the captives were sent as presents to the Tongsa *pönlop*.

The British had scarcely repulsed the incursions in Bijni, when new outrages were committed in the Darrang district from the Khaling duar in November 1835. This was followed by a major raid into the flourishing district of Kamrup from the Banska duar in January 1836. As usual, most of the depredations were perpetrated by lawless thugs operating under the clandestine protection of and with partial benefit to the delinquent local chieftains. The local officers managing the duars perhaps thought they could allow these depredations with impunity because the Bhutanese government was situated many weeks away from them and was itself seriously encumbered by internal strife and the British were reluctant to use any force, which could jeopardize their relationship with Bhutan. The situation may have seemed favourable for quick amassment of wealth for these individuals.

The British were not totally blameless as their accounts may have us believe. On their part, they exacerbated the situation by oppressing the people in the duar for money and this provoked more marauding of their subjects. We get a glimpse of this in an admission by F. Jenkins. Difficulties with Bhutan, the British agent wrote, were 'in some measure occasioned by the officers who held charge in our part'.[2] Unfortunately, we do not have any surviving records from the Bhutanese officers or their Indian representatives serving in duars giving their accounts of the conflicts to counterbalance the onesided view we have from the British sources. It is very plausible that the British contributed their share in stirring the problems as it was in their interest to gain full control of the highly productive tract of duars. We see their inclination to take over the duars for both its economic value and smooth administration of their frontier districts.[3] The Court of Directors in London even held the view that the duars were an integral part of Assam, and, thus, a possession of the British government.[4]

At any rate, the British agent decided to show a more robust response to the fresh raids into the Darrang and Kamrup districts although any overture to tackle the problem with full force was still resisted by the Governor-General with the fear of provoking Bhutan into a full conflict. By now, the new Assam Sebundies Corps has been formed, mainly from local recruits who were familiar with the hostile terrain and unhealthy climate of the duars, with a specific aim to deal effectively with troubles along the tracts. With sixteen men from this new corps, Captain Mathie marched into the Khaling duar and forced the local officer appointed by Bhutan to surrender some twelve perpetrators.

Soon after this, the British agent also dispatched a detachment of Assam Sebundies under Captain Bogle to the Banska duar to redress the depredations committed from there. The detachment crossed the border on 14 February 1836 and marched on Hazaragong, where the Boora Talookdar, the local manager of the Banska duar, was based. Talookdar had by then left for the Dewathang hills where his immediate master, the *drungpa* of Dungsam or the Dewangiri Rāja as he was known to the British, resided. With conclusive evidence that Talookdar was involved in the raids, Captain Bogle proclaimed the temporary annexation of the Banska duar and sent letters to the Dewangiri Rāja and the Tongsa *pönlop* demanding them to surrender the offenders including Talookdar, make reparations for the losses and to pay the arrears of tribute owed to the British. While internal conflict and border incursions went on, the Tongsa *pönlop* and the local officers responsible for the duars often neglected making the annual payments to the British leading to the arrears.

The Dewangiri Rāja responded first by sending two persons to persuade the British to leave the duar and when that failed, he descended from the Dewathang hills to negotiate with the British but Captain Bogle declined to meet him until the notorious offenders were surrendered. On 1 March 1836, the Dewangiri Rāja surrendered nineteen of the offenders and entered the British camp to meet Captain Bogle accompanied by twenty bodyguards on horses and 600 followers carrying matchlocks, arrows, bows, swords and spears. 'Their appearance in their gay dresses and their shining helmets of brass and iron' Captain Bogle noted, 'was much more imposing than could have been anticipated.[5] Captain Bogle demanded the surrender of Talookdar and several leading raiders who accompanied the Dewangiri Rāja and insisted that no further negotiation could take place without fulfilling this condition. The Dewangiri Rāja refused to give up Talookdar arguing that it was beyond his power to surrender an officer directly appointed by the Desi. The negotiation reached a dead end and the Dewagiri Rāja returned to the hills.

A few days later, in the evening of 7 March 1836, the Bhutanese troops made up of some 600 men under the Dewangiri Rāja clashed with the British detachment of some seventy-five men under Captain Bogle at Soobankhatta. This was the first of the major military clashes Bhutan was to have with the British in the nineteenth century. Both the Dewangiri Rāja and Captain Bogle were commanding their troops riding elephants. In spite of their numerical superiority, the Bhutanese forces were easily and quickly dispersed and defeated by the fire power of the British muskets. However, the main reason for the quick retreat of the Bhutanese despite being about ten times stronger than their enemy in manpower, it was thought, was the belief among the Bhutanese men that their leader was acting without the proper authorization from the government.[6] The men were not fully behind the Dewangiri Rāja's attempted assault on the British. The clash resulted in twenty-five dead and twice as many wounded on the Bhutanese side. The Dewangiri Rāja escaped to the hills and Talookdar and some ringleaders from the plains voluntarily surrendered themselves to the British, who then took formal control of the Banska duar and wrote to the Desi to that effect.

The collision with the British and the annexation of the Banska duar no doubted alarmed the government in Punakha. A month after the clash, two *zingup* officers arrived to investigate on behalf of the Desi and the Dharmarāja. The Desi was Chökyi Gyaltshen in his second term and the Dharmarāja was the young incarnate hierarch Jigme Norbu, the 4th Thugtrul. We have seen above how Jigme Norbu from Drametse was installed in 1834 on the throne of the Gyaltshab or prince regent, whom the British called the Dharmarāja. The two officers were then followed by a more formal delegation of four *zingup*s in May 1836. They represented the Desi, the Dharmarāja, the father of the Dharmarāja and the Tongsa *pönlop* under whose jurisdiction the duars in Assam fell. They must have also brought with them arrears of revenue and ponies, which the Tongsa *pönlop* sent.

The four *zingup*s also brought with them two letters from the Tongsa *pönlop* and the father of the Dharmarāja, both admitting in very friendly and courteous tones how they were totally unaware of the outrages committed by the border officers and how such trivial incidents should not damage the good friendship the British enjoyed with Bhutan. They claimed not to have received any of the letters which the British have sent prior to the annexation of the duar. 'I have never received any of your letters,' wrote the Tongsa *pönlop*. In a shrewd twist, they politely placed the moral onus on the British for jeopardizing a longstanding friendship due to minor mishaps caused by some reckless individuals. He further wrote:

At any rate, considering the great friendship subsisting between the Company and Bhutan, I beg you will not withhold your kindness from me, and that you will be well disposed every way . . . It would be sinful on your part were you to act otherwise; you know everything that is right. You will kindly pay attention to all that has been said, and remember you are for me, and I am for you. If you have a mind to listen to what enemies may say, and do things such as never was done; of course there is nothing that would prevent your doing so. You are however acquainted with all that is just and fair.[7]

Similarly, Tenzin Chögyal, the father of the Dharmarāja who was deputed to negotiate with the British wrote:

People between us by much backbiting cause confusion. Do not listen to any such tales, nor will I attend to what may be told me . . . You understand everything that is good and proper; you have many countries, let that suffice; should you by injustice think proper to deprive me of my little country, what is there to prevent?[8]

Although he was officially appointed by the state to lead the negotiations and deliver the payments, Tenzin Chögyal stayed in the temperate hills of Dewathang and did not travel to Gauhati to meet the British agent. Instead, the four *zingup*s represented Bhutan without a real mandate to carry out negotiations. They were actually assigned only to receive the duar from the British. Fortunately, the British agent F. Jenkins had been appeased by the congenial tone of the letters and he was only willing to resolve the issue. He quickly returned the granaries the British troops had seized but agreed to release the duar only after Bhutan had signed an agreement about future management of the duars and surrender all offenders. This, the *zingup*s, had no authority to do. So, they returned to Dewathang to consult Tenzin Chögyal, who sent them again with his seal on a blank paper which they subsequently filled with the eight-point agreement. According to the agreement adopted on 2 June 1836, Bhutan was to engage in putting down dacoity, deliver offenders or allow British troops to pursue them across borders, make the payments on time by a *zingup* in person, and if arrears accumulated to the size of one year's tribute, allow the British to seize the respective duar. With this, Jenkins returned the duar to Bhutan but the agreement was never ratified by the Desi or Tongsa *pönlop* and, therefore, remained officially invalid.

The fear of the unknown and the Pemberton mission

The unratified agreement of 1836 certainly marked the last chapter of the pro-Bhutan policy adopted by the British. Generally, the British approach to Bhutan since its first encounter with the country in 1773 had been a positive and favourable one. Apart from the military intervention on behalf of Cooch Behar, concerted efforts were made throughout the decades to avoid any hostilities and to gain increased access to Bhutan. The initial reason for this was primarily the trade interest, which was at the heart of the East India Company, and the promise Bhutan offered of being a small trading partner and, more importantly, a convenient trade route to Tibet and from there to China. The reason had changed slightly in the nineteenth century although trade still remained an important factor for pro-Bhutan policies. During the Anglo-Nepalese war, there were also political considerations to adopt a pro-Bhutan policy; they did not want the anti-British intrigues to spread across the sub-Himalayan foothills. It was reassuring for the British to have Bhutan stay out of the conflict.

With the British annexation of Assam in 1826, Bhutan and the British entered a whole new but complicated phase of relationship. The management of the duars as it was inherited from the Ahom rulers was no doubt inconvenient for both countries and the outrages committed by lawless dacoits who exploited the shaky situation seriously vexed the British. Yet, the British generally persisted in adopting a pro-Bhutan policy and avoided any direct hostilities with the state. Their military campaigns across the border were all targeted at delinquent local chieftains and went only as far as the foothills, mostly to penalize the offenders. Caution was taken at all levels to avoid provoking the Bhutanese state into military confrontation. There were several reasons for the British restraint.

Trade was still an important factor to maintain good relations with

Bhutan although it was not so much the benefit from Bhutan itself. The British still cherished the hope of reaching Tibet and China via Bhutan. A stable government and system in Bhutan was also advantageous to the British, especially in the smooth governance of the fertile plains of Assam bordering Bhutan. The lack of strong control of the duars indirectly affected the peace and productivity of the neighbouring areas in Assam. This has become a particularly important concern for the British with the discovery of indigenous tea in upper Assam in 1834. The land and climate of Assam was found to be suitable for growing tea and as the project of cultivating tea took off, Assam gained a new economic position. It had the potential to relieve the British of their dependency on China for tea trade.

However, the most important reason why the British persisted with a pro-Bhutan policy was their lack of knowledge about the country and its political leanings. After almost three quarters of a century of dealings with Bhutan, the British knew very little about Bhutan and its sociopolitical circumstances. They did come to know vaguely about the political instability and civil wars but their correspondences with the Bhutanese government had been intercepted by the border officials, who were largely working against them. They did not have direct contact with the Bhutanese government and had no confirmed knowledge of Bhutan's political situation. What little they knew must have been gathered haphazardly from the border officials and traders who visited the plains briefly. The Bhutanese knew even less about the British. Thus, an atmosphere of mutual apprehension and fear arising from the unknown existed between the two although they superficially claimed to be on friendly terms.

The big fear the British harboured about Bhutan from such ignorance was China's influence on Bhutan via Tibet. The British were worried about provoking China's wrath should they seriously attack Bhutan in retaliation for the depredations committed by the border officers. They were already aware of the two small neighbours of Bhutan, Sikkim and Tawang, being protectorates of Tibet, and thus indirectly linked to China. The British also knew about the communications between Nepal and China and almost certainly had heard of Nepal's diplomatic link with Bhutan. It is also likely that they came across rumours of the Chinese soldiers who were sent by the Amban in Lhasa to help the rebel Dorji Namgyal before he became the Desi. Pemberton mentions this in his report.[9] Under these circumstances, the last thing they wanted was to upset Bhutan and drag China into the anti-British intrigues, which, as it is, were already spreading along the sub-Himalayas.

Tension between the British and the Chinese Qing emperor was also already at the point of erupting into the famous Opium War.

However, in reality, China had no influence on or interest in Bhutan, and Bhutan's relations with Tibet were also at a very low point with no significant exchanges. If at all, the Bhutanese government would have viewed China and Tibet adversely. Jenkins, the British agent in Assam, got a rough idea of these situations but he, like his government, stood much in need of proper confirmation. Thus, he persuaded the new Governor-General, Lord Auckland, to open a direct contact with Bhutan by sending an envoy. Jenkins argued that a direct mission was the only way to overcome the misunderstanding caused by the frontier officers and to find out the actual status of Bhutan's connection to China.

Bhutan, however, was not willing to receive a British mission. When the British proposed to send a mission after the negotiations in 1836 over the Banska duar, the Bhutanese government politely declined to receive it, stating that there was no need until further problems arose. But the opportunity for the Governor-General to insist on sending a mission came again when Bhutan faced a revolt by Hargovind Katham, a landlord who controlled large parts of Bhutan's Mainaguri duar on the border with Bengal. This landlord inherited control over large parts of the duar from an uncle, who is said to have served the government of Bhutan in some ministerial capacity. However, with vicissitudes in Bhutanese politics, the landlord fell out of favour with the ruling government and was subjected to harassment by *zingup* officers. Until modern times, it was common practice in Bhutan for the government to send *zingup*s to penalize recalcitrant people and the *zingup*s would make outrageous demands and extort both goods and services according to their whims. Enraged by the harassment, Hargovind Katham put a couple of *zingup*s to death and revolted against the Bhutanese government with the help of some armed personnel from India and Nepal. He also sought military support from the British in return for a substantial tribute.[10] In order to thwart this revolt, Desi Chökyi Gyaltshen sent an officer to Calcutta to dissuade the Governor-General from providing any military support to the rebel landlord. The Governor-General acquiesced to the request and also grabbed the opportunity to announce that an envoy was being sent to Bhutan.

The chosen envoy was Captain Pemberton, accompanied by the botanist Dr Griffiths and Ensign Blake commanding an escort of twenty-seven men from the Assam Sebundies Corps. The objective of the mission was to assess Bhutan's political situation, particularly the presence of Chinese influence.

Pemberton was even instructed to proceed to Tibet if possible to revive the links started over sixty years ago. He also carried a letter from the Governor-General, which was to be sent to Tibet, if the mission failed to proceed to that country. The mission also aimed to gain a better understanding of the extent, resources and structure of Bhutan's physical country, in other words, to carry out an unauthorized survey. Much of central and eastern Bhutan was still a blank space to the British. Thus, the mission planned to start from as far east as possible and traverse the entire country, which it successfully did from Dewathang to Punakha despite Bhutanese reluctance to allow this.

Pemberton and his party entered Bhutan on 3 January 1838 and travelled via Dewathang, Tashigang, Tashi Yangtse, Kurtoe, Bumthang, Tongsa and Wangdi to reach Punakha on 1 April 1838. The mission had to take a detour along Tashi Yangtse and Kurtoe in order to avoid the rebel territory of Zhongar. The *dzongpön* of Zhongar in collaboration with his brother, the *pönlop* of Dagana, was at that time engaged in a rebellion against the government in Punakha. Pemberton was told that all able men of Zhongar region were conscripted to fight for their *dzongpön*[11] and it was advisable to 'avoid passing through the territories of these disaffected chieftains'. He, however, wrongly suspected that it was a ploy to impress on them 'the extremely difficult nature of the country' in case the British contemplated on a conquest. Little did he know that even the straight route through Zhongar had the same steep topography as the one they took and the rebellion was as serious as it could be. We shall turn now to this rebellion, which not only rendered Pemberton's mission fruitless but also led to two contending Desis ruling simultaneously from Punakha and Thimphu for half a decade.

Chakpa Sangay's rebellion and an unaccomplished mission

Chökyi Gyaltshen's second term as the Desi ended as tumultuously as his first one with a rebellion from the east. He was no more in control of Bhutan by the time Pemberton arrived in Punakha. By then, the rebels had already stormed Punakha. We don't know the precise reason for the rebellion led by the two brothers Chakpa Sangay, the *dzongpön* of Zhongar, and Dorji Norbu, the *pönlop* of Dagana. Pema Tshewang hints that it was the rivalry between people of the upper and lower Wang area which triggered the rebellion.[12] This is perhaps true if we are to follow the pattern of shifting power between the leaders from these areas. Apart from the short spells of rule by the incarnate hierarchs and by members of the Bönbji and Dungkar families, political power in the eighteenth and nineteenth centuries lay mostly in the hands of men from the Wang region, so much so that credulous visitors such as Bose and Eden even thought Wang referred to a caste of rulers.[13] Out of forty Desis who ruled from 1651 to 1851, more than half were from the Wang region, and the leaders from upper and lower parts of this region seem to have held the power alternately. The revolts and counter-revolts of this period in general ensued from strong sense of regionalism and desire to retain power in the family. Thus, it is highly likely that the rebellion by Chakpa Sangay and his brother from lower Wang against Chökyi Gyaltshen of upper Wang was inspired by regional rivalry.

The revolt led by Chakpa Sangay may also have a personal reason. Chakpa Sangay was the protégé of the 33rd Desi Dorji Namgyal, who ousted Chökyi Gyaltshen at the end of his first term and who was in turn killed by Chökyi Gyaltshen's men in 1833. It was perhaps to avenge his master's death and also to wrest power into his family that Chakpa Sangay started the rebellion. Whatever the reason, the rebels reached Punakha by March 1838. In the night of 11 March 1838, the rebels managed under the cover of darkness to penetrate into the Punakha *dzong* with the help of a tall flag pole.[14] Pemberton, however, reports that the door-keeper of the Punakha *dzong* assisted the rebels to enter and later got a promotion for his treachery.[15] Once the rebels were inside the *dzong*, the subsequent overthrow of Chökyi Gyaltshen's government was sharp and swift. In the commotion caused by the coup, Chökyi Gyaltshen managed to seek refuge in the company of the Je Khenpo Sherab Gyaltshen and the monks while other members of his faction fled from the *dzong*, thus ending Chökyi Gyaltshen's second term as the Desi. Soon after the take-over, Chakpa Sangay installed his elder brother, Dorji Norbu, on the throne as the 37th Desi. He himself took the post of both the chamberlain to the Desi and the *dzongpön* of Wangdi, thereby indirectly holding the reins of power.

Chökyi Gyaltshen and his faction were, however, unrelenting and far from conceding defeat. In order to settle the dispute without further bloodshed, the senior monastic figures and the retired Desi Tenzin Drukdra began negotiations between the two parties in earnest. As a result, Chökyi Gyaltshen was allowed to safely leave the Punakha *dzong* and retire in Wangditse but this did not end the strife. The supporters of Chökyi Gyaltshen found a new leader in the person of Tashi Dorji, the *dzongpön* of Thimphu, and held full control of Thimphu. They installed Tashi Dorji on the throne of the Desi in

Thimphu and blocked the new Desi and his government from making the seasonal migration to Thimphu. With the two blocs controlling each capital and vying for supremacy, a protracted war ensued although military clashes were temporarily suspended with the arrival of the British mission.

The mission arrived in Punakha on 1 April 1838 and met the new Desi Dorji Norbu on 9 April and the reigning incarnate or Dharmarāja Jigme Norbu a few days later. Pemberton described Dorji Norbu as about 'forty years of age, of rather dark complexion, mild manners and pleasing address' and 'a person of more than ordinary intelligence'. Jigme Norbu, he recorded, was 'a child of about nine years of age, and has held the present office for four years'.[16] He writes:

> His countenance possesses all the characteristics which so peculiarly mark the Mongolian race. The face is rather oval in its form, the eye very much elongated and very prominent, the nose short and rather flat. His complexion is fair, and he has a profusion of flowing black hair. On the occasion of our presentation, he was neatly and elegantly attired in a silken robe, and wore a pointed cap rather richly embroidered. The extreme neatness and cleanliness of his person and dress presented a very remarkable contrast to the filth which peered through the half-worn silk dresses of the motley group about him.

Griffiths, on the other hand, described the Desi as 'an ordinary-looking man in good condition' and the Dharmarāja as 'good looking, particularly when the looks of his father, the Tongsa Pillo [*pönlop*], are taken into consideration'.[17] Despite the cordial meetings, the British mission did not manage to carry out any serious negotiations and discussions with Desi. The political atmosphere was tense and the state of the new government still very precarious. The new Desi was as keen to have their company, perhaps to legitimize his rule in the public eyes, as the old Desi wanted to receive them for the same reason. However, Pemberton was exasperated by the Bhutanese disunity and the Desi's inability to sign the twelve-point agreement he had drafted. The Desi reiterated that the terms of the treaty were acceptable but he avoided ratifying it with frivolous excuses because the Tongsa *pönlop* seems to have objected to it.

Unable to achieve a breakthrough in negotiations, Pemberton finally embarked on his return journey on 9 May 1838 via Talo Sa-ngag Chöling, where the mission was cordially received by the ousted Desi. From there, the mission travelled through Thimphu, Chukha and Buxa to India. He neither managed to have a treaty signed by Bhutan nor have any successful overtures to Tibet. The Bhutanese outright refused to even forward his letters to Lhasa. His mission, nevertheless, was not utterly fruitless for the British because he produced one of the most detailed reports on Bhutan, which the Court of Directors desired all British officers concerned with Bhutan to read. Equally, Griffiths produced a journal with details of Bhutan's geography, flora and fauna although his remarks about the country and people were generally negative, and Ensign Blake produced a map of the mission's route.

The Pemberton mission marked the end of the forbearing and pro-Bhutan policy the British adopted and the beginning of a strict and punitive approach. In his concluding observations of his report, he noted that 'negotiation is utterly hopeless' while 'the nominal head is powerless and the real authority of the country is vested in the two Barons of Tongso and Paro, who divide it between them. A rigid policy under such circumstances would justify the immediate and permanent resumption of all the Dooars'.[18] However, he also argued that there are powerful reasons to pursue 'a less severe course of policy than that which stern justice and insulted forbearance demand'. He made two main suggestions; one of which was to take over the Assam duars under the jurisdiction of Tongsa *pönlop* so that 'the weight of punishment should fall more heavily upon him than upon those members of the Bootan Government whose conduct evinced a greater respect to the moderate demands and wishes of the British Government'. The aggressions on British subjects in Assam, he stated, were committed by people under the jurisdiction of Tongsa *pönlop*, who also prevented the ratification of the treaty. The other suggestion was to propose appointing a British representative in Bhutan, who would 'watch and counteract the evil consequences of unfriendly external influence and of internal misrule'.

Pemberton was right in lamenting the impotency of the government and the sad effects of contest for supremacy. Bhutan was gravely torn apart with civil unrest. The British were barely out of sight in the morning of 9 May when the fighting resumed in Punakha. As if the protracted civil strife were not enough of a tragedy for beleaguered Bhutan, another misfortune struck the country that spring. The Wangdiphodrang *dzong*, which was built by Zhabdrung in 1638, was destroyed by fire after two hundred years of being a prominent power base. The cause of the fire is not known but the Je Khenpo lamented that it was heartbreaking to hear about the destruction of Zhabdrung's seat due to the bad breath of heretics, perhaps referring to the British visitors. The British mission had by then left Bhutan without accomplishing the mission's objectives.

Two capitals, two rulers and oaths of reconciliation

The new Desi Dorji Norbu, who could not move his court to Thimphu that spring, set on the task of rebuilding the dzong in the same year. The young incarnate Jigme Norbu was also held back from travelling with the monk body to Thimphu and spent his summer in Khothangkha, where he had the rare experience of watching the Dolung Mani festival. He also met in Wangdiphodrang the 7th Peling Sungtrul who had come from Tibet to carry out the funerary rites for the 5th Gangteng Trulku. It is quite clear that as the incumbent prince-regent, Jigme Norbu's presence was important for Desi Dorji Norbu and his government. Having the incarnate hierarch on his side as the supreme figurehead gave the Desi and his government legitimacy. Meanwhile, the Thimphu bloc strengthened its position with the appointment of their own Desi Tashi Dorji; the ex-Desi Chökyi Gyaltshen had by now retired in Wangditse. Tashi Dorji and his court effectively controlled Thimphu and were also courting the 4th Tritrul Thinley Gyatsho, the incarnation of Tenzin Rabgay, as potential incarnate figurehead.

Since the unification of the country in the seventeenth century, Bhutan was for the first time seriously divided into two polities with two competing rulers. We may remember that Bhutan was mildly divided into two administrative polities between 1730 and 1735 with the secession of Paro to Kabji Dhondup. But the Desi at that time retained control over most of the country and the two capitals. The internal division this time was much worse with one group controlling the summer capital and the other the winter capital. The Punakha government under Dorji Norbu could not move to Thimphu for summer and Tashi Dorji and his court could not move to Punakha for winter when the monk body carried out their seasonal migration. Dorji Norbu partially used Wangdiphodrang as his summer base and Tashi Dorji came as far as Talo, where he established his winter office.

It appears that the powerful *pönlop* of Paro, Agay Haapa alias Tshultrim Namgyal, was on the side of the Thimphu government. He was a close ally of the ousted Desi Chökyi Gyaltshen. The government in Punakha under Dorji Norbu and Chakpa Sangay had control of Punakha, Wangdiphodrang and Dagana. The office of the powerful Tongsa *pönlop* changed hands at the peak of the rebellion, perhaps as a consequence of the power transfer in

Punakha. Ugyen Phuntsho of Tamshing, the shrewd official who wrote to the British earlier in 1836 and vetoed the treaty Pemberton presented to the Desi, was replaced by Tenzin Chögyal, the father of the reigning incarnate, Jigme Norbu. The former, Griffiths found, was 'the most aristocratic personage' he saw in the country and the latter 'a mean looking, bull-necked individual' but they were uncle and nephew.[19] Tenzin Chögyal previously worked as the chief official in Mongar under the *dzongpön* of Zhongar. We may recall that he was deputed to negotiate with the British in 1836 under Chökyi Gyaltshen's government. He may have previously remained neutral or mildly allied with the rebel forces and the Punakha bloc but his allegiance changed suddenly after his visit to Punakha, which cost him his life.

Some time in the winter of 1839, the Tongsa *pönlop* came to Punakha to mediate between the two warring governments. He set his camp at Medagang but even before any effort of mediation began, he was won over by the Thimphu bloc, probably through the persuasion of the Paro *pönlop*, Agay Haapa.[20] His son Jigme Norbu regretfully remarked that Tenzin Chögyal joined the Thimphu bloc after he was 'instigated by some bad people'.[21] Tenzin Chögyal's first move following his alliance with Thimphu was to remove his ten-year-old son, Jigme Norbu, from the Punakha *dzong*. The young incarnate was at that time occupying the throne of prince-regent and was symbolically at the helm of the Punakha bloc. Besides wishing familial solidarity, Tenzin Chögyal would have understood the political importance of having the symbolic leadership of the reigning incarnation for his own party. The presence of the regal incarnations as a figurehead gave the rulers legitimacy and moral authority for their military campaigns and rule in the prevailing public perception. On the eighteenth day of the twelfth Bhutanese month, 21 January 1840, Jigme Norbu's personal tutor was first taken out of the *dzong* under the pretext of being invited to perform a ritual outside the *dzong*. Then, young Jigme Norbu was put in a sack and smuggled out disguised as fruits by a courtier faithful to his father. Jigme Norbu later sarcastically remarked that although he had attained the precious humanhood, he was tied up in a small black leather bag and labelled as fruits. The 'whole experience was beyond words' for the young lama whose was brought to his father's camp. 'The joy of seeing old papa issued like flames, the worldly commotion at the dusty settlement whirled like winds and the thoughts of terror from worldly combats and cries such as "strike!" and "kill!" rushed like waterfalls,' he wrote.[22]

The conflict reached its pinnacle with the abduction of Jigme Norbu from the headquarters in Punakha. The turmoil and confusion even vexed the enlightened and peace-loving Je Khenpo making him deliver a public reprimand.[23] No doubt the power in Punakha must have considered Jigme Norbu's departure as a major blow to its campaign to assert supremacy in the country. The regime lost the most important incarnate figurehead but not all was lost as they still had with them the fourth speech incarnation, Jigme Dorji, from Bumthang. Soon after Jigme Norbu's departure, Desi Dorji Norbu installed Jigme Dorji on the golden throne of the prince-regent. The move demonstrates how important it was to have a regal incarnation as the figurehead.

As for Jigme Norbu, he was taken from his father's military camp to Talo Sa-ngag Chöling where the Desi of Thimphu bloc received him. Although he may have enjoyed the reunion with his father, that too was short-lived for the young incarnate. Some time in early spring of 1840, his father was stabbed to death in an ambush by the men of the Wangdi *dzongpön* while on his way to fetch more forces from Tongsa. His body was brought to Thinleygang, where the incumbent Je Khenpo Sherab Gyaltshen and his successor Yonten Gyatsho conducted the cremation. After this, young Jigme Norbu travelled to Thimphu, where the monk body soon joined him. Here, he resumed religous training under his master, Je Khenpo Sherab Gyaltshen, who shortly afterwards stepped down from the post of Je Khenpo to return to his hermitage in Gorina. Jigme Norbu spent his summer in Thimphu and winter in Talo Sa-ngag Chöling, closely accompanied by Desi Tashi Dorji but his family's tribulation was not yet over as we shall see below.

By the middle of 1840, the Punakha–Thimphu conflict reached a form of stalemate with the two Desis controlling a capital each but unable for both to impinge on the other. The public meanwhile bore the main brunt of this disunity at the power centres, probably with growing lawlessness in some areas and double imposition of taxes in others. Many may have felt insecure, confused and let down by their leaders and many men, needless to say, may have been exhausted fighting in the civil war. The country was getting sick of the contesting Desis and their pugnacious ways. It was perhaps out of such exasperation that a large number of headmen gathered in Kyerchu in some form of a public protest against the disruptive rulers. They petitioned the clergy and the former Desi Tenzin Drukdra to find an end to the conflict for the sake of public welfare. The clergy and ex-Desi sent two *pönlop*s to talk to the community leaders and the furore was diffused after a cordial meeting in Jagarthang although we don't know what exactly transpired.[24]

Sherab Gyaltshen's biography vaguely suggests that the headmen desired the leaders on both sides to take oaths in the presence of religious shrines and figures to end the conflict and work for the greater good of the country.[25] They may have pleaded the leading figures such as the Je Khenpo Sherab Gyaltshen and former Desi Tenzin Drukdra to make efforts to talk the rulers into taking such oaths. Whatever the agenda and outcome of the gathering in Kyerchu, we see an interesting series of atonement and oath-taking unfold in the next few years. During these ceremonial events, it seems the main political players and contestants were made to apologize for their transgressions in the presence of holy shrines and spiritual heavy weights and to take an oath to abandon political ill will and grudge, to reconcile with their enemies and to work for the general welfare of the country. This extraordinary tactic of mediation and diplomacy through the use of spiritual force and sociomoral pressure eventually helped resolve the differences between the conflicting governments and put an end to the civil war triggered by Chakpa Sangay's rebellion.

The first such ceremony took place in Talo Sa-ngag Chöling some time in 1840 when Desi Tashi Dorji and his court were perhaps made to take the oath in the presence of Sherab Gyaltshen, who had by then stepped down from the post of Je Khenpo, his successor the 26th Je Khenpo Yonten Gyatsho and the former Desi Tenzin Drukdra, who acted as witnesses. However, this first session of oath-taking scarcely lessened the strife as the Punakha group under Desi Dorji Norbu and Chakpa Sangay was still relentlessly fighting for dominion. In the autumn of 1841, political turmoil even blocked the seasonal migration of the state monks from Thimphu to Punakha, which in previous years took place in spite of the strife. Sherab Gyaltshen and the former Desi immediately intervened and travelled to Punakha to negotiate the smooth passage of the monk body. The state monks thus moved to Punakha in the middle of winter.

The strife had by then also spread to the eastern districts and was once again wrecking havoc on Jigme Norbu's family. His uncle, Drukdra Senge, and elder brother, Sonam Dhöndup, were at that point holding the posts of *dzongpöns* in Lhuntse and Zhongar respectively, these areas being directly under the jurisdiction of the Tongsa *pönlop*. Their appointments to these posts may have been made through Tenzin Chögyal's backing, which they had now lost. To make things worse, the new Tongsa *pönlop* allied with Chakpa Sangay and the Punakha bloc and they seem to have turned their full force on Jigme Norbu's uncle and brother.[26] Jigme Namgyal, who later became the

Desi and father of the first king, was at this point serving under the Tongsa *pönlop* and seems to have led some of the troops on this expedition to the east.[27] Apart from the districts of Lhuntse and Zhongar, the new *pönlop* seems to have had all other six eastern districts on his side. Faced with an overwhelming enemy and impending defeat, Jigme Norbu's uncle and brother escaped eastward to the regions of Tawang and Assam. The enemy soldiers arrested Jigme Norbu's mother and ransacked their family home in Drametse. The family's properties were looted and the servants dispersed. His mother was brought as prisoner to Wangdiphodrang, from where the 27th Je Khenpo Pema Zangpo eventually helped her move to Thimphu to be with Jigme Norbu. By 1843, his uncle and brother also returned to Bhutan and the family was reunited in Thimphu.

The exemplary luminaries in the midst of this period of civil strife were the 25th Je Khenpo Sherab Gyaltshen and the 31st Desi Tenzin Drukdra. Both had officially retired from their offices to devote their lives to spiritual pursuit, the former to his hermitage in Gorina and the latter to his retirement home in Semtokha. Both of these personages certainly held a high stature among the Bhutanese public and enjoyed good relations with dissenting parties. Sherab Gyaltshen, in particular, visited both parties repeatedly and gave teachings to the two Desis and young incarnate lamas although it is not clear how much influence he had on their political decisions. They appear to have maintained their neutrality and worked tirelessly for the greater welfare of the country, whether it was through numerous religious prayers and rituals they conducted or through persuasive acts of mediation. In the next few years, we see two of these luminaries busily engage in mediation trying to unite warring parties and promote unity and peace in the country.

The second chapter of mediation and ceremony of oaths took place in early 1842. Firstly, a meeting of all headmen was called by the two luminaries and other monastic elders in Khyime lhakhang. They explained their plans for reconciliation, which included a decision to bring the two Desis face to face. The two Desis were then invited to Bardrong (Bajo) Lhakhang where rituals of confession and reparation were conducted in their presence. The venue was perhaps chosen for its neutrality. From there, the assembly moved to Talo Sa-ngag Chöling, where in front of the remains of Jigme Drakpa II, a ritual feast was offered. This was followed by rituals of confession and atonement in the chamber of tutelary deities and the actual oath-taking for which the two luminaries acted as witnesses. We do not know exactly what such ritual of oath-taking involved but it is likely that Sherab Gyaltshen had devised a liturgical piece to be read out publicly. Following this ceremony, the assembly then climbed down to Punakha and everyone, including Desi Tashi Dorji of the Thimphu bloc, entered the *dzong* in the spirit of genuine harmony.

After this act of conciliation, fighting between the two blocs must have ended but the two Desis continued with their separate rule from their bases. The ice was not fully broken and another effort had to be made to bring them fully into a harmonious relationship and reunite the country. This third effort of oath-taking and reconciliation took place in Thimphu in 1845 through the initiative of the 27th Je Khenpo Pema Zangpo with the Thimphu bloc playing the host. Sherab Gyaltshen, who was now seventy-three years old and was losing his eyesight and hearing, was once again asked to come from his hermetic seat in Gorina to bear witness to the reconciliation and oath. The first delegation from Punakha was led by Chakpa Sangay, who stayed at Wangditse, the base of his former enemy ex-Desi Chökyi Gyaltshen, who perhaps acted as the host. The conciliation programme began at Semtokha on the ninth of the sixth Bhutanese month, 13 July 1845 with Sherab Gyaltshen, Tenzin Drukdra, the incumbent Je Khenpo Pema Zangpo, four monastic masters and some other elders as witnesses. After prayers of confession and reparation to the state protector deities, the representatives of the two blocs pledged to 'cast away former differences and grievances like the old scale of a snake and to sincerely reconcile and commit to the cause of the Buddhist teachings'.[28]

From here the assembly, including Chakpa Sangay, proceeded to Tashichödzong, where they were all very cordially received. Perhaps, now fully convinced by the sincerity of the conciliation efforts, Chakpa Sangay returned to Wangdiphodrang, where the Punakha government was based for summer, and returned with the two supreme figures of the Punakha bloc, the regal incarnation Jigme Dorji and Desi Dorji Norbu, who were warmly welcomed by the Thimphu government in Tashichödzong. A three-day ceremony of atonement and reparation began in the chamber of protector deities in Tashichödzong led by Sherab Gyaltshen, the incumbent Je Khenpo Pema Zangpo, the mind incarnation Jigme Norbu and the speech incarnation Jigme Dorji. The former Desi Chökyi Gyaltshen and the two current Desis, Dorji Norbu and Tashi Dorji, made together hundreds of prostrations during the ceremony to atone for their past deeds. On the final day, the leaders and all officials once again took an oath that 'no one will be allowed to instigate conflicts and perpetrate evil plots but everyone will promote noble deeds which maintain the peace of the Southern land of four entrances'.[29] The oaths were also written down and copies distributed to all concerned individuals.

This event temporarily ended the civil strife which started with Chakpa Sangay's rebellion and divided the country under two rival Desis based in the two capitals. It was primarily due to the initiative and encouragement of spiritual heavy weights such as Sherab Gyaltshen and Pema Zangpo, who had a great deal of influence on both sides that the rivalry was resolved and country reunited. Dorji Norbu and Tashi Dorji ruled Bhutan jointly after this reconciliation without major disagreements and the three leading incarnate lamas, Jigme Norbu, Jigme Dorji and Thinley Gyatsho, also shared a very cordial relationship.

The loss of the luminaries and re-ignition of strife

Civil strife ceased for the time being giving Bhutan a short respite from internal conflicts. With the disputes settled, Sherab Gyaltshen departed from Thimphu for his seat in Gorina for the last time. In the following year, Pema Zangpo retired from office making way for his successor, the 28th Je Khenpo Rinchen Zangpo. In 1846, Desi Tashi Dorji started the annual ritual of *sridpa chidoe* (སྲིད་པ་སྤྱི་མདོས་) and also launched the project of building a large Buddha statue in Punakha. Jigme Norbu meanwhile went on a tour of Paro and also received his full monastic ordination from Sherab Gyaltshen in Gorina but happy times for him and the country were not to last long. Firstly, he lost his beloved mother in the middle of 1847 causing him immense grief. Then, while in retreat, he received the grave news that his mentor and spiritual guide Sherab Gyaltshen passed away on the eighteenth of the eleventh Bhutanese month, 24 December 1847. Prior to this, he received two letters from his master, the first one to console him after his mother's death, asking him to reflect on the impermanence of life and the second one announcing Sherab Gyaltshen's own illness. The last letter was written poorly by the scribe with a lot of omissions. Jigme Norbu later remarked that these were ominous signs of the approaching demise of his master, which he had failed to read.

Jigme Norbu was in strict retreat when the news of his master's illness and subsequent demise reached him in Sa-ngag Chöling. He felt frustrated as he could neither end his retreat to go to his master's seat in Gorina nor focus on his meditation with the sad turn of events. He and Sungtrul Jigme Dorji, who was also in retreat in the Punakha *dzong*, decided in a joint deliberation to bring the master's body to Tashichödzong for cremation. Thus, word was sent to Paro that the body should be kept in Gorina undisturbed until the following spring. The former *pönlop* of Paro, Agay Haapa alias Tshultrim Namgay, was at the time the main person managing the rites having been the most trusted patron and disciple of Sherab Gyaltshen in his last days.

The following spring, Sherab Gyaltshen's body was brought to Thimphu and given a grand cremation, which was fitting for his stature and achievements, in the courtyard of Tashichödzong.[30] Jigme Norbu acted as the host and master of ceremony for the cremation while Jigme Dorji presided over the religious rituals; the ashes were strewn in the Thimphu river. The dignitaries of the country converged to mourn the death of a great leader. The demise of Sherab Gyaltshen meant not only the loss of a great master for the two incarnates and thousands of others who directly benefited from him. The country lost the most trusted leader and spiritual luminary of the time. Sherab Gyaltshen was unmatched in his influence as a spiritual master, political mediator and a patron of religious projects in his final years. Whatever offering he received in cash or kind, he spent on religious projects, redistributing a staggering figure of 2,39,816 *matram* coins according to Jigme Norbu's calculation. Sherab Gyaltshen's biography is to a great extent a detailed register of the monetary distribution he made for his religious works.

Sadly, for the joint government of the two Desis and the people of Bhutan, Sherab Gyaltshen's death was not the only one for them to mourn that year. Even as preparations were being made to bring Sherab Gyaltshen's body to Thimphu, the incumbent Je Khenpo Rinchen Zangpo passed away in Thinleygang in the spring of 1848 on his way to Thimphu. His body was cremated just before Sherab Gyaltshen's was brought to Thimphu. The former Je Khenpo Pema Zangpo took the office of Je Khenpo once again.

Not long after Sherab Gyaltshen's cremation, Bhutan saw the death of another leading figure. The 31st Desi Tenzin Drukdra, who had retired in 1822 to pursue a religious life but had since been actively engaged in reconciliation as a leading mediator alongside Sherab Gyaltshen, passed away in the summer of 1848. Jigme Norbu presided over the cremation of this statesman. His cremation was soon followed by the death of Desi Dorji Norbu in Punakha in the winter of 1848. We do not know what caused the untimely death of Dorji Norbu but it left Tashi Dorji for the first time as the sole Desi to rule over Bhutan. Later historians would enumerate Tashi Dorji as the 37th Desi of Bhutan. Following the death of his formal rival,

Tashi Dorji made a nationwide distribution of gifts to the people in an act of sumptuous generosity.

Tashi Dorji, however, scarcely enjoyed his independent rule before another tragedy struck his rule. As if the deaths of many leaders were not enough to expiate the earlier wrongdoing of schismatic conflicts, which angered the protector gods in Bhutanese belief, the Punakha *dzong* was destroyed by fire for the fifth time on the twenty-third of the eighth Bhutanese month, 9 October 1849.[31] Tashi Dorji was devastated by the incident. Jigme Norbu reports that the old Desi entered into a state of grief and lamentation shedding tears non-stop.[32] Senior figures including Jigme Norbu himself consoled the Desi by pledging to help him in rebuilding the *dzong*. The work of rebuilding the Punakha *dzong* began in earnest that autumn and the monk body spent the winter in Thimphu.[33] Carpenters, masons and labourers were summoned from all over the country to work on the construction. The workers from eastern Bhutan were at that point led by the chamberlain of Tongsa, Jigme Namgyal, whose reputation for physical strength and dexterity was rising. We shall see below how Jigme Namgyal saved his master, the Tongsa *pönlop* Tshokye Dorji, from harassment and perhaps from a fatal assault around this time.

By the spring of 1850, the *dzong* was largely completed and the four leading incarnate lamas including Jigme Norbu, Jigme Dorji, Tritrul Thinley Gyatsho and Jamtrul Dudjom Gyaltshen and Je Khenpo Pema Zangpo presided over the consecration of the new *dzong*. The new *dzong* was to remain one of the lasting legacies of Tashi Dorji although oddly he is only remembered today for the set of exceptionally melodious cymbals, which is named after him and which he donated to the monk body for use during sacred dances. By the spring of 1850, Tashi Dorji was too ill to hold the office of the Desi; he retired and Wangchuk Gyalpo, the *dzongpön* of Thimphu was made the 38th Desi. Tashi Dorji passed away in Thimphu that summer. Twenty-one days after his death, Jigme Dorji, the speech incarnation also passed away aged barely nineteen.

Wangchuk Gyalpo was an uncharismatic and unlucky ruler, as the spiritual master Jangchub Tsondrue noted.[34] His three-month reign saw the re-ignition of the civil war which the great luminaries worked hard to suppress a few years ago. The initial spark for the conflict this time came from Paro, where the former *pönlop* of Paro, Agay Haapa, and the incumbent *pönlop*, Yonten Rinchen alias Tazi Dronma, clashed in a serious dispute. Our sources do not record the bone of contention but Desi Wangchuk Gyalpo passed a verdict which evidently displeased the party of Agay Haapa. The *dzongpön* of

Thimphu and the brother of Jigme Norbu, who were on Agay Haapa's side, stabbed the Desi and a few of his men to death, accusing the Desi of a biased verdict. The supporters of the late Desi held possession of the Semtokha *dzong*, where Chakpa Sangay, the *dzongpön* of Wangdi, also joined them. Chakpa Sangay was initially on his way to Paro in order to mediate between the warring *pönlops* but the sudden assassination of the Desi by one party must have spurred him to join the Desi's faction. Serious fighting between the two parties, which were based separately in Tashichödzong and Semtokha dzong, took place throughout the summer. 'Conflict surged like torrents and the people were subjected to suffering,' wrote a contemporary witness. As if war was not enough, 'an epidemic of smallpox spread like wind and even the monk body had to disperse'.[35]

While the fighting continued in the Thimphu valley, the party in Tashichödzong, in an attempt to gain supremacy, installed Jigme Norbu on the throne of the Desi as both the spiritual and temporal ruler of Bhutan. It was thought that this appointment would appease the spirits, who had caused the epidemic of smallpox out of displeasure at the turn of events. Smallpox was described as 'the bad breath of *mamo* spirits'.[36] Barely nineteen years old, Jigme Norbu thus became the 39th Desi in the summer of 1850. He facetiously compared his appointment to being made 'a horse-herder even before he was capable of being a goat-herder'.[37] Despite the appointment of the most important incarnate hierarch at the helm of the government, neither the conflict nor the epidemic abated. During the Tshechu festival in autumn, the *dzongpön* of Thimphu was killed by Chakpa Sangay's men having been treacherously deserted by his soldiers in Lungtenphu. Chakpa Sangay put his corpse on stake and summoned his old mother to identify him, when the old lady sharply remarked that the corpse indeed was of her physical son but, now that he was dead, Chakpa Sangay had the obligation to be her surrogate son. A filial relationship is said have developed between this lady and Chakpa Sangay, who killed her son.[38]

The fate of Jigme Norbu and the fall of Chakpa Sangay

Jigme Norbu's nominal rule as the Desi in Thimphu was largely ignored by Chakpa Sangay and his group, who took control of the Punakha *dzong*. Instead, Chakpa Sangay took for himself the post of the Desi in Punakha once again dividing the nation's administration into two camps. Later historians would enumerate Chakpa Sangay as the 40th Desi. Like in the previous division, the Thimphu court could not move to Punakha in the winter. While the monks moved to Punakha, Jigme Norbu stayed in Thimphu where he conducted several rituals of expulsion and was joined by the Paro *pönlop*, Agay Haapa. But in the tenth month at the end of one such ritual service, Jigme Norbu fell seriously ill with smallpox. The illness was kept secret and Jigme Norbu fortunately recovered in a month and survived the disease unlike his friend Thinley Gyatsho, the incarnation of Tenzin Rabgay, who succumbed two months later to the disease. Thinley Gyatsho passed away in the beginning of 1851 followed by the former Desi Chökyi Gyaltshen, who died in Wangditse. Jigme Norbu, who was now the only regal incarnate still alive, presided over funerals of both these figures.

That winter, Jigme Norbu also survived another serious accident. He fell off a tall staircase in Tashichödzong and for a moment thought he was to going to die but miraculously landed with only a minor bruise on the right hip. These two incidents left a significant mark on Jigme Norbu's mind, which was already becoming increasingly tired of worldly stress and bent on religious pursuit. By 1851 and only twenty years old, Jigme Norbu had gone through a great deal of trials and tribulations. His father was killed in a battle and his mother died after a humiliating experience of imprisonment. He had already overseen the funerals of his two main teachers, five main patrons, two incarnate lamas and many friends and survived two fatal incidents. Although he was hailed as the leading hierarch of the country, his was by any standard a harsh and traumatic youth. He wrote in one of his poems:

Since my birth, until now
Twenty whole years have passed.
A hundred tribulations of others
Couldn't compare to a single cause for my angst.
Should [tragedies] fall on others
As they fall on me,
This body would crumble into a heap of dust.[39]

Almost everybody, who was close to him, was now dead and the task of holding the reins of a country which was severely divided did not appeal to him. He seemed to be hardly interested in holding the political reins and spent much of his time presiding over religious rituals. He felt his life was wasted at the capital and wished to leave for another place.

Meanwhile, fighting between the two factions continued sporadically with no end in sight and the rival Desi Chakpa Sangay took full control of power in Punakha. The Thimphu faction vehemently objected to this but they were unable to vanquish Chakpa Sangay. Thus, Agay Haapa, who was one of the main leaders of the Thimphu faction then, sent for help from the Tongsa *pönlop*. Jigme Namgyal, a close relation of Jigme Norbu, was now the chief of protocol of Tongsa and the second most powerful man in Tongsa after the *pönlop* Tshokye Dorji. He and his two brothers led a contingent of troops from the east to fight against Desi Chakpa Sangay and on the side of their relative Jigme Norbu. We don't exactly know if the forces took part in any military confrontation against the forces of the Desi in Punakha but as soon as they arrived in Punakha, the three brothers started contriving a plan to eliminate Tapön Migthol, the strongman who was the chief bodyguard of Chakpa Sangay and main muscle behind the Punakha troops.

Migthol was known to be a *nyagö*, a rare category of people with Herculean physical strength. He was born to a lady in Tangsibji in Tongsa, who was believed to have been impregnated by a local deity. Such stories of beautiful maidens being impregnated by local gods and spirits were well known in medieval Bhutan and often used for explaining the unusual physical strength and agility of some men. These children with non-human fathers are often referred to as bastards or *drang* (འདྲང་) of the particular deity or spirit and their formidable strength attributed to their non-human paternal origin. Migthol was believed to be one such cross-breed, who was blessed by his non-human father to be nearly invincible. Chakpa Sangay on one of his journeys through Tongsa recognized Migthol's strength and made him a trusted confidante and Migthol gradually reached the position of a *tapön* or in-charge of horses.

Jigme Namgyal was fully aware of Migthol's power and the blow Migthol's death could cause to the morale of Chakpa Sangay's forces. He had already encountered Migthol during the construction of the Punakha *dzong* in 1849 and they had challenged each other in friendly contests. On a more serious note, Migthol had ridiculed Jigme Namgyal with names such as 'bison's horn' or 'black skin' in reference to his complexion and Jigme Namgyal had previously questioned Migthol about his allegiances and why he worked so faithfully for a western master though he was himself from eastern Bhutan. To this, Migthol is said to have replied: 'The dog growls from where it eats.' Migthol was indeed Chakpa Sangay's faithful watchdog and Jigme Namgyal and his brothers also knew about the difficulties in overcoming him.

Sending the troops back to Tongsa under the pretext of returning home, the three brothers secretly stayed back in Punakha and plotted an assault.

Finally, one evening they waited in hiding on the roadside near Laptsakha in order to attack Migthol in an ambush. Migthol was returning home on a horse having finished his daily duty when the three brothers suddenly pounced on him. While his brothers forcibly held Migthol's hands, Jigme Namgyal stuck the fatal blow and after some struggle Migthol was toppled from the horse. Jigme Namgyal then pointed his sword on Migthol's forehead and poured out earlier grievances as Migthol lay seriously maimed and dying on the roadside. Migthol showed his last act of bravery and cried out, 'cut the crap and give me an adequate blow!'[40] Jigme Namgyal perhaps wished Migthol to die a painful and slow death but Dorji, the eldest brother, quickly drew a dagger through Migthol's armpit. He was worried that Migthol may use the time to say malicious prayers.[41]

While the combat went on at the roadside, Migthol's pony man escaped to call for help from the Desi's forces. Being hunted by the Desi's army, Jigme Namgyal and his brothers thus had to seek refuge in Talo with Sonam Dhendup, the brother of Jigme Norbu. After three nights in secrecy at Talo, their host and Agay Haapa arranged sixty bodyguards of Jigme Norbu to escort them as far as the northern border of Bhutan. As the direct route to Tongsa was fully under Chakpa Sangay's control, the three brothers took a detour via Tibet and reached their destination safely. The sixty bodyguards, who escorted them until Gasa were not so lucky. On their return, the house in which they halted was surrounded by the army of the Desi. The army set the house on fire with the sixty men trapped in it. Only one of them managed to escape to safety; the rest were burnt to death.

Chakpa Sangay seems to have remained unvanquished even after the loss of Migthol but that was not to last long. Agay Haapa used a nefarious ploy to eliminate him under the pretext of reconciliation. As a token of the hoax reconciliation, he made a robe from very fine silk and had it worn by someone infected with smallpox. He then packed the robe, still warm and now thoroughly impregnated with the disease, and sent it to Chakpa Sangay asking him to try it on, adding that there was more silk left if the robe was too small. Chakpa Sangay is said to have bought the trick and soon died from smallpox some time in the middle of 1851.[42] Jigme Norbu had by then also practically resigned from the office of the Desi in Thimphu. The post of the Desi was now, in effect, vacant but the conflict persisted as regional magnates vied for supremacy.[43] It was only in the winter of 1851 that concerted efforts were made by the clergy to bring an end to the division.

At the helm of the mediation was the 31st Je Khenpo Yonten Gyaltshen, who had been invited by Jigme Norbu to take the post in the summer of 1851. Under his guidance, the state monks moved from Thimphu in the winter but did not go as far as the Punakha *dzong*. They stayed in Talo but the Je Khenpo proceeded to Punakha and convened a meeting of headmen to bring an end to the division. The clergy, including Jigme Norbu, Yonten Gyaltshen, his precursor the 30th Je Khenpo Jampal Gyatsho and other monastic elders, lectured the headmen on the need for reconciliation and an end to civil strife.[44] On the seventh of the twelfth Bhutanese month, 28 January 1852, the headmen reached a general consensus and appointed the monastic elder, Barchung alias Damchö Lhendup, as the 41st Desi. Barchung was trained as a monk and had reached the position of a tantric master (རྡོ་རྗེ་ སློབ་དཔོན་), from which he resigned to lead a hermetic life by the time he was asked to take the office of Desi.

Two days after Barchung was appointed the Desi, Jamyang Tenzin, the third incarnation of Ngawang Gyaltshen, was also installed on the golden throne, the apex of the Bhutan's administrative system established two centuries ago. This was an unprecedented move as the occupants of the golden throne of Gyaltshab were until then always one of the four regal incarnations connected to Zhabdrung's family, the mind and speech incarnations of Zhabdrung, incarnations of his son Jampal Dorji and of Tenzin Rabgay. These four incarnate hierarchs alternated as the Gyaltshab or prince-regent and what the British called the Dharmarāja. Jamyang Tenzin's ascension broke this longstanding tradition. For the first time, someone who was not one of the four regal incarnations ascended the golden throne. Although, by now, the political power lay completely in the office of the Desi, the title of prince-regent still came with profound religious significance and no doubt carried immense political weight. Thus, it is not clear what motivated the Bhutanese clergy and court to depart from the established tradition and install Jamyang Tenzin on the golden throne. Perhaps, the prevailing situation partly occasioned the change. Jigme Norbu was the only surviving regal incarnation and he was generally disinterested in the affairs of the state. The speech incarnation and Tenzin Rabgay's incarnation died in 1850 and 1851 respectively and the incarnation of Zhabdrung's son was not recognized after the last one died in 1833.

It is also plausible that the politicians and public were gradually losing faith in the regal incarnations. Despite their devotion to the regal incarnations, none of the incarnations in the nineteenth century lived a successful life and managed to hold the country together peacefully. In contrast, they often became a cause of conflicts and players in the complicated power struggles between various magnates. Consequently, towards the end of nineteenth century, we see a gradual decline of their prestige and influence leading to their total eclipse by civil rulers in the twentieth century. The events which unfold around Jigme Norbu's life in the subsequent years clearly suggest that not all was going well for the regal incarnate.

Not long after the appointment of the new Desi Barchung and installation of Jamyang Tenzin on the golden throne, Jigme Norbu left the seats of government in Thimphu and Punakha and retired to Gorina, the monastic seat of his late teacher Sherab Gyaltshen in Paro. From here, he travelled to many places giving teachings to religious gatherings or presiding over religious rituals but by then a rift seems to have emerged between him and the court. His departure from the capital may have been triggered by an incident which concerned a close attendant of his named Kopi. This young monk was caught wearing an inappropriate garment by the monastic disciplinarian on his way to the latrine at night. The disciplinarian meted out the due punishment by flogging him at the entrance of the assembly hall the next morning, as was the custom. Later that evening, the young monk stabbed the disciplinarian in revenge and this provoked the monastic elders to deliver a very harsh sentence. Kopi was thrown into the river to the great annoyance of Jigme Norbu, who intervened to save his attendant but was unsuccessful.

To make things worse, during one of his religious tours, Jigme Norbu met his female consort, Dechen Tshomo, from Athang. Despite his resignation from the affairs of state, Jigme Norbu was still the highest religious figure in country and also perceived to be a fully ordained monk. Thus, his liaison with this newfound sweetheart and the birth of a daughter caused a scandal and an outcry among the monastic elders and precipitated the rupture between him and two most senior figures in Punakha: the Desi and Je Khenpo. Je Khenpo Yonten Gyaltshen, who was briefly Jigme Norbu's personal tutor, was a champion of Buddhist monasticism. Besides being a very strict monk himself, he ordained numerous others and even played an important role in the ordination of Jigme Norbu in Paro some years earlier. Thus, Jigme Norbu's fall from celibacy was heartbreaking for the puritanical abbot and he could not come to terms with it.

The abbot reproached Jigme Norbu following the two incidents and in course of doing so, perhaps out of frustration, blurted out that Jigme Norbu 'may go where he wished, be it India or Tibet'.[45] Unfortunately, the incarnate hierarch did not take the abbot's criticism and reaction lightly and it resulted in a total fall out between the master and disciple. In 1854, Jigme Norbu prepared a statue of the Yonten Gyaltshen and in 1855 Yonten Gyaltshen wrote, at the behest of Jigme Norbu, a monastic code of conduct based the earlier code by Zhabdrung. After this, Jigme Norbu seems to have totally stopped contact with him except for one letter he wrote to him and the Desi jointly. In this letter and in several other writings of his, he expresses strong displeasure at the way he was treated and even insinuates that Yonten Gyaltshen was an arrogant rogue in monk's robe.

The rupture aggravated further in the following years as the court removed some fifteen monk attendants of Jigme Norbu from the monastic register and stopped providing them with their maintenance allowances. This was followed by the loss of Jigme Norbu's quota of income from the duars some time in 1858. The loss of tithes from the duars may not have been entirely at the hands of the elders in the capitals but caused by the endless aggressions along the southern borders and the gradual British takeover of the duars, to which we shall return later. At any rate, Jigme Norbu was deeply upset by the sad turn of events and he left for Tibet in 1859 purportedly on a long pilgrimage. He wrote:[46]

With crafty power of speech,
They say this land belongs to you.
In effect, through canny designs, they rob me
Of wealth, power and domain.
When such shameless bad people fill this country,
What choice do I, a lowly mendicant, have
Other than occupy myself with the tour of holy sites?

In Tibet, the regent Rwatreng Ngawang Yeshe (1816–63), who ruled during the minority of the 12th Dalai Lama, granted him generous hospitality and Jigme Norbu also received the title of Drukpa Erdeni from the Manchu Emperor Xianfeng. From his base in Lhasa, he wrote several sentimental and poetic epistles to his patrons, students and friends in Bhutan, some of which captures the tragedies and the bitter-sweet memories of his life in Bhutan. In an imaginary dialogue with a cuckoo, which brings him news from Bhutan, he writes:

Listen! O cuckoo, who sings melodious tunes
From the top of turrets of the splendid palace.
Let me narrate with honesty my story,

A lazy man without *dharma*, who wanders in distant lands.
My native home is in the east of Mon country,
Which, now, I can merely hint with my finger.
Tenzin, my father of the luminous Nyö lineage,
Died being subjected to a weapon while at war.
My kind old mother, Yungdrung Gyalmo,
Entered dissolution some years back and is no more.
Having met my sublime teacher of three-fold kindness
I have received the rare instructions for the peak of diamond path.
Yet at a young age, when I had no self-control,
My sole protector and teacher passed away into the sphere of truth.
Without reaching the crux of meditation but with laziness
This stage has come, where I have crossed thirty.
Dechen Tshomo, the sweetheart I have embraced with much longing,
I have no fortune of being together with in this lifetime.
So has time passed for me to hold on my lap with love,
Rinchen Tshomo, my daughter of karmic connection.
Though I wish to live in delightful Kunang Ösal
This body, a karmic product, has been transported to Tibet.
Saddened by the fear and terror of horrifying cannibals
Who fill the southern land abundant in enjoyments such as food and drink,
I now reside peacefully in the palace of Tsemonling
By the lotus feet of the sole protector [Rwatreng] Dorjichang.[47]

The cuckoo flies away and as winter approaches, he turns to the cranes to carry his message to Bhutan. He writes:

O Listen, young cranes!
Along your journey's route
Is the hidden land known as sandalwood country,
Where Chenrezi sought enlightenment.
...
On the other side of Sharzel pass in the east,
In the peaceful village of Athang valley
Is my love Dechen Tshomo and her child,
Linked to me by our past actions and aspirations.
Convey this message to them, who depend on me
And others who miss me from their hearts.[48]

The message for his friends, family and devotees in Bhutan was one of despair and unfulfilled hopes and an exhortation to earnestly follow the spiritual path of religion. It was a message that he may never return to Bhutan and they may see each other again in the pure realms of the Buddha. Jigme Norbu's life was as turbulent and tragic in the end as it was in the beginning. His was a life torn apart by love, politics and piety and the struggle to fulfil different, almost opposing, expectations. If starting a family made him fail in his religious leadership, it was his religious proclivity which made him shy away from a successful political career and perhaps also from family life. The prevailing political factionalism certainly did not make it easy for him to successfully combine piety, politics and love in his life.

Despite the tumults and tragedies in his life, or perhaps because of them, Jigme Norbu turned out to be literary star in his milieu. He was the most erudite of the regal incarnations and his writings give us a direct insight into one of the most chaotic chapters of Bhutan's history as well as his own turbulent life. Ranging from religious counsels to tragic comedies and often written in difficult styles fitting a literary genius, his poems capture his troubled spirit and emotions, embittered feelings and frustrations, relentless devotion to his guru and affection for his people and above all, his deep spiritual approach to life. Jigme Norbu is said to have returned to his master's seat at Gorina in Paro and probably passed away in 1861.[49] His body, against his wishes to be kept in Gorina, was brought to Punakha and cremated.[50]

The incessant conflicts

Meanwhile the monk ruler Barchung did not enjoy an easy reign as the Desi due to the continued factional squabbles between the magnates in Thimphu and Punakha. He was said to be a person of immense integrity and compassion but his fall out with Jigme Norbu may have affected his authority. After two years as ruler, he resigned in 1854 and was replaced by Jamtrul Jamyang Tenzin as the 42nd Desi. This hierarch, the incarnation of Ngawang Gyaltshen, was then occupying the golden throne of the prince-regent. He now became Desi and vacated the golden throne to make way for the 5th Sungtrul or speech incarnation, Yeshe Ngodup. Yeshe Ngodup was born in 1851 in the Tang valley of Bumthang, just like his precursor Jigme Dorji. In the summer of 1854 after Jamyang Tenzin became the Desi, Yeshe Ngodup was brought to Thimphu and installed on the golden throne of the prince-regent under the supervision of the Je Khenpo Yonten Gyaltshen.[51]

Around this time, Yonten Gyaltshen tried hard to settle the conflict which erupted soon after the appointment of Jamyang Tenzin as the Desi. Jamyang Tenzin was the choice of the clergy for the post of the Desi but Umadewa, the *dzongpön* of Thimphu, refused to recognize the new Desi. We don't know clearly why Umadewa did not accept Jamyang Tenzin as the Desi or who were involved with or against Umadewa. What we know is that Yonten Gyaltshen's effort of mediation failed to appease Umadewa and the state administration was once again split between Thimphu and Punakha. As a last resort to end the violence, an agreement was reached to request former Desi Barchung to return to the throne and rule alongside Jamyang Tenzin. Whether or not Barchung liked it, this was accepted by Umadewa and this momentarily suppressed the violence but hardly resolved the conflict.

The accounts get very murky and vague at this point but it seems that the reappointment of Barchung provoked the *dzongpön* of Wangdi, who supported Jamyang Tenzin, into the conflict. He attacked the Punakha *dzong* where Barchung was back again as the Desi alongside Jamyang Tenzin. The bridges were guarded by Umadewa and the minister Kasha on Barchung's side and sporadic fighting seems to have occurred between them and the *dzongpön* of Wangdi. But after over a year, Jamyang Tenzin passed away in Punakha and Kuenga Palden, the *dzongpön* of Wangdi became the new Desi in Punakha in the beginning of 1856. Tired of the rivalry, Barchung, who was still occupying the post of the Desi in Thimphu, stood down for the second time and made his final exit from politics to leave for his hermitage. The Thimphu faction under Umadewa, however, was not ready to accept the sole leadership of Kuenga Palden as the Desi. Thus, Umadewa forcibly ascended the throne of the Desi in Thimphu, bringing the state administration back to a vicious split. Later historians enumerate Kuenga Palden alias Sonam Tobgay as the 43rd Desi and Umadewa alias Sherab Tharchin as 44th Desi.

The clergy led by Yonten Gyaltshen once again intervened to mediate and this time managed to get an agreement between the two factions to allow both Desis to rule jointly and move between Thimphu and Punakha. Another influential mediator in the scene around this time was Jigme Namgyal, who had become the Tongsa *pönlop*. He came purposely on a peaceful mission to negotiate between the warring factions of Thimphu and Punakha. In gratitude for his efforts, he was exempted from paying the annual tribute of four sacks of coins, which the Tongsa *pönlop* had to earlier pay the Desi. From then on, the Tongsa *pönlop* was also given the prerogative to appoint the other senior officials under his jurisdiction, who were earlier appointed by the Desi.

The truce reached by the negotiations, however, did not last long. Umadewa was killed in 1857 by the chamberlain of Kuenga Palden. After Umadewa's death, Kuenga Palden ruled as the only Desi and western Bhutan saw a brief respite from civil strife. But a new political conflict broke out in Tongsa and Bumthang between the Tongsa *pönlop* Jigme Namgyal and Jakar *dzongpön* Tsondru Gyaltshen, the son of Jigme Namgyal's former boss, Tshokye Dorji. The conflict sparked from arguments over the post of the Tongsa *pönlop*, as we shall see below. Tsondru Gyaltshen appealed to Desi Kuenga Palden for military help, which the Desi despatched promptly but the joint forces of the Desi and Jakar *dzongpön* failed to vanquish Jigme Namgyal. The protracted fighting caused a great deal of misery to the people of central Bhutan. Thus, a team of monastic elders led by Yonten Gyaltshen and a few senior civil officials from the west made their journey to Tongsa in 1858 to negotiate a settlement between the two rulers.[52] The conflict was resolved amicably after Tsondru Gyaltshen was promoted from *dzongpön* to the *pönlop* of Jakar, this office being a unique case in history.

Due to an illness, Desi Kuenga Palden retired from office in the beginning of 1861 and passed away soon after that; his nephew Nagzi Pasang, the *dzongpön* of Wangdiphodrang became the 45th Desi.[53] Barely a year in office, Nagzi Pasang soon saw his share of rebellion when he appointed his own nephew Sigay to his former post of the Wangdi *dzongpön*. Darlung Tobgay, who was married to a relation of Nagzi Pasang's wife, hoped Nagzi Pasang would bestow him the post because of this marital connection. It is not clear why Darlung Tobgay, who was already the Punakha *dzongpön,* wanted the post of the Wangdi *dzongpön*. The reason may be the direct access to Tsirang or Sidlee duar and the relatively higher autonomy the Wangdi *dzongpön* enjoyed compared to the *dzongpön*s of Thimphu and Punakha, where half of the year the central government and state court were based. Besides, there may have been a greater volume of rice tax collected under the Wangdi *dzongpön*.[54] When the post did not come his way as he wished, he staged a rebellion in coalition with Kawang Mangkhel, the chief minister of state and Tashi, the state chief of protocol, in 1862. The rebellion did not succeed in inflicting major damages on the Desi as the Desi had on his side the *dzongpön*s of Thimphu and Wangdi and the *pönlop* of Paro.

Darlung Tobgay then turned to Tsondru Gyaltshen, the *pönlop* of Jakar for military support. The latter and Jigme Namgyal had by then resolved their differences and were on very friendly terms. Thus, both Jigme Namgyal and Tsondru Gyaltshen, the *pönlop*s of Tongsa and Jakar, heeded Darlung

Tobgay's call and led their troops to Punakha to fight against the Desi. The main reasons for this war remain unknown but it surely cannot be merely the allocation of the post of the Wangdiphodrang *dzongpön*, which drew all the civil leaders of Bhutan to a war. On the Desi's Thimphu side were the Paro *pönlop*, the Thimphu *dzongpön* and Wangdiphodrang *dzongpön* and in opposition, on Punakha's side, were the *dzongpön* of Punakha, two *ponlöps* of Tongsa and Jakar, state chief councillor and the state chief of protocol. The only important official not listed in the conflict is the *pönlop* of Dagana.

The Punakha party marched into Thimphu under the shrewd command of Jigme Namgyal. Some time in 1863, the two troops clashed in Lungtenphu but before long the forces of Thimphu were on the retreat. The superior power of the Punakha coalition finally cornered the commanders of the Thimphu forces in a house but there was still one obstacle to full victory. The main champion of the Thimphu forces, Chudra Gyatsho, defended the Thimphu party with his flair for swordsmanship. Taking his position at the surrounding wall, he killed and maimed many attackers until Jigme Namgyal shot him in the knee with a rifle. Now, without the defence offered by their champion and trapped in a house, the *dzongpön*s of Thimphu and Wangdi cried out to Jigme Namgyal for mercy. They admitted defeat and explained that they had no ill feeling towards Jigme Namgyal, who had merely come to help the Punakha forces. The *dzongpön* of Punakha, however, wanted the enemies to be exterminated. Jigme Namgyal argued for leniency in an internecine conflict and set the *dzongpön*s free with the condition that they would remain in their homes and not take part in public affairs any more.

Throughout this conflict, the senior members of the clergy carried out a series of mediation but without much success. The monastic negotiation team was again led by Yonten Gyaltshen, who had by now resigned from the office of Je Khenpo, and his successor, the 32nd Je Khenpo Tshultrim Gyaltshen.[55] Yonten Gyaltshen's biographer claims that the old monk was entreated by the losers to come to their rescue, which he did successfully by protecting their lives and properties. The war had several direct outcomes for the leading positions. Desi Nagzi Pasang was forced to resign in 1863 and Tshewang Sithub, the former Thimphu *dzongpön*, became the 46th Desi. Darlung Tobgay got his coveted post of the Wangdi *dzongpön* and Tashi, the state chief of protocol, became the *dzongpön* of Punakha. Khasar Tobgay, a cousin of Jigme Namgyal, was appointed the *dzonpön* of Thimphu. No doubt, the internal conflict among western rulers gave Jigme Namgyal a wonderful opportunity to gain a major foothold in the domain of western politics.

Bhutan also saw a spate of flash floods in 1863 as the war was being fought. Many structures built close to the river, including the Punakha *dzong*, were seriously affected. Nothing is known about the natural causes, but it was widely believed that the floods were a result of the displeasure and sorcery of Jigme Norbu, who was then living in exile in Tibet. Jigme Norbu is said to have made a small heap of *tsampa* flour in his teacup in the shape of the Punakha *dzong* and then poured little tea over its side remarking, 'If I wished, I could make Punakha *dzong* wash away like this.'

The new Desi Tshewang Sithub belonged to the lower Wang region and almost immediately after he took office, the leaders of upper Wang staged a revolt. Fighting began to spread again. The clergy led by Yonten Gyaltshen once again negotiated a settlement and Tshultrim Gyaltshen, the former monastic disciplinarian, was installed on the throne on behalf of the upper Wang people in the same year. He became the 47th Desi and an agreement was reached for the two Desis representing upper and lower Wang to jointly hold the position of the Desi. However, it would be too good a story for a medieval polity entrenched with regional feuds if such an arrangement worked for long. The appointment of the upper Wang candidate provoked Nagzi Pasang, the Desi who was ousted earlier after the war in 1863, to plot his downfall. Nagzi Pasang is said to have won over the incumbent Je Khenpo to carry out an extensive programme of rituals of sorcery and magic aimed at the new Desi. The new Desi Tshultrim Gyaltshen died before finishing even a year in office and his partner, Desi Tshewang Sithub, also stood down from the post.

Kagyu Wangchuk became the 48th Desi in the beginning of 1864. This monk had served as resident lama in the Bhutanese temples in the Kathmandu valley and Kailash and also collected a transmission of rare teachings before he returned to Bhutan. His reign was, however, short and insignificant as he passed away in office a few months after taking the office. Surprisingly, his death was not followed by a surge of competition for the post of the Desi. The leaders of Bhutan requested Yonten Gyaltshen to take the position but the leading monastic hierarch kindly declined, giving his old age as the reason and advised that a senior monk who was both able and committed to promoting the welfare and peace in the country be appointed as the Desi.

Yonten Gyaltshen, like Ngawang Gyaltshen and Sherab Gyaltshen before him, was an outstanding luminary of his time. He was a learned monk with extensive knowledge in traditional sciences and monastic arts and a consummate meditation master. With a strong zest for religious study and practice, he gave countless religious teachings. Thus, most religious hierarchs in the generation after him were products of his teaching programmes. Above all, Yonten Gyaltshen was a strict monk committed to the promotion of monastic celibacy and discipline. He wrote an expanded version of the monastic code of etiquette based on the earlier one by Zhabdrung and also gave monastic ordination to numerous postulants. It was unfortunately this relentless commitment to monastic chastity, which spoiled his relationship with his most important disciple, Jigme Norbu. However, Yonten Gyaltshen's contribution to the country was not merely in the spiritual and religious domain. He was also a spiritual advisor and guru for most leading politicians of his time and, as an influential public figure, Yonten Gyaltshen worked tirelessly to mediate between warring factions and to foster peace in the country. There is no doubt that in the last decades of his life, he became the most respected figure in country looked up to as a leader with outstanding integrity, wisdom and compassion. Thus, he was certainly the best choice for the post of the Desi in 1864 when the post became vacant but in the true spirit of selflessness and non-attachment to power, he declined to take the position. He died in 1870 aged sixty-six and his body was cremated in the Punakha *dzong*.

Following Yonten Gyaltshen's polite rejection of the post, the master of dialectics (མཚན་ཉིད་སློབ་དཔོན་), Tsondru Pekar, was appointed as the 49th Desi in 1864 with the consensus of the clergy and senior leaders. He was described as a learned person with a loving heart and wont for giving but he died shortly after taking the office.[56] Tshewang Sithub, who stood down in 1864, once again ascended the throne of the Desi. With the country beleaguered by both external and internal wars, it is not clear who was behind the reappointment of Tshewang Sithub. It is plausible that Jigme Namgyal played a major part in it. Although Tshewang Sithub held the post for a much longer duration in his second term than the first, we know very little about his rule and the role he played in the political tumult which developed in the south leading to the Duar Wars. It was Jigme Namgyal who became almost the *de facto* ruler by this time and was also the chief player in the dealings with the British. It is to his story we turn now.

The rise of Jigme Namgyal

Much has already been written on Jigme Namgyal and I direct readers particularly to Damchö Lhendup's biography, Lama Sa-ngag's account of Jigme Namgyal and Michael Aris's chapter on him in his *Raven Crown* for those interested in more detail. The first two are in Dzongkha and the third in English. Here I present the gist of the story of Jigme Namgyal's rise in Bhutan's political scene as a prelude to the Duar Wars, his short tenure as the Desi and the introduction of the monarchy. Jigme Namgyal came from Dungkar in the Kurtoe district. His father, Pila Gyonpo Wangyal, was a descendent of Kuenga Wangpo, one of the sons of Pema Lingpa. Pila Gyonpo Wangyal and his brother, Pala, served as escorts of Jigme Drakpa II during the conflict of 1809 due to a family connection. Their cousin, Tenzin Chögyal, was married to Jigme Drakpa II's sister, Druk Gyalmo. After this conflict was over, Pila returned to Dungkar with a bride from Gangteng named Lhadron but she died a few years later.[57] Pila then married Sonam Dolma, a daughter of his family's serfs in Jangsa.[58] They produced three sons and a daughter. Jigme Namgyal was the second son and born in 1825.

Early in his youth, Jigme Namgyal embarked on a journey to Tongsa, purportedly triggered by a dream. His aim certainly would have been to join the court and being the second son in the family, he probably did not have the obligations to look after the family establishment and continue the lineage. Crossing over the Rudongla Pass, he reached the Tang valley and spent a few months herding the cattle and sheep for the family of the village chief in Naru. Later when he became the Tongsa *pönlop* and the chief came to seek an audience, he is said to have asked if the pot in which they prepared the skimpy buckwheat broth was still in use.

From Tang, he came to Chumey where he met the lama of Buli. The lama, after discovering Jigme Namgyal's predilection for court life, sent Jigme Namgyal with one of his attendants to Tongsa, where Jigme Namgyal first met his new master at an archery ground. The accounts are divided on the identification of this master but most likely he was Tshokye Dorji, the chief of protocol in Tongsa at that time. Jigme Namgyal joined him as a retainer or *tozen* (ཏོ་ཟན་). For his physical vigour and sociopolitical aptitude, Jigme Namgyal rose rapidly in his career and became a senior courtier by 1845. He was responsible for the organization of the religious ceremonies in Tongsa and Bumthang. His master, Tshokye Dorji, was also by then the Tongsa *pönlop* and he was soon promoted to be the merchant of Tongsa. His duty as district merchant, like other state, district and private merchants, was to trade local products such as textiles, rice, paper, etc. with Tibetan products including salt, wool, rugs, statues, etc. at the trade marts along the border with Tibet. It was during his term as merchant that he met his future wife, Pema Chöki some time around 1847 at the Lhalung monastery in southern

Tibet. She was there with her brother Tanpai Nyima, who was the 8th Peling Sungtrul.

Jigme Namgyal was promoted to the post of the chamberlain of the Tongsa *pönlop* in 1849 and soon after that made to simultaneously hold the post of the *dzongpön* of Lhuntse. It was during his journey from Tongsa to take over the post of the *dzongpön* of Lhuntse that he met his spiritual master, Jangchub Tsondru. Jangchub Tsondru was a Gelukpa lama from the Wensa tradition who had a very strong proclivity for an ecumenical approach to Buddhist practice. The *rimé* movement of religious ecumenism was at its height in eastern Tibet led by major Nyingma and Sakya figures, partially to overcome the Gelukpa dominance but it is highly intriguing that a figure with a Gelukpa background was ardently following religious ecumenism in south and central Tibet and seeking teachings from other schools of Buddhism, particularly the Kagyu and Nyingma schools which thrived in Bhutan. Jangchub Tsondru travelled through Bhutan several times and found devoted patronage in the magnates of Bumthang.

His biography tells us that Jigme Namgyal's first encounter with the lama took place in Tashi Peling, when the latter was conducting an empowerment ritual for elongating life to a group of patrons who were mostly Jigme Namgyal's in-laws. The lama was ready to bestow the blessings but waited, chanting a verse of prayer until Jigme Namgyal, who was on his journey to Lhuntse, arrived. The biographer concludes that the lama must have waited for Jigme Namgyal with the clairvoyant knowledge of the auspicious connection which they were to develop in the following years.[59] Jangchub Tsondru went from Bumthang to Tongsa at the invitation of the Tongsa *pönlop* and then returned to enter into a long retreat at Kurjey in order to say prayers for the good health of the 11th Dalai Lama. Jigme Namgyal, who had quickly taken over the Lhuntse *dzong* and appointed a deputy, hurried back to Kurjey to see Jangchub Tsondru again. According to Jangchub Tsondru's biography, the lama gave him numerous teachings with a clear view of Jigme Namgyal's future. He gave specifically the teachings pertaining to the worship of the horse-headed deity, Hayagrīva.[60] A prophetic text, composed in the style typical of a hidden treasure text, seems to have appeared claiming that 'the sun of peace and happiness will shine on the country for seven generations if Jangchub Tsondru gave the teachings and Jigme Namgyal took up the practice of the deity Hayagrīva'.[61] Following this exchange, the lama returned to Tibet and Jigme Namgyal to Tongsa but they had now formed a strong bond as priest and patron.

Religious piety was, however, not the defining strength of Jigme Namgyal. By the time he became the chamberlain of the Tongsa *pönlop* at the age of twenty-four, Jigme Namgyal was well known in his milieu for his physical stamina, valour and political shrewdness. He was considered one of the *nyagö* or men with exceptional strength in Tongsa. His debut in the state political arena in western Bhutan took place in 1849, when he led the workers from eastern Bhutan to rebuild the Punakha *dzong* destroyed by fire earlier that year. The magnates of Bhutan assembled here with their retinue of strong bodyguards and during the intervals of work, the labourers and strongmen often engaged in friendly contests of shot put, weightlifting, long jump, etc. Jigme Namgyal proved his superiority over his rivals in many of these contests but not all was jovial play. There was an undercurrent of regional tension between the east and west, which could easily erupt into a conflict with the slightest provocation. The officers of the west were said to have been looking for an excuse to provoke and attack Jigme Namgyal and his men.

One such opportunity came when the labourers were working on the roof of the *dzong*. The chamberlain of Punakha demanded that nine layers of shingles to be laid, which inevitably put extra strain on the labourers from the east, who were fewer in number and also running out of their ration stock. Jigme Namgyal thus protested and pushed away the top two layers with his stick, leaving only seven layers. The chamberlain of Punakha immediately seized the chance to pick up a fight and rushed toward Jigme Namgyal with his hand on the hilt of the sword. Jigme Namgyal shrewdly proposed to his opponent that they both jump from the roof of the *dzong* to prove their valour instead of causing an unnecessary conflict between the people of east and west. His opponent evidently backed out.

Another plot to attack the party from Tongsa was planned at the archery match between the eastern and western teams during the celebrations which followed the completion of the *dzong*. The western team was about to reach the final score and win the match. The western magnates planned to assassinate the Tongsa *pönlop* in the uproar of celebrating victory, when the morale of opponents would be low. This however did not happen as the Tongsa *pönlop* hit the bull's eye and denied victory to the western team. Or did he? An alternate version of the account has it that Jigme Namgyal got wind of the imminent attack and managed to raise enough eastern men to create a human fence around their leader.[62]

The third attempt to bring down the Tongsa *pönlop* and his party is believed to have happened after the celebrations as the Tongsa *pönlop* was taking his leave from the Desi. Suspecting a plot by the western magnates to kill his boss, Jigme Namgyal accompanied his master up to the courtroom and waited at the door. It was at this time that Migthol, the champion whom Jigme Namgyal later killed, ridiculed him with the hope of provoking him into a combat. Jigme Namgyal maintained his composure and alertness, fully aware of the ploy. Peeping from behind the door curtain, he saw his master standing in the courtroom, shaking in trepidation and sweating with fear as the high officials of the state berated him. It is not clear on what accounts the Tongsa *pönlop* was scolded. It is possible that the misrule of the duars under the Tongsa *pönlop*'s jurisdiction, which was causing havoc to the country's economy, was one of the issues. Surprisingly, one account has it that the issue was actually the uncontrollable and insolent character of Jigme Namgyal. The Tongsa *pönlop* was reprimanded for having no control over his bellicose chamberlain.[63] Whatever the case may have been, Jigme Namgyal was fully convinced that there was an imminent attempt on his master's life. He burst into the courtroom and with one hand on his sword hilt, he led his master out of the courtroom to safety.

It is not clear how many of the stories about east–west rivalry and Jigme Namgyal's valour really took place and to what extent the descriptions are accurate as there are no contemporary reports of these events. The laudatory stories of Jigme Namgyal's bravery and strength all come from much later sources, which are nuanced to embellish the origins of the monarchy. We also do not know the motives for the alleged plot to assassinate the Tongsa *pönlop*. The contemporary records of that time do not mention any rift between eastern and western Bhutan and the ploys to kill the Tongsa *pönlop*. Instead, the political power in western Bhutan in these years was severely divided between the Thimphu and Punakha blocs as we have already seen and there was no solidarity among the magnates of the western Bhutan. One source argues that the Tongsa *pönlop* was at that time very powerful and a serious contender for the post of the Desi, which gave enough reason for other contenders to eliminate him.[64] This is possible in the light of the incessant rivalry for regional supremacy in Bhutan's medieval polity. Whatever the nature of threat may have been and whoever posed it, Jigme Namgyal successfully foiled a coup on his master's life. In gratitude for saving his life, Tshokye Dorji promised to appoint Jigme Namgyal as the next Tongsa *pönlop* although Tsondru Gyaltshen, as his son, was the heir apparent.

In 1850, Jigme Namgyal was promoted to the post of chief of protocol of Tongsa and almost immediately after this appointment he was sent eastward to consolidate Tongsa's control over the eight districts under its jurisdiction. Several of the *dzongpön*s in the east are said to have rebelled against the Tongsa *pönlop* but we have no further information on what caused the rebellion or who exactly were involved. Jigme Namgyal suppressed the dissent and rounded up the rebellious leaders and had them march to Tongsa. Then, in 1851, Jigme Namgyal and his two brothers, Gyaltshen and Dorji, led the eastern forces to Punakha against Chakpa Sangay and killed the notorious strongman Migthol in an ambush. The killing of Migthol, whom some believed was invincible because of his non-human paternity, must have certainly enhanced Jigme Namgyal's reputation for his physical strength and shrewd tactics. After the ambush, he and his brothers barely escaped the Desi's forces to return to Tongsa via the northerly route through Tibet.

Back in Tongsa, Jigme Namgyal heard rumours that his master, the Tongsa *pönlop*, was planning to go back on his words and appoint his son, Tsondru Gyaltshen, as the next *pönlop*. Out of displeasure, Jigme Namgyal stayed away from the court under the pretext of ill health but his master soon found out the actual reasons for Jigme Namgyal's absence. Thus, with an understanding that Jigme Namgyal shall pass on the position of the Tongsa *pönlop* to Tsondru Gyaltshen after three years in office, Tshokye Dorji installed Jigme Namgyal as the Tongsa *pönlop* in 1853. In the meantime, Tsondru Gyaltshen took the post of the *dzongpön* of Jakar and Tshokye Dorji retired to Ogyen Chöling. Soon after the transfer of power in Tongsa, the Jakar *dzong* was destroyed by fire. The task of rebuilding the *dzong* started in earnest in the same year and, when it was finished, Jigme Namgyal invited his teacher, Jangchub Tsondru, to consecrate the new *dzong*.

Following the consecration of the Jakar *dzong*, Jigme Namgyal invited his teacher to Tongsa, where he was now the supreme boss. Jangchub Tsondru performed numerous religious services in the *dzong* and also gave religious blessings and teachings to Jigme Namgyal, who was at that time accompanied by Sonam Dhendup, the brother of and chamberlain to Jigme Norbu. It was at this time that he bestowed upon Jigme Namgyal the initiation of the deity, Gönpo Jangdü, which, combined with the Raven-headed Legön, would later become a major protecting deity for Jigme Namgyal. It is quite likely that Jangchub Tsondru also designed and blessed the raven-headed helmet which Jigme Namgyal wore to war and subsequently became the prototype of Bhutan's raven crown.

According to Jangchub Tsondru's biography, he also made predictions about Jigme Namgyal's future but the biographer does not tell us what the predictions were. We can perhaps assume that the predictions and instructions concerning the construction of a statue of the deity, Cakrasaṃvara, facing westward in Tongsa were given at this time. The lama is said to have instructed Jigme Namgyal to create the statue and also to chant the root mantra of the deity a hundred million times in order to subjugate the warring chieftains to the west and to bring the whole country under his control. Jigme Namgyal duly built a shrine dedicated to this deity and also created a silver statue of the female deity, Vajravarahi, into which he put a special relic. This relic was a miniature figure of Vajravarahi believed to have been formed from one of the vertebrae of Tsangpa Gyare, the founder of the Drukpa Kagyu School, like the chief relic of the state in Punakha.

It was also around 1853 that Pema Chöki became Jigme Namgyal's wife. According to later accounts, Jigme Namgyal is said to have consulted his lama about whether or not he should become a celibate monk, just as the early occupants of the position of the Tongsa *pönlop* had become. Jangchub Tsondru advised him against celibacy explaining that the couple are partners of mutual aspirations and actions in previous lifetimes and if a good son is born from this wedlock, he will benefit the country. It is not at all surprising that Jangchub Tsondru gave this advice as he was himself a married priest with children and a tacit practitioner of sex yoga. More importantly, the nuptial bond with Pema Chöki was very advantageous for Jigme Namgyal's political career. In addition to the prestigious pedigree of being a direct descendent of Pema Lingpa from the Tamshing line on her father's side and granddaughter of the 30th Desi on her mother's side, she came from households with some significant wealth and assets, which would have been useful to fund Jigme Namgyal's military campaigns. Jangchub Tsondru may have encouraged the wedlock not merely on the basis of spiritual concerns but with due consideration of the economic and political portfolios.

Jangchub Tsondru left Tongsa for Ogyen Chöling and from there he went to Tibet. In the next few years, Jangchub Tsondru would remain in Tibet, travelling to different places, meeting patrons, teaching students and writing various texts but showing no interest in returning to Bhutan. Instead, he was keen on visiting Nepal and Sikkim although he failed to do this due to the prevailing political situation. By the end of 1855, Jigme Namgyal was dying to see his lama and sent one Karma Lhawang purposely to invite the lama but Jangchub Tsondru declined the invitation. The dejected Tongsa *pönlop* embarked on a campaign of spiritual purification by having two sets of Buddhist scriptures printed. He also proclaimed that all citizens in his domain shall observe the five Buddhist precepts of eschewing killing, lying, stealing, sexual misconduct and intoxicating drinks and, in order to protect life 'sealed the mountains and rivers' from hunting, fishing and the like. This was a significant sacrifice to prove his spiritual commitment as Jigme Namgyal was himself a hunter.[65] Jigme Namgyal once again extended his invitation and the lama was obliged. The author of his biography, a learned Bhutanese student of Jangchub Tsondru, was also instrumental in persuading the lama to make his last journey to Bhutan.

In the early part of 1856, Jangchub Tsondru and his party travelled to Bhutan via Paro after visiting his brother in the neighbouring area. Jigme Namgyal had organized a reception at the border, including a gift of a beautiful mule possessing the same colour as the goddess Palden Lhamo's riding mule. Jangchub Tsondru remarked that the mule was an auspicious omen that Jigme Namgyal would have a good son in the near future. His eldest son, Thinley Tobgay, was born in 1856. Perhaps analogous to a mule, Thinley Tobgay became a monk and left no heir although there is even today a family in Bumthang believed to be direct descendents of him. Jangchub Tsondru was received in Paro by the leading religious and civil hierarchs of the region including Agay Haapa, the former *pönlop* of Paro. Jangchub Tsondru gave them various teachings and from Paro, he travelled to Thimphu via Phajoding, where the lama felt at home and happy. Sadly, he could not stay there long as the whole entourage insisted that they move on as Jigme Namgyal was eagerly waiting for him in Tongsa. Jangchub Tsondru was very reluctant to travel eastward. 'I feel like being dragged to death,' he said. 'If I stay in the west, I can benefit others widely; in the east, I feel like I will benefit only one learned person,'[66] he said, perhaps referring to his Bhutanese biographer, Zhanphan Rolpai Dorji, whom he always called *lopön khepa* (སློབ་མཁས་པ་) or 'the learned master' and who was also serving Jigme Namgyal as his secretary.

Passing through Thimphu and Wangdiphodrang, Jangchub Tsondru's party made their way to Tongsa. Along the journey, he gave numerous teachings and blessings to the devotees who gathered on the route to see him. While passing through the Shar valley, Jigme Norbu, who was at that time living with his consort in Gangteng, sent an invitation to Jangchub Tsondru to travel via Gangteng but he declined because the protector deity of Tongsa appeared to him and asked him to proceed to Tongsa in haste. Jigme Namgyal received his master in Tongsa on the thirteenth of the fourth Bhutanese month, 17 May 1856. Jangchub Tsondru immediately started giving Jigme Namgyal and his court a host of religious teachings and also conducted several ceremonies for their welfare. As an exceptionally rare privilege, Jangchub Tsondru also made the offering of prayers for longevity and prosperity to Jigme Namgyal. Normally, it is the patron who would offer such prayers to the lama, not vice versa. Jangchub Tsondru passed away in the watch tower of Tongsa one month after his arrival and his body was cremated in Jampa Lhakhang in Bumthang.

The year his master passed away, Jigme Namgyal also made his first important trip to the Punakha as the Tongsa *pönlop*. The mission was to mediate between the two factions of Punakha led by Desi Kuenga Palden and Thimphu led by Desi Umadeva. His mediation aided by the intervention of the clergy brought a brief pause to the conflicts in Bhutan's capitals. In return for his efforts, the Desi cancelled the tribute of four bags of coins which the Tongsa *pönlop* annually paid to the government and Jigme Namgyal was also given the full prerogative to appoint all senior officials under his jurisdiction. Sadly, the truce which Jigme Namgyal's efforts of mediation started did not last long although it enhanced Jigme Namgyal's own profile in the country and brought him economic benefits.

The truce ended with the assassination of Umadeva by Kuenga Palden's chamberlain in 1857 but this left only Kuenga Palden in power as the Desi and western Bhutan saw a short spell of peace. However, a new trouble erupted in Jigme Namgyal's his own court and domain towards the end of that year. Tshokye Dorji, who retired to Ogyen Chöling in 1853, had appointed one Pasang as second in command under Jigme Namgyal in Tongsa to ensure that Jigme Namgyal passed down the post of *pönlop* to his son, Tsondru Gyaltshen, after three years. This forceful officer was, unfortunately, disliked by Jigme Namgyal's supporters and at the peak of tension, Jigme Namgyal had him killed by one of his strong bodyguards.[67]

A war thus erupted between Jigme Namgyal on one side and his former master, Tshokye Dorji and his son, Tsondru Gyaltshen on the other. The main bone of contention between the warring parties was clearly the position of the Tongsa *pönlop*, which Jigme Namgyal had held, by now, for three years and was reluctant to give up according to the agreement. The death of Pasang was merely an incidental spark which triggered the war. There may have also been another reason if we are to believe local oral sources. Jigme Namgyal is said to have fancied Tshokye Dorji's daughter but she was not interested in him and escaped to avoid his attention. This snub, if it was true, could have exacerbated the political tension. The historian Tshering Dorji states that Jigme Namgyal initially laid total siege to Ogyen Chöling and allowed nothing either to enter or to leave the house.[68] Even the water offered at the altar was measured by cups and passed each morning. It was the wit and courage of a nun, who was Tshokye Dorji's sister, which eventually broke the siege. She is said to have picked up a rock with the shape of a pig's head, drawn eyes and mouth on it and threw it on a sling toward Jigme Namgyal's camp. Through the power of the family's protecting deities, the rock landed next to Jigme Namgyal and nearly hit his cup during breakfast. Reading it as a foreboding sign of the divine displeasure, Jigme Namgyal stopped the siege and moved to Jakar to fight against the forces of Tsondru Gyaltshen. He stationed his troops on the plains of Shamkhar below the Jakar *dzong*. This venue later became the premise of his royal palace of Wangdichöling.

Meanwhile, unable to challenge Jigme Namgyal with the available power, Tsondru Gyaltshen sought the support of Desi Kuenga Palden in Punakha but even the joint forces of the Desi, Jakar and Ogyen Chöling did not manage to suppress Jigme Namgyal. The war dragged on for a year and in 1858, the clergy led by Yonten Gyaltshen came to negotiate and the dispute was amicably resolved. Jigme Namgyal retained the post of the Tongsa *pönlop* but Tsondru Gyaltshen was promoted from the *dzongpön* to *pönlop* of Jakar and the eastern districts and duars were almost equally divided between the two. By this time, the Assam duars were already annexed by the British and Bhutan was paid annually Rs10,000, which the Desi allowed Jigme Namgyal to keep in 1856 as token of gratitude for his mediation in western Bhutan. So, it is not clear how Tsondru Gyaltshen benefited financially from this division of the duars. The outcome was for Jigme Namgyal a symbolic victory as he continued to retain the post of the Tongsa *pönlop* but it reduced his domain drastically and deprived him temporarily of a substantial base of power and source of income. The following passage by Dasho Lama Sa-nga provides an amusing glimpse of Jigme Namgyal's stubbornness and Yonten Gyaltshen's negotiation at Tongsa.

Calling Jigme Namgyal to his presence, the Je [Yonten Gyaltshen] scolded: 'The hook on which your fortune hangs comes from Tshokye Dorji. Now, you are defecating in the plate from which you ate." Jigme Namgyal, who was standing in front [of the Je] with his scarf held low, straigtened his scarf briskly and walked out, waving his hands like beating handheld drums and saying: "This Je is not impartial.' Then Tshokye Dorji was called in and [Yonten Gyaltshen] reprimanded: 'When you were about to lose your head and hands in Punakha, Jigme Namgyal saved your life and head risking his own. Now, you are repaying his good work with evil waging a war against him. You have no shame and it is not right both for this life and the next.' When these words were said, Jigme Namgyal, who stood behind the door listening, nodded his head and remarked: 'This Je is very impartial.'[69]

Whatever Jigme Namgyal's immediate responses may have been, the reconciliation effort by the clergy was hugely successful as Jigme Namgyal and Tsondru Gyaltshen shed off their previous grudges and made up fully. The two *pönlop*s of Tongsa and Jakar now presented a united front from the east and fought side by side in the subsequent conflicts. Their first united appearance took place in 1863 when Darlung Tobgay sought help from Tsondru Gyaltshen to fight against Desi Nagzi Pasang. We have already discussed this story and the strong foothold this mission gave Jigme Namgyal in the centre of Bhutanese politics.

Following the victory over Desi Nagzi Pasang and the appointment of a new Desi, Tshewang Sithub, Tsondru Gyaltshen not only held the post of the Jakar *pönlop* but also became the chamberlain to the Desi. Similarly, Jigme Namgyal continued as the Tongsa *pönlop* but also became the chamberlain to the prince-regent or Dharmarāja. Yeshe Ngodup, the speech incarnation from Bumthang, was now occupying the golden throne of the prince-regent and he and Jigme Namgyal, who shared a close regional, ethnic and linguistic affinity, would have found good reason to be allied together. By becoming the chamberlains to the Desi and the prince-regent, the two leaders of eastern Bhutan effectively controlled the two highest offices in Bhutan's political system. It is quite clear that Jigme Namgyal was by now the *de facto* ruler of Bhutan and he had a major part to play in the quick rise and fall of Desis in the two capitals. It was however the enemies to the south who would put Jigme Namgyal to his ultimate test and leave a major dent on Bhutan. It is to this story of relations and war with the British that we shall turn again.

The Duar War and the Black Regent

THE ENDLESS CIVIL STRIFE and political instability had serious consequences for Bhutan. On the domestic front, the political volatility led to serious stress in terms of both economic and human resources. Undoubtedly, the battles between the magnates brought about unnecessary loss of lives. In addition, the lack of stability in the centre led to misrule in the peripheral regions, particularly in the duar areas to the south. This resulted in severe strains in relations with the British. Despite the diplomatic efforts made after the 1836 clash through negotiations with the British agent in Gauhati and the Pemberton mission, the cross-border raids along the southern border continued unabated. The agreement presented by Jenkins in 1836 in Gauhati and the treaty drafted by Pemberton in 1838 in Punakha in order to curb the cross-border outrages were never ratified by Bhutan, let alone implemented.

Continued frontier outrages

These frontier outrages involving theft, robbery and kidnapping of people, including women and children, were mostly the work of petty officers, land managers and lawless gangsters in the duar areas. Taking advantage of the political instability in the centre, the local officers became a law unto themselves and committed the outrages with open or clandestine support of border officials, who often shared the booties of the culprits. Some of the booties, including people kidnapped for slavery, were also sent as presents to superiors in central Bhutan. However, the outrages were not merely committed by Bhutanese subjects or local officers appointed by Bhutan as most sources would have us believe. British subjects also tried to fish in the troubled water, as Majumdar puts it.[1] Rennie presents an unbiased contemporary account of how these outrages were mutual.[2] Many offences were launched from the British protectorate of Cooch Behar and Sikkim on Bhutanese territory while some were perpetrated by people who had absconded from Bhutan to settle in Indian territories. No doubt, Bhutan's inability to control and rein in the frontier officials and regulate the duars was mainly to be blamed for the aggressions from Bhutanese soil.

However, one cannot discount the role played cunningly by the British frontier officers in provoking or exacerbating the aggressions. It was no secret that British India was at the height of its imperialistic expansion. After the Gorkha War, neighbouring Sikkim has become a protectorate of the British and Darjeeling, which the British East India Company had received from the King of Sikkim, had become a British colony. Assam was now fully part of British India and also the plains of Assam and the duars had just been discovered to be conducive for the cultivation of tea. The East India Company had also lost its monopoly over tea from China in 1833 and their attention for cultivation of tea, one of the highest sources for the Company's revenue, now turned to Assam. Thus, it was only very opportune for the British interest that there were disturbances along the duars, giving the British officers a good excuse to annex them. Meanwhile, the incessant raids and state of lawlessness led to a serious depopulation of the areas around the border. The duars were a sparsely populated fertile ground which was too good to be wasted.

The opportunity indeed came barely months after the Pemberton mission returned from Bhutan in 1838. Bhutanese from the Khaling duars carried off some twelve people from the Darrang district of India. A Kacchari land manager, who worked under Bhutan but was planning to leave Bhutan to settle in Indian territory, was also killed. On these accounts and also on the account of arrears of tribute for the duars, Colonel Jenkins, the British agent in Gauhati, proposed the permanent annexation of the Khaling duar to his superiors in Calcutta. The Governor-General of India, Lord Auckland, sounded caution because the fear of China's interference still loomed large in the British mind. The British government was at that time fighting the first Opium War with China and anything which may aggravate the situation was to be avoided. Thus, it was decided that the duars would be annexed temporarily until the arrears are paid. The arrears of tribute occurred partly due to the disorganization in the capital but in part also due to the British insistence on receiving only Narainee Rupees, which Bhutan could not readily produce. Jenkins wrote to the Desi about plans to annex the Assam duars but did not receive any reply. In November, 1839, the British once again annexed the Khaling and Buri Gumar duars without any resistance or clamour from the Bhutanese side.

It is not surprising that there was no immediate protest from Bhutan against this annexation. Tenzin Chögyal, the incumbent Tongsa *pönlop* under whose jurisdiction the Assam duars fell, was busy in Punakha, embroiled in a conflict between the Thimphu and the Punakha blocs. He was stabbed to death some time in the beginning of 1840, after getting his son, Jigme Norbu, out of the Punakha *dzong*. Before this happened, it appears that the Punakha bloc under Desi Dorji Norbu sent the tantric master (རྗེ་རྗེ་སྒྲུབ་དཔོན་) to assign the management of some of the western duars to their preferred local land manager, arguing that the prince-regent or Dharmarāja Jigme Norbu was with them in Punakha. A large per cent of duar tracts was allocated as a source of income for the prince-regent and whoever occupied the golden throne of the prince-regent was entitled to its revenues. However, not long after this, Jigme Norbu was smuggled out of the Punakha *dzong* to be taken to join the Thimphu bloc under Desi Tashi Dorji. Tashi Dorji thus wrote to the British in 1840 claiming that the Dharmarāja was now with him and the rights over the duars were with the Thimphu bloc. He even invited an envoy to confirm this.

The British learnt from the lack of strong reaction to the annexation of Bhutan's eastern duars and as well as two duars belonging to the King of Tawang that China and Lhasa were not interested in the affairs of the duars to the south. The British fear of provoking a greater force by entering into a dispute with Bhutan had now been generally quelled although full annexation of all the Assam duars was still not to take place without the express approval from London and also because of the heavy military commitments to the northwestern frontiers. The Great Game between Britain and Russia to control central Asia has just begun and Britain was waging the first Anglo-Afghan war. Nonetheless, Jenkins was convinced that the full annexation was the only solution to the frontier troubles and Bhutan must be persuaded to give the British full control over the duars. By repopulating the area and farming the fertile lands, the duars would not only become of 'inestimable importance to all Eastern Bengal',[3] but Bhutan could be paid a portion of the revenue generated from the areas. This, it was thought, would not only keep the Bhutanese leaders happy but also make Bhutan entirely dependent on the British. Moreover, if the payment was made to the political party acknowledged by the British, this party would naturally become stronger and that could eventually end the anarchy, which had long gripped Bhutan.

The Bhutanese duar officers however, learnt nothing from the British annexation of the Khaling and Buri Gumar duars. Even as the British were contemplating sending an envoy to Bhutan to negotiate the attachment of the duars in lieu of an annual tribute, there were reports of fresh outrages in which five villages were plundered. Similarly, the leaders in the capitals scarcely realized the consequences of their neglect of the duars. The power in Bhutan at this time was deeply split with the Thimphu and Punakha blocs at the height of their conflict. Given the situation, the Governor-General in Calcutta saw no prospects for sending an envoy and remarked that 'fruitless Missions of this kind will only aggravate our embarrassment and are not creditable to the British power'.[4] Thus, he issued the final order to take control of the remaining duars and, by 11 November 1841, all seven Assam duars were annexed by the British forces without much resistance. It was decided that Bhutan would be paid Rs 10,000 per year for the 1600 square miles of land which were now added to British India.

Frontier troubles were not limited to just the Assam duars. On the far-western end of the Bengal duars, two land managers working for Bhutan locked horns in a contest over control of Bhutan's duar area. Hargovind Katham, whom we have encountered earlier, closely allied with the Thimphu bloc and exercised control over the duars on the eastern side of the Teesta river. His rival, Durga Dev, who was a scion of Raikat of Baikunthapur, managed the Bhutanese enclave of Ambari-Falakata on the western bank of Teesta and allied with the Punakha bloc. This enclave came under Bhutan's control perhaps as early as the reign of the 4th Desi Tenzin Rabgay but it was formally passed to Bhutan by Warren Hastings in 1774, to the great displeasure of the family of Raikat of Baikunthapur, who claimed it to be their homeland. Durga Dev, thus, had an historical axe to grind and was bent on expanding his domain of control and regaining his ancestral land. The backing of the Desi in Punakha gave him the precious opportunity to do this and eliminate Hargovind Katham.

The British were not completely faultless spectators of the conflict between the two local chieftains. While fighting against each other with the legitimacy granted by the rival governments in Bhutan, the two land managers also seem to have played a treacherous game of seeking British protection in return for substantial tributes. The British did not yield to these offers but sealed the border of Rangpur in order to avoid disturbances along the frontier. However, this went in favour of Durga Dev, who was an Indian citizen working as a land manager for Bhutan and owning property on both sides. He could raise men and resources from India to fight his enemy on Bhutanese soil. Katham, in contrast, could not even attack Ambari-Falakata without passing through British territory. The Desi in Thimphu pointed out this anomaly to the British agent and asked him to stop the British subjects joining Durga Dev's forces but before this was done, Katham was killed in September 1841. The Desi in Punakha now conferred the territories formerly under Katham to Durga Dev but the Thimphu bloc responded by inciting the officers of Dalingkha and Chamurchi against Durga Dev. The conflict between Thimphu and Punakha, in this way, effectively spilled over to the southwestern corner of Bhutan.

In early 1842, the British sent Dr Campbell, the superintendent of Darjeeling, to investigate the situation and subsequently barred Durga Dev from entering Bhutan's territory without written permission from the local magistrate. Meanwhile, a rigorous programme of reconciliation between the two blocs was in progress in Bhutan and the resultant coalition government transferred the management of Ambari–Falakata to the British for an annual rent of Rs 800. With the cause of dispute now controlled by the British, both Durga Dev and the family of Hargovind Katham went to live in obscurity under British protection. Troubles along the Bengal duars, however, did not end with the closure of rivalry among local land managers. Most of the border between Bhutan and India was not clearly demarcated and this led to frequent conflicts between people living along the border regarding ownership. The British generally did not desire the demarcation as they held the view that permanent annexation of duars was the only solution for peace along the frontiers. When they did agree to demarcate, they questioned the authority of the Bhutan's frontier officers and insisted on the presence of higher officials, who never came.

Besides, Bhutan's relation with the British protectorate of Cooch Behar was not going well with outbreaks of incursions and counter-incursions. The incursions agitated the British frontier officers but they were asked by their government 'to interfere as little as possible in the matters belonging to foreign territories'[5] as the British attention was drawn by problems in the northwestern frontiers. If the central authority of Bhutan was too indecisive and weak to be able to take any decisive actions on the outrages, the British central power was occupied with more pressing issues in the northwestern frontiers to come to any decision. Moreover, there were no mutually accepted formalities between the two countries on the extradition and trial of the culprits who committed the outrages. Thus the perpetrators got away with impunity as soon as they crossed the border. Such passivity, indecision and negligence on the part of the two governments emboldened the frontier officers and their under-agents to carry out more offences. Thus, the series of cross-border raids and counter the raids continued unabated throughout the 1840s and 1850s. Villages were plundered, crops, elephants and cattle stolen and people kidnapped.

Throughout this time, Bhutan remained gripped by factional politics and frequent outbursts of fierce fighting apart from the brief spell of respite brought by the reconciliation efforts. Its leaders were not happy with the British annexation of Assam duars and Rs10,000 they received as compensation but there was little they could do with the country still seriously encumbered by factious governance. In 1853, Jigme Namgyal became the Tongsa *pönlop*, the governor under whose jurisdiction the Assam duars fell. In March, 1854, he sent a mission led by the Dewathang *drungpa*, a brother or a close relation of his, to Gauhati to obtain an increase in the amount of the annual tribute. The mission failed to obtain this and, on its way back, was alleged to have committed several robberies, which the British magistrate of Kamrup stopped. The magistrate directly accused the Dewathang *drungpa* of the several cases of dacoities, which the *drungpa* and Jigme Namgyal denied commiting. Jenkins, the British agent, then wrote directly to the Desi about the offences and the Desi, as a punitive measure, ordered Jigme Namgyal, the Tongsa *pönlop*, to pay twice the value of the plundered goods to the state treasury.

Jigme Namgyal was infuriated by the arrogance and contempt of Jenkins to bypass his authority and to write directly to the Desi. This set Jigme Namgyal, the rising Bhutanese leader, at a bad start with the British. Following the Desi's order, the Dewathang *drungpa* was removed from his office but a discourteous exchange of letters unfolded between Jigme Namgyal and Jenkins, who were both equally shrewd and unrelenting figures. Jigme Namgyal wrote to Jenkins that the culpable officer had been dismissed and asked Jenkins to send a British officer to investigate into the case of plunder. He also demanded Jenkins pay half of the fine imposed on him by the Desi while also accusing Jenkins of slimy evasiveness. Jigme Namgyal pointed out that it was not in Bhutanese practice to snub the relevant authority and instigate a higher one.

As can be expected, Jenkins found the tone of Jigme Namgyal's rejoinder very rude and offensive. Furthermore, he was exasperated by the Tongsa *pönlop*'s demands to pay half of the fine. This was outrageous and he proposed to his government to punish the *pönlop* by the immediate annexation of the

Bengal duars. Lord Dalhousie, who was now the Governor-General, generally agreed with Jenkins but showed restraint. Instead of an outright annexation, he asked Jenkins to demand a formal apology from the Tongsa *pönlop* for the insolence shown to the government of British India in the person of Jenkins. If the apology was not forthcoming, the Bengal duars were to be annexed and the annual payments withheld. The amount equivalent to the value of plunder was to be deducted from the annual payment anyway. Letters were sent to the Desi and the Tongsa *pönlop* about this decision of the British government and a letter of apology was received from Bhutan eventually. When the British made the annual payment in 1855, Rs 2868 was deducted as the value for plundered property.

The wounds inflicted by the exchange had hardly healed when a fresh dispute broke out concerning a certain Arun Singh. Arun Singh, who was a subject of Bhutan and hereditary land manager of the Guma duar, defected from Bhutan and settled in British Indian territory, from where he was carried off by Bhutanese men. The Bengal government treated the issue as a minor problem requiring a proper explanation from Bhutan but Jenkins and Lord Canning, the new Governor-General, refused 'to take the friendly and moderate tone'.[6] They saw this as a serious breach of British territorial integrity and, using the threat to annex the Bengal duars, they demanded an apology for the act and punishment for its perpetrators. If the authorities of Bhutan made a satisfactory apology and amendments, Lord Canning was willing to increase the subsidy from Rs 10,000 to Rs12,000. The Desi politely replied that Arun Singh had always been a servant of Bhutan and the British need not worry about him. The letter was probably written jointly by the two Desis, Kuenga Palden and Umadewa, who occupied the post at that time.

The evasive response from the Desi did not satisfy Jenkins, who now pleaded with his government for total annexation of the Bengal duars. Even as Jenkins was placing his views and requests before his government, a British subject named Salgram Oswal was arrested by the Bhutanese in Mainaguri on charge of holding property of a deceased Bhutanese subject. Furthermore, some fifty Bhutanese men entered Cooch Behar and carried away three men, three women and their properties. The endless outrages perplexed the British authorities and they decided to move two regiments to the frontiers. In early 1857, Sir F. Halliday, the Lieutenant Governor-General, visited the frontiers and submitted his impression of the situation after consulting Jenkins, who in turn obtained information from two Bengali ex-officers of Bhutan.

The Desi, to their knowledge, enjoyed only a nominal rule and the control over the duars remained clearly divided between the *pönlop*s of Paro and Tongsa. Withholding the revenue for the Assam duars under the Tongsa *pönlop*, they realized, was not going to solve the problems in the Bengal duars under the jurisdiction of the Paro *pönlop*. Besides, they suspected that the authorities in the capital were not fully aware of the misdeeds of frontier officials, and even doubted if the revenue paid by the British reached the central authorities. Thus, it was decided that direct communication with the Desi, Dharmarāja and the two *pönlop*s would have to be resumed to obtain reparations for the outrages. It was decided that the areas of Ambari-Falakata and Jalpesh would be fully annexed if Bhutan failed to respond. Meanwhile in February 1857, a new military cantonment was set up in Jalpaiguri, right next to the border. Full hostility with Bhutan was still to be avoided as far as possible, particularly because British India was in the wake of the Indian Mutiny. The government had no troops to spare for the Bhutan frontiers to carry out the threat should Bhutan choose to defy the British requests.

The Bhutanese authorities, however, were embroiled in an internecine conflict between Jigme Namgyal and Tsondru Gyaltshen in central Bhutan and were perhaps totally oblivious to the problems posed by the mutiny against the British Indian government. Neither were they fully aware of the magnitude of the problems caused by the frontier officers. In this state of affairs, the cross-border outrages continued without inhibition. Some thirty cases of Bhutanese raids were reported in Cooch Behar alone during 1857–58. Outrages were also committed against Bhutan by British subjects. On 31 January 1860, Lord Canning ordered Jenkins to occupy Ambari-Falakata which was to be released only after British demands were met. Jenkins, however, went further to claim the occupation of Ambari-Falakata as permanent and threatened to seize more territory.

In 1861, Nagzi Pasang became the 45th Desi but there was neither an outcry at the British annexation of Ambari-Falakata, nor any attempt to end the outrages along the border on the Bhutanese side. Around this time, the relations between Sikkim and British India were also seriously strained, mainly over Darjeeling. This hill station, which had passed to the EIC in 1835, had turned into a thriving safe haven for defectors from Sikkim, Nepal and Bhutan. This annoyed the prime minister of Sikkim and consequently precipitated the British invasion of Sikkim in 1861. Given the hostilities with Sikkim, the British government did not want to antagonize Bhutan any further, lest they might join forces. Thus, the British did not carry out further threats. Their indecision and reluctance to deal with the outrages continued while Bhutan remained engulfed in another spate of internal war as Darlung Tobgay rebelled against Desi Nagzi Pasang.

By the end of 1861, the Government of India, the regional government of Bengal and the new British agent, Hopkinson, who replaced Jenkins, all agreed on sending a fact-finding mission to Bhutan. Hopkinson was convinced that the frontier officers intercepted the communications, influenced opinion in the capitals and, even worse, answered the British letters themselves in the Desi's name. With their mind set on sending a high-level envoy, extreme care was taken to avoid any incidents which Bhutanese authorities could use as an excuse to delay or reject the mission.

In 1862, the new Governor General, Lord Elgin, began to make preparations for the mission and a native messenger named Mukunda Singh was first sent to relay the news about it. Mukunda Singh arrived in Tashichödzong and received an audience from Desi Nagzi Pasang on 21 September 1862 but the Desi was not really keen on receiving a mission and sent Mukunda Singh with an elusive reply. He indicated that a proper enquiry needed to be conducted over the duars but a mission was not viable as the cold winter was setting in. Moreover, he argued that frontier outrages were a trifling issue not worthy of being discussed before the Dharmarāja. The Dharmarāja or prince-regent, Yeshe Ngodup, was only eleven years old then and the Desi must have said this merely as a ploy to avoid the mission. However, he proposed to send *zingup* officers to the duars soon to discuss the issue but in reality, the officers were never sent.

Lost in their own internal conflicts, the Bhutanese authorities seem to have no clear directions, policies or strategies to deal with the British, who were increasingly becoming a major nuisance to them. Their best tactic appears to be one of avoidance and elusiveness, trying as much as possible to keep the foreigners at bay and avoid discussing the issues as long as the income from the duars kept coming. In doing so, they were perhaps following the example of neighbouring Tibet, which closed its border to the white man and was going through an era of a self-imposed isolation since the end of the eighteenth century. However, the geo-political scenarios for Tibet and Bhutan were very different and in adopting this short-sighted strategy and in hoping the 'trifling' problem would go away with persistent elusion, the Bhutanese authorities badly underestimated the seriousness of the frontier outrages as well as the good will of the British and the consequences of losing it.

The government of British India meanwhile earnestly planned the mission. The frontier British officers were instructed to show tact and moderation in dealing with their Bhutanese counterparts, so that no incident arose which could jeopardize the plan. Most of the dealings along the border during this period went in favour of Bhutan. The Governor-General waited nearly a year for the *zingup* officers to arrive and listen to Bhutan's version of the story before despatching the mission but they never arrived. This is not surprising as the joint forces of Darlung Tobgay, Jigme Namgyal and Tsondru Gyaltshen were then wrecking havoc on Desi Nagzi Pasang. By the middle of 1863, Nagzi Pasang was ousted from office and Tshewang Sithub was appointed as the new Desi. Jigme Namgyal had now become the supreme force behind the removals and appointments in the seats of power.

The humiliation of Ashley Eden

On 11 August 1863, Lord Elgin appointed Ashley Eden as the British envoy to Bhutan. Eden had led the invasion of Sikkim in 1861, which resulted in a favourable treaty with the King of Sikkim. After he reached Punakha, he was to explain in a friendly manner the circumstances which led to the British annexation of Ambari-Falakata and retention of its revenue and the British offer of a subsidy of Rs 2000 or a sum equal to one-third of the total revenue annually if Bhutan redressed all British grievances concerning outrages along the duars. He was also to enquire into complaints from Bhutan of aggressions committed by British subjects and to work on an acceptable arrangement of rendition of criminals from either country. In addition, he was also to inform Bhutan that Sikkim and Cooch Behar were British protectorates and any aggression against them would be considered by the British government as unfriendly acts. Having fulfilled these conditions, Eden was also to explore free trade opportunities and the prospects for placing a British agent in Bhutan.

The main objective of the mission was to have a treaty between Bhutan and the British. So, Eden was furnished with a draft of this treaty but also given the freedom to use his judgement and discretion to negotiate and adjust minor points. The Governor-General also wrote two letters to the Desi and the Dharmarāja, which Eden was to deliver accompanied by presents when he presented his credentials. Eden was accompanied by Chibu Lama, the prime minister of Sikkim as the interpreter, Dr Benjamin Simpson as medical officer, Captain Austen and Captain Lance to command the escort of some hundred men, and Rs 10,000 was provided as expenses for the mission. Before the mission started, messages were sent to the Desi and Dharmarāja on 10

September 1863 announcing their departure but no replies came. Eden sent another round of messages two months later from Darjeeling asking them to instruct the Daling *dzongpön* to meet him at the border with porters to carry the baggage. He added, 'If they did not do this I should be compelled to report to my Government that no arrangements had been made, and their neglect would be considered a breach of friendship'.[7] Such threats showing self-importance would have almost certainly put the mission and a Bhutanese reception on an unpromising start.

The mission set off on 4 January 1864 from Darjeeling and it faced problems right at the outset as coolies started to desert them in large numbers, unwilling to cross the Teesta river into Bhutanese territory. The mission was received in a formal reception with some pomp at Dalingkha after some hesitance on the part of the local *dzongpön* but almost the entire journey after that was ridden with troubles. A detailed account of the mission can be found in Eden's own *Report on the State of Bootan and on the Progress of the Mission of 1663–64*; only a few salient points are provided here. Eden learnt that Bhutan was in a terrible anarchy and that even his host, the *dzongpön* of Dalingkha, was caught in the conflict. The *dzongpön* sided with the supporter of the new Desi but his immediate boss, the Paro *pönlop*, was a staunch supporter of the previous Desi. The *pönlop* thus sent his men to remove the *dzongpön* and laid a siege but the *dzongpön* successfully held the fort and repelled the forces. While in Dalingkha, Eden received a letter from the Desi vaguely saying that Eden should tell the *dzongpön* of Dalingkha what he had come for. Neither did the Desi spell out a refusal to receive the mission, nor did Eden recognize the deep reluctance of the government to welcome him. After a few days, in spite of the *dzongpön*'s hesitance to let him go, Eden pushed on, leaving behind nearly half of his escorts due to a shortage of porters.

The mission took the route to Haa via Sibsoo, where coolies again deserted them and Eden had to reduce his escort to fifteen men. The main reason for desertion, Eden says, was the fear of the Bhutanese, whom 'they looked upon as a race of murderers and robbers'.[8] The mission trekked from Sibsoo to Haa in snow via Sangbekha, where Eden had traditional shoes made out of hide and woollen cloth for his coolies, Dr Simpson removed a tumour on an old man's face and the party saw three albinos whom the locals thought were European. Eden says that due to oppressive rulers, some of the villages were deserted and people along the route were anxious to come under British rule and begged him to take them with him to Darjeeling. Eden also discovered, by opening a letter addressed to the *dzongpön* of Dalingkha that the *dzongpön* was penalized for letting the mission into the country and they were not welcome. The mission nevertheless continued in heavy snow to Haa, where two men died of the cold.

Upon hearing that there was a deputation on its way to stop them, Eden once again pushed on from there to Paro in deep snow over the Chelela Pass. This leg of the journey turned out to be most gruelling as the men and horses sank in snow up to the neck. The party reached the village they aimed for only at 1a.m. There, they were once again stopped by *zingup* officers and asked to proceed no further but Eden defied them and threatened to directly return to Darjeeling if he could not proceed to Punakha. The mission continued to Paro, where Eden met the ex-*pönlop* Nyima Dorji, who still held the reins of power, and the incumbent *pönlop* Thinley Zangpo, his stepson. Eden learnt from Nyima Dorji the incapacity of the ruling council to reach any decisions without the agreement of the Tongsa *pönlop*, who was the *de facto* ruler. The Desi and Dharmarāja were mere puppets in his hand. Nyima Dorji was not on good terms with the Tongsa *pönlop* and thus sympathized with Eden on the indecision of the government but it was beyond his power to either reject or reinforce the mission.

After sixteen days and without any message from the government, the mission set off for Punakha while the Paro *tshechu* festival was in progress. A day after leaving Paro, Eden was once again stopped by messengers from Punakha asking them to return to Paro but Eden was thoroughly tired of these requests, which he perceived as 'endeavours to wear out my patience by delays and obstacles, and induce me to return'.[9] He did not for once wonder if the Bhutanese would have a genuinely good reason to delay the mission. In fact, the court in Punakha was in disarray and not ready to receive an important envoy. Tshewang Sithub became the Desi around the time Ashley Eden was appointed as the envoy in 1863 but he had to share the post with Tshultrim Gyaltshen after a few months. Tshultrim Gyaltshen, however, passed away in office and Tshewang Sithub also stepped down. The monk administrator, Kagyu Wangchuk, was then appointed as the Desi just before Eden's arrival in Paro. In the light of such instability, it is quite likely that the Bhutanese authorities were not ready to receive the mission and earnestly wished to delay it. Eden, however, only saw things from his own supercilious perspective and expected a reception befitting the great British empire he represented. In all honesty, he did not even know who the Desi and Dharmarāja, the two leading figures, were and what role they played. On the contrary, he barged in against all refusals and requests, threatening the Bhutanese officers with the severe consequences Bhutan would face if he had to return without fulfilling his mission.

The mission arrived in Punakha on 15 March 1864 but there was no sign of a welcome reception, which Eden expected. Instead, a messenger arrived to tell them that they could not enter by the main gate and he showed them to a back entrance. No notice was taken of the mission except for the small quantity of poor-quality rice sent by the Punakha *dzongpön*. At least, that was the case according to Eden's official report submitted on 20 July 1864. However, in a private letter he wrote a couple days after his arrival, he says *zingup* officers came to meet and bring them into the camps, supplies were regularly sent and ordinary civilities shown.[10] Thus, it is with a pinch of salt that we will have to take the accuracy of his words although British writings are our only sources on the mission.

Two days after arrival, the envoy was summoned to meet the State Council or what was known as the Amlah in a house near the *dzong*. The envoy and his team were ushered through a disorderly crowd, who threw stones and sticks at them. Present at the meeting were Khasar Tobgay and Tashi, the *dzongpöns* of Tashichödzong and Punakha respectively, the state chief of protocol whose name we do not have, Tsondru Gyaltshen, the Jakar *pönlop* who was also the chamberlain to the Desi and Jigme Namgyal, the Tongsa *pönlop* who was also chamberlain to the prince-regent. None of the ceremonial formalities preceding an important meeting was observed and the supercilious Jigme Namgyal, according to Eden, occupied the main seat and took charge of the proceedings. Jigme Namgyal proposed that Chibu Lama, as an interpreter, visit him daily with Eden's proposals and Chibu Lama could then inform the mission of the council's response.

Eden agreed to this proposal and, upon returning to his quarters, sent Chibu Lama with the full draft treaty, which included many provisional articles for negotiation. This was a grave mistake as he hardly knew the Bhutanese stance and how they would react to the British proposals. Jigme Namgyal and the Bhutan authorities may have been alarmed by the demands. Had Eden sounded out the British proposals and then discussed the various alternatives, the mood might have been different and the meeting would have taken a different course. For the next couple of days, they discussed the treaty and on 20 March, the party was granted an audience with the Desi and Dharmarāja. Unlike previous audiences to the British visitors which took place in the *dzong* with solemn formalities, the audience this time took place outside the *dzong*. Eden and his group were hustled from one tent to another, jostled by a mob and made to stand in the sun before they saw the Desi and a bit later, the Dharmarāja. There was no interview with either of them and the Tongsa *pönlop* assumed the role of their spokesperson. Eden wrote that 'every opportunity was taken of treating us with indignity' and the jostling and jeering certainly appear to be orchestrated or a calculated act of aggression. It is unlike any Bhutanese attitude to visitors. To add to the embarrassment, Eden did not have any of the presents, which he was to deliver to the two leading figures. Due to a complication in the transport, the presents arrived only some days after the audience.

Following the audience, negotiations on the treaty continued between Eden and the Council and Eden, at one point, even thought that he was at the end of a successful negotiation. The two last articles of the treaty concerning the appointment of a British agent in Bhutan and free trade were dropped and a fresh copy of the treaty was made. Then, the negotiations fell on an unexpected stumbling block when the Tongsa *pönlop* insisted on inserting a new article about the return of all the Assam duars, which the British had annexed in 1841. Eden was taken aback by both the proposal and the Tongsa *pönlop*'s overbearing manners. He protested, stating that the Assam duars were a closed issue. Certainly, they did not fall in the purview of his mission and he had no authority to return them. The Tongsa *pönlop* crumpled the treaty and declared that he would rather have a war than sign a treaty if the Assam duars were not returned. As far as he was concerned, the British could keep Ambari-Falakata, which was anyway in the domain of the Paro *pönlop*, but as long as the British retained the Assam duars, there was no point of discussing anything. With negotiations at a dead end, the mission prepared to leave but other members of the council asked Eden to postpone his departure, hoping that the demand of the Tongsa *pönlop* could be resisted. In pushing the return of the Assam duars, the Tongsa *pönlop* was promoting his own interests and perhaps those of Tsondru Gyaltshen because only they benefited from the income of the Assam duars. The other members were fully aware of this but no one dared oppose the Tongsa *pönlop* openly. Eden insisted that the Assam duars issue should not be raised again and that the Tongsa *pönlop* be excluded from the discussions. He believed that demanding the Assam duars, which had been long annexed by the British, while the larger Bengal duars were at stake would only result in more harm than good. Some of the Bhutanese authorities seem to have concurred with Eden.

On 22 March, the mission had another meeting with the Council. This time, two members who were previously absent, Darlung Tobgay, the *dzongpön* of Wangdi and Kawang Mangkhel, the *zhung kalön* or chief councillor of state, were also present and, to Eden's utter surprise, the Tongsa *pönlop* walked in to take the head of the table. The draft treaty was read out with the exception of the two last articles. A similar meeting took place again on 24 March, when Eden was hopeful that the treaty would be finally signed but that was not to be. After reading out the first two articles, the Tongsa *pönlop* again stated that the Assam duars should be returned as soon as the treaty was signed with the revenue collected since 1841 to him. Eden was astonished by this brazen demand and appealed to other members of the Council but they 'were laughing and talking and did not pay the slightest attention to what was passing'.[11] Eden and his party were then told to go to another tent and in the middle of a large crowd were ridiculed by the Tongsa *pönlop* and Wangdi *dzongpön*. Jigme Namgyal rubbed Eden's face with a piece of wet dough and pulled his hair. Darlung Tobgay told Dr Simpson to eat some betel and areca nuts he had been chewing and when the latter refused, he threw it on the face, which Dr Simpson did not wipe off to show the insult. Darlung Tobgay then pulled the watch off Chibu Lama's neck.

Whatever may have triggered such brash and disgraceful behaviour, the two Bhutanese leaders went too far. It is the single most deplorable case of Bhutanese court behaviour and diplomatic failure, which has no semblance to the usual Bhutanese forbearance, court decorum and etiquette. The incident appears even more damning as the other leaders either condoned the behaviour or remained as indifferent spectators. After the insult, Eden and his party were allowed to leave and the Tongsa *pönlop* shouted after them: 'I want nothing but the Assam duars and if I don't get them it is better to have war than a treaty.'[12] The party planned to set off for India the next day but before they did, Chibu Lama was summoned and given the treaty to be signed. It proposed that the British should return the Assam duars along with the revenue calculated at Rs 3000 per year and all runaway slaves who took refuge in British territory. The Tongsa *pönlop* threatened to imprison Eden and Chibu Lama; the Wangdi *dzongpön* even to kill them if they failed to sign. Meanwhile, the presents from the Governor-General finally arrived and the Bhutanese authorities seem to have been briefly placated by the gifts distributed to them.

The mission received a civil reception on 27 March followed by a formal audience with the Desi and Dharmarāja two days later. However, Jigme Namgyal persisted with his demand that the British should relinquish all of the duars and that Eden should sign the treaty to that effect. Eden was now presented with a revised treaty, which omitted the demand for Rs 3000 per year and but added a new paragraph saying that if the British were ever again to encroach on Bhutanese territory they would be punished by the combined powers of Bhutan, Sikkim and Cooch Behar. The Bhutanese seem to have either underestimated the British imperial power or exaggerated the strength of the three little states. After much deliberation with his party about the possible options and due consideration of the safety of the mission and its dependents, Eden eventually yielded to pressure and signed the treaty adding the words 'under compulsion' after his signature. However, for fear of reprisals, he did not make this clear to the Bhutanese, who were left thinking it was a voluntary endorsement.

The mission left Punakha on the evening of 29 March by moonlight as soon as the Tongsa *pönlop* departed for his region. Despite the threats of the Wangdi *dzongpön* to stop them, they continued their march to Paro, where the old ex-*pönlop* was 'friendly and attentive', having heard of the sad turn of events in Punakha. He seems to have genuinely wished for the negotiations to take a friendly course as he had much to lose if the British annexed Ambari-Falakata and the Bengal duars. The young *pönlop* was also friendly but Eden found him 'an importunate beggar' trying to obtain possession of everything the mission had. The mission left Paro on 2 April on the final leg of their journey and the *pönlop*s in Paro were already busy preparing for another insurrection. Eden submitted a detailed report on Bhutan and his mission, covering the country's history, governance, religion, economy, culture, nature and his poor estimate of Bhutan's military strength.

With the return of Eden's mission, all friendly relations with Bhutan were suspended. The failure of the mission became a heated topic of discussion and debate among officers in India as well as some British press. While some criticized Eden of making the British name suffer in his hands as never before in the East and of timidly making over British territory to the enemies by relenting to pressure and signing a treaty, others applauded Eden's forbearance and dexterity in bringing home all members of the mission safely under trying circumstances. The critics accused Eden of not having kept the officials well informed of his progress, of being obstinate in pushing on despite not being welcome, of lacking judgement in presenting the entire draft treaty in the first instance of negotiation, of delivering presents long after opening the talks, although he was instructed to open talks with the presents, of being lenient in allowing the Tongsa *pönlop* to take part after it was decided he should be excluded and of lacking courage and straightforwardness in signing a treaty under compulsion without letting his counterparts know that he did so. No doubt, the diplomatic breakdown and the subsequent disaster of the war could have been avoided if only Eden had done things differently.

The British government and Eden should have accepted the reality and acknowledged the position of Jigme Namgyal in the country. Instead of seeing Jigme Namgyal as an illegal usurper and undermining his importance, Eden should have treated him as the main counterpart. The British approach to solving the Bhutan problem by dealing with the *de jure* ruler and ignoring the *de facto* ruler was impractical. The internal squabbles within Bhutan certainly did not help the mission but almost all British missions arrived in Bhutan in the course of insurrections and those in the past were generally successful. Thus, the failure of the mission was largely due to mutual intransigence and the discordant personalities of the two main players, aggravated by their fears and assumptions. Eden appears to have lacked the humour, congeniality and tact, which were manifest in visitors such as Bogle and Turner. He began the mission with a supercilious attitude and a very negative opinion of the Bhutanese and finished it with a damning impression and a diplomatic debacle. Nonetheless, he went on to have a successful career in British India and was subsequently even knighted.

The ultimate reason for the diplomatic breakdown and the consequent war, however, lay with the Bhutanese authorities and almost singularly with the Tongsa *pönlop*, whom Eden described as 'utterly reckless of human life . . . an avaricious, treacherous and unscrupulous robber.'[13] Like Eden, he was uncompromising and had a low opinion of his opponents. If Eden was stubborn in pushing his way to Punakha despite repeated resistance, Jigme Namgyal was equally stubborn in insisting the British return the Assam duars. All views of the greater good, honour and friendship took a blurred backstage as they focused single-pointedly on their personal pride and achievements; in the case of Eden that of reaching Punakha and accomplishing his mission in spite of inconvenience to Bhutan and in the case of Jigme Namgyal of retrieving the Assam duars even at the stake of greater loss of land. Despite the rising glory of Victorian imperialism, the British government on the whole genuinely professed good will and an accommodating policy towards Bhutan. Apart from securing its border from lawless raids, the British did not have ulterior motives to invade Bhutan or annex its duars, as Jigme Namgyal might have feared. The British genuinely sought Bhutan's friendship and the cooperation in combating the menace along the frontiers.

Thus, the mission presented a wonderful opportunity for Bhutan to mend the broken links with the British and consolidate the duar territories. Even the return of Assam could have been discussed after reining in the unruly men in the frontiers. The British were primarily interested in a peaceful and productive frontier area and Jigme Namgyal with his almost unchallenged power in Bhutan could have enforced law and order in the duars. Unfortunately, this did not happen but Jigme Namgyal remained fixated on the return of the Assam duars, short of which he was not willing to negotiate. It seems that Jigme Namgyal was influenced by a certain Indian advisor in his anti-British sentiments and harsh treatment of the mission. This man, perhaps a fugitive from the Indian mutiny, presented himself as General Nundanum Singh, grandson of the Sikh ruler Ranjit Singh. He became known in Bhutan as Padshah Rāja, acted as an advisor to Jigme Namgyal, spoke in a Bhutanese language, dressed in Bhutanese robes and later even took part in the military campaign against the British. According to Eden, he arrived in Bhutan with claims of close connections to the rulers of Delhi, Lahore and Nepal and proposed that Bhutan join a general war against the British. Eden writes that he ran into trouble with the Paro *pönlop* as he sided with the Dalingkha *dzongpön* in a rebellion and was consequently imprisoned in Paro. From there, he escaped and joined Jigme Namgyal in Tongsa and is believed to have slandered Jigme Namgyal against the British.

At any rate, Jigme Namgyal was almost singularly the stumbling block for the mission. If his overbearing presence in the meetings did not augur well for the mission which was intended to strengthen friendly relations, the insolence with which he and Wangdi *dzongpön* treated the British mission nailed the coffin. There have been some attempts by writers to exonerate Jigme Namgyal but the damage was irrefutable.[14] The rashness and insolence with which Jigme Namgyal and his coterie treated the mission resulted in a serious diplomatic rupture and precipitated the Duar War and ultimately the loss of about one-fifth of Bhutanese territory. It is to these consequences and the Duar War, one of the least known British imperial wars, we shall turn now.

The Duar War

The proceedings at Punakha had bruised the British imperial ego and serious discussions now followed on how recalcitrant Bhutan must be punished. On 7 May 1864, Eden suggested three options of actions to secure British frontiers from Bhutanese aggression: (1) to occupy the whole country permanently, (2) to occupy the country temporarily and destroy the *dzong*s and (3) to annex all the remaining duars. The Government of India, however, took a lenient approach to first annex Ambari-Falakata permanently and withhold payment for the Assam duars. A letter was sent to the Desi informing him of this punishment for the insult to which the British mission was subjected. Bhutan was also asked to deliver all British subjects and goods carried away from British soil in the last five years or face annexation of the Bengal duars. A letter was received in response, ostensibly from the young Dharmarāja, asking for fresh negotiations as the Tongsa *pönlop* had now left for his country.[15] A separate letter, with a threatening tone, was also received by Chibu Lama asking the British to honour the treaty.

Seeing no hope of meaningful negotiation, the British now made preparations for a full assault and annexation of all the duars. On 12 November 1864, the Governor-General made a proclamation of war and a force of some 3000 men and 600 elephants were assembled to attack Bhutan from four areas. The left column advanced from Jalpaiguri on Dalingkha, the left centre from Cooch Behar on Pasakha, the right centre from Goalpara on today's Sarpang area and finally, the right column from Gauhati on Dewathang. Brigadier-General Mulcaster commanded the entire operation but stayed with the right and right centre columns while Colonel Dunsford remained with the left and left centre columns. All inhabitants of the duar areas were asked to submit to the British and assist the invading forces; they were promised justice and protection of life and property. The aim was to annex the entire duar plains leading up to the foothills and occupy the border forts, and compensate Bhutan with an annual subsidy of Rs 25,000 in the first year gradually increasing it to Rs 50,000. The proclamation was also sent to British residents in Kathmandu and Peking and to authorities in Lhasa primarily with the aim of dispelling any doubts Nepal, Tibet and China may harbour about the British motive to occupy areas in the Himalayas.

At the end of November, the British troops began their advance towards the four main border forts. The left column marched toward Dalingdzong and took it over after ten hours of heavy firing and use of ammunition against the Bhutanese frontier guards who fought with arrows, stones and matchlocks. When they went in, the invading troops found only three wounded men, one of whom was a Bengali; the rest of the Bhutanese soldiers had retreated. On the British side, however, two soldiers were killed and twenty wounded in combat. Seven more, including three British officers, were killed and many others seriously mutilated in an accidental explosion of mortar due to a defective fuse. After taking over

Dalingdzong, the left column advanced toward Samtse via Tendu. Meanwhile, the centre left column under Colonel Watson took possession of Pasakha without any resistance. On 10 December, the right column under Colonel Campbell, who was also accompanied by Brigadier-General Mulcaster, advanced on Dewathang and captured it after some resistance and the death of a few Bhutanese frontier guards. After occupying Dewathang, Mulcaster led some of the troops westward to join the right centre column under Colonel Richardson. The two groups met at Sidli and marched on the hill fort of Bishensing in the modern Sarpang area with some 2000 men and 150 elephants. When they arrived, they found only a single stone house occupied by an old lama. By the end of January 1865, all the duar forts from Dalingkha to Dewathang were taken over by the British. The British occupation of duars was swift and sweeping and the main body of the army was withdrawn to the plains leaving only a smaller number to guard the hill forts. Little did they realize that the Bhutanese forces were yet to arrive and the men who resisted them thus far were probably only the soldiers posted at the frontiers. It was only a temporary silence before the storm.

While the British forces advanced, the Bhutanese were busy recruiting new forces to counteract the invaders. A proclamation, purportedly from the prince-regent but most likely authored by Jigme Namgyal, was sent out on 19 December, exhorting Bhutanese *pönlop*s, *dzongpön*s and others to defend the country from the invading forces and to prepare for the attacks.[16] On 27 December, the Desi Kagyu Wangchuk sent a letter to the Brigadier-General accusing the British of jeopardizing friendly relations, in which the Desi and Queen of England were like a brother and sister. The invasion, he argued, violated the treaty Eden signed and was a cunning and cowardly act to rob a small country of its land without even formally declaring the war and fixing the time and the venue of the battles.[17] He asked the British to withdraw or face the wrath of a long list of Bhutanese protector deities.

The wrath did come soon as Bhutanese leaders invoked their protector deities and descended upon the foothills. There are no detailed written records of Bhutan's military preparation and deployment but a couple of late twentieth-century sources mention three divisions of defence troops. One division approached Pasakha led by the Thimphu *dzongpön* and chief councillor of state to counter-attack the British left centre column and another on the western front along Samtse and Chamurchi area led by the Paro *pönlop* and state chief of protocol against the British left column.[18] By far the strongest was the division which marched to Dewathang under the commandership of Jigme Namgyal, the Tongsa *pönlop*, to counter-attack the British left column. He was assisted by Tsondru Gyaltshen, the Jakar *pönlop* and Sonam Dhendup, the brother of the former Dharmarāja Jigme Norbu. There probably was another division to counter-attack the British right centre column as David Rennie, the author of *Bhotan and the Story of the Doar War,* mentions an assault on Bishensing fort in the Sarpang area. Going by the other divisions, this would have been led by the Wangdi *dzongpön* and the Dagana *pönlop* as this area was under their jurisdiction.

There was probably no proper co-ordination among the Bhutanese leaders, most of whom were on bad terms with each other. Although the external enemy helped suspend their internal differences for a short period and aroused a sense of solidarity, it appears that the leaders were made to defend their own domains. Apart from the eulogized accounts of the eastern division under Jigme Namgyal, which were told and retold as part of the monarchical narrative in the twentieth century, we have no information on Bhutanese counter-attacks. Jigme Namgyal, as the Tongsa *pönlop* and the most powerful leader, no doubt raised and led the strongest force alongside his comrades. British sources confirm that there were about 5000 men including about 1500 warriors, porters to carry the wounded, servants to carry provisions and build stockades and other supporting staff. Each fighting men carried 'in the fold of his dress, a circular powder flask containing from 100 to 150 bullets, about three seers (six pounds) of rice and dried meat, and in addition to this from ten to twenty stones of a size sufficient to stun a man'.[19] Help was probably sought from Nepal and Tibet but these countries chose to stay out of the bilateral conflict although some Khampa mercenaries most likely fought alongside the Bhutanese.

Jigme Namgyal, according to the oral accounts, set off from Tongsa with propitious omens. As he made his supplications to his tutelary war gods, the shrine resonated with a noise and a raven flew out of the *dzong* and followed him on his route.[20] This was interpreted as a sign that the Raven-headed Mahākāla, whom Zhabdrung used as protector deity and the Bhutanese repeatedly used to threaten the British, was accompanying him. If Jigme Namgyal was a poor diplomat, he made up for it with his valour and upright character as a brave warrior. First, a week before the planned attack, Jigme Namgyal sent a letter warning the British and urging them to withdraw from Dewathang. Unfortunately, no one among the British regiment could read the letter written in Tibetan and it was sent to Darjeeling to be translated. In the meantime, Jigme Namgyal and his men made a surprise attack before dawn on 30 January 1865. The British heard a noise like that of stampeding cattle and the ropes of their tents were cut off by the time they realized it was an enemy attack.

The superior fire power of the British managed to fend off the Bhutanese from taking over the camp but they lost five men and thirty-one were wounded. Among the five dead was one British officer, Lieutenant Urquart of the Royal Engineers, who was killed by a jingal bullet.[21] It is perhaps in reference to this killing that almost all Bhutanese historians narrate the following hyperbolic account.

> Then, the commanding sahibs of the British were gathered at a table in Dewathang in a meeting. Padshah Rāja, who had escaped from military service [in India] and wandered to Bhutan, using a telescope pointed out Shalpa Lagdum,[22] the highest British commander. While the supplication to the protector deities Jangdu and Jarog Dongchen composed by His Holiness Jangchub Tsondru was chanted by his chaplain, Jigme Namgyal, the Tongsa *pönlop*, with a single pointed concentration and aspiration for the welfare of Buddhism and the sentient beings, fired his gun. Through the power of the deities, the shots hit the generals sitting in a row over the ear and killed them at the same time. The British soldiers took flight in the middle of their eating and drinking.[23]

It is quite likely that Jigme Namgyal, who was at the forefront of the Bhutanese troops, fired the shot which killed Urquart and the Bhutanese legend grew out of it. If this was the case, one of Urquart's hands was later chopped off and brought to Tongsa to be hung in the chamber of the protector deities as a token of gratitude to the war gods. The Bhutanese lost about sixty men including one fine old secretary of the Tongsa *pönlop*. According to Rennie, he was wounded in the chest, taken prisoner and made to translate some papers into Assamese before he died. It is possible that this was Lopen Gangchen or Zhalphan Rolpai Dorji, who served as a secretary to Jigme Namgyal.

The British temporarily managed to take positions and repel the Bhutanese forces but the Bhutanese warriors were far from defeated. In a strategic move, the Bhutanese next cut off the water supply to the British camp and the communication line to the backup forces in the plains by taking over the main pass. Meanwhile, the warriors closed in on the British camp, building stockades closer and closer to the British camp. Unable to hold the camp,

Colonel Campbell eventually ordered his troops on 4 February to silently evacuate and leave for the plains using another pass under the cover of the night. In their frantic retreat in darkness, they left behind their properties and their wounded, and threw away two Howitzer guns down a ravine, which the Tongsa *pönlop*'s men later retrieved. It is very likely that Urquart's body was also left behind and, as he was the only white officer to fall into their hands, the Bhutanese used it as trophy of their victory.

Soon after the Bhutanese took over Dewathang, the Tongsa *pönlop* sent a message to the British asking about the welfare of Bhutanese prisoners and informing that prisoners with him were in satisfactory condition. He even included some money for the expenses which might be incurred to send a reply. The strength of the Bhutanese forces, their dexterity in combat in spite of inferior weapons and the commandeering skill and upright character of the Jigme Namgyal in war proved to the British that Eden's opinions of Jigme Namgyal and Bhutanese soldiery were not all accurate. Eden portrayed Jigme Namgyal as an unscrupulous villain and speculated that he may have around 600 men under his command, although without much military skills. The British soldiers serving in Dewathang formed a very different impression of Jigme Namgyal. He was found to be a very astute leader and an understanding opponent.

It was, however, Eden's terrible underestimation of Bhutan's military strength and skill which annoyed his superiors the most. The fighting capacity of Bhutan was far stronger and more organized than Eden made the British authorities believe and the evacuation of Dewathang with the loss of two Howitzer guns seriously injured the imperial pride. It was a painful experience for the mighty British power to lose to little Bhutan. The operation was described by one general as 'so cowardly a conception, so bad a management and so disastrous a result'. British defence positions in Sarpang, Pasakha and Samtse were also seriously threatened by the other Bhutanese divisions but they generally managed to repel the Bhutanese and hold their positions. The Bhutanese under the Paro *pönlop* temporarily succeeded in occupying the forts in Tazagong and Samtse. A sense of Bhutanese nationalistic fervour and solidarity is captured in the letter from the Wangdi *dzongpön* to a general serving the Paro *pönlop*, which the British found in a captured stockade in Samtse.

I am aware the place is getting warm, but if you return without gaining a decided victory, the great Chiefs and Lamas will surely hold you in great disgrace. So resolve never to come back but die in war. If you now come back, then what avail the hardship you have undergone so long in fortifying the position? What was the good of undergoing labour so hard that you have reckoned one as ten? What is the consequence of your lying in the open air whole nights, and sleeping upon the grass, having only a stone for your pillow? . . . I am also informed that four men were killed in a battle. Do not be afraid on account of it, but remember that they were killed for the sake of their country. Resolve that we must take vengeance for it, by punishing the ambitious English, at the expense of our own lives. It is better to have our bodies cut into pieces than to come back without punishing the enemy. He who is the most prudent and careful can never be defeated. The Paro Penlow is determined to fight at all hazards, and retain one side of the country. Resolve that we should work hard, so as to cut the hardest stones and iron to pieces.[24]

The British made an immediate appeal for reinforcement and the Government of India called troops from Meerut, Lucknow and Calcutta to the duars and in March 1865, operations were resumed to recover earlier positions. The forces are now divided into the right and left columns under the commandership of Brigadier-Generals Tytler and Tombs respectively. Over 3000 soldiers in addition to the large force already fighting in the duars were deployed to recover British prestige and the areas reoccupied by the Bhutanese. What initially looked like a quick and easy invasion now turned into a protracted war and the Government of India was already worried by the potential for further embarrassments and the expenses the conflict could incur. Bhutan was no longer the small country which the British could punish and tell off at will but a significant, irritable force to reckon with.

In March, the forces of the Left Brigade under General Tytler advanced to regain control of Samtse and Pasakha, which they did with little difficulty. Some forty-four Bhutanese men under Paro *pönlop* died defending their stockades at the Balla Pass. At the same time, the Right Brigade under General Tombs marched towards Dewathang. The British troops at Bishensing near Sarpang were withdrawn after destroying the stockades and the forces were now concentrated to attack the Bhutanese division in Dewathang. Jigme Namgyal was still actively commanding the Bhutanese troops and wrote to General Tombs a very cordial letter enquiring about his health and the treatment of prisoners while also stating:

You are wanting Dewangiri again, but from whom did you receive permission to take possession of it, when you first captured it? . . . There is no quarrel at all between us, if you will allow us to possess the lands on the former boundaries.[25]

On 1 April 1865, over 1500 men under General Tombs ascended the hills of Dewathang and the following day, they stormed the three stockades from which the Bhutanese retaliated. Tragedy struck the Bhutanese forces when the British Native Infantry composed of Sikhs and Pathans managed to infiltrate into the stockade. These ruthless native soldiers indiscriminately butchered some 120 Bhutanese in the stockade. The Bhutanese narrative of the attack however differs significantly from British accounts. Dasho Lama Sa-nga writes:

Besieged by the sheer number of Indian soldiers, they went inside the stockade and closed its door. But [the enemy] climbed into the stockade from outside; [the Bhutanese] used their swords to strike them from above. The corpses of [dead enemies] piled up as tall as the stockade. However, being beaten by sticks from behind, [the enemy soldiers] were not allowed to back off. Climbing on the pile of corpses, they reached the top, then they closed their eyes, lowered their heads and forced in, in a suicidal manner. After a while, although the Bhutanese took turns to kill, there was no end to the enemy soldiers. Worn out, Sonam Dhendup, the Lama's chamberlain, went downstairs to *pönlop* Tsondru Gyaltshen and said: 'Lord! We cannot hold it any longer. Let's get out.' Despite repeated requests, Tsondru Gyaltshen refused. 'See you later,' said Sonam Dhendup. Wielding their swords high, he and his attendants jostled through the enemy soldiers and corpses, under a hailstorm of bullets, which mostly hit the enemy's own men. Many of his friends lay still amid the corpses of both sides feigning death but a few stood up and ran before the British left scene. Thus, in order to distinguish the dead and those feigning dead, the British came back and pierced them with spears and killed them. Some of those left behind escaped to the Chötse camp [of Tongsa *pönlop*]. Then, elephants were brought in to demolish the stockade and Jakar *pönlop* was either killed or captured. Dead bodies of others were recovered but his was not found. The body of Lhuntse *dzongpön* had swollen beyond recognition but he was identified through the golden ring he wore on one of his left fingers.[26]

The British sources mention only about thirty casualties on their side. They contain no accounts of serious losses, let alone of directing their native infantry to march on the Bhutanese stockade and get killed. Rennie states that the British officers unsuccessfully restrained the Sikhs and Pathans from indiscriminately killing the defeated enemies. There is no mention of spearing to death those Bhutanese soldiers feigning death even by the unruly native soldiers, as the Bhutanese account has us believe. Whatever the truth, this was by far the biggest clash and the *pönlop* of Jakar, Tsondru Gyaltshen, almost certainly was killed or captured at this time. Even Jigme Namgyal was wounded in the right foot and carried by a soldier until Yongla.[27]

The British occupation of Dewathang was purely for recovering pride and prestige because a few days after the place was captured, the general ordered the troops to destroy the fortification and withdraw to the plains. The monsoon was already on its way and the place would be untenable for the British as the heavy rain would make the paths treacherous and the swelling streams would cut off the supply line with their headquarters in the plains. The Bhutanese had also by then withdrawn to the hills. As the letter found in Samtse suggests, many Bhutanese may have already left the warm foothills with the fear of rising heat and malaria, known as 'heat disease', before the second British campaign. They generally avoided the lowlands and rarely descended to the plains after winter. This may be the reason for the absence of Bhutanese retaliation on the British forces after the second campaign. Despite the ultimate victory of the British in occupying the duars, Jigme Namgyal never accepted defeat and marched to Tongsa with his men claiming victory and carrying the hand of the British officer and the two Howitzer guns as trophies.

The British now cut off Bhutan from the plains and installed a police force to guard the frontiers. With the military defeat and annexation of duars, the Governor-General hoped the government of Bhutan would plead for peace and enter a formal treaty. He wrote to the Desi on 5 June, threatening to send troops into Bhutan if the entire duars and Ambari-Falakata were not relinquished, the copy of treaty signed by Eden under compulsion was not handed over with an apology and the two guns not surrendered. In response, the Desi only made reference to the return of all the duars to Bhutan and the Wangdi *dzongpön* continued the campaign to intensify the fight against the British. Only the Paro *pönlop* appears to have made some overtures for negotiation and settlement but he alone did not have sufficient power. Meanwhile, the British forces suffered a slow defeat at the hands of the inhospitable climate of the terai region. The forces across the duars were decimated by malaria followed by an outbreak of cholera. A fifth of 1300 men at Pasakha were in hospital and by July 1865, there was virtually no army left.

The Governor-General was both embarrassed by Bhutan's persistent defiance and worried by the condition of the troops and the costs of life and money if the defensive arrangements had to continue for an indefinite period of time. Although the permanent occupation of the duars and invasion of interior Bhutan were never considered as an option by his government, the Governor-General now used it as a threat to bring Bhutan to the negotiating table. Plans were made, perhaps ostensibly, for the troops in Pasakha to march on to Punakha and those in Dewathang on to Tongsa. The British even started building a road from Pasakha to Punakha. In reality, the Governor-General could not afford a full-scale invasion of Bhutan; the difficulties of penetrating into hostile territory and the financial expenses would be enormous. Thus, it was a great relief to the Governor-General when the threat worked and Bhutan turned to a peaceful settlement.

Bhutan's leaders, unfortunately, did not know about the dismal situation of the British troops in the duars and the anxiety of the Indian government throughout the summer of 1865. If they did, they would have considered this as a propitious work of their war gods, as they had done with the accidental explosion in Dalingkha which killed seven British soldiers. This would have certainly boosted the morale of the Bhutanese and they may have used the opportunity to wreck further havoc on the British. Unaware of the very vulnerable situation of the British troops and taking the Governor-General's threat seriously, the Desi finally sent two *zingup* officers in July to meet Colonel Bruce, the officiating political officer. His wish was to negotiate a peace deal by surrendering the Bengal duars in return for a cash subsidy and resumption of trade. Desi Tsondru Pekar, who succeeded Desi Kagyu Wangchuk, was probably in office then. He and the western Bhutanese magnates were in favour of a peaceful settlement but the Tongsa *pönlop* once again was opposed to the settlement. Jigme Namgyal wanted to continue the fight.

In response, the British threatened a full-scale invasion and advanced their troops into the hills above Pasakha and occupied Dewathang for the third time. This was done merely to put pressure on the Tongsa *pönlop* as there was really no hope of undertaking full operations for invading central Bhutan. The Tongsa *pönlop* eventually acquiesced with the decision of the Desi and the treaty of Sinchula was signed on 11 November 1865. The British agreed to suspend hostilities but the road-building process continued for some months. The treaty provided for (1) perpetual friendship between the two countries, (2) the permanent British annexation of all duars and an area on the left of Teesta river, (3) release of British subjects in Bhutan, (4) a subsidy of Rs 25,000 rising to Rs 50,000 in three years, (5) the right of the British to withhold the payment if Bhutan failed to check future frontier outrages, (6–7) mutual restitution of criminals, (8) arbitration of the Government of India in disputes between Bhutan and the British protectorates of Cooch Behar and Sikkim and (9) free trade.

The treaty of Sinchula marked a new chapter for Bhutan and came to define its historic relationship with its big neighbour to the south. Bhutan lost over 3433 square miles, nearly one-fifth of its area, but started receiving a subsidy from the Government of India, a practice which would continue into the twenty-first century. The ratification of the treaty, however, did not end the problems immediately because Bhutan and the British could not easily agree on the demarcation of the border and the Tongsa *pönlop* was still reluctant to deliver the two guns, the retrieval of which was very important to the British imperial prestige. The British troops continued to advance into Bhutan, still making the threat to take over Punakha and Tongsa.[28] Eventually, the guns were returned, the subsidy paid and the war came to a complete end with the exchange of the ratified treaties on 3 January 1866. The British withdrew all their troops and stopped the road construction after over twenty miles. The Duar War of 1864–65 was the last war Bhutan fought against a foreign sovereign power.

Resumption of civil war

The unity among Bhutanese leaders offered by external adversity crumbled as soon as the war with the British was over. Internal turmoil gripped Bhutan once again as the magnates resumed their feudal conflicts. Curiously, one of the feuds among the leading figures around this time was over a woman. Such a cause of war was totally unknown in the past when public offices were dominated by celibate monastics but as political power slipped into the hands of laities, women and fidelity in relationships among leaders became a significant issue. In the first of such cases, Khasar Tobgay, the *dzongpön* of Thimphu and Tashi, the *dzongpön* of Punakha are said to have 'stolen' Tshewang Chözom, the wife of Darlung Tobgay, the *dzongpön* of Wangdi. The historians are ambivalent on whether this 'stealing' was a case of abduction or infidelity but the act incensed Darlung Tobgay enough to kill Khasar Tobgay. If Eden's informant is correct, this incident took place soon after Eden's departure from Punakha in 1864.[29] Kawang Mangkhel, the chief councillor of state, then occupied the post of the Thimphu *dzongpön* after Khasar's death and the joint forces of Kawang Mangkhel and Darlung Tobgay fell on Tashi.

This row over a woman altered the existent power paradigm in Bhutan. Now, the political centre was split with Darlung Tobgay, the incumbent Wangdi *dzongpön* and Kawang Mangkhel, the new Thimphu *dzongpön*, on one side and Tashi, the Punakha *dzongpön* and Sigay, the former Wangdi *dzongpön* on the other. We may recall that Sigay was set free in 1863 by Jigme Namgyal with the understanding that he would remain homebound and not take part in state politics. This injunction did not last and he was back brewing trouble against his enemy, Darlung Tobgay. Unable to challenge Darlung Tobgay on their own, Tashi and Sigay sought the help of Jigme Namgyal, who was only too willing to come and avenge the death of his cousin, Khasar Tobgay. We may recall that Jigme Namgyal earlier fought alongside Darlung Tobgay against Desi Nagzi Pasang but the friends had now turned into foes, because Darlung Tobgay killed Khasar Tobgay, who was Jigme Namgyal's cousin and appointee at Thimphu. Jigme Namgyal arrived with his troops in Thimphu to take revenge on Darlung Tobgay and dislodge his ally, Kawang Mangkhel, the new Thimphu *dzongpön*.

Even the Paro *pönlop* joined the forces against Darlung Tobgay and Kawang Mangkhel although his real intention was suspect. The former Paro *pönlop* Nyima Dorji superficially affiliated with Jigme Namgyal but in fact he was against the Tongsa *pönlop*, if we are to go by what he told Eden. Bhutanese historians maintain the two were on good terms.[30] Moreover, the incumbent Paro *pönlop*, Thinley Zangpo, the stepson of Nyima Dorji, was a relation of Darlung Tobgay. So, it was only ostensibly that the Paro forces joined Jigme Namgyal's troops to help the Punakha *dzongpön*. The Tongsa troops under Jigme Namgyal set up their base in Zilukhar while the Paro forces camped in Kawajangsa but failed to penetrate the *dzong* and defeat Mangkhel. This was because the Paro *pönlop*, while pretending to fight against Mangkhel, secretly supplied him with firearms at night whenever he ran out of stock. The conflict dragged on and the clergy once again intervened to negotiate a settlement. However, it was the urgent call of the British invasion from the south, which helped suspend this conflict in 1864 and temporarily united the Bhutanese magnates.

However, when the war with the British ended, old enmities surfaced again

and the internal conflict resumed along former lines. By now, Desi Tsondru
Pekar has passed away and the 46th Desi Tshewang Sithub was reappointed as
the 50th Desi. He was, however, a weak leader and not much is known about
him. In 1869, he made a request to Colonel Haughton, the commissioner of
Cooch Behar, for military support although it is not clear which of the two
groups he sided with. Colonel Haughton declined to give any support on
the grounds of refusal to interfere in internal affairs. The Wangdi *dzongpön*
followed suit in asking the British for military help but his plea was also
turned down on the same grounds. However, one of his officers appears to
have recruited a large number of Nepali labourers in Buxa as fighters, which
vexed Colonel Haughton. This came to the notice of the two *pönlop*s of Paro
and Tongsa and the *dzongpön* of Punakha, who were now united against the
Wangdi *dzongpön*. They protested and requested the British to stay away
from interfering in internal matters. The British, they argued, should not be
concerned by Bhutan's internal conflicts where 'enemies turned into friends
and friends into enemies in a moment'.[31] Yeshe Ngodup, the prince-regent,
also wrote to the British, perhaps at their suggestion, asking them not to
entertain any appeals for military help and the British replied that they had
no intention of doing so.

Jigme Namgyal had in the meantime curiously retired in Wangdichöling
having installed his elder brother Dungkar Gyaltshen as the Tongsa *pönlop*.
Darlung Tobgay had also officially resigned from the post of the Wangdi
dzongpön after installing his nephew on it but these resignations were only a
temporary lull or perhaps a disingenuous withdrawal. As the fighting between
the two groups continued in Wangdiphodrang, Jigme Namgyal returned with
even more ruthless tactics. When Dungkar Gyaltshen made new overtures
to reach a friendly settlement with the party of the Wangdi *dzongpön*, Jigme
Namgyal feared that it would only create a bigger internal enemy but using
the opportunity, he appears to have devised a plot to overcome his opponents
and pave his way to the highest office in the country.[32]

In early 1869, Jigme Namgyal approached the Wangdiphodrang *dzong*
riding a black horse and wearing a black robe and a black hat. The *dzong*
was then gripped by fighting but Jigme Namgyal made proposals for peace,
perhaps ostensibly, and even celebrated some days of reconciliation with an
archery game. His main opponents, Darlung Tobgay and Kawang Mangkhel,
were probably relieved by the peace proposal but they did not know that
Jigme Namgyal had sent two trusted followers with ammunition to secretly
blow up Tashichödzong. With the news that Tashichödzong was on fire,

Kawang Mangkhel, the Thimphu *dzongpön* left Wangdi in a hurry. Darlung Tobgay and his nephew, the new *dzongpön* of Wangdi, were now left without their strong ally and at the mercy of their enemies. Persuaded by two of his attendants who held grievances against Darlung Tobgay, Jigme Namgyal put Darlung Tobgay to death. Darlung's nephew, the incumbent *dzongpön* of Wangdi, was killed by Jigme Namgyal's attendants.

With Darlung Tobgay out of the way and the rest of the leaders submitting to him, Jigme Namgyal was now indisputably the unchallenged leader in the country. At the request of the clergy and the leaders, Jigme Namgyal finally took the highest political office and became the 51ˢᵗ Desi in early 1870. Jigme Namgyal had a dark complexion, wore mostly a black robe in public and rode a black horse. Thus, he became known as Depa Nagpo (རྗེ་ པ་ནག་པོ་) or Black Regent. Felicitations were received from all corners of the country and from the regent of Tibet. The British understandably did not congratulate Jigme Namgyal but a steady relationship between him and the British began to emerge. On 9 March 1870, Colonel Haughton received a letter from Jigme Namgyal announcing his election to the post of the Desi and asking Haughton to send his interpreter, Fentok, to Bhutan. This officer, who spoke both English and Dzongkha or Tibetan, was honoured by Jigme Namgyal as a *dzongpön* and consulted on frontier issues. The demarcation of the new southern boundaries was completed during Jigme Namgyal's rule by Colonel Graham. At home, Jigme Namgyal began earnestly to rebuild Tashichödzong, which he ordered to be set alight the previous year. The *dzong* was completed and fully replenished with religious objects on time for the *drubchö* festival in the autumn of 1870. Its *dzongpön* Kawang Mangkhel resigned from office and his younger brother Lam Tshewang filled the post.

Jigme Namgyal's ascension to the highest political office did not lead to the complete end of internal strife as we are often led to believe. Factional intrigues erupted even while he was the Desi but he managed to stop or control them as we shall see. In 1872, Jigme Namgyal saw a brief rebellion from the new Paro *pönlop*, Tshewang Norbu. His cousin, Kitshalpa Dorji Namgyal, was sent to suppress the rebellion but the latter did not succeed and asked Jigme Namgyal to send Kawang Mangkhel, the ex-Thimphu *dzongpön* for support. Kawang Mangkhel gladly accepted the task but asked Jigme Namgyal to confer the office of Paro *pönlop* on him if he managed to dislodge the rebel. This, Jigme Namgyal nonchalantly accepted. Having arrived in Paro, Kawang Mangkhel, who knew the Paro *pönlop* very well, persuaded him to give up the revolt against the powerful Desi and run away while he could do so safely. The latter agreed and Kawang Mangkhel assumed the office of the Paro *pönlop* without spilling any blood. This, however, disturbed Kitshalpa, who was worried that there was a chance of grooming internal enemies if Kawang Mangkhel were allowed to remain the Paro *pönlop* while his brother was the Thimphu *dzongpön*. This was giving too much of a power base to the two brothers, who could easily turn into rivals, and he suggested to Jigme Namgyal to get rid of Kawang Mangkhel. Jigme Namgyal shared his cousin's concerns and sanctioned Kitshalpa to eliminate Kawang Mangkhel. Kitshalpa sent to Paro a strongman named Töpa Chuzhing, who was a *nyagö* and believed to be an illegitimate offspring of a non-human spirit. He struck Mangkhel on the head with his sword in an ambush and threw him out of the *dzong* while he was still alive. The post of the Paro *pönlop* was then given to the former Paro *pönlop*, Nyima Dorji.[33]

With the death of Darlung Tobgay and Kawang Mangkhel, Jigme Namgyal had got rid of two of his most powerful contemporaries and former allies. It did not take him long to lose another staunch ally, Sonam Dhendup, the brother of the 4th mind incarnation Jigme Norbu and now the grandfather of the new 5th mind incarnation Jigme Chögyal. Sonam Dhendup, who fought alongside Jigme Namgyal against the British and was by now one of the seniormost figures, had a case to settle with a certain Gup Panglep, who enjoyed the backing of Kitshalpa. When the case was brought before the Desi, the Desi passed a verdict, allegedly an unjust one, in favour of Gup Panglep, perhaps through the influence of his half-brother, Kitshalpa. As a result, Sonam Dhendup was unfairly made to pay an enormous fine. This displeased the Zhabdrung incarnate and his family and is said to have started the tension between the Zhabdrung line and Jigme Namgyal's family, which would be aggravated in the next century. The wrath of Zhabdrung's deities is believed to have caused the tragic accident which ended Jigme Namgyal's life later.[34]

In October 1873, Jigme Namgyal stood down from the post of the Desi and retired to Semtokha. His chamberlain Kitshalpa Dorji Namgyal, who was also the son of his uncle, Pala Gyaltshen, became the 52nd Desi although Jigme Namgyal was still the power behind the scene. The relationship with the British continued to stabilize. There were in fact only two minor cases of frontier problems recorded in Bhutanese sources. Three Bhutanese dacoits were caught in northern Sikkim but, before they were delivered to the Bhutanese authorities, one was killed and another committed suicide. In the ensuing exchange, the Bhutanese authorities demanded reparation for loss of life while the Sikkimese demanded return of stolen properties. Such exchanges regarding extradition of criminals, reparation and borders were in fact quite common between Sikkim and western Bhutanese officials of Haa and Paro.[35] The case ended with Sikkim paying 517 measures of silver to Bhutan as a fine and a bilateral agreement to solve cross-border problems mutually.[36] The second one was also a case of dacoity committed by some Bhutanese visiting the Kamrup district of Assam. The Desi immediately promised to hold an enquiry into it and posted officers along the border to keep watch upon the Bhutanese entering Indian territories. The relationship between Bhutan and the British was further strengthened by the meeting of Desi Kitshalpa and Sir Richard Temple, the Lieutenant-Governor of Bengal, in Buxa. This was in fact the first high-level meeting to take place between the two countries. The Desi even granted the British permission to build roads through Bhutan to Tibet.

However, this ambitious plan never took off as Bhutan's leaders once again got engulfed in feudal battles. Jigme Namgyal was still holding the reins of power when Damchö Rinchen, the *dzongpön* of Punakha, rebelled against the Desi. We do not know the reasons for his rebellion but this *dzongpön* had a chamberlain named Tag Namgyal (Victorious Tiger) and a gatekeeper called Domchung (Little Bear). He is said to have thus asserted himself to be invincible with 'a tiger' at his bedroom door and 'a bear' at his gate. Jigme Namgyal, however, brought him to his knees in three days resulting in the local saying: 'Damchö Rinchen's wrangle lasts only three days.' The rebel was ousted and Ngodup appointed as the new *dzongpön* of Punakha.

Meanwhile, a more sinister internecine conflict was brewing in Bumthang and Tongsa, in the same manner as it did some fifteen years earlier between Jigme Namgyal and Tsondru Gyaltshen. Jigme Namgyal's brother, Dungkar Gyaltshen, had become the Tongsa *pönlop* around 1867 with the agreement that he would pass on the office to Jigme Namgyal's brother-in-law, Pema Tenzin, after three years.[37] Pema Tenzin was then the *dzongpön* of Jakar and overlord of Bumthang. Under the influence of his wife, Dungkar Gyaltshen did not honour the agreement. He continued in the office of the Tongsa *pönlop* and instead decided to eliminate Pema Tenzin. With this aim, he led an invasion of Jakar but his Tongsa troops failed to defeat Pema Tenzin's forces even after five attempts. In contrast, Pema Tenzin's Bumthang troops infiltrated into the Tongsa *dzong* at night with the help of a monk who opened the door for them, and they occupied the fort. Dungkar Gyaltshen was thus forced out of the *dzong* to take residence in the watchtower. He now turned to his brother Jigme Namgyal for help but the latter refused to even negotiate between his brother and brother-in-law saying nonchalantly: 'I will take the side of the winner.'[38] Jigme Namgyal's indifference to the internecine conflict caused a dangerous rupture in the familial solidarity and opened fresh grounds for political contest.

The magnates of western Bhutan, who disliked Jigme Namgyal, were quick to take the opportunity of the rupture; revolts erupted one after the other in Paro, Punakha and Wangdiphodrang against Jigme Namgyal's power base. In Paro, Tshewang Norbu, who rebelled against Jigme Namgyal in 1872, was back in office as the *pönlop* and he killed Sharchung, the steward who was placed there by Jigme Namgyal to represent him and check his opponents. Jigme Namgyal marched on to Paro with the state troops to put down the rebellion some time in 1876.[39] Fighting on his side were his cousin and incumbent, Desi Kitshalpa, his son, Ugyen Wangchuk, and Lama Tshewang, the *dzongpön* of Thimphu. Ugyen Wangchuk was then only fourteen years old and accompanied by Phuntsho Dorji, one of his childhood friends. After some skirmishes, Jigme Namgyal's side managed to take over the watchtower above the Paro *dzong*.

In the meantime, in Wangdiphodrang, Angdruk Nyim, the chief of protocol usurped the post of the Wangdi *dzongpön*, having killed Kawang Sangay. Kawang Sangay was a confidante of Jigme Namgyal and appointed as *dzongpön* by him after the death of Darlung Tobgay in 1869. Similarly, in Punakha, Ngodup, who was earlier appointed by Jigme Namgyal as *dzongpön* after ousting Damchö Rinchen, now went against Jigme Namgyal and joined the side of Tshewang Norbu, who was related to him by marriage. In a move to destabilize Jigme Namgyal, Ngodup made two appointments. Although Kitshalpa was still the Desi, Ngodup installed Yeshe Ngodup, the speech incarnation of Zhabdrung, in the office of the Desi. He also appointed Galdum Tshewang as the chamberlain to the Desi. The insurgency against Jigme Namgyal and the Desi turned out to be a calculated and well co-ordinated scheme. It was essentially a coup.

Faced with a far more serious threat in the winter capital, Jigme Namgyal proceeded with the Thimphu *dzongpön* Lam Tshewang and some troops to Punakha, leaving behind Kitshalpa, Ugyen Wangchuk and Phuntsho Dorji in Paro to continue the assault on the Paro *pönlop*. While Jigme Namgyal made his preparation in Semtokha, Lam Tshewang advanced with his troops to Punakha, where the forces of the Punakha *dzongpön* and new Wangdi *dzongpön* were gathered. However, when he began his assault on the enemies, Lam Tshewang was easily outnumbered by the joint forces of the Wangdi and

Punakha *dzongpön*s. In a bitter switch of alliances, even Jigme Namgyal's own brother, Dungkar Gyaltshen, the incumbent Tongsa *pönlop*, had now joined the insurgents from Wangdi, Punakha and Paro against Jigme Namgyal and his Thimphu party. He sent his troops from Tongsa led by Dawa Peljor, who was then the chamberlain to the Tongsa *pönlop*, at the request of the *dzongpön*s of Wangdi and Punakha.

In sending his troops to fight against his own powerful brother, Dungkar Gyaltshen was returning the favour Angdruk Nyim has previously shown him by sending military support from Wangdi to fight on his side against Pema Tenzin of Jakar. When Dungkar Gyaltshen was waging a war against Pema Tenzin, Angdruk Nyim is said to have sent a contingent from Wangdi under the command of his chamberlain Pemai Tshewang Tashi to fight for him in Tongsa. The warriors from Wangdi, however, were routed and the chamberlain was himself hunted down by the soldiers of Pema Tenzin until he jumped off the Thumangdra cliff near Tongsa. The story of this chamberlain's fateful journey eastward and the tragic end he met after being chased by the enemies has been captured in one of Bhutan's most well-known ballads in the Dzongkha vernacular.[40]

Thus, it was in reciprocation of the earlier support he received that Dungkar Gyaltshen sent his troops to fight on the side of Angdruk Nyim and Ngodup. The combined forces of Punakha, Wangdi and Tongsa effectively resisted the Thimphu forces under Lam Tshewang, who was even briefly captured by the enemy. There was even a rumour that Lam Tshewang, the only western leader fighting on Jigme Namgyal's side, had also defected to the side of the insurgents but the rumour turned out to be false. The assault on the coalition forces at Punakha resumed as soon as Jigme Namgyal joined Lam Tshewang with his troops. The conflict protracted for many months with no clear victory on either side but the stronghold in Punakha was seriously weakened when Jigme Namgyal succeeded in cutting off the link between Punakha and Wangdi.

The coalition of the insurgents at this point appealed to the British for help. A letter signed by the leading figures of Paro, Punakha, Wangdi and Dagana was received by the deputy comissioner of Darjeeling in 1877. They played on the British fear of Chinese and Tibetan influence on Bhutan by reporting that a Chinese and a Tibetan officer came to Thimphu to offer assistance to the government to resist the British plans to build roads through Bhutan. The Chinese offer, according to the letter, had made Jigme Namgyal overconfident and high-handed in all his dealings, which naturally led to the insurgency. The insurgents professed their loyalty to the Bengal government and expressed full support for the road project. But British assistance was not forthcoming. Although the influence of China and Tibet still loomed large in their eyes and they were keen to see the road project implemented, the British declined to support the insurgents. As far as they were concerned, it was an internal affair. Besides, Jigme Namgyal had proved to be their only chance of having Bhutan as a united neighbour under a single power. So, the conflict went on without British interference.

As the hostilities continued in Punakha, Damchö Rinchen, the *dzongpön*, whom Jigme Namgyal had forced out of office the previous year, travelled to Paro under the pretext of a pilgrimage to Tibet. There, he managed to infiltrate into the watchtower and hold Ugyen Wangchuk and Phuntsho Dorji hostage. When news reached Jigme Namgyal that his son was held hostage by Damchö Rinchen, he immediately arrested twelve relatives of Damchö Rinchen in Punakha. He then sent a message to Damchö Rinchen to choose between losing twelve members of his relations and releasing Ugyen Wangchuk. Damchö Rinchen relented and hostages on both sides were set free. By then, Desi Kitshalpa had also succeeded in taking over the fort controlling the water supply for the Paro *dzong*. With the water supply cut off by the enemies, the Paro *pönlop* Tshewang Norbu once again faced defeat and escaped to India.

When the monks departed for Thimphu in the spring of 1877, Jigme Namgyal launched a full-scale attack on the Punakha *dzong* from the hillsides. Unable to hold the fort any longer, the *dzongpön* of Punakha and the speech incarnation Yeshe Ngodup fled with their troops downstream toward Wangdi but their route was blocked by forces loyal to Thimphu. They then turned westward but the forces under Jigme Namgyal caught up with them in Lobesa where there was a bloody clash, resulting in many deaths. The Punakha forces were routed but the two main leaders of Punakha managed to escape. The speech incarnation returned to his seat of Sa-ngag Chökhor in Paro and the *dzongpön* of Punakha fled to India. The chamberlain Galdum Tshewang was not so lucky; he was found hiding in nearby forests and put to death.

Jigme Namgyal's reprisal on the insurgents in Paro and Punakha resulted in about 125 Bhutanese refugees in India under British protection. They included the *dzongpön* of Punakha and the *pönlop* of Paro, who were even given an allowance of Rs 60 per month by the government of Bengal. The refugees were settled on 500 acres of land near Kalimpong with Rs 300 to improve their homes and Rs 1000 as seed money to engage in trade. When

Bhutan asked the British to handover the insurgents, the government of Bengal declined, adding that the Sinchula treaty of 1865 applied only to rendition of criminals and not to political dissidents.

Angdruk Nyim, the *dzongpön* of Wangdiphodrang, was not as fortunate as the two co-insurgents of Paro and Punakha. After defeating the forces of Punakha and Paro, Jigme Namgyal turned to Wangdi and laid siege to the *dzong*. Overpowered by his enemies, the *dzongpön* decided to blow up the *dzong* with ammunition before his enemies took it over. The master of ritual and music (དབྱངས་པའི་སློབ་དཔོན་) of the State Monk Body, however, managed to talk him out of it by promising him protection and escape to safety. Sadly, the monk master failed to deliver his promise when Angdruk and eight of his men were captured by Jigme Namgyal's men. Jigme Namgyal decreed their execution but inwardly wished for the Je Khenpo and other senior monastic figures to come begging for pardon on behalf of the insurgents. This would have saved him his warrior's pride and also helped him to let the men go with lesser punishment. Jigme Namgyal waited for twelve days but the monastic mediators did not come. Thus, the men were led to the bridge in an executional procession, fed their last sumptuous meal and thrown off one by one to be drowned in the river. Jigme Namgyal came to regret this act for many years to come, adding that only if Je Khenpo Shedrub Özer was in office, the hierarch would have stopped him from such a heinous act.

With the execution of Angdruk, the insurrection was effectively brought to an end. Jigme Namgyal had vanquished all those who dared to challenge his power and authority. His brother, the *pönlop* of Tongsa, who joined the enemy forces, had also lost his campaign against Pema Tenzin of Jakar. The latter took over the office of the Tongsa *pönlop* and Dungkar Gyaltshen was forced to retire in the village of Tekhazhong in Bumthang.[41] To fill in the vacant positions left by the insurgents, Jigme Namgyal summoned his eldest son, Thinley Tobgay, from Lhalung in Tibet and appointed him the *dzongpön* of Wangdi. His second son, Ugyen Wangchuk, became the *pönlop* of Paro and Phuntsho Dorji was appointed as the state chief of protocol. Jigme Namgyal had once again brought the country fully under his control and thereby paved the way for the future supremacy of his son and descendants.

His cousin, Kitshalpa however, did not last long on the throne of the Desi. He passed away in 1879 allegedly due to black magic performed against him by the 39th Je Khenpo Lodoe Gyaltshen. While the Je Khenpo went on a trip to enjoy the thermal bath upstream from Punakha, Desi Kitshalpa assisted a contender to the post of Je Khenpo to usurp it. This incensed the Je Khenpo, who resorted to occult practice to eliminate both the contender and the Desi. The contender, who became the 40th Je Khenpo, died from smallpox as Desi Kitshalpa may have; this episode is perhaps the only case of explicit violence and rivalry for the seat of Je Khenpo, unlike the unending feuds for the office of the Desi. Desi Kitshalpa's main cultural legacies are the temple in Phajoding named after him and a shrine in Tashichödzong dedicated to the Buddha Akṣobhya. He also built the permanent reserves of textiles, salt, tea and mineral colours in the two capitals.

He was succeeded by Chögyal Zangpo, the 53rd Desi and another loyal supporter of Jigme Namgyal. We can safely surmise that he was appointed by Jigme Namgyal, who controlled the reins from behind the scene. For this role, people sarcastically nicknamed Jigme Namgyal Debi Dasho, the boss of the Desi.[42] Chögyal Zangpo was a nephew of the 43rd Desi Umadewa, who was assassinated by the chamberlain of his co-ruler Desi Kuenga Palden in 1857. He avenged the death of his uncle by killing the chamberlain and escaped to Tongsa via the northern border to seek asylum under Jigme Namgyal. Ever since, he had remained loyal to Jigme Namgyal and was mainly responsible for persuading Jigme Namgyal to exterminate Darlung Tobgay and his nephew who exercised control over Wangdi. When Jigme Namgyal became the Desi, he served as the state chief of protocol and perhaps held this office under Desi Kitshalpa until the latter died and he became the Desi in 1879. After two years, Chögyal Zangpo passed away in office some time in 1881.

Around the same time, Jigme Namgyal also had a tragic accident on his way to Semtokha from Punakha. Soon after crossing the Dochula Pass, the yak he was riding went astray. Jigme Namgyal fell off and fractured his skull. He was carried on a stretcher to Semtokha where he passed away after five days. It was an unexciting end for a man renowned for his physical strength and valour and who had survived endless feuds unharmed. From his death bed, he made his last exhortation to four young men—his two sons, Thinley Tobgay and Ugyen Wangchuk, and two foster sons or protégés, Phuntsho Dorji and Alu Dorji—to support each other and remain united in the face of adversity.[43] This wish would not, however, come true due to their family backgrounds and prevailing tendency for internecine rivalry and shifting allegiances as we shall see below. A sustained solidarity would prove hard to come by but Jigme Namgyal since his appointment as the Tongsa *pönlop* in 1853 until his death in 1881 had effectively laid the foundations for a unitary power and authority to rule over the country, which was being continually ruined by internal fighting among the magnates.

The Emergence of Ugyen Wangchuk and End of Civil War

JIGME NAMGYAL'S DEATH neither ended nor exacerbated the internal conflicts in Bhutan but the country was beginning to witness a new chapter of history with the emergence of Ugyen Wangchuk as a leader and successor to his father. The geo-political situation of the region and the power patterns within Bhutan were both favourable for the rise of a unifying ruler and constitutional change. This unifying force and change came in the person of Ugyen Wangchuk with his sagacity and leadership skills. Ugyen Wangchuk's life and Bhutan's political transformation during his lifetime are discussed here and in the following chapter, using both local and British sources.[1]

The Rise of Ugyen Wangchuk

Ugyen Wangchuk was born in 1862 in Wangdichöling as the second son to Jigme Namgyal and Pema Chöki. Under his uncle, the 8th Peling Sungtrul, he had some training on how to read and write but no formal education. Like most other children who joined court life in his time, he started at the lowest rung of officialdom and was made to work his way up the ladder of responsibilities. Bhutanese believed in the benefit of hardship in youth and his father made it a point that he worked and ate as other courtiers of his group did. In fact, Ugyen Wangchuk was made to work even harder by carrying out the outdoor duties of a *zingup* officer during the day and performing the indoor duties of a *changup* attendant at night. He had to collect firewood, dig fields and build roads as others did and was prohibited from receiving any privileges, even some extra food from his mother. A rigorous upbringing and training in his father's court was thus his education.

The high demands of court life and the practical training under his father's guidance no doubt prepared Ugyen Wangchuk well for statecraft and the numerous court intrigues that he was to face. At barely fourteen, he was already playing an active role in the expansion and consolidation of his father's power and authority. We have already seen how in 1876, he was fighting alongside his father in Paro against the rebellious *pönlop* Tshewang Norbu. This is the earliest and perhaps one of the most defining moments for young Ugyen Wangchuk in his early political career, which was fraught with vicious feuds. Ugyen Wangchuk was nearly killed when taken hostage by his father's enemy, Damchö Rinchen. We have seen earlier how Jigme Namgyal departed from Paro to put down the rebels in Punakha in early 1877, leaving Ugyen Wangchuk, Desi Kitshalpa and Phuntsho Dorji to guard the watch tower in Paro and continue the assault on the *dzong*. Taking advantage of Jigme Namgyal's absence there, Damchö Rinchen travelled to Paro under the pretext of a pilgrimage to Tibet, infiltrated the watchtower, looted it and held Ugyen Wangchuk hostage. Only when Jigme Namgyal threatened to kill twelve members of Damchö Rinchen's sister's family was Ugyen Wangchuk set free. This must have been a traumatic but a useful learning experience for Ugyen Wangchuk. In the end, his father triumphed and he was appointed the *pönlop* of Paro in 1878 at the young age of sixteen, or seventeen by Bhutanese reckoning.

Two years after appointing him to this post, his father Jigme Namgyal passed away. His elder brother, Thinley Tobgay, who was earlier a monk in the Lhalung monastery in Tibet and now the Wangdi *dzongpön*, was not particularly a able person. So, the onus of holding the power base his father had built and leading the country under a unitary power fell on Ugyen Wangchuk's young shoulders. He resembled his father in being a commanding leader and shrewd strategist but he surpassed his father in his diplomatic skills, political judiciousness and tact for promoting peace and friendship before recourse to violence. He was a broadminded, compassionate, honest and straight person as we shall see from the testimonies of many of his British counterparts below. He was influenced by his strong faith in the Buddhist religion, which informed his thoughts and activities. For this, the scholar Karma Ura calls him, a strategist of faith.[2] He was even believed to be the incarnation of a holy man from eastern Tibet.[3] The following description by Michael Aris effectively captures Ugyen Wangchuk's character and approach to state politics:

Ugyen Wangchuk inherited the strengths and weaknesses of his father, but he seems to have rearranged these into a decisive new pattern. He consolidated the hold his father had gained on the country, using to begin with some of his father's methods, but early in his career he turned, crucially, from tactics of blunt coercion to those which promoted harmony and consensus. By doing so at a time when the shifting balance of power in Asia favoured the emergence of Bhutan as an independent buffer between India and Tibet, he was able to introduce constitutional changes that left him and his heirs triumphant and the country's survival as a sovereign state assured. As the founder of the Bhutanese monarchy he certainly ranks equal with the Shabdrung as the creator of the theocracy.[4]

Ugyen Wangchuk's accommodating and conciliatory approach can be seen in his activities immediately following the death of his father in 1881. A good example is his attitude and approach to the 5th mind incarnation of Zhabdrung. By the time of Jigme Namgyal's death, Jigme Chögyal, the rebirth of Jigme Norbu and, therefore, the 5th mind incarnation of Zhabdrung, was occupying the golden throne of the prince-regent. He was born in 1862 in the *chöje* family of Drametse, like his precursor. This is not surprising as political and social connections played a significant role in the search, nomination and selection of the incarnations. We may remember that the 4th mind incarnation Jigme Norbu was himself born to the sister of the 3rd mind incarnation Jigme Drakpa II. The seemingly spiritual manifestation and reappearance of the high lamas had a lot of sociopolitical undercurrents which largely influenced the final selection. Jigme Chögyal's father was a son of Tamshing, who was invited as a groom for the daughter of Sonam Dhendup in Drametse. Sonam Dhendup was a prominent figure in Bhutan by the middle of the nineteenth century but he fell out with Jigme Namgyal after an allegedly unfair court verdict passed against him by Jigme Namgyal as the Desi. This verdict against Sonam Dhendup, which we touched on earlier, appears to have incensed young Jigme Chögyal and subsequently, relations between the incarnate hierarch and Jigme Namgyal seem to have remained strained. The hierarch stayed mostly in his seat of Sa-ngag Chöling and did not dwell in the capitals, where Jigme Namgyal held supreme power in the years preceding his death.

When Jigme Namgyal died in Semtokha, some rowdy monks living in the vicinity even shouted in jubilation. Whether they were supporters of Zhabdrung or one of Jigme Namgyal's lay enemies is not clear but Ugyen

Wangchuk tolerated the discourteous behaviour. Then, as part of the funerary rites which include making offerings to lamas and temples, Ugyen Wangchuk travelled to Sa-ngag Chöling with various items of offerings to see the Zhabdrung incarnate and absolve any wrongdoing on the part of Jigme Namgyal. The lama refused to see Ugyen Wangchuk or accept the offering and remarked that he had no regret for Jigme Namgyal's death. Ugyen Wangchuk humbly piled the offering at the doorsteps and returned, saying that he had no wish to challenge the lama.[5] His overtures for reconciliation and patience certainly led to a very close relation between the two in the years to come. By 1904, Jigme Chögyal wrote about their meeting in Punakha in his biography:

> Due to the yearning induced by long deferral of a direct meeting
> When we met, our minds merged, like the meeting of a father and son.[6]

Another act of accommodation and tolerance was shown in the case of the steward Byamo Sermo and a man called Ashang Wang. The steward killed Samten Dorji, the *pönlop* of Dagana appointed by Jigme Namgyal, and sought refuge under Zhabdrung Jigme Chögyal in Sa-ngag Chöling. Ashang Wang was an enemy of Jigme Namgyal and had escaped to India while Jigme Namgyal was alive. Upon the death of Jigme Namgyal, both Byamo Sermo and Ashang Wang brazenly returned to the capitals. Although Ugyen Wangchuk was capable of taking revenge on these enemies of his father, he showed forbearance and kindness and took them under his fold. This open-hearted character of Ugyen Wangchuk seems to have deeply impressed Lam Tshewang, a staunch ally of his father, and the latter gave his daughter, Ludrong Drolma, to Ugyen Wangchuk as his wife. She was the first of the four women in Ugyen Wangchuk's life. One source even mentions that Ugyen Wangchuk and she had a daughter named Bida who later became a nun.[7] Lam Tshewang's steadfast support to and admiration of Ugyen Wangchuk was duly rewarded when the 53rd Desi Chögyal Zangpo passed away in 1881. He was appointed as the 54th Desi. We can surmise that Ugyen Wangchuk had a major say in his appointment.

Not all of Ugyen Wangchuk's adversaries and problems were pacified and solved by an accommodating heart and reconciliatory tone. A year after Jigme Namgyal's death, a bitter feud broke out in Bumthang, which drew Ugyen Wangchuk's attention. History repeated itself when a fresh conflict erupted in the court of Tongsa *pönlop* due to a broken promise. This was the third such conflict in a quarter of a century. The first one was between

Jigme Namgyal and Tsondru Gyaltshen and the second between Pema
Tenzin, Ugyen Wangchuk's maternal uncle and Dungkar Gyaltshen, Ugyen
Wangchuk's paternal uncle. When Pema Tenzin fought against Dungkar
Gyaltshen because the latter did not honour his promise to pass on the post
of the Tongsa *pönlop* to Pema Tenzin after three years as agreed, one Sengay
Namgyal led the forces of Pema Tenzin. Pema Tenzin promised to make
him the chief of protocol in Tongsa if the war was won. Sengay Namgyal
fought valiantly and Pema Tenzin's side came out victorious. However, when
Pema Tenzin became the Tongsa *pönlop*, he appointed his brother-in-law
Pema Tashi as chief of protocol and denied Sengay Namgyal the honour.
This embittered Sengay Namgyal, who waited for an opportunity to take
his revenge.

The opportunity came when Pema Tenzin was building the palace of
Lamai Gönpa in Bumthang. His brother-in-law and chief of protocol, Pema
Tashi, was made to supervise the work, which the latter did highhandedly.
The courtiers working on the site protested against the Pema Tashi's heavy-
handed management and as a result Pema Tenzin dismissed from his court
two men who led the protests. The two were leaving Bumthang when they met
Sengay Namgyal on the way. Together, the three disgruntled men hatched a
plot to get rid of *pönlop* Pema Tenzin. On the fifteenth of the sixth Bhutanese
month, 1882, Pema Tenzin was killed in the early hours of morning after
spending the entire night playing dice with Sengay Namgyal. The murder
took place in the Jakar *dzong*, a short distance from Wangdichöling where his
sister, Pema Chöki, was living. She sent a runner to inform her son, Ugyen
Wangchuk, who was then the *pönlop* of Paro, of his uncle's death.

Meanwhile, Sengay Namgyal assumed the post of the Tongsa *pönlop*
and, in order to win local support, proclaimed the abolition of all taxes in
Bumthang for one year, except those of fodder and firewood. Pema Tenzin
was said to have brought his own downfall by refusing to pay any part of
the revenues of eastern Bhutan to the central government. This, he is said to
have done, in response to the refusal of authorities in Thimphu and Punakha
to pay him the Tongsa *pönlop*'s share of the British subsidy. The payments
from Tongsa traditionally funded the butter lamps and other kinds of offering
in the shrines of protector deities in Punakha and Thimphu. By withholding
the payments, he had provoked the wrath of the country's guardian deities. It
is said that running short of things to offer, priests taking care of the shrines
of the deities would turn the chalices and altar bowls upside down and exhort
the deities 'to get their offerings from Tongsa'. In other words, the priests

prayed to the deities to regain the revenues from Tongsa. The guardian deities, many Bhutanese believed, caused the death of Pema Tenzin.

If his death was due to divine wrath, the brutal end of his killers was seen as an act of divine vengeance. His brother, the 8th Peling Sungtrul, who was at that time in Lhalung in southern Tibet, is said to have learnt about his assassination almost immediately through spiritual vision and started in earnest a ritual to destroy his murderers. In fact, it was believed that Pema Tenzin's consciousness reached Peling Sungtrul, seeking vengeance and redemption. The divine intervention did come quickly, in the form of the power and design of Ugyen Wangchuk and other members of Pema Tenzin's family. Ugyen Wangchuk led an attack on Sengay Namgyal in the Jakar *dzong* and managed to capture the water source. However, Sengay Namgyal and his men held the fort firmly. Moreover, he also held the wife and children of Pema Tenzin as hostages. Unable to defeat Sengay Namgyal through open war, Ugyen Wangchuk and his mother plotted a scheme to infiltrate the *dzong* and kill Sengay Namgyal.

Firstly, Pema Chöki approached Sengay Namgyal alone in order to propose a reconciliation. She convincingly argued that her brother, Pema Tenzin, had brought his death upon himself and Sengay Namgyal was now the only refuge for her and her family. She vouched for Ugyen Wangchuk's acceptance of a peaceful resolution and even ostensibly offered her daughter Choden's hand in marriage to Sengay Namgyal.[8] Suspecting some treachery, Sengay Namgyal made her take an oath using his holy reliquary, which she did with no sign of hesitation. He thus believed her and negotiations for reconciliation began. He was told that he would remain the Tongsa *pönlop* and rule over eastern Bhutan while Ugyen Wangchuk held his sway over western Bhutan as the Paro *pönlop*. A line of people carrying bags and baskets were despatched from Wangdichöling to give Sengay Namgyal a false impression that Ugyen Wangchuk's men and belongings were already being moved to Paro. But it was just a show and the bags actually contained only rocks and clods.[9]

In the meantime, a long file of people entered the Jakar *dzong* from Wangdichöling under the pretext of carrying food and drinks for the reconciliation party. Sengay Namgyal's officers grew suspicious but he remained convinced that there was a sincere effort of reconciliation. After the meal was finished and when the course for drinks was announced, Ugyen Wangchuk's men entered the courtroom to strike down Sengay Namgyal. He tried to defend himself but Ugyen Wangchuk, who was sitting on his right, held him down and Sengay Namgyal was hacked to death. Some of his men were also killed while others escaped. His body and the bodies of the two men who killed Pema Tenzin were dragged to the banks of Chamkhar river. There, their heads, hearts and hands were buried under a new stūpa, which was built in order to suppress all future offences. The 8th Peling Sungtrul performed the ritual of suppression and consecrated the stūpa.

Having got rid of Sengay Namgyal, Ugyen Wangchuk took over the post of the Tongsa *pönlop* in early part of 1884. His first task as the Tongsa *pönlop* was to clear the arrears of payment to the central government, which his late uncle had refused to make. The payments certainly helped placate any ill will held by the priests and leaders in the power centres of Punakha and Thimphu. Like his father, he seems to have also simultaneously assumed the post of chamberlain to the Desi, who was at that time his closest ally, Lama Tshewang. This position was crucial for access to and control of the highest political office. Next, his brother Thinley Tobgay was appointed in his place as the Paro *pönlop* and made to hold both the positions of the Paro *pönlop* and Wangdi *dzongpön*. However, Thinley Tobgay died soon after becoming the Paro *pönlop* due to a fatal fall from his riding pony below the Paro *dzong*. He left no heir although some people in Bumthang point out a family in Shingnyer village who directly descend from him. In his place, one Jampa, who was also the son of Jigme Namgyal, was appointed as the Wangdi *dzongpön* and Dawa Peljor was appointed as the Paro *pönlop*. Dawa Paljor was the son of Jigme Namgyal's brother, Dorji, but when his uncle, Dungkar Gyaltshen, joined the Punakha forces in 1877 against the Thimphu forces led by Jigme Namgyal, he was sent as the commanding officer of the Tongsa troops to fight against the Thimphu side. This made him fall out of Jigme Namgyal's favour and, when Dungkar Gyaltshen was defeated, he was forced to an early retirement in Norbugang in Bumthang. Ugyen Wangchuk, however, pardoned him for his past defection and appointed him as the Paro *pönlop*.

Bhutan's last internal strife and the battle of Changlingmethang

Consolidation of power over the country through appointment of his trustworthy relations at key positions was not the only strategy Ugyen Wangchuk employed to enhance his power and control over the country. After Pema Tenzin's death and the revenge on Sengay Namgyal, he appeared to actively strengthen his familial solidarity. Around 1884, Ugyen Wangchuk married his first cousin Rinchen Pemo, the daughter of Pema Tenzin, and his sister, Choden, married Pema Tenzin's son, Chimi Dorji, who was now appointed as the *dzongpön* of Jakar. The Wangdichöling house of Jigme Namgyal and Lamai Gönpa or Palri house of Pema Tenzin were thus fully joined in a double matrimonial link. This kind of arranged consanguineous marriages of cross-cousins was popular and is still common among many families of central and eastern Bhutan. The marital bonds helped the family present a strong and united front besides keeping the property intact. Although Ugyen Wangchuk moved out of the Wangdichöling household to live with his wife in Lamai Gönpa and his sister inherited Wangdichöling and its assets in accordance with the matrilineal tradition of the region, the two households were practically fused 'like water and milk' as one of his grandson put it.[10] With this merger, we see the emergence of a ruling household and the foundations being laid for the future royal family.

However, not all things were to go smoothly for Ugyen Wangchuk, both at home and at the level of state politics. His mother suffered a stroke and passed away soon after the feud with Sengay Namgyal was over. Her death, it was alleged, was brought about by the deceitful oath she took in front of a holy object to fool Sengay Namgyal. This loss was followed by a discovery that his two trusted friends, Phuntsho Dorji and Alu Dorji, the *dzongpön*s of Punakha and Thimphu respectively, were plotting against him. Phuntsho Dorji was his childhood friend, who was born in the village of Wangdichöling the same night Ugyen Wangchuk was born in the Wangdichöling palace. His mother was a sister of Damchö Rinchen, an officer who previously served Jigme Namgyal but later rebelled against him. Ever since his birth, Phuntsho Dorji was brought up in the company of Ugyen Wangchuk. We have seen how the two friends fought together in Paro in 1877 and he was subsequently appointed to the post of the state chief of protocol.

Alu Dorji was a son of Kawang Mangkhel, who was an ally of Jigme Namgyal until he was killed after usurping the position of the Paro *pönlop*. After his father's death, he was brought up by his father's younger brother, Lam Tshewang, who guided him and kept him a faithful supporter of Jigme Namgyal. He fought heroically on the Thimphu side during the 1877–78 conflict. By 1883, the two loyal friends had risen to the posts of the Thimphu and Punakha *dzongpön*s and were the only two powerful figures who were not blood relations of Ugyen Wangchuk. However, in a political climate filled with subterfuge, betrayals and shifting allegiances, such loyalties rarely lasted, particularly because the two friends had plenty of axes to grind with Jigme Namgyal's family. Alu Dorji's father, Kawang Mangkhel, was beheaded with the full consent of Jigme Namgyal and Phuntsho Namgyal's uncle, Damchö Rinchen, was an enemy of Jigme Namgyal. Damchö Rinchen had even taken Ugyen Wangchuk hostage and contemplated killing him in Paro in 1877.

The first sign of their dissent perhaps came when Lam Tshewang, the 54th Desi passed away in office and Alu Dorji installed his candidate, a monk named Gawa Zangpo, as the 55th Desi and his brother as the chamberlain to the Desi. Phuntsho Dorji, the Punakha *dzongpön*, and other authorities in Thimphu and Punakha must have endorsed this appointment without consulting Ugyen Wangchuk. The relationship was also strained between the authorities in the capitals and Ugyen Wangchuk because the latter was denied his rightful share of the British subsidy. This was the main cause of rupture between Ugyen Wangchuk and his rivals, according to John Claude White.[11] The immediate cause of the bitter breach in their friendship and cooperation, however, was a certain beauty named Dechen Zangmo of the wealthy house of Dongka.[12] Ugyen Wangchuk is said to have spotted her when he came to receive his formal appointment as the Tongsa *pönlop* from the Desi. He had a brief affair with her but when he was returning to Tongsa, Phuntsho Dorji asked him if he (Phuntsho Dorji) could take over Dechen Zangmo, as Ugyen Wangchuk was by then already married to his cousin, Rinchen Pemo. Ugyen Wangchuk gave no answer but Phuntsho Dorji went ahead with his plans to marry Dechen Zangmo. At around this time, his sister also married Alu Dorji thereby bringing them closer through a marital link. Overcome by their desire for a woman and power and emboldened by their new unity, the two now seemed to have plotted to exterminate Ugyen Wangchuk.

It is not clear what made the two think that the second in command in Tongsa, the regional chief of protocol, would carry out a coup against Ugyen Wangchuk. They sent to the officer 800 coins and a letter instigating him to assassinate Ugyen Wangchuk but this officer was loyal to his master and candidly exposed the treacherous scheme to Ugyen Wangchuk. One source blames Damchö Rinchen, who was still active, for persuading his nephew Phuntsho Dorji to rise against Ugyen Wangchuk. He and Phuntsho Dorji were said to have put the seal of the Thimphu *dzongpön* Alu Dorji on the letter without the latter being aware of it.[13] Whatever the truth may be, Ugyen Wangchuk responded judiciously. Pretending to be unaware of the plot and desiring to find out the truth for himself, he invited his two friends to a meeting in Shar valley, halfway between Tongsa and Thimphu, where he went to meet them with gifts. The two did not show up and Ugyen Wangchuk was now convinced of their dissension and scheme to get rid of him. He returned to Tongsa and began the preparations for what was to become the last civil war in the medieval history of Bhutan.

Having gathered a force of about 2140 men and made prayers and offerings to protector deities in all major temples in Bumthang and Tongsa, Ugyen Wangchuk marched with his troops to Punakha in the beginning of 1885. His cousin Dawa Paljor and half-brother Jampa also joined him with their troops from Paro and Wangdi respectively. As the forces advanced on Punakha, the clergy led by the 41st Je Khenpo Ngawang Donden came out to dissuade Ugyen Wangchuk from attacking Punakha but they failed to deter him. Ugyen Wangchuk requested the monks to return to the *dzong* and carry out, with expenses paid by him, a three-day supplication to the state gods, exhorting the deities to be the impartial jury to vindicate the right side and to punish those who are wrong. On one side were the Tongsa *pönlop*, Paro *pönlop*, Wangdi *dzongpön* and most other minor *dzongpön*s and on the other, the two *dzongpön*s of Thimphu and Punakha, the chamberlain to the Desi, the chief state councillor, the former *dzongpön* Damcho Rinchen and the *dzongpön*s of Gasa and Lingshi.

The deities, later historians tell us, were clearly on Ugyen Wangchuk's side as a fresh rupture occurred among the enemy camp in Punakha for no good reason. A baseless rumour spread that Alu Dorji's chief warrior was covertly supporting Ugyen Wangchuk and not his boss, Alu Dorji. Thus, Alu Dorji's men tried to corner the warrior but he escaped to the residence of the state chief of protocol for protection. When they pursued him there, the bodyguards of Zhabdrung Jigme Chögyal thought it was an attack on the state chief of protocol and joined in to fight off Alu Dorji's men. The Punakha and Thimphu forces were thrown into an internal chaos even before they confronted Ugyen Wangchuk's forces.

The incumbent Desi Gawa Zangpo was an ineffectual ruler, who could not give any support to the *dzongpön*s of the two capitals in their fight against what may have been seen as a rebellion by the Tongsa *pönlop*. He appealed to Lord Dufferin, the Viceroy of India, perhaps on behalf of the two *dzongpön*s for military support, which was politely refused. The two *dzongpön*s then planned to replace him with Konchö Wangdi, the father of Zhabdrung Jigme Chögyal, with the hope of getting military support from the officers and guards of the Zhabdrung. They requested Konchö Wangdi to become the

Desi and even offered him 3600 coins but he declined either to take the post of the Desi or to take part in the conflict against Ugyen Wangchuk.

The forces of Ugyen Wangchuk and his enemies finally clashed for two days. On the first day of battle at Zomphakha, only one soldier was killed and another injured on the side of the two *dzongpön*s. The second day clash at Jiligang saw again the death of four men on their side but Ugyen Wangchuk's party suffered no casualties. Jigme Chögyal, who was then holding the golden throne of prince-regent and teaching in Punakha, wrote about the conflict:

> As for the lords of the centre, east and west,
> Time ushered the fruits of their actions induced by five poisons.
> Thinking 'I am great and high', their hatred blazed like fire,
> Jealousy and rivalry among them flurried like wind.
> Intoxicated by the poisonous water of pride and arrogance,
> They destroyed the peace and happiness of the southern land.
> The country is turned for once into a real city of *asura*s.[14]
> In this capital resembling a nest of snakes
> I shed tears from the fuming smoke of attachment and hatred.
> Having concluded the sermons for my dependents,
> I returned to Sa-nga Chöling, the happy grove of *vidyadharas*.[15]

The poetic account of Jigme Chögyal, albeit a first-hand report, may be slightly misleading in portraying the conflict as widespread and tumultuous for the whole country. From the number of men killed and injured, we may assume the battle was a symbolic contest rather than a full-scale combat and loss of lives was kept to the minimum. The civil wars of Bhutan were not generally so rampant as to directly disrupt the daily lives of ordinary people although there were indirect consequences through levies of tax, corvée, conscription and looting. It is surprising, if the accounts are correct, that not a single man among over 2000 men fighting on Ugyen Wangchuk's side was even injured.

At the end of the second day, the forces of two *dzongpön*s were on the retreat. Unable to hold Punakha any longer, they departed for Thimphu, where they put up a strong defence. Ugyen Wangchuk and his men now pursued their enemies to Thimphu but as they descended from the slopes, Alu Dorji's men set fire to the forest near Langjophakha to hinder their advance. The invading troops were held in the hills for one night with no camps or resources. Even Ugyen Wangchuk did not have anything to eat and had to share the dry buckwheat bread, which one of his servants called Sampala carried in the fold of his dress.[16] The next day, Ugyen Wangchuk and his men marched southward and took over the Semtokha *dzong* with little difficulty as its *dzongpön* was absent. With this *dzong* as their base, the forces of Ugyen Wangchuk now launched their attack on the forces of the two *dzongpön*s. Before doing so, according to John Claude White, Ugyen Wangchuk first made a bold overture by visiting his adversaries at Tashichödzong with his demands but they refused to listen to him.[17]

The two parties clashed in Lungtenphu on the first day of the conflict in Thimphu, when, we are told, two leading warriors of the Thimphu party were shot dead and the rest 'instantly fled like a flock of birds struck by a stone'.[18] Once again, the clergy intervened to negotiate a peaceful settlement. The two parties agreed to have a truce and started negotiations on the knoll in Changlingmethang the following day. Ugyen Wangchuk's party was represented by Dawa Paljor, the *pönlop* of Paro and Phuntsho Dorji represented the Thimphu—Punakha coalition. Ugyen Wangchuk's party offered to provide a luncheon during the meeting. Unfortunately, Phuntsho Dorji's day had a bad start when his riding pony hesitated to cross the stone bridge over the brook in Chubachu. His servants interpreted this as a bad omen and asked him to cancel the meeting but he persisted and came to it.

At the meeting, the monastic mediators and the two representatives with their teams sat in a row and, after some discussion, lunch was served. Among those serving the meal were the chamberlains and chief of protocols of Wangdi, Paro and Tongsa, all six officials fully prepared for combat. After the meals were served and while the guests were enjoying the food, Ugyen Dorji, the chief of protocol of Wangdi, under the pretext of serving whey approached Phuntsho Dorji and struck him with his sword. The strike did not immediately incapacitate Phuntsho Dorji as he managed to hit back. Luckily for Ugyen Dorji, he was hit not by the cutting edge but the spine of the sword, which caused a superficial bleeding. Meanwhile, his companions joined him to hack Phuntsho Dorji to death. The attack caused a commotion and several men on both sides were killed in the skirmish. It is not clear if Ugyen Wangchuk was behind this treacherous plot to curtail the peaceful negotiations or was even aware of it. It is also not clear if this was a premeditated treacherous scheme, as most Bhutanese sources present, or a skirmish that flared up by accident among the lower ranks during the interval of the negotiation.

At any rate, Phuntsho Dorji was killed, the negotiations stopped and fighting spread quickly in the area. Ugyen Wangchuk, who was waiting not far from the venue with his forces, now actively joined the battle. At one point, his side was beginning to waver and he was surrounded by his enemies but Ugyen Wangchuk was unrelenting. He fought with renewed vigour and courage and killed about half a dozen enemy warriors. His brave leadership inspired his men to fight as it impressed those against him with fear. By the end of the day, the enemy forces were routed and their leaders fled from the scene. The enemy soldiers, who were caught, were brought to the Changlingmethang ground, disarmed and made to crouch through the arch of weapons. Such a humiliating act is believed to dispossess the enemies of their luck and good fortune.

The battle of Changlingmethang and the last fully armed conflict between Bhutanese magnates was over with a decisive victory to Ugyen Wangchuk in 1885. His adversaries Alu Dorji, the *dzongpön* of Thimphu, Damchö Rinchen, the former *dzongpön* of Punakha, Tandin Ngodup, the chamberlain to the Desi, Ngawang Sherab, the chief councillor of state, Pusola, the *dzongpön* of Gasa and Kawang Dorji, the *dzongpön* of Lingshi fled to Tibet via Gasa. The turn of events in Thimphu were recorded by two leading religious figures of the time, the 43rd Je Khenpo Tenzin Lhendup and the 5th mind incarnation Jigme Chögyal, in their contemplative poems. Tenzin Lhendup wrote:

By the force of common *karma* and fruition of negative actions,
Wars of attachment and hatred raged like the waves of a sea.
The congenial friend, who was dear to my heart,
Phuntsho, the *dzongpön* of Punakha had entered the path of death.
Having lost his power, Dorji, the *dzongpön* of Thimphu,
With his following had departed for the realm of Tibet.[19]

The turn of events, which Tenzin Lhendup sadly lamented, was for Jigme Chögyal a source of some pride and joy:

When the gust of heat of the four elements
Was about to destroy the crops of human body,
The lords of all directions, with their retinues,
Converged on Thimphu to wind up their battles.
There, they showed spectacles of arrows, spears and swords,
And filled the day and night with roaring noise of guns.
Chila Ugyen Wangchuk [was like] the god Indra.

The sun of his body radiated on the eastern ridge;
The lotus of his ministers and subjects blossomed.
Through the power of infallible truth,
He was victorious in war against his foes.
The banner of victory from all quarters was raised;
The aeon of warfare and weaponry came to an end.[20]

As Jigme Chögyal noted, the conclusion of the Changlimethang battle brought an end to the incessant internal strife in Bhutan and ushered in a new political paradigm. If his father started the centralization of power in his hands, Ugyen Wangchuk now fulfilled the task of firmly consolidating it with no rivals. Political power was now totally in the hands of Ugyen Wangchuk as he took control of all power centres and, like his father, filled them with his trusted relatives and friends. However, like his father, Ugyen Wangchuk took the back seat and did not immediately occupy the highest office for himself. The ineffectual Desi Gawa Zangpo was made to resign with full benefits and, in his place, the master of monastic ritual and arts, Sangay Dorji, was installed as the 56th Desi in August, 1885. He was a faithful supporter of Jigme Namgyal and acclaimed as a sound and benevolent monk. Ugyen Wangchuk's relatives and confidantes filled all other posts.

The fate of Dechen Zangmo, the beauty who partly incensed this conflict, turned into an interesting tale of feminine wit and deception. On his return from Thimphu to Tongsa, Ugyen Wangchuk ordered six *zingup* officers to bring her to Bumthang and also to confiscate her properties, such being the normal course of punishment in those days. When the officers approached her, Dechen Zangmo put on a show of extragavant hospitality with food, drinks and female companions for the officers. She convinced them, though misleadingly, that she did not regret her husband's death and was keen to depart for Bumthang only if they gave her a week to organize the trip. The officers could not refuse given the lavish hospitality shown to them. Meanwhile, Dechen Zangmo secretly hid all imperishable valuables in the ground and sent other things and her infant son to the border town of Phari with her trusted servants. Finally, on the sixth night when the officers were in their drunken slumber, she took off hidden in a basket carried by one of her trusted servants. Local stories from her village have it that she dropped clothes on the wrong paths to mislead her pursuers. She met up with the other fugitives from Bhutan in Phari and went on to live with Alu Dorji as his wife.

Once in Tibet, Ugyen Wangchuk's enemies turned to the regent Ngawang

Palden Chökyi Gyaltshen of Kundeling for help. This hierarch was ruling Tibet from 1875 to 1886 in the minority of his student, the 13th Dalai Lama. He may have agreed to support the Bhutanese fugitives, Alu Dorji and his friends, but nothing came out of it as he died in 1886. His death, the Bhutanese were quick to point out, was the work of Bhutan's protector deities. The Bhutanese dissidents then turned to the Chinese Amban in Lhasa; the Amban and the Tibetan government sent a joint mission to Phari, where they summoned Ugyen Wangchuk. There may have been even a threat of Tibetan invasion, which the Bhutanese sources allude to. During these years, the Chinese Amban and Tibetan government appear to have claimed some suzerain control over Bhutan although there was no influence of any sort in practice. Anyhow, Ugyen Wangchuk did not present himself but sent Dawa Paljor, the *pönlop* of Paro, and Tshewang Norbu, the state chief of protocol, to negotiate with the dissidents and their Tibetan and Chinese supporters.

The negotiations resulted in the restitution of the Bhutanese fugitives and allocation of appanages for the leaders with the condition that they would live under Bhutanese law and not reunite to create any opposition. Alu Dorji was given Dungnak although he chose to live in Phari, perhaps due to the remoteness of this place given to him. Haa was given to his brother, the former chamberlain to Desi, Paro Lamgong was given to the former chief councillor of state, Gasa was given to Damchö Rinchen and Lingshi to Kawang Dorji. The internal dissidents were subdued and the conflicts fully resolved in 1886. The reins of power now lay in the hands of Ugyen Wangchuk, who was the Tongsa *pönlop* but the *de facto* ruler of Bhutan. He was only twenty-four.

Ugyen Wangchuk as king-maker and mediator

Bhutan enjoyed peace during the years following the battle of Changlingmethang. Although officially he was only the Tongsa *pönlop* and still twenty years away from being crowned king, Ugyen Wangchuk was for all intents and purposes the ruler of Bhutan. With political power now concentrated in his hands, Ugyen Wangchuk ruled the country combining the Buddhist qualities of wisdom and compassion. He was kind to his subjects and forgiving to his enemies, most of whom, including the former Paro *pönlop* Tshewang Norbu, subsequently returned to Bhutan. In his leadership, Bhutan saw a refreshingly new trend of politics, driven not by the selfish desire for power and supremacy as it was previously, but by a genuine concern for the security of the nation and welfare of its citizens. Not only had Bhutan mended its own internal ruptures, under Ugyen Wangchuk it began to play a significant role in mediating between its warring neighbours.

In 1887, after refusing admission to the Macaulay Mission from British India, Tibetan forces occupied a part of the Chumbi valley under Sikkim, which was a protectorate of British India. The British retaliated with 2000 men and expelled the Tibetan soldiers in 1888. Tibet, which was then trying to delink itself from China, looked to Nepal and Bhutan for support but Ugyen Wangchuk, fully aware of the British strength, adopted a neutral stance. Ugyen Wangchuk's non-aligned position and indifference to some of the Tibetan and Chinese biddings around this period at last laid to rest the British fears of a significant Chinese and Tibetan influence on Bhutan. A whole new relationship based on good will and mutual trust began to grow between Bhutan and the British from then on, in a sharp contrast to the serious ruptures that appeared in relations between India and Sikkim as well as India and Tibet.

While Ugyen Wanchuk retained a stable relationship with Tibet, his relationship with British India was improving tremendously. A vital player in this development was Ugyen Dorji, a successful businessman based in Kalimpong. Ugyen Wangchuk heard of him and his rich offerings to Jigme Chögyal in Talo and thus summoned him. When they met, not only did the two get along very well, they turned out to be second cousins. Ugyen Dorji's father was an illegitimate son of Pala Gyaltshan of Dungkar, the brother of Ugyen Wangchuk's paternal grandfather. With his knowledge of the British, Tibet and English language, Ugyen Dorji became Ugyen Wangchuk's main envoy to the neighbouring countries of India, Tibet and Sikkim. For his abilities, the British also appointed Ugyen Dorji as their Bhutan agent in 1897 and sent their messages to both Bhutan and Tibet through him. Later in 1900, he was also appointed by Ugyen Wangchuk as the Bhutanese representative or *kutshab* (སྐུ་ཚབ་) for all affairs concerning the southern borders. He was in particular given the responsibility to settle Nepali migrant labourers, clear the forests and levy taxes along the southern border. Ugyen Dorji's role as a go-between would become increasingly significant as the British became ever more determined to open links with Tibet, as we shall see below.

In 1890, Ugyen Wangchuk's uncle, the 8th Peling Sungtrul, passed away in Lhalung. While conducting the funerary ceremonies for his uncle in Lhalung, Ugyen Wangchuk met the 8th Bakha *trulku* Khamsum Yongdrol, who was presiding over the funeral services. Later, Ugyen Wangchuk received from him the prophecies of the two most renowned contemporary lamas of Tibet, Jamyang Khyentsei Wangpo (1820–92) and Kongtrul Lodoe Thaye (1813–99) exhorting Ugyen Wangchuk to build a large statue of Padmasambhava in Kurjey. By doing so, it was believed that the internal strife which encumbered Bhutan for so long would be fully pacified. Thus, in 1894, Ugyen Wangchuk embarked on the cultural project of building the large temple in Kurjey housing the grand statue of Nangsi Zilnon, a form of Padmasambhava in the intense mood suppressing the world. Khamsum Yongdrol, who was now invited to Bumthang as Ugyen Wangchuk's court priest through the arrangement by one Bhutanese monk scholar called Mindu, acted as the main supervisor and consecrated the shrine during its completion.

The statue is said to have been built with mud mixed with a large quantity of powdered precious stones, much of which was contributed by Ugyen Wangchuk's wife, Rinchen Pemo. Many sacred relics were also collected from across Bhutan to be inserted in the statue. The main sculptors, Tenzin and Nidup, were local Bhutanese as was the artist Monlam Rabzang, who did the wall paintings of the temple. The temple was Ugyen Wangchuk's greatest cultural and artistic project and, today, his main material legacy. Around this time, Ugyen Wangchuk also started his visionary initiative of promoting education, which he would continue more robustly later in his life. He sent about seven Bhutanese students to study under the great scholars in Kham in eastern Tibet. Unlike Bhutan, where monastic life had now largely degenerated into routinized chores of rituals, Kham was buzzing with scholastic activity through its new fervour of the ecumenical *rismé* movement and proliferation of scholastic colleges known as *shedra*. Through the many Bhutanese scholars who made it to these centres and returned as learned masters, Bhutan would see a scholarly and intellectual revival in the twentieth century through the establishment of many *shedra*s.

Ugyen Wangchuk spent most of his time in Bumthang and Tongsa after the war of 1885. There were no political disruptions which needed his immediate presence in the two capitals and his spiritual pursuits kept him most of this time in Bumthang. According to a recent account, at this time, overcome with the joy of having completed his shrine in Kurjey, he is said to have given away everything he owned as alms to the people.[21] With nothing left, his wife one evening had to pick the rice from the crevices of the store to cook dinner for the two of them. Ugyen Wangchuk remarked that it was the best meal he had in his entire life. Whether or not such a story of generosity and austerity is true, it is clear that Ugyen Wangchuk had strong spiritual leanings which kept him in the cloisters of Lamai Gönpa. Beside his religious calls,

Ugyen Wangchuk also by then had two daughters, Sonam Peldon and Chimi Yangzom, born respectively in 1887 and 1889, to keep him in Bumthang.

His peaceful and quiet days in Bumthang were, however, disrupted in 1897 by a series of sad incidents. Firstly, on the evening of 2 June 1897, the Great Assam Earthquake, at about 8.8 on the Richter scale, reduced many buildings in Bhutan to rubble. Jigme Chögyal recounts that a comet appeared some time before the earthquake, portending the natural disaster. At that time, some parts of Bhutan were already hit by an epidemic of smallpox. About the earthquake, he writes:

> The earth shook with eighteen great tremors.
> The temples, houses and villages,
> Towns, cities, royal treasuries and so forth,
> Without exception were destroyed and crumbling.
> The earth was filled with the haze of dust.[22]

We do not know much about its affect on human lives but most of the large buildings were seriously damaged by this earthquake. Jigme Chögyal mentions without any detail that many great masters died as a result of the earthquake. Following the earthquake, the country was busy with task of rebuilding homes and public structures.[23] Under his direct supervision, Ugyen Wangchuk renovated the shrines in Tongsa and Jakar *dzong*s and largely rebuilt his residential palaces of Lamai Gönpa in Bumthang and Yungdrung Chöling in Tongsa.

This natural calamity was followed by a personal illness and loss. In that same year, Ugyen Wangchuk fell seriously ill with fever but he recovered with timely medical and religious intervention. Sadly, he was barely well when his wife, Rinchen Pemo, was struck with a similar problem. After nearly four years of protracted illness, she passed away in 1900 in spite of a numerous efforts of medical treatment and religious rituals performed by Khamsum Yongdrol and treasure-discoverer Namkha Dorji, who had been invited from Tibet. Grief-stricken, Ugyen Wangchuk entered a period of mourning and retreat above Lamai Gönpa while funerary services were conducted throughout the region. It was the end of his first marriage and perhaps a traumatic one. According to Ugyen Wangchuk's grandson, they had thirteen children, out of which only two daughters survived.[24]

Following the death of Rinchen Pemo, Ugyen Wangchuk paid a brief visit to Tibet to offer butter lamps and prayers in the famous Jokhang temple for his deceased wife and on this trip also met some important lamas of Tibet. Back in Bhutan, when one party from Kurtoe came to pay condolences to him, another woman caught his eyes. This was Tsondru Lhamo, a daughter of the nobility of Kholma in Kurtoe. She was perhaps living with one Singayla from Kurtoe when she first met Ugyen Wangchuk.[25] Ugyen Wangchuk's betrothal to her took place at the behest of religious masters and court officials, particularly the scholarly monk, Mindu from Dur. This monk, who received a thorough Buddhist training in the Drepung monastery in Tibet, was a highly respected priest in Ugyen Wangchuk's court and he played a major role in arranging Ugyen Wangchuk's second marriage.

When Rinchen Pemo passed away in 1900, she is said to have made a death bed wish. The most popular version states that she pleaded Ugyen Wangchuk to remarry and produce a male heir.[26] However, a lesser known account states that she died peacefully only after making Ugyen Wangchuk take an oath, using a religious scripture, that he would not remarry or neglect her two daughters.[27] We will never know what actually transpired but it seems that barely a year after the death of Rinchen Pemo, Ugyen Wangchuk and his court were looking for a new bride. His grandson mentions three other women who were considered before the mantle fell on Tsondru Lhamo of Kholma.[28] She was a relation of Ugyen Wangchuk on her father's side and a scion of Kholma nobility on her mother's side. Tsondru Lhamo, popularly known as Ashi Lemo, was formally presented to Ugyen Wangchuk in 1901 through the persuasion of several religious figures and encouragement from his eldest daughter, Peldon.[29] It was perhaps the oath he took at Rinchen Pemo's death which made Ugyen Wangchuk reluctant to take his new wife and necessitated the persuasion of religious figures to help him override the oath. One Tibetan lama is said to have even gone so far as to take upon himself all blame and consequences of breaking the oath.[30] About two years after their nuptial ties were made, Tsondru Lhamo gave birth to a son in 1903 but he died an infant, sending his parents into a spell of grief.[31] The 15th Karmapa Khachab Dorji consoled the couple predicting the birth of another, a better, son, who was duly born in 1905. Meanwhile, Ugyen Wangchuk's attention was drawn to the growing hostility between Bhutan's two neighbours, Tibet and British India.

Since the collision in the Chumbi valley in 1888, the relations between the two countries had deteriorated. The British tried to resolve the frontier problems with Tibet by dealing directly with the Chinese government, which claimed Tibet to be an integral part of China. Without the participation of either Tibet or Sikkim, the Sikkim–Tibet Convention was signed in March 1890 between the Chinese Amban and British Viceroy in Calcutta. It laid down the arrangements for the alignment of the Sikkim–Tibet border with the understanding that Tibet was part of China and Sikkim a protectorate of British India. This was followed by the Trade Regulation of 1893 which provided for the establishment of a rade mart at the border in Yatung and unobstructed access to traders from both Tibet and India. This was indeed a major achievement for the British, who had endeavoured to open a direct trade link with Tibet since the early days of the East India Company. It was also an achievement for China as her influence on Tibet at that point was waning.

The Tibetan government, under the young 13th Dalai Lama, disregarded the Anglo-Chinese agreements. Although Tibet did not have the power to formally challenge the Anglo-Chinese agreements, she enforced her own policy when a mart was opened in Yatung and ignored the Anglo-Chinese trade regulations, to which she was not a signatory. Tibet imposed restrictions on both the location and range of goods besides imposing a ten per cent duty. China witnessed this helplessly while the British now realized that any issues regarding Tibet must be directly discussed with Tibet itself. Annoyingly for the British, Tibet adopted an introvert policy to maintain a distance from both China and British India. Tibet was only eager to shed off China's control over it and defy the British intrusion into Sikkim, which it claimed to be under her protection. Under the strong and dynamic leadership of the 13th Dalai Lama, Tibet was just beginning to witness a new fervour of anti-Chinese nationalism and independence. The Great Thirteenth, as the Tibetans called him, was perhaps also looking for support from a different power to resist the perceived threats from the neighbouring powers of China and British India. At the turn of the twentieth century, some correspondence between Tsar Nicholas II of Russia and the Dalai Lama was already taking place through the intermediation of the Buryat monk, Dorjiev.

At the same time, India saw in 1899 the arrival of a strong new leader in the person of Lord Curzon, who abandoned the passive policy of his precursor concerning the frontiers. His precursor Lord Elgin was satisfied with a growing trade at the border but Lord Curzon wanted more. He wanted the British to penetrate Lhasa, the Forbidden City. With the Great Game or rivalry for supremacy in Central Asia between the British Empire and Tsarist Russia at its height, control over Tibet was both militarily strategic and commercially beneficial. Lord Curzon was convinced, without any evidence, of a Russian presence in Lhasa and that the Tsarist Russian hegemony was spreading to

Tibet at the invitation of the 13th Dalai Lama. Thus, for both military and commercial reasons, he earnestly desired to open communications with Tibet and reach Lhasa while at the same time Tibet persisted with its isolationist policy and blatantly refused to open any communications with him. It was in such political climate that Lord Curzon appointed Colonel Francis Younghusband, an earnest adventurer and ambitious imperial officer, to head a civil mission to Lhasa escorted by a large army of some 3000 soldiers and 7000 support staff under Brigadier James Macdonald.

The British desire to enter Tibet at all costs and the fierce Tibetan resistance to it unfolded into a bloody war on the Roof of the World but it offered Ugyen Wangchuk and Bhutan a rare opportunity to play an important role in the regional politics and gain political milieage, which would benefit Ugyen Wangchuk and Bhutan in unexpected ways.[32] By the end of 1903, Younghusband had already spent about half a year in the Gamba *dzong* frustratingly waiting for the Tibetan and Chinese counterparts to come for negotiations. When they finally came, the officers turned out to be of inadequate ranks and only insisted the British exit Tibet before any negotiations start. Thus, with Lord Curzon's full backing but lukewarm support from London, the Younghusband Expedition, as it was known, advanced into Tibet in December 1903 turning itself into a *de facto* invasion of Tibet.

While the British expedition to Tibet with its large armed escort made its way to Tibet, there was also an exchange of letters with Bhutan to make sure that Bhutan did not join Tibet against the British. The British were anxious about Bhutan's position and reaction to the mission, especially because Bhutan and Tibet shared a close religious and cultural affinity. The British suspicion of Bhutanese support to Tibet was perhaps correct as there may have been some plans to help the Tibetans in response to the Dalai Lama's appeal for help. The Paro *pönlop* was, particularly, not friendly to the British. But whatever clandestine support there may have been initially, Bhutan dropped them when Britian used the threat of withholding the annual subsidy. Instead of taking sides, Ugyen Wangchuk, it seems, have decided to play the prestigious role of a mediator between Tibet and the British, through the wise counsel of Ugyen Dorji who had a very sound understanding of both Tibetan and British administrations and was the main channel for their correspondences.

However, when the British invited him to negotiate, Ugyen Wangchuk first judiciously sent his cousin Kunzang Thinley, the *dzongpön* of Thimphu, to meet the British. Kunzang Thinley left a very positive impression on

Younghusband, who described him as 'the first sensible man I have met on this frontier'.[33] He started the negotiations between the British and Tibetans but the Tibetan officers obstinately insisted that no negotiations could happen until the British returned to the border. While the Kashag or Council of Ministers was a little flexible on the issue of opening links with the British, the Tshogdu or Assembly adopted a very defensive approach to stop the British by fighting 'to the last men and if necessary even deploy women'. Unable to broker any deal, Kunzang Thinley returned to Bhutan but before his return, he gave the British permission to build a road from India to Tibet along the Amochu river within Bhutan as a proof of Bhutan's genuine wish for a peaceful settlement and lack of anti-British intrigues. The road would have been useful for transporting goods for the mission and also for subsequent trade.

The public perception of the British invasion of Tibet in Bhutan was different from the political neutrality adopted by the authorities. Most people seem to have decried the mission as an invasion of the Buddhist realm of Tibet by barbaric forces of British India.[34] The hierarch Jigme Chögyal even spent a large amount of money to carry out rituals and prayers to stop the invasion. Thus, there were serious questions asked about, perhaps both the safety and the appropriateness of, Ugyen Wangchuk's mediation when he and his team had planned to leave for Tibet. Against such strong opposition, Ugyen Dorji, it seems, managed to convince Ugyen Wangchuk of the political benefit of the opportunity and persuaded him to travel to Tibet. Of course, the mediation also had the good intentions of genuinely wishing to save Tibet as Tibet was in eyes of the Bhutanese elders the hub of the Buddhist civilization. Ugyen Wangchuk set off for Tibet in the third Bhutanese month accompanied by some fifty officers, including Ugyen Dorji and Kunzang Domchung, who was the Wangdi *dzongpön* and a leading merchant called Dargay. The Zhabdrung incarnate Jigme Chögyal recounts Ugyen Wangchuk's departure for Tibet in his biography:

> News came, like a blast of wintry wind,
> That the Indian forces arrived in Gyantse.
> Then, the ocean-like congregation of abbots and masters,
> The rulers and I held discussions.
> In order to save many lives of India and Tibet,
> There was no one else to be found
> More appropriate to negotiate a settlement

Than the lord, who is established by merit and prophecy.
He set out on virtuous day of the third month
And arrived at the conference of India and Tibet.[35]

The British forces under Brigadier Macdonald had already wrecked its greatest havoc on Tibetan resistance by the time Ugyen Wangchuk and his team started from Bhutan. On 31 March 1904, some 625 Tibetans were killed in Guru when the British opened fired on the Tibetan army who were virtually disarmed under the impression that there was some truce. Sparked by an accidental firing, the British soldiers mowed down the Tibetan forces with quick-firing Maxim guns, some men killed even as they fled. It was a ruthless massacre intended by the general to leave 'as big an impact as possible to impress the Tibetans into submission.' Perhaps unaware of the actual nature of the massacre, the Bhutanese promptly congratulated the British for their victory. In spite of the loss, the Tibetan resistence was far from subdued as they continued to fight back.

The British gradually fought their way from Guru to Gyantse, destroying temples and houses and looting valuables. Here, they waited for senior representatives of the Dalai Lama to come to talk before they stormed the fortress. Ugyen Wangchuk was still away from the battle scene but he was now in active communication with the Tibetan government, warning them of the futility of armed resistence. He persuaded the Tibetan government to send high-ranking officials to negotiate a peaceful settlement. Unfortunately, the Tibetan government and the Dalai Lama remained obstinate with their demands for the British to withdraw to the border and sent Serkhang Trulku with a letter asking Ugyen Wangchuk to negotiate with the British to that effect. They feared that the British commercial overtures came with a hidden agenda of colonization, as was the case with the Indian subcontinent, and were willing neither to open trade links nor accept the mission. The British, on the contrary, insisted on their wish to establish trade links and open communications and asked Ugyen Wangchuk to use his good offices to persuade the Tibetan authorities to accept the British mission.

Ugyen Wangchuk met Younghusband first in Chumbi in the beginning of June 1904 and later that month joined him in Gyantse. The British found him a straight, honest, dignified, astute and jovial character. Although the British refused his role as mediator, he was for all practical purposes now acting as the main go-between and negotiator, with a genuine wish to peacefully resolve the conflict. He won the trust and respect from both sides and they both tried to use his influence on the other to obtain their demands. The Tibetan representative often consulted him before meeting the British. This was an impressive success for Ugyen Wangchuk as only some months earlier the British would have suspected him of colluding with Tibet due to cultural and religious affinities and the Tibetans would have thought of him as a puppet of the British. He managed to change this and he was now trusted and sought by both sides to further their demands.

As the British laid siege to the Gyantse *dzong*, Ugyen Wangchuk tried to broker a deal but both sides persisted with their positions. Eventually, the Gyantse *dzong* was stormed and occupied by the British troops and the Expedition now marched on to Lhasa despite further Tibetan resistence. The 13th Dalai Lama sent another desperate request to Ugyen Wangchuk to use his influence to stop the British from advancing to Lhasa. By that time, the British were already in Nagartse fighting their way to Lhasa. At this stage, Ugyen Wangchuk visited the Ralung monastery, the home of Zhabdrung Ngawang Namgyal, which is located between Gyantse and Nagartse. Another high delegation of Tibetan authorities met Younghusband in Nagartse and requested him to return to Gyantse to start negotiations but he refused to listen and continued his advance to Lhasa.

The British reached Lhasa on 3 August 1904 and Ugyen Wangchuk entered the city with them wearing his raven crown. The Dalai Lama had by then fled from Lhasa and appointed the Gaden Tripa as his regent. Younghusband did not find any Russian presence to substantiate his theories of Tsarist conspiracy but negotiations began in earnest on a treaty for trade and indemnity of war imposed by the British on Tibet. Ugyen Wangchuk, who was based in Tengyeling, and the Nepali representative played the role of chief negotiators in order to reach a mutually acceptable terms of the treaty and the amount of indemnity. The treaty between the British and Tibet was finally signed in Potala on 7 September 1904 and Ugyen Wangchuk, who was dressed in his ceremonial regalia and sitting in the inner circle, witnessed the outcome of the negotiations. He returned with the British forces having won the gratitude of both sides. Younghusband noted that his help was 'highly instrumental in effecting a settlement. A year ago the Bhutanese were strangers, today they are our enthusiastic allies'.[36] The Tibetans thanked him for his services with a token offering of a pair of shoes and a headgear but Ugyen Wangchuk chose to stick to his Raven Crown and did not wear the Tibetan gift.

The final years of a religious republic

Ugyen Wangchuk received a grand welcome when he returned to Bhutan. The success of his mission became a reason for a triumphant celebration and even a eulogy to his journey to Tibet was composed and sung by one Jamo Tshewang Peldon.[37] Back in Bhutan, the last Desi Yeshe Ngodup, the 5th speech incarnation of Zhabdrung, was on the throne as the Desi. In fact, he was installed as the Desi by Ugyen Wangchuk even before the latter travelled to Tibet. The 56th Desi Sangay Dorji passed away in 1903 after seventeen long years in the office of the Desi without any significant achievements. He was merely a figurehead and the real power lay in the hands of Ugyen Wangchuk, who was the Tongsa *pönlop* as well as the chamberlain to the Desi. After his death, Yeshe Ngodup was appointed as the 57th Desi at the behest of Ugyen Wangchuk.

Yeshe Ngodup, we have already seen above, was born in Bumthang in 1851, recognized as the 5th speech incarnation of Zhabdrung in 1854 and installed on the golden throne of the prince-regent in the absence of the mind incarnation.[38] He was the prince-regent or Dharmarāja whom the Eden mission saw briefly in Punakha in 1864 and he held this position until 1869 when Jigme Chögyal, the 5th mind incarnation of Zhabdrung, was installed on the throne.[39] Yeshe Ngodup was an exceptionally talented monastic artist as well as learned and accomplished master. He became particularly well known for the famous record of giving the extensive *thri* (ཁྲིད) sermons on the quintessential teachings of the Drukpa Kagyu tradition thirteen times and for his exquisite paintings and sculptures. Many of his artistic legacies can still be seen in his temples in Paro and Haa.

The religious luminary was, however, an ineffectual statesman and politician. As the prince-regent, he was largely a puppet of Jigme Namgyal but his relations with Jigme Namgyal soured at the wake of the united insurgency against Jigme Namgyal by leaders of Paro, Punakha and Wangdi in 1876. The Punakha *dzongpön* made Yeshe Ngodup the Desi while the incumbent Desi Kitshalpa, who was Jigme Namgyal's appointee, was busy waging a war against the Paro *pönlop*. The Punakha *dzongpön* perhaps did this to win public support by having the regal incarnation on his side. The consequence was Yeshe Ngodup, who enjoyed good relations with Jigme Namgyal, now fell out of his favour and his appointment as the Desi did not really take off as Jigme Namgyal attacked Punakha with full force. Yeshe Ngodup neither occupied the post of the Desi long nor exercised any influence and when the

Punakha troops were vanquished by Jigme Namgyal in 1877, he escaped to his seat of Sa-ngag Chökhor in Paro, where he retired temporarily. He took no part in state politics after that, partly due to a personal request from Jigme Namgyal's wife, Pema Chöki, at the height of the insurgency in 1877 to stay out of the political feuds.

In 1903, Ugyen Wangchuk brought Yeshe Ngodup back to the political arena by appointing him the 57th Desi. The appointment was certainly an act of reconciliation on behalf of Ugyen Wangchuk to make up with people who fell out with his father. But it was also an effective way of stabilizing his own position and power. We have already seen many times how important it was for the temporal rulers to have the support and blessing of the regal incarnations in order to legitimize their rule. This was partly due to the belief that the state protector deities were on the side of incarnate lamas and those who supported them. As divine support and sanction were very important in Bhutanese politics, it was important for Ugyen Wangchuk to win the support and approval of the religious hierarchs, particularly the regal incarnations. The reconciliation with Yeshe Ngodup and his appointment as the Desi was thus politically advantageous for Ugyen Wangchuk. However, for Yeshe Ngodup, the appointment was merely symbolic. Ugyen Wangchuk held the post of the Desi's chamberlain and kept the reins of power in his own hands. Yeshe Ngodup held the nominal post as the last Desi and *de juris* ruler of Bhutan from 1903 until the new chapter of monarchy opened at the end of 1907.

Ugyen Wangchuk also managed to win the blessing and support of Jigme Chögyal, the 5th mind incarnation of Zhabdrung, who, by the time of Ugyen Wangchuk's return from Tibet, has already passed away. Jigme Chögyal was born in the family of Drametse in 1862 and brought to Punakha and installed on the golden throne in 1869 as the incarnation of Jigme Norbu, his granduncle. His life was not very different from the life of his precursor and grand-uncle. During his youth in Sa-ngag Chöling, he witnessed much conflict, first between Jigme Namgyal and his enemies and later between Ugyen Wangchuk and his opponents. Even his own family was imbroiled in the disputes and his seat, Sa-ngag Chöling, did not remain undisturbed by these events. We have already discussed how a rift developed between Jigme Namgyal and his grandfather, Sonam Dhendup, when Jigme Namgyal was the Desi and he even refused to see Ugyen Wangchuk in 1881 when the latter came to make funerary offerings to him after the death of Jigme Namgyal.

It is quite clear that there was a tension between Jigme Chögyal's family of Drametse and Ugyen Wangchuk. In 1885, the enemies of Ugyen Wangchuk even asked his father, Köncho Wangdi, to take up the office of the Desi and join them against Ugyen Wangchuk. Köncho Wangdi wisely declined and this perhaps helped close the rift between the Drametse family and Ugyen Wangchuk although the main credit must perhaps go to Ugyen Wangchuk's own reconciliatory approach and diplomatic skills. In any case, by 1904, Jigme Chögyal and Ugyen Wangchuk enjoyed a very cordial relationship. When they saw each other in Punakha before Ugyen Wangchuk's departure for Tibet, Jigme Chögyal compared their meeting to one between a father and son.

A close relationship with Jigme Chögyal was particularly important for Ugyen Wangchuk's political career. Firstly, the blessings and the support of one of the Zhabdrung incarnations were vital for any political authority. By the end of the nineteenth century, the Bhutanese perception of the institutions of the four regal incarnations had significantly changed. Of the four incarnations, who traditionally occupied the golden throne, the Gyalse Trulku (རྒྱལ་སྲས་སྤྲུལ་ སྐུ་) or prince-incarnation line originating in Zhabdrung's son Jampal Dorji had come to a complete halt. After Jampal Dorji II, the 5th in the line, had passed away in 1833, no efforts seem to have been made officially to find his reincarnation. Similarly, the line of incarnation beginning in Tenzin Rabgay, known as Tritrul, (ཁྲི་སྤྲུལ་) was also practically forgotten after the death of Thinley Gyatsho in 1851. Two reincarnations were said to have been found after 1851 but neither of them lived a full life or were duly installed in Tenzin Rabgay's seat of Tango. The institution was, thus, for all practical purposes dead until it was resurrected at the end of the twentieth century.

Of the two main lines of Zhabdrung incarnations which were still active by the end of the nineteenth century, the institution of the mind incarnation was being increasingly perceived as the chief embodiment of Zhabdrung. By the middle of the eighteenth century, it was a common practice to refer to the mind incarnation as the Zhabdrung. The speech incarnation was often referred to as the incarnation of Chogley Namgyal (ཕྱོགས་ལས་རྣམ་རྒྱལ་སྐུ་), and not necessarily directly linked to the person of Zhabdrung. Jigme Chögyal was thus referred to as the Zhabdrung incarnation and Yeshe Ngodup as the incarnation of Chogley Namgyal. Perhaps, the nuances in the use of such epithets for the two incarnations indicate some informal choice among some people to have only one Zhabdrung incarnation. Jigme Chögyal, as the main Zhabdrung incarnation, obviously enjoyed a supreme position in Bhutanese religious hierarchy. It was crucial, therefore, for Ugyen Wangchuk to have Jigme Chögyal's blessing to legitimize his rule in the eyes of the pious populace.

In addition, the Drametse family of Jigme Chögyal had gained a highly prominent stature since the time of Jigme Drakpa II, the 3rd mind incarnation. The family's support would be very useful to Ugyen Wangchuk. The sister of Jigme Drakpa II, we have seen earlier, was the lady of Drametse and married to Tenzin Chögyal, who briefly became the Tongsa *pönlop*. Her son, Jigme Norbu, was identified as the reincarnation of her brother, Jigme Drakpa, II and thus as the fourth mind incarnation. After Jigme Norbu's death, his grandnephew Jigme Chögyal, who was born to his niece Senge Drolma, was recognized as his incarnation and therefore the 5th mind incarnation. Beside Jigme Chögyal, Senge Drolma had also given birth to two other preeminent incarnations of his time: the Tango Trulku Kuenga Drakpa and the 7th Gangteng Trulku Tenpai Nyinjed. Furthermore, Jigme Chögyal's father was also married to the younger sister of Jigme Chögyal's mother. This sister was the mother of another incarnation, Nyizer Trulku. Thus, Jigme Chögyal had two brothers and one half-brother, who were eminent religious incarnations. With three consecutive Zhabdrung incarnations and three other important incarnations directly associated with it and a noble descent from Pema Lingpa, the Drametse household was highly respected in the Bhutanese society by the end of the nineteenth century. Two further lamas would be born in this family in the next generation.

It is, therefore, not surprising that Drametse's prolific production of reincarnate lamas aroused some criticism. The scepticism it generated in some quarter is perhaps beautifully captured in the following verse, which implies that not all those who can recognize the personal belongings of a former lama are incarnations of lamas because even stable boys who have been in the service of the lama can do so:

At Drametse in the east,
Many lamas are born.
Indeed, many lamas are born,
But more horse-keepers are born.[40]

The membership of incarnate lamas was not the only strength of Drametse. Beside the four incarnations, the Drametse family also produced in that generation three officials including a *pönlop* of Dagana. The household was in its heydays and a centre of considerable influence. It was politically prudent to win its support and Ugyen Wangchuk did so successfully, particularly by winning the goodwill of Jigme Chögyal, the most eminent member of Drametse.

Jigme Chögyal's own life was however fraught with successive problems and losses. In his early youth, he experienced the disturbance of the civil wars of Bhutan. As we have seen earlier, he put in writing the horrors of the last one in his verse biography. In 1876, his main teacher, Shakya Gyaltshen, passed away. This was followed by the death of his mother and grandfather, Sonam Dhendup in 1877, when he was fifteen. Soon after this, there were problems in Dagana, where his half-brother was the *pönlop* and some relatives were killed. Then, in 1894, his father, Koncho Wangdi, died in Drametse. He travelled to Drametse and carried out the funerary services. On his return, he looked back at Drametse with a heavy heart and said prayers knowing too well that it was going to be his last trip home. This was followed by an epidemic of smallpox and the great earthquake of 1897. While he was busy fixing the damages caused by the earthquake to his centre of Sa-nga Chöling, he received the news in 1899 that his youngest sister, who was looking after the family home in Drametse, had died. The following year, his half-brother, the *pönlop* of Dagana, fell seriously ill during the consecration of the Gangteng temple. The half-brother was brought on a stretcher to Sa-ngag Chöling and was deteriorating when suddenly his brother Tenpai Nyinjed, the 7th Gangteng Trulku, passed away in 1900.

Like the life of his precursor Jigme Norbu, Jigme Chögyal's life was marred by a series of tragedies. It is perhaps these tribulations which kept him, like his former incarnation, deeply bent on spiritual work and away from state politics. During the times he was not occupied by misfortunes, he gave religious sermons, observed meditation retreats or undertook cultural projects. When he was free from these activities, he travelled passionately on pilgrimages to various places in Bhutan. He was also interested in travelling to Tibet on pilgrimage toward the end of his life but the authorities discouraged him, perhaps considering it unsafe for him as the British invasion of Tibet was about to unfold. Jigme Chögyal died some time in the middle of 1904, aged only forty-two, while Ugyen Wangchuk was away in Tibet. Kunzang Thinley, the *dzongpön* of Thimphu and his brother Kuenga Drakpa, the Tango Trulku, supervised the funerary services. Like his precursor, Jigme Chögyal also left for posterity an insightful autobiography, written in eloquent verse.

Ugyen Wangchuk must have been saddened by the early demise of the Zhabdrung hierarch when he returned from Tibet. However, his own fortunes were on the rise. The success of his mediatory mission during the Younghusband Expedition had won him great applause and recognition from all sides. The Bhutanese partook in the pride of his achievement and the Tibetans showed deep appreciation. The best recognition and honour, however, came from the British in the following year, when the Government of India sent John Claude White, the political officer in Sikkim, to honour Ugyen Wangchuk with the insignia of the Knight Commander of the Indian empire. White was accompanied by F.W. Rennick of the Intelligence Department, A.W. Paul, the previous British representative in Sikkim who travelled all the way from England at the invitation of Ugyen Wangchuk, and an escort of twenty-four sepoys. They left Gangtok on 29 March 1905 and travelled over the Nathula Pass and entered Bhutan from the Chumbi valley via Haa. Details of this and White's subsequent journeys in Bhutan can be found in his *Sikhim and Bhutan*.

In sharp contrast to the last British mission led by Eden, the mission was showered with warm reception and hospitality throughout its journey. Ugyen Dorji, who was working as a dual agent for Bhutan and the British, accompanied them from Chumbi and the jovial chief of protocol of Tongsa welcomed them in Damthang in Haa. The latter travelled with the British guests throughout their time in Bhutan, having been assigned by Ugyen Wangchuk to look after them. From Haa, the mission made its way to Punakha, where it was received with much pomp and ceremony and a grand investiture was held to present the knighthood to Ugyen Wangchuk. The ceremony was presided by the Desi and attended by all leading monastic and state officials of Bhutan. White, in his full uniform and attended by Rennick and the escorts, presented the insignia to Ugyen Wangchuk before the solemn congregation in the decorated hall of Punakha. 'With a few words appropriate to the occasion, I placed the ribbon of the order round his neck, pinned on the star, and handed the warrant to Sir Ugyen Wang-chuk,' he wrote. The rest of the mission also offered congratulatory greetings and presents to Sir Ugyen Wangchuk. This was followed by a very long file of congratulatory offerings from the local Bhutanese felicitators and the usual Bhutanese rituals of celebration.

After the investiture, the mission travelled to Tongsa and Bumthang, where Sir Ugyen Wangchuk and his family received them. White described his visit to Bumthang as 'the most beautiful part of our expedition, as we were received as honoured guests by Sir Ugyen in his private capacity'.[41] He and his friends were the first Europeans to spend some time in Chokhor

Sir Ugyen Wangchuk with his family in 1905

Thinley Rabten, the residence of the 1st Druk Gyalpo

The 1st Druk Gyalpo (photograph by John Claude White)

and tour the valley. They stayed both at Lame Gönpa and Wandichöling and saw the renovation of the Wangdichöling *dzong* after it was destroyed by the earthquake of 1897. Here, Sir Ugyen Wangchuk also found time to discuss national issues and intellectual topics with White and his party. 'Sir Ugyen is the only Bhutanese I have come across who takes a real and intelligent interest in general subjects, both foreign and domestic, and he neither drinks nor indulges in other vices,' wrote White. 'I held many long private conversations with the Tongsa [*pönlop*], and was deeply impressed by his sense of responsibility and genuine desire to improve the condition of his country and countrymen. I gave him what advice I could, and made an attempt to lay the foundation of a close friendship between him and the British Government.'[42]

Above all, White was overwhelmed by the warmth and hospitality shown by Sir Ugyen Wangchuk and his family. When it was time for departure, White wrote with a heavy heart: 'We then wished our kind hosts good-bye with sincere regret, for we had thoroughly enjoyed the natural, open-hearted hospitality with which all at Wang-du-choling had entertained us.' Sir Ugyen Wangchuk came to see them off as far as Pelela. 'Sir Ugyen waved us a last salute as we turned the corner and went out of sight,' wrote White. 'I think he really felt our departure as much as I can honestly say I did, and I cannot help repeating myself and saying again that no host could have been more courteous, more hospitable, and more thoughtful of his guests than Sir Ugyen Wang-chuk.'[43] The mission returned to Sikkim following a northerly route from Thimphu via Lingshi, where the Bhutanese hosts bid them final goodbye.

The friendship and hospitality White enjoyed with Sir Ugyen Wangchuk could not have been more different from the reception of Eden by Jigme Namgyal. Under Sir Ugyen Wangchuk, the Anglo-Bhutanese relations took a new course. In the beginning of the following year, 1906, Sir Ugyen Wangchuk was invited to Calcutta to meet the Prince of Wales, who was on a tour in India. The Māharāja of Sikkim and Panchen Lama of Tibet were also present but Desi Yeshe Ngodup declined his invitation. This trip was the first of Sir Ugyen Wangchuk's two visits to India and an important event in Bhutan's history. He was received with the same reverence shown to a mid-level Indian prince, with the salute of fifteen guns, which was also the number accorded to the Māharāja of Sikkim. Indian princes, altogether about 565, came with states of all sizes and shapes and were given salutes of twenty-one, nineteen, seventeen, fifteen, thirteen, eleven and nine guns.

There was a delicate relationship between the British as 'Paramount Power' and the princely states and such protocols were zealously observed. Sir Ugyen Wangchuk seems to have happily accepted the role when he was treated like a prince of a British colony. The visit and the tour brought Sir Ugyen Wangchuk and his Bhutanese team in direct contact with the outside world, of which, apart from Tibet, they have seen very little previously. Sir Ugyen Wangchuk took a keen interest in development programmes and industries he saw in India. Bhutan's relationship with the British had now gained a very firm footing and it began to look more southward and operate within the British sphere of influence.

The close personal rapport between Sir Ugyen Wangchuk and White also augured well for the emerging relationship between the two countries. Later in the spring of 1906, White again travelled across Bhutan to join Sir Ugyen Wangchuk in the Lhalung monastery in Tibet. This time, he entered from Dewathang in the east and travelled through Dungsam (now Pema Gatsel), Tashigang, Tashi Yangtse, Kurtoe and exited via Senge dzong to meet Sir Ugyen Wangchuk in Lhalung. Ugyen Wangchuk was then visiting his nephew, Chökyi Gyaltshen (1894–1925), who was now the head of the Lhalung monastery. He was recognized as a reincarnation of his granduncle Tanpai Nyima and, therefore, the 9th Peling Sungtrul. At Lhalung, Sir Ugyen Wangchuk again spent time with White 'discussing the affairs of Bhutan and talking over his projects for improvements, roads, developments, etc., all very interesting subjects.'[44]

In Sir Ugyen Wangchuk, Bhutan had now found a new and refreshingly different leadership from what was known since Sherab Wangchuk's days. He was forward-looking and progressive. Bhutan's relations with its neighbours had also reached a stable condition and the people enjoyed relative peace and security. The time was ripe for a new era and a sound political transition. It was about time the king-maker was made the king.

Jamgon Ngawang Gyaltsen, the
religious ambassador. He led embassies
to Derge and Ladakh (courtesy:
Yonten Dargye).

Shakya Rinchen, the 9th Je Khenpo
and great scholar and biographer
of medieval Bhutan

Tenzin Chogyal, Bhutan's 1st national
historian and the 10th Je Khenpo

Zhabdrung Jigme Norbu, the romantic
and poetic lama and
prince regent

The manor house of Bönbji in upper Mangde valley, which produced many religious and secular leaders

The manor house of Ogyenchöling, the home of Tongsa Pönlop Tshokye Dorji (with permission from Walter Roder)

The Drametse religious establishment today, as a monastic centre

Wangdichöling Palace, with the Jakar *dzong* in the background. The palace
has remained neglected in recent times and efforts are being made to
turn it into a museum.

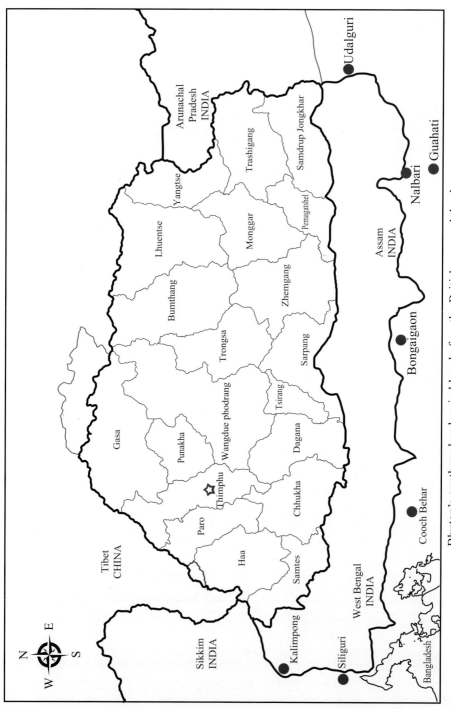

Bhutan's southern borders in blue, before the British annexed the duars

Thimphu Tashichödzong, the headquarters of the government, and
Gyalyong Tshogkhang, the Parliament building

The stupas on Dochula pass, built to memorialize Bhutan's latest
victory over Indian militants in 2003

Archers, with bamboo bows, and female dancers, in 1933.
Archery is the national sport and played with festive spirit.

Archers today, using imported compound bows (courtesy: Gerard Tardy)

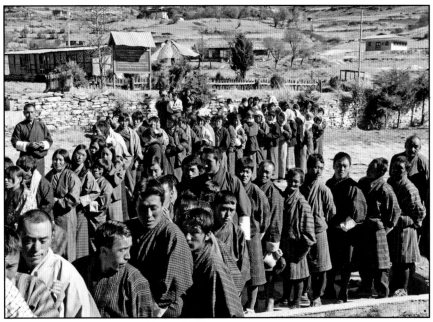

Men and women queue to vote during the first democratic elections
in 2008 when nearly 80 per cent of the electorate turned up to vote

The National Flag flying in front of Punakha *dzong*

The crowning of the 5th Druk Gyalpo

Celebrations during the coronation

Early Modern Period:
The Introduction of Monarchy

THE NEW CENTURY USHERED in a new political era for Bhutan. Over two centuries of tumultuous theocratic republican rule had worn out the Bhutanese public by the time Sir Ugyen Wangchuk rose to an eminent stature. The nation was exhausted by the recurrent factional fighting in the absence of a unifying authority. Moreover, Bhutan had seen significant changes in the power structure and relations both within the country and with neighbouring countries, largely due to the military dexterity of Jigme Namgyal and Sir Ugyen Wangchuk's political shrewdness and diplomatic skills. It is against the backdrop of these sociopolitical changes that we must appreciate Sir Ugyen Wangchuk's ascension to the throne as the King and the introduction of the hereditary monarchy in Bhutan, at a time when monarchies were collapsing in other parts of the world.

The sociopolitical setting

The political system initiated by Zhabdrung Ngawang Namgyal had changed significantly by the turn of the twentieth century. Firstly, the strong political leadership which the Zhabdrung institution provided in the seventeenth century had long ebbed away. Although the Zhabdrung figure still loomed large in the religious consciousness, the Zhabdrung institution was no more a pivotal point of Bhutan's political structure by the beginning of the twentieth century, in the way it was conceived during the formation of the state. The Zhabdrung institution now did not carry the same political weight as it did two centuries ago. The first stumble in this fall occurred when plans to establish a hereditary system based on the Ralung family failed to take off. The plans came to a dismal end with Tenzin Rabgay's death in 1696. The state elders then resorted to the incarnation line to continue Zhabdrung's legacy. This too failed to provide a unifying leadership for Bhutan as multiple candidates for Zhabdrung's incarnation appeared simultaneously. The candidates were skilfully accommodated, using the religious hermeneutics of multiple incarnations being possible for a single enlightened person but the problem of political fragmentation persisted as they vied for supremacy among each other. Even worse, the young and incompetent incarnations were frequently used by shrewd politicians to further their own political interests and goals.

In the eighteenth and nineteenth centuries, four incarnation lines originating in Zhabdrung, his son Jampal Dorji and Tenzin Rabgay, occupied the golden throne and held some sway over Bhutan's political course. By the beginning of the twentieth century, two of these incarnation lines, as we seen in the last chapter, were practically dead. Only the two lines which were initially linked to the person of Zhabdrung Ngawang Namgyal as his mind and speech incarnations were still active. There was a general decline in the influence of the Zhabdrung incarnations and also a tendency to streamline the institutions. Of the two remaining, the Sungtrul or speech incarnation was increasingly being referred to as the incarnation of Chogley Namgyal and not always directly linked to Zhabdrung or treated on par with the Thugtrul, the mind incarnation. The stature of the speech incarnation was diminishing and the political inaptitude of Yeshe Ngodup, the person holding the mantle of the speech incarnation at this period, did not help it.

At any rate, the mind incarnation had come to be perceived as the chief Zhabdrung incarnation by the end of the nineteenth century and was the most respected and dominant line. This is in a sharp contrast to the preponderance of the other three lines about two centuries earlier when the incarnation lines began. Nonetheless, Jigme Chögyal, who was the mind incarnation at this time, was an ineffectual leader politically. Despite being seen as the supreme leader or Dharmarāja, he never really exercised any political influence, at least to the degree of posing a challenge to Ugyen Wangchuk. Thus, neither of the two incarnations who carried some statutory weight at this time really provided an alternative political leadership and Ugyen Wangchuk was virtually unrivalled. Moreover, Jigme Chögyal, the main Zhabdrung incarnation, passed away in 1904, leaving the golden throne vacant. Time was just right for a systemic change.

The Bhutanese political perception had also changed in the two centuries of theocratic republican rule. It would have been inconceivable to have a lay person, especially from outside the Zhabdrung circle, to rule over the country in the early eighteenth century. Zhabdrung's dual system of religious and political authority, symbolized respectively by the silken knot and the gold yoke, was combined in the person of a religious figure, especially one directly associated with the Zhabdrung institution. The office of the Desi was only an adjunct to the golden throne and initially the post of a steward. Over time, with the political inefficacy of the incarnations, the office of the Desi became the strongest and highest political office and was also increasingly sought by lay contenders. This happened particularly because many monk candidates, despite being held in high esteem by the Bhutanese public, turned out to be weak and incompetent rulers. At the same time, the lay rulers began to rise and thrive because they were less inhibited in using force to wrest power.

By the nineteenth century, political authority lay mostly in the hands of ruthless magnates who wrested power through sheer force and military strength. Political leadership was no more the domain of the religious hierarchs. It was now acceptable to have a political supremo, who was neither a religious figure nor directly associated with the Zhabdrung institution. Similarly, the dual system of governance was also not limited to political space of the *dzong* structure, which combined both monastic and administrative communities. In fact, throughout much of the later half of the nineteenth century, Jigme Namgyal and Ugyen Wangchuk mostly controlled the country from outside the arena of traditional *dzong* establishments. They were occasionally in the two capitals and not regularly even in the Tongsa *dzong*, their official base. The physical sphere of political operation had changed as much as the perception of the operators.

Beside the transformation in the perception of the ruler, there were also other socio-political changes. Regionalism, which marred Bhutanese state politics in the eighteenth and nineteenth centuries, was now generally over. The rivalry between the upper and lower Wang regions of the Thimphu valley had ceased since Jigme Namgyal's assertion of political power in the middle of the nineteenth century. The last remnants of western political power were removed with the defeat of Alu Dorji and Phuntsho Dorji at the battle of Changlingmethang. The east–west regional rivalry, which existed in Tshokye Dorji and Jigme Namgyal's time, also ended with Ugyen Wangchuk becoming the unrivalled leader in 1885 supported by his relatives in key positions across the country. Political power was now in the hands of a new ruling family coming from Dungkar in Kurtoe but tracing its origins to Pema Lingpa of Bumthang.

There were also important changes in the power and condition of the leading families, which produced the ruling magnates in the past. The leading households in western Bhutan, including those of Obtsho, Kabji and those in Wang, were either totally debilitated or in decline by the end of the nineteenth century. Bönbji, the most powerful establishment in central Bhutan in the eighteenth century, was also politically at a low point after the death of the 52nd Desi Kitshalpa in 1879. Another powerful household in central Bhutan, particularly in the nineteenth century, was Ogyen Chöling, the home of Tshokye Dorji and Tsondru Gyaltshen. Tsondru Gyaltshen died in the battle against the British in Dewathang in 1665 without leaving a male heir and, the political prominence of this establishment also came to an end.

We have seen how Drametse was an influential family in eastern Bhutan towards the end of the nineteenth century. However, its fortune also rapidly changed at the turn of the twentieth century, with the death of several members, including Jigme Chögyal, his father, sister and brother.[1] In a few years, the establishment would be left without a capable heir to carry on its legacy. In contrast, Sir Ugyen Wangchuk's family in Bumthang was in ascendance. His sister and daughters were thriving in the family establishments of Wangdichöling and Lamai Gönpa and a new son, Jigme Wangchuk, was also born in 1905. Through family connections, Sir Ugyen Wangchuk enjoyed the support of most nobilities in central Bhutan. He also had the spiritual backing of three eminent Tibetan lamas—Khamsum Yongdrol, Zilnon Namkha Dorji and Serkhang Trulku—and the clergy of the State Monk Body. For a very devout Buddhist nation, such religious support was crucial.

Bhutan's relations with its neighbours were also favourable to Sir Ugyen Wangchuk. With the British to the south, he struck a very close and cordial relationship. Although the British did not actively promote him, or make him King as we are often wrongly told, the British, observing neutrality in Bhutan's internal affairs, happily accepted the course of events in Bhutan. When Sir Ugyen Wangchuk asked the British some time after receiving the knighthood to assist him in making the post of the Tongsa *pönlop* hereditary, Lord Curzon noted that it was 'most unwise to support one of the Pönlops (even the ablest) against either the [Dharma or Deb] Rajas. If he is the strongest man, he will support himself'.[2] There was certainly no open British campaign or directive for the appointment of Sir Ugyen Wangchuk as hereditary ruler but British support was implicit in the knighthood he was given, the close ties he enjoyed with the British representative in Sikkim and the promise of an increment in the cash subsidy.

To the north, Sir Ugyen Wangchuk enjoyed a very good priest–patron relationship with some of Tibet's leading lamas but there appears to be very little official link with the Tibetan government after the conclusion of the Younghusband Expedition. In the aftermath of this British mission, Tibet saw an increased interference from China. The Amban assumed greater control with the help of armed troops and the British were withdrawing their presence in Tibet. There was no exchange worth noting between Tibet and Bhutan at this time except for one Tibetan remonstrance against Sir Ugyen Wangchuk for allowing John Claude White to travel through southern Tibet in the spring of 1906. To this Ugyen Wangchuk is said to have responded somewhat as follows:

> Living as I do in the wilds of Bhutan, I am but a simpleton and have no doubt committed a serious mistake. But, as the Tibetan Government had permitted several hundred British soldiers, as well as some thousands of Indian soldiers under British Officers, to come to Lhasa, the heart of Tibet, I thought that there could be no harm in a solitary Englishman travelling through an out-of-the-way corner of your country.[3]

Charles Bell adds that Sir Ugyen Wangchuk said, with a twinkle in his eye, that he received no reply to this. It is quite clear from this response and earlier correspondences that Tibet did not have any influence on Bhutan and Sir Ugyen Wangchuk conducted his relations with Tibet as an independent and equal power. In fact, apart from the above, there appears to be no official exchange and what little existed was perhaps neither hostile nor particularly cordial. Occupied with its own problem of growing Chinese presence, Tibet had little time and power to interfere in Bhutan's affairs. Bhutan, on the other hand, remained untouched by the Chinese menace in Tibet and enjoyed full freedom of self-determination. There were no external hindrances; the internal and external conditions were conducive to the big step Bhutan was to take.

However, the most important factor leading to Sir Ugyen Wangchuk's installation as a monarch was his personal traits. Sir Ugyen Wangchuk possessed the characteristics of a king even before he was crowned as one. From the testimonies of his contemporaries, Sir Ugyen Wangchuk, we know, was a person of very endearing qualities. Younghusband described him as a 'jolly, astute individual' and 'straight and possessed of a natural authority',[4] and Waddell as a 'shrewd middle-aged man of strong character'.[5]

Even Landon's unflattering description portrays him as a 'cheerful but not particularly distinguished adjunct to the Mission'.[6] Bell, who knew Sir Ugyen Wangchuk better, wrote that 'His Highness is not only a very able Ruler, but is also universally respected both by his subjects and by his foreign friends. Though he has only twice in his life quitted his hermit land, he has all the broadminded tolerance of one who has lived a cosmopolitan life.'[7] Indeed, we have seen many instances of Sir Ugyen Wangchuk's military dexterity as well as his diplomatic skills, reconciliatory and magnnimous approach and genuinely benevolent and good nature.

The most flattering comments from a visitor perhaps come from White, who knew him very well. White wrote: 'I have never met a native I liked and respected more than I do Sir Ugyen. He is upright, honest, open, and straightforward, and I wish it had been possible to remain in India till he had at least commenced some of his schemes of reform.'[8] Sir Ugyen Wangchuk naturally possessed the qualities of a leader. Besides, he was a deeply spiritual man; 'he was more than a lama' as some of his followers described him to White. This spiritual proclivity went down well with his milieu, which was made of devout citizens. If there was a need for a new leader to take the helm of Bhutan, he fitted the bill. Only a call for it was wanting.

This call came at the end of 1906 from Sir Ugyen Wangchuk's most trusted friend and supporter, Ugyen Dorji, who was appointed as the *drungpa* of Haa by Sir Ugyen Wangchuk. He wrote a letter addressed to the council of the state explaining the benefit and appropriateness of appointing Sir Ugyen Wangchuk as the King of Bhutan.[9] Sir Ugyen Wangchuk was already known since the mission to Tibet as Druk Chichab or Overlord of Bhutan. The proposal now was to crown him as the King. It is difficult to see what inspired Ugyen Dorji to put forth this bold proposal. It is likely that he was drawing on the examples of the princely titles of India and Sikkim, with which he was familiar, and possibly even got the idea from Sir Ugyen Wangchuk himself if we are to take the cue of the latter's proposal to make the post of Tongsa *pönlop* hereditary. Ugyen Dorji explained that the absence of a King and clear procedures for appointing the Desi have made it very difficult for Bhutan to maintain the rule of religious and secular laws. Moreover, there had been of late an increase in foreign relations and the need for a capable figure to represent Bhutan.

Conferring the title of Druk Gyalpo or King of Bhutan on Sir Ugyen Wangchuk would not only benefit his descendants and relations but help protect the state legacy of Zhabdrung. The post of the Desi could continue for domestic affairs but the new appointment of Sir Ugyen Wangchuk would

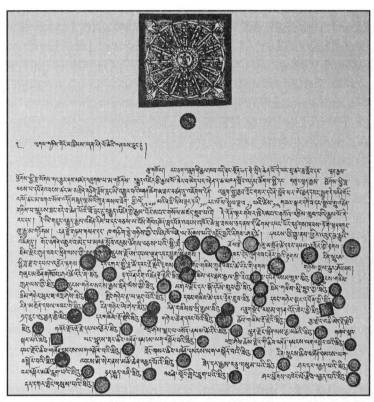

Contract for the new monarchy

Coronation of Ugyen Wangchuk as the 1st Druk Gyalpo

secure British support, the annual subsidy and Bhutan's territory. His most emphatic argument was that Sir Ugyen Wangchuk had been honoured by the greatest power in the world and Bhutan's State Council could not afford to 'remain ignorant' but recognize this and honour him with the title of King. The letter was written as an open proposal but clearly intended to test the waters. Its intended audience would include the Desi, the Je Khenpo, the four monastic masters, the three *dzongpön*s of Punakha, Thimphu and Wangdi, the three *pönlop*s of Paro, Tongsa and Dagana, the chamberlain to the Desi, the chief state councillor, the state chief of protocol and the various officials under them. We have no record of the reaction it received from the clergy and state administration. Most people to whom the letter was addressed were appointees of Sir Ugyen Wangchuk and it is probable that no strong objection came from any quarter. To use the Buddhist idiom, the *tendrel* or auspicious concurrence of causes and conditions for the installation of Sir Ugyen Wangchuk as King was now fully present. The only misfortune to take place was the fire, which destroyed the Paro *dzong* in 1907, barely weeks before the great event in Punakha.

The King is crowned

Roughly a year after the proposal was put forth by Raja Ugyen Dorji, Sir Ugyen Wangchuk was crowned as the hereditary monarch of Bhutan in Punakha on 17 December 1907. The venue was the main congregation hall of Punakha which was gaily decorated with wall hangings, banners and silk brocades. Three thrones were installed: one in the centre for King Ugyen Wangchuk, one to his right for John Claude White, the British representative, and another to his left for the 50th Je Khenpo Jampal Shenyen. They were flanked by the rows of clergy led by Tango Trulku Kuenga Drakpa, of the state officials led by the Paro *pönlop* Dawa Peljor and other members of the British team. Except for the broad aisle, the hall was thronged with officers and spectators and many people watched from the gallery above. As the venue was the chapel of protector deities and off limits to women, there was perhaps no woman partaking in the ceremony in the hall but the female spectators watched from the upper gallery. The proceedings started with the formal presentation of gifts from the Government of India followed by local gifts. The Je Khenpo did not get up from his throne to present his gifts but the Tango Trulku made three prostrations, perhaps to the shrine, before presenting his gifts as did the councillors after him. After this, the traditional *zhugdrel* ceremony of inauguration was conducted and 'three kinds of tea, rice, and pan were each offered in turn'.[10]

The pinnacle of the ceremony was the endorsement of the document containing the contract for the new monarchial system. The state clerk read out aloud the oath of allegiance to the new King written on a scroll. Then, the Je Khenpo put the large seal of Zhabdrung's Ngachudrukma at the top of the document in vermillion. The other lamas, councillors, governors, officers, people's representatives followed suit to put their seals on the document in black ink. The document bore altogether fifty different seals, including the two at the top.

To the feet of the precious and high judge of the dual system,

It is submitted that in our country, Bhutan, in former times whoever came forth from among lamas and master of the monastery, councillors and regional governors served as the great Desi. Apart from this, there was no hereditary monarch. Now, therefore, the abbot, monastic masters, the congregation, state council, regional governors and all officials and subjects unanimously and sincerely endorse firmly and conclusively the unalterable oath, the purport of which is, Bhutan's overlord, the Tongsa pönlop Sir Ugyen Wangchuk is enthroned as the hereditary monarch, through common agreement and as evident to all gods and men, in the Palace of Great Bliss of Punakha on 17 December 1907, 13th day of the 11th month of our own year of Earth Monkey, coinciding with an auspicious astrological conjunction. In pursuant to this, we, the above mentioned, lamas and officials, subjects and followers, all great and small, place our integrity as witness in order to offer service and support to the king who has been enthroned on the golden throne and to the succession of his royal heirs. Apart from this, if there are issues arising due to new talk from evil intention and duplicitous accusations, then such a person will expelled from the common fold. In acceptance of the unalterable [conditions] above, the common seal of the abbot, masters and congregation, ... the seal of the three regions of Darkar.

The state seal showing Zhabdrung's Ngachudrukma was impressed with great care at the top of the document to indicate that the new kingship was in service of Zhabdrung's rule and not a replacement for it. The appointment was perhaps seen at that time as a hereditary administrative post, adjunct to the office of Zhabdrung incarnate or Dharmarāja but not as an overhaul of the existent system. The Zhabdrung figure was still prominent in the Bhutanese religiopolitical consciousness and could not have been easily substituted by a new civil leadership. The kingship was most likely intended as a replacement for the office of the Desi although even this was not quite clear. The founding of the monarchy did not clearly nullify the office of the Desi in the eyes of everyone at that time, as we shall see below. One historian enumerated King Ugyen Wangchuk and the 2nd King as successive Desis even as late as the middle of the twentieth century. [11]

No doubt, there was high regard and deference shown to the founder of the nation, Zhabdrung Ngawang Namgyal, at the time of the coronation but the actual relationship between the new kingship and the Zhabdrung institution was perhaps becoming strained. The undefined and delicate power sharing brought with it tensions which would aggravate into hostile ruptures between the two in the decades to come. Even at that time, cracks in the relation were visible in the absence of the only surviving Zhabdrung incarnation during the enthronement ceremony. Sungtrul Yeshe Ngodup was not only the sole Zhabdrung incarnation around but he was also the last Desi. He presided over the investiture for awarding the KCIE to Sir Ugyen Wangchuk from a high throne only two years ago. However, this eminent figure was curiously absent during the enthronement of King Ugyen Wangchuk. Where was he and why was he not present at one of the most defining moments of Bhutan's history?

Yeshe Ngodup was certainly active in the country. In addition to his religious services, he also built the new establishment of Kuenga Chöling, just below his main seat of Sa-ngag Chökhor. When the Paro *dzong* was rebuilt after the fire of 1907, he took up the responsibility of designing the art work in its shrine rooms. In 1915, he became the 53rd Je Khenpo and occupied the office until he died in 1917. On 25 January 1910, when Charles Bell met him, he was on the way to ask King Ugyen Wangchuk to make him the Desi again. The King did not see the need for Desis any more as he carried out their work.[12] Yeshe Ngodup perhaps felt sidelined by the new kingship and, as a result, a rift was developing between him and King Ugyen Wangchuk.

The rift certainly intensified toward the end of his life. Some time in 1917, Yeshe Ngodup and his confidante Kuenga Gyaltshen boldly undertook the restoration of the mummified remains of Zhabdrung Ngawang Namgyal and the bone relic of Tsangpa Gyarey.[13] Such an undertaking was symbolically a powerful political act as access to and control over the state relics meant ultimate power and legitimacy over the state. The bodily remains, treasured as state relics, are said to have fallen into some disrepair and, in the previous century, Jigme Norbu and Agay Haapa tried to restore them but had to quickly stop the project when they felt the tremors of an earthquake. They interpreted the earthquake as a sign of divine wrath. Yeshe Ngodup, however, ignored this precedence and undertook the restoration successfully but he is also said to have kept a small piece for himself as a token of blessing. This act or the disturbance caused to the sacred relic, our sources tell us, incensed the deities, who caused a major landslide along the Mochu river course, an epidemic of smallpox among the state monks and the death of Yeshe Ngodup in the same year. The government under King Ugyen Wangchuk is said to have annulled Yeshe Ngodup's status and privileges and even banned further recognition of the speech incarnation after Yeshe Ngodup's death.[14]

Despite the tricky and tense relationship with the Zhabdrung institution, the monarchial system gained quick momentum and Bhutan experienced a new political order. The new system, in which the apex of the state administration was the hereditary King and not a Zhabdrung incarnation, took off with relatively little hiccups for a systemic political transformation. In a way, Bhutan had now come full circle and achieved hereditary leadership, which it sought at the beginning of its existence as a unified country. Back then, the plan was to have a hereditary monarchy from the Ralung family through its exiled scion Zhabdrung Ngawang Namgyal and his cousin, Tenzin Rabgay. This failed miserably when no male issue came forth one generation after it was commenced. In its place, Bhutan now obtained a new hereditary ruling line from a family of nobility, which was local and home-grown. With the establishment of the hereditary monarchy and endorsement of the oath of allegiance, political control over the country lay centralized in the hands of King Ugyen Wangchuk and a fresh sense of law and order prevailed.

King Ugyen Wangchuk's reign ushered Bhutan into a new, modern era. Although serious programmes of modernization were to only take place half a century later, we see the inception of plans for modernization during this phase of history, which I call the Early Modern Period. In addition to the political shift from a theocratic republic to a hereditary monarchy (which may not itself be seen as a modernizing trend), Bhutan witnessed several other sociopolitical changes which paved the way for modernization. We see the beginning of the two processes of modernization: the active pursuit of socioeconomic development and the passive reception of external influence through exposure and globalization. We will see how these processes take off in the second half of the twentieth century but foundations were already being laid by the time Ugyen Wangchuk was crowned King. We know from his conversations with John Claude White that King Ugyen Wangchuk was deeply concerned with the socioeconomic welfare of the people. White wrote:

[In 1905] I held many long private conversations with the Tongsa [*pönlop*], and was deeply impressed by his sense of responsibility and genuine desire to improve the condition of his country and countrymen . . .

[In 1906] I also spent much of my time with the Tongsa [*pönlop*], discussing the affairs of Bhutan and talking over his projects for improvements, roads, developments, etc., all very interesting subjects and I often wonder now how he is carrying out all his schemes . . .

[In 1907] I remained behind, at the urgent request of the new Maharaja and his council, to discuss with them many projects and schemes for the welfare and improvement of the country. These covered a large area— schools and education, population, trade, the construction of roads, the mineral resources of the country and the best method of utilising them, the desirability of tea cultivation on the waste lands at the foot of the hills, which are excellent for the purpose and equal to the best tea land in the Duars.[15]

It was the dawn of a new state politics in which the leader fully assumed the responsibility for the betterment of the country. The ruler was no longer occupied with squabbles and feuds to attain or retain power for himself. King Ugyen Wangchuk was keen to develop roads, education and health services and to improve the economic conditions of the people. Simultaneously, Bhutan was also beginning to open up to foreign ideas and influence although it would take another century to be swamped by globalizing trends. The country was just starting to creep out of isolation and have unprecedented exposure to the outside world, beyond the known world of the Buddhist Himalayas. The visits of King Ugyen Wangchuk and his royal team to Calcutta in 1906 and to Delhi in 1911 were two significant events in this respect. The Bhutanese leaders saw for themselves the cultures, economic conditions and technological advances of British India.

Another significant change the modern era saw was Bhutan's position in terms of political alignment and foreign relations. While relations and exchanges were primarily of a northward orientation in the past, Bhutan now increasingly looked southward to India as both a political ally and trading partner. This accorded well with Bhutan's south-facing geographical situation and the British policy to keep Bhutan as a stable buffer state between India and China. This southward political orientation initiated in King Ugyen Wangchuk's time would gradually develop into a very strong friendship between India and Bhutan many decades later. In contrast, Tibet was going through tough political challenges with increasing Chinese control as China pursued an aggressive policy to consolidate its grip on Tibet. By early 1910, 2000 Chinese troops entered Lhasa and the 13th Dalai Lama escaped to India. This would be repeated in 1959 with the full-scale invasion and occupation of Tibet by China, bringing Bhutan's northerly relations to a complete stop. Thus, the incipient socioeconomic and political steps taken during the reign of King Ugyen Wangchuk distinctly marked Bhutan's journey to modernity and the boundary between the pre-modern Medieval Period and the modern monarchial Bhutan.

King Ugyen Wangchuk's deeds and devotion

King Ugyen Wangchuk ruled for nearly twenty years as the first Druk Gyalpo or Dragon King. One of his first deeds as monarch was the amnesty he granted to all Bhutanese political and criminal fugitives who had sought refuge outside Bhutan. They were allowed to return to Bhutan and were given free land to settle. Some relatives of his former enemy, Aloo Dorji, were also restituted in this process and Bhutan's chapter of internal dissension among local magnates was now fully closed. Aloo Dorji himself passed away in Tibet and his body was brought to Bhutan but it was not allowed beyond Haa, where it was cremated and a stūpa built to hold his remains. The territories in western Bhutan, which were ceded to the rival chieftains after the 1886 war, were reinstated under state control. He also earnestly sought ways of increasing Bhutan's revenue for most of his ideas of development were stalled by lack of funds. Much of the taxes collected within the country were in commodities, as we shall see below, but some Rs 3,00,000 were received from Raja Ugyen Dorji around that time as tax in cash from southern districts and from sale of tea, timber, elephants, lac, etc. Apart from this, the annual British subsidy of Rs 50,000 was the only major cash revenue and King Ugyen Wangchuk was eager to ask for an increment.

In 1910, King Ugyen Wangchuk achieved this increment and took his relations with British India to a new level in yet another milestone in southerly relations. Since the Younghusband mission, the Chinese had returned to Tibet with renewed force and also claimed suzerainty over Bhutan. The Amban in Lhasa was reported as having said that 'Bhutan is the gate to the south to prevent entry (by the British).'[16] Even as early as 1890, the Amban in Lhasa proposed to the Emperor of China to appoint the Tongsa *pönlop* as the chieftain and the Paro *pönlop* as the vice-chieftain of Bhutan and the emperor approved this but these Chinese proceedings were merely their own rituals and had no real bearing on the situation in Bhutan as no one in Bhutan took notice of them and there were never any Chinese officials stationed in Bhutan. A seal and hat with an imitation coral button (the insignia of an official in second rank) and peacock's feather were sent to Bhutan, which the Bhutanese perhaps received out of politeness but they were locked away, were never used, and were eventually eaten by insects. In 1907, the Amban went beyond the symbolic suzerainty when he wrote to the Bhutanese leaders that 'the Bhutanese are the subjects of the Emperor of China, who is the Lord of Heaven'. He also sent Popon, the Chinese officer in the Chumbi valley to Paro with twenty soldiers 'to inspect climate, crops, etc.'[17] The Bhutanese reception was lukewarm and the officer met the Paro *pönlop* and the Thimphu *dzongpön* but the meeting was of no consequence to Bhutan. The Amban also wished Chinese currency to be accepted in Bhutan but this too was met with cold response.

In the light of the Chinese takeover of Tibet, which was partly of British making as they conceded Tibet to China in the successive Anglo-Chinese treaties, and the persistent Chinese overtures to Bhutan, the British were seriously worried about retaining Bhutan as a buffer zone. If Bhutan decided voluntarily to turn to China for help, there was nothing the British could do to stop it. If Bhutan did turn northward and the Chinese were allowed into Bhutan, it could have easily brought the mighty Chinese forces right up to the northeastern frontiers of British India. The new political officer in Sikkim, Charles Bell, who replaced White in 1908, now pursued a rigorous plan to stabilize the status quo and keep the Chinese out of Bhutan. While his precursor, White, only sought to retain Bhutan's allegiance with an increment in the annual subsidy and ask the rights for the British to intervene in the case of Bhutan's disputes with neighbouring countries, Bell proposed to his government that Bhutan should be persuaded to put its foreign relations under the British with the condition that the British would not interfere in Bhutan's internal affairs. This was his move to prevent any Chinese advance into Bhutan and the British government accepted the proposal.

With the intention to secure Bhutan's agreement to this, Charles Bell travelled to Bhutan with Captain Kennedy and Rs 1,00,000 in the beginning of 1910. His journey was hastened with a rumour that five Chinese spies were travelling ahead of his party. In reality, there was no Chinese spy or any serious Chinese threat to Bhutan. It was a figure of British imagination just like their fear of Russian presence in Tibet some years ago. Charles

Bell was warmly received with some pomp and ceremony in Punakha by the King and his council. Negotiations soon started with the few members of the council who were reluctant to sign the treaty and place the external relations of Bhutan under the British government. King Ugyen Wangchuk, it appears, was fully in favour of the British proposal. On 8 January 1910, the treaty of Punakha was signed and Bhutan agreed 'to be guided by the advice of the British Government in regard to its external relations'. We don't know how far King Ugyen Wangchuk and his council understood the political implications of this article in the treaty and also other panegyric letters of submission they wrote or statements they made to the British. But Charles Bell took this much further than the literal sense of words and declared: 'Thus, with the consent of all and with the blessing of its all-powerful priesthood, Bhutan was joined to the British Empire.'[18]

Generations of Bhutanese would deny that Bhutan ever was under the British empire and the British, on their part, also remained equally muddled about Bhutan's status. In their official administration, the British neither considered Bhutan to be under their rule nor gave Bhutan the kind of benefits received by princely states in the region. Today, it is not part of the Commonwealth of Nations. However, their general treatment of Bhutan was not very different from Indian princely states. In fact, even before Ugyen Wangchuk became King when he travelled to Calcutta in 1906, the British showed him the same reverence which they showed to a mid-level Indian prince with a salute of fifteen guns. He seems to have happily accepted this status and vaguely viewed Bhutan as one among the array of nations under the supreme British government.[19] King Ugyen Wangchuk had the wisdom to foresee that Bhutan's future lay with the British to the south and this move was particularly appreciated later when China made some concerted effort to claim control over Bhutan.

In 1911, King Ugyen Wangchuk travelled with thirteen officials of his court to Delhi to attend the durbar for the King-Emperor George V, whom he had earlier met in Calcutta as Prince of Wales. This was his second trip to India and by now Bhutan's alignment with British India was irrefutable. China persisted with its claims over Bhutan for a short while more and even sent a letter warning Bhutan that Chinese troops would be posted in Bhutan and they should not be resisted. The King forwarded the letter to Charles Bell and a sharp exchange ensued between Peking and the British, the former claiming Bhutan to be a vassal state paying annual tributes and the latter citing a considerable body of evidences to argue that China had no say whatsoever over Bhutan's politics. This was further supported by a copy of the Punakha treaty. The British deftly used China's shaky grounds for their control over Tibet. So long as Britain respected China's presence in Tibet, the British made it clear that Chinese interference in the state so remote from direct Chinese interest and clearly aligned with British India would not be tolerated. However, the dispute over Bhutan soon vanished as China saw the downfall of the Manchu rule in 1912, bringing an end to over 2000 years of its imperial rule and ushering in the new republican system. That same year, the Chinese troops were expelled from Lhasa after a successful Tibetan uprising and Chinese claims of suzerainty over Bhutan came to a perpetual end.

Meanwhile, Bhutan enjoyed peace and stability under King Ugyen Wangchuk. The new monarchial system gradually began to grow its roots although there were no concerted efforts made for any structural change. King Ugyen Wangchuk ran the country using the existent political and administrative structures from his base in Bumthang. Despite being crowned as King, he personally continued to play the role and use the seal of the Tongsa *pönlop*. The only stark change in domestic policy he made was perhaps the reduction of interest on loans from twenty-five per cent to twenty per cent per annum. State and monastic organizations which loaned out resources in cash and kind earlier charged one-fourth of the capital as interest but King Ugyen Wangchuk reduced this to one-fifth and paid the difference from his private treasury to make up for losses incurred by the state and monasteries through this change in interest rate. Despite his best intentions to improve, the mode of governance and tax structure and the harsh imposition on the people generally remained the same as before.

By now, a child from Domkhar Melong in Arunachal Pradesh, just outside of Bhutan's eastern border, had been recognized as the rebirth of Jigme Chögyal and therefore the 6th mind incarnation of Zhabdrung. This child, Jigme Dorji, was born in 1905 and brought to Punakha and installed on the golden throne in 1912.[20] This was the first time Bhutan had simultaneously at its helm the main Zhabdrung hierarch and a hereditary King. This was a potential recipe for political friction and a serious rupture did develop some decades later. But at that time, the appearance of the new Zhabdrung incarnation did not alter the political power structure or undermine King Ugyen Wangchuk's new position. If anything, King Ugyen Wangchuk seems to have happily endorsed the candidate and resumed the amiable relationship he had with the former incarnation Jigme Chögyal. The infant incarnation, as a sign of memory of his past life, is said to have even reminded the King of the pledge the King had made to offer a bull to the previous incarnation. This was now happily granted by the King to the new incarnation.[21]

King Ugyen Wangchuk had many plans for Bhutan's development but most of them did not actualize, mainly due to lack of funds. His most effective initiative of development was perhaps the foundation he laid down for modern education in Bhutan. Group education was until then imparted only in religious centres such as monasteries and accessible almost only to priests. Others who had education, especially the children of elites, received their education through tutorials at home. King Ugyen Wangchuk introduced school education by starting a small school in Bumthang, which was attended by Prince Jigme Wangchuk and some fourteen other students. Beside *chökey* or classical Tibetan, the children were taught Hindi and even some English by Ugyen Dorji, who had by then been given the title of Rāja by the British for his services to them and appointed to the office of *gongzim* or chamberlain to the King by King Ugyen Wangchuk.

Gongzim Ugyen Dorji became instrumental in establishing another school in Haa around 1912–13, with the help of Mr Sunderland of the Church of Scotland Mission in Kalimpong. The school was attended by some forty-six students, who initially spent their summer in Haa and travelled to Kalimpong for six months in the winter. Many of these students had by then already started their education in Kalimpong and one Do Thinle was perhaps the first Bhutanese to matriculate in 1923 followed by five others the following year.[22] One of them reminisced that when they met King Ugyen Wangchuk, the old King with flowing white beard, 'advised them to study hard to serve Bhutan and not to disgrace the nation with their bad behaviour'.[23] This typical affectionate Bhutanese advice did its work as many of these pioneers in modern education returned to start various professions. In the subsequent decades, hundreds of Bhutanese youth would follow their footsteps to study in Kalimpong and Darjeeling.

The two schools in Bumthang and Haa opened during King Ugyen Wangchuk's reign continued in the following decades but it would take another half a century for Bhutan to see the nationwide implementation of the school education programme. King Ugyen Wangchuk also wished to train Bhutanese in biomedicine, forestry, agriculture, animal husbandry and introduce mining and industries but most of these wishes did not realize in his lifetime.[24] The main stumbling block to advancement, as White noted,[25] was lack of funds. King Ugyen Wangchuk hoped to raise funds from the Government of India through the help of successive British political officers in Sikkim and about a dozen British visitors who toured Bhutan during his reign. But their requests for funding fell on deaf ears in Delhi and London, partly because Britain faced severe constraints on its resources as it was then fighting the First World War. On the contrary, King Ugyen Wangchuk toured his country to raise funds to help Britain during war times and contributed Rs 100,000 to the Indian Relief Fund.

The funding King Ugyen Wangchuk hoped to obtain from the British was not forthcoming even after the war was over. He and the new Sikkim political officer F.M. Bailey made a request in 1921 to the Government of India to raise the subsidy, as the value of the subsidy was by now much less than it was before the war, but this request was also rejected.[26] The British, however, accepted funding the training of three prospective teachers, two doctors, two veterinary assistants, four forest rangers and three boys in agriculture and dairy farming and one each in weaving, tanning, mining, engineering and civil engineering, from among the Bhutanese school boys.[27] King Ugyen Wangchuk himself was further adorned with the titles of Knight Commandership of the Order of the Star of India in 1911 and again the Grand Cross of the Indian Empire in 1922.

King Ugyen Wangchuk's pursuit of modernization was matched by his commitment to traditional education. We have already seen how early in his rule, he sent several young Bhutanese northward to Tibet to undertake advanced Buddhist studies. These students returned to Bhutan after finishing their studies, mainly in the great monastic centre of Drepung, and played important roles in Bhutan. King Ugyen Wangchuk sent another batch of students to study in Śrīsiṃha college at Dzogchen in the Kham region of eastern Tibet. These monks would also later return as learned Buddhist scholars to regenerate Buddhist scholarship in Bhutan.

A hallmark of King Ugyen Wangchuk was his spiritual devotion, which he showed through both patronage of religious masters and personal practice. A deeply religious man, King Ugyen Wangchuk sent regular offerings to leading Buddhist figures in Tibet including the 15th Karmapa Khachab Dorji, whom he regarded as his spiritual guru. He despatched each month an envoy to offer butter lamps in Jokhang and Ramoche temples in Lhasa on new moon and full moon days. When Togden Śakyaśrī renovated the Swayambhunath temple in Kathmandu, King Ugyen Wangchuk also sent an envoy with a total donation of Rs 70,000. His patronage of religious lamas and institutions extended as far as the famous monasteries of Dzogchen, Palpung, Zurmang, Dzigar, etc. in eastern Tibet.

King Ugyen Wangchuk carried out even more intensive religious patronage at home. In addition to the renovation of many temples, he established the annual religious ceremonies of *soldeb bumde* (གསོལ་འདེབས་ འབུམ་སྡེ་) in Kurjey and *lhenkye dungjur* (ལྷན་སྐྱེས་དུང་ཕྱུར་) in Punakha and made an extensive offering of cash to the state monks. Among the leading spiritual figures presiding over King Ugyen Wangchuk's religious ceremonies was Serkong Ngawang Tshultrim Donden (1856–1918), one of his main gurus. Like Jigme Namgyal's guru, Jangchub Tsondru, Serkong was a revered Gelugpa master with a special interest in the Nyingma tradition. During his time in Kurjey, this master composed several religious liturgies and performed various services at the behest of King Ugyen Wangchuk. Curiously, he also had a vision of Zhabdrung, who in the vision indicated that Ugyen Wangchuk was his outstanding patron and was destined to be reborn in Shambala.

King Ugyen Wangchuk was, as some of his followers intimated to White, more than a lama. His devotion became his main occupation in the latter part of his life. He spent a great deal of his time in seclusion, first, in a small hermitage above Lamai Gönpa and, later, in his new residence of Thinley Rabten, which was built in the vicinity of the holy site of Jampa Lhakhang. With only one or two attendants, he spent much of his time in deep prayers in these places, partly in order to expiate the violence he committed in his youth. Almost all affairs of state were delegated to his family members and subordinates, whose faithful support he enjoyed. Among them, his eldest daughter, Peldon, acted as the *de facto* Tongsa *pönlop* during some years of King Ugyen Wangchuk's hermetic life.

Despite his zest for spirituality, the devout monarch was not on good terms with all spiritual figures of his time. We have already seen how the relationship between the new King and the speech incarnation Yeshey Ngodup was not very cordial in the initial years of the monarchy. The rupture aggravated towards the end of Yeshe Ngodup's life and King Ugyen Wangchuk is said to have even officially banned the recognition of the next speech incarnation. Whether or not the ban was strictly implemented, Yeshey Ngodup returned two years later in 1919 in the person of Jigme Tenzin, a grandson of Yeshey Ngodup's niece and nephew of Zhabdrung Jigme Dorji. Jigme Tenzin was recognized as the reincarnation of Yeshe Ngodup and formally installed as the 6th Chogley incarnation by some members of the clergy in 1923 but King Ugyen Wangchuk seems to have not approved this recognition. He and the incarnation perhaps never met and, as we shall see later, Jigme Tenzin spent much of his short life away from the capitals and out of royal favour.

Another spiritual figure, who ran into problems with King Ugyen Wangchuk's court, was Khachab Namkha Dorji, the incarnate lama of Buli in Bumthang. Although the accounts of the dispute are fuzzy, the lama's brother Sangay Thinley, who served King Ugyen Wangchuk as a courtier, seems to be the main reason for the problem. Sangay Thinley, it was alleged, was attempting to assassinate the King under the influence of a malevolent local spirit. As punishment for this treacherous act, the family was banished from their home in Bumthang and three sons of the family were said to have been killed by the troops of Wangdichöling in the process of expulsion. This is the only case of a serious dissent and intrigue against King Ugyen Wangchuk we come across after he became King. Yet, we have no details to confirm what actually led to the intrigue, the death of three brothers of Buli Lama's family and the family's banishment.

Another version of oral accounts gives a more human cause for the conflict. In a typical cross-cousin marriage, King Ugyen Wangchuk's eldest daughter, Peldon, was betrothed to his nephew, Dorji, the son of Ugyen Wangchuk's sister, Choden.[28] Their liaison resulted in one son, Tshering Peljor, who later became the Paro *pönlop* but the marriage went sour after a while and Peldon started an affair with Sangay Thinley of Buli. This angered Dorji and his mother in Wangdichöling and led to the expulsion of Sangay Thinley's family from Bumthang. According to this version, it was the King's sister, Choden, and the Wangdichöling house, who were chiefly responsible for the expulsion and death of members of Buli Lama's family.

The elimination of Sangay Thinley, however, failed to mend the royal marriage. When the marriage with Peldon failed, King Ugyen Wangchuk sent Yangzom, the second daughter from his first wife, to be the wife of Dorji and to fill the marital gap left by the first daughter. Yangzom arrived in Wangdichöling when Dorji was making invocations to a local spirit. 'I am a princess; I do not want to become a shaman's wife,' she is said to have remarked when she saw him.[29] She returned to her home in Lamai Gönpa and refused to marry her cousin, Dorji. Her father, King Ugyen Wangchuk, did not take her refusal lightly and confined her to the central tower of Lamai Gönpa, where she fostered her spiritual leanings. While her sister, Peldon, played an active administrative role, Yangzom was strongly inclined to a religious life, like her father. Later, she started a new relationship, which resulted in a son, but this also did not receive the much needed royal blessing.

Apart from the lone intrigue with the Buli Lama's family and marital problems at home, King Ugyen Wangchuk's last years of rule from Bumthang were generally peaceful and quiet. As more and more people close to him passed away, he became increasingly immersed in spiritual practice. His most faithful officer, Raja Ugyen Dorji, had passed away in 1916 leaving behind the modern educated and able son, Sonam Tobgay, whom he appointed as the *drungpa* of Haa. The British also accorded the title of Rāja to Sonam Tobgay and passed him his father's post of British agent. In 1918, King Ugyen Wangchuk's slightly troublesome cousin, Dawa Peljor, the *pönlop* of Paro also passed away and the King's grandson, Tshering Peljor, was then appointed as the new *pönlop* of Paro. Tshering Peljor was the son of King Ugyen Wangchuk's daughter, Peldron, and his sister's son, Dorji. The appointment was made partly to quell the power struggles between the different branches of his family.

By now, the royal household was vaguely divided into at least three groups. King Ugyen Wangchuk's two daughters from the first wife took over the Lamai Gönpa palace while his sister, Choden, and her children took ownership of the Wangdichöling palace. These two establishments, often known as Pelri and Wangling respectively, began to have their own estates, serfs and appanages. The King lived in the modest residence of Thinley Rabten with his own private resources. The Pelri and Wangling establishments were no doubt very close and in order to reinforce the familial solidarity, King Ugyen Wangchuk's daughter was betrothed to his sister's son, Dorji. Until the birth of Jigme Wangchuk in 1905, King Ugyen Wangchuk even considered passing down the hereditary line through Dorji, his nephew and son-in-law, and Dorji seems to have also seriously harboured the hope of inheriting the throne. Unfortunately, for Dorji, the marriage failed and with the birth of Jigme Wangchuk, his hope of inheriting the throne was dashed. For some reason, he also fell of out the King's favour for a while. The appointment of his son, Tshering Peljor, was certainly a move on King Ugyen Wangchuk's part to reassure his nephew and his sister, Choden, who had now risen to be a powerful woman in Bumthang.

In April 1922, King Ugyen Wangchuk suffered another serious loss with the death of his 2nd Queen, Tsondru Lhamo. She passed away in Yungdrung Chöling, the winter palace in the Mangde district, and her body was brought to Bumthang for cremation. Extensive funerary ceremonies were carried out, which exhausted the King's private resources. The King expected his daughter, Peldon, of the Pelri house to come to his rescue but her help was not forthcoming. Instead, his nephew, Dorji, who had temporarily fallen out of favour, promptly delivered the requisites from his Wangdichöling treasury.

This service to the King in the hour of need helped Dorji revive his close relationship with the King. While the funerary services were in progress, King Ugyen Wangchuk received news that one of his important gurus, probably the 5th Karmapa Khachab Dorji, passed away in Tibet. Due to this, the cremation of Tsondru Lhamo was postponed and when F.M. Bailey and his team arrived in Bumthang on 22 July 1922 to offer King Ugyen Wangchuk the insignia of the Grand Cross of the Indian Empire, the King was still in mourning and with the body of his Queen.

The British honour came at a sad time for King Ugyen Wangchuk. In the previous year, Lord Ronaldshay planned to offer the insignia during his visit to Bhutan but failed to do so due to an epidemic. Now, the King was mourning the demise of his Queen and his guru. Nevertheless, an investiture for presenting the insignia took place with F.M. Bailey as the British representative in the large temple of Kurjey, which King Ugyen Wangchuk had built some decades ago. The procedures were more or less the same as the ceremony for the KCIE in Punakha in 1905; the only notable difference was the performance of mask dances at the end of the ceremony. After the investiture, the British team left Bumthang for Gyantse in Tibet over the Monlakarchung Pass. This was the last meeting between King Ugyen Wangchuk and F.M. Bailey, who strongly supported the King's proposals for modernization and development and in whom the King put his trust for support to ensure the continuity of the hereditary line after his death. Bailey visited Bhutan again in 1924 as far as Punakha to attend the formal appointment of Sonam Tobgay as the *drungpa* of Haa.

King Ugyen Wangchuk's health took a downturn after the death of his Queen. Rituals and prayers were conducted for his health and long life but he knew his death was approaching and began to prepare for it. When his courtiers insisted that he should live many more years and no stone should be left unturned to do so, he is said to have replied: 'I am a sinful King. I have no control over living and dying. Even if I live one more night, I may only accumulate negative actions proportionate to the time.'[30] On 21 August 1926, King Ugyen Wangchuk passed away in Thinley Rabten on the lap of his eldest son, Jigme Wangchuk. The medical cause of his death is said to be a problem of bile. However, people in Mangde narrate an account that the fatal illness was triggered by the malevolent spirit of the forest facing the King's winter residence of Yungdrung Chöling. The King ordered his courtiers to clear the forests to make fields and this allegedly angered the local spirit, who took the form of a bee and avenged the King with a fatal sting.[31]

His death, like his life, was marked by spirituality. At the time of his death, there were many signs of his spiritual achievement. Following his personal wish, his body was kept in Bumthang to be cremated near the holy shrine of Kurjey and an extensive and long programme of funerary rites began in earnest led by many important lamas. However, King Ugyen Wangchuk's demise left Bhutan's young monarchy with a slight uncertainty. Although almost all eyes now turned to his eldest son, Jigme Wangchuk, as the rightful heir, the Wangdichöling family of his sister, Choden, was very strong and both his nephew, Dorji, and grandson, Tshering Peljor, might have entertained hopes of inheriting the throne. Dorji most likely had such hope until Jigme Wangchuk was born. Tshering Peljor, who was the Paro *pönlop*, even wore the raven crown in official meetings with his guests. The judicious King knew the potential dangers posed to the security of the country and the burgeoning monarchy by both external threats from China and internal contention among rivals in the family.[32] He thus tried to secure British support for his son, Jigme Wangchuk, and also prepared him for any eventuality. Indeed, the relations between Jigme Wangchuk and Dorji were at a low point when King Ugyen Wangchuk passed away. To avoid any internecine contention, Jigme Wangchuk, through the support of Sonam Tobgay, now made haste to assume the hereditary title of the King. He postponed his father's cremation and journeyed to Punakha in the beginning of 1927 to be crowned as the 2nd Druk Gyalpo. It is to his story and reign that we shall turn now.

The reign of Jigme Wangchuk

Jigme Wangchuk was born to King Ugyen Wangchuk's second wife, Tsondru Lhamo, in 1905 in the royal residence of Thinley Rabten. Tsondru Lhamo gave birth to four sons (Chag Dorji, Jigme Wangchuk, Jigme Dorji[33] and Jigme Lhendup[34]) and one daughter (Konchö Wangmo) but the first son died at birth. We may recall that after the death of his first Queen, King Ugyen Wangchuk's court officials and priests made arrangements for him to marry again in order to beget a male heir. The most active agent who facilitated this liaison was the monk scholar Mindu of Dur, who King Ugyen Wangchuk earlier sent to Tibet for advanced Buddhist education while he was the Tongsa *pönlop*. The monk scholar died soon after Ugyen Wangchuk married Tsondru Lhamo and when Jigme Wangchuk was born in 1905, it was widely believed that the child was an immediate rebirth of Mindu. Thus, the King even sponsored the renovation of the parental home of late Mindu in Dur.[35]

The 2nd Druk Gyalpo Jigme Wangchuk was an avid archer.

Prince Jigme Wangchuk got his initial instruction in literacy from a personal tutor. When he was nine years old, Jigme Wangchuk attended the new school in Wangdichöling with some fourteen friends. In this school, he also learnt Hindi and some English under the two teachers: Norbu, who was appointed as the Bhutanese agent in Pasakha, and Phentok from Sikkim. The most notable outcome of this school education was Jigme Wangchuk's ability to communicate with his Indian and British counterparts directly in Hindi, a skill which would come handy in the years to come. In addition, he also received religious teachings and instructions from numerous religious masters and became well versed in monastic rituals.

However, his main education was the traditional upbringing and grooming he had, like his father before him, by going through the rigours of court life starting at the lowest rung and waiting on his father. By thirteen, he was appointed as chief of protocol in Tongsa under his father King Ugyen Wangchuk, who still held the office of the Tongsa *pönlop*. In this capacity, he was primarily responsible for the management of the appointments visitors sought with his father. Some time in 1923, at the age of eighteen, Jigme Wangchuk was formally promoted to position of the Tongsa *pönlop*. In the same year, his nephew and first cousin once removed, Tshering Peljor, was also appointed as the Paro *pönlop*.

It was around this time that an internecine marital alliance was again made to reinforce kinship ties and consolidate family relations. Jigme Wangchuk was married to Phuntsho Choden, the fourteen-year-old daughter of his first cousin, Demchö, who in turn was a daughter of his aunt, Choden. This was an unusual nuptial practice even by the local norms of cross-cousin marriage. According to local concepts of kinship, her mother, as a direct cross-cousin, would have been the appropriate candidate for Jigme Wangchuk and Phuntsho Choden would be his niece. However, this marriage enhanced the familial relationship both within the royal branches and with other leading families. Phuntsho Choden's father was Jamyang, a scion of a family in Ura and the *zhelngo* family of Prakhar which descend from one of the sons of Pema Lingpa.[36]

By the time Jigme Wangchuk became the Tongsa *pönlop* and married Phuntsho Choden, King Ugyen Wangchuk was seriously preparing for a smooth succession of hereditary kingship. It seems he had even thought of abdicating the throne as soon as Jigme Wangchuk was ready to take over the reins.[37] By doing so, King Ugyen Wangchuk would have ensured the safe passage of the throne to his son and quelled any ambition to become the King, which his grandson, Tshering Peljor, may have had with support from his (Tshering Peljor's) father, Dorji. However, King Ugyen Wangchuk's health failed before he could see this through and he passed away in 1926. Before his death, King Ugyen Wangchuk had successfully liaised with the British and his representative Sonam Tobgay to secure their backing for Jigme Wangchuk. It was thus with their support and with some urgency that Jigme Wangchuk now made plans to ascend the throne even before the remains of his father were cremated and the funerary rites completed.

Jigme Wangchuk and his entourage travelled to Punakha in the early part of 1927 bearing gifts for the State Monk Body, which included a copy of the Buddhist *kanjur* (བཀའ་འགྱུར) and *tanjur* (བསྟན་འགྱུར) canons, sets of silk costumes for mask dances and a *mithun* bull. On 14 March 1927, Jigme Wangchuk was formally installed as the 2nd Druk Gyalpo or Dragon King in Punakha in the presence of Jigme Dorji, the 6th mind incarnation of Zhabdrung, Sizhi Namgyal, the 58th Je Khenpo and almost all leading dignitaries of Bhutan. His cousin and brother-in-law, Dorji, was conspicuously absent but Dorji's son, Tshering Peljor, attended the coronation. The British representatives were led by F.M. Bailey, who also presented on that occasion the insignia of Companion of the Indian Empire to the new King. Bailey noted about the coronation: 'The fact that the Paro Pönlop's father did not attend the ceremony of installation points, I think, to his dislike of the present position and it is always possible that he himself or the Paro Pönlop under his instigation may give trouble. One of the chief factors likely to prevent this is the fact that they have very few arms.'[38] Indeed, the King had a significant collection of firearms in possession to resist any rebellion.

It is difficult to say if the British accounts of brewing tension between King Jigme Wangchuk and his cousin are accurate or exaggerated but with successful completion of the coronation, Jigme Wangchuk became the undisputed ruler of Bhutan. The hereditary monarchial system, which failed to take off in the seventeenth century, was now in full swing and with the issue of succession fully resolved, King Jigme Wangchuk turned his attention to the extensive funerary ceremonies he carried out for his late father. As part of his offering, he built a copper turret on the central tower of Punakha and gilded this and all statues in the Punakha *dzong* with gold. Offerings were also sent to all monastic establishments and temples in Bhutan and the Jokhang temple in Lhasa, where a new butterlamp chalice made of gold (the largest one in this temple at that time) was also donated. Finally, the cremation of the remains was held on the grounds of the Kurjey temple in Bumthang with many high lamas conducting the rituals and prayers.

The new King took the opportunity of the British presence at the coronation to reinforce the close relationship which existed between his father and British India. Both in Punakha and in Dewathang in the following year, he resumed the discussion with Bailey about Bhutan's development, which his father had pursued, and made further requests for British support. King Jigme Wangchuk could now conduct these discussions directly with his counterparts in Hindi and also had the unflagging assistance of Sonam Tobgay in these endeavours, just as his father had the assistance of the latter's father. King Jigme Wangchuk also enthusiastically continued the southward orientation of Bhutan's diplomatic association, which his father had developed since the beginning of the century. The British were only too happy to continue the existent political connections and to see a strong government in Bhutan for the sake of stability in their own Bengal and Assam frontiers. They also kept a close watch over the strained relations between King Jigme Wangchuk and his cousin, Dorji and his nephew, Tshering Peljor, who was the Paro *pönlop*, but the relationships improved and all fears of disputes over succession disappeared soon after the coronation.

In 1928, in course of the meeting in Dewathang, King Jigme Wangchuk was taken to Gauhati, where he 'for the first time, saw a motor car, a train, a river steamer and machinery of various kinds in which he took great interest'.[39] In the same year, Phuntsho Choden gave birth to a son in Trhuepang while the royal couple was living in Tongsa. In fact, this was her second child and the only one who survived. The first one was a daughter who died soon after birth causing much grief to the Queen.[40] The birth of Jigme Dorji Wangchuk in 1928 further secured the hereditary line of succession and the news was greeted with jubilant celebrations. In the following year, the King built the new palace of Kuenga Rabten in a place half-way between the Tongsa *dzong* and the Yungdrung Chöling palace built by his father. The spot was earlier given to his granduncle, Dungkhar Gyaltshen, when the latter was forced to resign after Pema Tenzin defeated him in their contest for the post of the Tongsa *pönlop*. The Queen's father took charge of designing and supervising the construction, which was undertaken by the King's officers and courtiers. The *dzong* became the main winter residence of the King throughout his reign.

King Jigme Wangchuk's married life took another turn in 1932. Although the royal couple had successfully produced a male heir, the King took the

Queen's younger sister, Pema Dechen, as his 2nd Queen. Such polygamous relationships, particularly with sisters, was common in the country, especially if the economy of the family permitted. Moreover, the new relationship was probably encouraged for socioeconomic purposes of reinforcing the closely knit family connections and retaining all property in the family. Following the matrilineal customs of the area, Pema Dechen in fact later inherited the palace of Wangdichöling from her grandmother, Choden, and this palace became the main summer seat of King Jigme Wangchuk's government. The union of the king and 2nd Queen resulted in the birth of four children: son Namgyel Wangchuk in 1943 and daughters Chökyi in 1937, Deki Yangzom in 1944 and Pema Choden in 1949.

As the 2nd Queen's family grew in Wangdichöling, the King built a separate summer palace for the senior Queen in Domkhar in 1937. The palace was built on the site of an earlier manor house, which the senior Queen used as her residence. It was named Tashichöling. Similarly, in the early 1930s, the King built the palace of Samdrupchöling as a winter residence for the 2nd Queen when the court spent its time in Mangde region. These *dzong* structures, including Wangdichöling, initially built by Jigme Namgyal, Lamai Gönpa and Yungdrung Chöling built during the time of the 1st King, Kuenga Rabten, Tashichöling and Samdrupchöling built by the 2nd King make up a new class of palace architecture. Unlike the *dzong*s built by Zhabdrung and his coterie in the seventeenth century as monastic fortresses, these late nineteenth- and twentieth-century *dzong*s were mainly constructed as royal residences. The seventeenth-century *dzong*s drew significantly on Tibetan forts and were designed with the dual purpose of being religious centres and fortified strongholds. Externally, they were designed to repel Tibetan invasions and internally they contained the space for intensive religious and monastic activity. Thus, the architectural style clearly reflected the existent utility of built space and the prevailing sociopolitical conditions at the time of their construction.

The new generation of *dzong*s built in the late nineteenth and early twentieth centuries drew largely on the local architectural tradition in their heavy use of timber and aesthetic designs. As they were mostly built by secular rulers at peace times, they contained much less space for religious activity and also had meagre fortification. Their primary function was as royal residences and quasi-administrative centres. The restriction of entry imposed on women after dusk for medieval *dzong*s did not apply to these new *dzong*s, in which the royal women played vital roles. Following the ancient transhumance pattern, King Jigme Wangchuk's court moved between Bumthang and Mangde districts staying in these various *dzong*s. No doubt, the migration resembled the movement of the state monks and the court between Thimphu and Punakha. The main difference was that the procession of people between Thimphu and Punakha was mainly monastic while the files moving between Bumthang and Mangde were composed of lay officials and porters.

In addition to the construction of new residential *dzong*s, King Jigme Wangchuk's reign also saw the restoration of the Tongsa *dzong* in 1930, the Tashigang *dzong* in 1936 and the Wangdiphodrang *dzong* in 1948. The King also commissioned the renovation and refurbishment of many temples, including Kurjey in Bumthang and Chitokha and Gogona in the Shar valley. Like his father and grandfather before him, he built a new shrine in the Tongsa *dzong* dedicated to the bull-headed deity Bhairava or Jigje (འཇིགས་བྱེད). The temple contains exquisite examples of wood carvings done by the master carver, Pap Yozer. King Jigme Wangchuk also commissioned the production of printing blocks, religious paintings and various other religious artefacts. He was a staunch patron of many cultural and educational projects, including the promotion of dances and revival of certain lost religious transmissions.

During his reign, the Tibetan lama Dzigar Chogtrul was invited to give teachings in Tongsa to a gathering of Bhutanese monks and the great scholar Minyak Chorpön to teach in Phajoding. He also sponsored a major religious sermon in Punakha, delivered by the 56th Je Khenpo Ngawang Thinley. His reign also saw the foundation of the scholastic colleges of Tharpaling and Nyimalung under the learned masters, Tenpa Rinchen and Doring Trulku respectively. Like his father, King Jigme Wangchuk also sent young Bhutanese students to pursue advanced studies in Tibet. This time, the four bright monks selected from Tongsa travelled to eastern Tibet to study under Khenpo Chogsel of Zurmang.

The school education programme, which started in Bumthang and Haa during his father's reign, now expanded with new schools in Paro, Wangdiphodrang and Tashigang. The first two schools in Bumthang and Haa were making very good progress and some of the students who received education in Haa and Kalimpong became teachers for the new schools. Similarly, King Jigme Wangchuk initiated the efforts to introduce biomedical services in the country by conducting vaccinations and dispensing medicines. The first Bhutanese who finished his medical training in India began practising in the country by 1932. In addition, a series of British medical officers, who visited the country during his reign, gave medical treatment to the people. They reported widespread cases of venereal diseases and the problem of goitre. Unfortunately, there was no fund to even defray the costs of a medical campaign against syphilis, let alone set up a proper medical system.

The King also took the initiative to build motor roads from India to Bhutan and set up wireless stations. He initiated the cultivation of cash crops in southern Bhutan and also tried growing rice in Bumthang. Generally, he laid the foundations for much of the development activities which took off in the second half of the twentieth century during the time of his son and grandson. The seeds of development which he sowed fully ripened only decades after his death, mainly due to the lack of funds and human resources in his days. Like his father, King Jigme Wangchuk was encumbered by the lack of funds to carry out his brilliant ideas of development. Since his coronation, he made repeated appeals to the Government of India to raise the subsidy but, despite the strong support from the successive political officers in Sikkim, he failed to gain an increase until 1942, when an increment of Rs 1,00,000 was granted. Funds were particularly needed for building the human capacity. When Basil Gould (later Sir Basil) visited Bhutan in 1938, the only people who received decent training outside the country were Gongzim Sonam Tobgay, one medical doctor, two veterinary surgeons, two schoolmasters, three forest rangers, one trained in mining and two in tannery.

King Jigme Wangchuk was a farsighted and savvy leader. Gould described him as 'a man of entire openness and honesty of mind and naturally inclined to seek good of his people.' He maintained a high level of order and decorum in his court. According to Gould, he had 'the gifts, as had his father, of picking out good men and sticking to them and their families.' Gould further noted: 'He treats them in a manner which gives them confidence and inspires loyalty . . . He talks freely with men and women of every class.'[41] King Jigme Wangchuk also liked to keep abreast with affairs of the world. He listened to radio regularly and engaged in intelligent conversations with his political companions. The King loved horses and enjoyed music. He even gave a solo at a singsong during an official dinner for Gould. He was an enthusiastic sportsman and has tried his hand even at golf during his sojourn in Calcutta. It was, however, archery, Bhutan national game, which was his best pastime. Karma Ura writes about his indulgence in archery:

Archery continued for about twenty days or so at a stretch. As the days wore on, they took a toll on the vigour of the players. Bow strings snapped and arrow shafts split down the middle. Players got sore bodies and black faces. They suffered from headaches and thirstiness due to the solar radiation striking from their heads over which—in keeping with etiquette— they did not wear hats. Blisters popped on the index, middle and ring fingers of the players . . . His Majesty himself was far from exhausted because he sat on a chair in the shade between bouts of shooting his arrows, and was plied on a rickshaw across the archery ground. When they were into the third week of the game, the players collected about four hundred betams amongst themselves, and with this offering, begged His Majesty to end the game for the time being. The Elder Queen often interceded on behalf of the players to bring an end to the prolonged game.[42]

The weight of the golden yoke

King Jigme Wangchuk initiated numerous cultural, educational and development projects. However, these were neither his most significant programmes nor his main contribution to country. Perhaps, his most important initiative was his programme of tax revision and his most lasting legacy Bhutan's sovereignty and national security at a time of serious political unrest and change in the region. Following his father's wish, King Jigme Wangchuk undertook a nationwide study and revision of tax structures which had continued since medieval times. The existent tax schemes were neither properly regulated nor just and equitable. In some areas, the existent tax impositions were oppressive to the extent that people fled from the country or moved to secluded places beyond the reach of the taxman. Yet, some people paid no taxes whatsoever and taxes differed significantly even between neighbouring districts with similar produces. The rulers and officialdom generally thrived on such an extractive and exploitative tax system. It is beyond the scope of this book to discuss ancient taxation schemes and their revisions in any detail. Readers can find some discussion of taxes elsewhere.[43]

The country was very broadly made up of three social classes of people. In the top stratum of the ancient feudal system were the political and religious elites, including the families related to the King. This class would generally include richly landed nobilities and gentries such as the families of *lama* (བྱ་མ་), *chöje* (ཆོས་རྗེ), *zhalngo* (ཞལ་ངོ), *khoche* (ཁོ་ཆེ), *pönchen* (དཔོན་ཆེན), *tsögan* (གཙོ་རྒན), *gup* (རྒེད་པོ) and *chukpo* (ཕྱུག་པོ). They normally owned large tracts of land for agriculture and pasture and often had some landless tenants and servants who worked for them on their land. The defining feature of this class was the family lineage (either male bone or female bloodline) and not so much material wealth. Thus, familial descent was the deciding factor for nuptial ties in this class, over and above political and economic considerations. Within the class, one could find very powerful and rich families such as those of Pelri/ Lamai Gönpa and Wangdichöling headed by the King's cousins as well as poor religious nobilities with very little wealth. The families of Lamai Gönpa and Wangdichöling did not have to pay regular taxes but instead had many appanages paying taxes to them in return for the protection they provided. Most nobilities paid taxes to the government or King but some of them were exempted by the King. Furthermore, some were even allowed to collect and keep the government's share of tax from certain areas.

Below them were the normal tax-paying households known as *trhepa* (ཁྲལ་པ་), who owned land and paid taxes to the government. Their status was mainly defined by their social and legal status as government tax-payers and their economic assets. As there was often very sparse difference between the upper rung of this middle class and the lower rung of the top class, the class boundaries faded in some cases allowing for social mobility between them. Some families in this class who could not pay full household tax often formed independent but downgraded subsidiary units called *zurpa* (ཟུར་པ་), which were not liable to pay full taxes. There were also many tax-paying families from eastern Bhutan, who paid their taxes to the families such as that of Pelri or Lamai Gönpa and Wangdichöling instead of the government. They were known as *srungma* (སྲུང་མ་) or protected appanages of these powerful houses. Such protection from a powerful house was useful at that time, as the state officials often exercised power at free will when they visited places away from the court.

In the lowest stratum were landless people made up of the two groups of *drap* (གྲཔ་) and *zap* (ཟཔ་). The first group originated in the circle of monks or lay priests who followed and camped around respected religious figures, such as a *lam* or *chöje*. They lived independently on a plot provided by the religious master, received teachings from him and spent some time serving and working for the master. Sometimes, the same arrangement was also adopted by non-religious families, who attracted landless dependents around them. The *zap* group, which is also known by other names such as *nangzen* (ནང་ཟན་), *jow* (ཇོཝ་) and *khyö* (ཁྱོལ་), lived mostly as in-house bonded labourers of the top class of people although the allocation of labour and benefits differed from place to place. The *zap* themselves or their ancestors were mostly people kidnapped from Tibet and India or bought in slave trades. Occasionally, people of other social groups are turned into a *zap* as a punishment. This bottom layer of people did not normally have to pay any taxes to the government or powerful houses but served their immediate feudal lords.

The items of taxes imposed on the citizens were mainly of two types: commodity and labour. Taxation in cash, understandably, was not a major component of the tax scheme in central and northern parts of Bhutan although it is clear to us from the accounts of medieval Bhutan that coinage was common in Bhutan. Some kind of silver coins was in circulation as early as the fourteenth century and coins minted in Cooch Behar were probably used in Bhutan by the sixteenth century.[44] We have seen in the previous chapters how coins were in wide currency in the eighteenth and nineteenth centuries. By the nineteenth century, coins were also made in Bhutan using local mints. The biography of the 13th Desi Sherab Wangchuk, which gives us a clear idea of coin usage in Bhutan in the eighteenth century, also suggests that there were many households paying tax in cash if we understand the medieval terms correctly.[45] Taxpayers, in this biography, are divided based on two kinds of taxes they paid: *löntrhel* (ལོན་ཁྲལ་) and *kamtrhel* (སྐམ་ཁྲལ་), which are understood to be commodity tax and cash tax respectively.

In the first half of the twentieth century, the major cash taxes were collected by Gongzim Sonam Tobgay from new settlers along southern foothills. Taxes in kind were imposed on all basic household items and village products including cereals like paddy, wheat, buckwheat, barley and maize, meat of various kinds, mustard oil, butter, textiles, paper, ash, soot, lac, dyes, firewood, timber, singles, gunpowder, iron, fodder, baskets, mats, ropes, leather and pelts. The estimate provided by Karma Ura after analysing a tax document from Kurtoe gives us a clear picture of the severity:

> The most conservative estimate of the important in-kind taxes paid by a typical tax paying household per year could be as follows: three hundred eighty five je (462kg) of paddy; 34 sangs (28kg) of butter; 120 pairs of wooden singles; 7 boobs [sets] of textiles; sixty baskets; 10 joey [= 6.66 kg] of bark for paper; 10 joey of ash; 1000 joey of paddy straw; 300 joey of dry grass; one je of mustard; 5 je of dry chillies and 5 jams of dry sliced pumpkins.[46]

Not all places paid the same tax as the commodity taxes were imposed in accordance with what the area produced. Thus, artefacts such as bamboo mats and baskets were collected as tax from Kurtoe while yak meat was collected from communities rearing yak. Even within one district, the Ura valley had to pay butter tax while Tang paid grains for the great Soldeb Bumde prayers, which King Ugyen Wangchuk started in Kurjey.

There were serious inconsistencies in the tax structure. For instance, people in Bumthang paid two kinds of cereal tax: the standard *wangyon* tax unrelated to landholdings and *thojab*, which was correlated to landholdings. *Wangyon* perhaps went back to the fees collected by the religious officials in the early days of Bhutan's nationhood while *thojab* was a later introduction and not imposed on people in Kurtoe and Mangde, where they grew cereals more abundantly than Bumthang. Similarly, the people in Bumthang paid two kinds of butter tax which did not apply to some districts with similar dairy farming. They also paid some forty-five cattles as meat tax to the officer in Jakar. These cattle would not be slaughtered but exchanged with carcasses of animals which had died from natural causes. Thus, it was mandatory for people to report the death of any animal and surrender the carcass. If a colt was born among the family's horses, the government immediately claimed it as tax.

The burden of tax got even worse with the labour tax. Free labour was required for construction of *dzong*s, roads, bridges, temples and transportation of official cargoes such as baggage of government officials and guests. The labour tax was mostly imposed on the basis of households but sometimes in relation to the number of male adults or fireplaces. Because most of the labour tax was imposed on each unit of household, young couples often lived in the same household as their parents without moving out to start new households. This resulted in a rampant extended family culture leading to congested and insanitary living conditions, which seriously worried British political officer, Frederick Williamson. He lamented that Bhutanese would be a dying race unless measures were taken to abolish the existing system of taxation.[47] Communities along the main national routes were imposed *sarim woola*, a labour tax, which required the people to deliver the message or goods immediately after its arrival at their borders. The villagers were required to carry it until the next village on the route whether it was day or night and the weather was fair or foul. Such express porterage no doubt expedited the delivery of urgent messages and goods but the people on the route suffered tremendously. In addition to providing food and basic items as tax in kind for the upkeep of the officialdom, the people were also required to work for the officials. They would have to till land, collect firewood, herd animals and weave clothes.

In places where cotton was grown, the government or a royal house would often simply provide a bag of cotton as *trothag* (སློད་ཐག་) or 'entrusted weaving' and demand that the household submit a woven textile within a certain period whether or not the raw material provided was sufficient for it. Often, people had to plant cotton merely to add to the cotton given to them and prepare the textile of the required size. The punishment for failing to deliver the textile would be severe. In some areas, people were given salt as token payments for growing cotton and weaving textiles with it. Labour tax was even worse for the *srungma* families, who owed allegiance to one of the royal households. They had to carry out the entire work of agricultural cultivation and submit the produce to their protectors. Failing to do so resulted in severe fines and punishments.

The burden of labour tax was particularly onerous for the public as there were several layers of officialdom for them to serve. The immediate official who exacted services from the people was the local *drungpa* (དྲུང་པ་) official. People in his jurisdiction carried out most of his farming and household work in rotation. Above him were many tiers of local and regional officials including the fodder in-charge, chief of stable, cattle in-charge, meat-keeper, gate-keeper, chief steward, secretary, chamberlain, flag-master, chief of protocol, governor and many other *garpa* officials, who would all exact their share of free service and tax in kind. The workload for a tax-paying household added up to a backbreaking and tortuous amount.

King Jigme Wangchuk engaged all his secretaries to study the prevailing tax schemes and to restructure them to make them less cumbersome and more equitable. Although the standard taxes may not have seen much reduction, there were many specific improvements which resulted from this programme. A palpable outcome was the reduction of the layers of officialdom and feudal lords who preyed on the masses. The number of *drungpa* officials was drastically reduced and the remaining officials were strictly warned against imposing any extra burdens on the people without the expressed sanction from the government. Similarly, the *sarim woola* labour tax and confiscation of colts was removed and people on the national route were given horses to help with the delivery of goods. The tax revision also saw the end of *tsatong* or vacant household tax. Formerly, when a household died out due to an epidemic or emigrated to other places, the rest of the village had to jointly pay its share of taxes. This was because the government demanded the same amount of tax from a village each year regardless of the fluctuation in the number of households. However, the government did not allow anyone to occupy the vacant property in place of the previous owner. King Jigme Wangchuk annulled this ludicrous imposition of the extinct household's taxes on other households of the village and also allowed new owners to own the property.[48]

King Jigme Wangchuk also made changes to some of the draconian laws, which existed in his days. For instance, if a person committed murder and was apprehended, the murderer was generally thrown into the river with the body of the victim. However, if the murderer was not apprehended, his family and village were imposed a hefty compensation and fine, which included fees and gifts to be paid to the thick layers of officialdom both at local and regional levels for handling the case. The total cost included the following amount of cash and textiles according to Pema Tshewang's calculation.

Recipients	Textiles	Matam coins	
Desi	3 pieces	2000	(as a token for information)
"	1	12000	(as fine)
Council of Ministers	1	...	(as token)
"		12000	(as fine)
Gongzim	1	3000	(as token and fine)
Dzongkhag official	1	...	(as token)
Dzongkhag official		12000	(as parting gift)
Zimpon official	1	3000	(as token and fine)
Chief of protocol	4	6000	(as parting gift)
Protocol officer	1	...	(as token)
"	2	1215	(as fine)
Funeral expenses	...	2000	
Zingap officer	...	12000	(as parting gift)
Bod officer	4	6000	(as parting gift)
Drungpa		3000	(as fine)
Victims of the family		6000	(as compensation)

No doubt, such a heavy penalty for the criminals and their families kept crimes to the minimum but the penalties were far beyond what most people could bear. King Jigme Wangchuk, according to Damchö Lhendup, cancelled the fees to some officials and also reduced the amount of fine listed above.[49] However, the legal framework for the execution of murderers by drowning or fire along with their victim's body appears to have continued during his reign as did other medieval laws and many forms of corporal punishments.

Similarly, serious burglars were meted with the punishment of having their Achilles' tendon cut to disable them for further break-ins. It is surprising that the harsh methods of chastisement were practised even during the reign of his deeply spiritual father, King Ugyen Wangchuk. The Kings themselves frequently flogged people in public and sanctioned dire reprisals for those who offended or failed them.

Notwithstanding the leniency in taxation, the golden yoke of secular law was not getting any lighter under the monarchy. One of the notorious punishments, which had severe economic consequences, was the custom of sending a *bangchen garpa* or a powerful officer to collect fines. The Kings often despatched a *bangchen garpa* to punish recalcitrant families who were well-to-do. The economic damage inflicted on the victim's family depended mostly on the royal order but partly on the character of the officer deputed to carry out the punitive mission. In its severest form, the officer would be ordered to confiscate the entire family assets of the target household. This was known as *zhichagni* or sweeping the estate clean and, in such cases, the victims lost all their properties, including household items. To make it worse, an opportunistic and nasty officer also used such temporary authority with no inhibition to extract all kinds of services and gifts from the family for himself. In most cases, the officer came with an official writ demanding a particular amount of fine or compensation. Even then, the officer would take liberty to make additional demands and extract more gifts. The following account of a former officer who was despatched as a *bangchen garpa* to punish a rich family in Paro gives us a general picture of this practice.

Changarp Drametsepa recalled arriving at the rich house carrying his long sword horizontally. When the sword obstructed his entry through the door, he and his companion complained about the size of the door until the family appeased them with a welcome gift. Then, when he was served the welcome drink, he berated the quality of the liquor after having one cup and had it all poured into a basin to wash his hands. When meal was served, he and his friend made similar complaints about the food until best dishes were prepared and new textiles given to wipe their hands. At bedtime, they had to be placated again with gifts to move them from the main living room to the bed prepared for them in the shrine room, the best room in a traditional house. Then, the family had to pay him fees to make him show the King's writ. In the morning, he packed all blankets and garments provided for the previous night and new ones had to be given for the next night.

The family slaughtered a pig to serve them pork but they again berated the size of the piece of pork they were served until the whole pig was given to them. Another pig had to be slaughtered for the second day. During the day, the officers ordered the family to pack all grains, textiles, jewellery and even crockery for forfeiture. Every night, village girls were called to entertain them and the family made to feed and tip the dancers. When they finally left, they took with them the entire wealth and livestock, leaving the family in penury.[50] The members of this family, like many others, escaped to Tibet.

The *bangchen* practice was a form of official spoliation and some avaricious officers took it to the extremes. Yet, for the ruler, it was a crafty means for destabilizing potential rivals and threats and maintaining control over the country. The king used it as an expedient method to keep a tight grip over the country. His leniency in taxation was skilfully complemented by his stringent enforcement of law and order and both of these contributed toward securing submission of the people and security in the country. In the eyes of a pious follower, even the violent and ruthless conduct of a ruler were seen as benevolent acts leading to the greater good of public security and peace. It is to these issues of security and peace that we shall turn next.

Securing the sovereignty

King Jigme Wangchuk was at the helm of the country at a very difficult stage of history. He faced the challenge of protecting the sovereignty of the nation and the nascent monarchy from both internal and external threats during the twenty-five years of his reign. Internally, the monarchy was not yet stable and the power dynamics between the King, the Zhabdrung and other players were far from defined and formalized when he ascended the throne at the age of twenty-three. Externally, his reign saw the region at the height of political struggles and volatile conditions. At that time, China went through the Nationalist—Communist conflict, Japanese occupation and subsequently the Sino-Japanese War (1937–45) while India was first seething with the independence movement and later engulfed in the troubles of Partition. This was in addition to the fervour of the First World War. Tibet, at least, briefly enjoyed *de facto* independence under the 13th Dalai Lama and the following interim government. Despite such a pervading sense of instability and uncertainty, King Jigme Wangchuk succeeded in strengthening the monarchy and steering the country towards a bright modern future.

If we are to believe the British reports, there were initial suspicions of internal threat and political rivalry to the King by his own cousin, Dorji, and nephew, Tshering Peljor, who allegedly harboured hopes for the throne around the time of King Ugyen Wangchuk's death. Such threats from relatives, if any ever existed as the British speculated, dissipated soon after King Jigme Wangchuk took the reins of power in his hands and emerged as the uncontested heir to the throne. Rather than being a threat, Tshering Peljor, who occupied the post of the Paro *pönlop* from 1923 to 1949, showed the King his undivided loyalty throughout his long tenure as the Paro *pönlop* as we shall see below in the royal fall-out with the mind incarnation of the Zhabdrung. In fact, the relations between him and the King and the royal advisor Sonam Tobgay were much more cordial than the ones between the former Paro *pönlop* Dawa Peljor and King Ugyen Wangchuk and the royal advisor Ugyen Dorji. The great degree of autonomy he enjoyed perhaps diminished his ambition for the throne. During his long tenure of twenty-six years as the Paro *pönlop*, Tshering Peljor ruled the areas within Paro district like a private fiefdom and never returned to Bumthang. He exercised unquestionable authority in his jurisdiction and generally did not have to forward the taxes to the King.

The British guests, numbers of whom he entertained in his residence and the new palace of Ugyen Pelri, described him as 'tolerant and unambitious', 'short, bald and very fat but unmarried' and as 'stout and inactive bachelor'.[51] Collister noted that he was known to be a benevolent administrator although some recent Bhutanese sources portray him as a highhanded and unscrupulous character.[52] The British reports described him as an unmarried bachelor although Tshering Peljor had several relationships and fathered many children. A gory oral account in Paro narrates how he ordered a lover of his partner to be killed and served his head to her on the breakfast plate.[53] Despite his allegedly autocratic character and despotic rule and the initial suspicions the British had, Tshering Peljor did not pose any threat to the monarchy. In fact, the real challenge to monarchy, which unfolded a few years after King Jigme Wangchuk's ascension to power, came from the people to whom Tshering Peljor was also seriously opposed—the family of Jigme Dorji, the 6th mind incarnation of Zhabdrung.

Tshering Peljor is said to have initially fallen out with the family of Jigme Dorji, the 6th mind incarnation, when he could not win the heart of the incarnate lama's sister.[54] However, this row took a more sinister turn when trouble broke out between the King, to whom he owed his allegiance, and the Zhabdrung incarnation. The relationship between the new monarchy and the ancient Zhabdrung institution was perhaps seen as a very problematic and sensitive issue even when King Jigme Wangchuk ascended the throne. There was no clear-cut understanding of power sharing or division of roles and responsibilities between the two leading institutions. The king continued to use the seal of the Tongsa *pönlop* for official endorsements although he was officially and practically the ruler of Bhutan.[55] The idea of the monarch as the head of state was yet to get deeply entrenched in the Bhutanese sociopolitical consciousness in spite of the consensual adoption of monarchy in 1907. A historian even in the middle of the twentieth century described the two first kings as the 57th and 58th Desi rather than opening a new era of monarchy.[56]

Moreover, the pious people seem to have continued to look up to the Zhabdrung incarnation as a supreme figurehead despite the fact that he was now practically deprived of any political power and privilege. Given this scenario, one wonders what kind of relationship, interaction and tension existed between the King and Zhabdrung incarnation when they met in person and the Zhabdrung incarnation presided over the coronation of the King. There was most likely some unseen tension and this perhaps finally erupted four years later in 1931. By then, the Zhabdrung incarnation, who was the same age as King Jigme Wangchuk, was also in his mid-twenties and his ambition as well as popularity must have been rising. The 6th mind incarnation of Zhabdrung is described as a strong, charismatic and domineering character.[57] Around such an age, important incarnations like himself generally presided over rituals, gave public sermons and exercised considerable influence on other people.

His stature naturally also gave his family a prominent position in Bhutanese society and this prominence was further enhanced by the appearance of another Zhabdrung hierarch in the family. Jigme Tenzin, one of the sons of Zhabdrung Jigme Dorji's sister, was recognized as the reincarnation of the Yeshe Ngodup, the 5th speech incarnation of Zhabdrung. The practice of finding the rebirth of an important lama among the lama's own family members had by now become a common trend and its political and economic significance was not lost on the Bhutanese public. This particular recognition became even more intriguing because Yeshe Ngodup, as we have seen earlier, did not enjoy a good rapport with King Ugyen Wangchuk towards the end of his life and the recognition of his reincarnation was allegedly banned by King Ugyen Wangchuk. We do not really know the reactions of the King to this act of recognition, if it was indeed banned, but the recognition could have exacerbated the tension between the family of Zhabdrung incarnations and the King and inadvertently increased the risk the Zhabdrung institution could pose to the nascent monarchy.

The simmering tension reached a boiling point in 1931. However, given its sensitivity and its tragic outcome, not much is found on this grievous affair in the written sources although oral accounts of it are on the lips of many senior citizens. The pious royal historians of the twentieth century, who did not want to discuss the conflict, either wholly ignored it or blamed it vaguely on the misfortune of the country and canny characters among Zhabdrung's circle.[58] Only one unpublished Bhutanese history[59] written around 1966 contains some account of the conflict defending the King's actions. However, secondary sources written at the end of the last century provide a fairly detailed account of the conflict both in English and Dzongkha.[60] I present here only a summary.

The immediate reasons for the eventual conflict in 1931 were multiple. Some time around 1928, the young Zhabdrung incarnation issued an edict in his name giving the rights of grazing lands within Bhutanese territory to members of his community who were living within Tibetan jurisdiction. The Zhabdrung incarnation, we may recall, was born just outside of Bhutan's eastern border in a pastoral community of Tawang. Although communities around here practised cross-border grazing and international borders would have meant little, it was a brazen act on the part of the Zhabdrung incarnation to issue an official edict granting land to his people. This deeply incensed King Jigme Wangchuk as the prerogative to grant land is deemed to lie totally in the hands of the King. It led to the suspicion that the Zhabdrung incarnation, under the influence of his family members, might be trying to regain temporal power which was lost to the new monarchy. The reprisal came when the King issued an edict granting the grazing lands around Punakha, which belonged to the institution of Zhabdrung to a member of Seula family. Just as their relationship was beginning to get strained over issues of land, an uncle of the Zhabdrung incarnate was killed by one of the King's men in cross-fire. The mother of the Zhabdrung incarnate asked the King to pay a *tong* or fine for her dead relative. This was a dangerous move. The King paid her 2000 coins but half of them turned out to be useless. When the chamberlain of the Zhabdrung incarnate returned the useless coins asking for replacement, the King's response was sharp: 'I did not mint the coins, the Tibetans did.'[61]

The rift between the King and Zhabdrung incarnation had now seriously widened. The King was under the impression that the Zhabdrung Jigme Dorji was conducting rituals and black magic against him and plotting to regain power. He claimed later in his letter to the British political officer that the Zhabdrung incarnation 'had been performing ceremonies calculated to do me harm, and had been invoking deadly maledictions upon me.'[62] Such information, whether or not there was truth in it, perhaps came from Tsetenla, a close attendant who was disgracefully banished from the court of the Zhabdrung incarnation in Talo. This disgruntled ex-attendant of the Zhabdrung incarnate joined the court of the Paro *pönlop* and is said to have fed him 'gossip and tales' against the Zhabdrung incarnation, according to Ashi Dorji Wangmo Wangchuck.[63] The Paro *pönlop* duly passed on the reports to the King, who had by now already lost much of his faith in the Zhabdrung incarnation for several reasons, including the latter's fall from celibacy.

The alleged performance of black magic and destructive rituals in order to regain power may have widened the rift between the King and the Zhabdrung incarnation but it was the news from India that the Zhabdrung had sent a team to seek support from Gandhi which finally brought the two into an open clash. Some time in spring of 1931, the Zhabdrung sent his cousin, Chökyi Gyaltshen, and two other attendants with many presents to meet Gandhi, who was leading the non-violent movement for independence. The team missed Gandhi in Calcutta and caught up with him in Borsad. The Mahatma was told that the Zhabdrung ruled Bhutan in the past but had no power now. His help was sought in restoring power to the Zhabdrung institution but the Mahatma simply said that he would pray for the Zhabdrung incarnation and gave a coconut in return. Utterly frustrated by the outcome, Chökyi Gyaltshen cut open the coconut with his knife and ate it when the team reached the border settlement of Pasakha.

In May 1931, a brief report about the meeting appeared in the Indian press, which Sonam Tobgay forwarded to King Jigme Wangchuk in Kuengarabten. The mission not only failed to recruit the much needed support from India but now alarmed the King. Some official enquiries seem to have been made almost immediately, leading to the arrests of some people, including the members of the mission. By now, the Zhabdrung incarnation perhaps also made arrangements to escape into exile. His baggage was transported as far as Pasakha from where they were brought back at the insistence of the monks of the State Monk Body. Fully aware of the damage the departure of Zhabdrung incarnation from the country could do to the prestige of the monarchy, the King asked the British to send him back if the Zhabdrung incarnation escaped to India but the Government of India said that they could not either stop him or return him like a criminal. He would be treated as a refugee if he came to India.

Next, the Zhabdrung incarnation might have planned to flee northward to Tibet or China. The King now made an appeal to the State Monk Body to use its influence on the Zhabdrung incarnation to keep him in Bhutan and stop him from leaving the country. According to one of our sources, the King was even willing to make apologies and mend the differences.[64] Meanwhile, an unsubstantiated rumour had spread from the Je Khenpo to the Paro *pönlop* that the Zhabdrung incarnation had already fled to Tibet. The Paro *pönlop*, who backed the King, sent his troops in pursuit of the Zhabdrung incarnation with an open order to arrest or kill him. The troops penetrated deep into Tibet but the Zhabdrung incarnation had not even left his residence of Sangag Chöling in Talo. Under royal command, three contingents of troops from Paro, Thimphu and Tongsa converged in Talo on 29 October 1931 and surrounded the residence of the Zhabdrung incarnate, ostensibly to confirm the Zhabdrung incarnation's whereabouts.

The fate of the Zhabdrung incarnation now perilously hung on the intervention of the clergy. Like during medieval times, the parties in dispute now waited for the clergy to mediate and avert bloodshed. That was the last traditional recourse to avoid both loss of life and loss of face. While Sangag Chöling and its residents were under siege, the senior monks of the State Monk Body met to write a petition to the King to spare the Zhabdrung incarnation. They proposed that the Zhabdrung incarnation be invited to live with them to keep him from causing further trouble. Sadly, the proposal did not get the consensual agreement it needed. Samten Gyatsho, the master of tantric rituals (དབུས་པའི་སློབ་དཔོན) and an influential appointee of the King, rejected the proposal and insisted that the clergy should have no say on the issue and leave it for the King to decide. A letter to this effect was sent to the King and, inadvertently, the fate of Zhabdrung incarnation was sealed.

In the night of 12 November 1931, Jigme Dorji, the 6th mind incarnation of Zhabdrung, passed away. Popular accounts have it that he was suffocated to death by the King's soldiers by thrusting a silk scarf down his throat in the middle of the night. Officially, his death was treated as a mystery, 'his passing not even noticed by the monks who were sleeping in the same room' according to the King's letter to the British political officer. The Tibetan government, instigated by the relatives of the Zhabdrung incarnation, however, suspected foul play and demanded an explanation for the hierarch's death as they claimed him to be a Tibetan subject. They were also justifiably angry at the illegal entry of Bhutanese troops into Tibet earlier in pursuit of the Zhabdrung incarnation. The Bhutanese effectively argued that the late Zhabdrung incarnation was a subject of Bhutan although born in Tibetan territory. As the issue with Tibetans was an international one and related to foreign affairs, the British political officer intervened and duly took it up with the Dalai Lama's agent in Gyantse. He produced the proof that the late Zhabdrung incarnation was a Bhutanese subject and thus any issue concerning the hierarch was an internal matter. This resolved the acrimony with Tibet.

With the mind incarnation of the Zhabdrung out of the picture, the major threat to the monarchy and internal stability was now evidently over. The mother of the deceased incarnate was released from confinement and allowed to live with freedom as was the family of his sister. Young Jigme Tenzin, the 6th speech incarnation of Zhabdrung and nephew of the deceased Zhabdrung incarnation, was perhaps not perceived as a serious threat to the existent power structure. He was only thirteen in 1931 and did not have a large following. Besides, we may recall that over centuries, the speech incarnations have come to generally hold less prestige and stature than the mind incarnations, who were identified with Zhabdrung Ngawang Namgyal. Nonetheless, even the speech incarnation was not totally outside the range of official scrutiny and suspicion; his family continued to endure vicissitudes resulting from the Paro *pönlop*'s aggravations for many years. Fearing for his life, he and his family spent long periods in exile and it was only towards the end of his life that he and his family were fully reconciled with the King and his court through the benevolent efforts of Gongzim Sonam Tobgay. Sadly, the speech incarnation passed away in 1949 soon after the reconciliation and just before his meeting with the king.

The mind incarnation appeared again twice in eastern Bhutan in the twentieth century. The 7th incarnation was born in Jangphu in Tashigang in 1939 but he was also hunted down by some men allegedly working for the King and subsequently killed in his early teenage years.[65] The next mind incarnation was again born in Jangphu in 1955. Immediately after his recognition at an early age, he was smuggled out of Bhutan. He spent the rest of his life in northern India under the protection of the Government of India until his death in 2003. By the end of the twentieth century, the prestige and the popularity of the Zhabdrung incarnations had subsided to an all-time low since their appearance in the eighteenth century. Although people's faith in the first Zhabdrung, the founder of the Bhutanese nation, remained undiminished, his 8th incarnation in exile did not command the same respect and devotion as his former incarnations. With his base in the valley of Manali in Himachal Pradesh, he lived a normal life, drawing some Bhutanese devotees but his existence was generally of no consequence to Bhutan and its politics.

The line of the speech incarnation, also known as the Chogley line, ceased to continue after the death of Jigme Tenzin, the 6th speech incarnation. No child was recognized as his reincarnation perhaps due to political sensitivity concerning the Zhabdrung incarnations which persisted for the rest of the century. Thus, three of the four main lines of ruling Zhabdrung incarnations were practically dead by the end of the last century. Meanwhile, the new monarchy began to take roots in the Bhutanese political psyche and the figure of the King successfully replaced the Zhabdrung institution as the head of state. The golden throne became directly associated with the civil monarchs; it was no more the sacred seat occupied only by the regal incarnations connected to Zhabdrung.

By the turn of the new century and a hundred years after the monarchy was established, the political legitimacy of the Zhabdrung institution had become a fading memory. While the Zhabdrung figure with a flowing white beard continued to loom large in Bhutan's spiritual and historical consciousness, the political prerogative and function of the Zhabdrung incarnations was now largely forgotten. Moreover, a new political paradigm of a constitutional democracy with the King at its apex had been introduced in 2008, opening another chapter of Bhutan's political story. With this transfer of power to the people and secularization of what was for most part of the history a religious state, the central role which the Zhabdrung incarnations and the clergy once played have come to a final end.

However, there has been a recent revival of interest of Zhabdrung incarnations as religious figures. A couple of children have been covertly recognized and declared to be the incarnations of the mind and speech incarnations of Zhabdrung amid fears and speculations of imprisonment and persecution. They are being clandestinely worshipped by people as this book is being written. Nonetheless, it is very unlikely that an erratic and late return of a Zhabdrung incarnation could pose any threat to the current power structure and the well-established institution of the monarchy. In this respect, King Jigme Wangchuk's proactive approach to the Zhabdrung problem in the early years of his rule has successfully secured the future of the nascent monarchy and contributed to the long period of internal peace. Furthermore, in an interesting development and in the fashion of combining religious prestige with political authority, the 70th Je Khenpo of Bhutan has identified the 4th King of Bhutan as an incarnation of Zhabdrung.

To return to the issue of security during King Jigme Wangchuk's rule, the Zhabdrung incarnation was not the only one who posed a challenge to the King's power base. There were probably many others with a vendetta or other reasons to undermine the King. One Zamsung Namgyal is said to have even attempted an assassination by carrying a gun in the fold of his *gho* during an audience with the King. But before he managed to take his shot, the King is said to have shot him straight in the forehead and killed him.[66] King Jigme Wangchuk kept a vigilant watch over families who could have posed threats to his authority. To this end, he shrewdly used the practice of *bangchen* to disempower any potential troublemakers and powerful families who showed signs of disobedience and recalcitrance.

An unexpected threat to the internal security of the country and monarchial power came from the south in 1946 when a protest by some of the Nepali settlers broke out in Dagapela. By then, the southern belt, which the Bhutanese from the northern valleys visited only occasionally and dreaded for its malarial climate, was widely occupied by new Nepali settlers. They were initially brought as labourers to clear the jungles for cultivation. The British may have initially encouraged the flow of ethnic Nepalis to Bhutan in order to counteract the Tibetan and Chinese influence from the north. However, by 1928, the British political officer who visited Bhutan noted that a major problem for Bhutan was the rising population of Nepali immigrants, which numbered about 50,000 then. Subsequent British political officers also reported the issue of uncontrolled growth of Nepali settlers. By 1946, the population of settlers had significantly increased. Besides, they could follow the political changes across the border in India, where the atmosphere was effervescent with the imminent Indian independence and the turmoil of Partition. King Jigme Wangchuk was apprehensive that the Gurkha leaders active in India, particularly one Danbar Singh Gurung, could incite dissidence among the Nepali population within Bhutan and that the trouble may spill over.[67]

It was perhaps with the foresight of such threat to the national security that King Jigme Wangchuk started to build the modern armed forces. Fifteen young men were sent to be trained under the Gurkha Rifles in Shillong around 1932 and upon their return, they recruited and trained about a hundred men, who formed the first Bhutanese modern army. By 1940, over a hundred men had been trained under the Gurkhas and there was a sizeable platoon of soldiers and some 1900 rifles. Using these new military forces, the demonstration in Dagapela in 1946 was successfully suppressed but history would repeat itself many decades later during the reign of King Jigme Wangchuk's grandson. A similar uprising, which rocked the central power in Thimphu, took place in 1990 leading to a sordid ethnic conflict. It temporarily shattered Bhutan's internal peace and caused a protracted refugee problem, which still continues to scar Bhutan's international image.

However, by far the most unsettling worry King Jigme Wangchuk may have had concerning Bhutan's sovereignty perhaps came from the political changes in India. As the Indian independence movement gained momentum and plans were made for the transfer of power from the British to the local Indians, the King was very anxious about the consequences this political change in India would have for Bhutan. Since the rise of Ugyen Wangchuk as the Tongsa *pönlop*, Bhutan's national security and sovereignty had become rather awkwardly dependent on the British support from the south. The British power in Delhi and the successive British political officers in Gangtok were the closest allies of the monarchy and the Punakha Treaty of 1910 gave Bhutan the much needed security and protection as long as the British ruled India. Beside, the subsidy of Rs 1,00,000 received in return for British occupation of the duars and another Rs 1,00,000 as the compensation for removal of liquor shops within ten miles from the border were the main source of revenue for the state. For the British, a stable government in Bhutan of which foreign relations were conveniently placed under them was to their best interest when they ruled India. Bhutan became a good buffer zone between their northeastern frontier and China. However, now that Britain was leaving India, Bhutan was not really their concern.

Uncertainty had arisen partly due to the ambiguous status of Bhutan *vis-à-vis* the British Raj, which we have discussed earlier. Bhutan was not a native state under British rule, the way the numerous Indian princely states were, although King Ugyen Wangchuk was treated like a native prince during the Delhi Durbar in 1911. Bhutan received neither the financial nor military benefits from Government of India which these princely states enjoyed. By the same token, the British had no obligation to be concerned about Bhutan's situation as a consequence of their withdrawal from India. Yet, Bhutan was not looked on as a fully foreign state. Even the King was usually referred to as the Mahārāja, a title profusely used for the Indian princes, and his relationship with the British was not one on an equal standing. Thus, the existent status and approaching Indian independence gave rise to many questions about Bhutan's future. Would Bhutan remain independent and even get the duars back or would it be usurped into the new Indian Union? Would it continue to receive the subsidy? What would be the attitude of new India towards Bhutan?

According to J.L.R. Weir, the British political officer who visited Bhutan in 1931 to present the insignia of KCIE, King Jigme Wangchuk expressed serious doubts about the future relationship with an independent India. Weir also noted that the King, like the Tibetans, utterly failed to understand the British policy towards what he (the King) saw as a rebellion against established authority. The King thought the execution of Gandhi would have solved the problem of the Indian resistance movement. Thus, the British effort to help India break away from Britain through the round table conferences in London was totally lost on him. Bhutan had been enjoying wonderful relations with the British for nearly half a century. Understandably, any change to this would have been perceived as a serious disruption, not only to its relationship with India but also to its domestic affairs.

The King's pro-British attitude and opinion at the time was perhaps also strongly influenced by the friendship he enjoyed with the British officers, as did his father before him. During his reign, he saw a series of British visitors to Bhutan including five political officers based in Gangtok. His visitors were overwhelmed by the warm reception and hospitality and remained staunch supporters of his rule and development initiatives. They almost incessantly entreated the central administration in Delhi for an increment in the subsidy and development aid for Bhutan but precious little came from either Delhi or London in response to their requests. The subsidy was increased by one lakh in 1942 after clamouring for many years. The total was still only three lakhs, much lower than the actual value of the land the British occupied. The lukewarm and muddled responses from Delhi, however, did not diminish King Jigme Wangchuk's friendly spirits. Like his father, he even made a contribution to the Viceroy's war fund and the Vicerine's Red Cross appeal when Britain was encumbered by the Second World War.

In 1934, the British reciprocated King Jigme Wangchuk's hospitality by inviting him with Queen Phuntsho Choden, Prince Jigme Dorji Wangchuk and a large entourage of 200 attendants to Calcutta. The group travelled by car to Jalpaiguru and then by train to Calcutta where they stayed with the Governor of Bengal and called on the Viceroy. In Calcutta, the King visited the zoo, the paper mills, ammunitions factory and warships and went on picnics accompanied by Frederick Williamson, the British political officer in Sikkim. The visit was full of fun and ceremony with two things a day to see and banquets in the evening. On their way back, the King took a flight to Bagdogra and from there travelled to Bhutan via Sikkim. Throughout this journey and the general intercourse with the British, Sonam Tobgay, who had now become his *gongzim* (གོང་གཞིས་) or chamberlain and had also been accorded the Rāja title by the British, accompanied and advised the King. Like his father, Gongzin Sonam Tobgay had come to win the trust and respect of both the Bhutanese monarch and the British officers and worked for both without any qualm of there being any conflict of interest. The families of the King and his chamberlain had also grown very close, auguring the intimate alliance which was to develop in the following generation. His daughter, Kesang Choden, married Prince Jigme Dorji Wangchuk in 1951, a year before they became King and Queen.

Worries in Bhutan increased as the Indian independence drew nearer. The worst fear was of Bhutan being forcibly shoved into the new republic along with the Indian princely states. Thus, when the British Cabinet Mission arrived in Delhi to draw plans for Indian independence, King Jigme Wangchuk was determined to point out to them that Bhutan had never been an Indian state and had always remained independent. A Bhutanese delegation was sent to Delhi perhaps with the desire to confirm the independent status, secure a place in the British Commonwealth and retrieve the duar areas but the Cabinet Mission did not have time to meet the delegation. Two officers of External Affairs Department in Delhi later heard their case and Arthur Hopkinson, the last British political officer in Sikkim, was asked to produce a memorandum on Bhutan and Sikkim. He advised his government that Bhutan, as well as Sikkim, fell in a category different from other Indian states geographically, historically and culturally. He argued that India needed a friendly and contented Bhutan within the Indian rather than the Chinese orbit. This was particularly important as Tibet was planning to reclaim suzerainty over both Bhutan and Sikkim on the eve of the British departure from India.

Hopkinson visited Bhutan in 1947 just before Indian independence to confer on King Jigme Wangchuk the insignia of KCSI. He was the last in a long line of British political officers to visit Bhutan. Like all his predecessors in the twentieth century, Hopkinson was very supportive to Bhutan and concerned that Bhutan may be left in a weak and dangerous situation when the British left India. On 15 August 1947, India became independent and Bhutan was left on its own to deal with the new republican system. The foreboding fear, however, turned out to be untrue when Pandit Jawaharlal Nehru, the prime minister of independent India, met the Bhutanese delegation in 1948 and agreed to consider their proposal. The delegation was led by Gongzim Sonam Tobgay and one of the key demands was the return of all forested areas of the duars that were not under tea cultivation or a significant increment to subsidy that reflected the true value of the land. On 8 August 1949, two years after India got independence, a new treaty was signed between Bhutan and India in Sikkim. A notable insertion was the title 'Druk Gyalpo' for the King instead of Mahārāja, which bore the connotation of being an Indian prince. The treaty was largely a reconfirmation of the earlier one signed in Punakha in 1910 and Bhutan agreed to be guided by India in its foreign affairs while it kept internal administration in its own hands.

India returned to Bhutan the thirty-two sq. km tract of Dewathang, which the British previously refused to return for reasons of prestige as that was where they suffered a humiliating defeat at the hands of the Bhutanese and lost two guns in 1865. Such vestiges of colonial pride and prestige were of no interest to India. The new Government of India also raised the subsidy to Rs 5 lakhs and agreed to allow free trade between the two countries. Thus, independent India pursued the pro-Bhutan policy, which successive British political officers had persuaded their leaders in Delhi to adopt. The treaty was the first milestone in the history of close Indo-Bhutan friendship, which went on to shape Bhutan through the second half of the twentieth century. It renewed Bhutan's southward orientation of political and economic relations and kept Bhutan within the orbit of Indian influence, as Hopkinson suggested.

This was strategically important for India in order to counteract the Chinese influence, which had begun to spread across Tibet by 1950. As Communist China began its occupation of Tibet, thousands of Tibetans fled to India and Bhutan and thereby exacerbated the political tension which was already building up in the region. By 1959, the Chinese military invasion reached the northern borders of Bhutan and consequently, Bhutan's border with Tibet was sealed, stopping the historic links with Tibet. As a result, Bhutan's southward orientation of political and trade relations now entered an unprecedented phase. India, which gradually assumed a big brotherly role, became the only country with which Bhutan had any real official intercourse and diplomatic relations. For the next few decades, Bhutan saw the outside world mostly through the Indian lens. India's role in Bhutan's security and development was so great that some people even mistook Bhutan for an Indian state or considered it a protectorate of India. Similarly, the treaty of 1949 opened the floodgate for Indian influence on Bhutan in the spheres of politics, development, economy and even culture. Although Bhutan now reaches out directly to many countries beyond India and the treaty of 1949 has been revised in 2007 and Bhutan is no more formally guided by India in its foreign affairs, the two countries continue to enjoy the close relationship launched by King Jigme Wangchuk.

The smooth transfer of good relations from the British to the local Indian leaders is perhaps the most significant achievement of King Jigme Wangchuk's rule. With this single act, King Jigme Wangchuk managed to both safeguard Bhutan's sovereignty and security at a critical time and usher Bhutan into a new modern era. The good relationship he had struck with India's political leadership continued during the reign of his descendents, ensuring a sustained good will and support from India. Financial assistance from India, where it was perceived as a continuation of the subsidy or as new aid, increased also dramatically in the following decades with India providing the lion's share of Bhutan's development budget. King Jigme Wangchuk had successfully recast with independent India the good relations which his father had commenced with the British and the ramifications of this deed continue well into our times.

At home, the monarchy was in a very stable position by the middle of the twentieth century. Potential threats have been long overcome and, for a change, there was no contention over the line of succession. King Jigme Wangchuk's brother, Jigme Dorji, died in 1933 from typhoid and his other brother, Nakhu, served him as his chief of protocol until he retired to pursue a religious career. According to one source, the King is said to have first made an offer to appoint Nakhu as the Thimphu *dzongpön* and later withdrawn the offer after Nakhu had already made some preparations for an official inauguration.[68] This offended Nakhu and the King's sister, Köncho Wangmo, and they left the court in Bumthang to live a religious life in the temple of Jangchubling in Kurtoe. After Nakhu's death in 1949, Köncho Wangmo departed for Tibet to live close to her teacher, the 16th Karmapa.

In the final years of King Jigme Wangchuk's reign, the future of the monarchy was secure and promising. The promise undoubtedly lay on the heir apparent, Prince Jigme Dorji Wangchuk. He received some modern education in Bumthang and Kalimpong and served as his father's chief of protocol before he was appointed as the Paro *pönlop* in 1950 following the death of his cousin, Tshering Peljor. Like his father and grandfather, he also went through practical training in court but, heeding to the call of time, he also had a spell in Scotland accompanied by Jigme Dorji, the son of his father's chamberlain. Jigme Dorji had already been appointed as the *drungpa* of Haa at the age of eight and later became the first prime minister of Bhutan under Jigme Dorji Wangchuk. The reign of Jigme Dorji Wangchuk would see the realization of his father and grandfather's dreams of developing Bhutan. As a visionary and benevolent monarch, he later led the nation on the path of modernization.

With the succession secure and the country in a stable condition, King Jigme Wangchuk passed away in 1952 after bouts of illness. The actual cause of his death is not clear but the King seems to have suffered from episodes of a psychotic problem. During his last days in Kuengarabten, the King often had hallucinations that Batru, one of his attendants, was attempting to assassinate him and chased his court officials with a gun in his hands. Fearing that the illness was caused by the protecting deities of Zhabdrung, his officials sponsored long rituals in Sa-ngag Chöling to appease the deities. The illness, however, got worse and the King passed away on the thirtieth day of the first Bhutanese month, 25 March 1952. His body was cremated in Kurjey, alongside that of his aunt, Choden, who also died around the same time.

The Modern Period:
The Dragon's New Journey

BHUTAN UNDOUBTEDLY was one of the last nations in the world to embrace modernity and launch the process of modernization. Bhutan's modern era effectively begins only in the middle of the twentieth century with the reign of the 3rd King, who is popularly remembered as the father of modern Bhutan. The Bhutanese world until that time was medieval in character, and vestiges of medieval life are even today easy to find in rural areas. The most prominent characteristic of the medieval polity was the role of religion in society. Bhutan's culture, art, governance and worldview were primarily informed by a spiritual ethos, and religion played an important part in both state administration and ordinary lives. It was essentially a church-state of the Drukpa Kagyu school as we have seen above. Its subsistence economy was managed through a feudal social structure and even taxes were mostly paid in kind. This changed in the second half of the twentieth century with the introduction of modern legislative, judiciary and administrative mechanisms, monetization of the economy, development of modern infrastructures such as roads and hospitals, enhanced communication with the outside world and, above all, the secularization of education. Bhutan saw in the second half of the twentieth century the arrival of the secular, urban, capitalist, industrial and technological developments associated with modernization.

Due to the rise of organized administration, literacy and education, the modern period of Bhutan's history is the most well-documented era. There are a great number of books and articles by both local and foreign authors on affairs and events in this era in addition to the innumerable press covers, reports and government dossiers. In 2008 alone, the various government departments and organizations in Bhutan produced over twenty books on the monarchial rule and development issues. Thus, no attempt will be made to consult all these sources and to put together a chronological narrative as I have done for the pre-modern eras. It is pointless to reinvent the wheel as much of the political narratives can be found in existent sources. Besides, the events of the later half of the twentieth century are in the living memories of a great number of people, who took part in it. For our purpose of winding up the historical narrative, I shall briefly discuss, *as an epilogue*, the sociocultural, governmental, political and economic transformations the country has gone through during the modern era. These transformations, which build on or replace the pre-modern historical constructions, currently shape and define the contemporary Bhutanese nationhood and personality.

Decentralization, democracy and dasho aspirants

As the medieval religious republicanism gave way to hereditary monarchy, we see two major phases of power appropriation in the twentieth century. The first half is marked by active and forceful assertion of power in order to gain full control over the country and to centralize power, which lay diffused in a segregated polity. Such unitary power and control was necessary to bring about systemic changes and ensure long-term peace and security in the country. By the end of the 2nd King's reign, this was fully achieved and the power lay concentrated in the hands of the monarch without any serious rival. Then, the approach changed from an active and assertive one to a placatory and participatory one. There was no further need to wrest power. The 3rd King Jigme Dorji Wangchuk (r.1952–72) was a true visionary and astute leader. He knew early on the inefficacy of unquestionable centralized authority to sustain the secure status of both the monarchy and the country. If genuine loyalty and stability were to be secured and sustained, it was crucial to win people's trust through interactive rule and consultative governance. In this respect, he was different from all past rulers in embracing a democratic approach. No doubt, his education outside Bhutan and exposure he gained in Britain and Switzerland must have contributed to this novel approach.

A year after ascending the throne, he opened the Tshogdu (ཚོགས་འདུ་) or National Assembly in Punakha to share the decision-making process with the elders in the country. It gave the people a platform to voice their concerns and the King one to share his aims and plans. The assembly of some 138 members including the representatives of the people, monastics and government discussed issues ranging from Tibetan immigration to reduction of horses in the royal stable. The political power, which the earlier kings secured through active campaigns, was now being redistributed and shared with the relevant groups. This helped the King to mobilize the people and create an efficient governing system within the country, which would be crucial for promoting Bhutan abroad. In 1965, he took another step by setting up the Lodoe Tshogde (ཨ་ཕོས་ཚོགས་སྡེ་) or Royal Advisory Council of eight members to advise the King and the government. This also served as a body of review and often deliberated the judicial appeals made to the King. The devolution of power under the 3rd King reached its pinnacle in 1969 when he removed the royal power to veto bills presented in the parliament. Furthermore, he proposed that the King be subjected to a vote of confidence every three years. The Tshogdu was given the power to remove the King with a two-third majority in favour of the next in line of succession. Interestingly, when the second vote of confidence was cast in 1971, only 133 out of 137, not all, were in favour of the King. The other four were perhaps made by the King to vote against him.

The National Assembly, which also included the members of the Royal Advisory Council when in session, functioned as the legislative body to develop new laws for the country. In the past, the main legal document was the law code which originated in Zhabdrung and was preserved in the 1729 history of Bhutan by Tenzin Chögyal. Beside this state legal code, most of the local polities also functioned on the basis of unwritten social contracts such as arrangement for grazing rights, distribution of water for irrigation and community services. Conflicts and contestations were traditionally resolved through mediation and consensual agreements, as we have seen in the chapters on medieval history. The establishment of the National Assembly as a legislative body formalized the process of enacting laws and the first outcome of this process was the adoption of Thrimzhung Chenmo (ཁྲིམས་གཞུང་) or the Supreme Laws in 1959. This was followed by many Acts and bye laws. As the written legal framework grew, the King also appointed judges or Thrimpöns (ཁྲིམས་དཔོན་), now called Drangpön, to implement them in every district. This set in motion the development of an independent judiciary system for which the High Court was established in 1967. The judiciary system would see further developments during the reign of the 4th King with some eighty-seven Acts passed, court procedures modernized and streamlined, and the establishment of the National Legal Course, the National Judicial Commission, and the Office of the Attorney General. During the 5th King's reign, the Supreme Court was established as the guardian of the Constitution.

In 1972, the King also formalized the burgeoning administrative body into Lhengye Zhungtshog (ལྷན་རྒྱས་གཞུང་ཚོགས་) or the Cabinet, which met every week under the chairmanship of the King to plan and pursue the development of the country. Although it shared the name with the administrative council of medieval times, its mode of work, frequency and structure were very different. The officialdom in medieval times almost entirely served in the courts of the rulers but the new Cabinet, which was supported by a fast-growing civil service, focused on the daily administration and development of the country. It became effectively the executive arm of the state. Thus, by the end of the 3rd King's reign, Bhutan saw a general separation of the legislative, judiciary and executive organs of the state although it will take several more decades to bring about a genuine separation. This was a drastic improvement from the medieval polity in which the ruler was largely the law, the ultimate arbiter of justice and the state administration existed to serve him. The concept of free media was still unknown but *Kuensel*, which later became the national newspaper, was also launched in 1967 as an internal government bulletin.

The reign of the 3rd King also saw in 1958 two other sociopolitical developments which would significantly change Bhutan's social structure and demography. The first was the emancipation of bonded labourers, whom we have discussed in the last chapter. Serfdom was officially abolished and the former serfs were given land by the state to start new lives. The former social order maintained through a hierarchical structure based on social class and familial descent was discarded in favour of a generally egalitarian system based on equal rights and opportunities. An egalitarian system would, however, prove hard to come by as a new class of bureaucratic elites emerged; most of the serfs were genuinely liberated. The second development concerned immigration and the official bestowal of citizenship to the Nepali immigrants who populated the southern lowlands. The Nepali immigrants had by 1958 grown to form about twenty per cent of Bhutan's population and a few of their leaders had also formed a group called the Bhutan State Congress, which led some demonstrations in the south demanding equal rights for Nepali settlers. The government successfully suppressed the disturbances but in order to diffuse the tension, the Nepali immigrants were given Bhutanese citizenship and strong encouragement was shown for their assimilation into mainstream Bhutanese culture. Meanwhile, Bhutan also saw a great number of immigrants pouring into Bhutan from the north as China's occupation of Tibet reached its bloody climax in 1959. The political upheavals connected to the influxes of Nepali and Tibetan immigrants would shake the hermitic kingdom in the following decades as we shall see later.

The noble initiative of sharing political power with the people started by the 3rd King continued during the reign of the 4th King in a gradual process. Like his father, the 4th King Jigme Singye Wangchuck (r.1972–2006) ruled with sagacity and foresight when the mantle of leadership fell on his shoulders at the young age of seventeen. The introduction of the civil service in 1973 was an important social and administrative milestone. Not only did it modernize the state bureaucracy and social services, it became the main employer of the growing number of the educated people who passed out from schools and colleges. The formation of this new administrative organ also broadened the set of career choices for Bhutanese youth and initiated a new work culture and social group. It led to the rise of a new middle class of administrators and professionals, who performed white collar jobs sitting at office desks in contrast to the manual work of the farmers. This was, however, not without implications. The divide between the commoners and civil servants and excessive regard for the office-based administrative work led to many unfavourable sociocultural trends, including loss of dignity in jobs involving manual work and migration to urban administrative centres. As the civil service replaced medieval officialdom and its officers became the immediate point of call for the citizens, the prestige and benefits of working as a civil servant increased and this subsequently changed the expectation of most young people. The school-educated youth of the twentieth century looked down on any work involving a tool heavier than a pen and the post of a *dasho* or a high-ranking official became a much desired ambition in life. In 2012, the civil service was still the largest employer with over 23,000 members, about a third of them women, and desired by most educated youth for its job security and perks. Another notable development around this time was also the introduction of Radio NYAB, which was the precursor of the Bhutan Broadcasting Service. Although it took several decades for Bhutan to have more radio stations, the introduction of the radio certainly heralded the arrival of the audio-visual media, which today thoroughly swamp the country.

The process of decentralization saw another step with the formation of the Dzongkhag Yargye Tshogchung (རྫོང་ཁག་ཡར་རྒྱས་ཚོགས་ཆུང་) or district development committees in 1981. Plans for development programmes were deliberated among people's representatives at the district level and their feedbacks and proposals fed to the Cabinet. Although the King and the circle of senior civil servants continued to have the final say on matters, this form of grassroots participation in decision-making and political processes helped enhance the human resources and social capital. Such a participatory process went a step further in 1991 with the formation of the Gewog Yargye Tshogchung (རྒེད་འོག་ ཡར་རྒྱས་ཚོགས་ཆུང་) or county development committee. This process included many more village elders and community leaders in the deciding the needs and implementing the programmes of development at the level of a county, at the centre of which was the office of *gup*. The *gup* or a head of the county, who was the most crucial administrative officer and link between the people and the government, was appointed in the past from a hereditary line or selected from among the elders. This fundamentally changed in 2002 with the election of the *gup*s, using a secret ballot. People could elect their immediate leader without any inhibition or fear. The election of *gup*s using a secret ballot was also the first instance of a nationwide practice of this voting method. Such a method has already been used within the parliament for the election of some of its members including the election of ministers in 1999. The King handed down the executive power of daily administration to the Cabinet of ministers who held the post of the prime minister in rotation.

Notwithstanding the gradual and calculated process of decentralization and devolution of power throughout the second half of the twentieth century, true power, for all intents and purposes, lay absolutely in the hands of the King for the rest of the century. His authority was unquestioned and no political dissent aimed at changing the *status quo* really succeeded to do so. The King was judicious and determined; Bhutan's political transformation was to happen in his own time as an initiative from the throne. It was to be a unique case of change with the King passing down the power to people while autocrats and politicians elsewhere only craved for more power. The 3rd King envisioned a democratic form of governance to secure the future of both the monarchy and the stability of the country, and this began to crystallize at the turn of the new millennium during his son's reign. In 2001, the King initiated the process of drafting the first written Constitution for the country. The drafting committee consulted a great number of Constitutions as references but produced a unique piece of legal documentation which would become the cornerstone of Bhutan's state administration. In an unprecedented and ironic move, the drafting committee of the democratic Constitution elevated and sacralized the institution of the monarchy as a unified symbol of both secular and spiritual powers, besides preserving most of the privileges and prerogatives the monarchy enjoyed before democratization. It was the first time in the history of Bhutan for a civilian ruler to be formally anointed as the embodiment of spiritual authority.

The Constitution laid out the formal procedures for a constitutional monarchy within a democratic system. It was, in its draft form, taken around the country to be discussed with the people in large consultation meetings. Yet, despite the best intentions, people made very few comments of substance during these gatherings, perhaps inhibited by the formal procedure and the presence of the leaders and media. Everywhere, they unanimously praised the royal initiative and voiced their reservations against the clause which required the reigning monarch to retire by the age of sixty-five. In contrast, anonymous comments posted in online forums provided more critical and constructive feedbacks. Just as the Constitution was being finalized, the King startled the nation at the end of 2006 with the announcement of his abdication from the throne to make way for the young Crown Prince to take the helm of a new democratic Bhutan. This was unexpected and shocking news, particularly because the people had been clamouring during the discussion on the draft Constitution for the monarch to be allowed to rule beyond sixty-five years of age. The King was only fifty-one when he abdicated. The 5th Druk Gyalpo Jigme Khesar Namgyal Wangchuck immediately ascended the throne to carry on his father's legacies although his coronation only took place two years later in 2008.

The process of parliamentary democracy gained quick momentum under the 5th King and even mock elections were conducted to familiarize the citizens with the electronic voting machine. By 2008, Bhutan was ready to kick off a new political chapter. The year marked a watershed in Bhutan's political history and was perhaps one of the most eventful years in its entire history. Firstly, the year saw Bhutan embrace its unique democracy with unexpected excitement and fervour as people enthusiastically took part in the election of the members of the bicameral parliament through secret ballot. The election ushered in a new set of political players as most of the members of the previous parliament were disqualified by the new electoral regulations. Formerly, the parliament was composed of the community representatives, members of the clergy and senior civil servants including district commissioners. Now, while the civil servants could not stand for elections without resigning from their jobs, the clergy were altogether excluded from even voting in the elections. Most of the community representatives were disqualified to stand for the parliament as the new regulations made a university degree a prerequisite for political candidacy.

Despite being seriously weakened by these regulations at the very outset, the election process was not without political vigour and effervescence. I have discussed this experience elsewhere and shall not repeat here.[1] Of the two parties which competed during the first election to form the government, the People's Democratic Party led by the King's uncle suffered an astonishing defeat while the Druk Phunsum Tshogpa won a landslide victory of forty-five seats out of forty-seven and went on to form the first democratically elected government.

The elections, surprisingly, ran very smoothly and efficiently for a first-time experience. On 18 July 2008, the newly elected parliament and the King formally adopted the new Constitution and turned Bhutan into a constitutionally democratic country. The political transformation which the 3rd King envisioned over half a century ago and which the 4th king nurtured throughout his reign was now fully realized. The Constitution became the legal framework for a democratic political system, which aimed 'to secure the blessings of liberty, to ensure justice and tranquillity and to enhance the unity, happiness and well-being of the people for all time.' As the fever of political transformation died down, Bhutan turned to its next momentous event of 2008. The last two months of the year were marked by a joyous mood for celebration with festivities running for weeks as the nation observed the coronation of the 5th king and the centenary commemoration of Ugyen Wangchuk's ascension as the 1st King a hundred years ago.

Security, sovereignty and the dragon's wrath

Bhutan's emergence from a medieval polity and her entry onto the global stage as a modern nation-state in the second half of the twentieth century took place in the midst of a very precarious chapter of regional politics. When the 3rd King ascended the throne in 1953, India had barely recovered from the ravages of Partition and its territorial boundaries were far from secured. In the following decades, India fought several wars with Pakistan to the west and lost a major war against China in 1962 along Bhutan's borders in the northeastern frontiers. Bangladesh, which was East Pakistan, broke away and emerged as a new state in 1971 while Sikkim, Bhutan's neighbouring Buddhist kingdom, got usurped by India in 1975. To the north, Bhutan's intercourse with Tibet was eclipsed by China's expansionist policy to 'liberate' and annex Tibet to its 'motherland'. As the People's Liberation Army marched into Tibet, Tibetan political refugees, like in ancient times, trickled into Bhutan throughout the 1950s. When the brutal occupation of Tibet by China reached its climax in 1959 and Tibet's leader, the Dalai Lama, fled to India, Bhutan saw an exodus of Tibetans into Bhutan. This led to the closure of Bhutan's northern border and brought an abrupt end to the historical exchanges with Tibet, which in the meantime went through a tumultuous period under the Communist occupation and the madness of the Cultural Revolution. Tibet's harrowing tribulation under a repressive China continues in our times as indicated by the incessant self-immolations.

In comparison, Bhutan enjoyed relative peace and security under the capable leadership of the Kings. The southward diplomatic relationship Bhutan had developed with India early in the twentieth century no doubt played a significant part in ensuring Bhutan's sovereignty and peace. While the explicit confirmation of Bhutan's independence in the treaty of 1949 helped Bhutan avoid too much Indian interference, the Article in the treaty allowing India to guide Bhutan in its external affairs certainly deterred any expansionist interests the Chinese in Tibet could have harboured. Bhutan was clearly in the orbit of Indian influence as far as international politics was concerned. This was definitely made clear by Jawaharlal Nehru's visit to Bhutan in September 1958 when he travelled to Paro on horseback and on yaks. His historic visit was later followed by his daughter and grandson as prime ministers and a host of other Indian dignitaries. To make communications with India easier, the King also moved his court from Bumthang and Mangde first to Paro and then to Thimphu. The 3rd King visited India many times as did his son and grandson and a very close friendship also developed between the royal family and the Gandhi family, which continues to this day. In addition to the close political rapport, independent India also became the main sponsor of Bhutan's development programmes. Following Nehru's visit, independent India provided both financial and technical support needed for socioeconomic development, which British India in the first half of the twentieth century was reluctant to give despite repeated requests.

India's role in Bhutan's affairs at the time of fervent political expansionism and territorial conflicts in the region was undoubtedly of great benefit to Bhutan as was the generous support it gave for development in Bhutan. Yet, it required shrewd diplomacy and political dexterity on the part of Bhutan's leaders to skilfully juggle with a chaotic power like India. India at times was only too keen to play a big brotherly role in the affairs of Bhutan and to exercise a form of suzerainty, especially in Bhutan's foreign relations. Such political suzerainty was possible with its powerful presence in Bhutan. The

Jawaharlal Nehru, his daughter Indira Gandhi and the
3rd Druk Gyalpo with his family

Indira Gandhi on a yak on the 1958 trip to Bhutan

main artery of motor roads in Bhutan was built and managed by an Indian para-military company, Bhutan's northern borders were guarded by Indian soldiers and some of the main advisors to the King were Indian. The fear of Indian expansion into Bhutan was quite real, particularly at the time of the annexation of Sikkim.

However, through the decades, Bhutan managed to assert more and more self-determination, even in its external relations, although India was duly consulted as required by the treaty of 1949. The shifting powers in Delhi in the last decades of the twentieth century also helped Bhutan to gradually shake off Delhi's grip. The first step for Bhutan to emerge out of the Indian fold on the international arena as an independent state took place when Bhutan became a member of Colombo Plan in 1962. This was followed by joining the International Postal Union in 1969 but by far the most important achievement in this respect was Bhutan's entry into the United Nations in 1971. Since then, Bhutan ventured out to join many other international bodies and also opened embassies and diplomatic missions in many countries beyond India such as Thailand, Kuwait and Switzerland. The introduction of direct flights from Bhutan to third-world countries in the 1980s allowed Bhutan to physically bypass India.

By the beginning of the new millennium, Delhi had no political control over Thimphu, which took all its decisions independently. Although India continued to give military protection and provide a lion's share of Bhutan's development budget, the two countries stood on an equal footing in the international forums. Thus, in 2007 the two nations revised the old treaty and dropped the Articles on India's guidance of Bhutan's external relations and importation of arms and ammunitions only from India. The new treaty promoted perpetual peace, close friendship and cooperation between the two countries as neighbours of equal standing. Officially, this marked a new chapter of the relationship with India and was in tune with changing times. In a highly globalized world, Bhutan's political and diplomatic connections had no need to be (in fact could not be) confined bilaterally as either northward or southward orientation since advanced communication facilities allowed direct diplomatic and trade relations with distant countries as easily as with immediate neighbours.

Bhutan's relationship to India today, to use the familial analogy given by a diplomat, is like that of successful daughter to a possessive mother. The daughter has come of age, found her independent voice and life, and moved out of the mother's cosy care but the mother finds it difficult to let her go as much as she prides in the successful maturation of the child into a capable woman. Even today, India persists in holding some core areas and exercising influence on political matters although it is aware that such interventions are no longer needed or even welcome. Yet, if Bhutan is indeed comparable to a successful daughter, the credit for her making is to no small degree owed to India. Today, the daughter has surpassed her mother in beauty and political wisdom, in integrity and the standards of life, but the mother still looms large in her life holding the purse strings for the dowry, without which no daughter of India could easily start her independent life. She offers a comforting lap to turn to in the event the daughter fails to make ends meet and in doing so regularly pokes her nose into the daughter's private affairs. However, it is in the modern cultural traits and habits and economic reliance, which the daughter inherited during her upbringing, that we see the most enduring and worrying influence of the mother that is India.

Meanwhile, the relationship to the north with China remains marginal with occasional official meetings to settle the unresolved border issues. Large swathes of mountainous area, which were used by herder communities to whom international boundaries meant very little, still remain contested areas claimed by both sides but only China has managed to build roads through them. A few travellers cross the Himalayan watershed along ancient routes as pilgrims and some clandestine trade takes place across the high passes illegally. However, like in many other parts of the world, Chinese goods, having reached Bhutan via the sea and from India, are now widely available in Bhutan. Beyond this, China's presence is almost non-existent so much so that the meeting of Bhutan prime minister with the Chinese premier along the sidelines of Rio+20 conference managed to raise eyebrows in the subcontinent. While China is said to be keen on diplomatic overtures, Bhutan remains cautious, like a shy daughter influenced by her mother to keep away from an unworthy suitor.

If Bhutan's leaders have played the right cards on the international front, they did so successfully in the domestic arena as well although there is no denying that there were times of struggle and uncertainty. Barely halfway through his reign, the 3rd King faced a spate of internal turmoil following the assassination of Jigme Palden Dorji, the King's brother-in-law who acted also as his prime minister in 1964. The King was already at that time suffering from poor health and was being flown in and out of the country for treatment of a serious heart problem. Rumours were rife about tension between the King and his court officials on the one hand and the Dorji family of the Queen and prime minister on the other. Rustomji, a royal family friend and advisor at this time,[2] whose book is the most detailed account of this turmoil, saw this tension as one between the conservative traditionalist members of the royal court and the modernist and pro-Indian Dorji family. Leo Rose rejects this and gives the account of internal marital intrigue to explain the troubles. He puts the blame of assassination almost squarely on the family and supporters of the Tibetan mistress of the King.[3]

Whatever the actual cause, the prime minister was shot by a sniper in the middle of a card game in Phuntsholing and the King's chief of army was implicated in the assassination and executed in public after a quick trial. Even with the execution, the matter was far from settled as some harboured suspicions that the King might have implicitly given the order to eliminate his prime minister while others feared the in-laws might be plotting to overthrow the King. Word went around that a serious rift had developed between the Wangchuck and Dorji families and if we were to believe Rustomji, who claimed to be close to both families, the royal marriage was at a very low point. In fact, some members of the Dorji family and their supporters even left Bhutan on self-imposed exile. To make things worse, there was also an attempt on the King's life in Paro in 1965. The King narrowly missed a grenade thrown at him although this was again suspected by some to have been staged by the King to highlight the perceived threat.

These tensions and rumours eventually passed and the King managed to maintain a firm grip on the affairs of the country. The brief turmoil was a good reminder of the precariousness of the political situation but was of no serious consequence to the rule of monarchy or Bhutan's political stability. The country, as a whole, was firmly behind the King but the position of the Tibetan mistress, however, did not diminish as she became a mother of royal children. Perhaps emboldened by this, she began to increasingly appear in public as a royal consort and her audacious ostentation certainly got on the nerves of the royal in-laws. Sadly, the frail health of the King took a downturn before he could fully resolve the problems in his private life. The King died in 1972 in Nairobi from heart failure, bringing an abrupt end to his visionary and benevolent rule. The seventeen-year-old Crown Prince now took over the charge of the country without recourse to the interim regency but not long after he came to power, a plot by the Tibetan mistress and her cohort to overthrow the King and blow up the Tashichödzong was said to have been uncovered just in the nick of time. The plot was successfully aborted but the mistress managed to flee to India. Following this, many Tibetan refugees, including a couple important figures, were arrested and questioned as were some Bhutanese officials, who were close to the mistress. The incident led to a sordid acrimony between Bhutan and the Tibetan refugees, who, the government felt, abused the hospitality extended to them. As a result, thousands of Tibetan refugees, who had previously settled in Bhutan, moved to India although a great many stayed in Bhutan enjoying the same privileges as Bhutanese citizens. While very little is recorded or available in the public domain about this unfortunate episode, the Dalai Lama long held that his people in Bhutan have been made a scapegoat of an internal Bhutanese conflict. On the contrary, the Bhutanese believed that even the Dalai Lama's older brother had a hand in a subterfuge to oust the King and replace him by one of the sons of the late King from the Tibetan mistress. Ironically, the first ever Tibetan hunger protest in Delhi is said to been staged against Buddhist Bhutan, not Communist China.

The acrimony with the Tibetans was almost forgotten towards the end of the 1980s and the last prisoners held for their involvement in the alleged coup were being set free when a much more serious problem of dissidence began to brew in southern Bhutan among people of Nepali origin. We have already seen in the previous chapter how some of the British officers expressed misgivings concerning the rising population of Nepali immigrants in Bhutan. The immigrants were brought at the turn of the twentieth century as labourers to clear the forest along the foothills and the programme was encouraged by the British in the hope of counteracting the Sino-Tibetan influence from the north and securing Bhutan under their influence but already by the middle of the century, the British saw how the growing population of immigrants from a different culture was turning into a problem for stability in Bhutan. Both the 2nd King and the 3rd King faced small acts of dissent by leading immigrants of Nepali origin, who had some exposure to the democratic processes in the subcontinent. However, the dissidence to take place during the 4th King's reign at the end of 1980s surpassed earlier protests in both scale and fervour. 'The hermit kingdom,' according to the current prime minister, 'was forcibly shaken out of its cloister'[4] by this and it led to a protracted international refugee issue which would scar Bhutan's peaceful face to the world for several decades to come.

A great deal has already been written on this issue presenting the stories of both the Bhutanese government and the Nepali-speaking dissidents. Much of these writings are available online including my own analysis and need not be repeated here.[5] The sordid conflict was essentially an ethnic collision although it was presented in extremes by the dissidents as a programme of an ethnic cleaning and by the government as an anti-national terroristic movement. The issue is a very complex one involving, among other things, problems of immigration which every nation slightly more prosperous than its neighbours faces. The immigrants of Nepali origin, who had already settled in Bhutan by 1958, were given full citizenship as we have seen above. With generous cash incentives for cross-cultural marriages, the government also undertook an active programme of integration for the immigrants to assimilate into the mainstream culture. Instead of referring to them as Nepali, a local term 'Lhotshampa' or southerner was used as a politically correct designation for those people of Nepali origin, who have legally settled in Bhutan.

Aware of the cultural and political malaise among the immigrant populace and their potential threat to the security of country, the government made special allowances but primarily to encourage them to assimilate into the mainstream culture rather than boost their own ethnic identity. For the latter, the immigrants looked up to Nepal, their land of origin. The southern population, however, did not consist merely of bona fide citizens. There were thousands more who had entered Bhutan illegally through the porous border or came to work legally on the development projects, particularly road-building since 1960, and illegally settled in Bhutan. This immigration scenario arose due to the demographic mess the Himalayan foothills were in with an enormous and uncontrolled mass of roaming population of Nepali origin looking for greener pastures. While Nepal was bursting with its fast-growing population, Bhutan had low population density, plenty of fertile land and better social services, including free education and healthcare which attracted a lot of illegal immigrants. It was the separation of the legal and illegal immigrants during the census of 1988 without a reliable system of evidence to prove either way, which finally triggered the southern rebellion.

The rebellion was no doubt also partly occasioned by the enforcement of Bhutan's conservative policies. The King came to a realization that Bhutan's unique cultural identity, in the absence of military might or economic power, was its defining strength for its sovereignty. Thus, Bhutanese culture was actively promoted through various programmes, including the enforcement of *driglam namzha*, a traditional code of etiquette. The most palpable example of this enforcement in its material form was the requirement to wear the national dress in public places, which did not go down well with the southern population, who were used to Nepali dress, and the modern

Bhutanese youth, who preferred Western trousers. The wound got deeper when the government removed the Nepali language, which was taught in some primary schools until then, from the school curriculum in 1989. No doubt, the southern population felt these cultural strictures particularly acutely as the Nepali culture and language was expanding unabated in other parts of the Himalayan foothills, even replacing other cultures. Sikkim, Bhutan's Buddhist neighbour, was a good example. It first suffered a cultural invasion and then lost its sovereignty due to uncontrolled Nepali immigration. Bhutan direly needed to avoid Sikkim's fate.

Therefore, the southern rebellion was not caused by merely domestic grievances. It was indirectly fuelled by the political changes in Nepal, where Nepal's king was stripped of his power by the new democratic uprising, and the rise of Nepali power in Sikkim and the hill stations of West Bengal. Moreover, some ideas of Nepali cultural expansionism across the foothills from Nepal to Burma and an associated nationalism to build a greater Gorkha state were also floating in the region. Such political dreams and the hope of getting support from the democratic Nepal undoubtedly contributed to the sudden outburst of demonstration along the southern districts of Bhutan. Anti-government protests were carried out in several places simultaneously in 1990 but the zealous rebels went overboard to burn the national flag, strip Bhutanese officers' of the national dress and destroy census records. If the protests were intended to be civil disobedience against an unfair rule of an authoritarian government, this was thwarted at the outset by its wayward advocates. Instead of seeing it as a democratic or human rights movement, the majority of the Bhutanese public viewed it as campaign against the very existence of Bhutan and its cultural and political integrity.

The rebels initially caught the government unprepared but it did not take long for Thimphu to prepare its military and raise militia from all parts of northern Bhutan to suppress the rebellion. A fairly bloody conflict between the Bhutanese military and the armed rebels supported by Nepal and Nepali diasporas in India unfolded along southern Bhutan as the government scoured the area of recalcitrant rebels. For Bhutan, this was a serious test as it had not experienced any political upheaval of such magnitude since its last war with the British in 1865, let alone from an ethnic group as well known for valour at war as the Gorkha was. The protracted conflict led to the suspension of all development programmes in the southern areas. The government accused the rebels of terroristic activities of arson, robbery, extortion of money, kidnapping and murder while the dissidents accused the government of a reign of terror, ethnic cleansing and genocide. Most of the innocent southern citizens of Nepali origin were trapped between the two sides, being suspected of treason by both, against their country by the government and against their own people by the rebels. On a personal level, it was a conflict between a person's political affiliation and cultural identity, which now apparently became difficult to reconcile. Caught between the devil and the deep sea, many of them emigrated in the hope of finding a safe home in Nepal, where the UNHRC and Red Cross opened refugee camps, but most stayed in Bhutan to rebuild their lives.

The conflicts in Bhutan subsided by the middle of 1990s in favour of Bhutan but they left behind a protracted refugee issue which remains unresolved even today. The UNHRC camps in eastern Nepal received about 6000 refugees from Bhutan at the height of the conflict but the number shot up in the following years reaching over 1,00,000 by the end of 1993. While Nepal and some international organizations claimed all of them to be Bhutanese refugees and demanded Bhutan to have them repatriated *en masse,* Bhutan contested that they were all Bhutanese citizens. With a generous daily allowance in refugee camps and poor process of verification, Bhutan argued that many stateless and landless people in the area joined the refugee bandwagon. In an attempt to resolve the crisis, the governments of Nepal and Bhutan held some fifteen rounds of bilateral talks by 2003, the most significant achievement of the negotiations being the formation of the Joint Verification Team.

This team undertook the verification of 12,173 residents of the Khudunabari refugee camp and declared that 293 were forcefully evicted from Bhutan, 8595 emigrated voluntarily and 347 fled after criminal activities. The remainder (2948, that is, almost a quarter of the total) were said to have no links to Bhutan. When the result was announced, the Bhutanese members of the verification team came under missile attack from the frustrated crowd. This incident sadly stalled the negotiations and, with Nepal beset by its own political turmoil, no further progress has been made in resolving the issue bilaterally ever since. Meanwhile, many Western countries have offered third-country settlements for some of the refugees with the US alone agreeing to take in about 60,000. By the end of 2011, over half of the refugees have left the refugee camps to begin new lives in these third countries and the rest are waiting for their turns. In Bhutan itself, notwithstanding the clear memories people have of the rebellion and conflict, the refugee issue has ceased to be of any significance, apart from the havoc it continues to cause to Bhutan's international projection as a happy country. At the height of the conflict, Bhutan saw a spate of nationalism, which was partially fuelled by the state with slogans such as 'One nation, one people'.[6] Such nationalistic fever and ethnic tension fully subsided by the beginning of the new political chapter in 2008. The Lhotshampas, who still make up about twenty-five per cent of the population, have integrated into the northern culture and the ethnic tension is disappearing while the new democratic system also allows for greater multicultural co-existence.

The rebellion from the south was barely over when Bhutan was challenged by another security threat and violation of its sovereignty. Throughout the 1990s, three heavily armed Indian militant outfits started to operate from Bhutanese soil. The United Liberation Front of Asom was a secessionist group fighting against India for an independent socialist country of Assam and the National Democratic Front of Bodoland was fighting for free Bodoland in the Indian areas north of the Brahmaputra river. The third and most recently formed of the three groups was the Kamtapur Liberation Organization, which aimed for a separate state for the Cooch and Rajbongshi tribes. These militant outfits, each seeking their own political objectives, based themselves in the Bhutanese jungles along the southern border and waged a guerrilla war against the Indian states of Assam and West Bengal. Whenever they were defeated and chased by the Indian security forces, these militants escaped to bases in Bhutan. In this manner, they continued their insurrection against India and ignored Bhutan's calls to evacuate the camps on Bhutanese soil. This exasperated the Indian security forces and there may have been increasing pressure from Delhi for Bhutan to dislodge the militants. In the autumn of 2003, Bhutan gave its final ultimatum, which fell on deaf ears.

On 15 December 2003, the 4th King, in the fashion of a classical leader, led the Bhutanese offensive to flush out the militants. In a dextrous ploy to fool the enemies, religious ceremonies were conducted in the days leading to the attack in areas close to the camps of the militants. Soldiers dressed as priests infiltrated the area carrying weapons which were disguised as religious scriptures. The Bhutanese attack, under the commandership of the 4th King, was swift and well co-ordinated. Some thirty-five camps were routed in two days and 485 insurgents flushed out into India where the Indian security forces waited to arrest them. Eleven Bhutanese lost their lives and many more were wounded but it was a small casualty list for an outright victory. Reminiscent of the conflict with the British 138 years earlier in the same region, this was the last military operation Bhutan undertook to safeguard its sovereignty and security. The victory was later memorialized through the construction of 108 stupas on the Dochula Pass.

Socioeconomic development and cultural transformations

In spite of the minor turbulences we have discussed above, Bhutan's political transformation from a medieval polity to a twenty-first-century democracy was, on the whole, a steady process. It neither caused any serious disruption to the continuity of life in the country nor led to any radical shift in the power paradigm. The successive leaders were very wise and farsighted to bring about a healthy and progressive change and the people were not totally unfamiliar or unprepared for the new political processes. However, we see a very different story in the case of the socioeconomic and cultural changes, which Bhutan went through as it shed its isolation and embarked on modernization. The sociocultural transformation was both quite rapid and chaotic with widespread ramifications. No doubt the socioeconomic developments brought Bhutan many benefits, especially in areas of health, education and living standards, but the process also opened the floodgate for sociocultural influences from outside both in terms of ideas and articles. It would not be an exaggeration to say that Bhutan went through a greater societal change in the last fifty years than it did in the 500 years before the modern era. The changes catapulted the country from a medieval polity of a traditional religious worldview, subsistence agricultural economy and largely oral society into a modern world of a secular scientific worldview, market economy and audio-visual culture.

Bhutan's socioeconomic and cultural changes can be said to have occurred through two main processes: active modernization which Bhutan enthusiastically sought through its development programmes and passive globalization, which reached Bhutan insidiously and spread across the country, particularly with fast communication. We have already seen in the previous chapter how the initial seeds for these two processes were sown as early as the turn of the twentieth century. It was, however, during the reign of the 3rd King that we see these processes take off fully and change Bhutan's sociocultural landscape. In this respect, the year 1959 marks the beginning of Bhutan's programme of modernization. Following the successful visit of Jawaharlal Nehru, Bhutan launched its large-scale development programmes in 1959 through Indian support. The calculated move to modernize in close relations with the southern neighbour also betrays the anxieties Bhutan had with its northern neighbour. The brutal occupation of Tibet by China reached its culmination in March 1959 after a failed uprising by the Tibetans and the departure of the Dalai Lama into exile.

The first major development project was the construction of motor roads from India to Thimphu, which we have seen was already seriously desired in the preceding decades but not realized due to lack of resources. The construction of roads began in earnest in 1959 although the plan for the east–west national highway was drawn only in 1961 when Bhutan launched its first five-year plan. This framework for economic development on the basis of five-year periods was a Soviet model used by most other Communist countries and also adopted by India, which Bhutan later emulated. The first five-year plan started in 1961 and the current tenth five-year plan is due to end in 2013. By the end of the first five-year plan in 1966, Bhutan had already achieved an impressive 1770 km of motorable roads and this increased gradually in the following decades to reach 9492 km in 2011. Today, most villages are connected by motor roads, and communication by road between the different parts of Bhutan and with India has improved immensely.

The introduction of the Drukair service in 1983 took the development of communication even further. Today, the domestic air service connects places in eastern and western Bhutan in twenty minutes, covering a distance which earlier took about twenty days by foot and twenty hours by car. Moreover, the introduction of international flights allowed Bhutan to directly reach countries beyond India. Simultaneously, more and more Bhutanese travelled abroad for work or study. Bhutanese today can be found from Australia to Alaska and even the majority of rural Bhutanese have ventured to India on pilgrimage at least once in their life. In a single generation, the Bhutanese conception and understanding of the world, time and space, has been utterly transformed and with it, the peoples' interests, outlooks and lifestyles.

The development in communication was not merely of physical movement and transport but also of exchange of ideas and information. A systematic postal service was introduced in 1962 to replace the old runner service and was quickly followed by telephone and telegraph facilities. This enhanced the communication within the country but Bhutan's exposure to the outside world was minimal in the initial years of development. As India was Bhutan's main source of both financial and human capital, whatever intercourse Bhutan had with the outside world was almost entirely with or through India. This began to change after Bhutan became a member of the United Nations in 1971 and with the launch of tourism in 1974. Yet, only about 1000 tourists arrived annually in the early days of tourism with a total of 7800 tourists before 1981. With improvements in infrastructure and ease of travel, this gradually increased to 6392 tourists in 2001 but the number of tourists visiting Bhutan shot up rapidly in the new century. According to *Kuensel*,[7] a record number of 105,414 tourists including 53,504 high-end visitors arrived in Bhutan in 2012. Despite serious anxieties among many people of the sociocultural implications of large-scale tourism, the current government is bent to rope in 100,000 high-end tourists each year from 2012. Bhutan's former policy of 'high value, low volume' is now being rephrased as 'high value, low impact'. A vivid sign of the ubiquitous and overwhelming presence of tourists is seen in some of the remote village festivals where tourists now outnumber the locals.

In addition to growing number of tourists, Bhutan's exposure to the outside world also drastically increased with developments in information technology. While previously only a few who travelled abroad had direct experience of the outside world, in 1999, the outside world came tumbling directly into people's homes in the form of a magic box. Television, which was kept at bay until then, spread quickly through the country. By 2007, 37.7 per cent of about 125,500 households of Bhutan had access to television and reports in 2011 suggest that, with Direct-to-Home TV services, over 50 per cent of the population spend at least two hours zapping through some 190 channels. Many families now take their meals in front of the box instead of around the hearth. Grandpas no longer have an occasion or an audience for their stories around the fireplace and even village grannies reschedule their daily prayers so as not to miss Indian TV serials and soaps.

The internet was introduced at the same time as TV and has had an equally invasive and rapid impact on society. This box fitted into a shoulder bag and could access information and direct communication in an instant. By April 2011, there were 97,955 internet subscribers and the government aims to connect all county offices to fibre optic broadband network by 2013. A significant number of Bhutanese youths today have Facebook accounts and spend hours logged onto chatrooms and online forums. The last major technology to arrive was mobile telephone in 2003. This magic box fitted inside one's pocket. Most Bhutanese homes and villages embraced mobile telephony without ever using the wired landlines. In April 2011, the prime minister reported that 419,926 people (59.3 per cent of the population) had mobile phones. After airlifting fifteen tonnes of equipment by helicopter into Lunana—the most northerly and remote valley in the kingdom—Bhutan

Telecom declared in October 2011 that mobile coverage in the country had reached 100 per cent.

The fast improvement in communication had a major impact on people's mobility and culture and led to an unprecedented sense of homogeneity, shared national identity and culture. Sixty years ago, there was no national language or shared cuisine as the country was deeply divided into numerous valley communities which rarely mixed with one another. The idea of chilli and cheese as a shared Bhutanese cuisine is a recent one as is the status of Dzongkha as a national language. We have already surveyed the linguistic and cultural diversity in traditional Bhutan in the second chapter. Much of this cultural and linguistic heritage is ebbing away with the homogenizing effect of modernization and globalization. Today, there is not only an intense fusion of local Bhutanese cultures but a widespread tendency to adopt a modern Western trend which is in vogue, as we shall see in some examples shown later.

The process of modernization no doubt brought developments in the social sectors such as health and education. Only a couple of dispensaries existed before 1959 but the government undertook an active campaign of immunization and construction of hospitals and dispensaries in the subsequent years. By the end of the first five-year plan in 1966, three hospitals and forty dispensaries were established. Today, there are about 250 hospitals and dispensaries across the country delivering health services to approximately 90 per cent of the population. However, the number of doctors remained dismally low at 181, roughly only three doctors for 10,000 people even by 2011. People generally have access to clean drinking water and free medical facilities. Life expectancy, before the modern era, was as low as forty-five years with infant mortality rate at about 20 per cent. This rate was slashed to around six per cent in the middle of 2000 and to about two per cent today and life expectancy has moved to about sixty-five years. A visible impact of the modern health programme is the disappearance of goitre, which was a familiar sight before iodized salt was distributed. Leprosy is another example. Traditionally, leprosy was considered a contagious disease and lepers were removed from communities and made to live in seclusion away from the main settlements. Such social exclusion is now unheard of and leprosy has been virtually eliminated as have several other health problems.

The living standards of the people also improved with Bhutan moving upward on the UN's Human Development Index and enjoying the highest per capita income in the region although about 25 per cent of the population was still living under income poverty line in 2010. Another major achievement of development which has brought significant changes to people's living conditions is electrification. Today, nearly all homes are connected to electricity and this has transformed the people's ways of time use, eating habits, social life and even dating practices. Yet, Bhutan's encounter with modernity was an apprehensive meeting with the strange and unknown. Modernization primarily involved the introduction of exogenous items and ideas which did not always blend well with the indigenous world. The use of plastic and synthetic materials is a case in point. As the arrival and widespread use of this new material coincided with the beginning of the modern period, this period can be rightly called the plastic era. People initially fell for the new, light, cheap and weather-proof materials but their attraction is slowly fading away as the non-biodegradable synthetic materials outlast their use, clogging drains or littering even remote sacred sites. Another example is the use of processed sugar in Bhutanese foodways. Prior to the modern era, Bhutanese did not have access to refined crystalline sugar but only to some sugarcane and raw sugar from India. Tea was synonymous with salty butter tea but today the Bhutanese have acquired a strong sweet tooth and tea is usually identified with 'sweet tea' (མངར་ཇ་). The new taste, however, is not without negative consequences to people's eating habits and public health. Even in the case of useful electricity, short circuit is said to have been the cause of most recent house fires including those which destroyed the temple of Pagar and the historic *dzong* of Wangdiphodrang in 2012.

By far the most dramatic and far-reaching of the changes Bhutan saw during the modern era can be attributed to the programme of education. The nationwide introduction of modern school education brought about fundamental changes in the social, cultural, political and economic structures, and has revolutionized the Bhutanese worldview, outlook and way of life. Before the modern era, education was largely imparted in monasteries and only the clergy and some elites had access to it. We have seen the efforts of the 1st and 2nd Kings to change this and modernize education to make it more universal. In 1959, eleven schools were established and about 440 students enrolled in them. By the end of the first five-year plan in 1966, there were 108 schools with 15000 students. Today, Bhutan has over 600 educational institutions with about 2,00,000 youth in full-time education. The adult literacy rate has risen from an estimate of 17 per cent before the modern era to about 60 per cent today and primary school enrolment has also nearly reached 100 per cent although the government is yet to make primary education compulsory.

The most pervasive and fundamental impact of education nevertheless was not as much from the accessibility of education as from the new content and worldview the modern school education introduced. Traditional Bhutan functioned primarily based on the cultural ethos derived from the Buddhist and pre-Buddhist belief and religious systems. The traditional worldviews, perceptions, attitudes, behaviour and practices in general and the pre-modern education system in particular were informed by religious values and principles. The traditional education system focused on the internal mind and was aimed at cultivating wisdom and other sublime qualities and reaching the soteriological goal of enlightenment. Internal values took precedence over external and material developments, and traditional education promoted worldviews such as the understanding of interdependence and impermanence of all things, the theory of *karma* and the dream-like illusory nature of existence. It was a value-driven liberal education imparted in the religious institutions or through regular upbringing.

With the introduction of modern school education, Bhutan saw the arrival of a new system of ideas. The modern school curriculum and method of instruction focused on the development of knowledge and skills with the ultimate aim of seeking human development and improving living conditions. It had limited traditional religious content and promoted the modern secular and scientific worldview, which explained the complex world and all life forms in it in terms of a material and chemical processes. With a stronger extrovert orientation to matter outside than to the mind inside, the new education system was a clear departure from the traditional worldview and it inadvertently promoted materialism. Furthermore, the new educational system was deeply embedded in the Western cultural concepts, outlooks and principles which stood in stark contrast to the traditional Buddhist ones.

If traditional education was *out of time* for not being up-to-date in the modern era, modern education was *out of place* for being an alien system haphazardly implanted in the Bhutanese society without sufficient adaptation. Even the textbooks were directly borrowed from India or written by people with poor understanding of the local cultural context. The adoption of English as the medium of instruction in schools took this even further. Only one out of the eight daily sessions at school contained a genuine Bhutanese education.

Thus, the children grew up learning in a Western language, absorbing Western ideas and emulating Western characters. They would have read about King Arthur but learnt nothing about King Gesar and read Sherlock Holmes but not even heard of Śāntideva.

The modern education ushered in a whole new set of ideas and outlooks which was largely alien to Bhutan. The rapid spread of modern education not only transformed the patterns of education but the whole cultural ethos of the country. In educational practice, it was a shift of focus from a sacred liberal training, which emphasized inner development, to a secular and technical education, which aimed at enhancing external material and socioeconomic development. But its main impact was the sociocultural disjunction it entailed beyond the school premises. It gave rise to a whole new generation of literati and a widening linguistic and cultural rift between the modern educated youth and the older generation who had traditional upbringing. While the old generation viewed the world and purpose of life from the traditional Buddhist perspective, the modern educated generation approached life and the world from a modern Western perspective.

The Bhutanese protégés of modern education today represent a culture in transition and change. Unlike the older generation who are mellow in the traditional context, they have neither a strong footing in the old traditional setting nor a firm ground in the new and modern affair of things. Yet, with one foot in modernity based on the Western model and the other in the traditional past, they live a diachronic life, which is at once very novel, chaotic and confused but also adventurous and dynamic. Their aspirations, expectations, values, and priorities in life vastly differ from those of their parents. It is a new order of life, which is somewhere between tradition and modernity, between the ancient roots of the East and new trends of the West but largely a shallow populist pursuit of life without a firm grounding in the artistic and intellectual traditions of either one. We have already seen this state of diachronic conundrum in the case of language in the second chapter. While a few may have succeeded to integrate the two seamlessly, thus having the best of both worlds, most modern Bhutanese are in a cultural limbo, having relinquished the old but not fully reached the new. Their cultural identity, formed from a shaky convergence of the two, is as amorphous as it is insecure. Symptoms of such insecurity and immaturity can be seen in the poor sense of aesthetic taste and a peculiar sense of sophistication and the hybrid culture which begins to emerge.

Much more can be said about the sociocultural affects of modernization on Bhutan and Bhutanese identity than space here will permit. Let me briefly illustrate the shift in people's worldview and perception through the examples of their approaches to nature and people. The Bhutanese approach to nature has the three phases inspired by three different worldviews. The first phase is based on the animistic and shamanistic beliefs found in their numerous localized forms. In this phase, nature represented a powerful and indomitable force to be reckoned with. Mountains, lakes, cliffs, rivers and forests were seen as formidable sites or abodes of a plethora of non-human spirits, who sometimes communicated with the people through shamans and oracles. The Bhutanese world was teeming with non-human agencies ranging from the benevolent gods to bloodthirsty demons, from ever-present mountain deities to roaming ghosts. The traditional Bhutanese life was marked by beliefs, behaviour and rituals to live in harmony with these invisible forces.

The second phase starts with the introduction of Buddhism. With its message of non-violence and transcendence, Buddhism brought about a great change in people's perception of nature. Buddhism did not annihilate the previous beliefs but incorporated them skilfully. With the focus on the internal mind, Buddhism argued the world is a creation of the mind and the power of the mind surpassed the power of external nature. The spread of Buddhism was not merely about the conversion of the people. It involved the conversion of nature from a formidable malevolent force to a wholesome habitat. Nature was tamed and transformed into spiritually conducive dwelling while the malevolent denizens in it were subdued and converted into righteous guardian deities. Nature's power, such as wind and water, was harnessed to be used for the greater good of merit-making and enlightenment. Wide stretches of nature were earmarked as spiritual sanctuaries in the forms of holy mountains, hidden valleys, sacred lakes and power spots. The pre-Buddhist and Buddhist worldview treated nature as a living organism and has been so far the main driving force behind Bhutan's rich ecology.

The Bhutanese today have entered the third phase of their intercourse with nature. The new secular scientific worldview promoted by modern education reduces nature to its material and chemical parts and processes and shuns the belief in supernatural force as superstitions. It removes the non-human players in nature and gives people the centrestage to deal with nature. This worldview, accompanied by the insidious growth of materialism and a consumerist lifestyle, has led to some unrestrained exploitation of nature. To combat this problem which originated in the Western secular worldview, the Bhutanese today turn to Western solutions. Nature conservation is now sought mainly through the Western environmentalist discourse, by promoting environmental education, legislations and establishments of protected areas. Spirituality may be on a decline but environmental awareness and state legislations are filling the vacuum left by the supernatural force as deterrents to exploitation. But will people fear the human state as much as the non-human spirits?

The shift in the attitude to nature is comparable to the changes in attitude towards people. The Bhutanese mode of social interaction and organization went through a sweeping change and continues to do so. The traditional village communities were God-fearing and their actions largely regulated by belief in unseen divine forces. They generally cherished all forms of life, particularly the precious human form (མི་ལུས་རིན་པོ་ཆེ), and faithfully adhered to moral values and principles such as the law of karma (ལས་རྒྱུ་འབྲས་) and moral integrity (མཐའ་དཀར་ཚིག་).[8] The traditional society was based on a hierarchical structure in which the superior and elder led by examples and the inferior and younger followed with obedience but the gap between the two was not too wide to cause a serious rift. Such a structure generally worked well for a secluded, close-knit community. Social cohesion was secured through unwritten bonds, obligations, norms and customs which were faithfully observed out of fear for a divine or karmic punishment. Moreover, money played very little role in the traditional economy and its absence, as Turner noted in 1783,[9] helped to avoid various vices associated with the monetized economy.

The modern Bhutanese diverged from most of these personal traits and situations. If the scientific and secular education made people less God-fearing and more materialistic, their materialistic tendency was further aroused by the lures of modern consumerism. Exposure to more expensive goods and higher standards of living is redefining people's interests, expectations and goals in life. Today, there is no dearth of enticements for the Bhutanese to unleash their greed and avarice. The growth of materialism is exacerbated by the rapid spread of consumerism. With subsistence farming and the barter system swiftly replaced by a cash economy and a large portion of the population living a non-agrarian life, cash has become the new blood of Bhutan's economic organism. After monetization of the economy, it did not take long for money to become the foremost objective of people's endeavours and for vices associated with money to appear in Bhutan.

The consumerist lifestyle based on a cash economy provided a conducive environment for the growth of another social phenomenon: individualism.

The traditional Bhutanese were a highly communal people with very little sense of privacy and personal space. Their attitude towards the other is marked more by its openness and accommodation than by reserve and concern for private space. This, however, began to change with the generation of modern Bhutanese, who have acquired a new notion of space and individualism through Western influence. Similarly, the traditional Bhutanese enjoyed a robust sense of humour and an easygoing approach to life and had few hang-ups but the modern Bhutanese have acquired a new kind of sensibility. They put on a peculiar show of sophistication and self-importance which sharply contrasts with the sincerity and simplicity prevalent among traditional people. The modern Bhutanese are less tolerant but more sensitive, less intrusive but more constricted.

If materialism, consumerism and individualism are like modern social pests, Bhutan's new urban settlements have become a perfect breeding ground for them. The urban townships, none of which really existed before the modern period, constitute a whole new Bhutan and this urban environment largely shapes the character of modern Bhutan. It is in the urban centres such as Thimphu, most of which were regrettably built in former rice bowls and are still growing at an alarming rate, that we see the collision of tradition and modernity and the emergence of a new Bhutanese personality and a hybrid culture. With better amenities and higher prospects for comfortable life, people are flocking to the towns, leaving many parts of the rural cultural and agricultural heartlands virtually empty. It is estimated that Thimphu, in particular, is growing at a staggering 10 per cent each year until recently. This is not only leading to severe decline of cultural and agricultural activity in the country but also putting immense pressure on the urban infrastructure. As fairly recent developments, the urban centres have little or no social organization or community support in place to either address their social ills or engage their members meaningfully. Without the closely knit social fabric known in traditional rural settings, problems such as crimes and substance abuse have become all too common. Places such as Thimphu have an alarming suicide rate with some eleven cases reported in the first half of 2010 alone.

Bhutan's sprawling towns represent an emerging society and its struggle to cope with the stresses of modern life. Pollution in the urban environment is high while the sense of civic responsibility is low. Unlike rural villagers, urban residents are yet to take ownership of their new surroundings. Cultural and social avenues to engage the large populations, apart from the commercial outlets, are few and far between. Due to constraints in space and resources, there is also an increase in nuclear families in place of large and extended families, leading to more individualism. Yet, the towns are the exciting meeting grounds of exogenous modernity and endogenous tradition and we see a new urban culture emerge out of this chaotic convergence. The urban architecture is a very good example of this. It attempts to have the best of both but often results in a crude mixture of the two having neither the benefit of modern facilities nor the aesthetics of traditional designs. Similarly, we see the fusion of modern Western practices with the local tradition in the area of intangible culture. For instance, the celebration of birthdays was unknown in Bhutan in pre-modern times. Instead, Bhutanese observed death anniversaries in remembrance of the deceased. Today, the practice of birthday celebrations, especially for children, has become a common practice but instead of blowing out candles (which is considered inauspicious in local culture), the Bhutanese ingenuously have the birthday child light a butterlamp.

Another example is the proliferation of wedding parties. Ceremonies for nuptial bonds were rare in the past and limited to certain areas and some aristocratic families who adopted Tibetan customs. The Buddhist tradition does not have wedding rituals. However, today, new wedding rituals incorporating an element of Buddhist prayers and a big luncheon are common in Thimphu and other urban centres. Such invention of tradition, inevitably, comes with its own set of problems and challenges. While most people still approach such public displays of affection and novel rituals with some discomfort, the rituals have led to economic pressures amongst peers to throw grander parties or give more expensive presents. In a small society where most people know each other, it is also causing a stigma for those who cannot have these ceremonies.

The modern habit of attaching the father's or husband's name to one's name in imitation of foreign cultures is another case of a modern accretion. Bhutanese traditionally received their names from religious figures individually and did not have the tradition of a family name. However, many parents today choose either the whole or part of their children's names, and some children and female spouses add the second name of the father as their surname. Trendy as it may seem, this has its own practical and social problems. Bhutanese first names are generally gender-neutral and one has to tell the gender of the person by their second name. This is now impossible in the case of a girl who adopts her father's second name as her second name. It is also a socially regressive practice in embracing a patriarchal symbol in favour of Bhutanese tradition with gender equality. There are many other examples of such cultural adoptions and adaptations.

As Bhutan's engagement with modernity is still in its exciting, romantic phase, it is still early to gauge the full impact of the unfolding relationship. Although the management and organization of the country on the state level appears to have found a general sense of direction and stability, the social fabric on the community level, in both rural and urban Bhutan, is seriously strained. The process of modernization and urbanization has certainly altered the social dynamics and ushered in a complicated and unpredictable relationship between the state and people and among people themselves. To deal with the complexity and uncertainty, we see a rapid increase in the number of legislations and rules to regulate the frenzy of change. Each year, many new acts are passed by the parliament but the institutions which enforce these laws are still not fully developed. Sadly, even when they become fully developed, they will not have the same restraining influence as the ubiquitous and unfailing spiritual forces did in the traditional past. Instead, the proliferation of laws and regulations is indirectly leading to further decline of common sense and traditional wisdom.

Even the economic progress, which has evidently improved the living standards, has posed a serious problem of disequilibrium with a growing disparity between the rural poor and urban rich and an unprecedented reliance on India. Before modernization, Bhutan had a self-sufficient economy with salt being perhaps the only essential item imported from Tibet or India. Today, over 60 per cent of Bhutan's essential goods, including rice, comes from India. Both as an exporter of hydroelectric power and importer of goods and raw materials, Bhutan has become dangerously dependent on India. This economic dependence no doubt also prolongs India's political and cultural influence on Bhutan and it was only a matter of time for such dependence to cause a serious problem. The first jolt of the problem was felt in the early months of 2012 when it ran out of its stock of rupees to buy goods from India even after selling several hundred million dollars from its foreign currency reserve to India.

On the political front, the process of democratization is generally progressing with no upheaval although a large number of citizens are yet to fully grasp the rights and responsibilities they have in a democracy. Three new political parties emerged to compete, alongside the ruling and opposition parties, in the second parliamentary elections in the spring of 2013. While traditional community systems are declining, Bhutan is today witnessing the emergence of a new type of social organization and social support in the form of civil society organizations. Since 2010 when the Civil Society Organization Act was passed, some twenty-eight groups have become registered civil society organizations and are playing an active role in supplementing the state programmes of development, filling the gaps left by the government or mitigating the impacts of changes in the society. Another major development since the 2006 was the rise of the media. Bhutan had only one newspaper and one radio and TV station in the beginning of 2006 but this increased drastically to twelve newspapers and news magazines, six radio stations and two local television channels in 2012. The proliferation of the media and critical journalism has changed the mode of public discourse and information although both the state and people are still grappling to understand the roles and responsibilities of the media.

The dragon's tryst with happiness

No story of Bhutan could end without the mention of Gross National Happiness, which is increasingly becoming the trademark of Bhutan to the outside world. A great deal has already been written on GNH and can be easily found online. Thus, apart from an introductory note on the topic, there is no need for a detailed account or analysis here. The concept has been variably described by its advocates as a development philosophy, guiding principle, overarching goal of development and, lately, as a new development paradigm. It is currently being used as the overall framework for Bhutan's development programmes and increasingly being presented to the outside world as a new model of development, which takes into account many other factors influencing human well-being beside economic growth.

The concept is commonly attributed to the 4th King, whose kaleidoscopic view of a holistic human development it is suppose to capture. It is commonly thought that the 4th King extemporaneously coined the term in response to a question from a journalist concerning Bhutan's GNP some time in 1979. His reply 'Gross National Happiness is more important than Gross National Product' has since gained proverbial status and forms the locus classicus of the entire GNH discourses and discussions which are in vogue today. The earliest printed discussion we have is a *Financial Times* article in 1987 from which we know that GNH remained the underlying ethos for the 4th King's approach to development and modernization. The King was convinced that Bhutan's aim of development should not be merely economic prosperity but contentment and happiness 'which includes political stability, social harmony and Bhutanese culture and way of life.' However, the exposition of GNH as a national goal of development began to emerge only towards the end of the twentieth century. The rise of the current prime minister, Jigme Y. Thinley as a leading statesman and the establishment of the Centre for Bhutan Studies as a government think tank facilitated the promotion of GNH as a national intellectual discourse.

It is a simple and well-known fact that happiness is desired universally. Since very ancient times, the pursuit of happiness has remained a central concern of human existence. This is particularly the case with the Buddhist tradition prevalent in Bhutan, in which happiness is emphatically sought as the ultimate goal of all worldly and spiritual endeavours. It is very common to hear in Bhutan the murmurs of daily prayers for happiness of all sentient beings by both young and old. Thus, there is nothing new or revolutionary in the idea of seeking happiness. Yet, it was visionary for a monarch to crystallize the ideas and practices which remained diffused in the society into a formal national policy in order to guide development programmes. The 4th King was farsighted and judicious enough to not lose sight of the ultimate goal in the course of the frantic process of modernization.

However, despite the pervasive presence of happiness in spirit and practice in Bhutan's communities, the notion of GNH as a technical concept was totally new to the people. To begin with, the term Gross National Happiness was coined from the economic term Gross National Product, which most Bhutanese have not even heard of, let alone understand. Moreover, there was no terminology for it in Dzongkha or other Bhutanese languages and the rough equivalent, Gyalyong Gakyi Pelzom (རྒྱལ་ཡོངས་དགའ་སྐྱིད་དཔལ་འཛོམས་), was coined only at the turn of this century. When this was first introduced, most people had no clue while some thought it was a new government department. It was also confusing because the term sounds like a feminine name. On being asked for his take on it by a radio journalist, a man replied: 'From what I hear, she seems beautiful but I have not yet seen her.'

This, however, changed quickly as the concept became a hot topic of discussion for the nation's literati by the end of the twentieth century. The discussion was mainly triggered by the new exposition of GNH by Jigme Y. Thinley, in whom the concept found a highly willing, capable and eloquent advocate. He took the construction of the GNH edifice further by providing it four concrete pillars of socioeconomic development, good governance, cultural preservation and environmental conservation. He launched this framework in 1998 during the Millennium Meeting for Asia and the Pacific in Seoul. Since then, GNH has been discussed and debated in no less than five major conferences and several publications. Leading development specialists and economists have taken interest in it. The Centre for Bhutan Studies under the stewardship of Dasho Karma Ura was put in charge of developing GNH index and indicators to make it accountable and assessable and internationally applicable.

The Centre for Bhutan Studies took GNH to the next level by breaking down the conditions for collective happiness and developing a complex and comprehensive set of seventy indicators under nine domains of psychological well-being, living standard, good governance, health, education, time use, community vitality, cultural diversity and ecological resilience. The conventional econometrics, which measured a country's progress only through its economic growth and consumption were not sufficient to capture the actual status of happiness. This is because external material comfort does not necessarily lead to internal happiness. The main thrust of the GNH index is to include all important social, cultural, economic and ecological factors determining human happiness, which is not reflected by the GDP or even covered by the UN's Human Development Index. It works with the premise that happiness is a collective public good and it can be sought through public policies.

The index and its method of measuring the state of happiness in the society are still in the process of being tried and tested in Bhutan. Two rounds of nationwide surveys have been conducted so far. Meanwhile, the GNH policy is also being experimented in practice through the adoption of a screening tool by the country's main planning authority, now renamed the GNH Commission. Every government project is in principle assessed for its GNH worthiness using a screening chart before it is approved.

Despite these attempts to make GNH philosophically and econometrically tenable, the initiative is not without problems and criticisms. Most people argue that happiness is a state of the mind and an internal subjective experience. What triggers the experience of happiness differs from person to person depending on their cultural background, individual interest and often on the point of comparison. Any attempt on the part of a state or government to provide, let alone impose, a uniform value or definition of happiness is futile. What the state must create are the conducive conditions required for the experience of happiness. While many agree that GNH is a useful framework for guiding development and giving it a sense of direction, they argue that for a developing country like Bhutan the government's priority must be in improving the basic conditions for happiness rather than excessively talking about happiness itself. These critics point out that even today over 20 per cent of the population live under the national poverty line, governance and public services are far from efficient, youth delinquency and crimes are rising while the cultural heritage is eroding and the economy is ever more precarious with too much dependence on imported goods. At such times, GNH dangerously veers to the point of being an ideological distraction from the real issues and problems. If the 4th King introduced GNH so that Bhutan will not miss the forest for trees, there is now a risk of missing the trees for the forest.

Being a misplaced priority or distraction is not the only problem associated with GNH. It is an initiative to define and measure happiness, which is essentially non-quantifiable and immeasurable. Even many of the conditions for happiness are qualitative states and not quantifiable. Many of its critics note that happiness may be best left to the individuals and that the state should focus on improving the basic needs of the people. Furthermore, it is not realistic to seek all components of GNH as some of them are not consistent with each other but are even mutually exclusive. For instance, the many symbols of hierarchy in the name of culture are not consistent with the egalitarian outlook required for good democratic governance. Similarly, the promotion of tourism for economic benefit may lead to an erosion of culture. Yet, the most serious question its critics raise relates to the commitment of its advocates beyond mere rhetoric. Questions are asked about how much do some of those who preach GNH sincerely take it to their heart and practice it? There is a perception among some quarters that GNH is merely an intellectual occupation for the elites, who enjoy all the benefits in life, and that it is a catchy branding for promoting Bhutan to the outside world while the ordinary and poor citizens struggle for their daily needs. No doubt, many questions are raised and GNH is also being increasingly bandied by the dissatisfied citizens to verbally bash the government and leaders for any failure. If it is an ideal the leaders have chosen for the country, they are now being earnestly expected to live up to it, however lofty it may be.

GNH has, however, captured the imagination of many developed countries, which are suffering from the affects of the recent economic recession and are disillusioned by the current economic model of measuring progress through growth and consumption. Many countries are now turning to Bhutan for a new order of life balancing material comfort with spiritual well-being and economic growth with ecological and cultural integrity. In 2011, the UN General Assembly unanimously passed a resolution initiated by Bhutan to place happiness on the global agenda. A high-level meeting was held in April 2012 on the sidelines of the UN General Assembly to draw a road map for GNH as a new global economic paradigm. In the past decade, Bhutan has been itself voted as the happiest country in Asia and the eighth and thirteenth happiest in the world according to two separate surveys conducted by institutions in the UK. Today, even while young Bhutanese eye an opportunity to travel to the US and engage in manual jobs to earn quick bucks, the rest of the world is looking up to Bhutan as a happy country—a postmodern Shangrila. It is indeed a very lofty position to reach and perhaps even loftier to maintain in the changing fortunes of time.

Bibliography

Anonymous (1865), 'The Truth about Bootan', Chakravarti, *A Cultural History of Bhutan,* Calcutta: Self Employment Bureau Publications, vol. II, pp. 139–74.

Anonymous (1966), *sMan ljongs 'brug rgyal khab chen po'i sde srid khri rabs dang brgyud 'dzin gyi rgyal po rim par byon pa'i rgyal rabs deb ther gsal ba'i me long,* manuscript. n.p.

Anonymous (n.d.), *sKyes bu dam pa rnam kyi rnam par thar pa rin po che'i gter mdzod,* n.p.

Ardussi, John (2008), 'Gyalse Tenzin Rabgye (1638–1696), Artist Ruler of 17th-century Bhutan' in Bartholomew and Johnston, *The Dragon's Gift: Sacred Arts of Bhutan*, Chicago: Serindia Publications.

—— (2004a), 'The Gdung Lineages of Central and Eastern Bhutan—A reappraisal of their origin, based on literary sources' in Karma Ura & Sonam Kinga, *The Spider and the Piglet,* Thimphu: Centre for Bhutan Studies, pp. 60–70.

—— (2004b), 'The 17th Century Stone Inscription from Ura Village', *Journal of Bhutan Studies,* Thimphu: Centre for Bhutan Studies, vol. 11, pp. 1–11.

—— and Karma Ura (2000), 'Population and Governance in mid-18th Century Bhutan, as Revealed in the Enthronement Record of *Thugs-sprul 'Jigs med grags pa I* (1725-1761),' *Journal of Bhutan Studies*, Thimphu: Centre for Bhutan Studies, vol. 2. no. 2, pp. 36–78.

—— (1999), The Rapprochement between Bhutan and Tibet under the Enlightened Rule of sDe-srid XIII Shes-rab-dbang-phyug (r.1744–63), *Journal of Bhutan Studies*, Thimphu: Centre for Bhutan Studies, vol. 1, no. 1, pp. 64–83.

—— (1977), *Bhutan before the British: A historical study,* Thesis submitted to the Australian National University.

Aris, Michael (1997), 'Himalayan Encounters', in Samten Karmay and Philippe Sagant, *Les Habitants du Toit du Tibet: Étude Recueillies en*

Hommage à Alexander W. Macdonald, Nanterre: Société d'ethnologie, pp.179–188.

—— (1995), *'Jigs-med-gling-pa's 'Discourse on India' of 1789,* Tokyo: The International Institute of Buddhist Studies.

—— (1994), *The Raven Crown: The Origins of Buddhist Monarchy in Bhutan,* London: Serindia Publications.

—— (1989), *Hidden Treasure and Secret Lives: A Study of Pemalingpa (1450–1521) and the Sixth Dalai Lama (1683–1706),* London: Kegan Paul International.

—— (1988), 'The Temple-Palace of gTam-zhing as Described by its Founder', *Arts Asiatiques,* xliii, pp. 33–39.

—— (1986), *Sources for the history of Bhutan,* Wien: Arbeitskreis für Tibetische und buddhistische studien universität wien.

—— (1982), *Views of Medieval Bhutan: Diary and Drawings of Samuel Davis 1783,* London: Serindia Publications.

—— (1979), *Bhutan: The Early History of a Himalayan Kingdom,* Warminster: Aris and Philips Ltd.

Ashi Dorji Wangmo Wangchuck (1999), *Of Rainbows and Clouds: The Life of Yab Ugyen Dorji as told to his Daughter,* London: Serindia Publications.

Baillie, Luiza Maria (1999), 'Father Estevao Cacella's Report on Bhutan in 1627', *Journal of Bhutan Studies,* vol. 1, no. 1. Thimphu: Centre for Bhutan Studies, pp. 1–35.

Barawa Gyaltshen Palzang (1970), 'rJe btsun ba ra wa rgyal mtshan dpal bzang po'i rnam thar mgur 'bum dang bcas pa', in *The Collected Writings of 'Ba'ra ba rGyaltsen dPal bzang,* Dehra Dun: Ngawang Gyaltsen and Ngawang Lungtok, vol. 14.

Bartholomew, Terese and Johnston, John (2008), *The Dragon's Gift: Sacred Arts of Bhutan,* Chicago: Serindia Publications.

Ba Salnang (1982), *sBa bzhed,* Beijing: Mi rigs dpe skrun khang.

Beal, Samuel (tr.) (1906), *Buddhist Records of the Western World,* London: Kegan Paul.

Bell, Charles (2000), *Tibet Past and Present,* New Delhi: Motilal Banarsidass.

Blochmann, H. (1872), 'Koch Bihar, Koch Hajo and Assam in 16th and 17th Centuries according to the Akbarnamah, the Padishahnamah and the Fathiya-i-Ibriyah', *Journal of Asiatic Society of Bengal,* vol. LXI, part I.

Blumer R. and Vial F. (1999), *Bathpalathang, New Archaeological Site near Jakar, Bhumtang District, Bhutan: Preliminary Report for the*

Investigations of April 1999, Zurich: Swiss-Liechtenstein Foundation for Archaeological Research Abroad.

Bose, Kishen Kant (2000), 'Account of Bootan', in Eden, *Political Missions to Bhutan*, New Delhi: Munshiram Manoharlal Publishers, pp. 187–206.

Chakravarti, B. (1992), *A Cultural History of Bhutan*, Calcutta: Self Employment Bureau Publications.

Chand, Raghubir (2004), *Brokpas: The Hidden Highlanders of Bhutan*, Nainital: People's Association for Himalayan Area Research.

Chogden Gönpo (1979), *sPrul sku rig 'dzin mchog ldan mgon po'i rnam thar mgur 'bum dad ldan spro ba skyed byed*, Paro: Ugyen Tempai Gyaltsen.

Chogdrub Palbar (n.d.), *Thugs sras 'gyur med mchog grub dpal bar bzang po'i rang tshul drang po'i gtam du brjod pa*, n.p. (Manuscript kept in Drametse temple.)

Collister, Peter (1996), *Bhutan and the British*, New Delhi: UBS Publishers Ltd.

Damchö Lhendup (2008a), *Gong sa 'jigs med rnam rgyal gyi rtogs brjod bpa' bo'i gad rgyangs*, Thimphu: Centre for Bhutan Studies.

—— (2008b), *'Brug brgyud 'dzin gyi rgyal mchog dang pa mi dbang o rgyan dbang phyug gi rtogs brjod*, Thimphu: Centre for Bhutan Studies.

—— (2008c), *'Brug brgyud 'dzin gyi rgyal mchog gnyis pa mi dbang 'jigs med dbang phyug gi rtogs brjod*, Thimphu: Centre for Bhutan Studies.

Das, B.S. (1995), *Mission to Bhutan: A Nation in Transition*, New Delhi: Vikas Publishing House.

Dewa Zangpo (1984), *Bla ma thang stong rgyal po'i rnam thar gsal ba'i sgron me*, Thimphu: National Library of Bhutan.

Dorji Lingpa and Choying Rangdrol (1984), *gTer chen rdo rje gling pa'i rnam thar dang gzhal gdams*, Delhi: Kunzang Tobgeyl.

Eden, Ashley (2000), *Political Missions to Bhutan*, New Delhi: Munshiram Manoharlal Publishers.

Ehrhard, Franz-Karl (2007), 'Kaḥ Thog Pa Bsod Nams Rgyal Mtshan (1466-1540) and the foundation of O Rgyan Rtse Mo in Spa Gro', in Ardussi and Pommaret, *Bhutan: Tradition and Changes*, Leiden: Brill Academic Publishers, pp. 73-96.

Gait, Edward (1933), *A History of Assam*, Calcutta: Thacker Spink & Co.

Gandolfo, Romolo (2004), 'Bhutan and Tibet in European Cartography (1597–1800)' in Karma Ura and Sonam Kinga, *The Spider and the Piglet*, Thimphu: Centre for Bhutan Studies, pp. 90–136.

Gedun Rinchen (1987), *dPal ldan 'brug pa rin po che mthu chen chos kyi rgyal po ngag dbang rnam rgyal gyi rnam thar rgya mtsho'i snying po,* Thimphu: Drolung Rithroe.

—— (1972), *dPal ldan 'brug pa'i gdul zhing lho phyogs nags mo'i ljongs kyi chos 'byung blo gsar rna ba'i rgyan,* Thimphu: Tango Drubde.

—— (1971), *'Gro ba'i* mgon po chos rje kun dga' legs pa'i rnam thar rgya mtsho'i snying po mthong ba don ldan, Kalimpong: dGe 'dun rin chen.

Gelong Ngawang (2003), *Sa skyong rgyal po'i gdung rabs 'byung khungs dang 'bangs kyi mi rabs chag tshul,* Thimphu: Centre for Bhutan Studies.

Gerner, Manfred (2007), *Chakzampa Thangtong Gyalpo: Architect, Philosopher and Iron Chain Bridge Builder,* Thimphu: Centre for Bhutan Studies.

Götshang Repa (1993), *Chos rje lo ras pa'i rnam thar,* Zining: mTsho sngon mi rigs dpe skrun khang.

Ghose, Jadunath (1874), *The Rājopākhyān or History of Kooch Behar,* Calcutta: C.B. Lewis.

Ghoshal, S.C. (2005), *A History of Cooch Behar* (translation of Caudhurī Āmānataullā Āhamada's *Kocabihārera itihāsa*), Siliguri: N.L. Publishers.

Gökyi Demthruchen (2005), *sBas yul spyi dang bye brag yol mo gangs ra'i gnas yig,* Kathmandu: Khenpo Nyima Dhondup

Griffiths, William (n.d.), 'Journal of the Mission to Bootan in 1837–38', in Eden (2000), *Political Missions to Bhutan,* New Delhi: Munshiram Manoharlal Publishers, pp. 125–86.

Guru Chöwang (1979), *The Autobiography and Instructions of Guru Chos-kyi dBaṅ-phyug,* Paro: Ugyen Tempai Gyaltsen, vols. I and II.

Gyurme Dechen (1976), *dPal grub pa'i dbang phyug brtson 'grus bzang po'i rnam par thar pa kun gsal nor bu'i me long,* Bir: Kandro.

Hasrat, Bikram Jit (1980), *History of Bhutan: Land of the Peaceful Dragon,* Thimphu: Education Department.

Hutt, Michael (2005), *Unbecoming Citizens: Culture, Nationhood, and the Flight of Refugees from Bhutan,* New Delhi: Oxford University Press.

—— (1994), *Bhutan: Perspectives on Conflict and Dissent,* Gartmore: Kiscadale Publications.

Imaeda, Yoshiro (2011), *Histoire médiéval du Bhoutan: établissement et évolution de la théocratie des 'Brug pa,* Tokyo: The Toyo Bunko.

Imaeda and Pommaret (1987), 'Le monastère de gTam-zhing (Tamshing) au Bhoutan central', *Arts Asiatiques,* xlii, pp. 19–30.

Jagar Dorji (2000), 'The Lhopus of Western Bhutan', *Tibet Journal,* vol. XXV, no. 2, Dharamsala: Library of Tibetan Works and Archives, pp. 52–59.

Jangchub Norbu (1985), *dPal ldan bla ma thams cad mkhyen gzigs chen po ngag dbang 'jigs med grags pa'i rnam par thar pa byang chen spyod pa rgya mtshor 'jug pa'i gtam snyan pa'i yan lag 'bum ldan rdzogs ldan dga' char sbyin pa'i chos kyi sprin chen po'i dbyangs,* Thimphu: National Library of Bhutan.

Jigme Chögyal (1985), *The biography and collected writings of the fifth Żabs-druṅ thugs-sprul of Bhutan, Jigs-med-chos-rgyal (1862–1904),* Thimphu: National Library of Bhutan.

Jigme Drakpa II (1811) *sKyabs mgon rdo rje 'chang dbang ngag dbang 'jam dbyangs rgyal mtshan gyi rnam par thar pa grub rigs bzhad pa'i rgyud mang thugs rje bskul ba'i chu 'dzin 'khrigs pa'i rang sgra,* n.p.

Jigme Norbu (1984), *The Collected Works of the Fourth Żabs-druṅ Thugs-sprul of Bhutan 'Jigs-med-nor-bu (1831–1861),* Thimphu: The National Library.

Jigme Y. Thinley (1994), 'Bhutan: A Kingdom Besieged', in Hutt (ed.), *Bhutan: Perspectives on Conflict and Dissent,* Gartmore: Kiscadale Publications, pp. 43–76.

Jñāna Vajra (1997), *'Bri gung skyob pa 'jig rten mgon po'i dngos slob 'phrin las rang mnyam mcu gsum las dpal gnyos rgyal ba lha nang pa'i rnam thar,* Dehra Dun: Drigung Kagyu Institute.

Kapstein, Matthew (2006), *The Tibetans,* Oxford: Blackwell Publishing.

—— (2000), *The Tibetan Assimilation of Buddhism: Conversion, Contestation, and Memory,* New York: Oxford University Press.

Karma Palbar (1984), *dPal ldan 'brug pa rin po che ngag dbang 'jam dbyangs shAkya bstan 'dzin gyi rnam par thar pa legs byas rgya mtsho'i sprin gyi sgra dbyangs,* Thimphu: National Library of Bhutan.

Karma Phuntsho (ed.) (2013), *The Autobiography of Pema Lingpa,* Thimphu: Agency for Documentation of Bhutan's Cultures.

—— (2008), 'Bhutan's Unique Democracy: a first verdict', at www.opendemocracy.net/article/institutions/bhutan_s_unique_democracy_a_first_verdict accessed on 20 August 2012.

—— (2006), 'Bhutanese Reforms, Nepali Criticism', at www.opendemocracy.net/democracy-protest/bhutan_nepal_3996.jsp, accessed on 20 August 2012.

—— (2004), 'Echoes of Ancient Ethos: Some Reflections on Bhutanese Social Themes', *The Spider and the Piglet,* Thimphu: Centre for Bhutan Studies, pp. 564–80.

Karma Ura (2010), *Leadership of the Wise: Kings of Bhutan,* Thimphu: Karma Ura.

—— (1997), 'Tradition and Development', in Schicklgruber and Pommaret, *Bhutan: Mountain Fortress of Gods*, London: Serindia Publications.

—— (1996), *The Ballad of Pemi Tshewang Tashi: A Wind Borne Feather,* Thimphu: Karma Ura.

—— (1995), *The Hero with a Thousand Eyes: a historical novel*, Thimphu: Karma Ura.

Kesang Choden Dorji (1997), *The Emergence of Modern Bhutan: Jigme Namgyal's life and career,* thesis submitted to the University of New Brunswick.

Khenpo Phuntsok Tashi (ed.) (2003), *Fortress of the Dragon: Recent Research on Dzongs*, Paro: National Museum of Bhutan.

Kholi, Manorama (1982), *India and Bhutan, A Study in Interrelations, 1772–1910*, New Delhi: Munshiram Manoharlal Publishers

Konchog Jigme Wangpo (2002), *Paṇ chen dpal ldan ye shes kyi rnam thar*, Beijing: Krung go bod rig pa dpe skrun khang, 2 vols.

Kongtrul Lodoe Thaye (1973), *gTer ston rgya rtsa'i rnam thar*, Tezu: Tibetan Nyingmapa Monastery.

—— (1976), *Rin chen gter mdzod,* Delhi: Ngodrup & Sherab Drimay.

Kuenga Gyaltshen (1985), *mTshungs med dpal ldan bla ma dam pa dam chos padma dkar po'i sde'i rnam par thar pa yon tan nor bu'i 'od kyi dkyil 'khor*, Thimphu: National Library of Bhutan.

—— (1970), *mTshungs med chos kyi rgyal po rje btsun dam chos pad dkar gyi rnam par thar pa thugs rje chen po'i dri bsung*, New Delhi: n.p.

Lama Sa-ngag (2005), *'Brug gi smyos rabs yang gsal me long*, Thimphu: KMT Publishers.

—— (1983), *'Brug tu 'od gsal lha'i gdung rabs 'byung tshul brjod pa smyos rabs gsal ba'i me long*, Thimphu: Lama Sa-ngag.

Lamb, Alastair (2002), *Bhutan and Tibet: The Travels of George Bogle and Alexander Hamilton 1774–1777,* Hertingfordbury: Roxford Books.

Lamitare, Devi Bhakat (1978), *Murder of Democracy in Himalayan Kingdom,* New Delhi: Amarko Book Agency.

Lhendup Tharchen (2013), *Protected Areas and Biodiversity of Bhutan,* Thimphu: Lhendup Tharchen.

Lobzang Chögyan (1969), *The Autobiography of the First Panchen Lama Blo-bzang-chos-kyi-rgyal-rgyal-mtshan,* Delhi: Ngawang Gelek Demo.

Longchenpa Drime Özer (n.d.), 'Bum thang lha'i sbas yul gyi bkod pa me tog skyed tshal', in *gSung 'bum*, Derge: sDe dge par khang chen mo, vol. 5, ff. 22v–26r.

Lopen Nado (1986), *'Brug dkar po*, Bumthang: Tharpaling Monastery.

Majumdar, A.B. (1984), *Britain and the Himalayan Kingdom of Bhutan*, Patna: Bharati Bhawan Publishers and Distributors.

Markham, Clements R. (ed.) (1879) *Narratives of the Mission of George Bogle to Tibet, and of the Journey of Thomas Manning to Lhasa*, London: Trübner and Co.

Michailovsky, Boyd and Mazaudon, Martine (1994), 'Notes on the Languages of the Bumthang Group' in Per Kvaerne (ed.) *Tibetan Studies: Proceedings of the 6th Seminar of the International Association for Tibetan Studies*, Fagernes: The Institute for Comparative Research in Human Culture. vol. 2, pp. 545–57.

Mullard and Wongchuk (2010), *Royal Records: A Catalogue of the Sikkimese Palace Archive*, Andiast: International Institute for Tibetan and Buddhist Studies.

Myers, Diana and Bean, Susan (eds) (2008), *From the Land of the Thunder Dragon: Textile Arts of Bhutan*, Chicago: Serindia Publications.

Namgyal Tenzin (n.d), *'Gro ba'i mgon po rig 'dzin sbyin pa rgyal mtshan gyi rnam par thar pa skal ldan dad gus can gyi dga' ston*, manuscript in Drangye Gönpa.

Ngawang Drakpa (n.d.), *sPrul sku ngag dbang grags pa'i rnam thar ngo mtshar nor bu'i do shal*, manuscript in Neyphug Temple.

Ngawang Chokyi Gyatsho (1985a), *rJe btsun bdag nyid chen po ngag dbang chos kyi rgya mtsho'i rnam par thar pa byang chen spyod pa'i me long*, Thimphu: National Library of Bhutan.

—— (1985b), *'Jam mgon bla ma ngag dbang kun dga' rgya mtsho'i zhabs kyi rtogs brjod rgyal sras rgya mtsho'i 'jug nogs*, Thimphu: National Library of Bhutan.

Ngawang Lhundup (n.d.), *mTshungs med chos kyi rgyal po rje rin po che'i rnam par thar pa bskal bzang legs bris 'dod pa'i re skong dpag bsam gyi snye ma*, n.p.

Ngawang Lobzang Gyatsho (2007), *rGyal ba lnga pa chen po'i gsum 'bum*, Dharamsala: Nam gsal sgron ma.

—— (1993), *rGya bod hor sog gi mchog dman bar pa rnams la 'phrin yig snyan ngag tu bkod pa rab snyan rgyud mang*, Zining: mTsho sngon mi rigs dpe bskrun khang.

—— (1991), *Za hor gyi ban de ngag dbang blo bzang rgya mtsho'i 'di snang 'khrul ba'i rol rtsed rtogs brjod kyi tshul du bkod pa du kU la'i gos bzang,* Lhasa: Bod ljongs mi dmangs dpe bskrun khang.

Ngawang Paldan Zangpo (1976), 'rDo rje 'dzin pa chen po bsod nams 'od zer gyi rnam thar snyan tshig 'dod 'jo'i 'khri shing', *The Lives of Three Bhutanese Religious Masters*, Thimphu: Kunsang Topgey, pp. 1–57.

Ngawang Pekar (2004), *rGyal sras gdung 'dzin sprul sku'i rnam thar sa bon tsam bkod pa,* Thimphu: Centre for Bhutan Studies.

Ngawang Tenzin (n.d.), *Pha jo 'brug sgom zhig pa'i rnam par thar pa byang chub thugs rje myur ba*, Thimphu: bDe chen lhun gyis grub pa'i rtse.

Ngawang Zangpo (2002), *Guru Rinpoche: His Life and Times*, Ithaca: Snow Lion Publications.

Nordrang Ogyen (1993), *Bod kyi deb ther dpyid kyi rgyal mo'i glu dbyangs kyi 'grel pa yid kyi dga' ston,* Lhasa; Mi rigs dpe skrun khang.

Nüden Dorji (1972), *Bod kyi jo mo ye shes mtsho rgyal gyi mdzad tshul rnam par thar pa gab pa mngon byung rgyud mangs dri za'i glu phreng,* Kalimpong: bDud 'joms rin po che.

Nyangral Nyima Özer (2007), 'Slob dpon padma 'byung gnas kyi skyes rabs chos byung nor bu'i phreng ba', in *Rin chen gter mdzod chen mo*, vol. 1, pp. 1–190, New Delhi: Shechen Publications.

—— (1988), *Chos byung me tog snying po sbrang rtsi'i bcud*, Lhasa: Bod ljongs mi rigs dpe bskrun khang.

Palden Gyatsho (1974), *dPal 'brug pa rin po che ngag dbang bstan 'dzin rnam rgyal gyi rnam par thar pa rgyas pa chos kyi sprin chen po'i dbyangs,* Delhi: Topden Tshering.

—— (1975), *Byang chub sems dpa' bstan 'dzin gyi skyes bu gtsang mkhan chen 'jam dbyang dpal ldan rgya mtsho'i rtogs brjod dbyangs can rgyud mang,* Thimphu: Kunzang Tobgay.

Pema Karpo (1992), *Chos 'byung bstan pa'i padma rgyas pa'i nyin byed,* Lhasa: Bod ljongs bod yig dpe rnying dpe skrun khang.

Pema Lingpa (1975), *The Rediscovered Teachings of the Great Pema Gliṅpa*, Thimphu: Kunzang Tobgay.

Pema Tshewang (1994), *'Brug gsal ba'i sgron me,* Thimphu: National Library.

Pemberton, R. Bolieau (1838), 'Report on Bootan', in Eden (2000), *Political Missions to Bhutan,* New Delhi: Munshiram Manoharlal Publishers, pp. 1–124.

Penjore, Dorji (2003), *On the Mule Track to Dagana*, Thimphu: Centre for Bhutan Studies.

Petech, Luciano (1972), 'The Rulers of Bhutan c.1650-1750', *Oriens Extremus*, Hamburg: Otto Harrassowitz, vol. 19, pp. 203–13.

Phuntsho Tshering (2000), *Deb ther kun gsal me long*, Lhasa: Bod ljongs mi dmangs dpe skrung khang.

Pommaret, Francoise (2007), 'Estate and Deities: A Ritual from Central Bhutan, the *bskang gso* of O ryan chos gling', in Ardussi and Pommaret, *Bhutan: Tradition and Changes*, Leiden: Brill Academic Publishers, pp. 135–58.

—— (1999), 'The Mon pa revisited: in search of Mon', in Toni Huber (ed.) *Sacred Spaces and Powerful Places in Tibetan culture,* Dharamsala: Tibetan Library of Works and Archives, pp. 52–73.

—— (1997), 'Ethnic Mosaic: Peoples of Bhutan', in Schicklgruber and Pommaret (eds.) *Bhutan: Mountain Fortress of Gods*, London: Serindia Publications.

Phuntsho Wangdi (2007), *'Brug chos srid kyi rabs*, Thimphu: National Library of Bhutan.

Rennie, David F. (1970), *Bhotan and the Story of the Doar War,* New Delhi: Mañjuśrī Publishing House.

Rhodes, Nicholas (1999), 'Coinage in Bhutan' *Journal of Bhutan Studies,* vol. 1, no. 1. Thimphu: Centre for Bhutan Studies, pp. 84-113.

Richardson, Hugh (1998), *High Peaks, Pure Earth: Collected Writings on Tibetan History and Culture*, London: Serindia Publications.

Richardson, Hugh and Snellgrove, David (1968), *A Cultural History of Tibet*, Boulder: Great Eastern Book Company.

Ronaldshay, Lord (2005), *Lands of the Thunderbolt: Sikhim, Chumbi & Bhutan*, Varanasi: Pilgrims Publishing.

Rongthong Kunley Dorji (2003), 'My understanding of Shabdrung' in *Bhutan Today*, http://www.bhutandnc.com/aprilmay03_3.htm, accessed on 20 August, 2012.

Rose, Leo (1977), *The Politics of Bhutan*, Ithaca: Cornell University Press.

Rustomji, Nari (1978), *Bhutan: The Dragon Kingdom in Crisis*, New Delhi: Oxford University Press.

Sa gnas lo rgyus zhib 'jug rtsom sgrigs tshogs chung (2000), *Myang stod dpal gnas rnying dgon pa'i lo rgyus*, Zhigatse: Sa gnas srid gros kyi rig gnas lo rgyus dpyad gzhi'i rgyu cha zhib 'jug rtsom sgrigs tshogs chung.

Sangay Dorji (1999), *dPal ldan 'brug pa rin po che zhabs drung ngag dbang rnam rgyal gyi rnam thar,* Thimphu: Dzongkha Development Commission.

Samgyal Khache (1975), "'Jam dbyangs kun dga' seng ge'i rnam par thar pa dgos 'dod kun 'bung yid bzin nor bu'i phreng ba' in *Rwa lung bka' brgyud gser phreng*, Palampur: Sungrab nyamso gyunphel parkhang, vol. Kha, pp. 363–488.

Shakabpa, Tsepon W.D. (1967), *Tibet: A Political History,* New Haven: Yale University Press.

Shakya Rinchen (n.d.), *sKu bzhi'i dbang phyug rje btsun ngag dbang rgyal mtshan gyi rnam par thar pa thams cad mkhyen pa'i rol mo*, Thimphu: Lhongtsho Tashigang.

—— (1976a), 'rDo rje 'chang chen po rje btsun ngag dbang 'phrin las kyi rnam par thar pa rgyal sras rtse dga'i 'khri shing', *Biographies of Three Bhutanese Prelates*, Thimphu: Kunzang Tobgey.

—— (1976b), 'sPrul pa'i sku ngag dbang bstan 'dzin mi pham dbang po'i rnam par thar pa bskal bzang rna rgyan' in *The Collected Works (gsung-'bum) of Sakya Rinchen, the ninth rje mkhan-po of Bhutan*, Thimphu: Kunzang Topgey, vol. 2, pp. 379–440.

—— (1976c), 'sPrul pa'i sku mchog ngag dbang phyogs las rnam rgyal gyi rnam par thar pa bskal bzang 'jug ngogs' in *The Collected Works (gsung-'bum) of Sakya Rinchen, the ninth rje mkhan-po of Bhutan*, Thimphu: Kunzang Topgey, vol. 2, pp. 447–92.

—— (1976d), 'Byang chub sems dpa' chen po kun tu dga' ba'i rgyal mtshan dpal bzang po'i rtogs pa brjod pa dpag bsam yongs 'du'i snye ma', *The Lives of Three Bhutanese Religious Masters*, Thimphu: Kunsang Topgey, pp. 59–309.

Sakyapa Sonam Gyaltshen (1996), *rGyal rabs gsal ba'i me long,* Beijing: Mi rigs dpe skrun khang.

Shakya Tenzin (1976), 'Byang chub sems dpa' ngag dbang pad dkar gyi rtogs pa brjod pa drang srong dgyes pa'i glu dbyangs gzhan phan bdud rtsi'i rlabs phreng', *The Lives of Three Bhutanese Religious Masters*, Thimphu: Kunsang Topgey, pp. 311–479.

Sharma, Deben (2005), *Lhops (Doya) of Bhutan: An Ethnographic Account*, New Delhi: Akansha Publishing House.

Sherab Gyaltshen and Jigme Norbu (1976), 'rJe bla ma rin po che'i rnam par thar pa zhal gsung ma bden gnyis 'grub pa'i shing rta,' *Biographies of Three Bhutanese Prelates*, Thimphu: Kunzang Topgey.

Sherab Palden (1984), *rJe grub thob chen po lcags zam pa'i rnam par thar pa ngo mtshar rgya mtsho,* Thimphu: National Library of Bhutan.

Sherab Palzang (2004), *The Gem Necklace of Short Biography of Hungral*

Dung Dung and His Descendants, Thimphu: Centre for Bhutan Studies.

Smith, Gene (2001), *Among Tibetan Texts*, Boston: Wisdom Publications.

Sonam Drakpa (1985), *rGyal rabs 'phrul gyi lde mig gam deb thar dmar po 'i deb gsar ma,* Mundgod: Drepung Loseling Library Society.

Sonam Gyaltshen (1979), *Shar kaḥ thog pa bsod nams rgyal mtshan dpal bzang po'i rnam par thar pa dri med yid bzhin nor bu'i phreng ba*, Gangtok: Dzongsar Jamyang Khyentsey Labrang.

Sonam Kinga (2004), *Ugyen Wangchuk & Younghusband Mission to Lhasa,* Thimphu: Galing Printing & Publishing.

Sonam Kinga (2009), *Polity, Kingship and Democracy: A Biography of the Bhutanese State*, Thimphu: Ministry of Education

Sonam Tobgye (2011), 'Heroes buried by time' in *Kuensel*, 11 and 12 November 2011.

Stein, M. A. (1961), *Kalhaṇa's Rājataraṅginī: A Chronicle of the Kings of Kaśmīr*, vol. I, Delhi: Motilal Banarsidass.

Stearns, Cyrus (2007), *King of The Empty Plain: The Tibetan Iron Bridge Builder Tangtong Gyalpo,* Ithaca: Snow Lion Publications.

Subedi, Raja Ram (2005), 'Historical Entity of Vijayapur State', *Voices of History*, vol. 20, no. 1, pp. 23–28. At http://www.nepjol.info/index.php/ VOH, accessed on 20 August, 2012.

Sungtrul Chogley Namgyal (1985), *mKhas btsun bzang po'i bdag nyid mtshungs med chos kyi rje ngag dbang rgyal mtshan gyi rnam par thar pa'i rgya mtsho ngo mtshar gyi rba rlabs rnam par g.yo ba,* Thimphu: National Library of Bhutan.

Sungtrul Tsultrim Dorji (n.d.), *rNam thar byang chub sems kyi me tog bstan pa mdzes par byed pa'i rgyan gcig*, manuscript with Dasho Sangay Dorji.

—— (n.d.), *sPrul sku tshul rdor gyi rnam thar rang tshul sgrib med ston pa'i me long*, manuscript with Dasho Sangay Dorji.

Taktshang Paljor Zangpo (1979), *rGya bod yig tshang mkhas pa dga' byed chen mo 'dzam gling gsal ba'i me long*, Thimphu: Kunsang Tobgay and Mani Dorji.

Tāranātha (?) (1983), *Myang yul stod smad bar gsum gyi ngo mtshar gtam gyi legs bshad mkhas pa'i 'jug ngogs*, Lhasa: Bod ljongs mi dmangs dpe skrun khang.

Teltscher, Kate (2006), *The High Road to China,* London: Bloomsbury.

Tenzin Chögyal (n.d.), *rGyal kun mkhyab bdag 'gro ba'i bla ma bstan 'dzin rin po che legs pa'i don grub zhabs kyi rnam par thar pa ngo mtshar nor bu'i mchod sdong,* manuscript. n.p.

—— (1759) *Lho'i chos 'byung bstan pa rin po che'i 'phro 'thud 'jam mgon smon mtha'i 'phreng ba zhes bya ba/ gtso bor skyabs mgon rin po che rgyal sras ngag dbang rnam rgyal gyi rnam thar kun gyi go bde gsal bar bkod pa bcas,* Thimphu: 'Brug zab don lhun rtse.

Tenzin Lhendup (1985), *ShAkya'i dge sbyongs bla dwags 'chang ba bstan 'dzin lhun grub gyis gtam blo gsal kun dga' bskyed pa'i rol mtsho,* Thimphu: National Library of Bhutan.

Thutob Namgyal and Yeshe Drolma (2003), 'Bras ljongs rgyal rabs, Gangtok: The Tsuklakhang Trust.

Tenzin Dorji (1988), *'Brug shar phyogs kyi rje dpon byung rabs blo gsar byis pa dga' ba'i rna rgyan,* n.p.

Tenzin Phuntsho (1870), *dPal ldan bla ma dam pa rje btsun gu Na dhava dza'i rtogs pa brjod pa rmad byung ye shes sgyu ma'i rol gar zab mo gsang ba mchog gi gtam skal bzang rna ba'i bcud len,* Talo: Sa-ngagchöling.

Tshering Dorji, (Gelong Nyerchen Drepa) (1963), *Lho 'brug rgyal rabs,* n.p.

—— (n.d.), *Rig 'dzin chen po a yu va jra'i 'khrungs rabs rnam thar,* manuscript in Dongkarla temple.

Tshering Tashi (2008), 'Druk Gyalpo Ugyen Wangchuck's Twenty Points Proposal to the British India to Modernise Bhutan', *Journal of Bhutan Studies,* Thimphu: Centre for Bhutan Studies, pp. 1–8.

Tshering Wangyal (1981), *dPal mi'i dbang po'i rtogs pa brjod pa 'jig rten kun tu dga' ba'i gtam,* Chengdu: Si khron mi rigs dpe skrun khang.

Turner, Samuel (1800), *An Account of an Embassy to the Court of the Teshoo Lama, in Tibet: Containing a Narrative of a Journey through Bootan, and Part of Tibet,* London: W. Bulmer and Co.

van Driem, George (2007), 'OB VIRULENTAS NONNULARUM HERBARUM EXHALATIONNES', in Ardussi and Pommaret, *Bhutan: Tradition and Changes,* Leiden: Brill Academic Publishers, pp. 65–71.

—— (2001), *Languages of the Himalayas: An Ethnolinguistic Handbook of the Greater Himalayan Region,* Leiden: Brill Academic Publishers.

—— (1998), *Dzongkha,* Leiden: School of Asian, African and Amerindian Studies.

Waddell, L. Austine (1988), *Lhasa and Its Mysteries: With a Record of the Expedition of 1903–1904,* New York: Dover Publications.

Wehrheim, John (2008), *Bhutan: Hidden Land of Happiness,* Bangkok: Serindia Publications.

White, J. Claude (2008), *Sikhim and Bhutan: Twenty-one years on the northeast frontier, 1887–1908,* Delhi: Low Price Publications.

Whytse, Brendan (2002), *Waiting for the Esquimo: An historical and doucumentary study of the Cooch Behar enclaves for India and Bangladesh,* Melbourne: University of Melbourne.

Yonten Dargye, Sorenson and Tshering (2008), *Play of the Omniscient: Life and Works of jamgön Ngawang Gyaltshen, An Eminent 17th–18th Century Drukpa Master (1647–1732),* Thimphu: National Library and Archives of Bhutan.

Yonten Dargye (2001), *History of the Drukpa Kagyud School in Bhutan (12th to 17th century AD)*, Thimphu: Yonten Dargye.

—— (ed.) (2009), *Life of King Sindha and the Clear Mirror of Predictions,* Thimphu: National Library and Archives of Bhutan.

Yonten Thaye (1985), *Paṇḍita bstan 'dzin chos kyi rgyal po'i rtogs pa brjod pa sgyu ma chen po'i gar stabs*, Thimphu: National Library of Bhutan.

—— and Kuenga Gyatsho (2003), *The Necklace of Pearls: Biography of the 13th Druk Desi Sherab Wangchuk (1697–1765)*, Thimphu: Centre for Bhutan Studies.

Zhanphan Rolpai Dorji (1859), *rDo rje 'dzin pa chen po 'phrin las mkha' khyab mchog gi rdo rje 'am byang chub brtson 'grus kyi rtogs pa brjod pa ngo mtshar nor bu'i snying po,* Tongsa: Chökhor Rabtentse.

Notes

The Country and its Names

1   Aris (1979), p. xvi.
2   See Beal (1906), vol. II, p. 198.
3   Ardussi (forthcoming), pp. 16–17. I am grateful to the author for sharing couple of the chapters of his manuscript in draft stage.
4   Sherab Palzang (2004), pp. 45–46.
5   Personal communication with Tshewang Dargay, who cited the late Chagkhar Lama Gyonpo.
6   See Ngawang Tenzin (n.d.) f. 22. If Ngawang Tenzin is citing the letter from Lhapa lama to Phajo Drukgom Zhigpo accurately, the letter describes Paro as Paro Menjong—Paro, the medicinal land. See also Sherab Pelzang (2004), p. 44 for the same description of Paro.
7   Personal communication with Tshewang Dargay. The story perhaps came about only in the twentieth century as the Mentsikhang or the Institute of Medical and Astral Studies in Lhasa was only opened in 1916 by Khyenrab Norbu (1883–1963) under the patronage of the 13th Dalai Lama.
8   Dorji Lingpa and Choying Rangdol (1984), p. 42.
9   Shakya Rinchen (1976b), p. 415.
10 Tshering Wangyal (1981), pp. 748, 753, 760.
11 See Lamb (2002), pp. 320–21 for the translation of Panchen Lama's letter and p. 374 for John Stewart's account based on Bogle's report that inhabitants of Bhutan called the country Ducpo.
12 Romolo Gandolfo (2004).
13 Chakravarti (1992), p. 1.

The Land and Its People

1 Gedun Rinchen (1972), pp. 117–18.
2 Tharchen (2013), p. 15.
3 Pommaret (1997), p. 55. See also Jagar Dorji (2000) and Sharma (2005).
4 Longchenpa Drime Özer (n.d.).
5 See Karma Phuntsho (ed.) (2013), p. 347.
6 Tenzin Chögyal (1759), f. 6v and Lopen Nado (1986), p. 7.
7 Pommaret (1997), p. 45.
8 Pema Lingpa (1975), p. 500. See Aris (1979), p. 75
9 Pommaret (1997), p. 54. See also Myers and Bean (2008), pp. 48 and 117.
10 Gelong Ngawang (2003), p. 41. See also Chand (2004) for a monograph on this group.
11 See van Driem (2007), pp. 65–72.

Many Tongues

1 van Driem (1998).
2 van Driem (1998), p. 30.

History and Prehistory

1 སྤྲ་བྱུང་གི་ལོ་རྒྱུས་མ་ཤེས་ན། །དགས་ཚལ་ནང་གི་སྟུ་དང་འདྲ།།
2 See Aris (1979), 37 and Penjore (2003), pp. 53–55.
3 van Driem (2001).
4 Ngawang Pekar (2004), pp. 94–95.
5 Pema Tshewang (1994), p. 22 and Gedun Rinchen (1972), p. 119.
6 Pema Lingpa (1975), vol. Tsa, p. 503.
7 Tenzin Chögyal (1759), f. 6r.
8 Karma Phuntsho (ed.) (2013), p. 221.
9 Lopen Nado (1986), pp. 3–5.
10 Chakravarti (1992), pp. 91–94.
11 See Beal (1906), vol. II, p. 198.
12 Lopen Nado (1986), pp. 8–9.
13 Aris (1979), p. 58–59. See Bose (2000), p. 187.
14 Eden, et al. (2000), pp. 187–88.
15 See Lopen Nado (1986), p. 8.
16 Tenzin Chögyal (1759), f. 7r.

17 Turner (1800), p. 11.

Early Historic Period: Early Diffusion of Buddhism

1 Tenzin Dorji (1988), pp. 4–8.
2 *rGya bod tshig mdzod chen mo*, p. 3197 puts Nyatri's installation as king in 126 BC.
3 Richardson (1998), p. 239.
4 Citation taken from Kapstein (2006), p. 66–67.
5 Ibid., p. 67.
6 See Rob Mayer, 'Padmasambhava in early Tibetan myth and ritual', accessed on 23 February 2012. http://blogs.orient.ox.ac.uk/kila/2011/05/06/padmasambhava-in-early-tibetan-myth-and-ritual-part-1/
7 See Kongtrul Lodoe Thaye (1973), pp. 548–49 and pp. 264–65 and 295–96 for brief biographies. For a brief discussion on Ugyen Zangpo's identity and dates, see Karma Phuntsho (2013), p. 5. Aris mistakenly identified him with Pema Lingpa.
8 Ibid., p. 548.
9 See Pommaret (1999). Oral communication with Tshewang Dargay, who cited Chagkhar Lama Gyonpo.
10 Tenzin Chogyal (n.d.), f. 15 and Choying Rangdol (1984), pp. 17–18.
11 Pema Lingpa (1975), vol. Tsa, pp. 397–517.
12 Kapstein (2006), p. 72.
13 Gökyi Demthruchen (2005), pp. 8–9.
14 Pema Lingpa (1975), vol. Tsa, pp. 464–65.
15 Ibid., p. 465.
16 As Khikha Rathö settled in Kyizom in Tang, it would make better sense if this temple is actually Anu Lhakhang, which is in the vicinity of Kyizom. It is possible that Genye was a scribal error as the two often appeared together and are believed to be from the same period.
17 Ba Salnang (1982), p. 32–33.
18 Nüden Dorji (1972), f. 4r.
19 Ba Salnang (1982), p. 30 and Nüden Dorji (1972), f. 66.
20 Nüden Dorji (1972), ff. 55–66 and Kongtrul Lodoe Thaye (1973), pp. 94–96.
21 Kongtrul Lodoe Thaye (1973) states Tashi Khyidren met Padmasambhava in Layag Monkharteng.
22 Pema Tshewang (1994), p. 45.

23 Tshering Dorji (n.d.), section cha, ff. 5–6.

24 Nyangral Nyima Özer (1988), p. 437.

25 See Aris (1979) and Ardussi (forthcoming).

Early Historic Period: Later Diffusion of Buddhism

1 Pema Tshewang (1994), p. 69–71.

2 Nyangral Nyima Özer (1988), pp. 458–59.

3 Guru Chöwang (1979), vol. II, p. 377: རྒྱུ་རྐྱེན་ཆོས་ཀྱི་དབང་ཕྱུག་ལ། མོན་བུམ་ཐང་ལྗུ་རའི་ཐད་ (sic བཙད་) པོས་གསོལ་བ། ཉིད་སྐྱོབ་དཔོན་པདྨ་ཡིན། དབྲི་སྲོང་ལྡེ་བཙན་བཙན་བུ་རྒྱུད་ (sic བརྒྱུད་) ཡིན།

4 Longchenpa Drime Özer (n.d.), f. 27v.

5 See Ardussi (2004b) for more information on this.

6 See Ardussi (forthcoming).

7 See Sonam Drakpa (1985), p. 429, Sakyapa Sonam Gyaltshen (1996), p. 248 and Phuntsho Tshering (2000), 132–34.

8 Richardson (1998), pp. 265–66.

9 See Taktshang Paljor Zangpo (1979), vol. II, pp. 105–12. Tāranātha (?) (1983), pp. 44, 86, Nordrang Ogyen (1993), pp. 431–35, section on Gyal mkhar rtse pa.

10 See Ardussi (2004), p. 64.

11 Ardussi (2004), pp. 60–70.

12 Aris (1979), p. 120.

13 Samgyal Khache (1975), p. 400, 438.

14 Barawa Gyaltshen Palzang (1970), p. 350.

15 Kongtrul (1973), p. 117.

16 Pema Tshewang (1994), p. 75.

17 Lama Sa-ngag (1983).

18 Ngawang Tenzin (n.d), f. 7r.

19 Ibid., ff. 23v–24r.

20 Sangay Dorji (1999), p. 94.

21 Götshang Repa (1993), p. 92.

22 Gedun Rinchen (1972), p. 180.

23 Ibid., p. 197.

24 Pema Tshewang (1994), pp. 116-9, Tenzin Chögyal (1759), ff. 15v–16r and Gedun Rinchen (1972), pp. 201–03.

25 See Wehrhiem (2008).

26 Chogden Gönpo (n.d.), pp. 178–79.

27 Smith (2001), p. 16. The original text contains transliteration of Tibetan names using the Wylie system. The phonetics are mine.

28 See Karma Phuntsho (2013), p. 94–95.

29 See Aris (1995).

30 See Karma Phuntsho (2013).

31 Ibid., p. 107.

32 Aris (1989), p. 76.

33 Karma Phuntsho (2013), p. 115.

34 Ibid., p. 200.

35 Lama Sa-ngag (1983), p. 232.

36 Karma Phuntsho (2013) p. 266–67.

37 Ibid., p. 327.

38 Ibid., p. 330.

39 Sherab Palzang (2004), p. 56.

40 Gedun Rinchen (1972), p. 141.

41 Dasho Lama Sa-nga (2008), vol. IV, p. 8.

42 Ehrhard notes that Zhagla Yeshe Bumpa (fifteenth century) must not be confused with Oyod Yeshe Bum (thirteenth century), both of Kathog. Michael Aris, who perhaps followed Gedun Rinchen, made this mistake and dated the introduction of the Lhomon Kathog tradition in the thirteenth century. See Ehrhard (2007).

43 See Dewa Zangpo (1984), p. 260–61. Other two biographies are by Gyurme Dechen (1976) and Sherab Palden (1984). For biographies in English, see Stearns (2007) and Gerner (2007).

44 Anonymous (n.d.), *sKyes bu dam pa rnam kyi rnam par thar pa rin po che'i gter mdzod* and Sa gnas lo rgyus zhib 'jug rtsom sgrigs tshogs chung (2000). See also Tāranātha (1983), pp. 74–75.

45 Ardussi (forthcoming), ch. 2, p. 2.

46 Ibid., p. ch. 2, p. 57.

47 Anonymous (n.d.), *sKyes bu dam pa rnam kyi rnam par thar pa rin po che'i gter mdzod*, vol. kha, ff. 40, pp. 50–51. See also Pema Tshewang (1994), pp. 88–89.

48 Aris (1979), p. 193.

49 Anonymous (n.d.), *sKyes bu dam pa rnam kyi rnam par thar pa rin po che'i gter mdzod*, vol. kha, ff. 48–53.

50 See Ardussi (forthcoming) ch. 2, pp. 34–35. for more information on the fortunes of this school after Barawa's death.

51 Gedun Rinchen (1972), p. 177.

52 See Gedun Rinchen (1972), pp. 176–77 and Pema Tshewang (1994), pp. 109–10 for their discussion of Gedan Shingtapa.

53 See Karma Phuntsho (2008), pp. 237–39.

54 Ibid., pp. 116–19.

55 Kongtrul (1973), p. 490.

56 Götshang Repa (1993), p. 102.

57 See, for instance, Jñāna Vajra (1997), pp. 99, 101.

58 Sonam Gyaltshen (1979), pp. 114–15.

59 Jñāna Vajra (1997), pp. 42–43.

60 It is not clear if the tiger and leopard skins are actual animal skins or a name of a certain kind of textiles. In Haa, people refer to the kira as zupa, very close to our zigpa (གཟིག་སྤགས་) or leopard skin.

61 Dewa Zangpo (1984), p. 270.

62 Chogden Gönpo (n.d.), p. 155.

63 Chogden Gönpo (n.d.), p. 143.

64 Sherab Pelzang (2004), p. 28: སྲས་མོ་མ་སྟོང་ཞིག །འབྲུག་པས་གདན་ས་བཏབ་འོང་། སྲུ་ཆུམ་ཟག ཞིག ཆུ་རལ་པས་རྩ་རག་བཙུགས་འོང་།

65 Ibid., pp. 21–22: སྙིན་བདག་ཁར་ཅང་དོལ་པོ་ཀུན། ཆུ་རལ་དྲང་དྲང་དབང་གནས་དོ། ཁྲིམ་རྒྱབ་སྲན་ཁྲར་ནས་ དབང་ལུ་སོག །

66 Dewa Zangpo (1984), p. 408.

67 Samgyal Khache (1975), p. 429.

68 Longchenpa Drime Özer (n.d.), ff. 22v–23r.

69 Karma Phuntsho (ed.) (2013), p. 347.

70 Barawa Gyaltshen Palzang (1970), p. 242.

71 Gedun Rinchen (1971), p. 160.

72 Sherab Palzang (2004), p. 46.

73 Barawa Gyaltshen Palzang (1970), p. 378.

74 See Gelong Ngawang (2003), Pema Tshewang (1994), pp. 171–87 and Sangay Dorji (1999), pp. 83–84.

75 Taktshang Paljor Zangpo (1979), p. 105.

76 Sherab Palzang (2004), pp. 45–47.

77 No author: *dKar chags mthong ba 'dzum shor*, a manuscript in Dongkarla temple, f. 2.

The Medieval Period: The Unification of the Dragon Country

1 Shakabpa (1967), p. 71.

2 Ngawang Lobzang Gyatsho (1991), vol. 1, pp. 55–57.

3 The geneology presented in the table is based on Pema Karpo (1992) and Gedun Rinchen (1972). Ardussi includes Dorji Lingpa Senge Sherab (1238–80) and Namkha Palzang (1398–1425) as the fifth and twelfth hierarchs respectively but I have excluded them here as they were neither throne-holders of Ralung nor in the direct lineage leading to Zhabdrung although both were important scions of the Ralung line. Both Pema Karpo and Gedun Rinchen explicitly state that the former did not hold the Ralung seat and the latter seems to have also missed it as his brother took the seat immediately after the death of his father. See Pema Karpo (1992), p. 453 and Gedun Rinchen (1972), p. 99 and pp. 102–03. For Ardussi's chart of the Gya family and incarnation line, see Bartholomew and Johnston (2008), pp. 373–75.

4 Aris (1979), p. 205. Aris wrongly identified her first husband as the Tsangpa ruler, Phuntsho Namgyal and speculated if this separation 'may have been a factor in the hostility that developed between him and the Zhabdrung' but this is untenable as the Tsangpa ruler was born only in either 1586 or 1598 and thus too young to father a daughter before 1594. Yonten Dargye repeats the same, reproducing Aris in Yonten Dargye (2001), p.176.

5 Ngawang Pekar (2004), p. 11.

6 Ngawang Pekar (2004), pp. 14–15.

7 Ibid., p. 18.

8 Sangay Dorji (1999), pp. 357–60.

9 Palden Gyatsho (1974), p. 360 and Sangay Dorji (1999), p. 126.

10 Shakya Rinchen (1976d), p. 231.

11 Sangay Dorji (1999), pp. 146–47: འབྲི་ཁུང་པ་ལུ་རྒྱ་མ་འགྲན། ས་སྐྱ་པ་ལུ་མི་མ་འགྲན། འབྲུག་པ་ལུ་མཐུ་མ་འགྲན།

12 Ngawang Pekar (2004), p. 40, Sangay Dorji (1999), pp. 176–77 and Maria Luiza Baillie (1999), p. 19.

13 Ibid., pp. 88–89, Sangay Dorji (1999), p. 180 and Maria Luiza Baillie (1999), p. 32.

14 Sangay Dorji (1999), p. 188 and Palden Gyatsho (1974), pp. 493–94.

15 Baillie (1999), p. 18.

16 Ibid., pp. 19–20, 32–33.

17 Ibid., p. 29.

18 Palden Gyatsho (1974), pp. 518–19.

19 Ngawang Pekar (2004), p. 45 and Palden Gyatsho (1974), pp. 497–98.

20 See Ngawang Pekar (2004), p. 60 and Sangay Dorji (1999), p. 232 for citations.

21 Palden Gyatsho (1974), pp. 520–23.
22 ibid., pp. 523–24.
23 Ngawang Pekar (2004), pp. 30–31.
24 Gedun Rinchen (1987), pp. 200–08 and (1972), p. 220.
25 Pema Tshewang (1994), p. 155.
26 Sangay Dorji (1999), pp. 276, 279 and Ngawang Pekar (2004), p. 63.
27 Sungtrul Tshultrim Dorji (n.d.a), f. 28v.
28 Palden Gyatsho (1975), vol. II, p. 5 and Sangay Dorji (1999), p. 272.
29 Ngawang Lobzang Gyatsho (1991), vol. I, p. 223.
30 Ngawang Pekar (2004), p. 72.
31 Shakabpa (1967), p. 112.
32 Ngawang Lobzang Gyatsho (1991), vol. I, p. 284.
33 Shakabpa (1967), p. 113.
34 Sangay Dorji (1999), p. 329.
35 Tenzin Chögyal (n.d.), f. 36ab and Shakya Rinchen (n.d.), f. 32b.
36 Ngawang Lobzang Gyatsho (1991), vol. I, p. 310.
37 Sungtrul Tshultrim Dorji (n.d.b), f. 24r.
38 Lopen Nado (1986), p. 170.
39 Ardussi (2004b)
40 Aris (1986), pp. 94–5. Yonten Dargye (2009), pp. 125–26

Zhabdrung's Legacy and the Early Monk Rulers

1 See Ngawang Pekar (2004), p. 82 and Palden Gyatsho (1974), pp. 564, 617.
2 A fifth one in Buddhist sciences was added recently.
3 Baillie (1999), p. 23.
4 Ngawang Lhundup (n.d.), f. 51v.
5 Ngawang Lobzang Gyatsho (1991), vol. 1, p. 495 and Palden Gyatsho (1974), p. 615.
6 Ngawang Lobzang Gyatsho (1991), vol. 1, pp. 497, 499, 507–08.
7 Lobzang Chögyan (1969), p. 314–16. See also Ngawang Lhundup (n.d.), f. 184.1v.
8 Lobzang Gyatsho (1991), vol. 1, p. 516.
9 For sources, see note 212.
10 Ngawang Lhundup (n.d.), f. 26 and Tenzin Chögyal (1759), f. 94r.

11 Ardussi (1977), p. 302.

12 See Ardussi (1977), chapter VI for a thoroughgoing analysis of the region's political situation at this time.

13 Kuenga Gyaltshen (1985), pp. 71–76.

14 Thutob Namgyal and Yeshe Drolma (2003), p. 68.

15 Ngawang Lobzang Gyatsho (1991), vol. 2, p. 127.

16 Ibid., vol. 2, p. 135.

17 Ngawang Lobzang Gyatsho (1993), pp. 351–54.

18 Ngawang Lobzang Gyatsho (1991), vol. 2, p. 135.

19 Ibid., vol. 2, p. 455.

20 Ibid., vol. 2, p. 508.

21 Ngawang Lhundup (n.d.), f. 98v.

22 See Blumer and Vial (1999), p. 238.

23 Ngawang Lobzang Gyatsho (1991), vol. 3, p. 365.

24 Ardussi (1977), pp. 327–28.

25 Ngawang Lhundup (n.d.), ff. 87v–88r.

26 Kuenga Gyaltshen (1970), p. 46.

27 For Indian sources, see Ghose (1874), Whytse (2002), Blochmann (1872), Gait (1933) and Ghoshal (2005). These are based on primary sources such as Caudhurī Āmānataullā Āhamada's *Kocabihārera itihāsa*, a history of Cooch Behar and Shihab al-Din Talish's *Fathiyah-i'-Ibriyah*, a Mughal account of North-East India. See also http://www.coochbehar.gov.in/ HTMfiles/history_book2.html#p1, accessed on 1 September, 2010.

28 Ardussi (1977), chapter VI and VII.

29 Gedun Rinchen (1974), p. 244 and Tshering Dorji (1963), p. 153. The sources do not give a date for the afflication of disease.

30 Tshering Dorji (1963), p. 153.

31 Ngawang Pekar (2004), p. 104 and Sangay Dorji (1999), pp. 332–33.

32 Ngawang Lhundup (n.d.), f. 109r.

33 Ibid., f. 14, 34.

34 Tshering Dorji (1963), p. 154.

35 Ngawang Lhundup (n.d.), f. 134r.

36 Ibid., f. 134v: ཕྱི་ཚར་ལས་ནང་ཐིགས་རླུབ་

37 See Aris (1982), pp. 119–21.

38 Shakya Rinchen (n.d.), f. 61r.

39 Ngawang Lobzang Gyatsho (1999), vol. 3, p. 365 and (2007), vol. 23, pp. 801–04 and vol. 25, pp. 715–16.

40 Ardussi (1977), p. 336–37 and 395.

41 Dargye, Sorenson and Tshering (2008), p. 112. See also Shakya Rinchen (n.d.), f. 97v.

42 Ngawang Lhundup (n.d.), f. 203.

43 Ngawang Tenzin (n.d.), f. 25r.

44 Ardussi (2008), p. 99.

45 Shakya Rinchen (n.d.), f. 90v and Pema Tshewang (1994), p. 275.

46 Tenzin Chögyal (1759), f. 61v and Gedun Rinchen (1974), p. 342. See Kuenga Gyaltshen (1970), p. 64

47 Kuenga Gyaltshen (1970), p. 65.

48 Shakya Rinchen (n.d.), f. 104.

49 See Kuenga Gyaltshen (1985) and (1970) for details about Damchö Pekar's life.

50 Ardussi (1977), p. 422.

51 Shakya Rinchen (1976a), p. 256.

52 Ngawang Lhundup (n.d.), f. 330v.

53 Ardussi (1977), pp. 403, 420 and see Bartholomew and Johnston (2008), p. 98.

54 Kuenga Gyaltshen (1985), p. 127. The recent work by Yoshiro Imaeda concurs with my argument that at the time Kuenga Gyaltshen was claimed to be the immediate incarnation of Zhabdrung himself. See Imaeda (2011), pp. 134–35. I have not managed to make full use of this work as much of my history was written by the time this came out.

55 Tenzin Chögyal (n.d.), ff. 80–84.

56 Ibid., ff. 85–86, 89.

57 Shakya Rinchen (n.d.), ff. 108–11 and Yonten Dargye, Sorenson and Tshering (2008), p. 119–30.

58 Kuenga Gyaltshen (1985), pp. 141–43.

59 Tenzin Chögyal (1759), f. 97.

60 Pema Tshewang (1994), p. 289.

61 Shakya Rinchen (n.d.), f. 130–31.

62 For details about his mission to Ladakh, see Shakya Rinchen (n.d.) ff. 131–71 and Dargye, Sorenson and Tshering (2008), pp. 133–76.

Multiple Incarnations and the Rise of Lay Rulers

1 Pema Tshewang (1994), pp. 291–92

2 Tshering Dorji (1963), p. 57.

3 For more details on Sungtrul Chogley Namgyal, see Shakya Rinchen (1976c), pp. 48–53.

4 Shakya Rinchen (1976d), p. 301.

5 See Tshering Wangyal (1981), pp. 227–32 for details.

6 Ardussi (1977), p. 432.

7 Thutob Namgyal and Yeshe Drolma (2003), pp. 60, 64–67.

8 Shakya Rinchen (n.d.), f. 201.

9 Thutob Namgyal and Yeshe Drolma (2003), p. 82.

10 Tshering Wangyal (1981), pp. 230–50.

11 Ngawang Lobzang Gyatsho (1991), pp. 514–15. See Kongtrul Lodoe Thaye (1973), p. 360.

12 See Kongtrul Lodoe Thaye (1973), p. 360.

13 Tshering Wangyal (1981), p. 749.

14 Tshering Dorji (1963), p. 175.

15 Shakya Tenzin (1976), p. 358.

16 Ardussi (1977), p. 445. Note his original contains transliteration, Pho-lha-nas, instead of phoneticized Pholhaney.

17 Shakya Rinchen (n.d.), ff. 216–17.

18 Chogdrub Palbar (n.d.), f. 27v.

19 See Shakya Tenzin (1976), pp. 365–75 and Shakya Rinchen (1976c), pp. 479–86 for general information on the escape, death and rebirth of Chogley Namgyal.

20 Shakya Rinchen (1976a), pp. 186–93.

21 Tshering Wangyal (1981), pp. 750, 758–60.

22 Ardussi (1977), p. 462, Shakya Rinchen (1976b), pp. 416–19 and Gedun Rinchen (1972), p. 262.

23 Shakya Rinchen (1976d), pp. 121, 133 and 296.

24 Tenzin Chögyal (1759), ff. 66–67.

25 For detail, see Yonten Thaye and Kuenga Gyatsho (2003) and Ardussi and Ura (2000).

26 Yontan Thaye (1985), pp. 43–44.

The Rise of Southward Relations and Internal Strife

1 Ngawang Chökyi Gyatsho (1985b), p. 307.

2 Karma Palbar (1984), p. 336.

3 Ghose (1874), pp. 91–92.

4 Ngawang Chökyi Gyatsho (1985b), p. 306.

5 Tshering Dorji (1963), p. 252.

6 Lamb (2002), p. 92.

7 Majumdar (1984), pp. 28–39.

8 Ngawang Chökyi Gyatsho (1985b), p. 307.

9 Majumdar (1984), p. 35.

10 Karma Palbar (1984), pp. 363–64.

11 Ghose (1874), pp. 93, 99.

12 Karma Palbar (1984), pp. 363–64.

13 Ibid., p. 365.

14 Pema Tshewang (1994), p. 374, Gedun Rinchen (1974), p. 352, Tshering Dorji (1963), p. 246.

15 Lamb (2002), pp. 37–38.

16 Ngawang Chökyi Gyatsho (1985b.), p. 312.

17 Lamb (2002), p. 48.

18 Lamb (2002), pp. 101–04, 317, 327

19 Ibid., pp. 104–05.

20 Konchog Jigme Wangpo (2002), p. 589.

21 Lamb (2002), p. 334.

22 Ibid., pp. 390 and 392.

23 Ibid., p. 90.

24 Ibid., p. 70.

25 For this rebuke, see Aris (1982), pp. 119–21 but readers must be cautious of some problems in translation.

26 Lamb (2002), p. 412.

27 Ibid., p. 333.

28 See Aris (1995).

29 Turner (1800), p. 81.

30 Tshering Dorji (1963), p. 262.

31 Lamb (2002), p. 128.

32 Ibid., p. 349.

33 Ibid., p. 404.

34 Ibid., p. 443 and also Teltscher (2006), pp. 228–29 and Markham (1879), p. 119.

35 Ibid., pp. 424–25.

36 Turner (1800), p. 153.

37 Ibid., p. 72.

38 Ibid., p. 82.

39 Ibid., p. 83.

40 Ngawang Chökyi Gyatsho (1985b.), p. 35.
41 See Lamb (2002), Markham (1879), Turner (1800) and Aris (1982).
42 His drawings and diary are reproduced in Aris's *Views of Medieval Bhutan* with a very good introduction although in this work, Aris was confused concerning the identification of the Desi Jigme Sengay.
43 See Tshering Dorji·(1963), p. 261 and Pema Tshewang (1994), p. 379 and Thutob Namgyal and Yeshe Drolma (2003), p. 117.
44 Tshering Dorji (1963), p. 268.
45 See Kaptein (2006), p. 159.
46 Pema Tshewang (1994), p. 385 and Ngawang Chökyi Gyatsho (1985a), pp. 78–79.
47 Jigme Drakpa II (1811), ff. 160–61.
48 Ibid., ff. 176–78. See also Jangchub Norbu (1985), pp. 283–84 and Sherab Gyaltshen and Jigme Norbu (1976), p. 308.
49 Jangchub Norbu (1985), p. 305
50 Ngawang Chökyi Gyatsho (1985a), p. 149 gives 1802, Male Water Dog as the year of this conflict and the fire of Punakha but Jangchub Norbu (1985), p. 305 has 1803, Female Water Hog.
51 Jangchub Norbu (1985), pp. 307–08.
52 Jigme Drakpa II (1811), f. 213b. His date for the fire and Jamyang Gyaltshen's death appears to be incorrect.
53 Turner (1800), p. 377. Lam' Ghassatoo in Turner's account must be Gyalse Trulku Jigme Namgyal although, as Aris rightly pointed out (Aris 1982, p. 94), the child Turner pointed out is a younger incarnate.
54 See Jangchub Norbu (1985) on these two incarnations.
55 Pema Tshewang (1994), p. 394.
56 See Sherab Gyaltshen and Jigme Norbu (1976), pp. 319–21.
57 Ngawang Chökyi Gyatsho (1985a), p. 166.
58 Jangchub Norbu (1985), p. 382.
59 Ibid., pp. 392–93.
60 Ngawang Chökyi Gyatsho (1985a), p. 177. Aris (1994), pp. 45 claims the Desi was killed by Norbu Rinchen but mixes up Jigme Drakpa II and Tshultrim Drakpa in his account.
61 Markham (1879), p. 214–16.
62 Jangchub Norbu (1985), pp. 493–94.
63 Lopen Nado (1986), p. 145 and Pema Tshewang (1994), p. 422.
64 Majumdar (1984), p. 71.
65 Ibid., p. 73.

66 Bose (2000), p. 196.

67 Ibid., p. 199.

68 Our sources only give the name Jampal Dorji. The ordinal epithet (Jampal Dorji II) is my addition to make a clear distinction with the son of Zhabdrung.

69 Pema Tshewang (1994), p. 430.

70 Sherab Gyaltshen and Jigme Norbu (1976), pp. 368–69.

71 Ibid., p. 370.

72 Ibid., p. 373.

73 Pema Tshewang (1994), pp. 432–33.

74 Sherab Gyaltshen and Jigme Norbu (1976), p. 383.

75 Sherab Gyaltshen and Jigme Norbu (1976)

Civil Wars and Frontier Troubles

1 Pemberton (1838), p. 13.

2 Majumdar (1984), p. 84.

3 Pemberton (1838), pp. 26–7, Majumdar (1984), p. 86.

4 Majumdar (1984), p. 90.

5 Pemberton (1838), p. 22.

6 Ibid., p. 24.

7 Ibid., pp. 104–05.

8 Ibid., pp. 105–06.

9 Ibid., p. 89.

10 Ibid., p. 33.

11 Ibid., p. 38.

12 Pema Tshewang (1994), p. 442.

13 Bose (2000), pp. 198–9 and Eden (2000), pp. 109–10.

14 Tshering Dorji (1963), p. 309. and Pema Tshewang (1994), pp. 436, 457. Tshering Dorji and Pema Tshewang's date for this assault is in line with the British sources but other sources put this attack in the preceding year. Pema Tshewang's date for Dorji Norbu's ascension is however problematic.

15 Pemberton (1838), pp. 53–54.

16 Pemberton (1838), pp. 51–52.

17 Griffiths (n.d.), pp. 145–46.

18 Pemberton (1838), pp. 97–98.

19 Griffiths (n.d.), p. 141.

20 Tshering Dorji (1963), p. 310.

21 Jigme Norbu (1984), p. 17.

22 Ibid., pp. 17–18.

23 Sherab Gyaltshen and Jigme Norbu (1976), p. 393.

24 Ibid., p. 395.

25 Ibid., pp. 398, 407, 418–19.

26 Jigme Norbu (1984), pp. 24–25. The new *pönlop* is either Ogyen Phuntsho of Tamshing, who probably briefly returned to office after Tenzin Chögyal's death, or Tshokye Dorji of Ogyen Chöling.

27 Damchö Lhendup (2008a), p. 43.

28 Jigme Norbu (1984), pp. 32–33.

29 Sherab Gyaltshen and Jigme Norbu (1976), p. 419.

30 Jigme Norbu (1984), p. 57.

31 Jigme Norbu (1984), p. 59.

32 Ibid., p. 59.

33 Ibid., p. 61. Tshering Dorji (1963), p. 307 and Pema Tshewang (1994), p. 443 state the monk body moved to Paro that winter.

34 Zhanphan Rolpai Dorji (1959), f. 179v.

35 Tenzin Phuntsho (1870), p. 519.

36 Jigme Norbu (1984), pp. 66, 69.

37 Ibid., p. 66.

38 Pema Tshewang (1994), p. 446.

39 Jigme Norbu (1984), pp. 223–23.

40 Lama Sa-ngag (2005), vol. II, p.79–81.

41 Damchö Lhendup (2008a), pp. 75–76.

42 Pema Tshewang (1994), p. 459 and Damchö Lhendup (2008a), p. 84 date his death in the first month of the Iron Pig (=1851) and the installation of his successor in the first month of the following year.

43 Tenzin Phuntsho (1870), p. 524.

44 Ibid., p. 525 and Jigme Norbu (1984), pp. 73–74.

45 Jigme Norbu (1984), p. 426.

46 Ibid., pp. 509–10.

47 Ibid., pp. 415–17.

48 Ibid., pp. 423.

49 Gedun Rinchen (1972), p. 250 and Eden (2000), p. 99 give the year of his death as 1861 but this is untenable if he was alive during the flood of Punakha in 1863. There is no contemporary source on his death or the date of the floods. Jigme Norbu mentions a flood in his own writing. See

Jigme Norbu (1984), p. 452. Phuntsho Wangdi (2007), p. 107 mentions his death in Tibet at 31.

50 Lama Sa-ngag (2005), p. 174.

51 Tshering Dorji (1963), p. 313.

52 Tenzin Phuntsho (1870), pp. 536–37.

53 Ibid., p. 547.

54 Karma Ura (2010), p.12 makes this speculation.

55 Tenzin Phuntsho (1870), pp. 548–49.

56 Ibid., p. 559.

57 Lama Sa-ngag (2005), vol. ii, p. 50 mentions he had a son from a lady of Bönbji. This is probably the same lady as the one from Gangteng as she appears to be a relation of the 6th Gangteng Trulku. See Phuntsho Wangdi (2007), p. 184.

58 Phuntsho Wangdi (2007), p. 184. This author is the great-grandson of Jigme Namgyal.

59 Zhanphan Rolpai Dorji (1859), f. 96r.

60 Ibid., f. 99v.

61 Phuntsho Wangdi (2007), p. 187.

62 Lama Sa-ngag (2005), vol. ii, p. 63, Damchö Lhendup (2008a), pp. 58, and Kesang Choden (1997), p. 75.

63 Kesang Choden (1997), p. 76.

64 Damchö Lhendup (2008a), p. 52 cites Brula Nyerpa Samdrup.

65 Pema Tshewang (1994), pp. 494–5 and Aris (1994), p. 66–67.

66 Zhanphan Rolpai Dorji (1859), f. 152v.

67 Pema Tshewang (1994), p. 487.

68 Tshering Dorji (1963), p. 327.

69 Dasho Lama Sa-nga (2005), vol. II, pp. 94–95.

The Duar War and the Black Regent

1 Majumdar (1984), p. 110.

2 Rennie (1970), pp. 358-62, 385–406.

3 Cited in Eden (2000), p. 21.

4 Ibid., p. 23 and Majumdar (1984), p. 126.

5 Cited in Majumdar (1984), p. 109.

6 Ibid., p. 113.

7 Eden (2000), p. 55.

8 Ibid., p. 70.

9 Ibid., p. 95.

10 See Anon (1865), pp. 153–54.

11 Cited in Collister (1996), p. 102.

12 Ibid., p. 103.

13 Eden (2000), p. 102.

14 See Collister (1996), Kesang Choden Dorji (1997) and Karma Ura (2010).

15 Rennie (1970), p. 165.

16 Ibid., pp. 175–76.

17 Ibid., pp. 181–82.

18 Tshering Dorji (1963), p. 329 and Damchö Lhendup (2008a), p. 121 has Dzaigong as the destination of the Paro *pönlop*'s column but this is probably a mistaken identification as the town of Jaigon, as we know it, is adjacent to Pasakha. It is probably a confusion with Tazagong, a stockade post on Balla Pass near Samtse, where there were serious attacks according to Rennie (1970), p. 204.

19 Rennie (1970), p. 202.

20 Khenpo Phuntsok Tashi (2003), p. 83.

21 Rennie (1970), p. 196.

22 The name Shalpa Lagdum was probably given retrospectively to the officer whose hand was cut off. Lag dum is literally 'amputated hand' and 'Shal pa' is a term used by the Bhutanese to refer to the British, perhaps a derivative of the term 'British pa', the 'pa' suffix denoting a person.

23 Pema Tshewang (1994), p. 491.

24 Rennie (1970), pp. 286–87.

25 Ibid., p. 290.

26 Lama Sa-ngag (2005), vol. II, pp. 99–100.

27 Ibid., p. 103.

28 Lama Sa-ngag (2005), vol. II, pp. 103–04 writes that some British force came as far as Saling in Mongar to recover the two guns but Tshering Dorji (1963), p. 330 concurs with the British records that they came up to Drangmechu. Lama Sa-ngag perhaps compounded the advance of British troops with the arrival of some Indian landlords to pay homage to the new Zhabdrung incarnate, Jigme Chögyal in Drametse, which Tshering Dorji mentions.

29 Eden (2000), p. 103.

30 Pema Tshewang (1994), p. 496, Lama Sa-ngag (2005),vol. II, p. 110 and Lopen Nado (1986), p. 185.

31 Cited in Majumdar (1984), p. 154.

32 Phuntsho Wangdi (2007), p. 203 and Lopen Nado (1986), p. 184.

33 Phuntsho Wangdi (2007), p. 204 and Lopen Nado (1984), p. 185 states that Tshewang Norbu was reinstated as he was the nephew of Nyima Dorji, who was on good terms with Jigme Namgyal.

34 Dashi Lama Sa-ngag (2005), vol. II, p. 129 and Damchö Lhendup (2008b), p. 48.

35 See Mullard and Wongchuk (2010), pp. 115–37.

36 Thutob Namgyal and Yeshe Drolma (2003), p. 177.

37 Damchö Lhendup (2008a), p. 180 states the post was to be passed on after five years and not three.

38 Lopen Nado (1984), p. 185, Phuntsho Wangdi (2007), p. 205.

39 None of the sources give the exact date for the conflict. Phuntsho Wangdi (2007), p. 205 states this conflict started when Jigme Namgyal was fifty-two. By Bhutanese reckoning, this would be 1876.

40 See Karma Ura (1996) for the English translation of this ballad.

41 Damchö Lhendup (2008a), p. 182.

42 Lama Sa-ngag (2005), vol. II, p. 128.

43 Pema Tshewang (1994), p. 504.

The Emergence of Ugyen Wangchuk and End of Civil War

1 My main local sources for the accounts of Ugyen Wangchuk's life, just as that of his father and son, are late twentieth-century historians, including Lopen Nado (1986), Pema Tshewang (1994), Lama Sa-ngag (2005), Phuntsho Wangdi (2007), Tshering Dorji (1963) and Damchö Lhendup (2008b.). Most sources share the main stories with some variation. I have used British sources to draw an external perspective. Michael Aris (1995) provides by far the most elaborate account of Ugyen Wangchuk in English.

2 Karma Ura (2010), p. 29.

3 Damchö Lhendup (2008b), p. 4 states Ugyen Wangchuk was a reincarnation of Drubchen Rinpoche from the Amdo province of eastern Tibet. However, Phuntsho Wangdi (2007), p. 208, records an oral account that Ugyen Wangchuk was a rebirth of one Gaap Karpo of Wang Sisina. Traditional historians also cite a prophecy of Padmasambhava which predicts the birth of Ugyen Wangchuk.

4 Aris (1994), p. 75.

5 Damchö Lhendup (2008b), p. 52.

6 Jigme Chögyal (1985), p. 177: རྡོས་འཛལ་ཡུན་འགྱུངས་སོ་བའི་དུན་སྲུང་གིས། །འཛལ་ཚེ་པ་དུ་ འཕད་སྲུང་རྒྱགས་ཡིད་འརྗེས།།

7 Lama Sa-ngag (2005), vol. II, p. 138.

8 Phuntsho Wangdi (2007), p. 212.

9 Damchö Lhendup (2008b), p. 42.

10 Phuntsho Wangdi (2007), p. 213.

11 White (2008), p. 132.

12 Local oral stories provide the name Pema of Dongka or Namgay Pema of Dongka while the literary sources give the name Dechen Zangmo.

13 Lama Sa-ngag (2005), p. 152, mainly blames Damchö Rinchen, who persuaded his nephew to rise against Ugyen Wangchuk.

14 Asuras are a class of beings in Buddhist cosmology, who are in constant hostility and war with the celestial realm of gods.

15 Jigme Chögyal (1985), p. 72. Vidyadharas are a category of saintly beings who have achieved certain supernatural powers and degrees of spiritual heights in Vajrayāna Buddhism.

16 Oral account by Aap Tshewang Dargay.

17 White (2008), p. 132.

18 Pema Tshewang (1994), pp. 523–24.

19 Tenzin Lhendup (1985), pp. 105–06.

20 Jigme Chögyal (1985), pp. 73–74.

21 Damchö Lhendup (2008b), p. 75.

22 Jigme Chögyal (1985), p. 148.

23 Ibid., p. 149.

24 Phuntsho Wangdi (2007), p. 224.

25 Damchö Lhendup (2008b), p. 131.

26 Pema Tshewang (1994), p. 532, Phuntsho Wangdi (2007), p. 224, Lama Sa-ngag (2005), p. 181.

27 Damchö Lhendup (2008b), p. 118.

28 Phuntsho Wangdi (2007), p.

29 Pema Tshewang (1994), p. 565 has 1903 for the year of her marriage to Ugyen Wangchuk.

30 Damchö Lhendup (2008b), p. 128.

31 Ibid., p. 132.

32 See Sonam Kinga (2004) for more details. This short monograph gives a comprehensive account of Ugyen Wangchuk's role in the Younghusband Expedition to Tibet.

33 Cited in Collister (1996), p. 138.

34 See Pema Tshewang (1994), pp. 533–34, Aris (1997), pp. 179–88 and Sonam Kinga (2004), pp. 94–97 for the poem by Nyizer Lhatshab and Jigme Chögyal (1985), pp. 174–81 in which they describe the British forces as barbaric and Tibet as a Buddhist realm.

35 Jigme Chögyal (1985), pp. 177–78.

36 Cited in Kohli (1982), p. 164.

37 See Sonam Kinga (2004), pp. 60–93.

38 Tshering Dorji (1963) p. 313 states he was installed on the golden throne of the prince-regent in 1854.

39 Jigme Chögyal (1985), p. 42.

40 Oral narration by Tshewang Dargay: པར་ཕྱོགས་སུ་མི་རྗེ་པ། །རྒྱ་མ་མང་པོ་འབྱུངས་པ། །འབྱུངས་ དགྲ་མ་འབྱུངས་པ། །ཨ་རུང་མང་སེ་འབྱུངས་ཅ། ། See Lama Sa-ngag (2005), vol. III, p. 185 for a slightly different version.

41 White (2008), p. 164.

42 Ibid., p. 165.

43 Ibid., p. 172.

44 Ibid., p. 206.

Early Modern Period: The Introduction of Monarchy

1 Many other establishments in eastern Bhutan, such as Tsakaling with Jigme Chögyal's uncle, Doshal Samdrup, at its lead, were thriving at this time but their influence was primarily in the religious domain and had a limited bearing on national politics.

2 Cited in Aris (1994), p. 90.

3 Bell (2000), p. 105.

4 Cited in Aris (1994), p. 88.

5 Waddell (1988), p. 269.

6 Cited in Aris (1994), p. 112.

7 Bell (2000), p. 104.

8 White (2008), p. 233.

9 A copy of this letter is reproduced in Pema Tshewang (1994), pp. 543–46 and Lama Sa-ngag (2005), vol. II, pp. 197–2003.

10 White (2008), p. 226.

11 Tshering Dorji (1963), pp. 348, 366.

12 Cited in Aris (1994), p. 102.

13 Ashi Dorji Wangmo Wangchuk (1999), p. 19.

14 Anon. (1966), p. 72, Lopen Nado (1986), p. 124, Aris (1994), pp. 101–02,

Damchö Lhendup (2008b), vol. II, p. 221 and Rongthong Kunley Dorji (2003), p. 1.

15 White (2008), p. 165, p. 206 and pp. 232–33.

16 Bell (2000), p. 101.

17 Ibid., pp. 101–02.

18 Ibid., p. 103.

19 Aris (1994), pp. 94, 100.

20 Tshering Dorji (1963), p. 347 gives Iron Dog (1910) but Ashi Dorji Wangmo Wangchuck (1999), p. 14 and Damchö Lhendup (2008c), p. 176 have 1912. The former is perhaps date for his trip to Punakha and the latter for the formal installation.

21 Ashi Dorji Wangmo Wangchuck (1999), p. 14.

22 Sonam Tobgye (2011), November 11, p. 5.

23 Ibid.

24 Ibid., 12 November, p. 13.

25 White (2008), p. 233.

26 See Tshering Tashi (2008) for King Ugyen Wangchuk's proposal to the British.

27 Collister (1996), p. 175.

28 Damchö Lhendup (2008b), pp. 74–75, 215–16.

29 Ibid. (2008b), p. 74–75.

30 Damchö Lhendup (2008c), p. 48.

31 Damchö Lhendup (2008b), p. 230.

32 Pema Tshewang (1994) and Damchö Lhendup (2008c), p. 50.

33 Phuntsho Wangdi (2007), p. 228 gives his name as Jigme Dorji, Damchö Lhendup (2008b), p. 135 as Chimi Dorji, Aris (1994), p. 50 as Gyurme Dorji.

34 Aris (1994), p. 50 gives his name as Karma Trinley alais Nakhu.

35 Damchö Lhendup (2008b), p. 135.

36 Jamyang's father was one Lamala, an illegitimate son of the Sumthrang *chöje* born to a woman in Ura village.

37 Damchö Lhendup (2008c), pp. 29–30.

38 Cited in Aris (1994), p. 116.

39 Collister (1996), p. 179.

40 Damchö Lhendup (2008c), pp. 71–72.

41 Cited in Collister (1996), p. 193.

42 Karma Ura (1995), pp. 87–88.

43 See Karma Ura (1995), pp. 123–41, Pema Tshewang (1994), pp

575–77 and Damchö Lhendup (2008b), pp. 190–93 and (2008c), pp. 144–63.

44 See Barawa Gyaltshen Palzang (1970), p. 242 and Dewa Zangpo (1984), pp. 268–9. See Rhodes (1999).

45 Yonten Thaye and Kuenga Gyatsho (2003), pp. 98–102. See also Ardussi and Karma Ura (2000), pp. 48–49.

46 Karma Ura (1995), p. 128.

47 Collister (1996), p. 189.

48 For these changes see Pema Tshewang (1994), pp. 575–77, Damchö Lhendup (2008c), pp. 146–51 and Karma Ura (1995), pp. 138–39 and (2010), pp. 49–52.

49 Damchö Lhendup (2008c), p. 150.

50 Damchö Lhendup (2008c), p. 152–54.Very few written histories record this practice but oral accounts of it are still widely narrated across Bhutan. Ashi Dorji Wangmo Wangchuck (1999), p. 51–52 recounts a similar anecdote of official extortion.

51 See Collister (1996), pp. 183, 187 and 191 for his citation of Weir, Williamson and Gould from *Political Collections*, Bhutan 1906–47.

52 Ashi Dorji Wangmo Wangchuck (1999), pp. 20 and 46 and Damchö Lhendup (1008c), pp. 42–44.

53 Damchö Lhendup (2008c), pp. 42–43.

54 Ashi Dorji Wangmo Wangchuck (1999), p. 20.

55 Karma Ura (1995), pp. 49 and 93.

56 Tshering Dorji (1963), pp. 348, 366.

57 Tshering Dorji (1963), p. 358 and Lopen Nado (1986), p. 128.

58 See Tshering Dorji (1963), p. 358 and Gedun Rinchen (1972), p. 251.

59 Anon. (1966), *sMan ljongs 'brug rgyal khab chen po'i sde srid khri rabs dang brgyud 'dzin gyi rgyal po rim par byon pa'i rgyal rabs deb ther gsal ba'i me long*.

60 Aris (1994), pp. 120–24, Ashi Dorji Wangmo Wangchuck (1999), pp. 24–32 and Damchö Lhendup (2008c).

61 Ashi Dorji Wangmo Wangchuck (1999), p. 27.

62 See Aris (1996), p. 120 for the citation.

63 Ashi Dorji Wangmo Wangchuk (1999), pp. 24–26.

64 Anon. (1966), p. 76.

65 Lopen Nado (1986), p. 129 and Rongthong Kunley Dorji (2003).

66 See Damchö Lhendup (2008c), pp. 160–61 for oral accounts by Dasho Karma Gelek.

67 See Damchö Lhendup (2008c), pp. 114–15 for the citation.

68 Damchö Lhendup (2008c), pp. 170–71.

The Modern Period: The Dragon's New Journey

1 See Karma Phuntsho (2008).

2 See Rustomji (1978).

3 See Rose (1977).

4 Jigme Y. Thinley (1994), p. 43.

5 See Hutt (1994) and (2005). The first one contains Bhutanese perceptions and the second a refugee perspective. See also papers on open democracy and other websites, including Karma Phuntsho (2006).

6 See Karma Phuntsho (2004).

7 *Kuensel*, 25 January 2013.

8 See Karma Phuntsho (2004) for a discussion of these traditional principles.

9 See Aris (1982), p. 54.

Index

Acknowledgements

SETTING ABOUT TO WRITE the first complete history of one's own country in a foreign language is as stupendous a task as making history itself. It would not have been possible without the support offered from various quarters in the form of institutional backing, time, resources, guidance and encouragement. I would like to thank Stephen Hugh-Jones and the team at the Mongolian and Inner Asian Studies Unit at Cambridge University for their open support during my time at Cambridge, when much of this was written.

I also owe immense gratitude to many colleagues and friends in the field of Bhutan, Buddhist and Tibetan studies, who shared their knowledge and information generously. In particular, I take this opportunity to pay my homage to all traditional and modern scholars, both past and present, who have paved the way for this book with their works on Bhutan history. Despite a high level of interest and enthusiasm, a student of Bhutan history would not know where to begin without their writings.

My friend Alex Mckay has given his time generously to read through the first draft of the manuscript. I am grateful to him for his critical remarks and feedback as I am to Meru Gokhale, Archana Shankar and the team at Random House India for the professional and friendly manner in which they transformed my manuscript into this book. The book is also the outcome of much encouragement and support from my friends, family members and colleagues, who are too numerous to be named here. Special mention may be made of Dawa, who became the inadvertent victim of my affair with this book. Her departure was a heavy price for the book and only her return could absolve the 'sin'. I am grateful to Elizabeth Chatwin, my 'mother' in the UK, for her sustained affection and the space I could call home in London, where the final chapters were written. I owe gratitude also to many friends, including Shane Suvikapakornkul of Serindia Publications and Yonten Dargye, who shared pictures although not all are used.

Due to the long span of history it covers and lack of reliable information for many periods, I am ruefully aware that I have not been able to do justice to some events and figures in Bhutan's history. It is my hope that future studies and projects will fill this gap.

Tibetan and Bhutanese terms are presented in simple phonetics to make them accessible to the general audience but staying as close to the orthographic form as possible. Dates in the common calendar, which corresponded to the Bhutanese dates from pre-modern times, are based on Edward Henning's excellent resource for calendrical calculation. All mistakes, shortcomings, obfuscations and defects are mine alone.

Karma
Losar Day, Water Snake Year, 17th Rabjung—11 February 2013